The Alphabet

This is our alphabet in capital (large) and lower-case (small) letters:

ABCDEFGHIJKLMNOPQRSTUVWXYZ
a b c d e f g h i j k l m n o p q r s t u v w x y z

There are 26 letters in the alphabet, and each has at least one sound that we use in our spoken language.

Write the lower-case of these capital letters. Two have been done for you.

A a	G ____	J ____	D ____
I i	K ____	B ____	L ____
E ____	C ____	H ____	F ____
O ____	N ____	M ____	P ____

Write the capital letters of these lower case letters from the box. Two have been done for you.

q Q	r ____	a ____
x X	f ____	w ____
g ____	y ____	d ____
b ____	c ____	z ____
k ____	i ____	n ____
o ____	m ____	j ____
h ____	e ____	l ____
p ____	s ____	t ____

A	B	C
D	E	F
G	H	I
J	K	L
M	N	O
P	Q	R
S	T	W
X	Y	Z

Write your name. ____________________

Matching Shapes

Draw an "X" through each one that is different. See example "A."

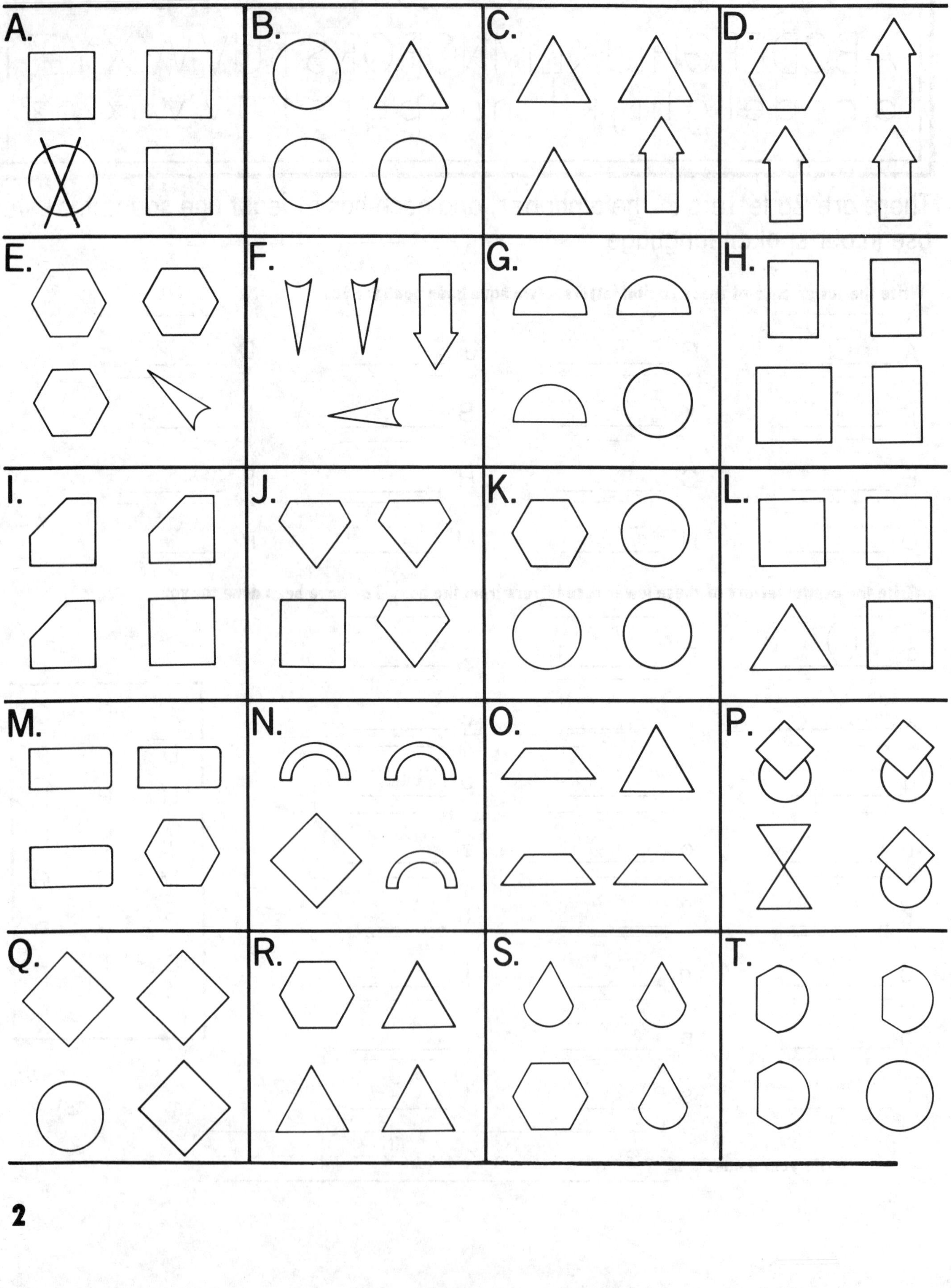

A. B. C. D.

E. F. G. H.

I. J. K. L.

M. N. O. P.

Q. R. S. T.

Lengths of Words

Draw a line under each word that is of a different length. See examples "1" and "2."

1.	here	no	come	2.	see	green	funny
3.	is	with	find	4.	father	dinner	the
5.	home	play	me	6.	chair	and	cakes
7.	go	down	here	8.	for	mother	sister
9.	said	to	fast	10.	house	not	water
11.	up	help	this	12.	staple	stores	far
13.	what	toys	we	14.	start	red	bride
15.	ride	it	have	16.	big	stored	hopped
17.	if	stop	blue	18.	stone	never	toy
19.	make	work	of	20.	women	you	often
21.	at	pool	diet	22.	point	bread	can
23.	back	be	vest	24.	get	sheep	begin
25.	in	pack	ring	26.	brown	put	older
27.	cane	neat	on	28.	was	thing	happy
29.	ball	or	next	30.	rabbit	helped	rod
31.	an	bill	line	32.	pet	garden	farmer

See, Say, and Write Words

Pick the word from the box that matches each picture, and write the word in the space. See sample "1."

car	bat	star	lady
apple	head	pan	flag
ant	lake	ball	barn

1. SAMPLE apple	**2.**	**3.**
4.	**5.**	**6.**
7.	**8.**	**9.**
10.	**11.**	**12.**

Number Recognition 1 — 5

Circle the numeral that shows the correct number of items in each set. See samples "A" and "B."

A. 0 1 2 3 4 5	B. 0 1 2 3 4 5	C. 0 1 2 3 4 5	D. 0 1 2 3 4 5
E. 0 1 2 3 4 5	F. 0 1 2 3 4 5	G. 0 1 2 3 4 5	H. 0 1 2 3 4 5
I. 0 1 2 3 4 5	J. 0 1 2 3 4 5	K. 0 1 2 3 4 5	L. 0 1 2 3 4 5
M. 0 1 2 3 4 5	N. 0 1 2 3 4 5	O. 0 1 2 3 4 5	P. 0 1 2 3 4 5
Q. 0 1 2 3 4 5	R. 0 1 2 3 4 5	S. 0 1 2 3 4 5	T. 0 1 2 3 4 5
U. 0 1 2 3 4 5	V. 0 1 2 3 4 5	W. 0 1 2 3 4 5	X. 0 1 2 3 4 5

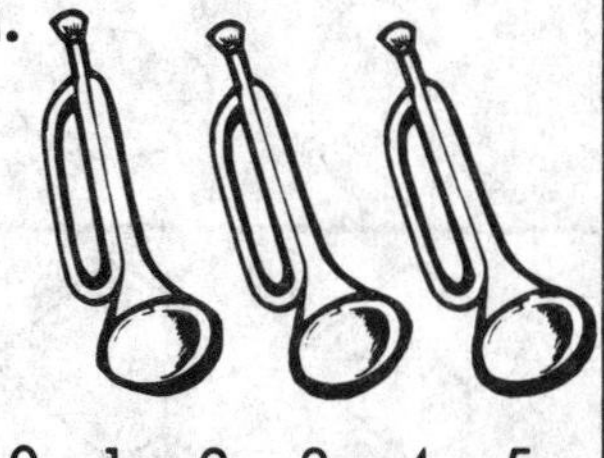

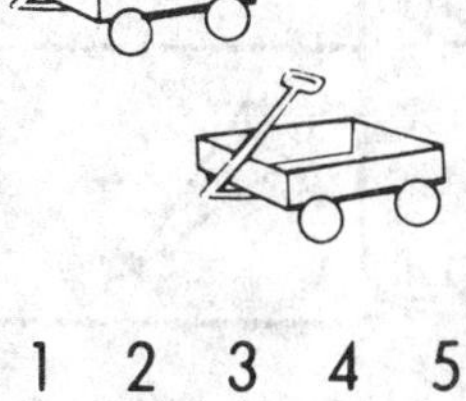

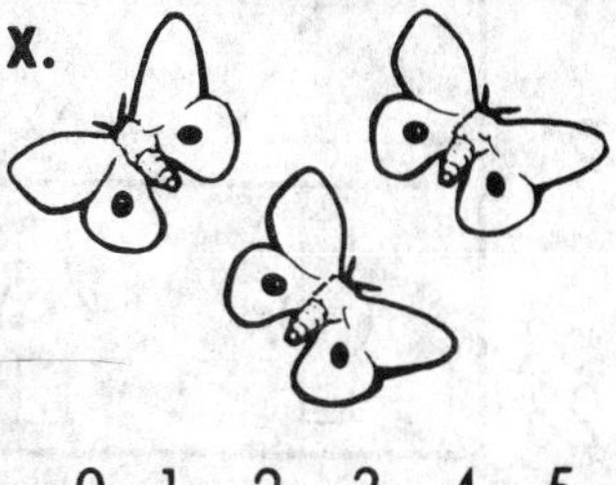

Direction Pointers

Draw an "X" through each one that points in the opposite direction. See examples "1" and "2."

1.

2.

3.

4.

5.

6.

7.

8.

9.

10.

11.

12.

13.

14.

15.

16.

17.

18.

19.

20.

21.

22.

23.

24.

"s" Endings

Draw a line under each word that ends in "s." See examples "1" and "2."

No.				No.			
1.	cake	cake	cakes	2.	works	work	work
3.	help	helps	help	4.	make	makes	make
5.	toys	toy	toy	6.	find	find	finds
7.	work	works	work	8.	boat	boats	boat
9.	hat	hat	hats	10.	feeds	feed	feed
11.	wants	want	want	12.	like	like	likes
13.	jump	jump	jumps	14.	rakes	rake	rake
15.	stop	stops	stop	16.	run	runs	run
17.	get	get	gets	18.	word	word	words
19.	seats	seat	seat	20.	boy	boys	boy
21.	look	looks	look	22.	girls	girl	girl
23.	farms	farm	farm	24.	cave	cave	caves
25.	cow	cows	cow	26.	dog	dogs	dog
27.	pig	pig	pigs	28.	boat	boat	boats
29.	cars	car	car	30.	hand	hands	hand
31.	ball	balls	ball	32.	goats	goat	goat

"m," "l" Sounds

A Listen to these words that have the "m" sound in them.

Beginning "m"	Middle "m"	End "m"
mittens	animal	room
moon	farmer	arm
mouse	woman	broom

Listen to these sounds of "m." If the "m" sound is at the beginning of the word, draw a line under the "B." If the "m" sound is in the middle of the word, draw a line under the "M." If the "m" sound is at the end of the word, draw a line under the "E."

EXAMPLES: meat B • M • E (B underlined) stomach B • M • E (M underlined) cream B • M • E (E underlined)

1. tomato B • M • E
2. morning B • M • E
3. men B • M • E
4. dream B • M • E
5. monkey B • M • E
6. lemonade B • M • E
7. bottom B • M • E
8. home B • M • E
9. medicine B • M • E
10. time B • M • E
11. money B • M • E
12. family B • M • E
13. Christmas B • M • E
14. mirror B • M • E
15. company B • M • E
16. umbrella B • M • E

B Listen to these words that have the "l" sound in them.

Beginning "l"	Middle "l"	End "l"
loud	alone	all
large	yellow	tell
long	hello	fall

Listen to these sounds of "l." If the "l" sound is at the beginning of the word, draw a line under the "B." If the "l" sound is in the middle of the word, draw a line under the "M." If the "l" sound is at the end of the word, draw a line under the "E."

1. pillow B • M • E
2. laugh B • M • E
3. eleven B • M • E
4. careful B • M • E
5. policeman B • M • E
6. line B • M • E
7. building B • M • E
8. leather B • M • E
9. shoulder B • M • E
10. live B • M • E
11. pail B • M • E
12. silver B • M • E
13. ugly B • M • E
14. bowl B • M • E
15. always B • M • E
16. pencil B • M • E

Which Are Words?

Circle the correctly spelled word that matches each picture.

See the example.

EXAMPLE:

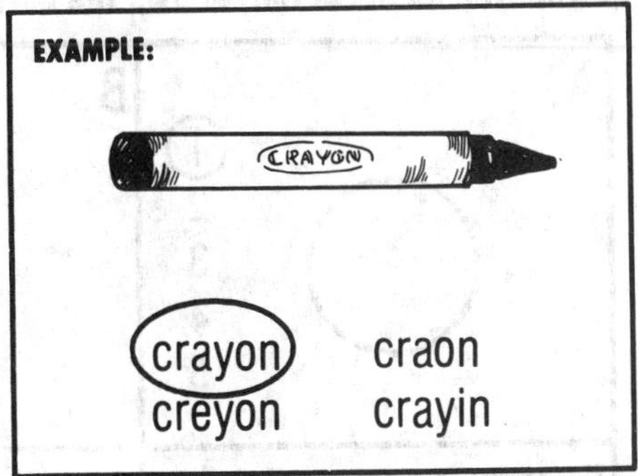

crayon craon
creyon crayin

1. appul appel
aple apple

2. lak lakke
lake laek

3. pan payn
pann paen

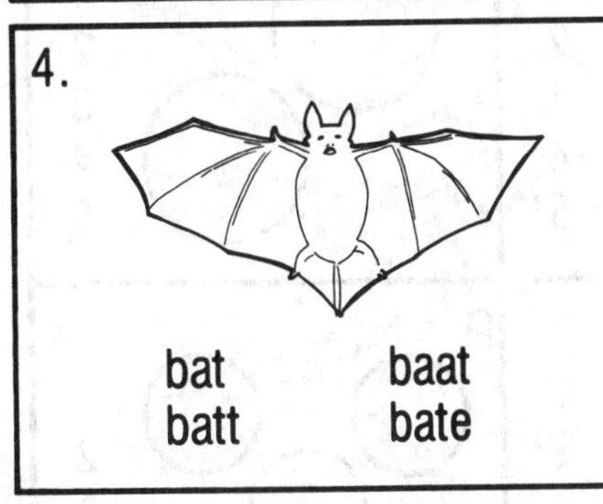

4. bat baat
batt bate

5. barne barnn
barrn barn

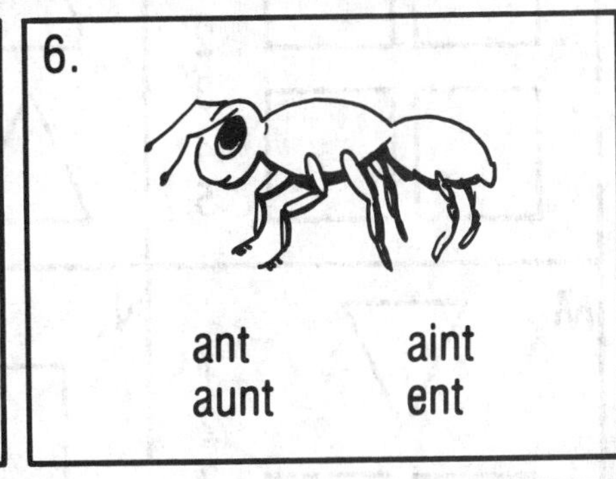

6. ant aint
aunt ent

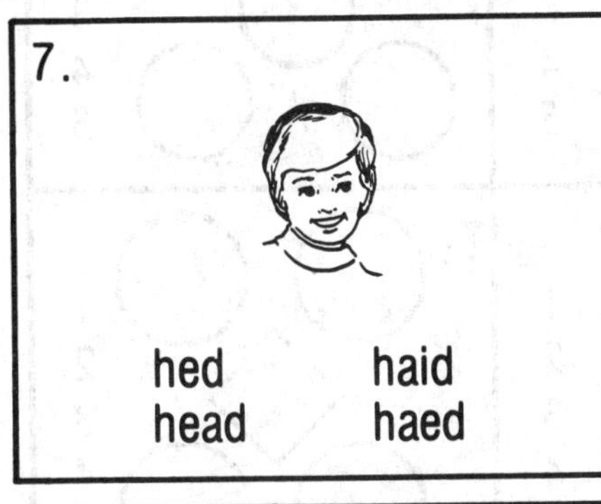

7. hed haid
head haed

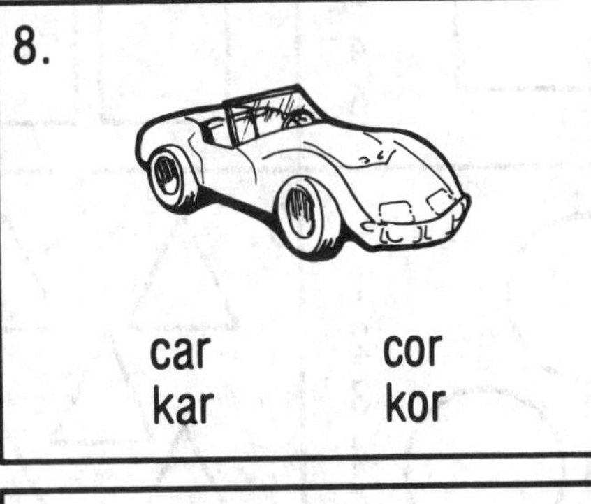

8. car cor
kar kor

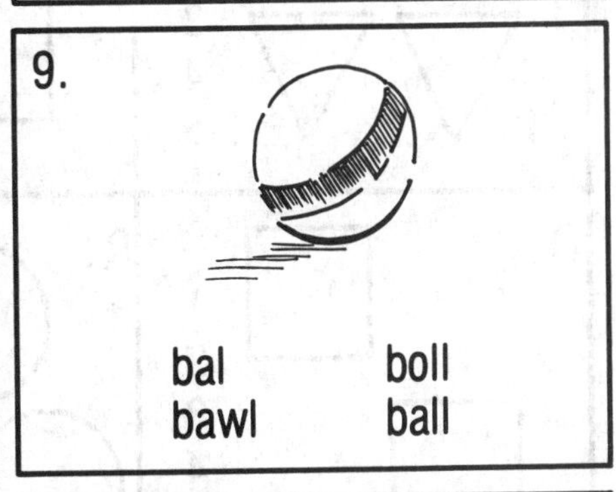

9. bal boll
bawl ball

10. fleg flag
flage falg

11. ladi lady
lade laddy

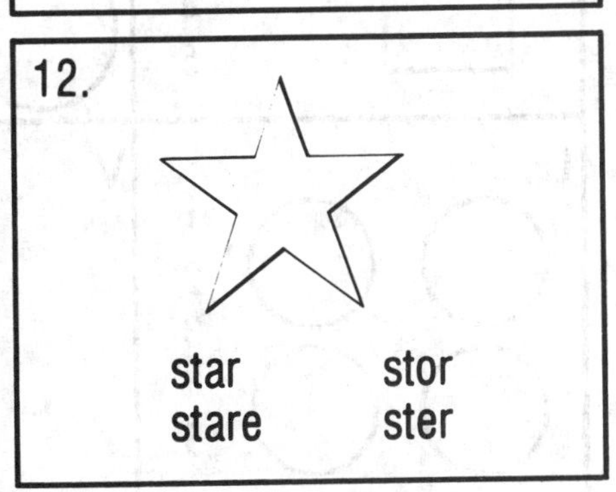

12. star stor
stare ster

Geometric Figures

Circle the numeral that shows the correct number of items in each set. See samples "A" and "B."

A. (1) 2 3 4 5	B. 1 (2) 3 4 5	C. 1 2 3 4 5	D. 1 2 3 4 5
E. 1 2 3 4 5	F. 1 2 3 4 5	G. 1 2 3 4 5	H. 1 2 3 4 5
I. 1 2 3 4 5	J. 1 2 3 4 5	K. 1 2 3 4 5	L. 1 2 3 4 5
M. 1 2 3 4 5	N. 1 2 3 4 5	O. 1 2 3 4 5	P. 1 2 3 4 5
Q. 1 2 3 4 5	R. 1 2 3 4 5	S. 1 2 3 4 5	T. 1 2 3 4 5
U. 1 2 3 4 5	V. 1 2 3 4 5	W. 1 2 3 4 5	X. 1 2 3 4 5

Descriptions of Words

Underline the answer that defines each word. Write your own sentence about each word.

1. **apple**
   a. a fruit that grows on trees
   b. a yellow vegetable
   c. a fruit that grows on the ground

2. **lake**
   a. rain water
   b. a body of water
   c. water from melted snow

3. **pan**
   a. something you drink out of
   b. something used to cook food in
   c. something you stir food with

4. **bat**
   a. a bird
   b. an insect
   c. a small animal that flies

5. **barn**
   a. a place where farm animals sleep
   b. a place where you park your car
   c. a place where money is kept

Size Discrimination

Draw an "X" through each one that is a different size. See examples "1" and "2."

1.		2.	
3.		4.	
5.		6.	
7.		8.	
9.		10.	
11.		12.	
13.		14.	
15.		16.	
17.		18.	
19.		20.	
21.		22.	
23.		24.	

(n) (p) Sounds

A Listen to these words that have the "n" sound in them.

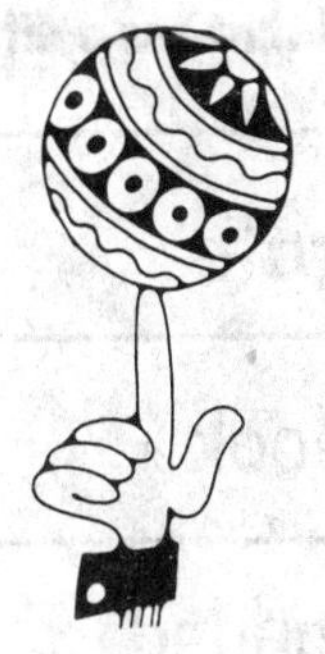

Beginning "n"	Middle "n"	End "n"
nap	candy	spin
nut	winter	sun
nest	picnic	rain

Listen to these sounds of "n." If the "n" sound is at the beginning of the word, draw a line under the "B." If the "n" sound is in the middle of the word, draw a line under the "M." If the "n" sound is at the end of the word, draw a line under the "E."

EXAMPLES: noise B • M • E (B underlined) money B • M • E (M underlined) spoon B • M • E (E underlined)

1. nail B • M • E
2. north B • M • E
3. pony B • M • E
4. dentist B • M • E
5. hen B • M • E
6. train B • M • E
7. corner B • M • E
8. nurse B • M • E
9. man B • M • E
10. funny B • M • E
11. chain B • M • E
12. balloon B • M • E
13. furniture B • M • E
14. nickel B • M • E
15. ribbon B • M • E
16. airplane B • M • E

B Listen to these words that have the "p" sound in them.

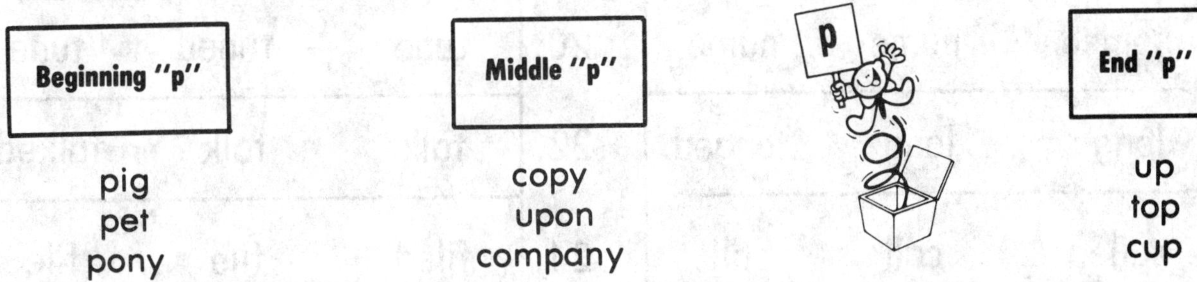

Beginning "p"	Middle "p"	End "p"
pig	copy	up
pet	upon	top
pony	company	cup

Listen to these sounds of "p." If the "p" sound is at the beginning of the word, draw a line under the "B." If the "p" sound is in the middle of the word, draw a line under the "M." If the "p" sound is at the end of the word, draw a line under the "E."

1. napkin B • M • E
2. sweep B • M • E
3. zipper B • M • E
4. paste B • M • E
5. penny B • M • E
6. expect B • M • E
7. sheep B • M • E
8. soap B • M • E
9. pocket B • M • E
10. sleep B • M • E
11. suppose B • M • E
12. happy B • M • E
13. puzzle B • M • E
14. captain B • M • E
15. stop B • M • E
16. paint B • M • E

Word Endings

Draw a line under each word that has a different ending. See examples "1" and "2."

1.	rate	rate	rated	2.	liked	like	like
3.	looked	look	look	4.	rake	raked	rake
5.	hand	handed	hand	6.	help	help	helped
7.	work	work	worked	8.	noted	note	note
9.	filed	file	file	10.	call	called	call
11.	talk	talked	talk	12.	long	long	longed
13.	tuned	tune	tune	14.	named	name	name
15.	want	want	wanted	16.	bake	baked	bake
17.	bake	baked	bake	18.	wanted	want	want
19.	named	name	name	20.	tune	tuned	tune
21.	long	long	longed	22.	talk	talk	talked
23.	called	call	call	24.	filed	file	file
25.	note	noted	note	26.	work	worked	work
27.	help	help	helped	28.	handed	hand	hand
29.	raked	rake	rake	30.	look	looked	look
31.	like	liked	like	32.	rate	rate	rated

More Than

Which set has more? In the following pairs of sets, write "X" in the blank of the set which has more. See sample "A."

A. 0 ____	1 __X__	B. 1 ____	2 ____
C. 1 ____	2 ____	D. 2 ____	0 ____
E. 2 ____	1 ____	F. 0 ____	2 ____
G. 3 ____	2 ____	H. 3 ____	1 ____
I. 4 ____	3 ____	J. 2 ____	4 ____
K. 5 ____	4 ____	L. 5 ____	3 ____

Word Meanings

Underline the answer that defines each word. Write your own sentence about each word.

1. **ant**
   a. a flower
   b. a small insect
   c. your uncle's wife

2. **head**
   a. the top part of the body
   b. the part of the body used for walking
   c. the part of the body next to the arms

3. **car**
   a. used to ride in on water
   b. has two wheels and driven on a road
   c. has four wheels and driven on a road

4. **ball**
   a. a round object used for games
   b. an object shaped like a box
   c. an object with three sides

5. **flag**
   a. a coin made of copper
   b. a cloth that stands for a country
   c. a cloth used to cover the head

Writing Words

Pick the word from the box that matches each picture, and write the word in the space. See sample "1."

broom	cube	bus	bird
cabin	boy	bow	bee
comb	tub	web	bear

1. sample

bee

2.

3.

4.

5.

6.

7.

8.

9.

10.

11.

12.

Less Than

Which set has less? In the following pairs of sets, write "X" in the blank of the set which has less. See sample "A."

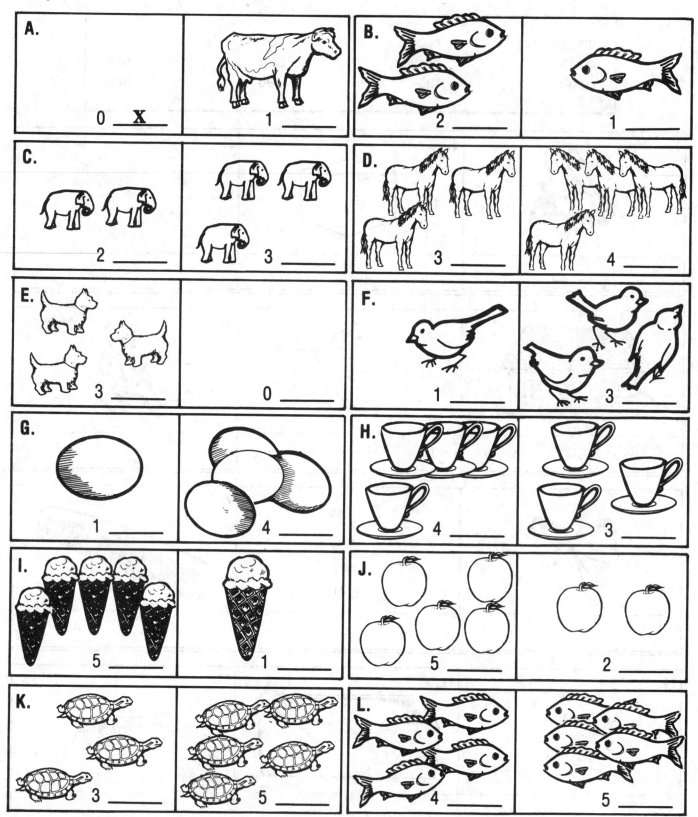

A.	0 X	1 ____
B.	2 ____	1 ____
C.	2 ____	3 ____
D.	3 ____	4 ____
E.	3 ____	0 ____
F.	1 ____	3 ____
G.	1 ____	4 ____
H.	4 ____	3 ____
I.	5 ____	1 ____
J.	5 ____	2 ____
K.	3 ____	5 ____
L.	4 ____	5 ____

Spelling Words

Circle the correctly spelled word that matches each picture.
See the example.

EXAMPLE:

angry (circled) | angri
angrey | angree

1.
be | bea
bee | bey

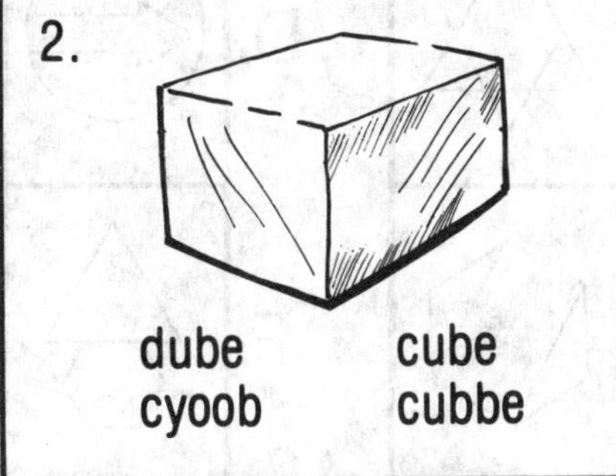

2.
dube | cube
cyoob | cubbe

3.
broom | brum
broome | brume

4.
kabin | cabbin
caben | cabin

5.
bird | berd
burd | byrd

6.
ber | beir
bear | bare

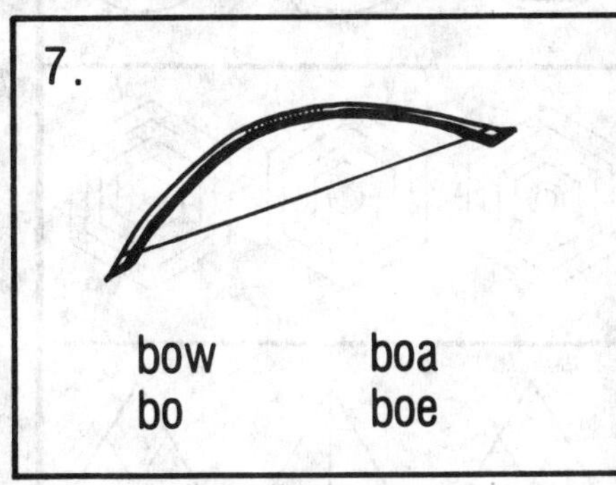

7.
bow | boa
bo | boe

8.
boi | boye
boiy | boy

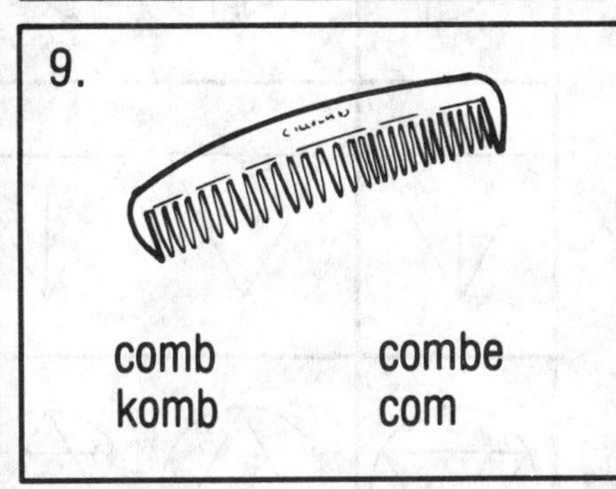

9.
comb | combe
komb | com

10.
webb | wib
web | wheb

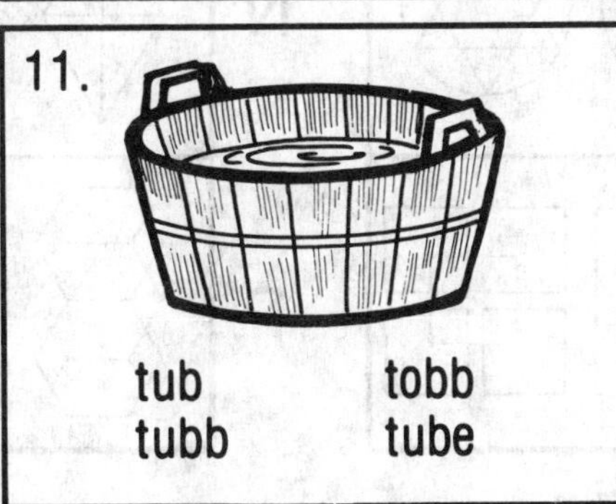

11.
tub | tobb
tubb | tube

12.
buss | bus
bos | busc

Which Is Like the First?

Draw an "X" through each one that is like the first. See example "A."

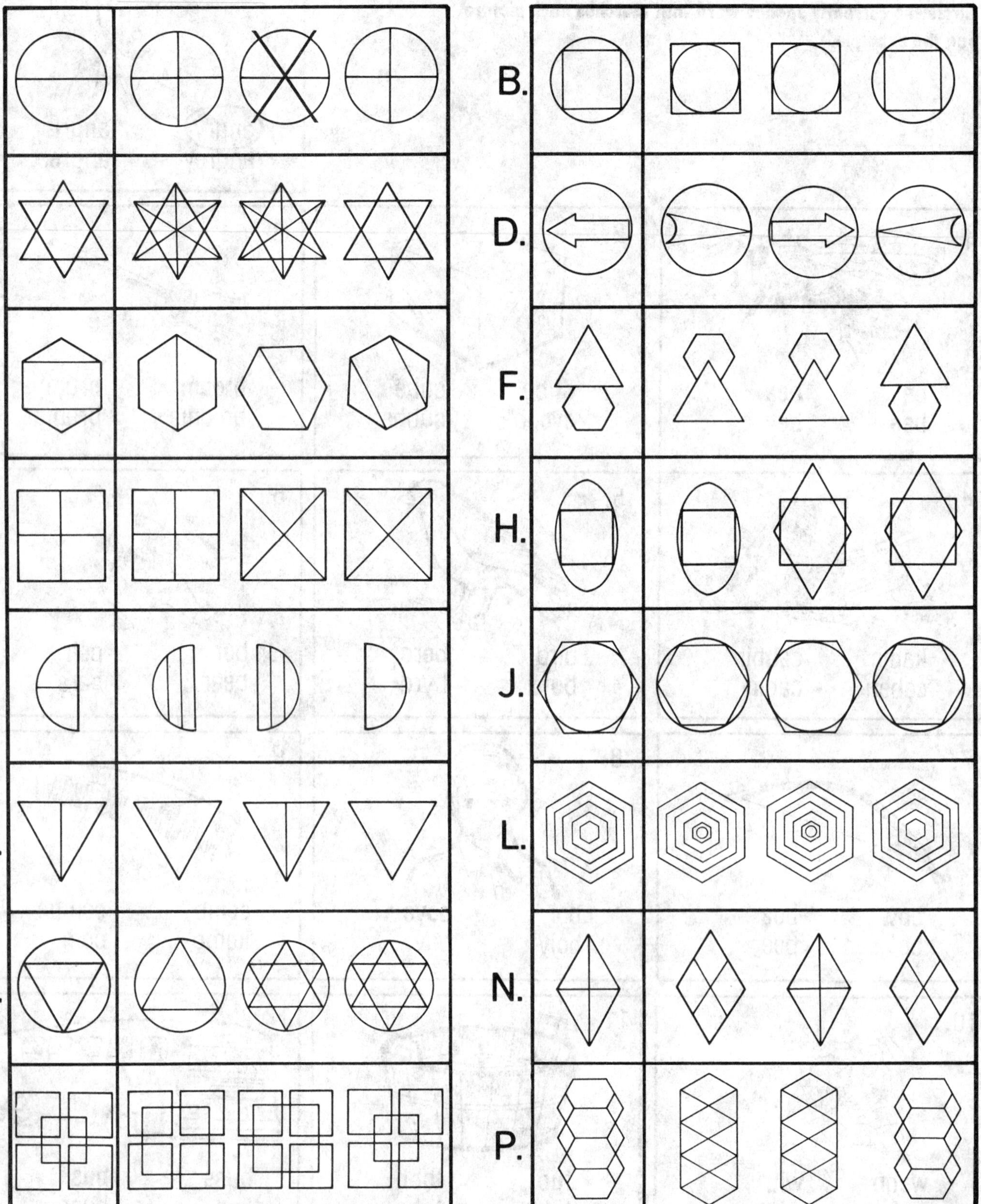

A.

B.

C.

D.

E.

F.

G.

H.

I.

J.

K.

L.

M.

N.

O.

P.

"q," "r" Sounds

A Listen to these words that have the "q" sound in them.

Beginning "q"	Middle "q"
quart	require
quick	square
quiz	request

Listen to these sounds of "q." If the "q" sound is at the beginning of the word, draw a line under the "B." If the "q" sound is in the middle of the word, draw a line under the "M." If the "q" sound is at the end of the word, draw a line under the "E."

EXAMPLES:

quantity	inquire	quick
<u>B</u> • M • E	B • <u>M</u> • E	<u>B</u> • M • E

quack 1. B • M • E	quail 2. B • M • E	frequent 3. B • M • E	quaint 4. B • M • E
esquire 5. B • M • E	quality 6. B • M • E	quarrel 7. B • M • E	queer 8. B • M • E
quell 9. B • M • E	earthquake 10. B • M • E	quest 11. B • M • E	quiet 12. B • M • E
equal 13. B • M • E	equip 14. B • M • E	equation 15. B • M • E	quit 16. B • M • E

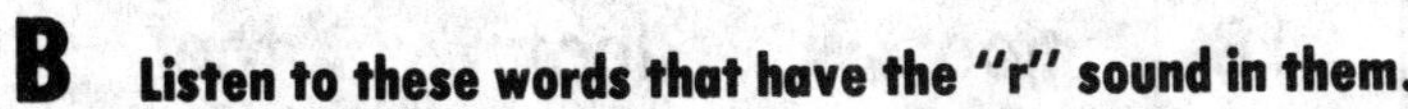

B Listen to these words that have the "r" sound in them.

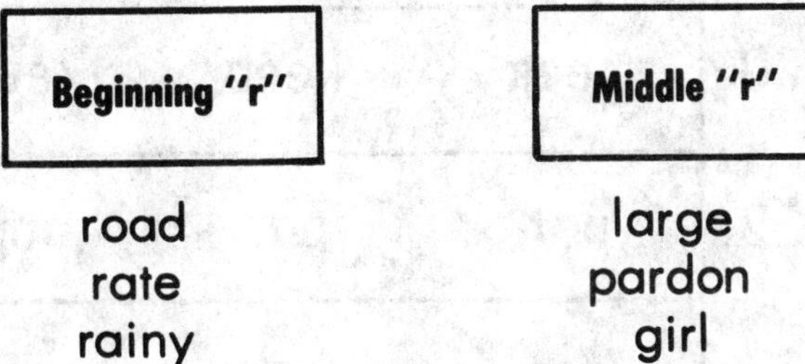

Beginning "r"	Middle "r"	End "r"
road	large	officer
rate	pardon	owner
rainy	girl	pear

Listen to these sounds of "r." If the "r" sound is at the beginning of the word, draw a line under the "B." If the "r" sound is in the middle of the word, draw a line under the "M." If the "r" sound is at the end of the word, draw a line under the "E."

orange 1. B • M • E	rag 2. B • M • E	marries 3. B • M • E	giver 4. B • M • E
radish 5. B • M • E	older 6. B • M • E	Saturday 7. B • M • E	ranger 8. B • M • E
scram 9. B • M • E	sport 10. B • M • E	gear 11. B • M • E	park 12. B • M • E
rust 13. B • M • E	curtain 14. B • M • E	afternoon 15. B • M • E	water 16. B • M • E

Word Reversals

Draw a line under each word that is reversed. See examples "1" and "2."

1.	wed	<u>dew</u>	wed	2.	tub	tub	<u>but</u>
3.	pan	pan	nap	4.	gas	sag	sag
5.	saw	was	was	6.	won	now	won
7.	not	ton	not	8.	pit	tip	tip
9.	top	top	pot	10.	nab	nab	ban
11.	tap	pat	tap	12.	gip	pig	gip
13.	peek	keep	peek	14.	war	raw	raw
15.	tool	loot	loot	16.	bad	dab	bad
17.	bad	dab	dab	18.	loot	loot	tool
19.	war	war	raw	20.	peek	keep	keep
21.	pig	gip	pig	22.	pat	pat	tap
23.	nab	ban	ban	24.	top	pot	pot
25.	pit	tip	pit	26.	ton	not	ton
27.	now	now	won	28.	saw	saw	was
29.	sag	gas	gas	30.	pan	nap	nap
31.	but	tub	but	32.	dew	wed	dew

Number Recognition 6 — 9

Fill in each blank with the number of items in each set. See samples "A" and "B."

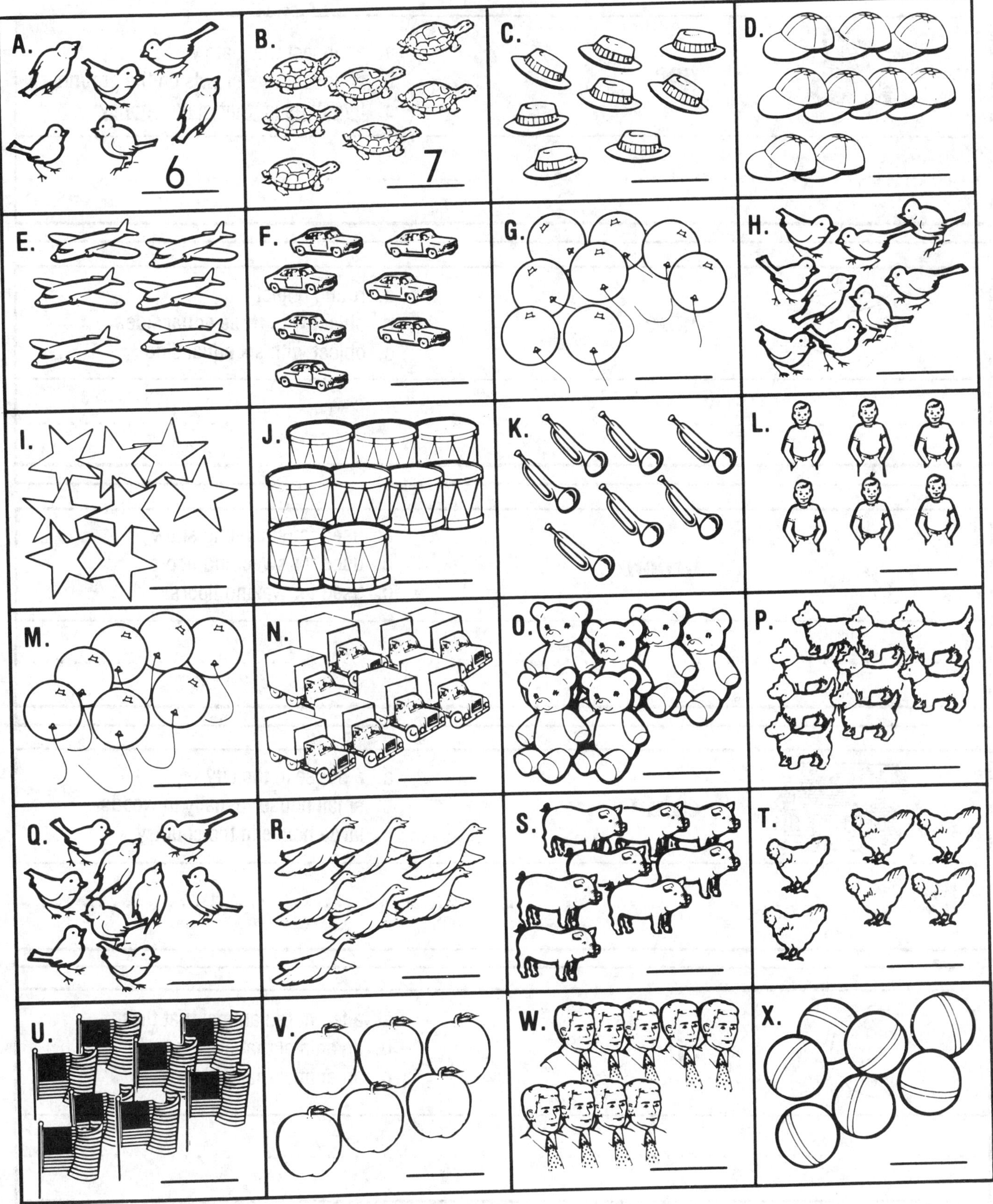

Word Descriptions

Underline the answer that defines each word. Write your own sentence about each word.

1. **bee**
   a. an insect that eats wood
   b. an insect that crawls on the ground
   c. flying insect that makes honey

2. **cube**
   a. round object
   b. object with three equal sides
   c. object with six equal sides

3. **broom**
   a. used for shoveling snow
   b. used for sweeping floors
   c. used for waxing floors

4. **cabin**
   a. a house in the city
   b. small house, usually in woods
   c. large house in the country

5. **bird**
   a. a feathered animal that flies
   b. an animal that crawls
   c. an animal that swims

Matching Capital Letter Forms

Draw an "X" through each letter that is different. See example "1."

1. A A / A ~~B~~
2. B C / B B
3. C C / D C
4. D D / E D
5. E F / E E
6. F F / G F
7. G G / G H
8. H I / H H
9. I I / J I
10. J J / J K
11. K L / K K
12. L L / M L
13. N O / N N
14. O O / P O
15. P P / P Q
16. Q R / Q Q
17. R R / S R
18. S S / S T
19. T U / T T
20. U U / V U

Number Words 1 — 5

Write in the blank the correct numeral for each word.

A. one 1	**B.** two ____	**C.** three ____	**D.** four ____
E. five ____	**F.** three ____	**G.** four ____	**H.** one ____
I. three ____	**J.** four ____	**K.** one ____	**L.** two ____
M. four ____	**N.** five ____	**O.** two ____	**P.** three ____
Q. two ____	**R.** one ____	**S.** five ____	**T.** four ____
U. one ____	**V.** two ____	**W.** three ____	**X.** five ____

"s," "t" Sounds

A Listen to the words that have the "s" sound in them.

Beginning "s"	Middle "s"	End "s"
see	beside	yes
sell	Easter	dress
sun	listen	case

Listen to these sounds of "s." If the "s" sound is at the beginning of the word, draw a line under the "B." If the "s" sound is in the middle of the word, draw a line under the "M." If the "s" sound is at the end of the word, draw a line under the "E."

EXAMPLES:

saw — B • M • E (B underlined)
outside — B • M • E (M underlined)
kiss — B • M • E (E underlined)

1. summer B • M • E	2. silver B • M • E	3. question B • M • E	4. glass B • M • E
5. whisper B • M • E	6. house B • M • E	7. city B • M • E	8. across B • M • E
9. medicine B • M • E	10. circle B • M • E	11. piece B • M • E	12. yesterday B • M • E
13. grocery B • M • E	14. soup B • M • E	15. mouse B • M • E	16. accident B • M • E

B Listen to these words that have the "t" sound in them.

Beginning "t"	Middle "t"	End "t"
town	sister	meat
toy	party	cat
tow	button	coat

Listen to these sounds of "t." If the "t" sound is at the beginning of the word, draw a line under the "B." If the "t" sound is in the middle of the word, draw a line under the "M." If the "t" sound is at the end of the word, draw a line under the "E."

1. basket B • M • E	2. rooster B • M • E	3. town B • M • E	4. fruit B • M • E
5. teacher B • M • E	6. kitten B • M • E	7. skirt B • M • E	8. tongue B • M • E
9. winter B • M • E	10. tired B • M • E	11. sweet B • M • E	12. afternoon B • M • E
13. towel B • M • E	14. night B • M • E	15. scooter B • M • E	16. butterfly B • M • E

Defining Words

Underline the answer that defines each word. Write your own sentence about each word.

1. **bear**
   a. an animal with no fur
   b. a small animal with a bushy tail
   c. a large animal with thick fur

2. **bow**
   a. a linked chain
   b. a looped knot
   c. a loose string

3. **boy**
   a. a male child
   b. a female child
   c. another word for ''man''

4. **comb**
   a. used to arrange the hair
   b. used to brush the teeth
   c. used to wash the hair

5. **web**
   a. a spider's home
   b. a fly's home
   c. an ant's home

Confusing Words

Draw a line under each word that is different. See examples "1" and "2."

1.	hammer	hammer	hamper	2.	hone	home	hone
3.	bread	beard	beard	4.	court	count	count
5.	brood	broad	brood	6.	dance	dance	dunce
7.	torch	torch	touch	8.	lower	lover	lower
9.	chew	chow	chew	10.	stick	stick	stuck
11.	clear	clean	clean	12.	warn	warm	warm
13.	soap	soup	soap	14.	moved	mowed	moved
15.	slain	slain	snail	16.	lion	loin	loin
17.	dared	dread	dread	18.	untie	untie	unite
19.	stored	stored	sorted	20.	board	broad	board
21.	indent	intend	indent	22.	bride	bride	bribe
23.	staple	staple	stable	24.	dump	dumb	dumb
25.	flap	flag	flag	26.	pack	pack	back
27.	scared	sacred	scared	28.	trails	traits	trails
29.	quiet	quite	quite	30.	fried	fried	fired
31.	house	house	horse	32.	daisy	dairy	dairy

Recognizing Shapes

Match the shapes on the left with the correct descriptions on the right. See the sample.

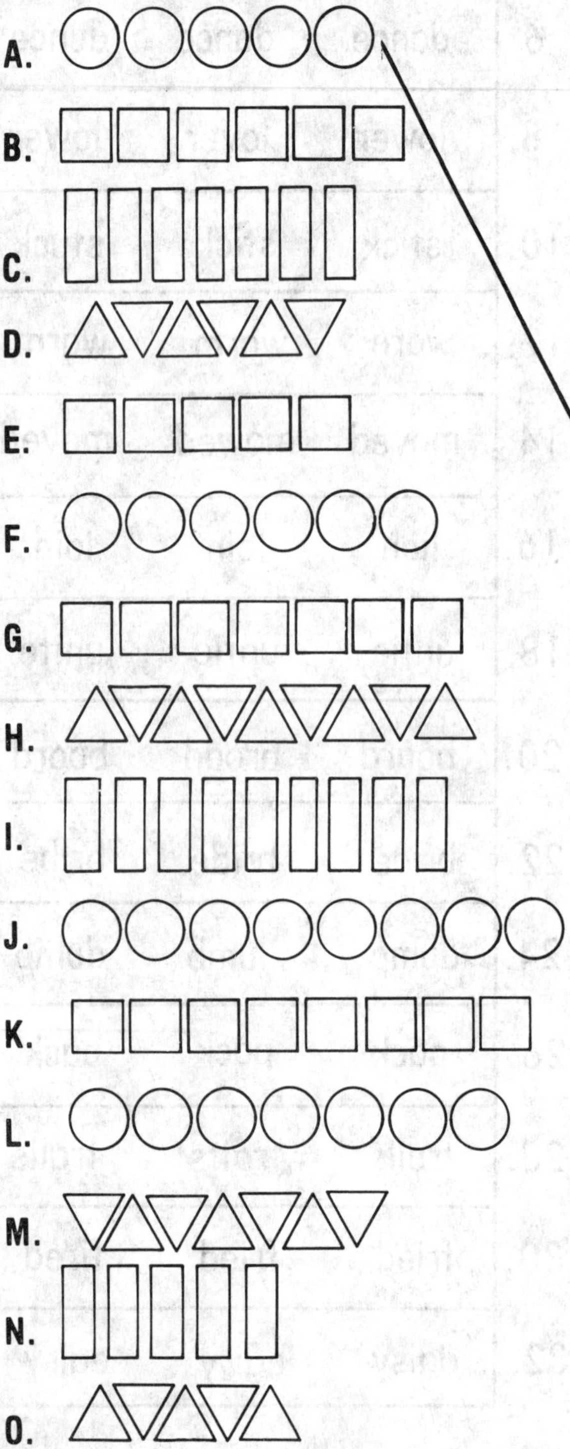

A.
B.
C.
D.
E.
F.
G.
H.
I.
J.
K.
L.
M.
N.
O.

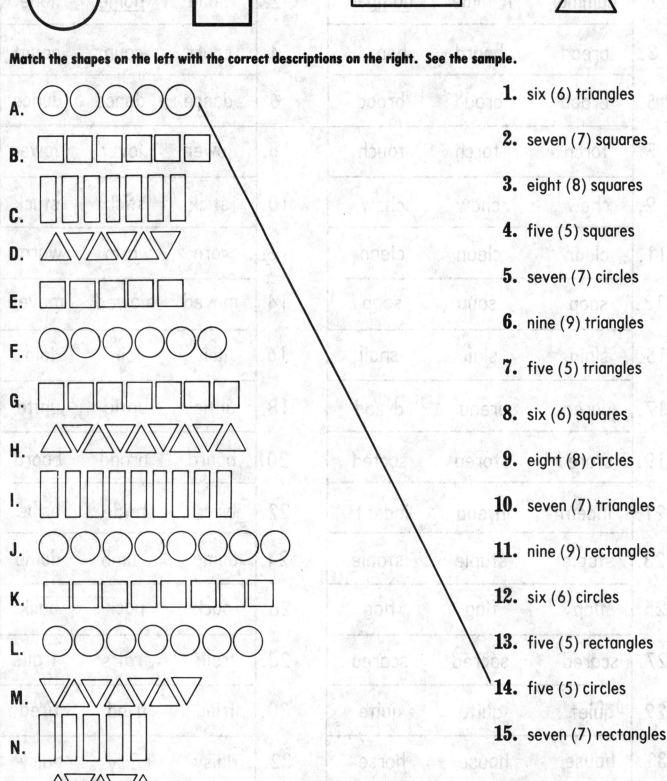

1. six (6) triangles
2. seven (7) squares
3. eight (8) squares
4. five (5) squares
5. seven (7) circles
6. nine (9) triangles
7. five (5) triangles
8. six (6) squares
9. eight (8) circles
10. seven (7) triangles
11. nine (9) rectangles
12. six (6) circles
13. five (5) rectangles
14. five (5) circles
15. seven (7) rectangles

What Are the Pictures?

Pick the word from the box that matches each picture, and write the word in the space. See sample "1."

cap	sack	cake	tack
sock	face	coat	ice
cage	cat	cup	cone

1. **SAMPLE**

coat

2.

3.

4.

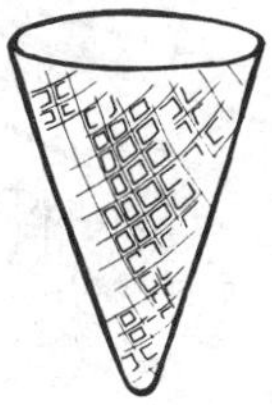

5.

6.

7.

8.

9.

10.

11.

12.

Spelling Words for Fun

Circle the correctly spelled word that matches each picture. See the example.

EXAMPLE:

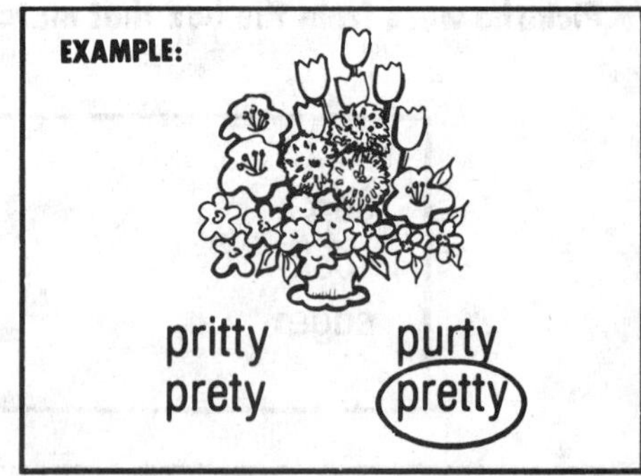

pritty purty
prety pretty

1.

koat cote
kote coat

2.

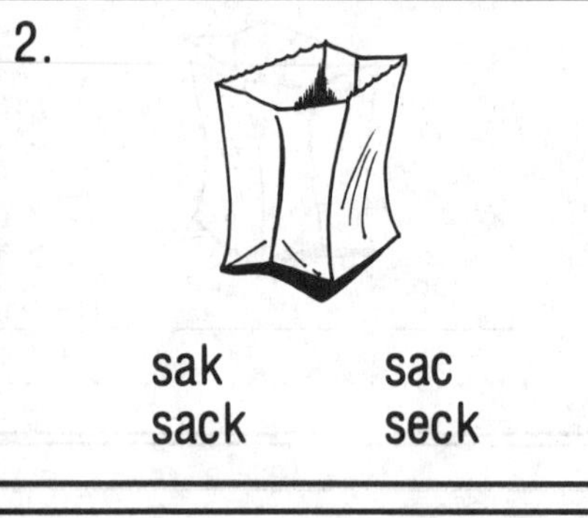

sak sac
sack seck

3.

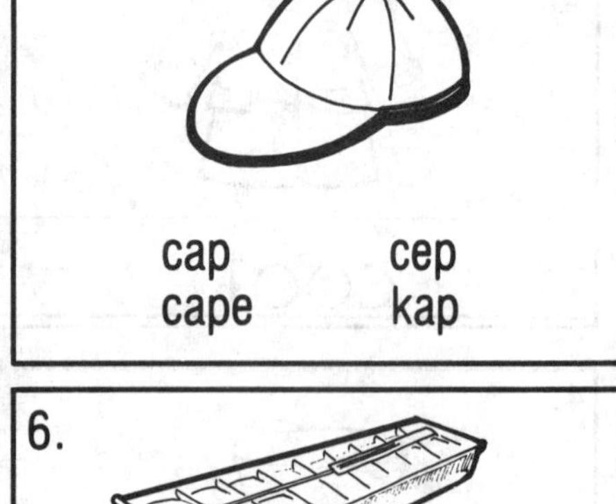

cap cep
cape kap

4.

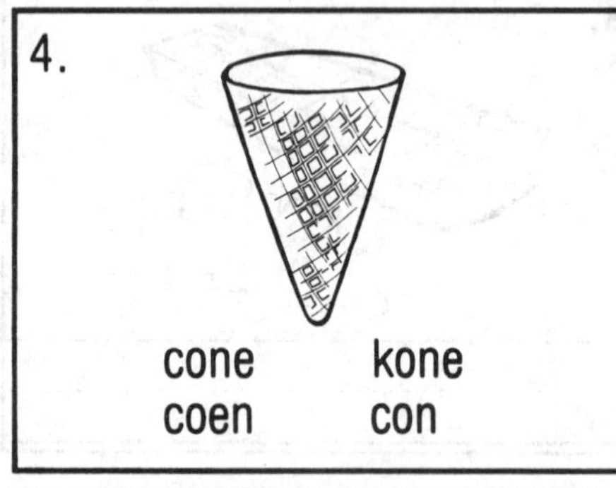

cone kone
coen con

5.

caek cake
kake cakk

6.

ice ise
iyc eice

7.

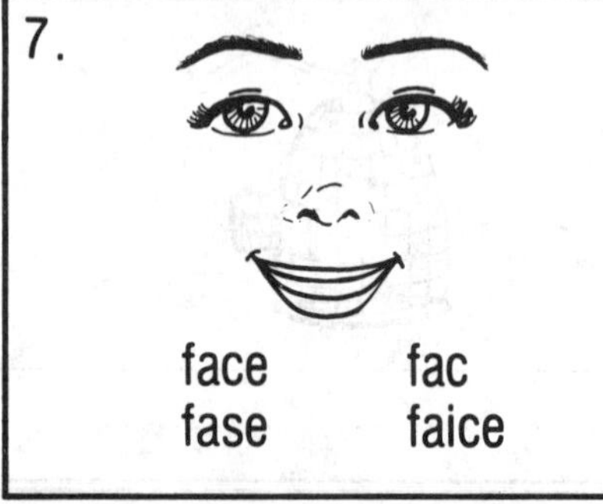

face fac
fase faice

8.

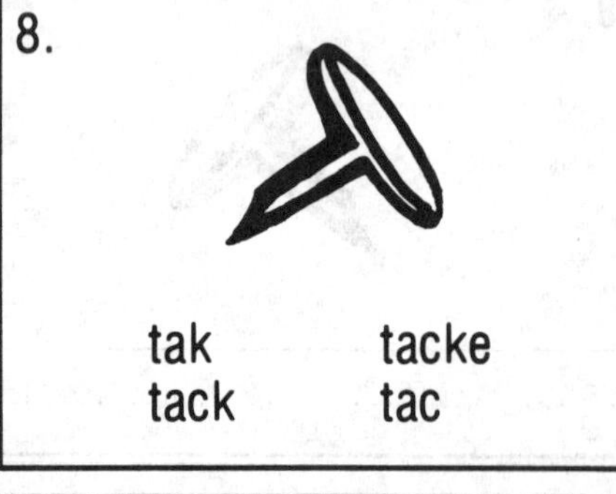

tak tacke
tack tac

9.

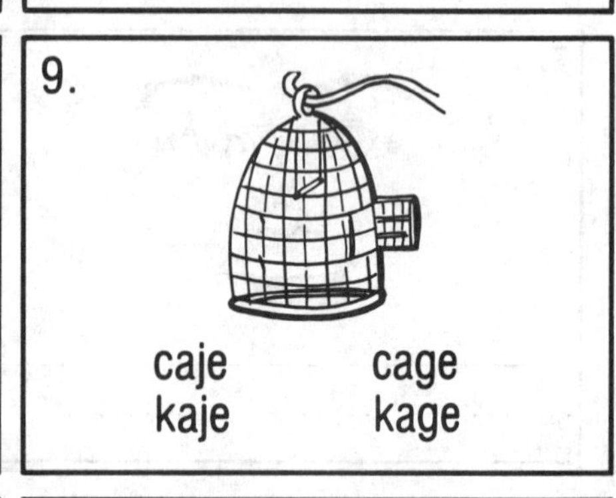

caje cage
kaje kage

10.

kup cup
kupp cupp

11.

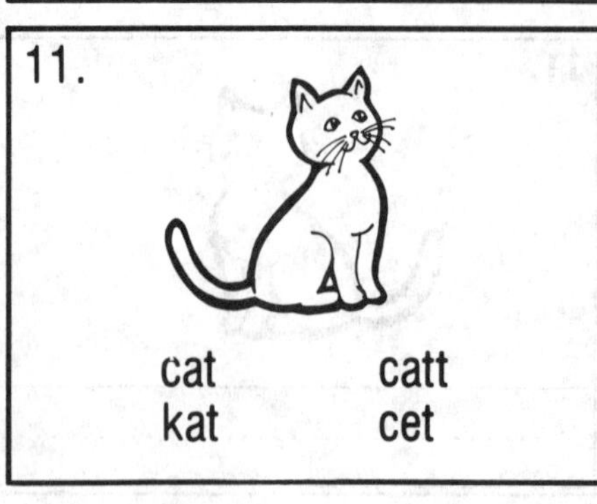

cat catt
kat cet

12.

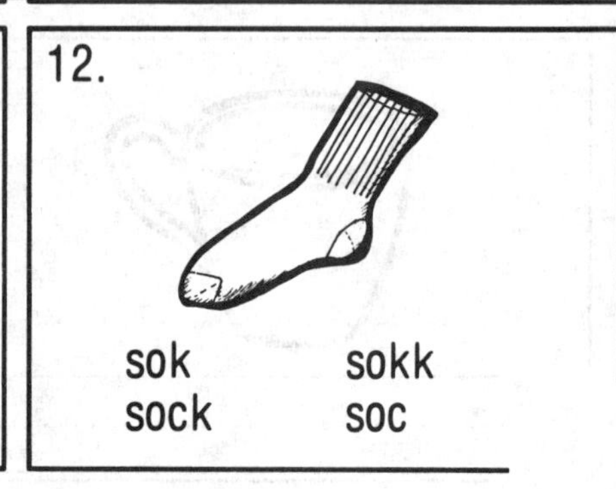

sok sokk
sock soc

Define Words

Underline the answer that defines each word. Write your own sentence about each word.

1. **coat**
   a. worn in very warm weather
   b. worn in place of a shirt
   c. worn over other clothes to keep warm

2. **sack**
   a. a bag made of metal
   b. a large bag
   c. a box made of thin paper

3. **cap**
   a. covering for the head
   b. a covering for the hand
   c. a covering for the foot

4. **cone**
   a. a round object
   b. a square object
   c. object flat on one end and pointed at other

5. **cake**
   a. a baked, sweet dessert
   b. a food eaten at breakfast
   c. a food eaten in place of vegetables

How Many?

A **Write the numeral in the blank beside each word. Then write the word in the blank underneath.**

1. eight 8 eight
2. five
3. four
4. nine
5. seven
6. six
7. three
8. two
9. zero
10. one
11. eleven
12. ten

B **How many elephants are in each of the following rows? Write the numeral in the first blank and the name of the numeral in the second blank.**

1. 1 one
2.
3.
4.
5.
6.
7.
8.
9.

Matching Lower-Case Letters

Draw an "X" through each letter that is different. See example "1."

1. a a / a b
2. b b / c b
3. c c / c d
4. d e / d d
5. e f / e e
6. f f / g f
7. g g / h g
8. h i / h h
9. i i / j i
10. j j / j k
11. k l / k k
12. l l / m l
13. m m / m n
14. n o / n n
15. o o / p o
16. p p / p q
17. q q / r q
18. s t / s s
19. t t / u t
20. u v / u u

"v," "x" Sounds

A Listen to these words that have the "v" sound in them.

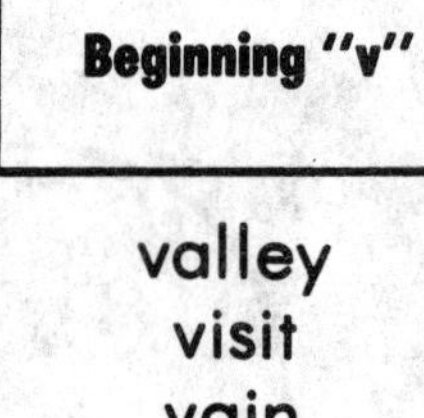

Beginning "v"	Middle "v"	End "v"
valley	river	above
visit	ever	give
vain	eleven	serve

Listen to these sounds of "v." If the "v" sound is at the beginning of the word, draw a line under the "B." If the "v" sound is in the middle of the word, draw a line under the "M." If the "v" sound is at the end of the word, draw a line under the "E."

EXAMPLES:

van	every	save
<u>B</u> • M • E	B • <u>M</u> • E	B • M • <u>E</u>

cover 1. B • M • E	drive 2. B • M • E	over 3. B • M • E	vault 4. B • M • E
everything 5. B • M • E	vail 6. B • M • E	love 7. B • M • E	village 8. B • M • E
heavy 9. B • M • E	Virginia 10. B • M • E	overalls 11. B • M • E	gave 12. B • M • E
evening 13. B • M • E	violent 14. B • M • E	waving 15. B • M • E	leave 16. B • M • E

B Listen to these words that have the "x" sound in them.

Beginning "x"	Middle "x"	End "x"
except	text	box
exchange	waxed	fox
excite	oxen	lax

Listen to these sounds of "x." If the "x" sound is at the beginning of the word, draw a line under the "B." If the "x" sound is in the middle of the word, draw a line under the "M." If the "x" sound is at the end of the word, draw a line under the "E."

excrete 1. B • M • E	sixth 2. B • M • E	flux 3. B • M • E	boxing 4. B • M • E
tuxedo 5. B • M • E	excitement 6. B • M • E	mix 7. B • M • E	hexagon 8. B • M • E
exclude 9. B • M • E	sandbox 10. B • M • E	texture 11. B • M • E	flex 12. B • M • E
Mexican 13. B • M • E	excise 14. B • M • E	fixation 15. B • M • E	taxable 16. B • M • E

Number Transposition

Draw a line under each number that is transposed. See examples "A" and "B."

A.	10	10	10	01	B.	12	21	12	12
C.	13	31	13	13	D.	14	14	41	14
E.	14	14	14	41	F.	51	15	15	15
G.	61	16	16	16	H.	17	17	17	71
I.	18	18	81	18	J.	19	91	19	19
K.	20	02	20	20	L.	23	23	32	23
M.	32	23	23	23	N.	24	24	24	42
O.	25	25	52	25	P.	62	26	26	26
Q.	27	27	27	72	R.	28	82	28	28
S.	29	92	29	29	T.	30	30	03	30
U.	30	30	03	30	V.	34	34	34	43
W.	53	35	35	35	X.	36	63	36	36
Y.	37	37	37	73	Z.	38	38	83	38
A.	39	93	39	39	B.	04	40	40	40
C.	45	45	54	45	D.	46	46	46	64
E.	74	47	47	47	F.	48	84	48	48

Number Words 6 — 9

Write in the blank the correct numeral for each word.

A. six 6	**B.** seven ____	**C.** eight ____	**D.** nine ____
E. seven ____	**F.** eight ____	**G.** nine ____	**H.** six ____
I. eight ____	**J.** nine ____	**K.** six ____	**L.** seven ____
M. nine ____	**N.** six ____	**O.** seven ____	**P.** eight ____
Q. seven ____	**R.** nine ____	**S.** six ____	**T.** seven ____
U. nine ____	**V.** six ____	**W.** seven ____	**X.** eight ____

Word Definitions

Underline the answer that defines each word. Write your own sentence about each word.

1. **ice**
   a. frozen water
   b. very warm water
   c. rain water

2. **face**
   a. the side of the head
   b. the front of the head
   c. the back of the head

3. **tack**
   a. a big needle
   b. a long thin nail
   c. a short nail with a flat, broad head

4. **cage**
   a. a door with no lock
   b. an open room
   c. a fenced-in area

5. **cup**
   a. a dish used for eating
   b. a dish used for drinking
   c. a dish used for baking

Naming Pictures

Pick the word from the box that matches each picture, and write the word in the space. See sample "1."

duck	cold	deer	hand
drum	bread	door	wood
candy	end	bed	card

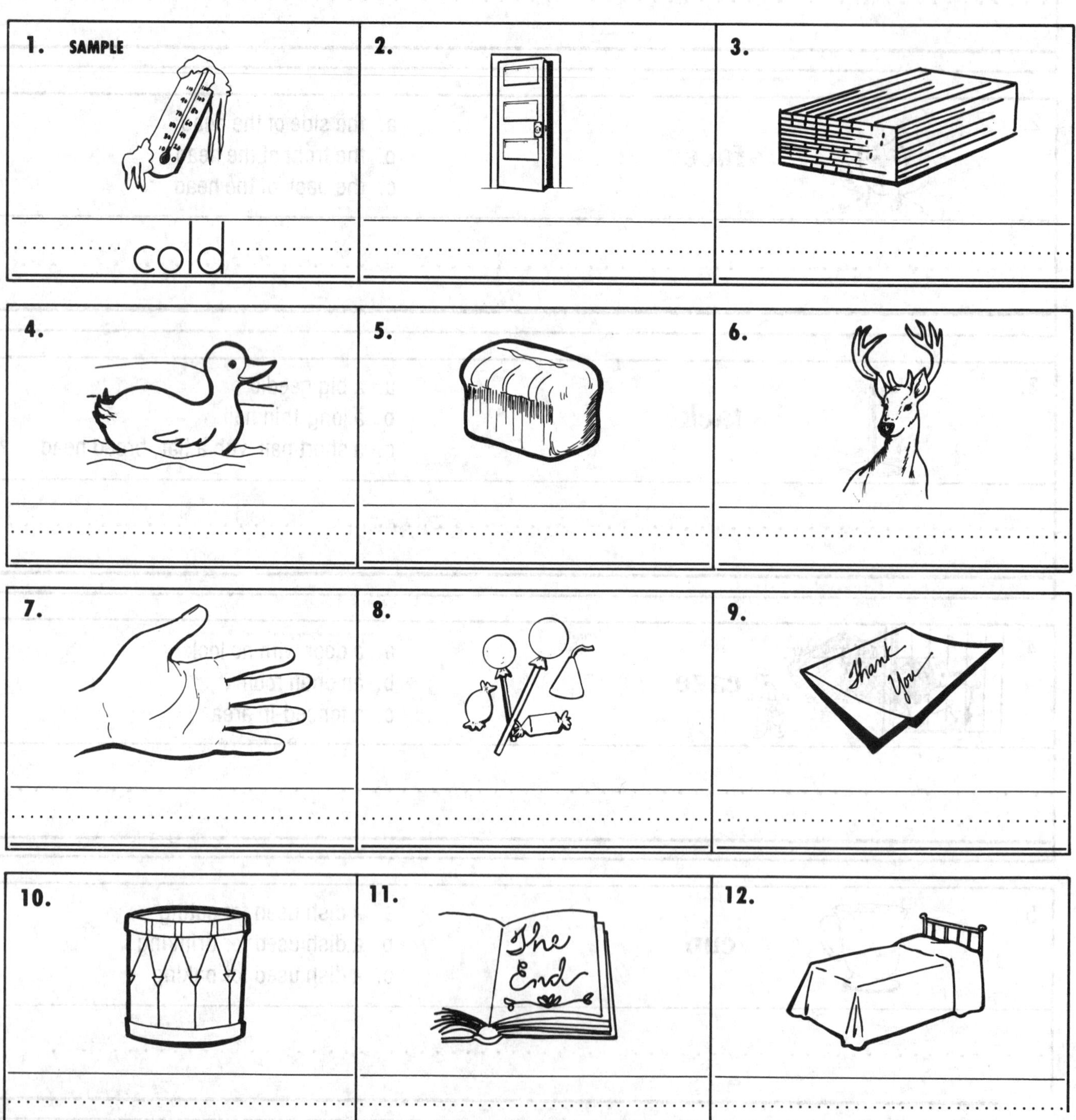

Spelling Words Correctly

Circle the correctly spelled word that matches each picture. See the example.

EXAMPLE:

hai hey
(hay) haye

1. 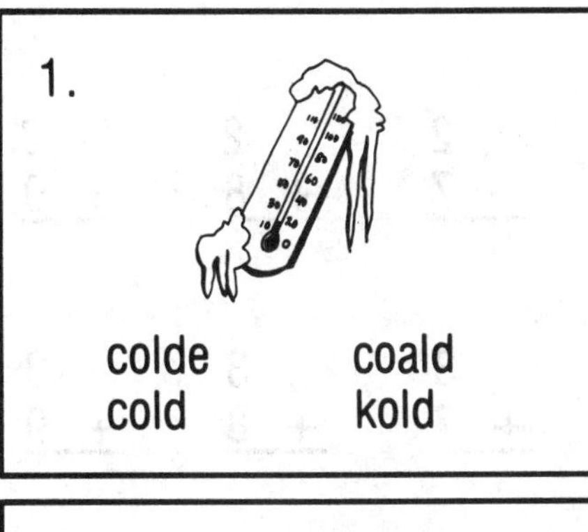

colde coald
cold kold

2. 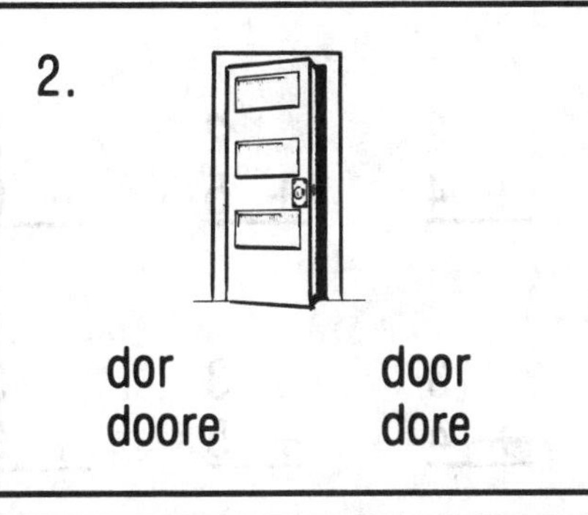

dor door
doore dore

3. 

wood wud
woud would

4. 

duck duc
duk dock

5. 

bred braed
brid bread

6. 

deer dear
dere dir

7. 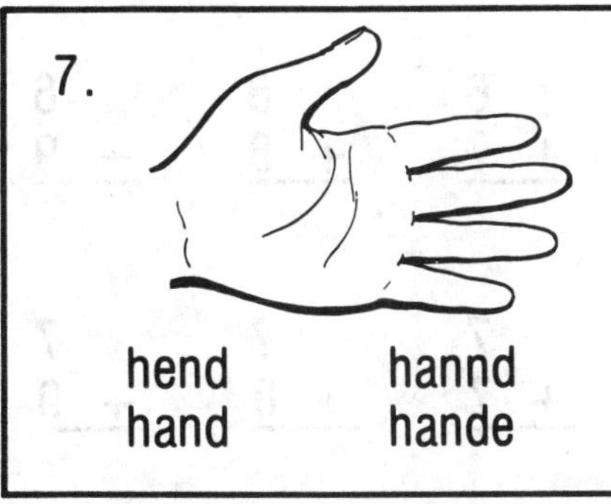

hend hannd
hand hande

8. 

candy kande
candee kandy

9. 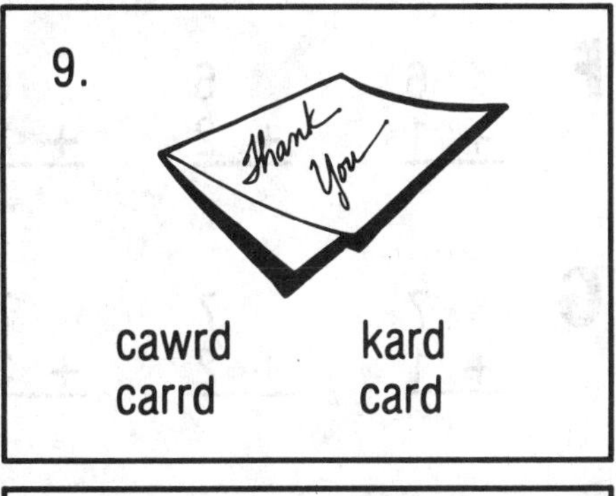

cawrd kard
carrd card

10. 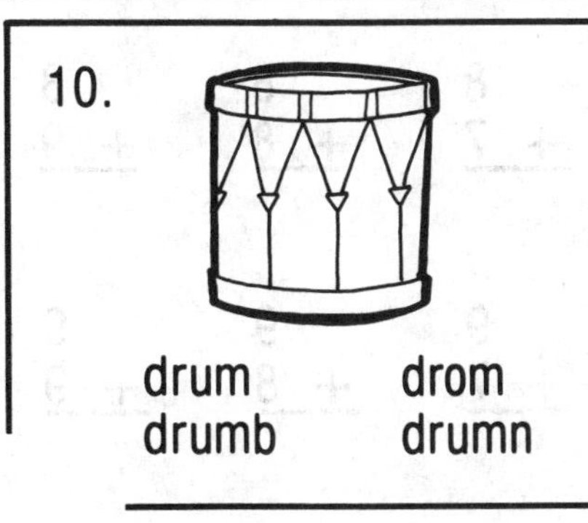

drum drom
drumb drumn

11. 

ennd innd
ind end

12. 

baed beid
bed bid

Addition Facts

You should learn the following facts so you can use them quickly and easily. You will be using these facts in your daily life.

Write the answer for each problem.

A	1 + 1 2	1 + 2	1 + 3	1 + 4	1 + 5	1 + 6	1 + 7	1 + 8	1 + 9
B	2 + 1	2 + 2	2 + 3	2 + 4	2 + 5	2 + 6	2 + 7	2 + 8	2 + 9
C	3 + 1	3 + 2	3 + 3	3 + 4	3 + 5	3 + 6	3 + 7	3 + 8	3 + 9
D	4 + 1	4 + 2	4 + 3	4 + 4	4 + 5	4 + 6	4 + 7	4 + 8	4 + 9
E	5 + 1	5 + 2	5 + 3	5 + 4	5 + 5	5 + 6	5 + 7	5 + 8	5 + 9
F	6 + 1	6 + 2	6 + 3	6 + 4	6 + 5	6 + 6	6 + 7	6 + 8	6 + 9
G	7 + 1	7 + 2	7 + 3	7 + 4	7 + 5	7 + 6	7 + 7	7 + 8	7 + 9
H	8 + 1	8 + 2	8 + 3	8 + 4	8 + 5	8 + 6	8 + 7	8 + 8	8 + 9
I	9 + 1	9 + 2	9 + 3	9 + 4	9 + 5	9 + 6	9 + 7	9 + 8	9 + 9

Upper- and Lower-Case Matching

Draw an "X" through each one that is different. See example "1."

1. V V / V W
2. W X / W W
3. X X / Y X
4. Y Y / Y Z
5. Z Z / A Z
6. v v / w v
7. w w / x w
8. x x / y x
9. y z / y y
10. z z / z a
11. V V / v V
12. W W / W w
13. X X / x X
14. Y y / Y Y
15. z Z / Z Z
16. v v / V v
17. w w / w W
18. x x / X x
19. y Y / y y
20. Z z / z z

Counting Sets

Count the dots in each set; then write the number in the box below. See examples "A" and "B."

A. 1	B. 2	C.	D.	E.	F.	G.	H.	I.
J.	K.	L.	M.	N.	O.	P.	Q.	R.
S.	T.	U.	V.	W.	X.	Y.	Z.	A.
B.	C.	D.	E.	F.	G.	H.	I.	J.
K.	L.	M.	N.	O.	P.	Q.	R.	S.
T.	U.	V.	W.	X.	Y.	Z.	A.	B.

"z," "b" Sounds

A Listen to these words that have the "z" sound in them.

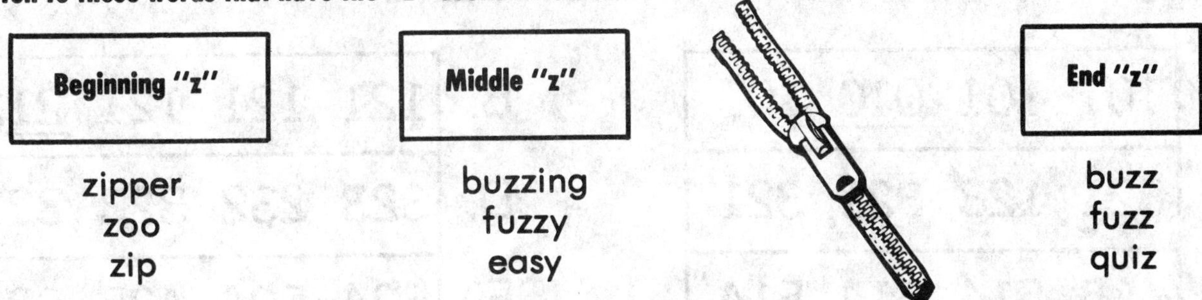

Beginning "z"	Middle "z"	End "z"
zipper	buzzing	buzz
zoo	fuzzy	fuzz
zip	easy	quiz

Listen to these sounds of "z." If the "z" sound is at the beginning of the word, draw a line under the "B." If the "z" sound is in the middle of the word, draw a line under the "M." If the "z" sound is at the end of the word, draw a line under the "E."

EXAMPLES:

zest B • M • E (B underlined)
quizzing B • M • E (M underlined)
whiz B • M • E (E underlined)

1. zing B • M • E
2. music B • M • E
3. please B • M • E
4. reason B • M • E
5. does B • M • E
6. toys B • M • E
7. suppose B • M • E
8. present B • M • E
9. zoom B • M • E
10. noise B • M • E
11. thousand B • M • E
12. zero B • M • E
13. peas B • M • E
14. visit B • M • E
15. choose B • M • E
16. buzzed B • M • E

B Listen to these words that have the "b" sound in them.

Beginning "b"	Middle "b"	End "b"
bat	carbon	drab
bake	cowboy	bulb
ball	doorbell	club

Listen to these sounds of "b." If the "b" sound is at the beginning of the word, draw a line under the "B." If the "b" sound is in the middle of the word, draw a line under the "M." If the "b" sound is at the end of the word, draw a line under the "E."

1. black B • M • E
2. cranberry B • M • E
3. club B • M • E
4. gobble B • M • E
5. benefit B • M • E
6. globe B • M • E
7. Robert B • M • E
8. job B • M • E
9. bulb B • M • E
10. December B • M • E
11. scrub B • M • E
12. bib B • M • E
13. neighbor B • M • E
14. snowball B • M • E
15. blob B • M • E
16. blackboard B • M • E

Number Changes

Draw a line under each number that is different. See examples "A" and "B."

A.	101	101	<u>010</u>	101
C.	321	123	321	321
E.	415	514	514	514
G.	181	181	181	188
I.	618	816	618	618
K.	545	545	454	545
M.	563	367	367	367
O.	584	584	584	485
Q.	779	997	779	779
S.	967	967	679	967
U.	876	678	678	678
W.	348	348	348	483
Y.	442	424	442	442
A.	336	336	337	336
C.	258	285	285	285
E.	556	559	556	556

B.	121	121	121	<u>212</u>
D.	323	232	323	323
F.	524	524	425	524
H.	242	242	242	422
J.	725	527	527	527
L.	627	726	627	627
N.	283	283	382	283
P.	823	823	823	328
R.	593	359	359	359
T.	667	676	667	667
V.	542	542	542	245
X.	262	262	626	262
Z.	727	772	772	772
B.	192	191	192	192
D.	364	364	364	346
F.	277	277	272	277

Proper Positions

Copy each statement on the line, and remember these rules for good handwriting habits.

1 Sit erect in your chair.

2 Keep feet flat on the floor.

3 Rest both arms on the desk.

4 Hold your head up.

5 Hold your pencil loosely between the thumb and the first two fingers.

6 Place your paper at an angle.

7 Keep your wrist straight.

Addition Facts 1's, 2's, and 3's

Write in the correct answers. See sample "A."

A + = 2   + = 3   + = 4

B + = __   + = __   + = __

C + = __   + = __   + = __

D + = __   + = __   + = __

E + = __   + = __   + = __

F + = __   + = __   + = __

G + = __   + = __   + = __

H + = __   + = __   + = __

I + = __   + = __   + = __

J 1 + 1 = __   2 + 1 = __   3 + 1 = __   4 + 1 = __

K 2 + 2 = __   3 + 2 = __   4 + 2 = __   5 + 2 = __

L 3 + 3 = __   4 + 3 = __   5 + 3 = __   6 + 3 = __

M 2 + 5 = __   1 + 7 = __   3 + 4 = __   2 + 3 = __

Proper Attitudes

Good writing depends on your frame of mind. Copy the attitude rules on the lines.

1 Think before you write.

2 Do not hurry. Take your time.

3 Apply the rules of handwriting.

4 Practice doing your best.

5 Try to improve each day.

6 Look forward to daily writing.

7 Writing is silent talking.

8 Your handwriting must be easy to read.

Meanings of Words

Underline the answer that defines each word. Write your own sentence about each word.

1. **cold**
   a. high temperature
   b. more warm than usual
   c. <u>less warm than usual</u>

2. **door**
   a. a movable part to close an opening in wall
   b. opening covered by glass
   c. the top of a room

3. **wood**
   a. the green part of a tree
   b. that which trees are made of
   c. the stem of a flower

4. **duck**
   a. a bird with no wings
   b. a bird with webbed feet
   c. a bird with no feathers

5. **bread**
   a. a food eaten with a spoon
   b. a food made of sugar and water
   c. a food made with flour

Recognizing Pictures

Pick the word from the box that matches each picture, and write the word in the space. See sample "1."

egg	rake	belt	ear
eye	bell	gate	leg
key	five	nose	ten

1. SAMPLE

bell

2.

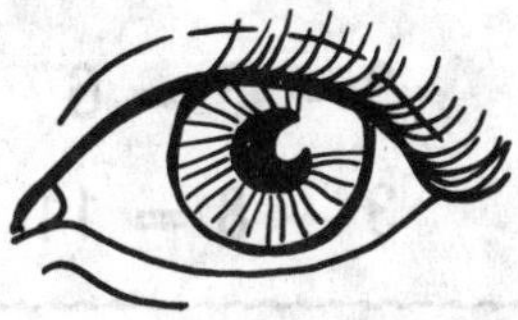

3.

10

4.

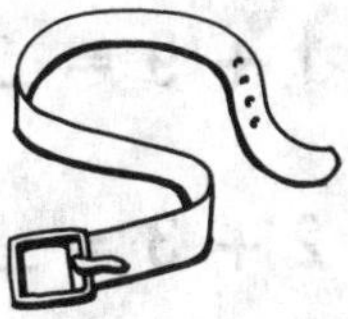

5.

6.

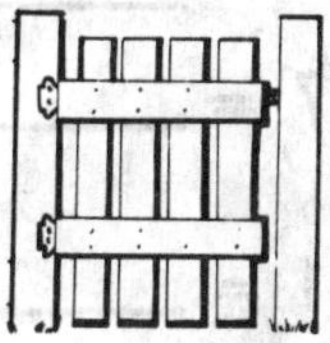

7.

8.

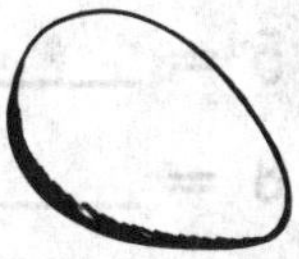

9.

10.

11.

5

12.

Addition Facts

A Draw a line under each addition fact as you read.

1. 1 + 1 = 2   1 + 2 = 3   1 + 3 = 4   1 + 4 = 5   1 + 5 = 6
   1 + 6 = 7   1 + 7 = 8   1 + 8 = 9   1 + 9 = 10

2. 2 + 1 = 3   2 + 2 = 4   2 + 3 = 5   2 + 4 = 6   2 + 5 = 7
   2 + 6 = 8   2 + 7 = 9   2 + 8 = 10   2 + 9 = 11

3. 3 + 1 = 4   3 + 2 = 5   3 + 3 = 6   3 + 4 = 7   3 + 5 = 8
   3 + 6 = 9   3 + 7 = 10   3 + 8 = 11   3 + 9 = 12

B Fill in the blanks.

4. 1 + 1 = ______   1 + 2 = ______   1 + 3 = ______
   1 + 4 = ______   1 + 5 = ______   1 + 6 = ______
   1 + 7 = ______   1 + 8 = ______   1 + 9 = ______

5. 2 + 1 = ______   2 + 2 = ______   2 + 3 = ______
   2 + 4 = ______   2 + 5 = ______   2 + 6 = ______
   2 + 7 = ______   2 + 8 = ______   2 + 9 = ______

6. 3 + 1 = ______   3 + 2 = ______   3 + 3 = ______
   3 + 4 = ______   3 + 5 = ______   3 + 6 = ______
   3 + 7 = ______   3 + 8 = ______   3 + 9 = ______

C Fill in the blanks.

7. ______ Mary received two dolls last Christmas and three dolls this Christmas. How many dolls does Mary now have?

8. ______ Bobby has three white rabbits, and Don has seven white rabbits. How many rabbits do they both have?

9. ______ Karen has two white kittens and three black kittens. How many kittens does Karen have?

10. ______ Jack has three green marbles and eight red marbles. How many marbles does Jack have?

Letter Discrimination

Draw an "X" through each letter that is like the first. See examples "1" and "2."

1.	F	E	E	F (crossed out)
3.	H	B	E	H
5.	E	E	F	H
7.	B	R	B	P
9.	P	B	R	P
11.	R	P	R	B
13.	W	N	M	W
15.	N	Z	N	H
17.	M	M	W	Z
19.	Z	N	Z	H
21.	A	R	K	A
23.	G	O	G	C

2.	K	R	K (crossed out)	P
4.	Q	O	Q	C
6.	C	O	Q	C
8.	O	Q	O	C
10.	a	o	a	c
12.	o	o	c	a
14.	h	b	h	k
16.	b	b	k	h
18.	n	r	n	u
20.	u	a	n	u
22.	P	B	P	D
24.	k	b	h	k

Underlining Answers

Underline the answer that defines each word. Write your own sentence about each word.

1. **deer**
   - a. a fast, graceful animal
   - b. a farm animal
   - c. an animal you can ride

2. **hand**
   - a. the end part of the neck
   - b. the end part of the arm
   - c. the end part of the leg

3. **candy**
   - a. sweets to eat
   - b. food eaten at breakfast
   - c. food eaten in place of meals

4. **card**
   - a. paper with long letter on it
   - b. paper which tells news
   - c. small piece of paper with message

5. **drum**
   - a. an instrument you beat to make sound
   - b. an instrument you blow on
   - c. an instrument with strings

Practicing Addition 1's, 2's, and 3's

Solve these problems. Write your answer below each problem.

A	1 +1 2	6 +1	2 +4	1 +8	3 +2	2 +6	2 +5	3 +7	8 +1	5 +2
B	1 +5	1 +6	7 +2	4 +1	3 +5	1 +4	1 +7	2 +6	2 +8	1 +3
C	4 +3	1 +2	1 +9	3 +8	1 +5	3 +6	1 +8	3 +4	9 +1	1 +4
D	1 +2	4 +5	3 +3	1 +7	2 +5	6 +3	2 +1	3 +1	1 +6	3 +7
E	1 +7	4 +2	8 +2	1 +8	2 +2	3 +1	1 +6	2 +4	8 +3	5 +3
F	1 +3	6 +2	2 +5	2 +8	3 +2	1 +4	3 +5	2 +2	9 +2	6 +3
G	4 +3	3 +6	9 +2	9 +3	3 +4	5 +1	2 +7	3 +3	3 +5	9 +1
H	2 +7	3 +8	1 +4	9 +1	3 +5	7 +3	1 +2	8 +2	4 +1	3 +6
I	4 +2	2 +6	1 +1	3 +9	7 +2	3 +5	1 +8	2 +3	1 +7	9 +2
J	7 +2	1 +2	3 +5	3 +1	1 +5	6 +2	1 +4	2 +2	1 +9	1 +8

"c," "d" Sounds

A Listen to these words that have the "c" sound in them.

Beginning "c"	Middle "c"	End "c"
cat	doctor	lilac
canal	bacon	basic
call	locate	magic

Listen to these sounds of "c." If the "c" sound is at the beginning of the word, draw a line under the "B." If the "c" sound is in the middle of the word, draw a line under the "M." If the "c" sound is at the end of the word, draw a line under the "E."

EXAMPLES: carry B • M • E (B underlined); because B • M • E (M underlined); traffic B • M • E (E underlined)

cousin 1. B • M • E	second 2. B • M • E	civic 3. B • M • E	decant 4. B • M • E
Colorado 5. B • M • E	secret 6. B • M • E	icicle 7. B • M • E	arithmetic 8. B • M • E
cuddle 9. B • M • E	politic 10. B • M • E	concave 11. B • M • E	citric 12. B • M • E
cocoa 13. B • M • E	pelvic 14. B • M • E	chocolate 15. B • M • E	create 16. B • M • E

B Listen to these words that have the "d" sound in them.

Beginning "d"	Middle "d"	End "d"
dance	under	bed
doctor	window	good
dog	garden	loud

Listen to these sounds of "d." If the "d" sound is at the beginning of the word, draw a line under the "B." If the "d" sound is in the middle of the word, draw a line under the "M." If the "d" sound is at the end of the word, draw a line under the "E."

outdoors 1. B • M • E	grade 2. B • M • E	crowd 3. B • M • E	deliver 4. B • M • E
dinner 5. B • M • E	medicine 6. B • M • E	food 7. B • M • E	goodbye 8. B • M • E
birthday 9. B • M • E	dentist 10. B • M • E	radio 11. B • M • E	parade 12. B • M • E
bandage 13. B • M • E	yesterday 14. B • M • E	indoors 15. B • M • E	divide 16. B • M • E

Internal Number Changes

Draw a line under each number that is different. See examples "A" and "B."

A.	1562	<u>1652</u>	1562
C.	2412	2142	2142
E.	3103	3103	3013
G.	2762	2672	2762
I.	4215	4215	4125
K.	3264	3624	3624
M.	5235	5235	5325
O.	2434	2344	2434
Q.	1725	1275	1275
S.	2348	2348	2438
U.	1482	1482	1842
W.	2252	2522	2252
Y.	3124	3214	3214
A.	2536	2536	2356
C.	1249	1429	1249
E.	2316	2136	2316

B.	<u>1054</u>	1504	1504
D.	2369	2369	2639
F.	1894	1984	1894
H.	2478	2748	2748
J.	2519	2519	2159
L.	3271	3721	3721
N.	4562	4562	4652
P.	3876	3786	3876
R.	2919	2199	2199
T.	3685	3865	3685
V.	2972	2972	2792
X.	3838	3388	3388
Z.	3641	3461	3641
B.	2895	2985	2985
D.	3217	3217	2127
F.	8543	8453	8543

Addition Facts 4's, 5's, and 6's

A **Draw a line under each as you read.**

1. 4 + 1 = 5   4 + 2 = 6   4 + 3 = 7   4 + 4 = 8   4 + 5 = 9
   4 + 6 = 10   4 + 7 = 11   4 + 8 = 12   4 + 9 = 13

2. 5 + 1 = 6   5 + 2 = 7   5 + 3 = 8   5 + 4 = 9   5 + 5 = 10
   5 + 6 = 11   5 + 7 = 12   5 + 8 = 13   5 + 9 = 14

3. 6 + 1 = 7   6 + 2 = 8   6 + 3 = 9   6 + 4 = 10   6 + 5 = 11
   6 + 6 = 12   6 + 7 = 13   6 + 8 = 14   6 + 9 = 15

B **Complete the number sentences by filling in the blanks.**

4. 4 + 1 = ______   4 + 2 = ______   4 + 3 = ______
   4 + 4 = ______   4 + 5 = ______   4 + 6 = ______
   4 + 7 = ______   4 + 8 = ______   4 + 9 = ______

5. 5 + 1 = ______   5 + 2 = ______   5 + 3 = ______
   5 + 4 = ______   5 + 5 = ______   5 + 6 = ______
   5 + 7 = ______   5 + 8 = ______   5 + 9 = ______

6. 6 + 1 = ______   6 + 2 = ______   6 + 3 = ______
   6 + 4 = ______   6 + 5 = ______   6 + 6 = ______
   6 + 7 = ______   6 + 8 = ______   6 + 9 = ______

C **Write each answer in the blank.**

7. ______ Joey is a cub scout. Last month Joey turned in five achievements. He has nine more achievements to turn in tomorrow. How many achievements will Joey have turned in altogether?

8. ______ Jerry had been to the store and bought oranges for his mother. One bag had seven oranges in it, and the other bag had six oranges in it. How many oranges in all did Jerry buy?

9. ______ Mary has four pencils, and Susan has seven pencils. How many pencils do both Mary and Susan have?

10. ______ Jane carried six books to school this morning, and Melissa carried five. How many books did Jane and Melissa both carry to school?

Spell the Words

Circle the correctly spelled word that matches each picture. See the example.

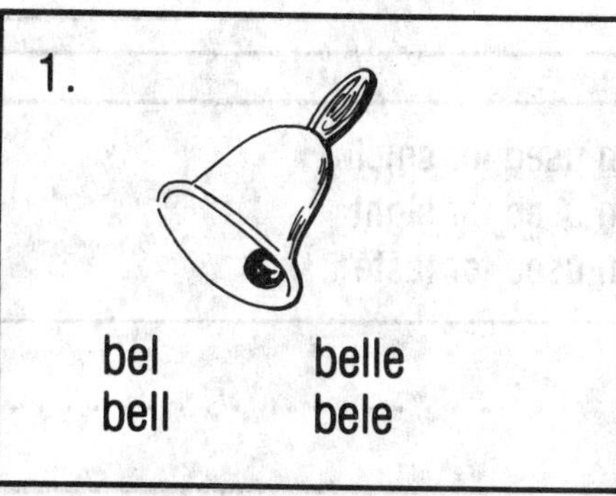

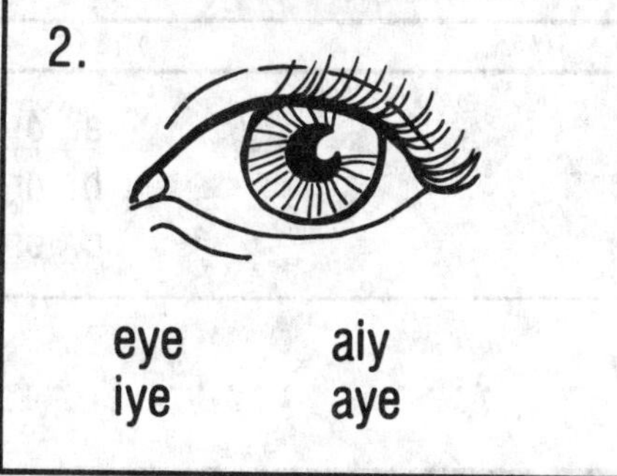

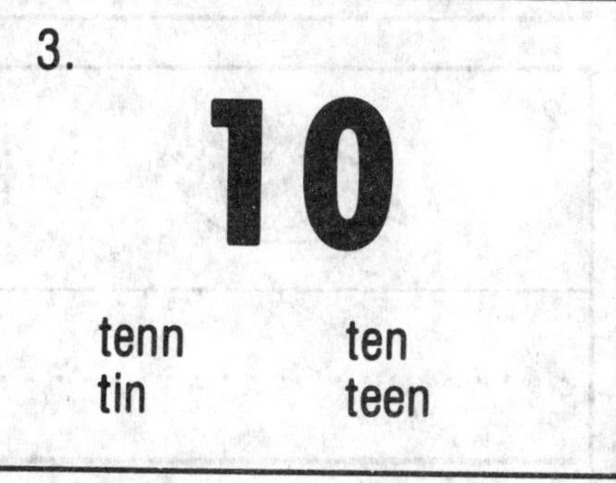

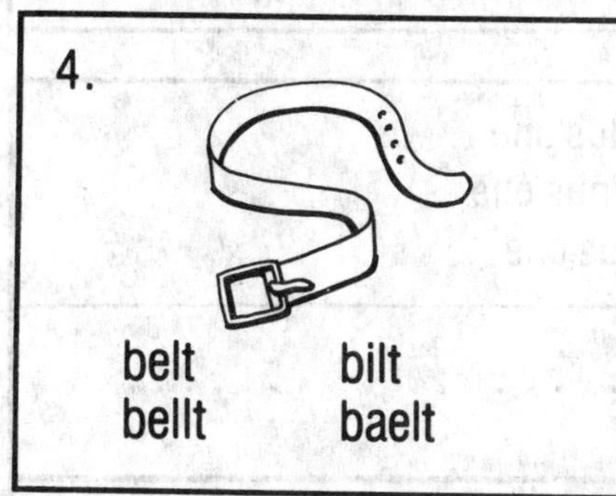

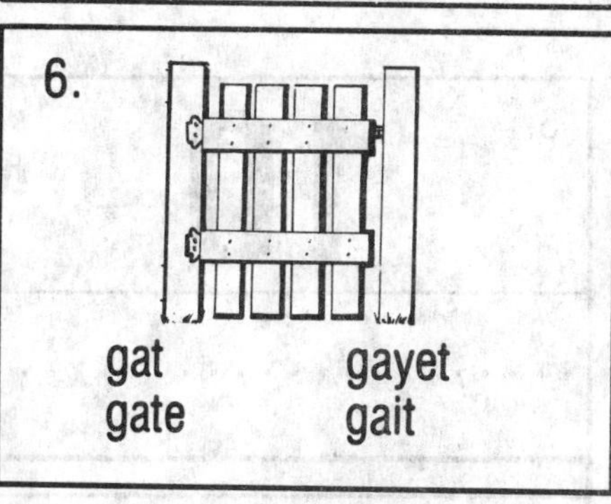

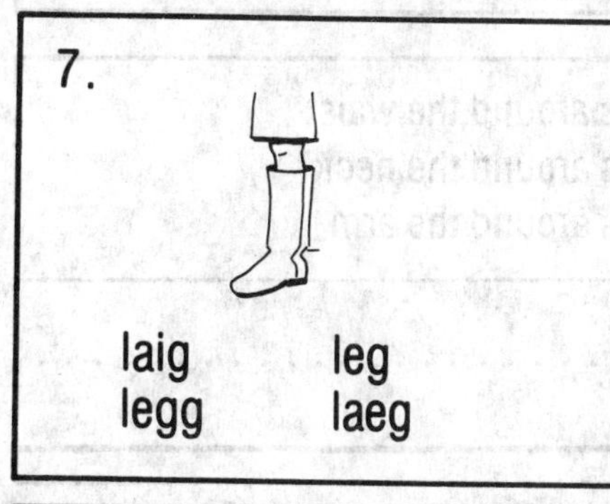

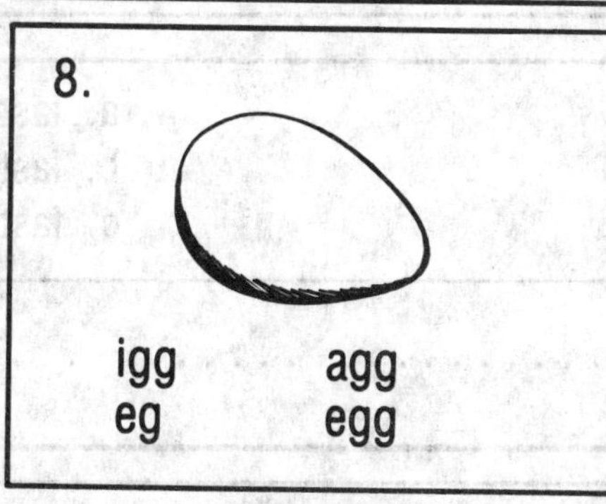

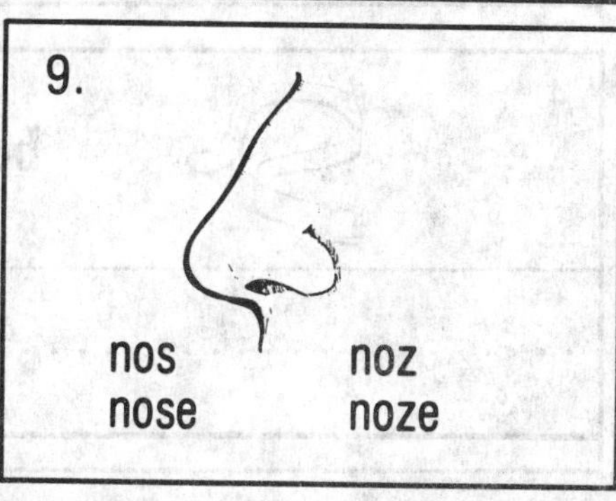

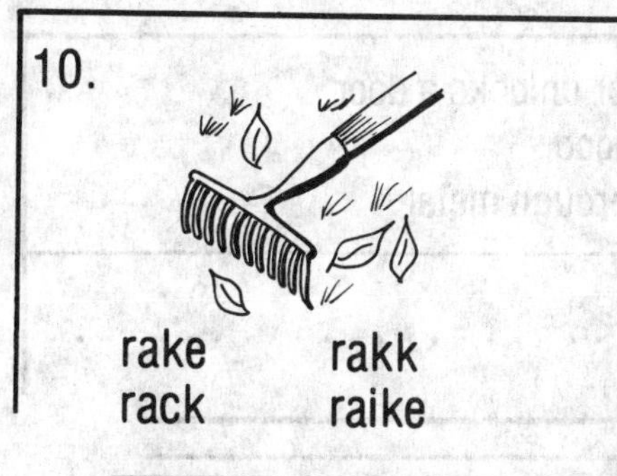

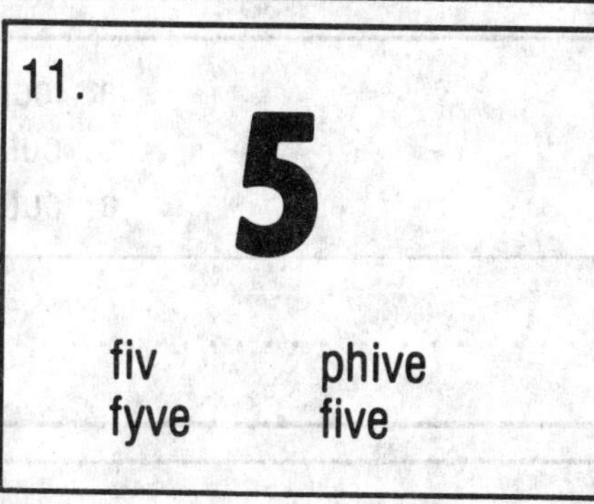

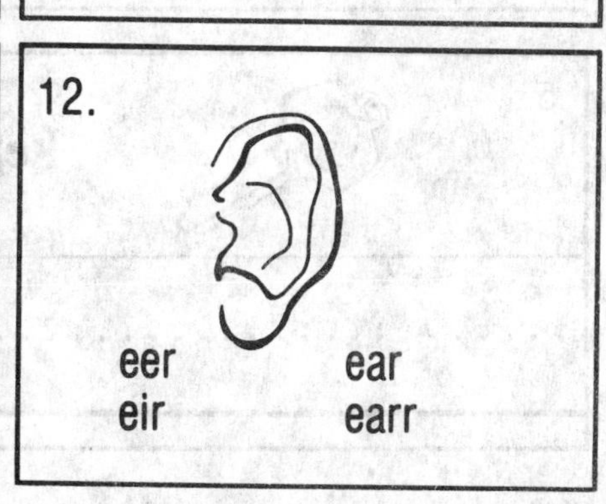

Can You Define the Words?

Underline the answer that defines each word. Write your own sentence about each word.

1. **bell**

   a. object that makes buzzing noise
   b. object made of paper
   c. metal cup that makes ringing sound

2. **eye**

   a. organ used for smell
   b. organ used for sight
   c. organ used for taste

3. 10 **ten**

   a. eight plus one
   b. nine minus one
   c. nine plus one

4. **belt**

   a. fastens around the waist
   b. fastens around the neck
   c. fastens around the arm

5. **key**

   a. locks or unlocks a door
   b. cuts wood
   c. cuts through metal

Practicing Addition 4's, 5's, and 6's

Solve these problems. Write your answer below each problem.

A	1 4 5	8 6	7 5	6 5	4 4	7 6	4 5	6 6	9 4	8 5
B	6 4	3 4	1 5	7 6	2 6	5 5	4 6	4 5	9 4	9 6
C	4 7	3 5	9 6	8 5	7 6	8 4	7 5	4 9	5 7	5 8
D	6 7	5 6	5 5	4 8	2 5	7 4	1 6	2 5	4 3	2 6
E	9 4	8 6	5 6	6 6	3 4	1 5	6 9	4 9	8 4	9 3
F	6 4	4 9	8 3	5 7	4 7	4 5	4 6	2 6	5 4	6 8
G	9 4	8 5	6 9	2 8	4 9	5 8	1 6	8 6	9 6	4 7
H	5 7	9 6	8 6	1 7	2 4	5 8	4 9	6 9	9 4	7 4
I	7 5	9 5	6 8	1 5	2 6	2 4	1 6	5 9	8 4	4 7
J	4 8	9 4	6 5	6 2	3 4	2 5	4 9	1 5	9 5	3 6

Seeing Difference

Draw an "X" through each one that is different. See examples "1" and "2."

1.	A	A	A	A	2.	R	R	R	R
3.	B	B	B	B	4.	T	T	T	T
5.	C	C	C	C	6.	U	U	U	U
7.	D	D	D	D	8.	V	V	V	V
9.	E	E	E	E	10.	W	W	W	W
11.	F	F	F	F	12.	Z	Z	Z	Z
13.	G	G	G	G	14.	A	A	A	A
15.	H	H	H	H	16.	B	B	B	B
17.	I	I	I	I	18.	C	C	C	C
19.	J	J	J	J	20.	D	D	D	D
21.	K	K	K	K	22.	E	E	E	E
23.	L	L	L	L	24.	H	H	H	H
25.	M	M	M	M	26.	F	F	F	F
27.	N	N	N	N	28.	E	E	E	E
29.	P	P	P	P	30.	L	L	L	L
31.	Q	Q	Q	Q	32.	M	M	M	M

"f," "g" Sounds

A Listen to these words that have the "f" sound in them.

Beginning "f"	Middle "f"	End "f"
fall	office	off
fix	after	calf
fat	often	roof

Listen to these sounds of "f." If the "f" sound is at the beginning of the word, draw a line under the "B." If the "f" sound is in the middle of the word, draw a line under the "M." If the "f" sound is at the end of the word, draw a line under the "E."

EXAMPLES:

farm	before	chief
B • M • E	B • M • E	B • M • E

gruff 1. B • M • E	careful 2. B • M • E	furniture 3. B • M • E	laugh 4. B • M • E
father 5. B • M • E	cliff 6. B • M • E	elephant 7. B • M • E	bluff 8. B • M • E
grandfather 9. B • M • E	cough 10. B • M • E	different 11. B • M • E	chief 12. B • M • E
breakfast 13. B • M • E	handkerchief 14. B • M • E	enough 15. B • M • E	fluff 16. B • M • E

B Listen to these words that have the "g" sound in them.

Beginning "g"	Middle "g"	End "g"
got	began	bag
gate	finger	dog
good	ago	rug

Listen to these sounds of "g." If the "g" sound is at the beginning of the word, draw a line under the "B." If the "g" sound is in the middle of the word, draw a line under the "M." If the "g" sound is at the end of the word, draw a line under the "E."

golden 1. B • M • E	eager 2. B • M • E	plug 3. B • M • E	stag 4. B • M • E
catalog 5. B • M • E	begun 6. B • M • E	grown 7. B • M • E	throng 8. B • M • E
popgun 9. B • M • E	geese 10. B • M • E	neglect 11. B • M • E	bang 12. B • M • E
Thanksgiving 13. B • M • E	again 14. B • M • E	hoeing 15. B • M • E	gagging 16. B • M • E

Addition Facts 7's, 8's, and 9's

A Draw a line under each fact as you read.

1. 7 + 1 = 8   7 + 2 = 9   7 + 3 = 10   7 + 4 = 11   7 + 5 = 12
   7 + 6 = 13   7 + 7 = 14   7 + 8 = 15   7 + 9 = 16
2. 8 + 1 = 9   8 + 2 = 10   8 + 3 = 11   8 + 4 = 12   8 + 5 = 13
   8 + 6 = 14   8 + 7 = 15   8 + 8 = 16   8 + 9 = 17
3. 9 + 1 = 10   9 + 2 = 11   9 + 3 = 12   9 + 4 = 13   9 + 5 = 14
   9 + 6 = 15   9 + 7 = 16   9 + 8 = 17   9 + 9 = 18

B Complete the number sentences by filling in the blanks.

4. 7 + 1 = ______   7 + 2 = ______   7 + 3 = ______
   7 + 4 = ______   7 + 5 = ______   7 + 6 = ______
   7 + 7 = ______   7 + 8 = ______   7 + 9 = ______
5. 8 + 1 = ______   8 + 2 = ______   8 + 3 = ______
   8 + 4 = ______   8 + 5 = ______   8 + 6 = ______
   8 + 7 = ______   8 + 8 = ______   8 + 9 = ______
6. 9 + 1 = ______   9 + 2 = ______   9 + 3 = ______
   9 + 4 = ______   9 + 5 = ______   9 + 6 = ______
   9 + 7 = ______   9 + 8 = ______   9 + 9 = ______

C Fill in the blanks.

7. ______ Jerry had nine nickels, and his mother gave him seven more nickels. How many nickels does Jerry have now?

8. ______ Mr. Ball has nine Jersey cows and nine Guernsey cows. How many cows does Mr. Ball have in all?

9. ______ Linda has eight Barbie dolls, and Susan has seven Barbie dolls. How many Barbie dolls do they both have?

10. ______ Jack has six white rabbits and seven black rabbits. How many rabbits does Jack have?

Definitions of Words

Underline the answer that defines each word. Write your own sentence about each word.

1. **gate**
   a. <u>opening in a fence</u>
   b. a hole in the ground
   c. a hole in a tree

2. **leg**
   a. something on which you stand
   b. something on which you sit
   c. something used to carry things

3. **egg**
   a. object used for games
   b. a small rock
   c. object laid by mother bird

4. **nose**
   a. used for hearing
   b. used for seeing
   c. used for breathing

5. **rake**
   a. a tool for cutting grass
   b. a tool for gathering leaves
   c. a tool for watering the lawn

Write the Words

Pick the word from the box that matches each picture, and write the word in the space. See sample "1."

fan	calf	roof	four
safe	knife	fist	fork
gift	fire	fish	fox

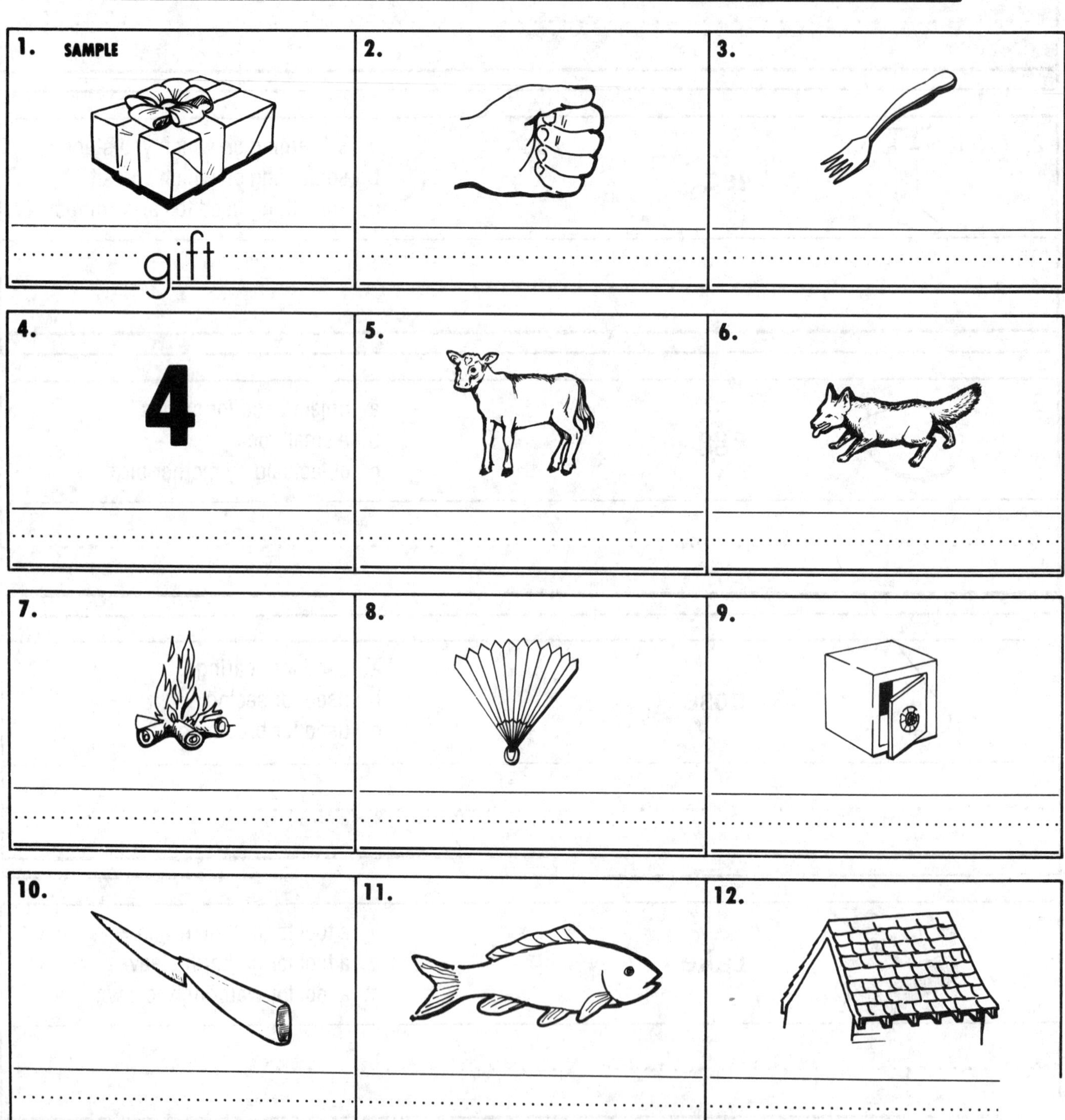

Practicing Addition 7's, 8's, and 9's

Solve these problems. Write your answer below each problem.

A	1 8 9	4 8	4 7	8 9	2 9	6 7	5 8	7 7	3 8	2 9
B	5 7	6 8	2 9	1 9	5 8	4 8	7 5	6 9	8 7	3 9
C	9 3	8 2	7 9	9 8	8 5	7 6	8 9	8 3	7 1	9 4
D	2 8	7 5	3 9	7 7	5 8	9 2	6 7	2 9	1 9	3 7
E	7 9	4 8	9 2	1 9	8 2	3 8	9 1	8 6	8 4	3 8
F	9 3	8 2	7 5	8 8	3 9	4 7	8 5	2 9	2 8	7 3
G	7 3	8 3	7 2	3 7	5 8	9 1	2 8	7 8	3 9	1 7
H	3 9	4 7	8 2	9 9	9 8	8 8	7 6	5 8	9 7	7 3
I	8 2	7 3	1 8	9 3	2 7	2 8	8 7	8 8	7 9	4 9
J	9 8	8 5	9 1	8 8	6 8	9 2	3 8	7 5	3 9	9 7

Letter Reversal

Draw an "X" through each one that is different. See examples "1" and "2."

1.	B	B	~~ᙠ~~	B	2.	a	a	a	~~ɒ~~
3.	C	Ɔ	C	C	4.	b	b	d	b
5.	D	D	D	ᗡ	6.	c	ɔ	c	c
7.	E	E	Ǝ	E	8.	d	d	d	b
9.	F	ꟻ	F	F	10.	e	e	ɘ	e
11.	G	G	G	ᘐ	12.	h	h	ᖹ	h
13.	K	K	ꓘ	K	14.	m	m	m	ɯ
15.	L	⅃	L	L	16.	n	ᴎ	n	n
17.	M	M	Ɯ	M	18.	p	p	q	p
19.	P	P	P	ꟼ	20.	s	ƨ	s	s
21.	R	Я	R	R	22.	u	u	u	ᴜ
23.	W	W	W	M	24.	k	ʞ	k	k
25.	Z	Z	Σ	Z	26.	b	b	b	d
27.	F	ꟻ	F	F	28.	c	ɔ	c	c
29.	E	E	E	Ǝ	30.	d	b	d	d
31.	K	K	ꓘ	K	32.	h	h	ᖹ	h

"h," "j" Sounds

A Listen to these words that have the "h" sound in them.

Beginning "h"	Middle "h"	End "h"
he	ship	fish
have	ahoy	wash
his	shoe	dash

Listen to these sounds of "h." If the "h" sound is at the beginning of the word, draw a line under the "B." If the "h" sound is in the middle of the word, draw a line under the "M." If the "h" sound is at the end of the word, draw a line under the "E."

EXAMPLES: head B • M • E (B underlined) — shot B • M • E (M underlined) — wish B • M • E (E underlined)

1. heart B • M • E
2. washer B • M • E
3. radish B • M • E
4. shave B • M • E
5. beehive B • M • E
6. brush B • M • E
7. cohabit B • M • E
8. relish B • M • E
9. house B • M • E
10. Mohawk B • M • E
11. torch B • M • E
12. behold B • M • E
13. hasten B • M • E
14. cohort B • M • E
15. behind B • M • E
16. harsh B • M • E

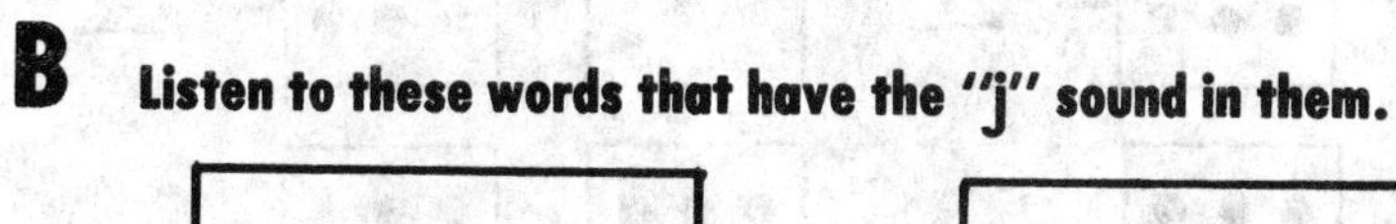

B Listen to these words that have the "j" sound in them.

Beginning "j"	Middle "j"	End "j"
juice	major	ridge
just	unjust	average
jar	enjoy	hinge

Listen to these sounds of "j." If the "j" sound is at the beginning of the word, draw a line under the "B." If the "j" sound is in the middle of the word, draw a line under the "M." If the "j" sound is at the end of the word, draw a line under the "E."

1. jangle B • M • E
2. object B • M • E
3. cage B • M • E
4. lodge B • M • E
5. jelly B • M • E
6. subject B • M • E
7. jackknife B • M • E
8. singe B • M • E
9. bridge B • M • E
10. pageant B • M • E
11. dodge B • M • E
12. majority B • M • E
13. infringe B • M • E
14. enjoyable B • M • E
15. disengage B • M • E
16. judge B • M • E

Addition of 4's, 5's, and 6's

Write in the correct answers. See sample "A."

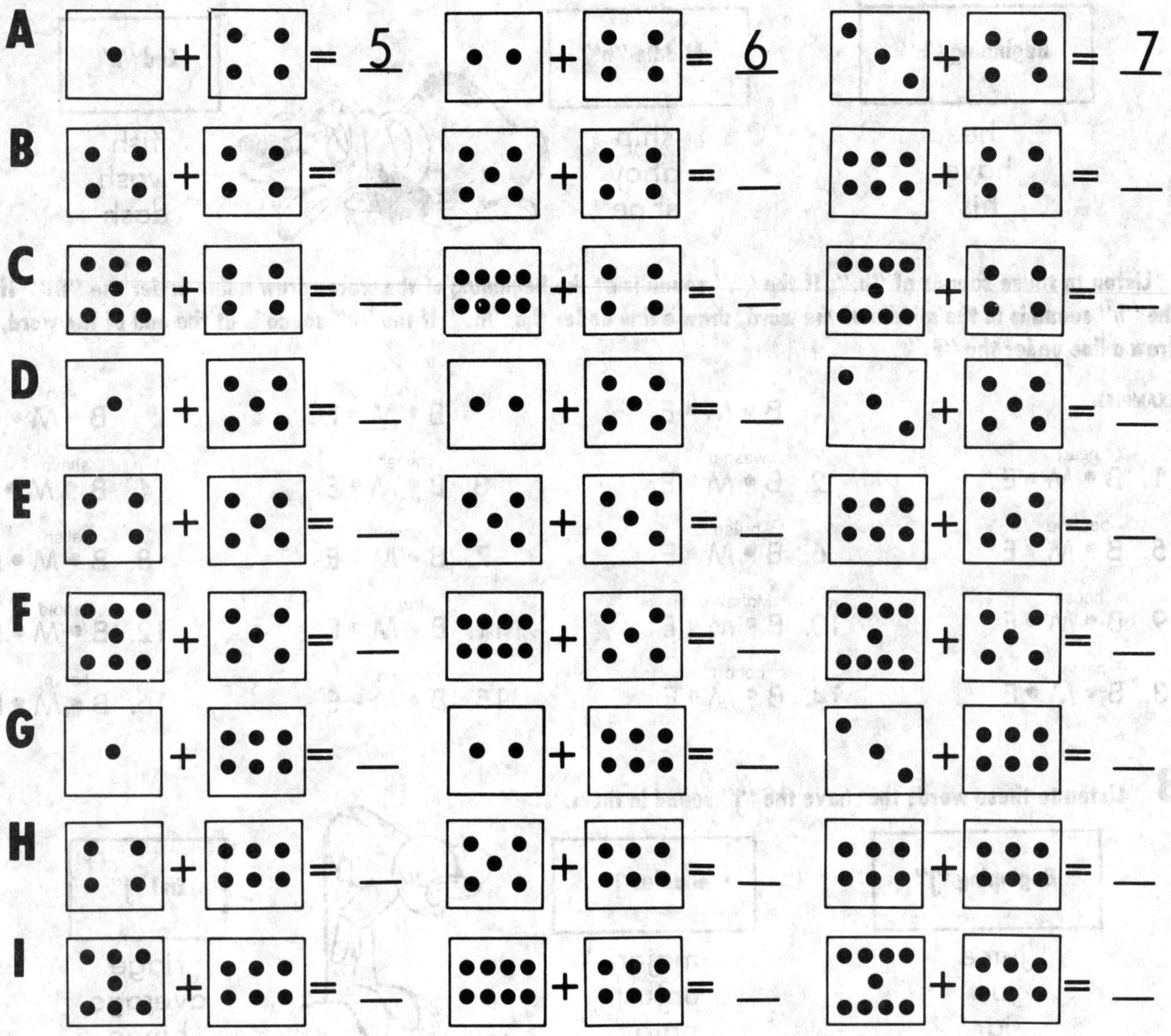

A + = 5 + = 6 + = 7

B + = __ + = __ + = __

C + = __ + = __ + = __

D + = __ + = __ + = __

E + = __ + = __ + = __

F + = __ + = __ + = __

G + = __ + = __ + = __

H + = __ + = __ + = __

I + = __ + = __ + = __

J 1 + 4 = __ 2 + 4 = __ 3 + 4 = __ 4 + 4 = __

K 6 + 4 = __ 7 + 4 = __ 8 + 4 = __ 9 + 4 = __

L 2 + 5 = __ 3 + 5 = __ 4 + 5 = __ 5 + 5 = __

M 7 + 5 = __ 8 + 5 = __ 9 + 5 = __ 1 + 6 = __

Spell

Circle the correctly spelled word that matches each picture.
See the example.

EXAMPLE:

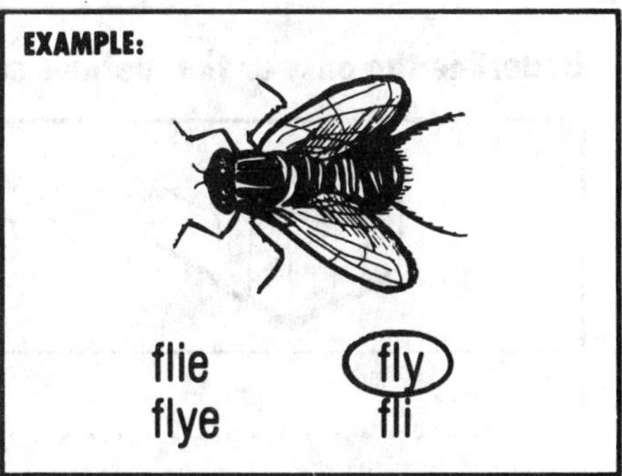

flie fly
flye fli

1.

gift geft
givt gevt

2.

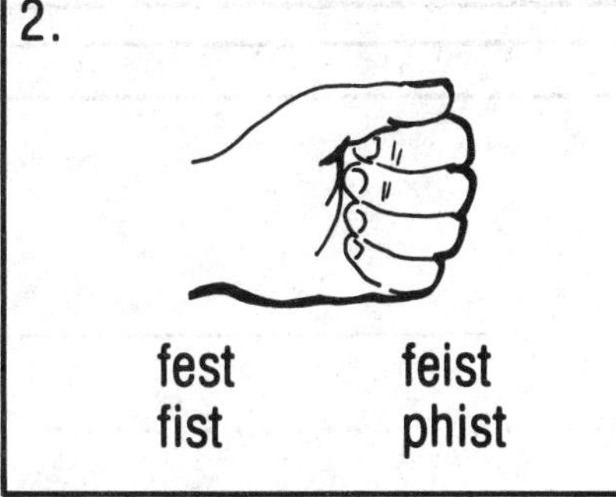

fest feist
fist phist

3.

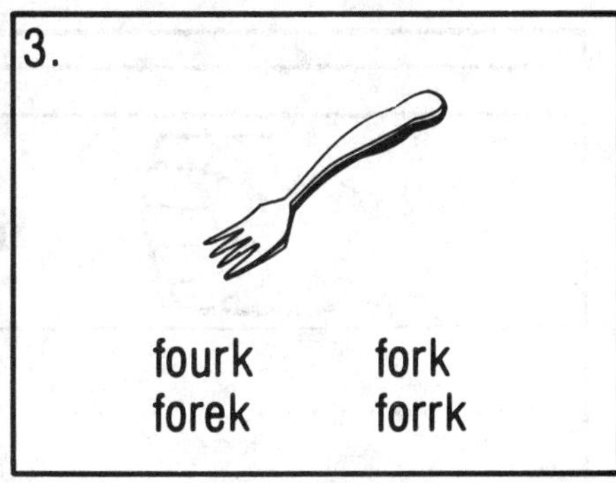

fourk fork
forek forrk

4.

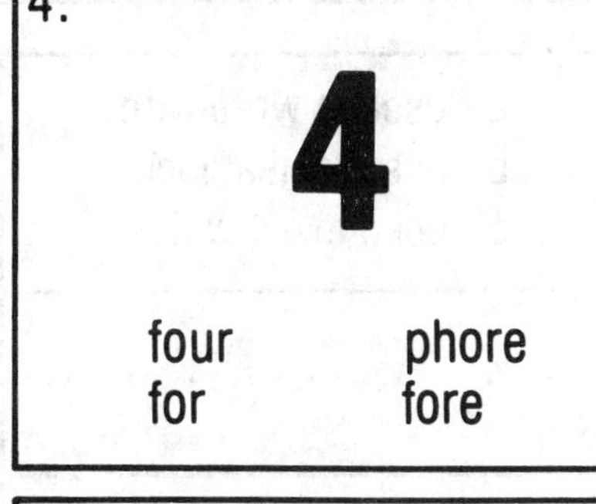

four phore
for fore

5.

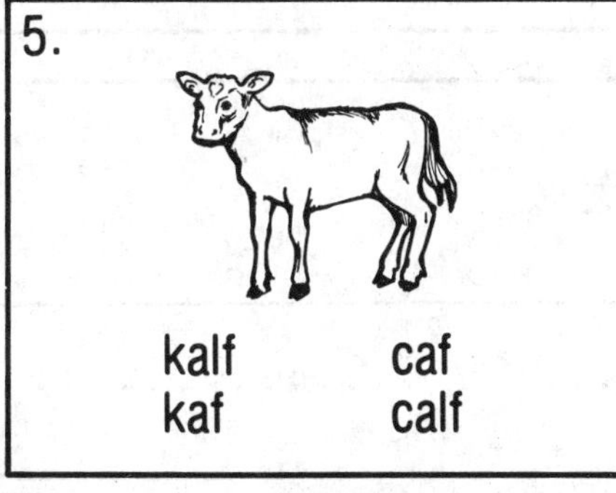

kalf caf
kaf calf

6.

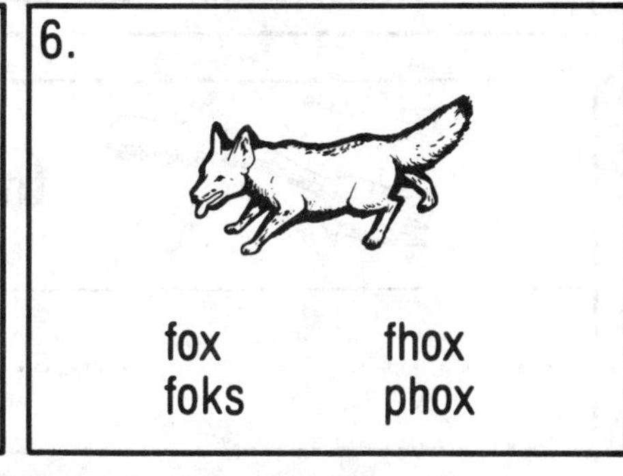

fox fhox
foks phox

7.

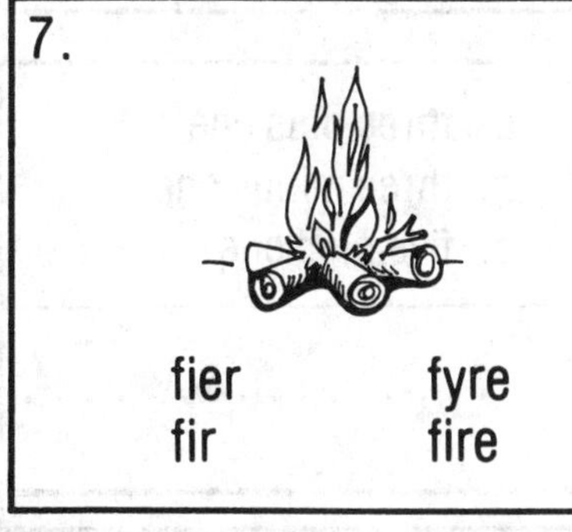

fier fyre
fir fire

8.

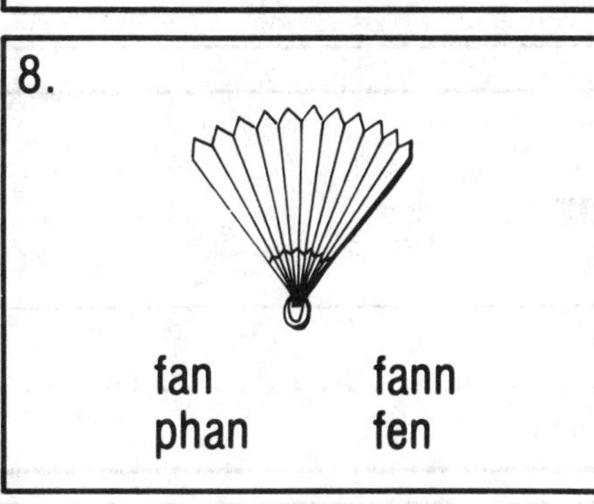

fan fann
phan fen

9.

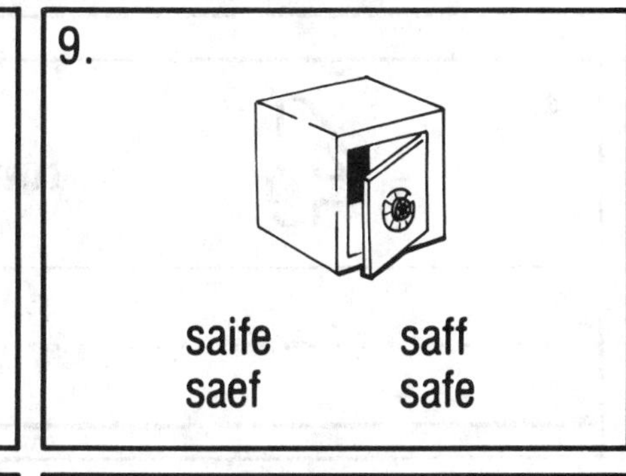

saife saff
saef safe

10.

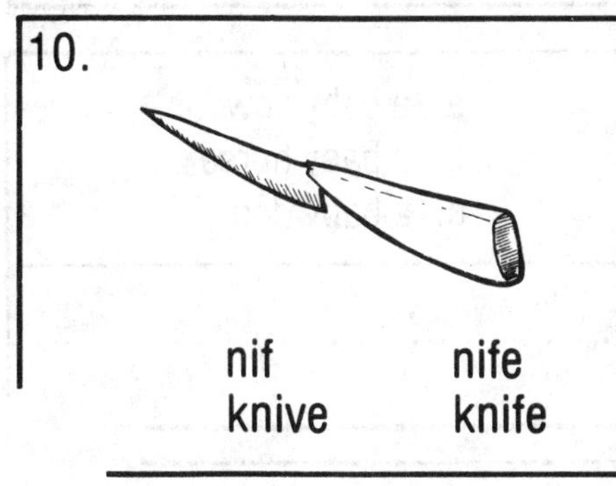

nif nife
knive knife

11.

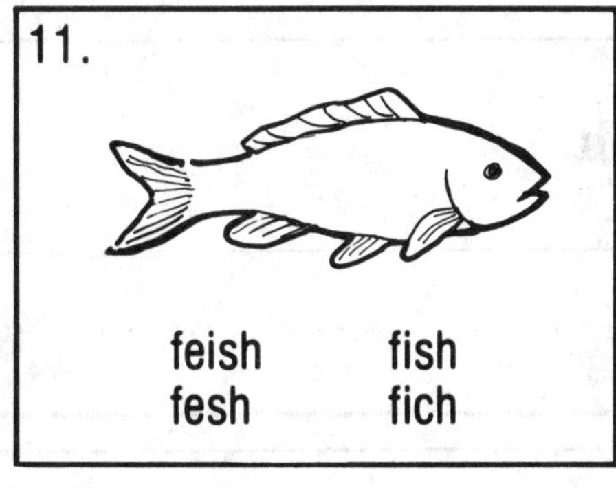

feish fish
fesh fich

12.

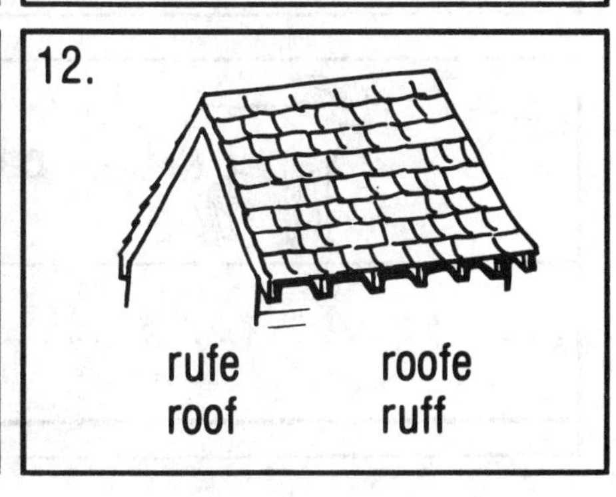

rufe roofe
roof ruff

Underlining Definitions

Underline the answer that defines each word. Write your own sentence about each word.

1. **gift**
   - a. a letter
   - b. <u>a present</u>
   - c. a greeting

2. **fist**
   - a. tightly closed hand
   - b. both feet
   - c. your knee

3. **fork**
   - a. used to write with
   - b. used to heat food
   - c. used to eat with

4. **four**
   - a. three plus one
   - b. three minus one
   - c. five plus one

5. **calf**
   - a. a baby cow
   - b. a baby horse
   - c. a baby dog

Addition of 7's, 8's, and 9's

Write in the correct answers. See example "A."

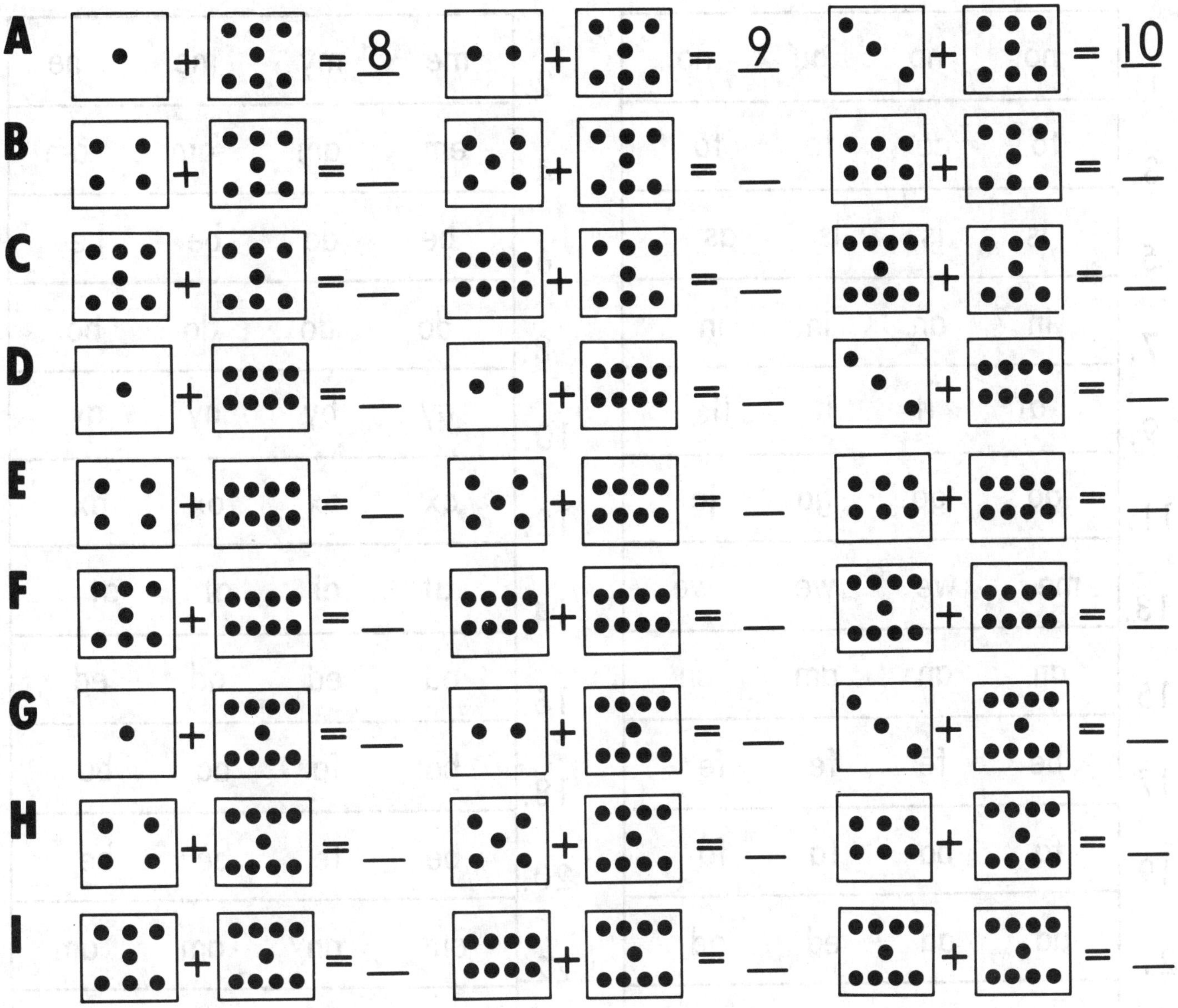

A + = 8 + = 9 + = 10

B + = __ + = __ + = __

C + = __ + = __ + = __

D + = __ + = __ + = __

E + = __ + = __ + = __

F + = __ + = __ + = __

G + = __ + = __ + = __

H + = __ + = __ + = __

I + = __ + = __ + = __

J 1 + 7 = __ 2 + 7 = __ 3 + 7 = __ 4 + 7 = __

K 6 + 7 = __ 7 + 7 = __ 8 + 7 = __ 9 + 7 = __

L 2 + 8 = __ 3 + 8 = __ 4 + 8 = __ 5 + 8 = __

M 7 + 8 = __ 8 + 8 = __ 9 + 8 = __ 1 + 9 = __

Differences in Words

Write an "X" through each word that is different. See the example.

1.	no	no	~~on~~	no
3.	to	do	to	to
5.	is	is	is	as
7.	in	an	in	in
9.	at	it	it	it
11.	go	go	go	jo
13.	me	we	we	we
15.	an	an	am	an
17.	be	fe	fe	fe
19.	fa	ba	fa	fa
21.	ad	ad	ed	ad
23.	ai	ai	ai	at
25.	ax	ax	ax	ox
27.	by	ay	by	by
29.	bo	bo	bo	do
31.	de	be	de	de

2.	me	my	me	me
4.	em	am	am	am
6.	be	de	be	be
8.	do	do	do	bo
10.	ay	by	ay	ay
12.	ox	ox	ox	ax
14.	at	ai	at	at
16.	ed	ed	ad	ed
18.	ba	fa	ba	ba
20.	be	fe	be	be
22.	am	an	am	am
24.	we	me	me	me
26.	jo	jo	jo	go
28.	it	it	at	it
30.	an	an	an	in
32.	as	is	as	as

"k," "oy," "oi" Sounds

A Listen to these words that have the "k" sound in them.

Beginning "k"	Middle "k"	End "k"
kiss	market	make
kid	skill	silk
keen	walker	desk

Listen to these sounds of "k." If the "k" sound is at the beginning of the word, draw a line under the "B." If the "k" sound is in the middle of the word, draw a line under the "M." If the "k" sound is at the end of the word, draw a line under the "E."

EXAMPLES:

kind B • M • E

monkey B • M • E

mark B • M • E

1. pocket B • M • E
2. kingdom B • M • E
3. book B • M • E
4. killed B • M • E
5. thank B • M • E
6. basket B • M • E
7. kindly B • M • E
8. black B • M • E
9. kitchen B • M • E
10. drink B • M • E
11. milking B • M • E
12. kept B • M • E
13. maker B • M • E
14. stocking B • M • E
15. breakfast B • M • E
16. kick B • M • E

B Listen to these words that have the "oi" sound in them.

Beginning "oi"	Middle "oi"	End "oi"
oil	voice	boy
oiler	voyage	toy
oiled	void	joy

Listen to these sounds of "oi." If the "oi" sound is at the beginning of the word, draw a line under the "B." If the "oi" sound is in the middle of the word, draw a line under the "M." If the "oi" sound is at the end of the word, draw a line under the "E."

1. avoidable B • M • E
2. alloy B • M • E
3. oink B • M • E
4. royal B • M • E
5. devoid B • M • E
6. broil B • M • E
7. oilproof B • M • E
8. convoy B • M • E
9. uncoil B • M • E
10. ointment B • M • E
11. disjoin B • M • E
12. troy B • M • E
13. exploit B • M • E
14. destroy B • M • E
15. royalist B • M • E
16. asteroid B • M • E

Picture Problems

How much do all the items in each problem cost? See sample "A."

A 

9¢ 8¢

9¢ + 8¢ = 17¢

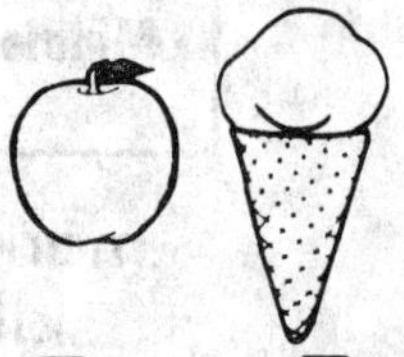

7¢ 7¢

7¢ + 7¢ = 14¢

B 

3¢ 6¢

3¢ + 6¢ = __¢

8¢ 4¢

8¢ + 4¢ = __¢

C

7¢ 5¢

7¢ + 5¢ = __¢

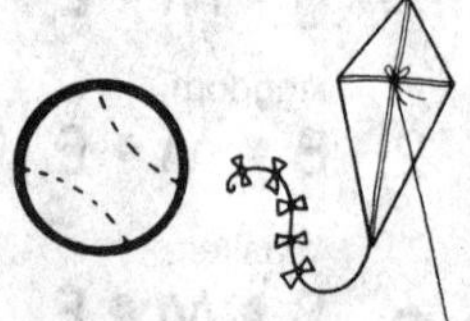

3¢ 9¢

3¢ + 9¢ = __¢

4¢ 2¢ 3¢

4¢ + 2¢ + 3¢ = __¢

9¢ 4¢

9¢ + 4¢ = __¢

5¢ 4¢

5¢ + 4¢ = __¢

1¢ 6¢ 5¢

1¢ + 6¢ + 5¢ = __¢

 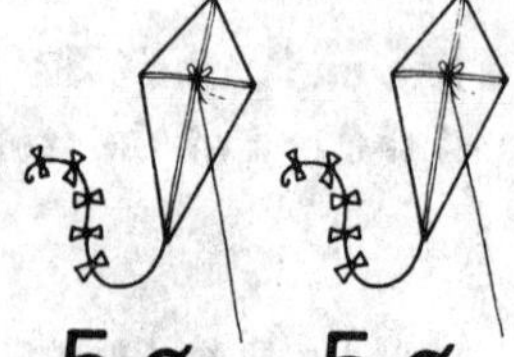

5¢ 5¢

5¢ + 5¢ = __¢

9¢ 5¢

9¢ + 5¢ = __¢

G 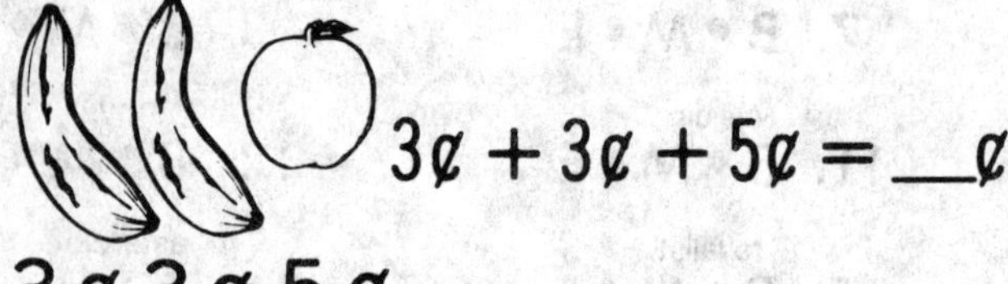

3¢ 3¢ 5¢

3¢ + 3¢ + 5¢ = __¢

4¢ 2¢ 7¢

4¢ + 2¢ + 7¢ = __¢

Underlining Correct Answers

Underline the answer that defines each word. Write your own sentence about each word.

1. **fox**
   a. a small animal with no tail
   b. an animal in the cat family
   c. wild animal with bushy tail

2. **fire**
   a. something burning
   b. something frozen
   c. something very cold

3. **fan**
   a. still
   b. used to move the air
   c. without movement

4. **safe**
   a. in danger
   b. metal box to keep things safe
   c. not protected

5. **knife**
   a. used for eating soup
   b. used for cutting
   c. used for stirring

Picture Names

Pick the word from the box that matches each picture, and write the word in the space. See sample "1."

girl	bag	hang	wagon
wag	goat	gun	sun
glove	gas	pig	glass

1. SAMPLE

bag

2.

3.

4.

5.

6.

7.

8.

9.

10.

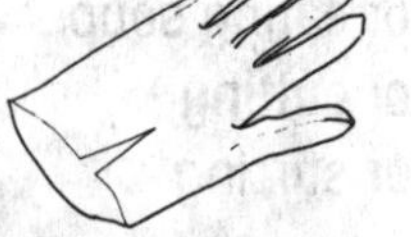

11.

12.

Subtraction of 1's, 2's, and 3's

Subtract the members of the second set from the members of the first set to make the third set. See sample "A."

A. — = 8 — = 7 — = 6

B. — = __ — = __ — = __

C. — = __ — = __ — = __

D. — = __ — = __ — = __

E. — = __ — = __ — = __

F. — = __ — = __ — = __

G. — = __ — = __ — = __

H. — = __ — = __ — = __

I. — = __ — = __ — = __

J. 9 − 1 = __ 8 − 1 = __ 7 − 1 = __ 6 − 1 = __

K. 4 − 1 = __ 3 − 1 = __ 2 − 1 = __ 1 − 1 = __

L. 8 − 2 = __ 7 − 2 = __ 6 − 2 = __ 5 − 2 = __

M. 3 − 2 = __ 2 − 2 = __ 9 − 3 = __ 8 − 3 = __

Internal Letter Changes

Draw a line under each word that is different. See examples "1" and "2."

1.	lost	<u>last</u>	lost	2.	then	<u>than</u>	then
3.	ride	ride	rode	4.	spat	spot	spat
5.	hone	home	home	6.	want	went	went
7.	time	time	tine	8.	whit	whit	what
9.	want	want	wont	10.	make	make	mike
11.	word	ward	ward	12.	coke	cake	coke
13.	find	fond	find	14.	came	come	come
15.	give	gave	gave	16.	lake	like	lake
17.	like	like	lake	18.	gave	give	give
19.	come	came	came	20.	find	find	fond
21.	cake	cake	coke	22.	ward	word	word
23.	make	mike	mike	24.	wont	want	wont
25.	what	what	whit	26.	tine	tine	time
27.	went	want	went	28.	home	hone	hone
29.	spot	spot	spat	30.	rode	ride	rode
31.	then	than	than	32.	last	last	lost

"th," "wh" Sounds

A

Listen to these words that have the "th" sound in them.

Beginning "th"	Middle "th"	End "th"
thin	mother	health
there	nothing	smooth
them	leather	fifth

Listen to these sounds of "th." If the "th" sound is at the beginning of the word, draw a line under the "B." If the "th" sound is in the middle of the word, draw a line under the "M." If the "th" sound is at the end of the word, draw a line under the "E."

EXAMPLES:

thanks — B • M • E (B underlined)
another — B • M • E (M underlined)
wealth — B • M • E (E underlined)

1. healthy B • M • E
2. threat B • M • E
3. width B • M • E
4. weather B • M • E
5. thing B • M • E
6. length B • M • E
7. feather B • M • E
8. thrash B • M • E
9. grandmother B • M • E
10. twelfth B • M • E
11. bathe B • M • E
12. whether B • M • E
13. thicket B • M • E
14. death B • M • E
15. thrift B • M • E
16. arithmetic B • M • E

B

Listen to these words that have the "wh" sound in them.

whale	whatever	whack
wheat	when	who
what	wheel	why

Listen to these sounds of "wh." If the "wh" sound is at the beginning of the word, draw a line under the "B." If the "wh" sound is in the middle of the word, draw a line under the "M." If the "wh" sound is at the end of the word, draw a line under the "E."

1. whistle B • M • E
2. rewhiten B • M • E
3. whip B • M • E
4. pinwheel B • M • E
5. whisper B • M • E
6. whirleybird B • M • E
7. awhile B • M • E
8. whittle B • M • E
9. paddlewheeler B • M • E
10. whether B • M • E
11. nonwhite B • M • E
12. whichever B • M • E
13. bewhiskered B • M • E
14. whipsaw B • M • E
15. anywhere B • M • E
16. whimwham B • M • E

Combining Members of Sets

Write in the correct answers. See example "A."

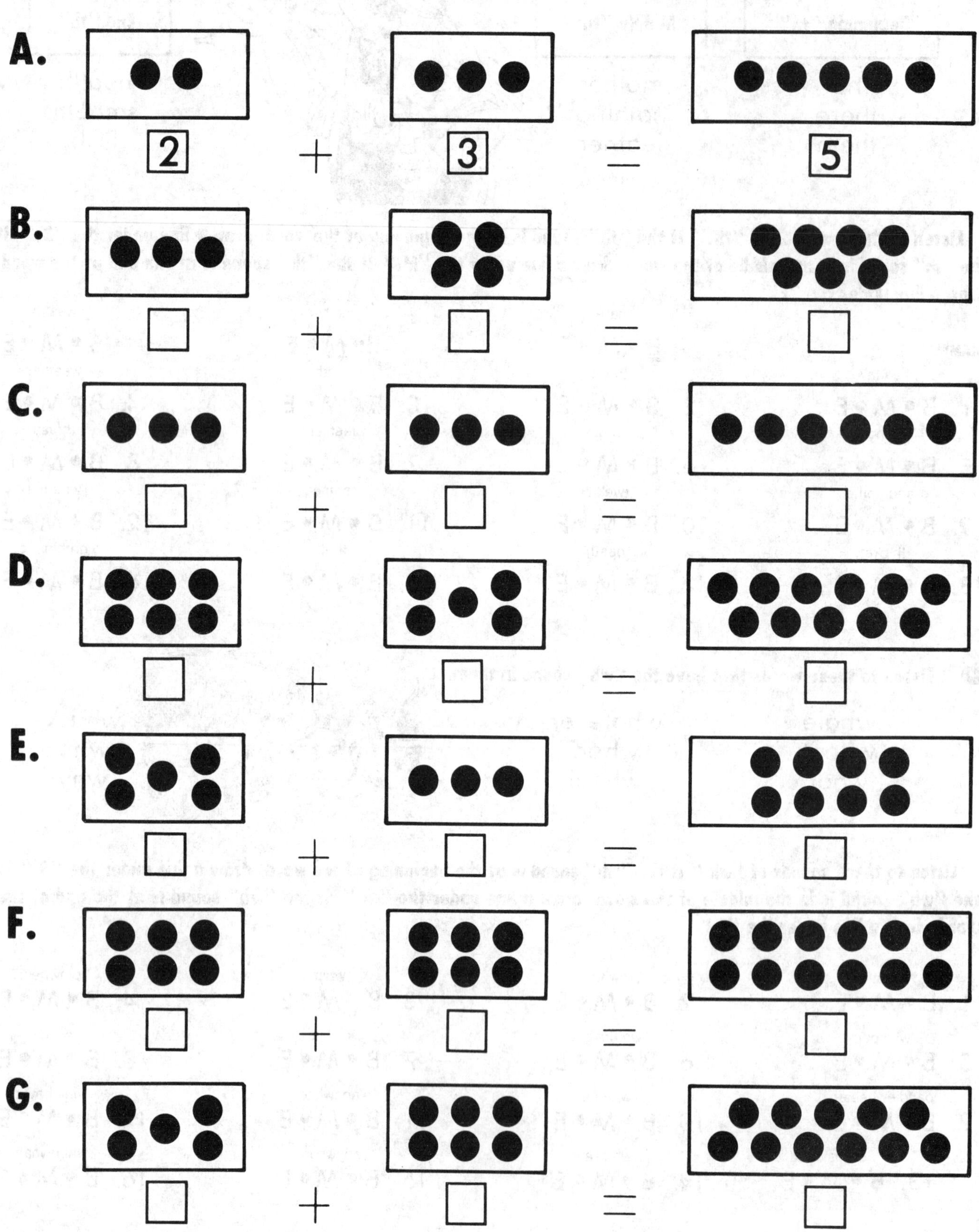

Correct Spellings

Circle the correctly spelled word that matches each picture.
See the example.

EXAMPLE:

heavy (circled) heavee
hevy hevie

1\.

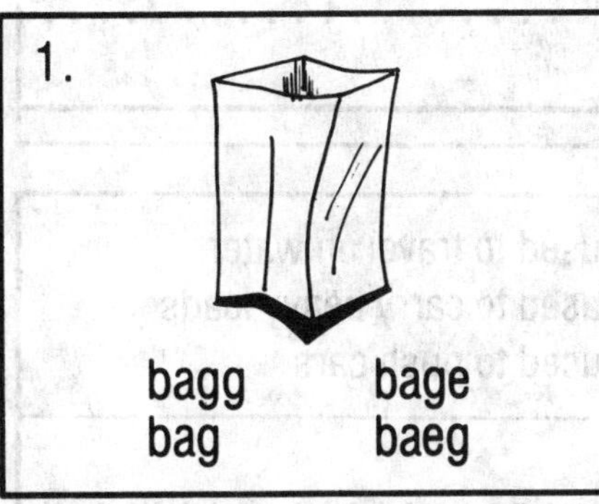

bagg bage
bag baeg

2\.

wagen wagon
wagin waggon

3\.

goat goet
gote got

4\.

gurl gerl
gyrl girl

5\.

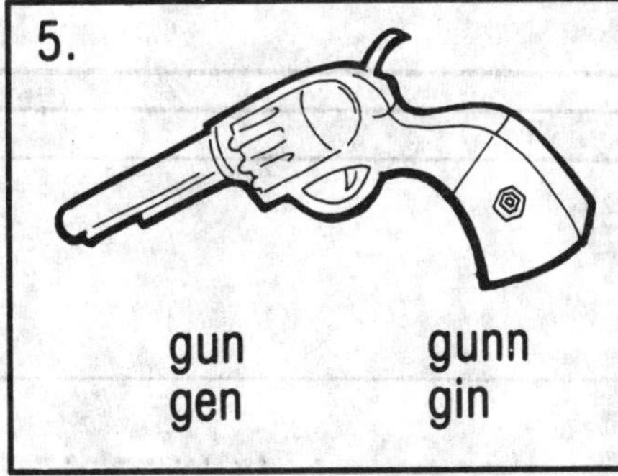

gun gunn
gen gin

6\.

wagg waeg
wag weg

7\.

glass gless
glas glaes

8\.

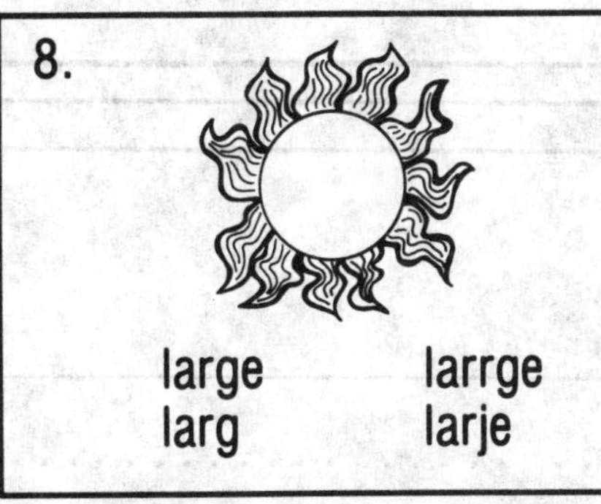

large larrge
larg larje

9\.

pigg pig
peeg pigge

10\.

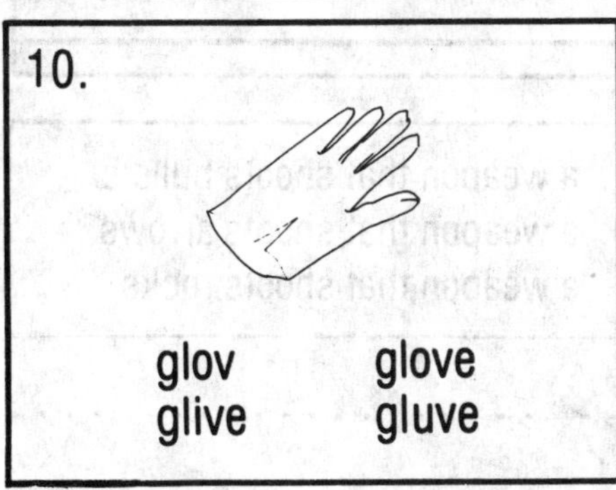

glov glove
glive gluve

11\.

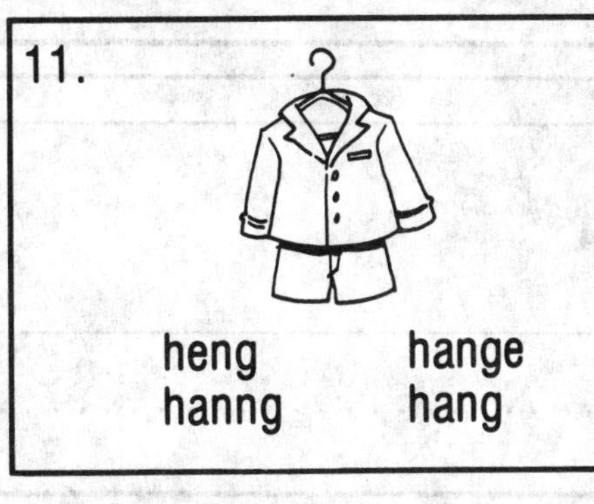

heng hange
hanng hang

12\.

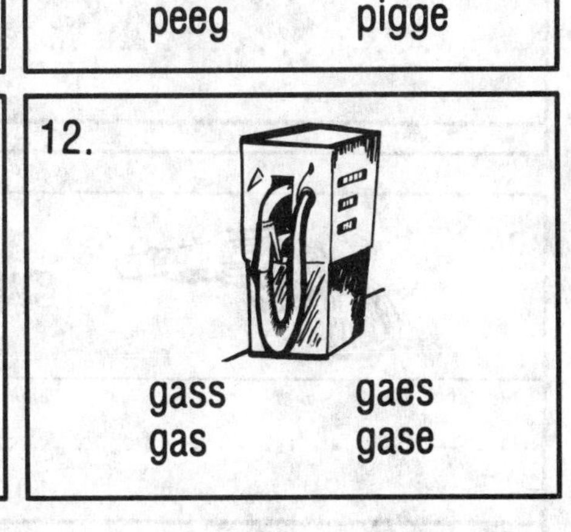

gass gaes
gas gase

Underline the Right Answers

Underline the answer that defines each word. Write your own sentence about each word.

1. **bag**
   a. a container made of steel
   b. a container made of wood
   c. a container made of paper

2. **wagon**
   a. used to travel on water
   b. used to carry heavy loads
   c. used to push cars

3. **goat**
   a. an animal similar to a cow
   b. an animal similar to a horse
   c. an animal similar to a sheep

4. **girl**
   a. a female child
   b. a male child
   c. another word for "woman"

5. **gun**
   a. a weapon that shoots bullets
   b. a weapon that shoots arrows
   c. a weapon that shoots rocks

Subtraction Facts 1's, 2's, and 3's

A Draw a line under each subtraction fact as you read.

1. 2 − 1 = 1   3 − 1 = 2   4 − 1 = 3   5 − 1 = 4   6 − 1 = 5
   7 − 1 = 6   8 − 1 = 7   9 − 1 = 8   10 − 1 = 9

2. 3 − 2 = 1   4 − 2 = 2   5 − 2 = 3   6 − 2 = 4   7 − 2 = 5
   8 − 2 = 6   9 − 2 = 7   10 − 2 = 8   11 − 2 = 9

3. 4 − 3 = 1   5 − 3 = 2   6 − 3 = 3   7 − 3 = 4   8 − 3 = 5
   9 − 3 = 6   10 − 3 = 7   11 − 3 = 8   12 − 3 = 9

B Complete the number sentences by filling in the blanks.

4. 2 − 1 = ____   3 − 1 = ____   4 − 1 = ____
   5 − 1 = ____   6 − 1 = ____   7 − 1 = ____
   8 − 1 = ____   9 − 1 = ____   10 − 1 = ____

5. 3 − 2 = ____   4 − 2 = ____   5 − 2 = ____
   6 − 2 = ____   7 − 2 = ____   8 − 2 = ____
   9 − 2 = ____   10 − 2 = ____   11 − 2 = ____

6. 4 − 3 = ____   5 − 3 = ____   6 − 3 = ____
   7 − 3 = ____   8 − 3 = ____   9 − 3 = ____
   10 − 3 = ____   11 − 3 = ____   12 − 3 = ____

C Fill in the blanks.

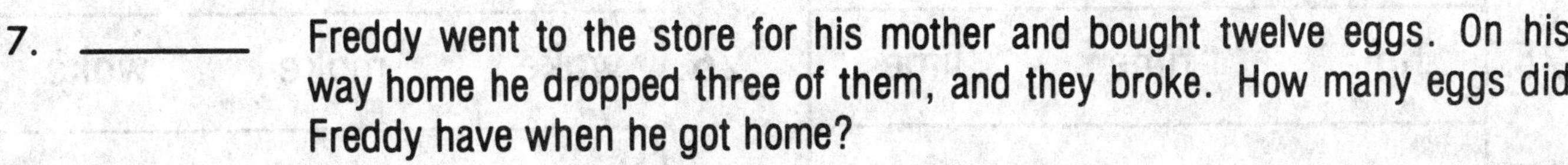

7. ____ Freddy went to the store for his mother and bought twelve eggs. On his way home he dropped three of them, and they broke. How many eggs did Freddy have when he got home?

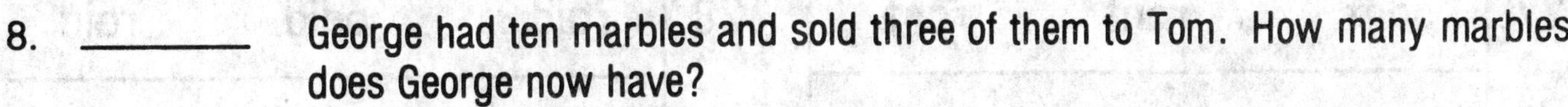

8. ____ George had ten marbles and sold three of them to Tom. How many marbles does George now have?

9. ____ Jerry had eight balloons. Two of them burst. How many balloons does Jerry now have?

10. ____ Joan brought nine cupcakes to school. She has already given three cupcakes to her friends. How many cupcakes does she have left?

First Letter Changes

Draw a line under each word that is different. See examples "1" and "2."

1.	look	book	look	2.	cone	cone	hone
3.	lake	lake	take	4.	rake	bake	rake
5.	raid	paid	paid	6.	rant	pant	pant
7.	make	make	wake	8.	lime	lime	time
9.	ball	tall	tall	10.	jump	pump	jump
11.	some	come	come	12.	side	ride	ride
13.	same	same	came	14.	went	went	sent
15.	cave	rave	rave	16.	dove	love	love
17.	dove	love	dove	18.	cave	cave	rave
19.	sent	sent	went	20.	came	same	came
21.	ride	side	side	22.	come	some	some
23.	jump	pump	pump	24.	ball	ball	tall
25.	time	time	lime	26.	wake	make	wake
27.	pant	rant	rant	28.	raid	paid	raid
29.	bake	bake	rake	30.	take	take	lake
31.	hone	cone	cone	32.	book	look	book

"ch," "sh" Sounds

A **Listen to these words that have the "ch" sound in them.**

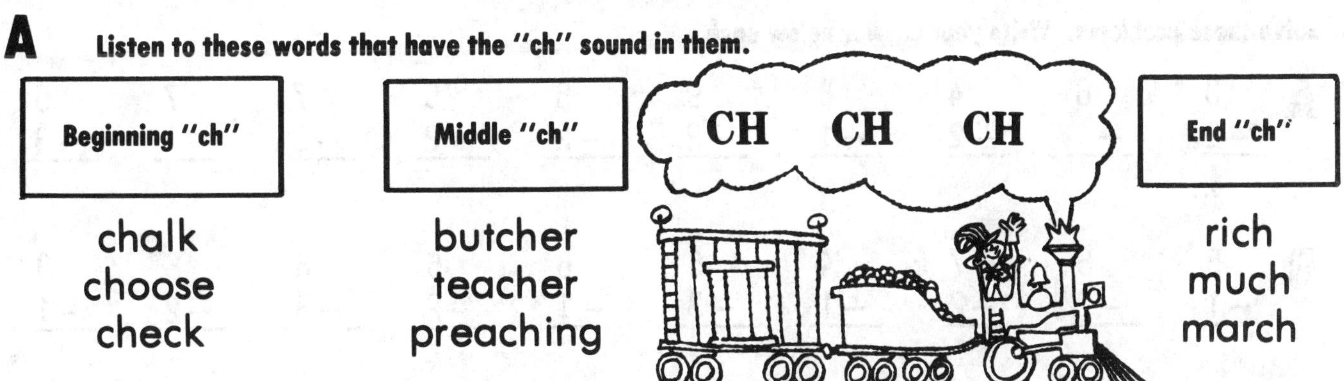

Beginning "ch"	Middle "ch"	End "ch"
chalk	butcher	rich
choose	teacher	much
check	preaching	march

Listen to these sounds of "ch." If the "ch" sound is at the beginning of the word, draw a line under the "B." If the "ch" is in the middle, draw a line under the "M." If the "ch" sound is at the end, draw a line under the "E."

EXAMPLES:

reach	child	reachable
B • M • E (E underlined)	B • M • E (B underlined)	B • M • E (M underlined)

checkers	peach	Charlie	screeching
1. B • M • E	2. B • M • E	3. B • M • E	4. B • M • E
choice	beseech	grandchild	catcher
5. B • M • E	6. B • M • E	7. B • M • E	8. B • M • E
discharge	scratch	quenching	cherry
9. B • M • E	10. B • M • E	11. B • M • E	12. B • M • E
attaching	exchange	handkerchief	spinach
13. B • M • E	14. B • M • E	15. B • M • E	16. B • M • E

B **Listen to these words that have the "sh" sound in them.**

Beginning "sh"	Middle "sh"	End "sh"
ship	dishpan	flush
shed	fishing	wish
shelf	washed	trash

Listen to these sounds of "sh." If the "sh" sound is at the beginning of the word, draw a line under the "B." If the "sh" sound is in the middle of the word, draw a line under the "M." If the "sh" sound is at the end of the word, draw a line under the "E."

blush	washer	dishpan	smash
1. B • M • E	2. B • M • E	3. B • M • E	4. B • M • E
washability	shower	bashful	plush
5. B • M • E	6. B • M • E	7. B • M • E	8. B • M • E
shotgun	dashboard	smash	fashionable
9. B • M • E	10. B • M • E	11. B • M • E	12. B • M • E
cashier	flourish	shampoo	Washington
13. B • M • E	14. B • M • E	15. B • M • E	16. B • M • E

Practicing Subtraction 1's, 2's, and 3's

Solve these problems. Write your answer below each.

A	$3 - 2$ 1	$6 - 1$	$4 - 2$	$8 - 1$	$9 - 2$	$6 - 2$	$5 - 2$	$7 - 3$	$7 - 1$	$5 - 3$
B	$5 - 1$	$6 - 2$	$7 - 2$	$4 - 1$	$5 - 3$	$6 - 1$	$5 - 2$	$6 - 3$	$8 - 2$	$3 - 1$
C	$4 - 3$	$2 - 1$	$7 - 1$	$8 - 3$	$5 - 1$	$6 - 3$	$8 - 1$	$5 - 3$	$9 - 1$	$4 - 1$
D	$2 - 1$	$5 - 4$	$9 - 3$	$7 - 1$	$5 - 2$	$6 - 2$	$4 - 1$	$3 - 1$	$6 - 1$	$7 - 3$
E	$7 - 1$	$4 - 2$	$8 - 2$	$8 - 1$	$9 - 2$	$3 - 1$	$6 - 1$	$4 - 3$	$8 - 3$	$5 - 3$
F	$3 - 1$	$6 - 2$	$5 - 2$	$8 - 2$	$3 - 2$	$4 - 1$	$5 - 3$	$9 - 2$	$7 - 2$	$6 - 3$
G	$4 - 3$	$6 - 3$	$9 - 2$	$9 - 3$	$5 - 3$	$5 - 1$	$7 - 2$	$8 - 3$	$4 - 1$	$9 - 1$
H	$7 - 2$	$8 - 3$	$4 - 1$	$9 - 1$	$5 - 3$	$7 - 3$	$2 - 1$	$8 - 2$	$4 - 2$	$6 - 3$
I	$4 - 2$	$6 - 2$	$7 - 1$	$9 - 3$	$7 - 2$	$5 - 3$	$8 - 1$	$3 - 2$	$7 - 3$	$9 - 2$
J	$7 - 2$	$2 - 1$	$5 - 3$	$3 - 1$	$5 - 1$	$6 - 2$	$4 - 1$	$3 - 2$	$9 - 1$	$8 - 1$

Practice Spelling Words

Underline the answer that defines each word. Write your own sentence about each word.

1. **wag**
   - a. to move from side to side
   - b. to move up and down
   - c. to hold still

2. **glass**
   - a. a material you can see through
   - b. a material you cannot break
   - c. a material that bends easily

3. **large**
   - a. very small
   - b. not big
   - c. very big

4. **pig**
   - a. an animal raised for racing
   - b. an animal raised for its fur
   - c. an animal raised for its meat

5. **glove**
   - a. covering for head
   - b. covering for hand
   - c. covering for foot

Writing the Words

Pick the word from the box that matches each picture, and write the word in the space. See sample "1."

ham	teeth	horse	light
chin	sharp	fight	shell
three	bath	house	shoe

1. ham

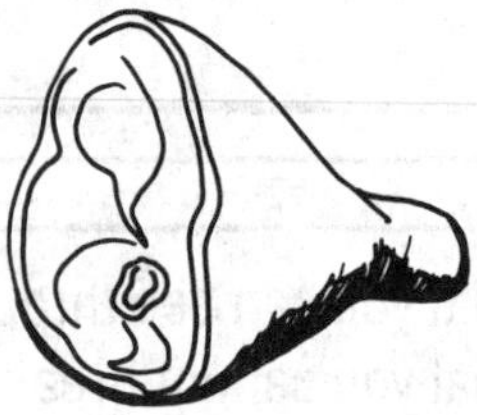

2.

3.

4.

5.

6.

7. 3

8.

9.

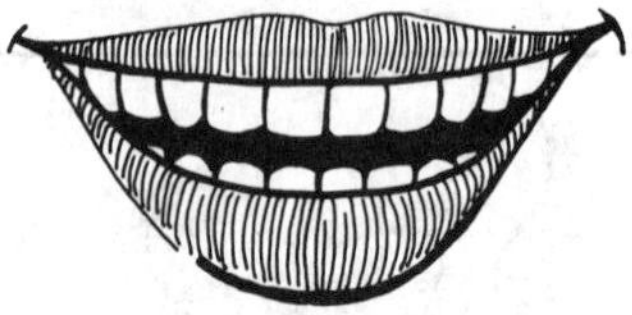

10.

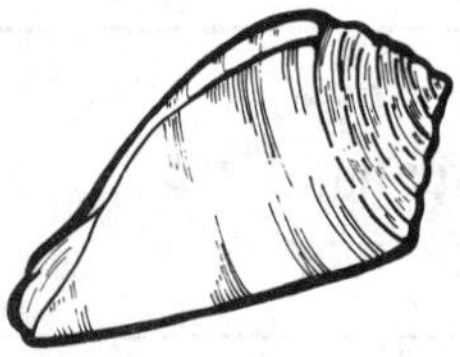

11.

12.

Subtraction Facts 4's, 5's, and 6's

Write in the correct answers. See example "A."

A 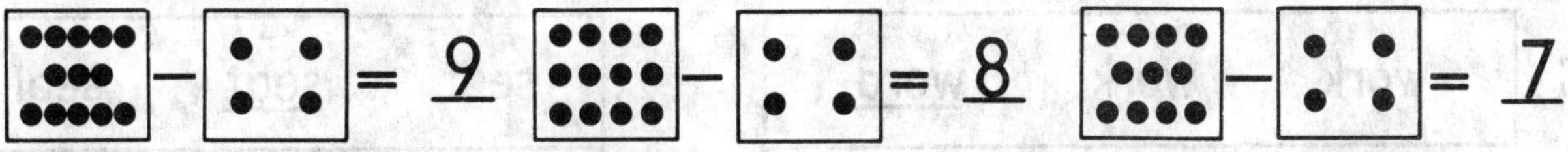

= 9 = 8 = 7

B 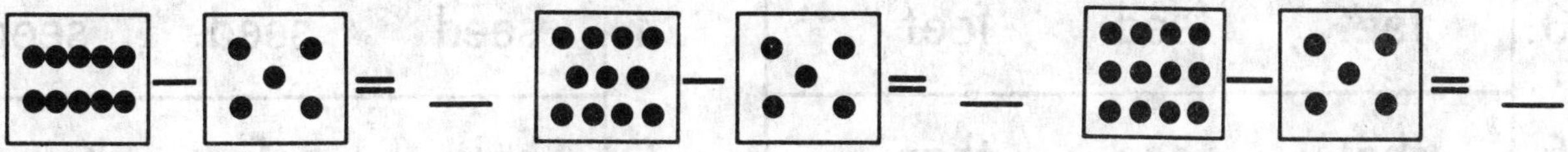

C 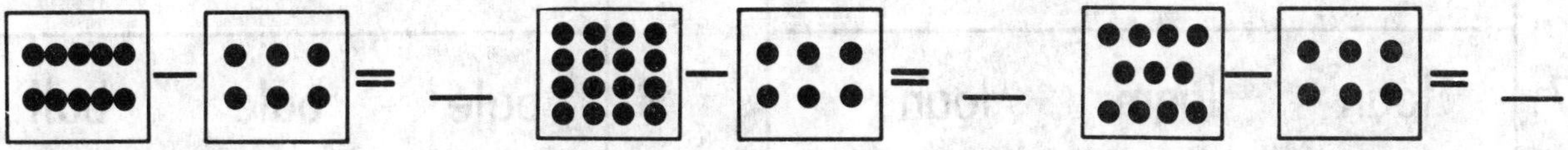

D 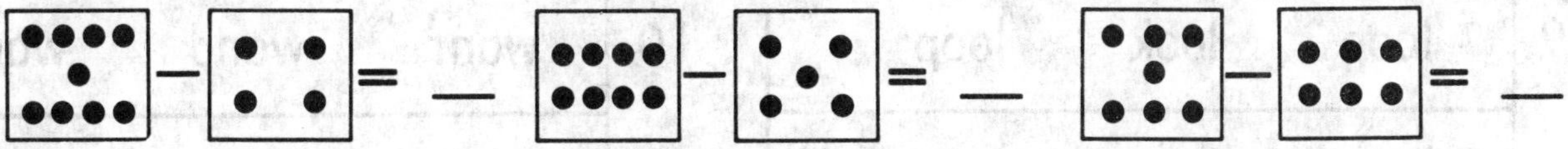

E 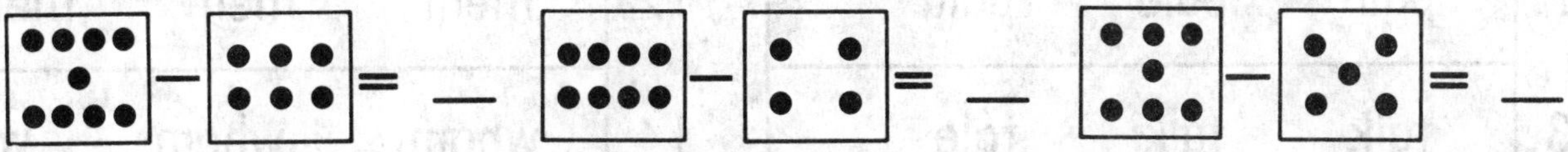

F 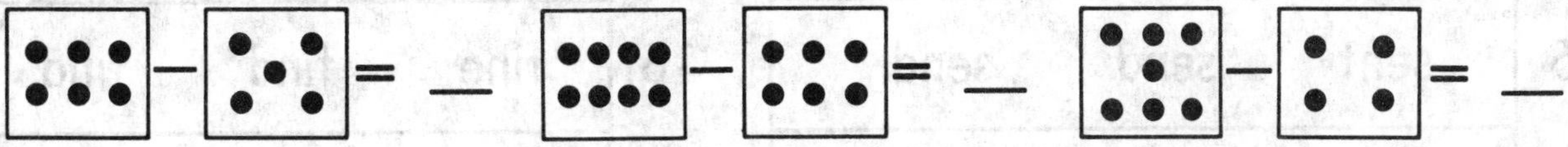

G 13 — 4 = __ 12 — 4 = __ 11 — 4 = __ 10 — 4 = __

H 8 — 4 = __ 7 — 4 = __ 6 — 4 = __ 5 — 4 = __

I 13 — 5 = __ 12 — 5 = __ 11 — 5 = __ 10 — 5 = __

J 12 — 6 = __ 11 — 6 = __ 10 — 6 = __ 9 — 6 = __

K 12 — 5 = __ 8 — 5 = __ 7 — 4 = __ 4 — 4 = __

L 11 — 4 = __ 7 — 4 = __ 12 — 6 = __ 10 — 4 = __

Last Letter Changes

Draw a line under each word that is different. See examples "1" and "2."

1.	work	work	<u>word</u>	2.	seal	<u>seat</u>	seal
3.	feet	feed	feet	4.	seed	seed	seep
5.	that	than	than	6.	held	help	help
7.	loan	loam	loan	8.	bale	bale	ball
9.	loop	look	loop	10.	want	wand	want
11.	pair	paid	paid	12.	them	then	then
13.	talk	talk	tale	14.	wham	wham	what
15.	sent	send	send	16.	fine	find	find
17.	fine	find	fine	18.	sent	send	sent
19.	what	wham	what	20.	talk	tale	tale
21.	then	them	them	22.	pair	pair	paid
23.	wand	wand	want	24.	look	loop	look
25.	ball	bale	ball	26.	loan	loam	loam
27.	held	help	held	28.	that	than	that
29.	seep	seep	seed	30.	feed	feed	feet
31.	seal	seat	seat	32.	word	work	word

"ng," "dr" Sounds

A Listen to these words that have the "ng" sound in them.

Middle "ng"	End "ng"	End "ng"
bingo	cling	gang
anger	bang	sing
tango	king	wing

Listen to these sounds of "ng." If the "ng" sound is at the beginning of the word, draw a line under the "B." If the "ng" sound is in the middle of the word, draw a line under the "M." If the "ng" sound is at the end of the word, draw a line under the "E."

EXAMPLES:

twang B • M • E (E underlined)	triangle B • M • E (M underlined)	buzzing B • M • E (E underlined)

spring 1. B • M • E	songster 2. B • M • E	building 3. B • M • E	bring 4. B • M • E
amongst 5. B • M • E	angle 6. B • M • E	blaming 7. B • M • E	twanging 8. B • M • E
language 9. B • M • E	hung 10. B • M • E	tangled 11. B • M • E	swung 12. B • M • E
tango 13. B • M • E	uncle 14. B • M • E	monkey 15. B • M • E	handkerchief 16. B • M • E

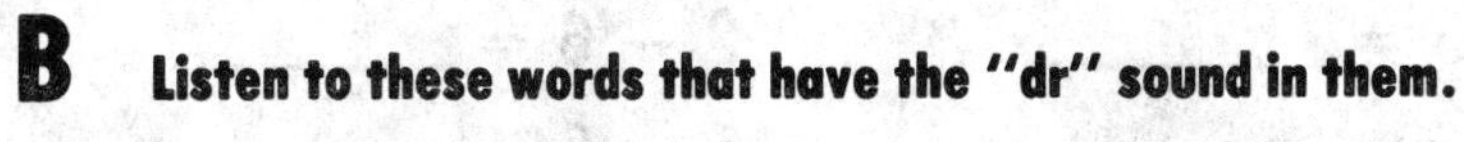

B Listen to these words that have the "dr" sound in them.

drank	hundred	drop
drew	withdraw	hydraulic
drip	undress	drum

Listen to these sounds of "dr." If the "dr" sound is at the beginning of the word, draw a line under the "B." If the "dr" sound is in the middle of the word, draw a line under the "M." If the "dr" sound is at the end of the word, draw a line under the "E."

dresser 1. B • M • E	drab 2. B • M • E	sundries 3. B • M • E	hidrosis 4. B • M • E
drew 5. B • M • E	teardrop 6. B • M • E	drink 7. B • M • E	dried 8. B • M • E
hindrance 9. B • M • E	dreamland 10. B • M • E	hydrochloric 11. B • M • E	dreadfulness 12. B • M • E
hydroscopic 13. B • M • E	dromedary 14. B • M • E	drumstick 15. B • M • E	humdrummed 16. B • M • E

Subtraction of 4's, 5's, and 6's

A **Draw a line under each subtraction fact as you read.**

1. 5 − 4 = 1   6 − 4 = 2   7 − 4 = 3   8 − 4 = 4   9 − 4 = 5
   10 − 4 = 6   11 − 4 = 7   12 − 4 = 8   13 − 4 = 9

2. 6 − 5 = 1   7 − 5 = 2   8 − 5 = 3   9 − 5 = 4   10 − 5 = 5
   11 − 5 = 6   12 − 5 = 7   13 − 5 = 8   14 − 5 = 9

3. 7 − 6 = 1   8 − 6 = 2   9 − 6 = 3   10 − 6 = 4   11 − 6 = 5
   12 − 6 = 6   13 − 6 = 7   14 − 6 = 8   15 − 6 = 9

B **Complete the number sentences by filling in the blanks.**

4. 5 − 4 = ______   6 − 4 = ______   7 − 4 = ______
   8 − 4 = ______   9 − 4 = ______   10 − 4 = ______
   11 − 4 = ______   12 − 4 = ______   13 − 4 = ______

5. 6 − 5 = ______   7 − 5 = ______   8 − 5 = ______
   9 − 5 = ______   10 − 5 = ______   11 − 5 = ______
   12 − 5 = ______   13 − 5 = ______   14 − 5 = ______

6. 7 − 6 = ______   8 − 6 = ______   9 − 6 = ______
   10 − 6 = ______   11 − 6 = ______   12 − 6 = ______
   13 − 6 = ______   14 − 6 = ______   15 − 6 = ______

C **Fill in the blanks.**

7. ______ If you had twelve pennies and you spent four of them, how many pennies would you have left?

8. ______ Melvin had eleven pencils at the beginning of the school year. He has used five of them. How many pencils does he have left?

9. ______ Jackie's mother has promised to buy her a membership in a book club when she has read a total of fifteen books from the library. Jackie has already read six books. How many more books does Jackie need to read to receive her membership?

10. ______ Joe had fourteen white rabbits and sold six of them. How many white rabbits does Joe have left?

Learn to Spell

Circle the correctly spelled word that matches each picture. See the example.

EXAMPLE:

curlee curly
curlly curley

1.

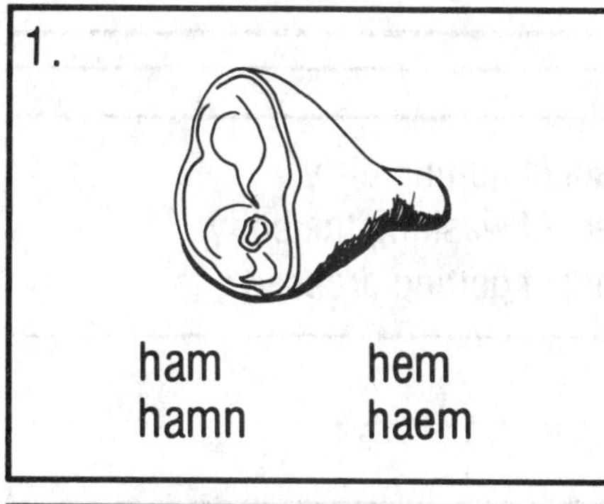

ham hem
hamn haem

2.

beth both
baeth bath

3.

figt fiht
fight fit

4.

shoo shoe
shu shue

5.

hoise howse
hous house

6.

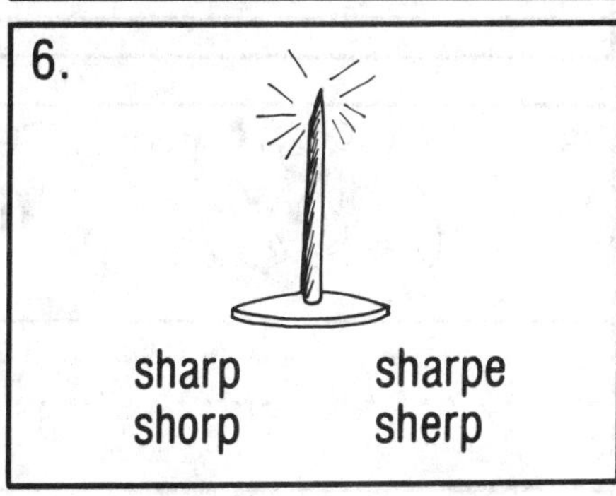

sharp sharpe
shorp sherp

7.

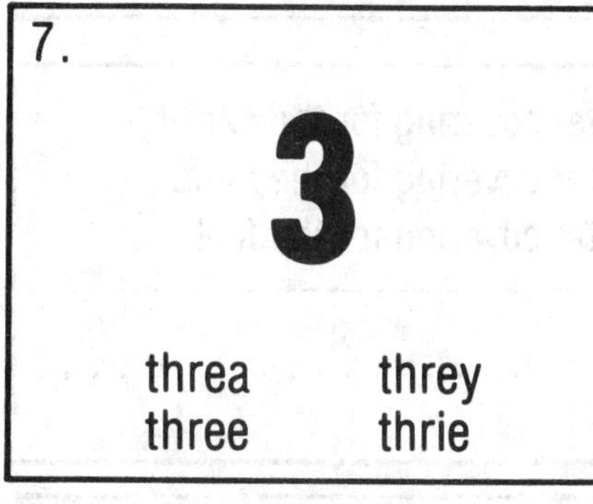

threa threy
three thrie

8.

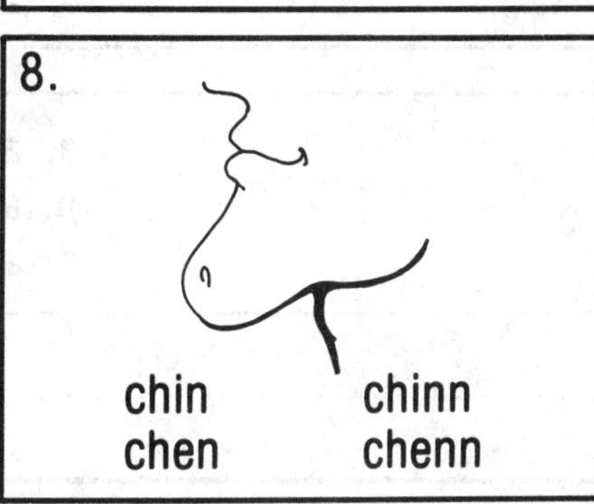

chin chinn
chen chenn

9.

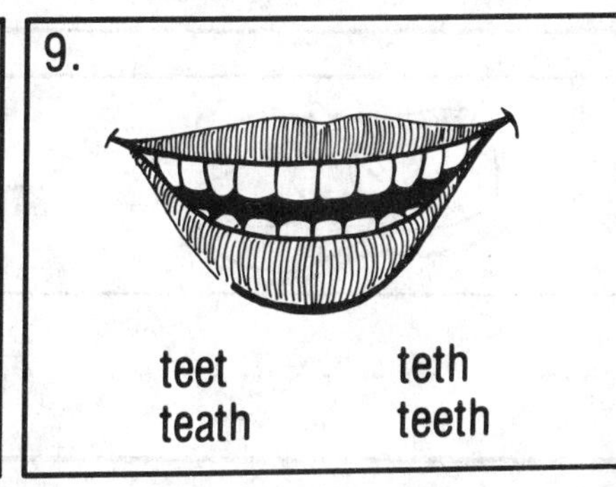

teet teth
teath teeth

10.

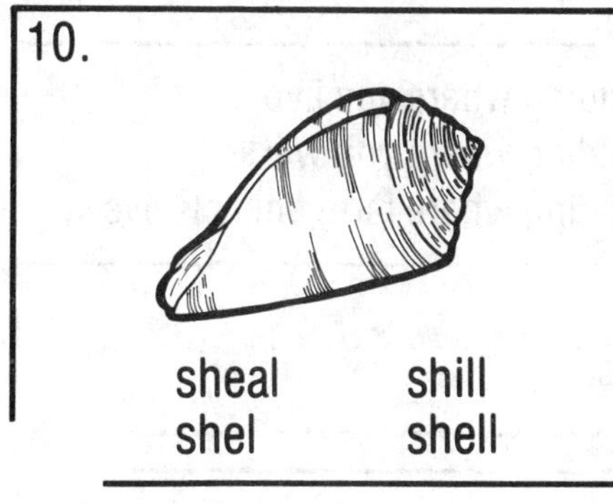

sheal shill
shel shell

11.

hors horsse
horse harse

12.

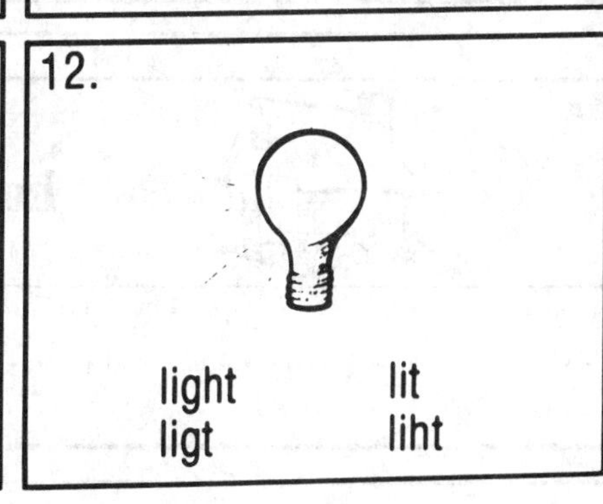

light lit
ligt liht

Practicing Spelling

Underline the answer that defines each word. Write your own sentence about each word.

1. **ham**
   a. meat from a hog
   b. meat from a cow
   c. meat from a chicken

2. **bath**
   a. the act of getting dirty
   b. the act of washing the body
   c. the act of getting dressed

3. **fight**
   a. a boxing match
   b. the act of making friends
   c. to think about

4. **shoe**
   a. an outer covering for the ear
   b. an outer covering for the hand
   c. an outer covering for the foot

5. **house**
   a. a building where you live
   b. a building where you work
   c. a building where farm animals live

Practicing Subtraction 4's, 5's, and 6's

Solve these problems. Write your answer below each.

A	$4 - 1 = 3$	$8 - 6$	$7 - 5$	$6 - 5$	$9 - 4$	$7 - 6$	$5 - 4$	$9 - 6$	$9 - 4$	$8 - 5$
B	$6 - 4$	$4 - 3$	$5 - 1$	$7 - 6$	$6 - 2$	$6 - 5$	$7 - 4$	$5 - 4$	$9 - 3$	$9 - 6$
C	$7 - 4$	$5 - 3$	$9 - 6$	$8 - 5$	$7 - 6$	$8 - 4$	$7 - 5$	$9 - 4$	$7 - 5$	$8 - 3$
D	$7 - 6$	$6 - 5$	$9 - 5$	$8 - 4$	$5 - 2$	$7 - 4$	$6 - 1$	$5 - 3$	$4 - 3$	$6 - 2$
E	$9 - 4$	$8 - 6$	$6 - 5$	$7 - 6$	$4 - 3$	$5 - 1$	$9 - 6$	$9 - 5$	$8 - 4$	$9 - 3$
F	$6 - 4$	$9 - 4$	$8 - 3$	$7 - 5$	$7 - 4$	$5 - 4$	$6 - 3$	$6 - 2$	$5 - 3$	$8 - 6$
G	$9 - 4$	$8 - 5$	$9 - 6$	$8 - 2$	$9 - 5$	$8 - 4$	$6 - 1$	$8 - 6$	$9 - 6$	$7 - 4$
H	$7 - 5$	$9 - 6$	$8 - 6$	$7 - 1$	$4 - 2$	$8 - 5$	$9 - 4$	$9 - 5$	$9 - 3$	$7 - 3$
I	$8 - 5$	$9 - 5$	$8 - 6$	$5 - 1$	$6 - 2$	$4 - 2$	$6 - 1$	$9 - 6$	$8 - 4$	$7 - 4$
J	$8 - 4$	$9 - 4$	$6 - 5$	$6 - 2$	$4 - 3$	$5 - 2$	$9 - 6$	$5 - 1$	$9 - 5$	$6 - 3$

Add a Letter

Draw a line under each word that is different. See examples "1" and "2."

1.	see	<u>seed</u>	see	2.	the	the	<u>them</u>
3.	you	you	your	4.	doe	does	doe
5.	care	car	car	6.	wind	win	win
7.	can	can	cane	8.	fun	fund	fun
9.	cape	cap	cap	10.	cute	cut	cut
11.	pin	pine	pin	12.	bit	bit	bite
13.	tear	tea	tea	14.	hate	hat	hat
15.	kit	kit	kite	16.	rat	rate	rat
17.	tap	tape	tap	18.	dot	dot	dote
19.	bush	bus	bus	20.	sea	seat	sea
21.	rod	rode	rod	22.	mad	mad	made
23.	hop	hop	hope	24.	here	her	her
25.	feed	fee	fee	26.	cop	cop	copy
27.	fin	fin	find	28.	rid	ride	rid
29.	too	toot	too	30.	sink	sin	sin
31.	war	war	ward	32.	boo	boo	book

"gl," "fl," "cl" Sounds

A Listen to these words that have the "gl" and "fl" sound in them.

Beginning "gl" and "fl"	Middle "gl" and "fl"	End "gl" and "fl"
flute	overflow	jingle
glass	underglaze	trifle
floor	trifling	pitiful

Listen to these sounds of "gl" and "fl." If the "gl" or "fl" sound is at the beginning of the word, draw a line under the "B." If the "gl" or "fl" sound is in the middle of the word, draw a line under the "M." If the "gl" or "fl" sound is at the end of the word, draw a line under the "E."

EXAMPLES:

flower — B • M • E (B underlined)
pitifulness — B • M • E (M underlined)
mingle — B • M • E (E underlined)

1. triangle B • M • E
2. glass B • M • E
3. overflow B • M • E
4. wonderful B • M • E
5. awful B • M • E
6. glorious B • M • E
7. pitiful B • M • E
8. butterfly B • M • E
9. wiggle B • M • E
10. glimpse B • M • E
11. flashlight B • M • E
12. flown B • M • E
13. trifling B • M • E
14. centrifugal B • M • E
15. painful B • M • E
16. playfully B • M • E

B Listen to these words that have the "cl" sound in them.

Beginning "cl"	Middle "cl"	End "cl"
clothes	incline	bicycle
classroom	declare	chicle
clock	inclose	popsicle

Listen to these sounds of "cl." If the "cl" sound is at the beginning of the word, draw a line under the "B." If the "cl" sound is in the middle of the word, draw a line under the "M." If the "cl" sound is at the end of the word, draw a line under the "E."

1. included B • M • E
2. cleaner B • M • E
3. clutch B • M • E
4. medical B • M • E
5. inclosure B • M • E
6. nickel B • M • E
7. decline B • M • E
8. cliff B • M • E
9. mechanical B • M • E
10. inclination B • M • E
11. honeysuckle B • M • E
12. climbing B • M • E
13. hydrochloric B • M • E
14. clink B • M • E
15. motorcycle B • M • E
16. crackle B • M • E

Subtraction Facts 7's, 8's, and 9's

Write in the correct answers. See the example.

A EXAMPLE: [18 dots] − [7 dots] = 11   [16 dots] − [8 dots] = ____

[16 dots] − [9 dots] = ____   [16 dots] − [7 dots] = ____

[13 dots] − [5 dots] = ____   [16 dots] − [9 dots] = ____

B 18 − 9 = ____ 17 − 9 = ____ 16 − 9 = ____ 15 − 9 = ____

C 17 − 8 = ____ 16 − 8 = ____ 15 − 8 = ____ 14 − 8 = ____

D 16 − 7 = ____ 15 − 7 = ____ 14 − 7 = ____ 13 − 7 = ____

E 17 − 8 = ____ 15 − 9 = ____ 12 − 7 = ____ 11 − 9 = ____

F	9 − 9	10 − 9	11 − 9	12 − 9	13 − 9	14 − 9	15 − 9	16 − 9
G	8 − 8	9 − 8	10 − 8	11 − 8	12 − 8	13 − 8	14 − 8	15 − 8
H	7 − 7	8 − 7	9 − 7	10 − 7	11 − 7	12 − 7	13 − 7	14 − 7
I	12 − 8	14 − 9	10 − 8	13 − 8	10 − 9	13 − 9	16 − 7	15 − 8

Write Sentences

Underline the answer that defines each word. Write your own sentence about each word.

1. **sharp**

a. coming to a point
b. rounded
c. having a dull edge

2. 3 **three**

a. one plus one
b. two plus one
c. two plus two

3. **chin**

a. place below the mouth
b. place about the eyes
c. place above the mouth

4. **teeth**

a. the roof of the mouth
b. the gums in the mouth
c. plural of "tooth"

5. **shell**

a. a soft outer covering
b. a hard outer covering
c. the inside of an egg

Word, Picture Matching

Pick the word from the box that matches each picture, and write the word in the space. See sample "1."

bib	king	milk	time
pipe	chair	train	stir
hit	nine	sit	pin

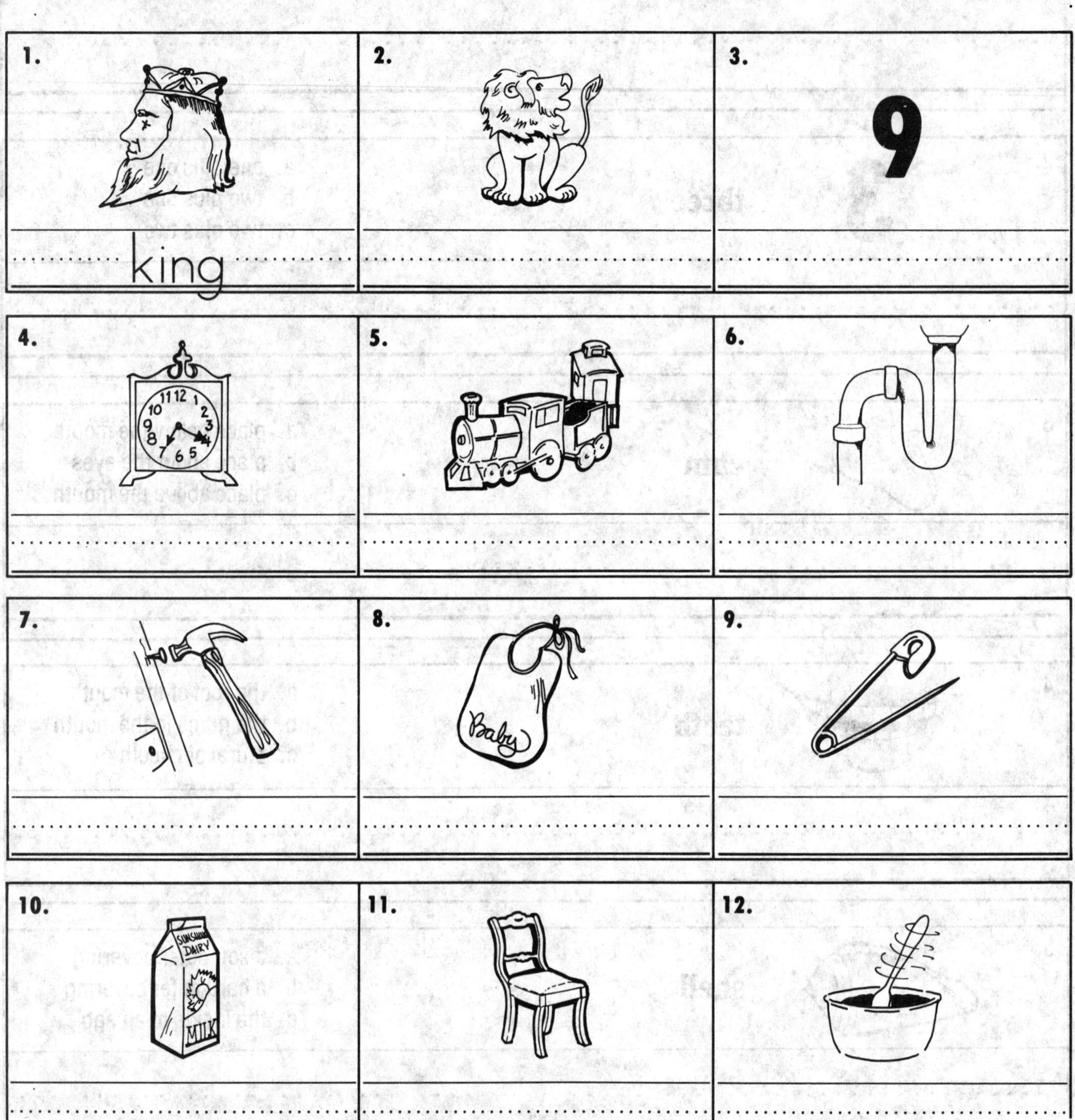

Subtraction Facts

A **Draw a line under each subtraction fact as you read.**

1. 8 − 7 = 1 9 − 7 = 2 10 − 7 = 3 11 − 7 = 4 12 − 7 = 5
   13 − 7 = 6 14 − 7 = 7 15 − 7 = 8 16 − 7 = 9

2. 9 − 8 = 1 10 − 8 = 2 11 − 8 = 3 12 − 8 = 4 13 − 8 = 5
   14 − 8 = 6 15 − 8 = 7 16 − 8 = 8 17 − 8 = 9

3. 10 − 9 = 1 11 − 9 = 2 12 − 9 = 3 13 − 9 = 4 14 − 9 = 5
   15 − 9 = 6 16 − 9 = 7 17 − 9 = 8 18 − 9 = 9

B **Complete the number sentences by filling in the blanks.**

4. 8 − 7 = ______ 9 − 7 = ______ 10 − 7 = ______
   11 − 7 = ______ 12 − 7 = ______ 13 − 7 = ______
   14 − 7 = ______ 15 − 7 = ______ 16 − 7 = ______

5. 9 − 8 = ______ 10 − 8 = ______ 11 − 8 = ______
   12 − 8 = ______ 13 − 8 = ______ 14 − 8 = ______
   15 − 8 = ______ 16 − 8 = ______ 17 − 8 = ______

6. 10 − 9 = ______ 11 − 9 = ______ 12 − 9 = ______
   13 − 9 = ______ 14 − 9 = ______ 15 − 9 = ______
   16 − 9 = ______ 17 − 9 = ______ 18 − 9 = ______

C **Fill in the blanks.**

7. ______ Ann rode seventeen miles Sunday. Today she rode only eight miles. How much farther did she ride Sunday than she did today?

8. ______ Bill's father has a roadside stand. Monday morning he sold fifteen bushels of apples. That afternoon he sold only nine bushels. How many more bushels did he sell in the morning than in the afternoon?

9. ______ Carla had fourteen cents and lost eight cents. How many cents does she have left?

10. ______ Jim had a score of twelve, and Mike had a score of seven. How much larger was Jim's score than Mike's score?

Number Discrimination

Draw an "X" through each number that is like the first one. See examples "A" and "B."

A.	1	2	~~1~~	3
C.	2	1	3	2
E.	3	3	2	1
G.	4	3	2	4
I.	5	4	5	3
K.	6	6	4	2
M.	7	8	7	6
O.	8	8	9	5
Q.	9	7	6	9
S.	0	1	0	2
U.	1	1	2	3
W.	2	4	3	2

B.	3	4	5	~~3~~
D.	4	4	5	6
F.	5	4	3	5
H.	6	7	6	8
J.	7	8	9	7
L.	8	8	9	0
N.	9	8	9	7
P.	0	0	1	2
R.	1	2	1	3
T.	2	2	3	4
V.	3	1	2	3
X.	4	3	4	5

"ed," "th" Ending

A Listen to these words that have the "ed" sound in them.

Beginning "ed"	Middle "ed"	End "ed"
Edward	greedy	graded
eddy	steadier	dedicated
edit	shedding	doubted

Listen to these sounds of "ed." If the "ed" sound is at the beginning of the word, draw a line under the "B." If the "ed" sound is in the middle of the word, draw a line under the "M." If the "ed" sound is at the end of the word, draw a line under the "E."

EXAMPLES: Edgar B • M • E (B underlined) dreadful B • M • E (M underlined) created B • M • E (E underlined)

1. leaked B • M • E
2. greed B • M • E
3. edify B • M • E
4. chided B • M • E
5. editor B • M • E
6. highbred B • M • E
7. contacted B • M • E
8. guarded B • M • E
9. deadbeat B • M • E
10. treed B • M • E
11. dusted B • M • E
12. editorship B • M • E
13. pleaded B • M • E
14. steady B • M • E
15. dreadfully B • M • E
16. beheaded B • M • E

B Listen to these words that have the "th" sound in them.

Beginning "th"	Middle "th"	End "th"
third	weather	earth
theater	brother	month
throat	bathtub	worth

Listen to these sounds of "th." If the "th" sound is at the beginning of the word, draw a line under the "B." If the "th" sound is in the middle of the word, draw a line under the "M." If the "th" sound is at the end of the word, draw a line under the "E."

1. thankful B • M • E
2. Smith B • M • E
3. mathematics B • M • E
4. berth B • M • E
5. wither B • M • E
6. thought B • M • E
7. feather B • M • E
8. tenth B • M • E
9. grandmother B • M • E
10. themselves B • M • E
11. mammoth B • M • E
12. wealth B • M • E
13. hundredth B • M • E
14. whether B • M • E
15. thousand B • M • E
16. mouth B • M • E

Practicing Subtraction 7's, 8's, and 9's

Solve these problems. Write your answer under each.

A	8 −1 = 7	8 −2	9 −7	9 −8	8 −5	7 −6	9 −6	8 −3	7 −1	9 −4
B	8 −2	7 −5	9 −3	9 −7	8 −3	9 −2	7 −6	9 −4	9 −1	7 −3
C	9 −7	8 −4	9 −2	9 −1	9 −3	8 −2	9 −2	8 −6	8 −5	8 −3
D	9 −3	8 −2	7 −5	9 −8	9 −6	7 −4	8 −5	9 −2	8 −3	7 −3
E	8 −7	8 −3	7 −2	7 −3	8 −5	9 −1	8 −2	8 −4	9 −3	7 −1
F	9 −3	7 −4	8 −2	9 −6	9 −8	9 −7	7 −6	8 −5	9 −5	7 −2
G	8 −2	7 −3	8 −1	9 −3	7 −2	8 −3	8 −7	9 −5	9 −2	9 −4
H	9 −8	8 −5	9 −1	9 −7	8 −6	9 −2	8 −3	7 −5	9 −3	9 −6
I	8 −2	8 −3	7 −4	9 −8	9 −3	7 −6	8 −5	9 −2	8 −1	9 −4
J	7 −5	8 −6	9 −2	9 −1	8 −5	8 −4	7 −3	9 −6	8 −7	

Improve Your Spelling

Circle the correctly spelled word that matches each picture. See the example.

EXAMPLE:

funny funnee
funnie funy

1\.

kenng kinng
king keng

2\.

sit sitt
cit site

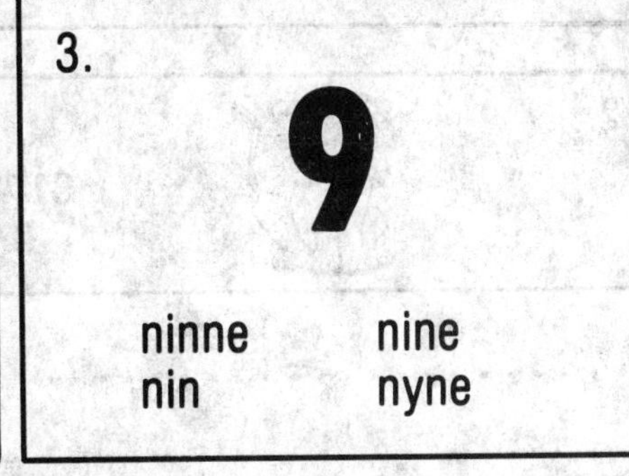

3\.

ninne nine
nin nyne

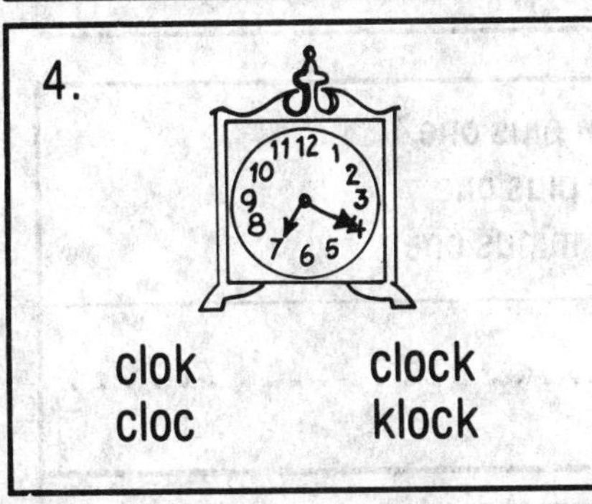

4\.

clok clock
cloc klock

5\.

trayn train
trane traine

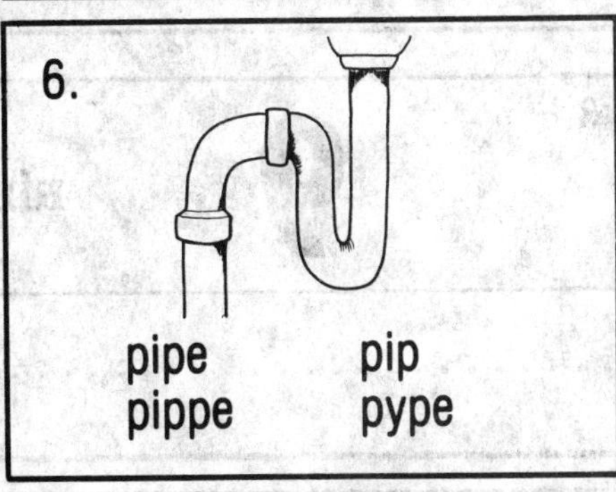

6\.

pipe pip
pippe pype

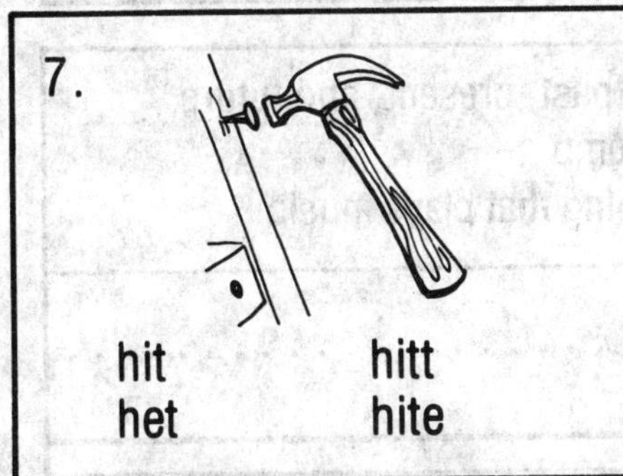

7\.

hit hitt
het hite

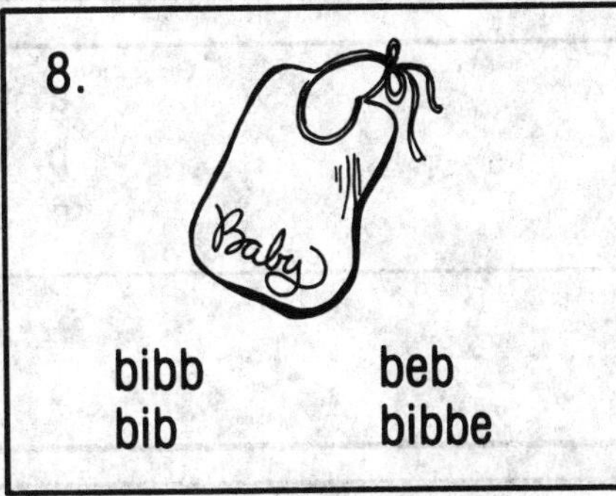

8\.

bibb beb
bib bibbe

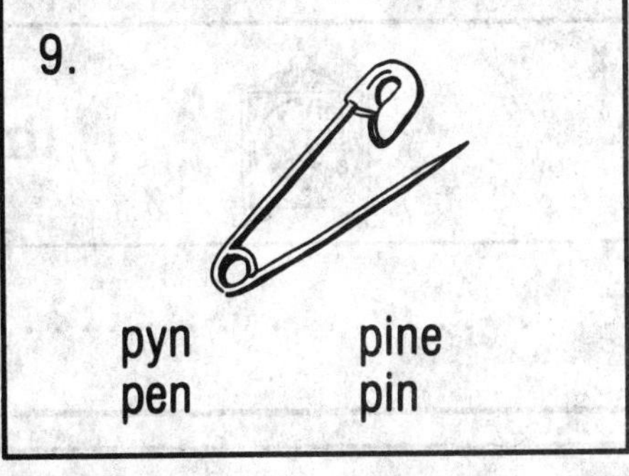

9\.

pyn pine
pen pin

10\.

millk milc
milck milk

11\.

chare chair
chaire cher

12\.

stir stur
ster stirr

Practice Spelling

Underline the answer that defines each word. Write your own sentence about each word.

1. **king**
   a. a woman who rules
   b. a man who rules
   c. the son of a queen

2. **sit**
   a. to play
   b. to work
   c. to rest

3. 9 **nine**
   a. seven plus one
   b. eight plus one
   c. eight minus one

4. **time**
   a. the past, present, and future
   b. a bomb
   c. a thing that plays music

5. **train**
   a. a car that moves through the air
   b. a car that moves on water
   c. many cars moving on a track

Add — Subtract Combinations Through 9's

Write in the correct answers. Watch for the "add" (+) or "subtract" (−) sign.

A	5	6	3	8	7	4	6	5
	−1	−3	−2	−4	−3	−1	−2	−3
	4							
B	4	8	5	9	6	7	3	9
	−2	−1	−2	−4	−1	−2	−1	−3
C	7	9	5	6	8	7	9	6
	−5	−2	−4	−4	−2	−1	−6	−5
D	4	8	9	3	7	6	9	5
	+3	+5	+3	+1	+2	+1	+4	+2
E	5	6	3	8	7	4	6	5
	+1	+3	+2	+4	+3	+1	+2	+3
F	8	6	9	9	4	5	4	8
	+7	+5	+2	+8	+5	+6	+6	+2

G	7 − 4 = __	5 − 1 = __	9 − 5 = __	6 − 3 = __
H	8 − 3 = __	4 − 2 = __	3 − 1 = __	7 − 4 = __
I	9 − 3 = __	8 − 5 = __	6 − 2 = __	5 − 2 = __

"z" Sounds and "l" Blends

A Listen to these words that have the "z" sound in them.

Middle "z"	End "z"	End "z"
baptised	breeze	cheese
comprised	ease	please
revised	freeze	seize

Listen to these sounds of "z." If the "z" sound is at the beginning of the word, draw a line under the "B." If the "z" sound is in the middle of the word, draw a line under the "M." If the "z" sound is at the end of the word, draw a line under the "E."

1. advertised B • M • E
2. squeeze B • M • E
3. tease B • M • E
4. authorized B • M • E
5. civilized B • M • E
6. criticized B • M • E
7. wheeze B • M • E
8. appease B • M • E
9. disease B • M • E
10. equalized B • M • E
11. idolized B • M • E
12. ideas B • M • E
13. exercised B • M • E
14. paradise B • M • E
15. sympathize B • M • E
16. recognized B • M • E

B Listen to these words that have the "l" blends in them.

sledge	place	blanket
sleepyhead	plaid	blame
slenderize	plain	blasting

Listen to these words that have the "l" blend in them. If you hear the "pl" blend, draw a line under the "P." If you hear the "sl" blend, draw a line under the "S." If you hear the "bl" blend, draw a line under the "B."

EXAMPLES:

slept B • P • S

plan B • P • S

bleachers B • P • S

1. sleuth B • P • S
2. plane B • P • S
3. blessing B • P • S
4. blind B • P • S
5. planet B • P • S
6. sliced B • P • S
7. plank B • P • S
8. blighted B • P • S
9. slight B • P • S
10. plantation B • P • S
11. blister B • P • S
12. slipstream B • P • S
13. plaque B • P • S
14. bloodhound B • P • S
15. platinum B • P • S
16. blooming B • P • S

Underline Definitions

Underline the answer that defines each word. Write your own sentence about each word.

1. **pipe**

   a. used for digging
   b. used to stop the flow of water
   c. a tube that water flows through

2. **hit**

   a. to let go
   b. to pull away
   c. to strike against

3. **bib**

   a. keeps the feet warm
   b. protects clothing while eating
   c. keeps the hands warm

4. **pin**

   a. used to hold things together
   b. used to open locks
   c. used to undo seams

5. **milk**

   a. a white liquid
   b. a clear liquid
   c. a dark-brown liquid

Sets of Ten

The total of the sets in each row is 10. Fill in the blanks for each equation at the right of each row. See samples "A" and "B."

A.	1 + 9 = 10
B.	8 + 2 = 10
C.	___ + ___ = 10
D.	___ + ___ = 10
E.	___ + ___ = 10
F.	___ + ___ = 10
G.	___ + ___ = 10
H.	___ + ___ = 10
I.	___ + ___ + ___ = 10
J.	___ + ___ + ___ = 10
K.	___ + ___ + ___ = 10
L.	___ + ___ + ___ = 10
M.	___ + ___ + ___ = 10
N.	___ + ___ + ___ = 10
O.	___ + ___ + ___ = 10
P.	___ + ___ + ___ = 10
Q.	___ + ___ + ___ = 10

Choosing Words

Pick the word from the box that matches each picture, and write the word in the space. See sample "1."

jar	juice	jet	Jell-O
jacket	jug	jelly	jump
jam	junk	judge	join

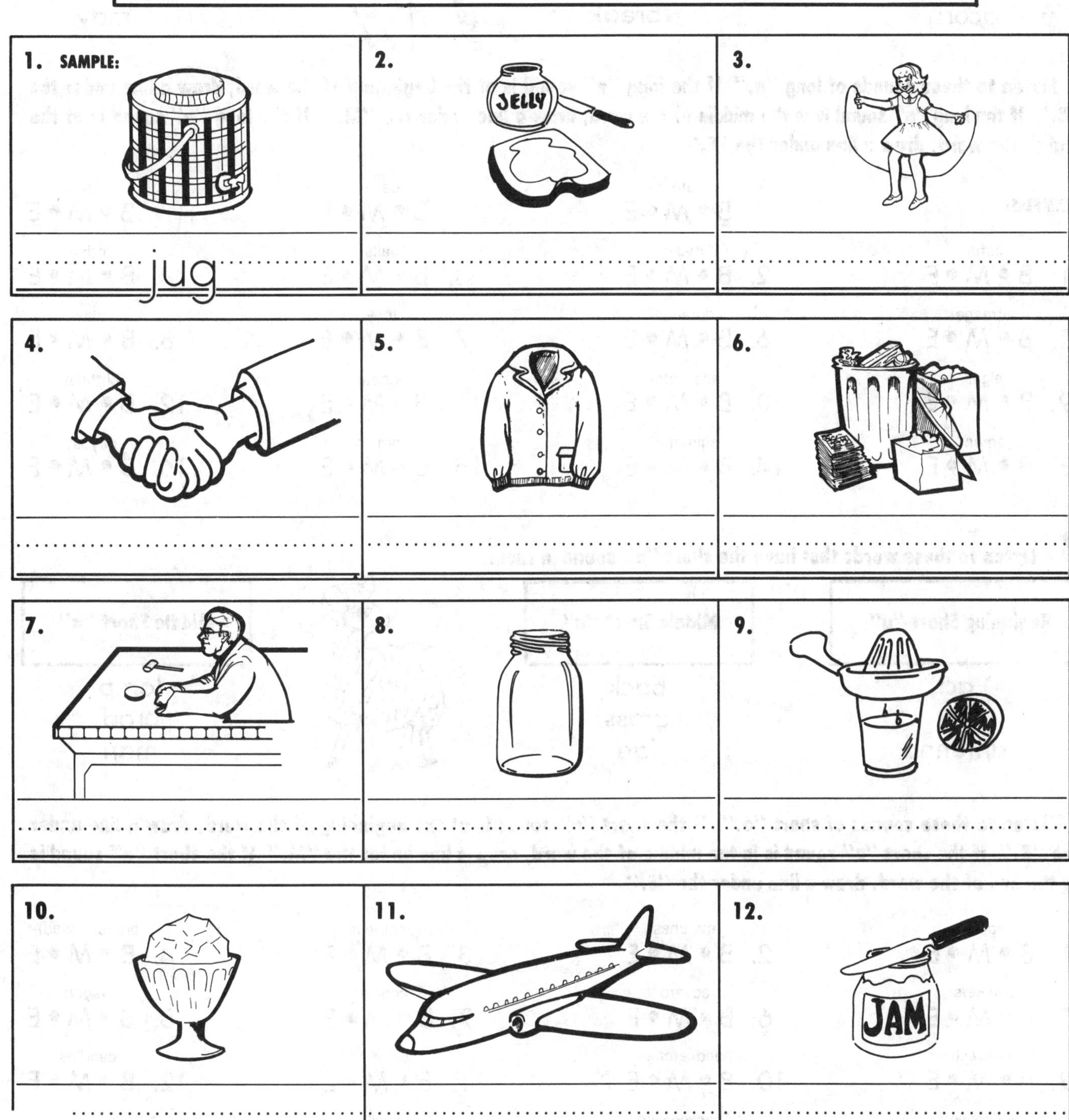

Long "a," Short "a"

A **Listen to these words that have the long "a" sound in them.**

Beginning Long "a"	Middle Long "a"	End Long "a"
ace	bathe	day
ape	brave	play
acorn	break	may

Listen to these sounds of long "a." If the long "a" sound is at the beginning of the word, draw a line under the "B." If the long "a" sound is in the middle of the word, draw a line under the "M." If the long "a" sound is at the end of the word, draw a line under the "E."

EXAMPLES:

ate — <u>B</u> • M • E

cake — B • <u>M</u> • E

lay — B • M • <u>E</u>

1. ache — B • M • E
2. maze — B • M • E
3. nails — B • M • E
4. today — B • M • E
5. acreage — B • M • E
6. duration — B • M • E
7. they — B • M • E
8. stay — B • M • E
9. eight — B • M • E
10. alternator — B • M • E
11. donate — B • M • E
12. birthday — B • M • E
13. amen — B • M • E
14. animated — B • M • E
15. domain — B • M • E
16. payday — B • M • E

B **Listen to these words that have the short "a" sound in them.**

Beginning Short "a"	Middle Short "a"	Middle Short "a"
act	back	lamp
ant	grass	brad
antenna	fad	man

Listen to these sounds of short "a." If the short "a" sound is at the beginning of the word, draw a line under the "B." If the short "a" sound is in the middle of the word, draw a line under the "M." If the short "a" sound is at the end of the word, draw a line under the "E."

1. apple — B • M • E
2. matches — B • M • E
3. accident — B • M • E
4. am (stressed) — B • M • E
5. crackers — B • M • E
6. adverb — B • M • E
7. annals — B • M • E
8. wagon — B • M • E
9. sandwich — B • M • E
10. handkerchief — B • M • E
11. animal — B • M • E
12. candles — B • M • E
13. antiseptic — B • M • E
14. Thanksgiving — B • M • E
15. anvil — B • M • E
16. baa — B • M • E

Supplying Missing Numerals

Fill in the missing numbers.

A.	1	2	3	4	5	6	7	8	9
B.	2	3		5	6		8	9	1
C.	3	4		6	7		9	1	2
D.	4	5		7	8		1	2	
E.	5	6		8	9	1		3	
F.	6	7		9	1	2		4	
G.	7	8		1	2	3		5	
H.	8	9		2	3	4		6	
I.	9	1		3	4	5		7	

Correctly Spelled Words

Circle the correctly spelled word that matches each picture.
See the example.

EXAMPLE:

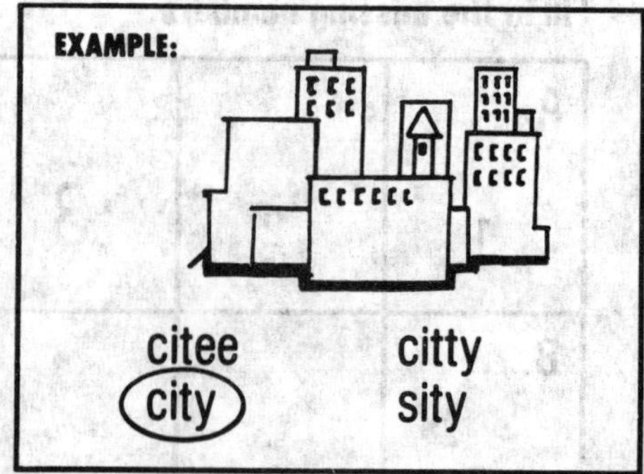

citee citty
city sity

1.

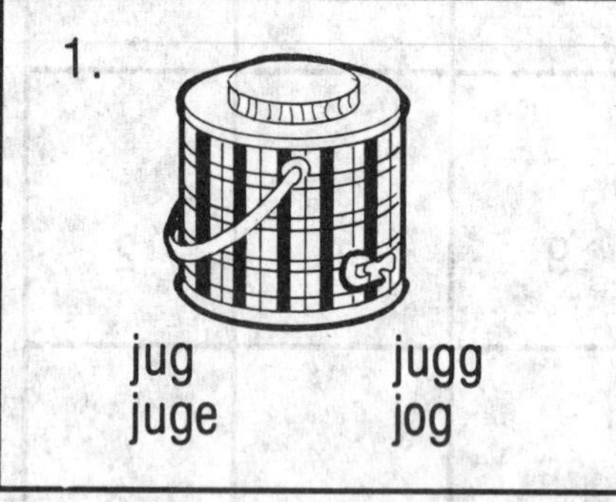

jug jugg
juge jog

2.

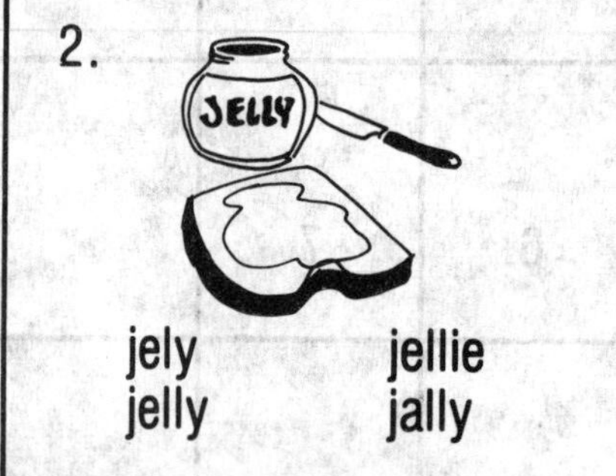

jely jellie
jelly jally

3.

jimp jump
jumpe jemp

4.

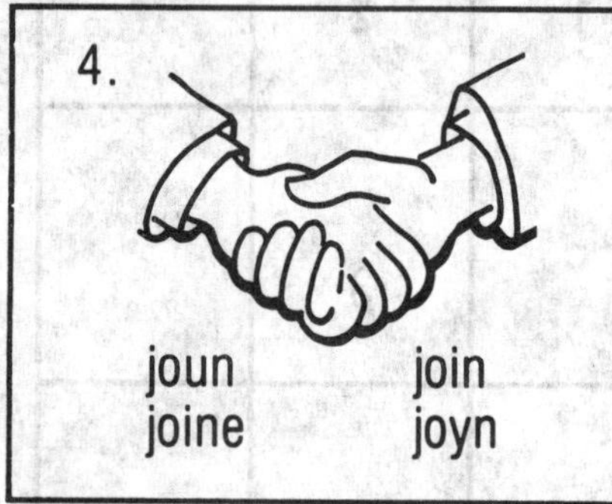

joun join
joine joyn

5.

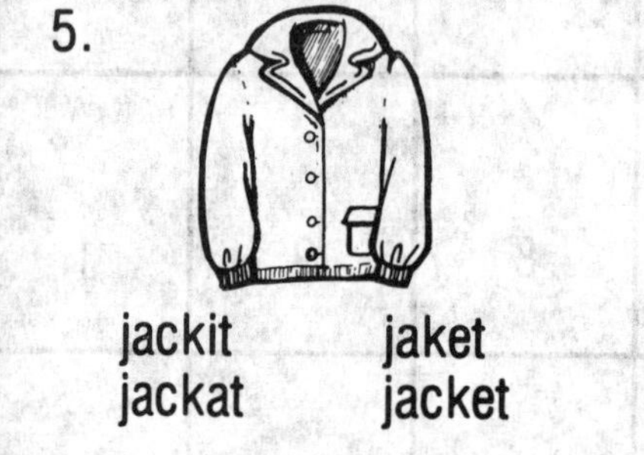

jackit jaket
jackat jacket

6.

junk junnk
junke jenk

7.

judge judje
juge judgee

8.

jor jar
jarr jer

9.

jooce jewce
juice juce

10.

Jillo Jelo
Jellow Jell-O

11.

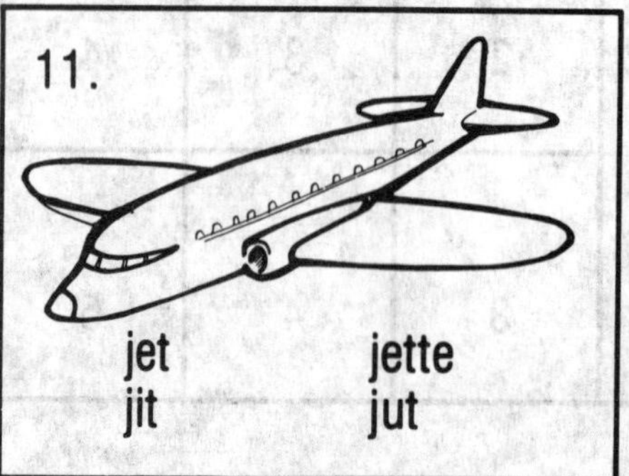

jet jette
jit jut

12.

jame jamm
jam jaim

Underline Word Meanings

Underline the answer that defines each word. Write your own sentence about each word.

1. **jug**
   a. a cup for tea
   b. a bowl for soup
   c. <u>a bottle for holding liquids</u>

2. **jelly**
   a. a sweet food usually made with fruit
   b. something you mix with milk
   c. something you eat with potatoes

3. **jump**
   a. to move slowly
   b. to move upward suddenly
   c. to move downward

4. **join**
   a. to break
   b. to take apart
   c. to bring together

5. **jacket**
   a. a short coat
   b. a very long coat
   c. a coat to wear in the summer

Watch That Sign

Solve each of the following problems. Watch for the add or subtract signs.

1. Some horses were in a pasture. After 8 horses joined them, there were 13 horses in the pasture. How many horses were in the field to begin with? __5__

2. Don was a car salesman. After he sold 3 cars, he had 9 left. How many cars did Don have before he sold any? ____

3.	6 + 5 = ____	____ + 8 = 13	8 + 4 = ____	13 − 8 = ____
4.	____ − 3 = 9	8 + 5 = ____	7 + 6 = ____	12 − 4 = ____
5.	____ + 4 = 13	13 − 6 = ____	____ − 7 = 5	13 + 4 = ____
6.	12 − 8 = ____	4 + 9 = ____	7 + 6 = ____	13 − 5 = ____
7.	13 − 6 = ____	5 + 8 = ____	9 + 3 = ____	13 − 9 = ____
8.	8 + 5 = ____	13 + 7 = ____	13 − 3 = ____	6 + 7 = ____
9.	9 + 4 = ____	____ + 5 = 14	____ − 6 = 8	5 + 9 = ____
10.	13 − 6 = ____	____ − 5 = 8	14 − 7 = ____	____ + 7 = 13
11.	9 + 5 = ____	____ − 8 = 6	13 − 7 = ____	14 − 9 = ____
12.	6 + 8 = ____	14 − 5 = ____	14 − 7 = ____	8 + 6 = ____
13.	14 − 5 = ____	14 − 7 = ____	____ + 6 = 14	13 − ____ = 5
14.	5 + ____ = 14	14 − ____ = 8	7 + ____ = 14	____ + 5 = 13
15.	14 − ____ = 5	13 − ____ = 9	6 + ____ = 14	14 − ____ = 8

16. John spent $8 for a jacket. Then he had $6. How many dollars did John have before he bought the jacket? ______

17. Linda found 8 stones. Then she had 14 stones. How many stones did she have before she found the 8? ____

18. 9 cartons of gum were on display on a table. Susan put 6 more cartons with them. How many cartons were on the table then? ____

Long "e," Short "e"

A **Listen to these words that have the long "e" sound in them.**

Beginning Long "e"	Middle Long "e"	End Long "e"
each	need	he
ego	bleed	me
Easter	cream	we

Listen to these sounds of long "e." If the long "e" sound is at the beginning of the word, draw a line under the "B." If the long "e" sound is in the middle of the word, draw a line under the "M." If the long "e" sound is at the end of the word, draw a line under the "E."

EXAMPLES:

eager — B • M • E (B underlined)

teen — B • M • E (M underlined)

tea — B • M • E (E underlined)

1. peach B • M • E
2. eke B • M • E
3. flee B • M • E
4. eyebeam B • M • E
5. extreme B • M • E
6. equal B • M • E
7. freedom B • M • E
8. entry B • M • E
9. eden B • M • E
10. bleach B • M • E
11. feast B • M • E
12. entity B • M • E
13. galaxy B • M • E
14. pinkie B • M • E
15. teeny B • M • E
16. peewee B • M • E

B **Listen to these words that have the short "e" sound in them.**

Beginning Short "e"	Middle Short "e"	Middle Short "e"
end	bed	red
em	hen	nest
elf	pet	met

Listen to these sounds of short "e." If the short "e" sound is at the beginning of the word, draw a line under the "B." If the short "e" sound is in the middle of the word, draw a line under the "M." If the short "e" sound is at the end of the word, draw a line under the "E."

1. enjoy B • M • E
2. enemy B • M • E
3. whet B • M • E
4. gazette B • M • E
5. entire B • M • E
6. sweat B • M • E
7. forget B • M • E
8. elephant B • M • E
9. duet B • M • E
10. cadet B • M • E
11. emerald B • M • E
12. embers B • M • E
13. alphabet B • M • E
14. except B • M • E
15. medicine B • M • E
16. expect B • M • E

Underline the Definitions

Underline the answer that defines each word. Write your own sentence about each word.

1. **junk**
   a. things of value
   b. something that costs too much
   c. unwanted things

2. **judge**
   a. someone who asks a question
   b. someone who makes a decision
   c. someone who is in trouble

3. **jar**
   a. a container with a wide mouth
   b. another word for ''box''
   c. a paper bag

4. **juice**
   a. the liquid part of a fruit
   b. the outside part of a fruit
   c. the solid part of a fruit

5. **Jell-O**
   a. a meat
   b. a vegetable
   c. a dessert

Telling Time

Write the correct time as shown on each clock. See sample "A."

A.

7:00

B.

C.

D.

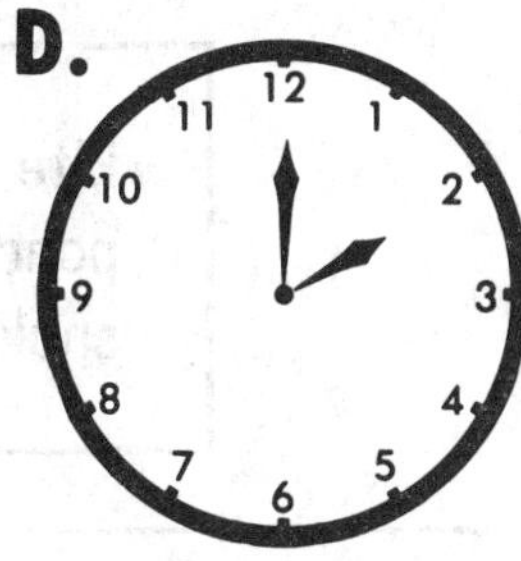

E.

F.

G.

H.

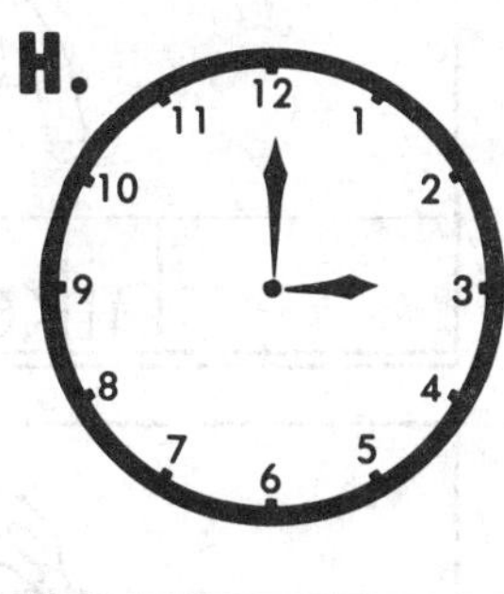

Draw the hands on these clock faces to show the time given below each. See sample "I."

I.

7:00

J.

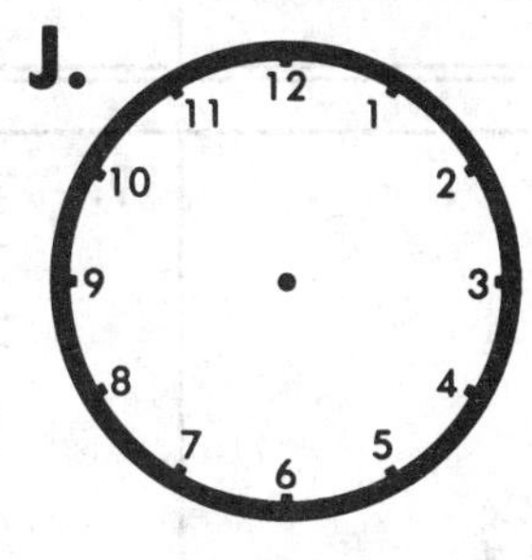

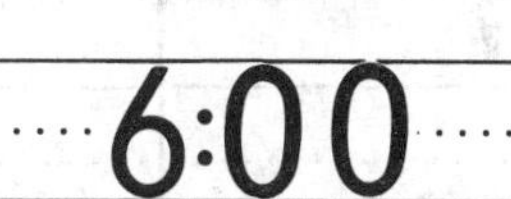

K.

4:00

L.

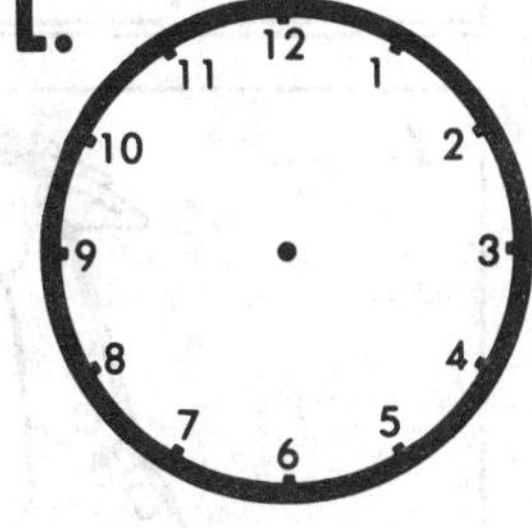

10:00

M.

11:00

N.

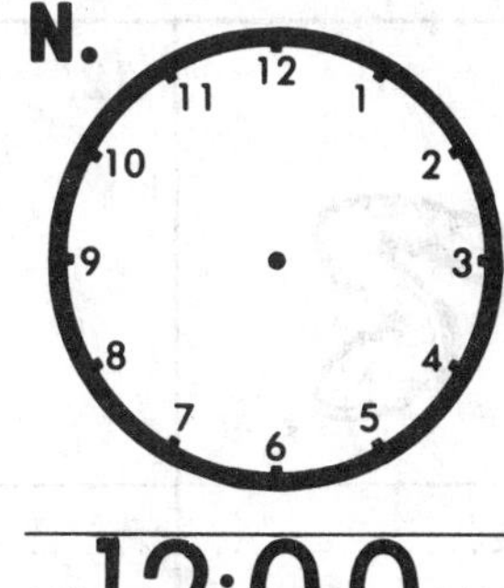

12:00

O.

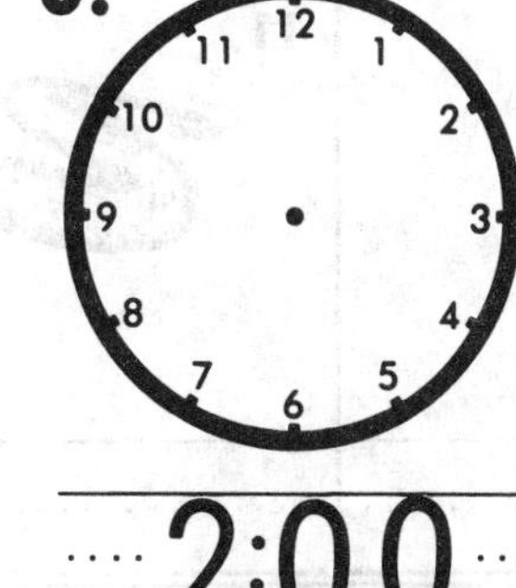

2:00

P.

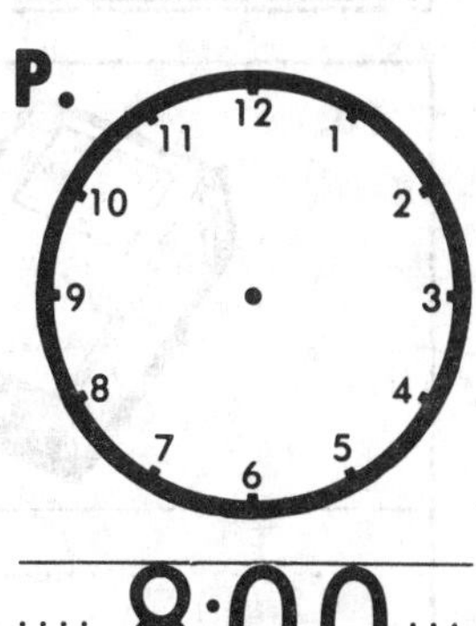

8:00

Choosing and Writing Words

Pick the word from the box that matches each picture, and write the word in the space. See sample "1."

kite	bank	hike	bake
pond	mark	neck	bike
snake	knee	dark	book

Long "i," Short "i"

A

Listen to these words that have the long "i" sound in them.

Beginning long "i"	Middle long "i"	End long "i"
ice	kite	pie
idol	invite	July
ivy	hike	buy

Listen to these sounds of the long "i." If the long "i" sound is at the beginning of the word, draw a line under the "B." If the long "i" sound is in the middle of the word, draw a line under the "M." If the long "i" sound is at the end of the word, draw a line under the "E."

EXAMPLES:

iron B • M • E (B underlined)

fight B • M • E (M underlined)

comply B • M • E (E underlined)

1. behind B • M • E
2. Isaac B • M • E
3. apply B • M • E
4. final B • M • E
5. gripe B • M • E
6. ivory B • M • E
7. icicle B • M • E
8. iodine B • M • E
9. might B • M • E
10. deny B • M • E
11. knight B • M • E
12. magnify B • M • E
13. highline B • M • E
14. flight B • M • E
15. beautify B • M • E
16. fortify B • M • E

B

Listen to these words that have the short "i" sound in them.

Beginning short "i"	Middle short "i"	Middle short "i"
it	sit	mill
in	Tim	kiss
if	fit	sin

Listen to these sounds of the short "i." If the short "i" sound is at the beginning of the word, draw a line under the "B." If the short "i" sound is in the middle of the word, draw a line under the "M." If the short "i" sound is at the end of the word, draw a line under the "E."

1. sill B • M • E
2. Miss B • M • E
3. fin B • M • E
4. ill B • M • E
5. indoors B • M • E
6. picture B • M • E
7. filter B • M • E
8. instead B • M • E
9. dimple B • M • E
10. children B • M • E
11. Iliad B • M • E
12. igniter B • M • E
13. Christmas B • M • E
14. illadvised B • M • E
15. indemnify B • M • E
16. Indian B • M • E

Writing Two Equations

Fill in the blanks to make two equations for each set. See sample "A."

A

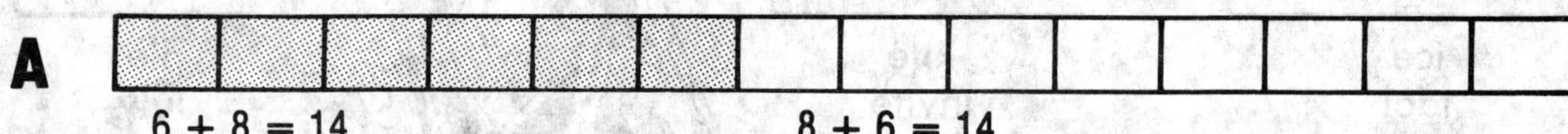

6 + 8 = 14 8 + 6 = 14

B

___ + ___ = ___ ___ + ___ = ___

C

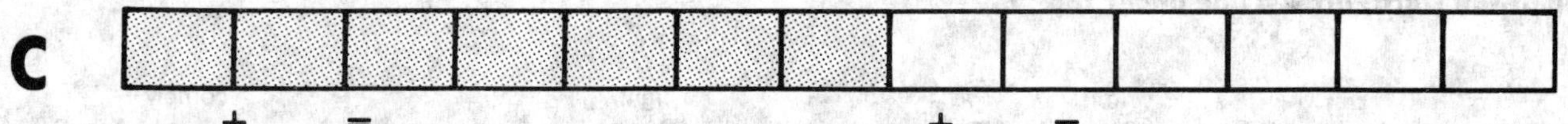

___ + ___ = ___ ___ + ___ = ___

D

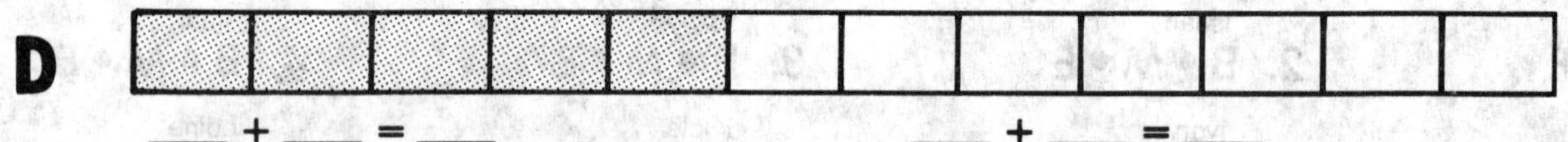

___ + ___ = ___ ___ + ___ = ___

E

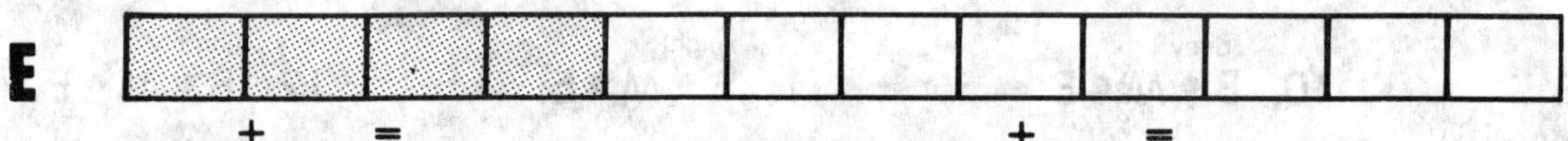

___ + ___ = ___ ___ + ___ = ___

F

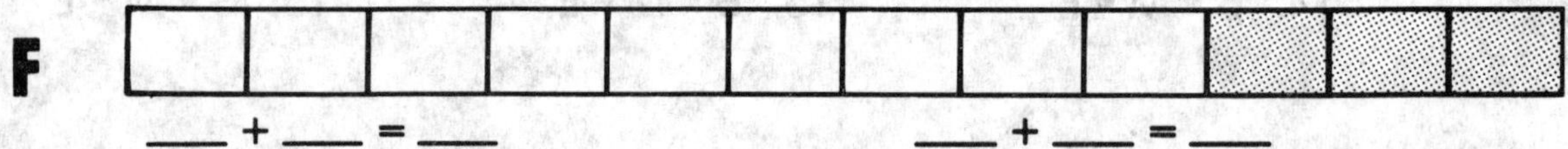

___ + ___ = ___ ___ + ___ = ___

G

___ + ___ = ___ ___ + ___ = ___

H

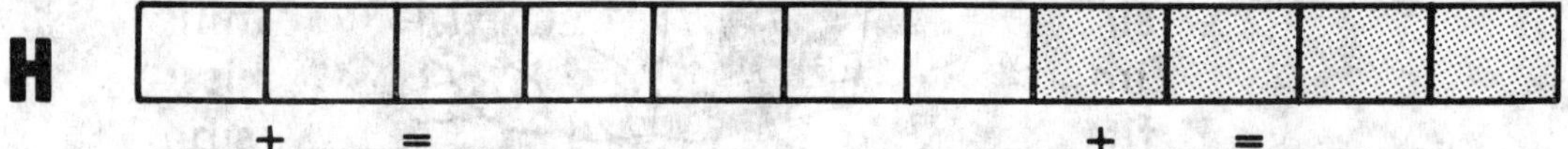

___ + ___ = ___ ___ + ___ = ___

I

___ + ___ = ___ ___ + ___ = ___

J

___ + ___ = ___ ___ + ___ = ___

K

___ + ___ = ___ ___ + ___ = ___

Spelling

Circle the correctly spelled word that matches each picture. See the example.

EXAMPLE:

urly erly
earlly (early)

1.

hike hyke
hikk hyck

2.

marrk mork
marke mark

3.

bik bike
byke hikke

4.

banke banck
bank bannk

5.

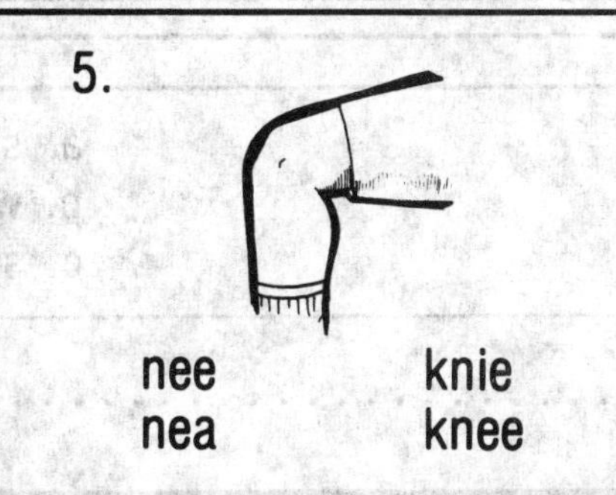

nee knie
nea knee

6.

bake bayk
baik bakke

7.

nick neck
nack nek

8.

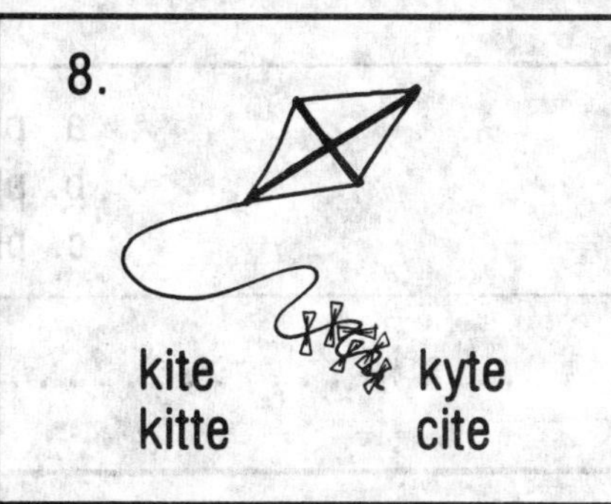

kite kyte
kitte cite

9.

ponde pund
pond ponned

10.

buk booke
bokk book

11.

snakke snaik
snache snake

12.

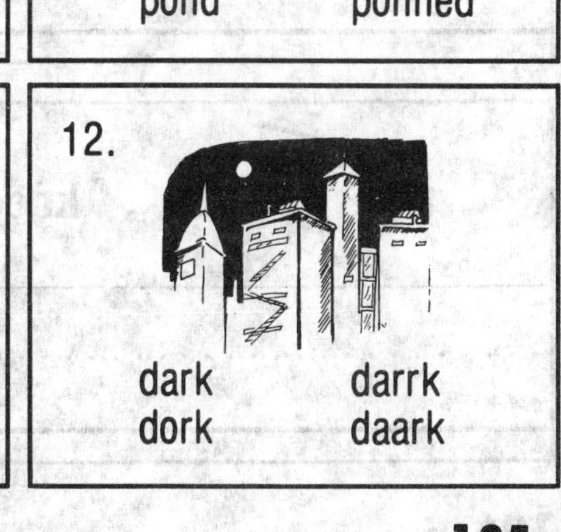

dark darrk
dork daark

Picking the Right Answers

Underline the answer that defines each word. Write your own sentence about each word.

1. **hike**
   a. a slow run
   b. a short walk
   c. a long walk

2. **mark**
   a. to make clear
   b. to rub out
   c. an impression made by a pencil

3. **bike**
   a. short for ''automobile''
   b. wagon with four wheels
   c. short form of ''bicycle''

4. **bank**
   a. place where money is kept
   b. place where food is sold
   c. place where clothes are sold

5. **knee**
   a. joint between upper and lower arm
   b. joint between upper and lower leg
   c. joint in finger

Writing Subtraction Equations

Complete the subtraction equations for each of the following sets. See samples "A" and "B."

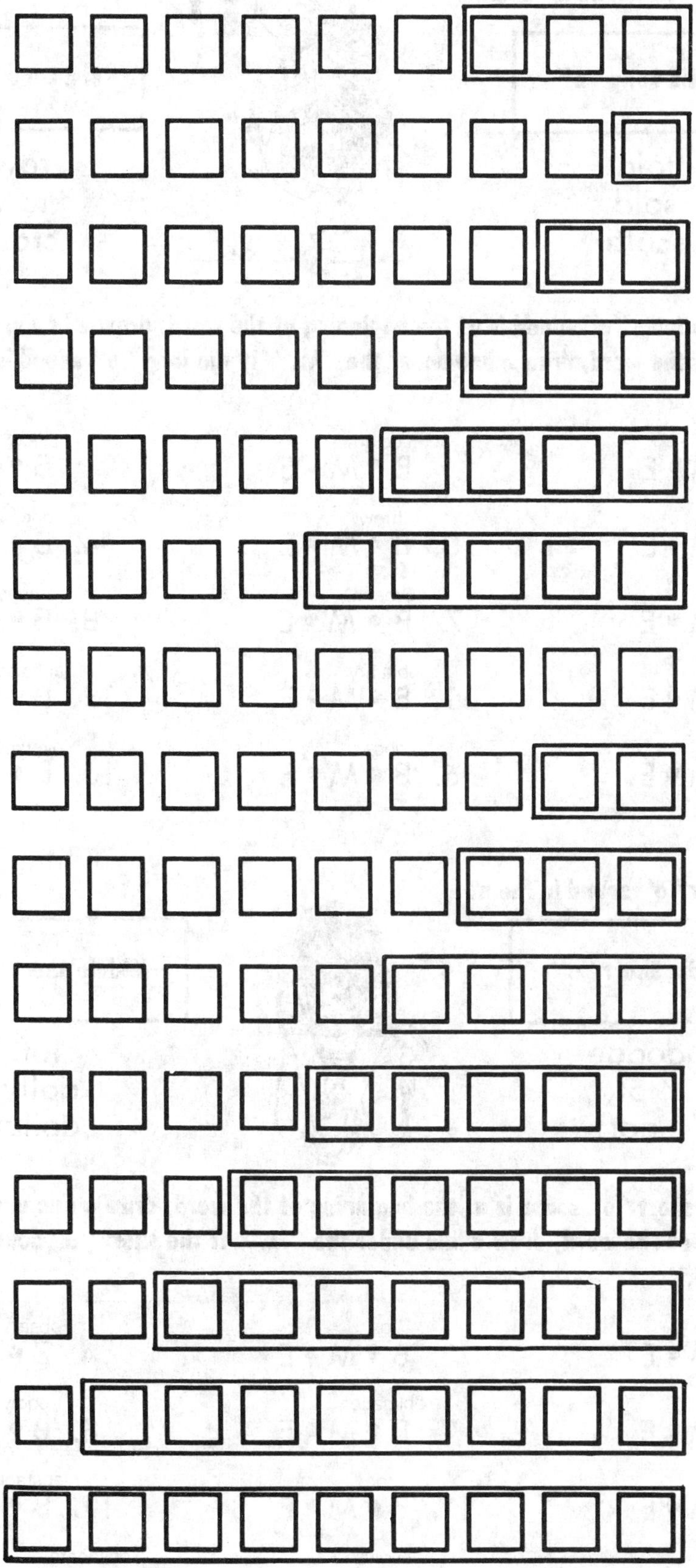

A 9 – 3 = 6

B 9 – 1 = 8

C 9 – ____ = ____

D 9 – ____ = ____

E 9 – ____ = ____

F 9 – ____ = ____

G 9 – ____ = ____

H 9 – ____ = ____

I 9 – ____ = ____

J 9 – ____ = ____

K 9 – ____ = ____

L 9 – ____ = ____

M 9 – ____ = ____

N 9 – ____ = ____

O 9 – ____ = ____

Long "o," Short "o"

A **Listen to these words that have the long "o" sound in them.**

Beginning Long "o"	Middle Long "o"	End Long "o"
old	told	row
over	sold	tow
opal	scold	crow

Listen to these sounds of long "o." If the long "o" sound is at the beginning of the word, draw a line under the "B." If the long "o" sound is in the middle of the word, draw a line under the "M." If the long "o" sound is at the end of the word, draw a line under the "E."

EXAMPLES: okra B • M • E (B underlined) cold B • M • E (M underlined) flow B • M • E (E underlined)

1. clover B • M • E	2. toe B • M • E	3. throw B • M • E	4. ocean B • M • E
5. hold B • M • E	6. over B • M • E	7. Omaha B • M • E	8. omega B • M • E
9. blow B • M • E	10. float B • M • E	11. obituary B • M • E	12. although B • M • E
13. ozone B • M • E	14. oleo B • M • E	15. oboe B • M • E	16. oversew B • M • E

B **Listen to these words that have the short "o" sound in them.**

Beginning Short "o"	Middle Short "o"	Middle Short "o"
on	dodge	lot
olive	tot	dolly
odd	not	dollar

Listen to these sounds of short "o." If the short "o" sound is at the beginning of the word, draw a line under the "B." If the short "o" sound is in the middle of the word, draw a line under the "M." If the short "o" sound is at the end of the word, draw a line under the "E."

1. clog B • M • E	2. obsolete B • M • E	3. job B • M • E	4. observe B • M • E
5. solved B • M • E	6. trolley B • M • E	7. obligation B • M • E	8. oddly B • M • E
9. solid B • M • E	10. catalog B • M • E	11. frog B • M • E	12. obstacle B • M • E
13. bionic B • M • E	14. stopper B • M • E	15. obolus B • M • E	16. obstinate B • M • E

Choosing the Correct Answers

Underline the answer that defines each word. Write your own sentence about each word.

1. **bake**
   a. to cook on top of the stove
   b. to cook without heat
   c. to cook in the oven

2. **neck**
   a. part between arm and hand
   b. part between head and shoulders
   c. part between leg and foot

3. **kite**
   a. paper frame that digs in snow
   b. paper frame that floats
   c. paper frame you fly in the air

4. **pond**
   a. a stream
   b. land with no water
   c. a very small body of water

5. **book**
   a. a card
   b. many printed pages put together
   c. a picture

Subtract the Facts

It is best for you to learn the subtraction facts so that you can recall them without stopping to work them out. You should use them to solve problems right away.

Write the answer for each problem.

A.	$2 - 1$	$3 - 1$	$4 - 1$	$5 - 1$	$6 - 1$	$7 - 1$	$8 - 1$	$9 - 1$	$10 - 1$
B.	$3 - 2$	$4 - 2$	$5 - 2$	$6 - 2$	$7 - 2$	$8 - 2$	$9 - 2$	$10 - 2$	$11 - 2$
C.	$4 - 3$	$5 - 3$	$6 - 3$	$7 - 3$	$8 - 3$	$9 - 3$	$10 - 3$	$11 - 3$	$12 - 3$
D.	$5 - 4$	$6 - 4$	$7 - 4$	$8 - 4$	$9 - 4$	$10 - 4$	$11 - 4$	$12 - 4$	$13 - 4$
E.	$6 - 5$	$7 - 5$	$8 - 5$	$9 - 5$	$10 - 5$	$11 - 5$	$12 - 5$	$13 - 5$	$14 - 5$
F.	$7 - 6$	$8 - 6$	$9 - 6$	$10 - 6$	$11 - 6$	$12 - 6$	$13 - 6$	$14 - 6$	$15 - 6$
G.	$8 - 7$	$9 - 7$	$10 - 7$	$11 - 7$	$12 - 7$	$13 - 7$	$14 - 7$	$15 - 7$	$16 - 7$
H.	$9 - 8$	$10 - 8$	$11 - 8$	$12 - 8$	$13 - 8$	$14 - 8$	$15 - 8$	$16 - 8$	$17 - 8$
I.	$10 - 9$	$11 - 9$	$12 - 9$	$13 - 9$	$14 - 9$	$15 - 9$	$16 - 9$	$17 - 9$	$18 - 9$

Picking Proper Words

Pick the word from the box that matches each picture, and write the word in the space. See sample "1."

lion	clown	smile	sail
walk	bowl	nail	plate
lamp	pail	play	tail

1. SAMPLE: clown

2.

3.

4.

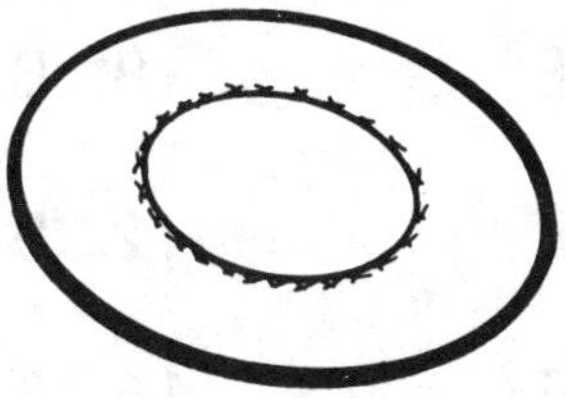

5.

6.

7.

8.

9.

10.

11.

12.

Long "u," Short "u"

A **Listen to these words that have the long "u" sound in them.**

Beginning long "u"	Middle long "u"	End long "u"
use	cube	Sue
union	flute	clue
unify	fruit	you

Listen to these sounds of long "u." If the long "u" sound is at the beginning of the word, draw a line under the "B." If the long "u" sound is in the middle of the word, draw a line under the "M." If the long "u" sound is at the end of the word, draw a line under the "E."

EXAMPLES:

uniform B • M • E (B underlined)

acute B • M • E (M underlined)

new B • M • E (E underlined)

suit 1. B • M • E	ukulele 2. B • M • E	residue 3. B • M • E	debut 4. B • M • E
unity 5. B • M • E	compute 6. B • M • E	subdue 7. B • M • E	flew 8. B • M • E
substitute 9. B • M • E	universal 10. B • M • E	parachute 11. B • M • E	through 12. B • M • E
university 13. B • M • E	rendezvous 14. B • M • E	nude 15. B • M • E	avenue 16. B • M • E

B **Listen to these words that have the short "u" sound in them.**

Beginning short "u"	Middle short "u"	Middle short "u"
up	cut	mud
us	cub	cup
utter	mum	much

Listen to these sounds of short "u." If the short "u" sound is at the beginning of the word, draw a line under the "B." If the short "u" sound is in the middle of the word, draw a line under the "M." If the short "u" sound is at the end of the word, draw a line under the "E."

mumble 1. B • M • E	ultraconfident 2. B • M • E	muffle 3. B • M • E	mug 4. B • M • E
udder 5. B • M • E	stuck 6. B • M • E	mullett 7. B • M • E	money 8. B • M • E
lumber 9. B • M • E	uproar 10. B • M • E	utterance 11. B • M • E	munch 12. B • M • E
umbilical 13. B • M • E	monkey 14. B • M • E	stomach 15. B • M • E	Monday 16. B • M • E

Writing Addition Equations

Complete the addition equations for each of the following sets. See samples "A" and "B."

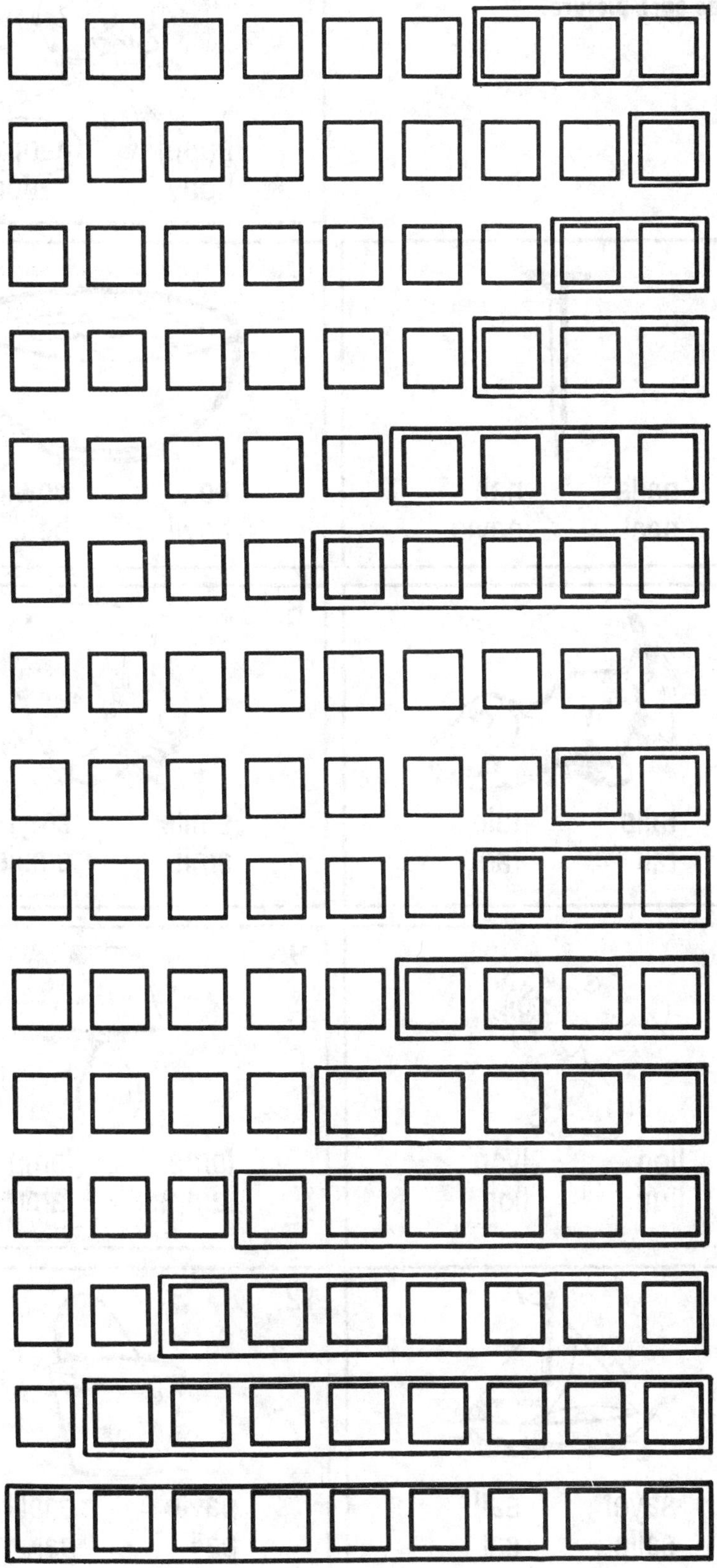

A. 6 + 3 = 9

B. 8 + 1 = 9

C. ___ + ___ = 9

D. ___ + ___ = 9

E. ___ + ___ = 9

F. ___ + ___ = 9

G. ___ + ___ = 9

H. ___ + ___ = 9

I. ___ + ___ = 9

J. ___ + ___ = 9

K. ___ + ___ = 9

L. ___ + ___ = 9

M. ___ + ___ = 9

N. ___ + ___ = 9

O. ___ + ___ = 9

Picture Fun

Circle the correctly spelled word that matches each picture.
See the example.

EXAMPLE:

happi (happy)
hpay happee

1.

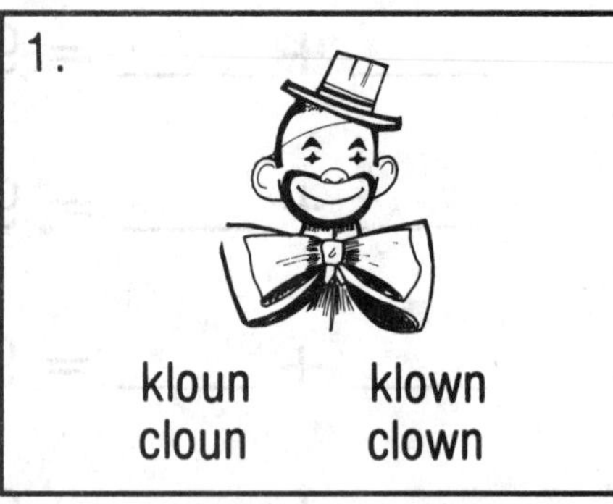

kloun klown
cloun clown

2.

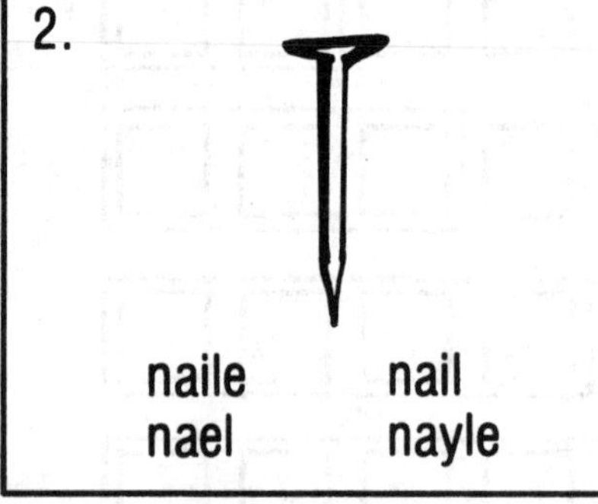

naile nail
nael nayle

3.

bole bowle
bowl boul

4.

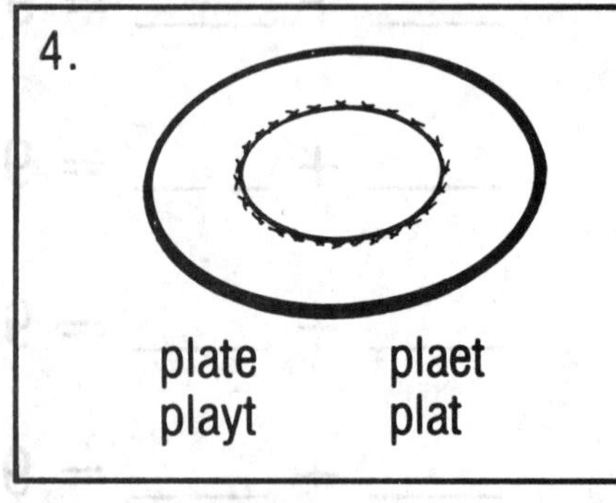

plate plaet
playt plat

5.

taile tale
tail tael

6.

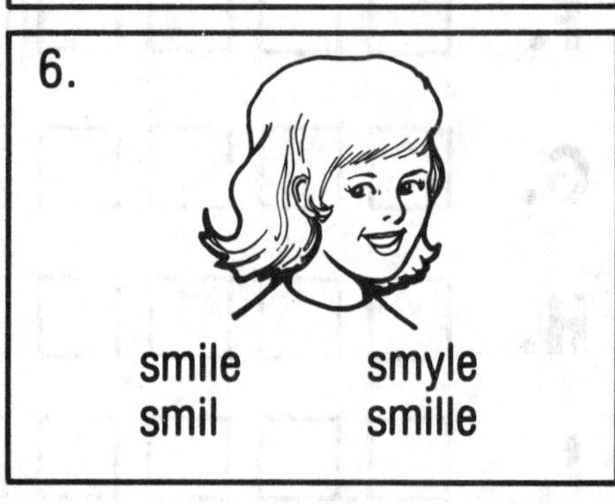

smile smyle
smil smille

7.

walk wolk
wak wok

8.

lien lyon
liun lion

9.

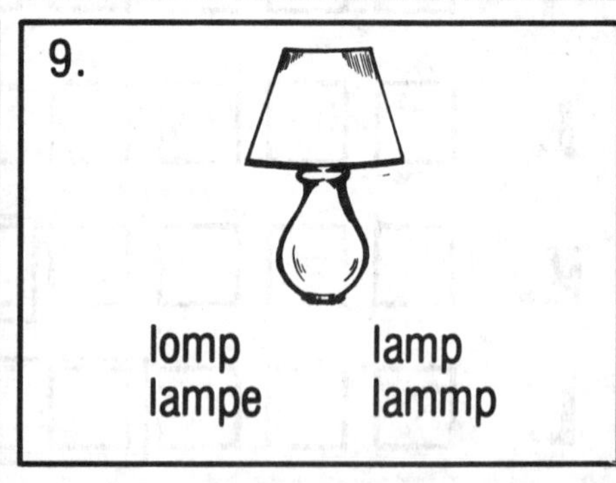

lomp lamp
lampe lammp

10.

play playe
plai plaey

11.

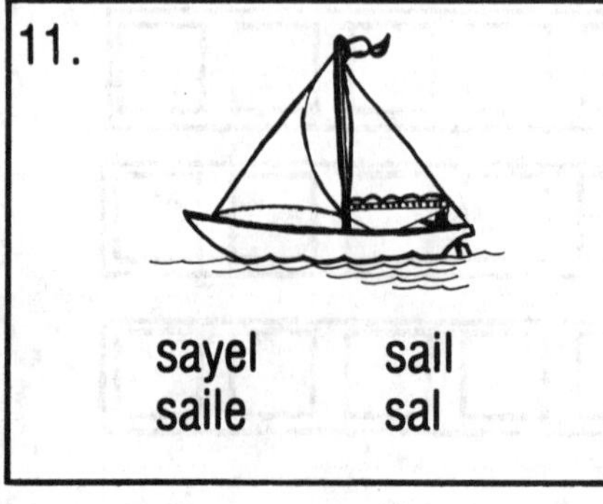

sayel sail
saile sal

12.

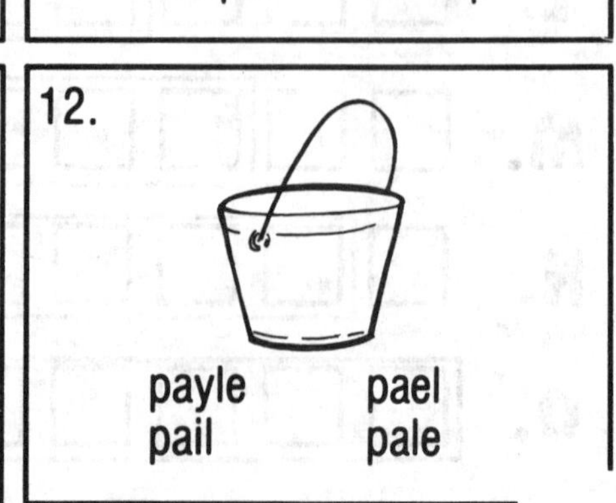

payle pael
pail pale

Can You Remember the Meanings?

Underline the answer that defines each word. Write your own sentence about each word.

1. **clown**
   a. angry person
   b. sad person
   c. funny person

2. **nail**
   a. metal object pointed at one end
   b. object pointed at both ends
   c. a piece of wood

3. **bowl**
   a. curved dish for eating soup
   b. curved dish for drinking
   c. curved dish for cooking on stove

4. **plate**
   a. a dish for cereal
   b. a dish for drinking hot tea
   c. flat dish for eating

5. **tail**
   a. the front part
   b. the end part
   c. the middle part

Likenesses and Differences

Write the missing numbers to complete each problem. If the shapes are different, the numbers must be different. If the shapes are the same, the numbers are the same. See samples "A" and "B."

A. 1 + 1 2	**B.** 1 + 2 3	**C.** + 1 3	**D.** + 4
E. 3 + 4	**F.** 3 + 5	**G.** 3 + 6	**H.** 4 + 6
I. + 4	**J.** 1 + 4	**K.** 1 + 3	**L.** 3 + 5
M. + 4 8	**N.** 5 + 6	**O.** 2 + 6	**P.** 4 + 7
Q. + 2	**R.** 6 + 7	**S.** 3 + 7	**T.** 5 + 7
U. 5 + 10	**V.** 7 + 8	**W.** 7 + 9	**X.** 6 + 9

Long "oo," Short "oo"

Listen to these words that have the long "oo" sound in them.

room
noon

soon
stool

boot
choose

Listen to these words that have the short "oo" sound in them.

book
wood

hoop
hood

took
stood

Listen to the sound of "oo" in these words. If the word has the long "oo" sound in it, draw a line under the "L." If the word has the short "oo" sound in it, draw a line under the "S."

moon 1. L • S	coon 2. L • S	cook 3. L • S	booth 4. L • S
snooker 5. L • S	spool 6. L • S	brook 7. L • S	smooth 8. L • S
good 9. L • S	toon 10. L • S	snoop 11. L • S	tooth 12. L • S
blood 13. L • S	hoof 14. L • S	coop 15. L • S	spook 16. L • S
school 17. L • S	snooze 18. L • S	boon 19. L • S	wool 20. L • S
scooter 21. L • S	hooky 22. L • S	root 23. L • S	mood 24. L • S
stood 25. L • S	spoon 26. L • S	smooch 27. L • S	goody 28. L • S
scoop 29. L • S	foot 30. L • S	cool 31. L • S	booster 32. L • S
swoon 33. L • S	moose 34. L • S	goodness 35. L • S	hook 36. L • S
look 37. L • S	troop 38. L • S	stoop 39. L • S	soothe 40. L • S
whoop 41. L • S	cookie 42. L • S	flood 43. L • S	goodbye 44. L • S

How Is Your Vocabulary?

Underline the answer that defines each word. Write your own sentence about each word.

1. **smile**
   a. to show fear
   b. to show anger
   c. to show happiness

2. **walk**
   a. to go on foot
   b. to go on your knees
   c. to move with wings

3. **lion**
   a. a wild horse
   b. a wild dog
   c. a wild animal in the cat family

4. **lamp**
   a. used to give light
   b. used to block out light
   c. used for heating

5. **play**
   a. to be unhappy
   b. to have fun
   c. to be sick

Going to the Store

Banana 6¢ | Candy 6¢ | Whistle 6¢ | Kite 9¢
Balloon 5¢ | Root Beer 6¢ | Apple 8¢ | Pencil 5¢
Ice Cream 10¢ | Lollipop 2¢ | Ball 8¢ | Gum 1¢

A group of students visited a store. Some items with prices that they saw are listed above. Each student bought a list of articles. Here is a list of what each student bought.

Write the price of each article the students bought; then add to see how much each one spent. See sample "A."

A. Susan
apple 8¢
pencil 5¢
gum 1¢
Total 14¢

B. Bill
root beer ____
kite ____
ball ____
Total ____

C. Jack
banana ____
whistle ____
balloon ____
Total ____

D. Patty
ice cream ____
lollipop ____
candy ____
Total ____

E. Jane
ball ____
ice cream ____
kite ____
Total ____

F. Sally
candy ____
pencil ____
ice cream ____
Total ____

G. Nancy
banana ____
ball ____
ice cream ____
Total ____

H. Peter
ball ____
root beer ____
apple ____
Total ____

I. Tom
whistle ____
apple ____
root beer ____
Total ____

Choose the Proper Words

Pick the word from the box that matches each picture, and write the word in the space. See sample "1."

arm	moon	smell	mill
mail	pump	mop	stump
aim	farm	seam	stamp

1. SAMPLE: arm	**2.**	**3.**
4.	**5.**	**6.**
7.	**8.**	**9.**
10.	**11.**	**12.**

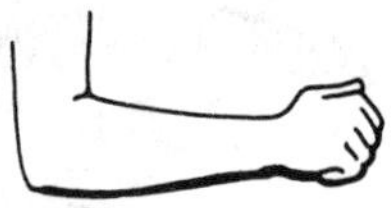

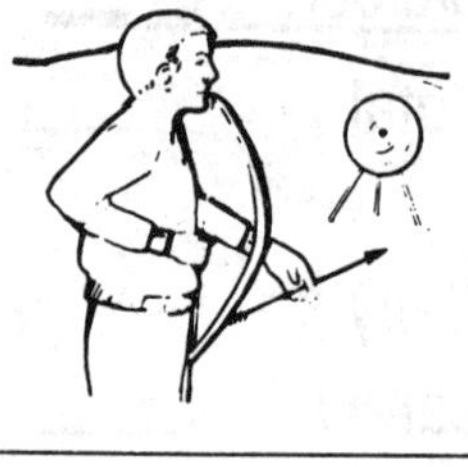

"aw," "au," "ow," "ou" Sounds

A Listen to these words that have the "aw" sound in them.

Beginning "ou"	Middle "ou"	End "ou"
awl	dawn	saw
auto	clause	flaw
audit	shawl	draw

Listen to these sounds of "aw." If the "aw" sound is at the beginning of the word, draw a line under the "B." If the "aw" sound is in the middle of the word, draw a line under the "M." If the "aw" sound is at the end of the word, draw a line under the "E."

EXAMPLES: aught <u>B</u> • M • E moral B • <u>M</u> • E raw B • M • <u>E</u>

more 1. B • M • E	straw 2. B • M • E	border 3. B • M • E	haul 4. B • M • E
aural 5. B • M • E	author 6. B • M • E	mortal 7. B • M • E	daub 8. B • M • E
squaw 9. B • M • E	order 10. B • M • E	mortar 11. B • M • E	fault 12. B • M • E
August 13. B • M • E	chalk 14. B • M • E	Bordeau 15. B • M • E	mackinaw 16. B • M • E

B Listen to these words that have the "ou" sound in them.

Beginning	Middle	End
our	loud	sow
out	about	now
ouch	mouth	cow

Listen to these sounds of "ou." If the "ou" sound is at the beginning of the word, draw a line under the "B." If the "ou" sound is in the middle of the word, draw a line under the "M." If the "ou" sound is at the end of the word, draw a line under the "E."

account 1. B • M • E	ours 2. B • M • E	meow 3. B • M • E	found 4. B • M • E
clown 5. B • M • E	pouch 6. B • M • E	outsider 7. B • M • E	mount 8. B • M • E
outworn 9. B • M • E	oust 10. B • M • E	pow 11. B • M • E	blouse 12. B • M • E
outwear 13. B • M • E	mouse 14. B • M • E	bough 15. B • M • E	thou 16. B • M • E

Adding, Number Line

Use the number line to solve each problem. See samples "A" and "B."

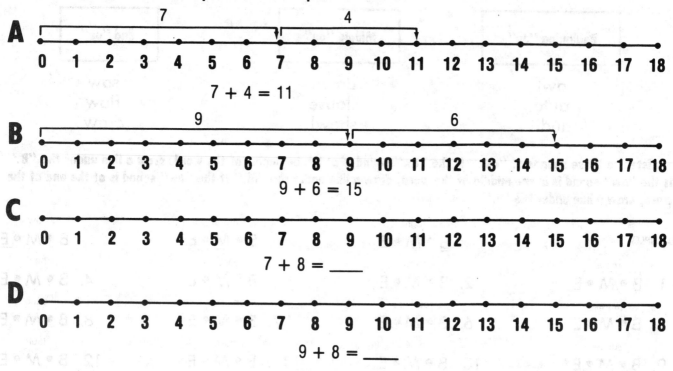

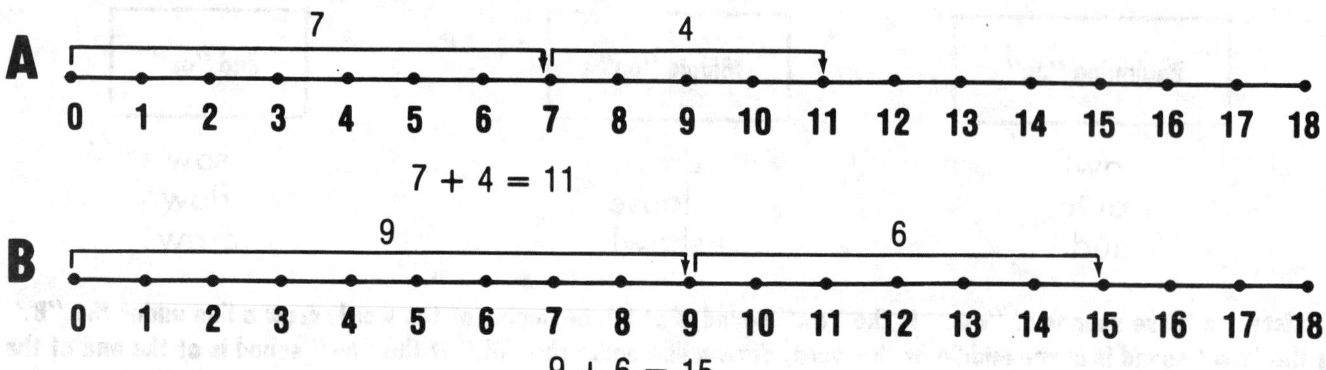

C

0 1 2 3 4 5 6 7 8 9 10 11 12 13 14 15 16 17 18

7 + 8 = ____

D

0 1 2 3 4 5 6 7 8 9 10 11 12 13 14 15 16 17 18

9 + 8 = ____

0 1 2 3 4 5 6 7 8 9 10 11 12 13 14 15 16 17 18

Use the above number line to work each of the following problems.

E	6 + 4 = ____	7 + 4 = ____	8 + 4 = ____	9 + 4 = ____	6 + 5 = ____
F	7 + 5 = ____	8 + 5 = ____	9 + 5 = ____	7 + 6 = ____	8 + 6 = ____
G	9 + 6 = ____	8 + 7 = ____	8 + 8 = ____	8 + 9 = ____	9 + 7 = ____
H	9 + 8 = ____	9 + 9 = ____	4 + 5 = ____	4 + 6 = ____	4 + 7 = ____
I	4 + 8 = ____	4 + 9 = ____	5 + 4 = ____	5 + 5 = ____	5 + 6 = ____
J	5 + 7 = ____	5 + 8 = ____	5 + 9 = ____	3 + 2 = ____	3 + 3 = ____
K	3 + 4 = ____	3 + 5 = ____	3 + 6 = ____	3 + 7 = ____	3 + 8 = ____
L	3 + 9 = ____	2 + 1 = ____	2 + 2 = ____	2 + 3 = ____	2 + 4 = ____
M	2 + 5 = ____	2 + 6 = ____	2 + 7 = ____	2 + 8 = ____	2 + 9 = ____
N	1 + 2 = ____	1 + 3 = ____	1 + 4 = ____	1 + 5 = ____	1 + 6 = ____
O	1 + 7 = ____	1 + 8 = ____	1 + 9 = ____	2 + 1 = ____	3 + 1 = ____
P	4 + 1 = ____	5 + 1 = ____	6 + 1 = ____	7 + 1 = ____	8 + 1 = ____

Can You Name the Pictures?

Circle the correctly spelled word that matches each picture.
See the example.

EXAMPLE:

dissy dizzy
dizy dezzy

1.
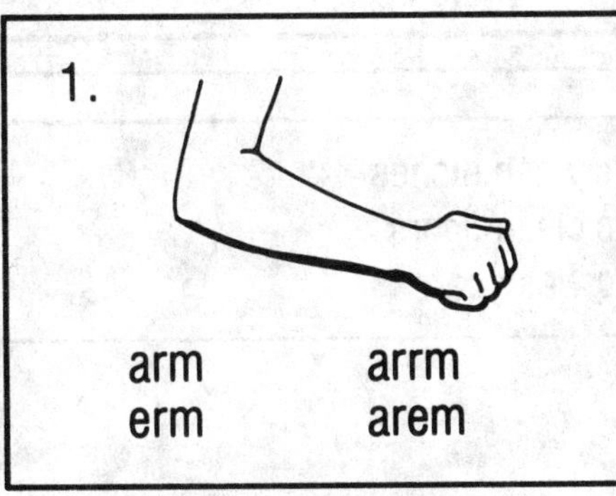

arm arrm
erm arem

2.
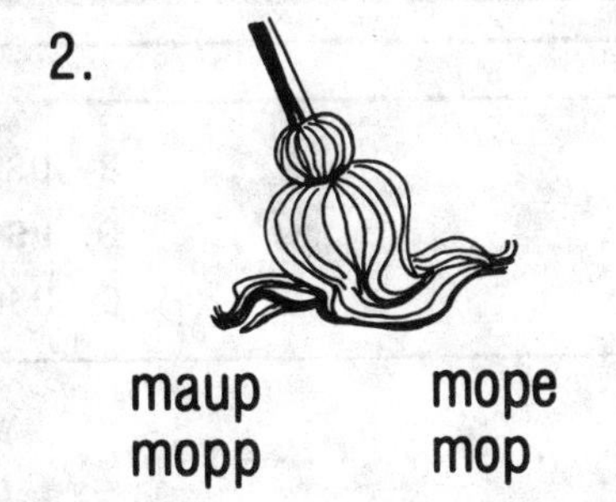

maup mope
mopp mop

3.
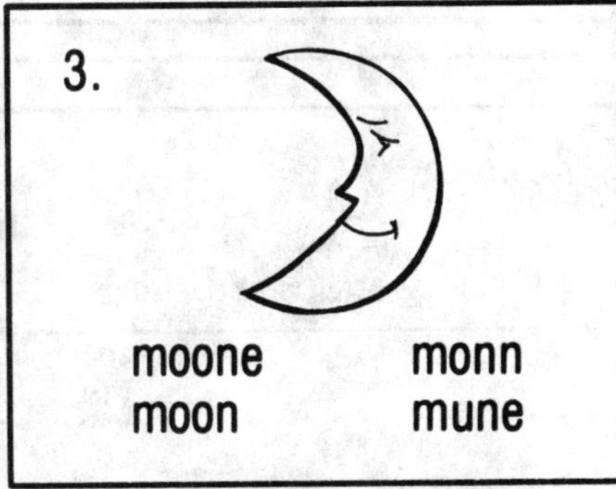

moone monn
moon mune

4.
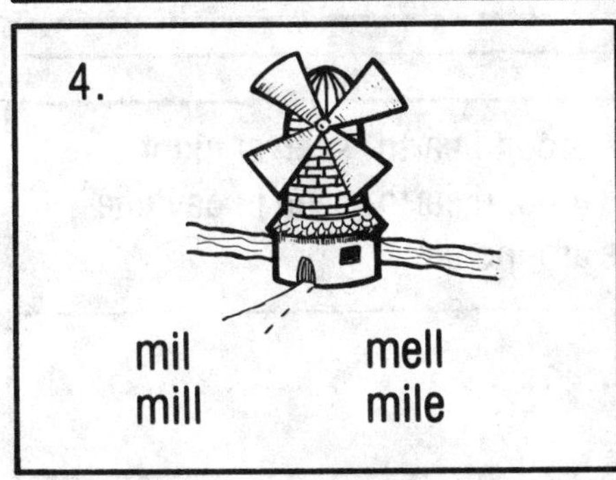

mil mell
mill mile

5.

farm farrm
farme forme

6.

stumpe stump
stumpp stomp

7.

aym ame
aime aim

8.

stamp stemp
stimp staimp

9.
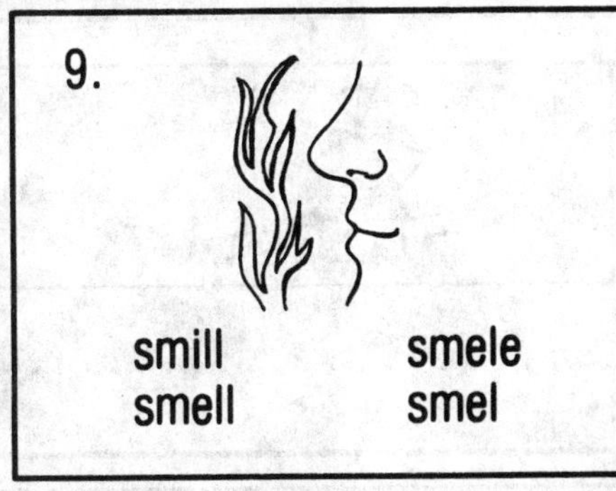

smill smele
smell smel

10.
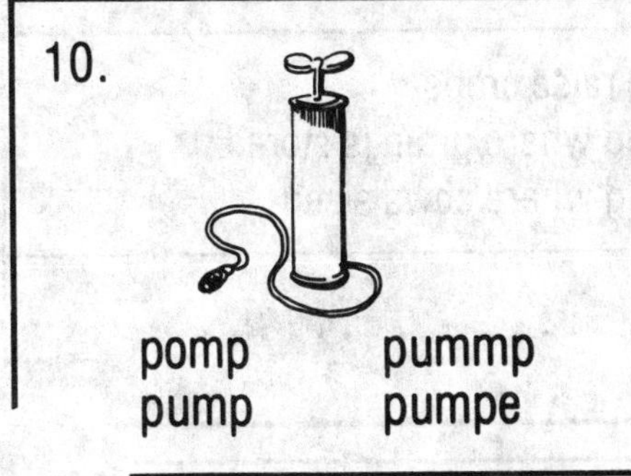

pomp pummp
pump pumpe

11.
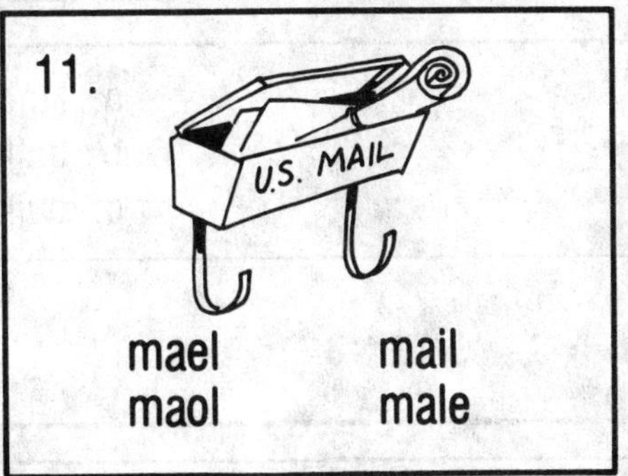

mael mail
maol male

12.
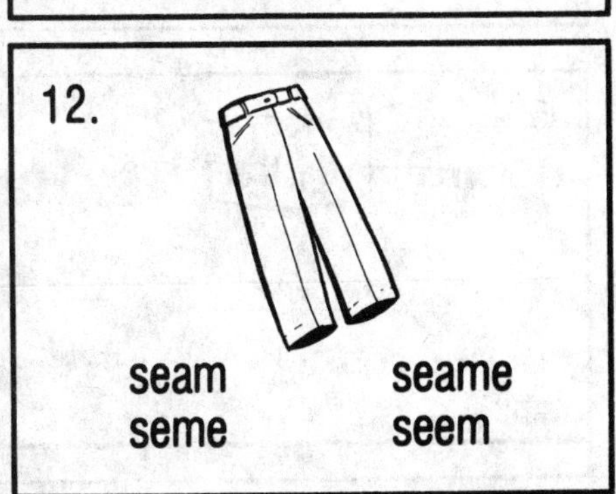

seam seame
seme seem

Word Description

Underline the answer that defines each word. Write your own sentence about each word.

1. **arm**
   a. part between shoulder and hand
   b. part between knee and foot
   c. part between head and shoulder

2. **mop**
   a. used to wash dishes
   b. used to clean floors
   c. used to wash cars

3. **moon**
   a. moves around earth, seen at night
   b. moves around earth, seen in daytime
   c. moves around sun

4. **mill**
   a. makes electricity
   b. pump water
   c. machine for grinding grain

5. **farm**
   a. land to raise crops
   b. building where grain is stored
   c. building where cows sleep

Money Problems

Give the missing numbers and amounts. See samples "A" and "B."

	NUMBER OF COINS			NUMBER OF CENTS			
							SUM
A.	2	1	2	2¢	5¢	20¢	27¢
B.	3	1	0	3¢	5¢	0¢	8¢
C.				3¢	5¢	10¢	
D.	4	2	2				
E.				5¢	10¢	30¢	
F.	7		1		15¢		
G.			3	4¢	10¢		
H.				2¢	15¢	30¢	
I.				3¢		20¢	38¢
J.					20¢	10¢	30¢
K.				5¢	15¢	10¢	
L.				1¢		10¢	16¢
M.				2¢	10¢		32¢
N.					15¢	20¢	39¢

"w," "y" Sounds

A Listen to these words that have the "w" sound in them. Notice the "w" is silent at the end of the words.

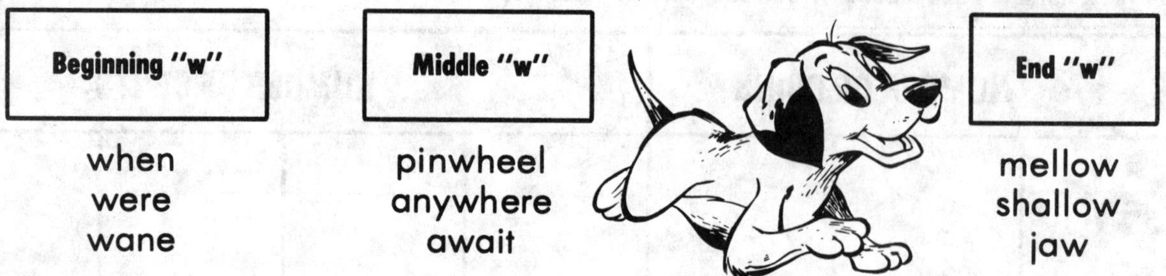

Beginning "w"
when
were
wane
Middle "w"
pinwheel
anywhere
await
End "w"
mellow
shallow
jaw

Listen to these sounds of "w." If the "w" sound is at the beginning of the word, draw a line under the "B." If the "w" sound is in the middle of the word, draw a line under the "M." If the "w" sound is at the end of the word, draw a line under the "E." Remember the "w" may be silent at the end of the word. If so, draw a line under the "E."

EXAMPLES:

	wife	buckwheat	narrow
	B̲ • M • E	B • M̲ • E	B • M • E̲

wipe	bullwhip	whittle	what
1. B • M • E	2. B • M • E	3. B • M • E	4. B • M • E
unwind	nowhere	fellow	forward
5. B • M • E	6. B • M • E	7. B • M • E	8. B • M • E
why	northward	wheelie	wham
9. B • M • E	10. B • M • E	11. B • M • E	12. B • M • E
awake	meadow	wept	willow
13. B • M • E	14. B • M • E	15. B • M • E	16. B • M • E

B The "y" at the end of a word often has the long "e" sound. The "y" is often silent in the middle of a word. Listen to these words.

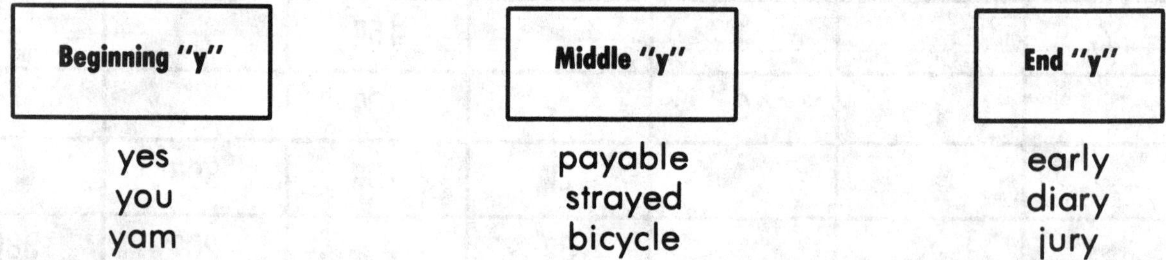

Listen to these words. If the "y" sound is at the beginning of the word, draw a line under the "B." If the "y" is in the middle of the word and is silent, draw a line under the "M." If the "y" is at the end of the word and has the sound of a long "e," draw a line under the "E."

yon	analyze	honey	youth
1. B • M • E	2. B • M • E	3. B • M • E	4. B • M • E
cherry	yard	beauty	year
5. B • M • E	6. B • M • E	7. B • M • E	8. B • M • E
played	yearn	yeast	buddy
9. B • M • E	10. B • M • E	11. B • M • E	12. B • M • E
straying	ferry	yummy	yoyo
13. B • M • E	14. B • M • E	15. B • M • E	16. B • M • E

Defining Words Is Fun

Underline the answer that defines each word. Write your own sentence about each word.

1. **stump**
   a. top part of a tree
   b. middle part of a tree
   c. lower end of a tree

2. **aim**
   a. to point at a target
   b. to close your eyes
   c. to look with one eye

3. **stamp**
   a. to put in a mailbox
   b. shows charge on a letter is paid
   c. to write a letter

4. **smell**
   a. to hear something
   b. to see something
   c. to recognize an odor

5. **pump**
   a. forces air into a tire
   b. stops the flow of air
   c. lets out too much air

Number Line Subtraction

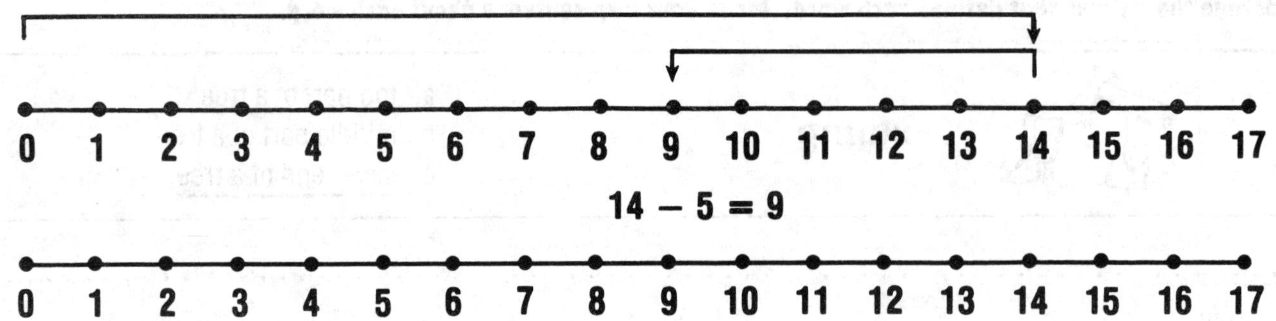

Use the above number line, and do the following subtraction. See sample "A."

A	17 − 8 = 9	16 − 5 = 11	17 − 9 = 8	17 − 5 = 12
B	15 − 7 = ____	15 − 6 = ____	15 − 9 = ____	15 − 8 = ____
C	17 − 3 = ____	17 − 2 = ____	17 − 4 = ____	17 − 6 = ____
D	15 − 5 = ____	14 − 3 = ____	14 − 5 = ____	13 − 2 = ____
E	12 − 7 = ____	11 − 3 = ____	14 − 4 = ____	15 − 4 = ____
F	10 − 4 = ____	10 − 8 = ____	9 − 4 = ____	8 − 6 = ____
G	12 − 3 = ____	16 − 7 = ____	16 − 3 = ____	17 − 6 = ____
H	13 − 4 = ____	12 − 5 = ____	11 − 5 = ____	10 − 6 = ____
I	4 − 2 = ____	6 − 4 = ____	5 − 3 = ____	7 − 5 = ____
J	8 − 3 = ____	8 − 5 = ____	9 − 6 = ____	13 − 5 = ____
K	12 − 4 = ____	16 − 8 = ____	17 − 7 = ____	16 − 4 = ____
L	15 − 3 = ____	14 − 6 = ____	10 − 5 = ____	11 − 4 = ____
M	12 − 6 = ____	11 − 7 = ____	10 − 7 = ____	6 − 6 = ____
N	5 − 2 = ____	7 − 4 = ____	8 − 2 = ____	9 − 5 = ____
O	13 − 7 = ____	16 − 6 = ____	15 − 2 = ____	14 − 6 = ____
P	13 − 3 = ____	12 − 8 = ____	11 − 2 = ____	10 − 3 = ____
Q	6 − 5 = ____	7 − 2 = ____	8 − 4 = ____	9 − 2 = ____
R	9 − 7 = ____	7 − 6 = ____	6 − 3 = ____	5 − 2 = ____
S	10 − 2 = ____	11 − 6 = ____	12 − 2 = ____	13 − 6 = ____
T	16 − 2 = ____	14 − 7 = ____	11 − 8 = ____	6 − 2 = ____
U	8 − 7 = ____	9 − 3 = ____	15 − 8 = ____	7 − 3 = ____
V	15 − 8 = ____	7 − 3 = ____	14 − 2 = ____	

Let's Match Words with Pictures

Pick the word from the box that matches each picture, and write the word in the space. See sample "1."

nurse	money	sing	nut
sun	nest	horn	run
can	phone	corn	wing

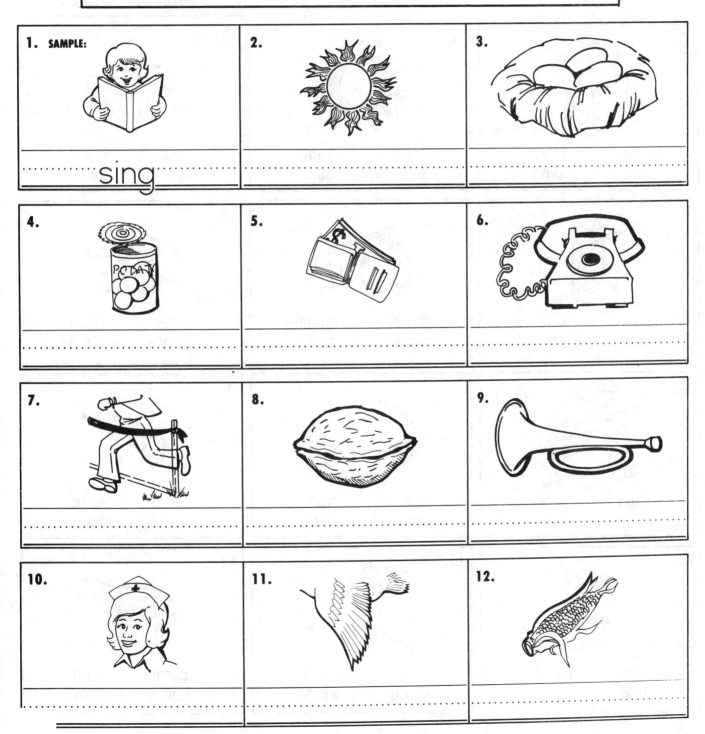

1. SAMPLE: sing

2.

3.

4.

5.

6.

7.

8.

9.

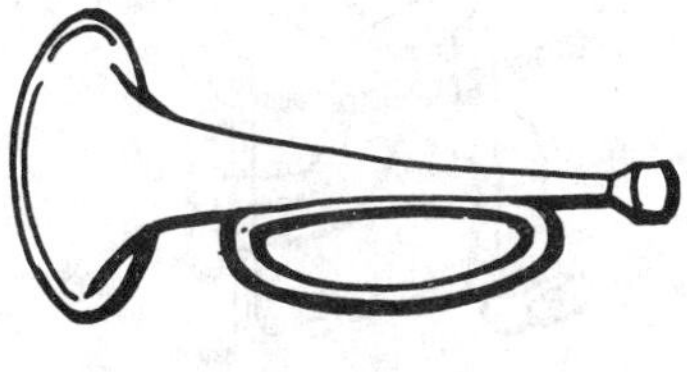

10.

11.

12.

Which Words Are Correct?

Circle the correctly spelled word that matches each picture.
See the example.

EXAMPLE:

dozen duzzen
duzen duzin

1.

singe cing
sing seng

2.

suun sunn
son sun

3.

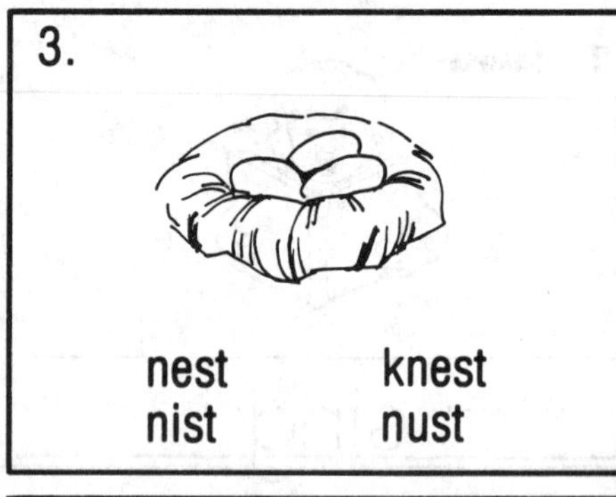

nest knest
nist nust

4.

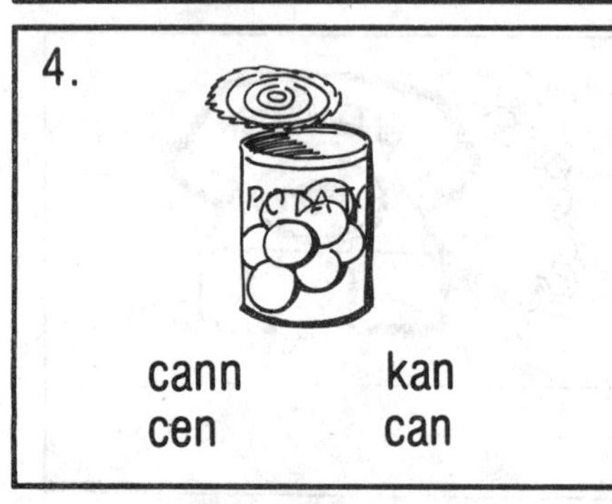

cann kan
cen can

5.

money munney
muney mony

6.

fone phon
phone phene

7.

rhun runn
rune run

8.

nut nutt
knut knutt

9.

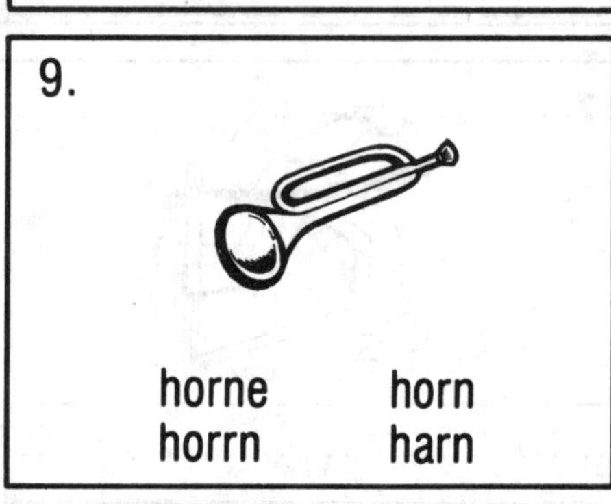

horne horn
horrn harn

10.

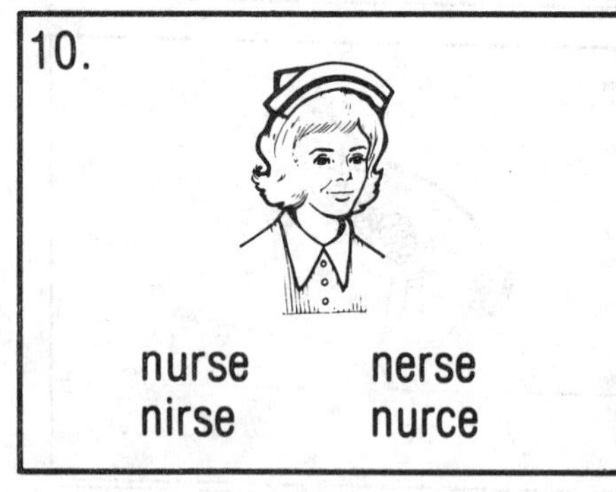

nurse nerse
nirse nurce

11.

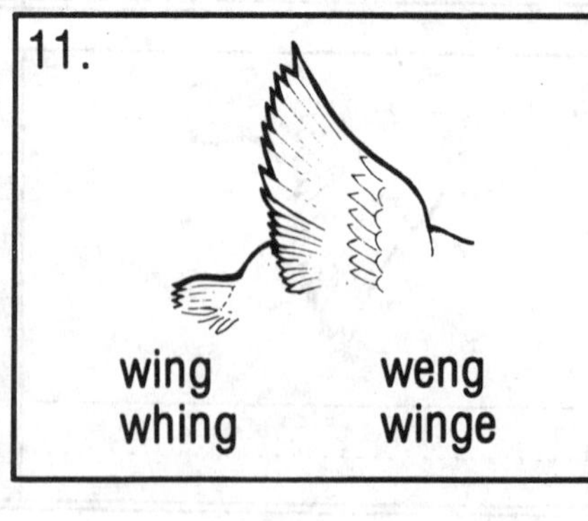

wing weng
whing winge

12.

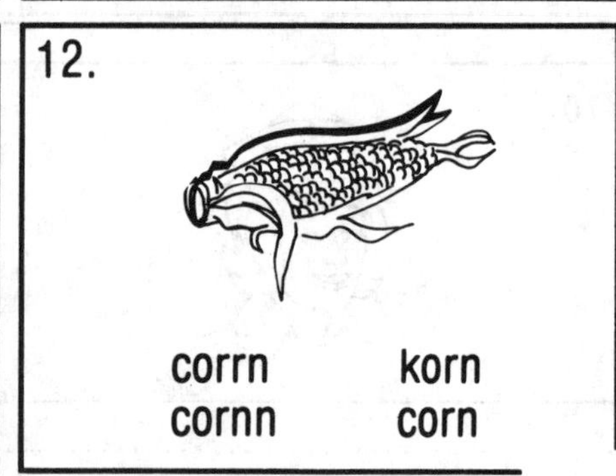

corrn korn
cornn corn

Sets Can Help

Write four equations for each set. See sample "1."

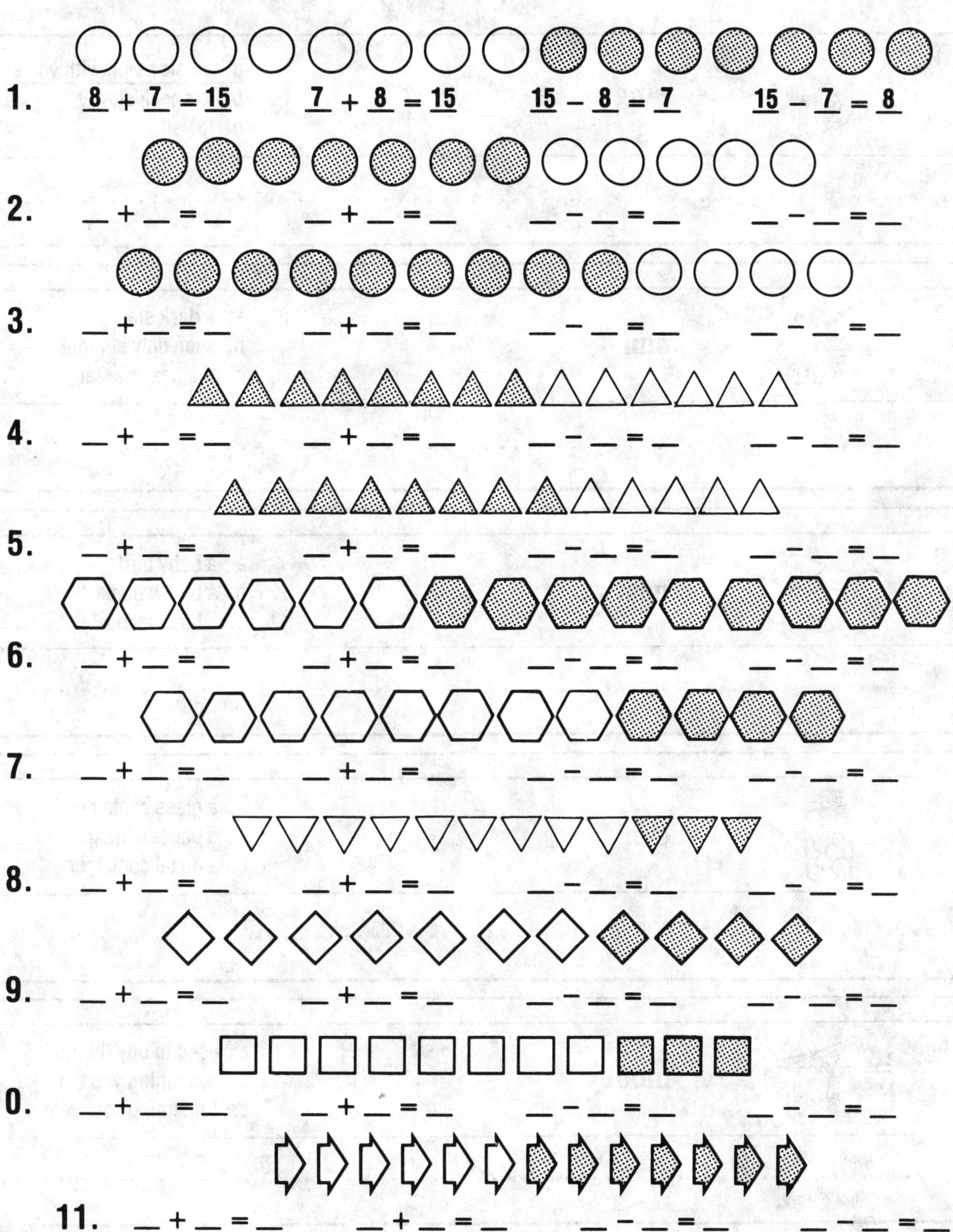

What Are the Meanings?

Underline the answer that defines each word. Write your own sentence about each word.

1. **sing**
   a. music made with voice
   b. to speak slowly
   c. to yell

2. **sun**
   a. a dark star
   b. seen only at night
   c. the nearest star

3. **nest**
   a. a baby bird
   b. a bird's home
   c. a bird's food

4. **can**
   a. a glass container
   b. a paper container
   c. a metal container

5. **money**
   a. used to buy things
   b. something you eat
   c. something you wear

Writing Time

What time is it? Write your answers in the blanks.

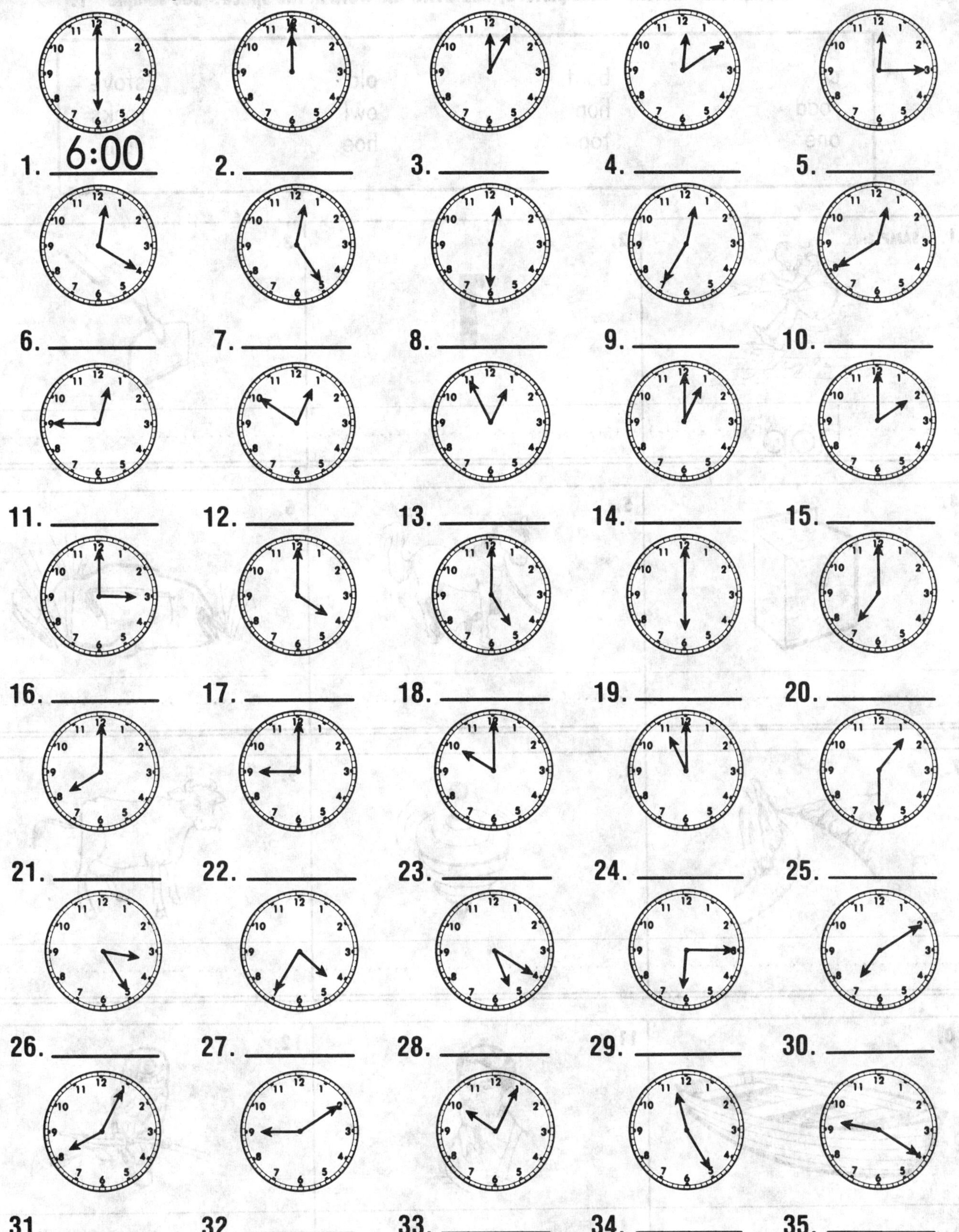

1. 6:00
2. ______
3. ______
4. ______
5. ______
6. ______
7. ______
8. ______
9. ______
10. ______
11. ______
12. ______
13. ______
14. ______
15. ______
16. ______
17. ______
18. ______
19. ______
20. ______
21. ______
22. ______
23. ______
24. ______
25. ______
26. ______
27. ______
28. ______
29. ______
30. ______
31. ______
32. ______
33. ______
34. ______
35. ______

Write the Correct Words

Pick the word from the box that matches each picture, and write the word in the space. See sample "1."

cow	boat	old	stove
road	hop	owl	rocks
one	top	hoe	pony

Vocabulary Development

Underline the answer that defines each word. Write your own sentence about each word.

1. **phone**
   a. short form of "telephone"
   b. short form of "television"
   c. something not real

2. **run**
   a. move the arms quickly
   b. move the legs slowly
   c. move the legs quickly

3. **nut**
   a. a flower
   b. a seed with a hard shell
   c. a seed with a soft shell

4. **horn**
   a. instrument sounded by blowing
   b. instrument sounded by beating
   c. instrument sounded by plucking

5. **nurse**
   a. works in a library
   b. teaches students to write
   c. helps care for the sick

Words and Pictures

Circle the correctly spelled word that matches each picture.
See the example.

EXAMPLE:

buzzurd	buzzard (circled)
buzzird	buzzerd

1\.

hop	hope
hopp	hup

2\.

won	whon
one	wone

3\.

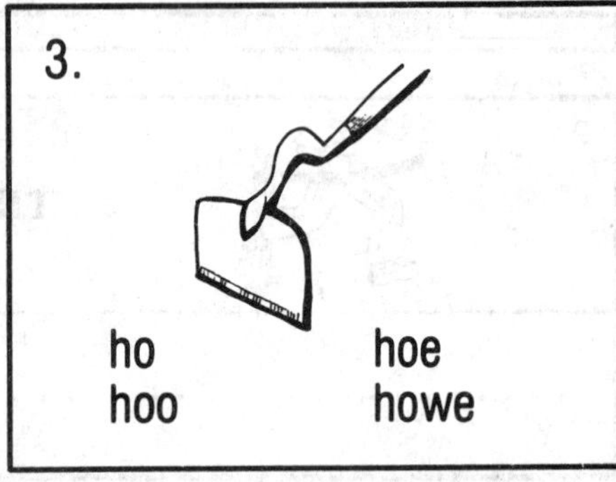

ho	hoe
hoo	howe

4\.

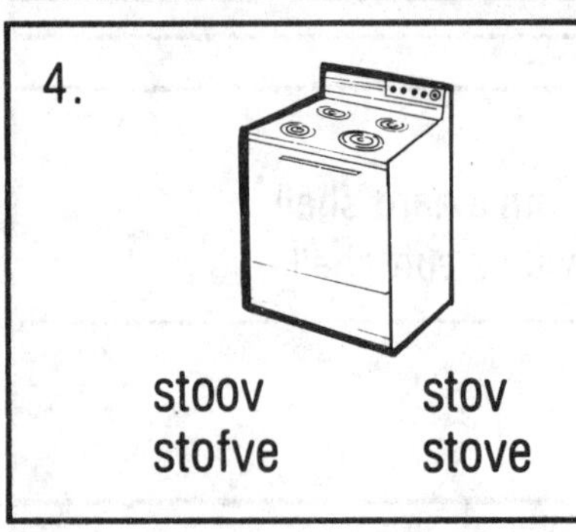

stoov	stov
stofve	stove

5\.

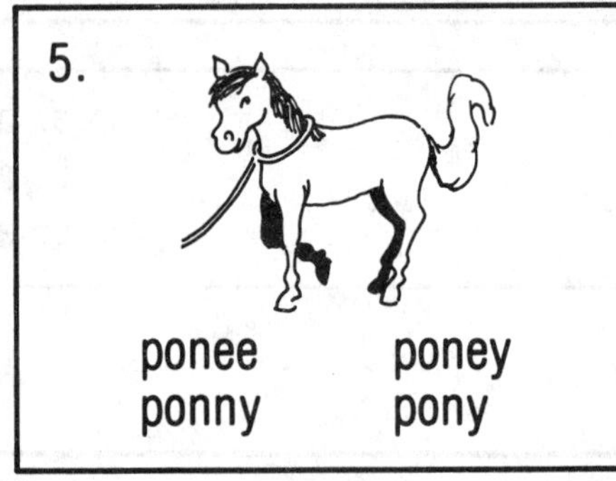

ponee	poney
ponny	pony

6\.

rocks	rucks
rocs	roks

7\.

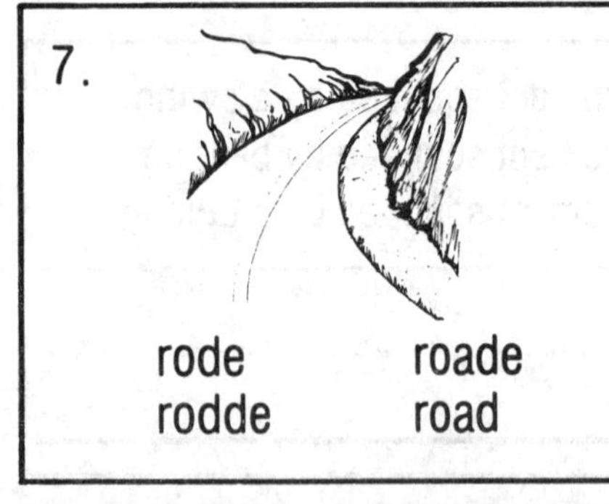

rode	roade
rodde	road

8\.

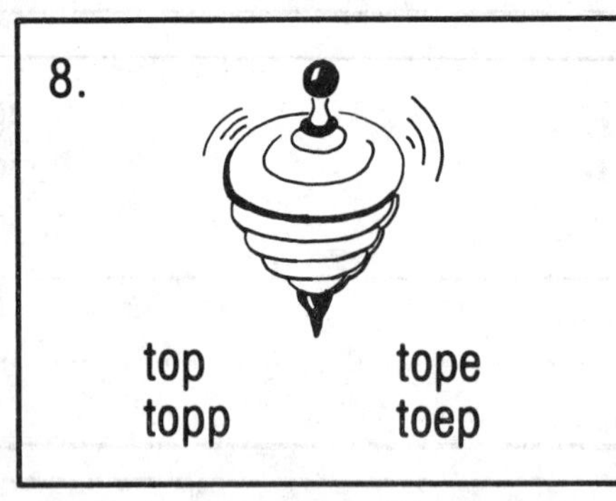

top	tope
topp	toep

9\.

kow	cowe
cow	cou

10\.

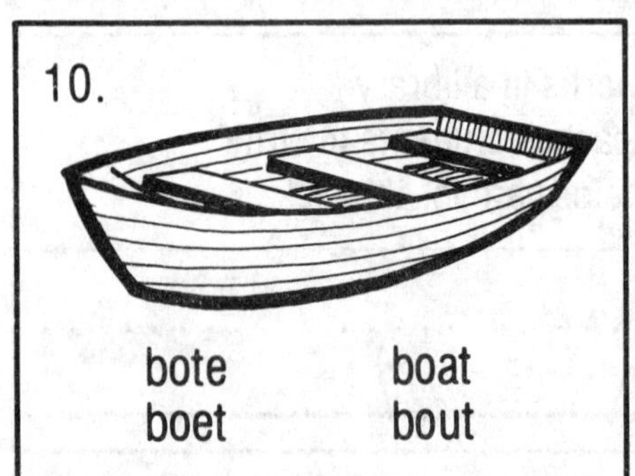

bote	boat
boet	bout

11\.

owld	ould
old	olde

12\.

oul	owl
ouel	owel

5 + 3 Puppies

Fill in the blanks.

A. Five puppies are playing. Three more puppies are coming to play with them. Then how many puppies will be playing?

✋ + ✋ = 8   5 + 3 = 8 $\begin{array}{r} 5 \\ +3 \\ \hline 8 \end{array}$

five + three = eight

B. Three puppies are playing. Five more puppies are watching them. How many puppies are there in all?

✋ + ✋ = ______   3 + 5 = ______ $\begin{array}{r} 3 \\ +5 \\ \hline \end{array}$

three + five = __________

C. Eight puppies were playing. If five of the puppies go away, how many puppies will be left?

8 − 5 = ______ $\begin{array}{r} 8 \\ -5 \\ \hline \end{array}$

eight − five = __________

D. Eight puppies were asleep. If three of the puppies woke up, how many were still asleep?

8 − 3 = ______ $\begin{array}{r} 8 \\ -3 \\ \hline \end{array}$

eight − three = __________

Give the Meanings

Underline the answer that defines each word. Write your own sentence about each word.

1. **hop**
   a. to crawl
   b. to walk on the hands
   c. to spring on one foot

2. **one**
   a. the number after "zero"
   b. the number before "three"
   c. the number after "two"

3. **hoe**
   a. used for cutting paper
   b. used for cutting weeds
   c. used for cutting bread

4. **stove**
   a. used to cook food
   b. used to keep food cold
   c. used to carry food

5. **pony**
   a. small dog
   b. small cow
   c. small horse

5 + 4 Geese

Fill in the blanks.

A. Five geese were flying in formation. Four more geese joined them. Then how many geese were flying in formation?

(hand) + (hand) = ______ $5 + 4 =$ ______

$$\begin{array}{r} 5 \\ +4 \\ \hline \end{array}$$

five + four = __________

B. Four geese were flying in formation. Five more geese joined them. Then how many geese were flying in formation?

(hand) + (hand) = ______ $4 + 5 =$ ____

$$\begin{array}{r} 4 \\ +5 \\ \hline \end{array}$$

four + five = __________

C. Nine geese were flying in formation. Five geese left the formation. How many geese were then flying in formation?

$9 - 5 =$ ______

$$\begin{array}{r} 9 \\ -5 \\ \hline \end{array}$$

nine − five = __________

D. Nine geese were flying in formation. Four geese left the formation. Then how many were still in formation?

$9 - 4 =$ ______

$$\begin{array}{r} 9 \\ -4 \\ \hline \end{array}$$

nine − four = __________

Pick the Proper Words

Pick the word from the box that matches each picture, and write the word in the space. See sample "1."

pants	paper	drip	paint
rope	drop	pear	peanut
soup	soap	map	ape

What Are the Descriptions?

Underline the answer that defines each word. Write your own sentence about each word.

1. **rock**
   a. a mountain
   b. a small stone
   c. a large stone

2. **road**
   a. where cars drive
   b. where airplanes land
   c. where people walk

3. **top**
   a. the highest part
   b. the middle part
   c. the lowest part

4. **cow**
   a. the male of cattle
   b. the female of cattle
   c. the young of cattle

5. **boat**
   a. used to travel in the air
   b. used to travel on land
   c. used to travel on water

Improve Your Spelling

Circle the correctly spelled word that matches each picture. See the example.

EXAMPLE:

sneaze sneez
(sneeze) sneze

1.

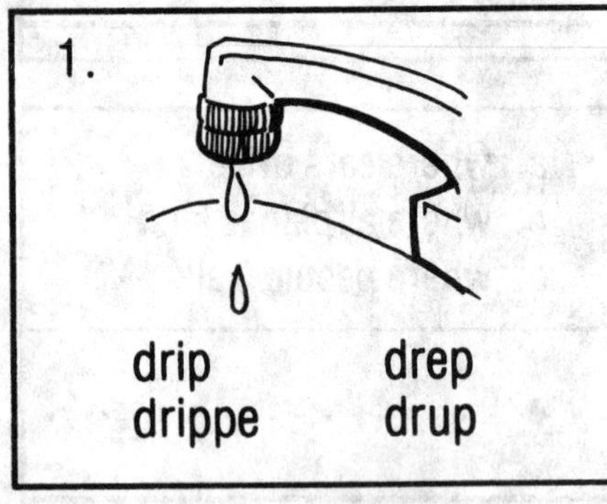

drip drep
drippe drup

2.

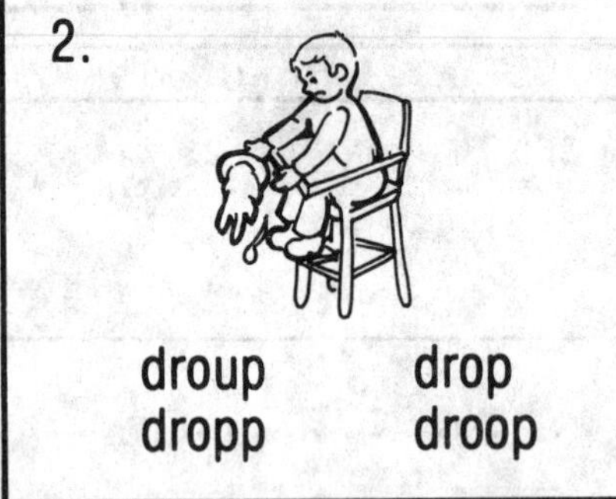

droup drop
dropp droop

3.

painnt peint
paint paynt

4.

aip appe
ape aap

5.

pantes pants
pantz pents

6.

soep soape
soap sope

7.

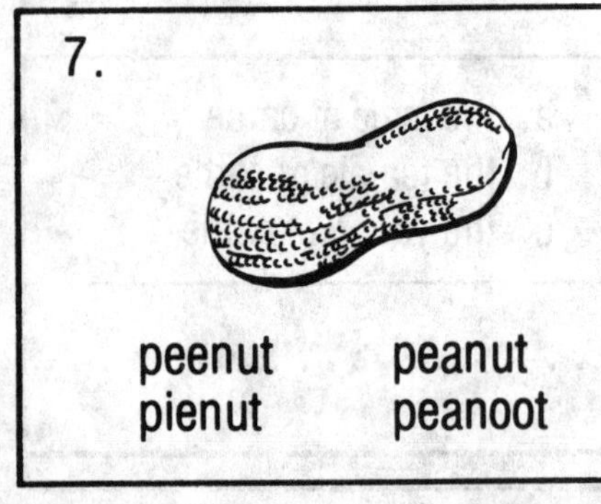

peenut peanut
pienut peanoot

8.

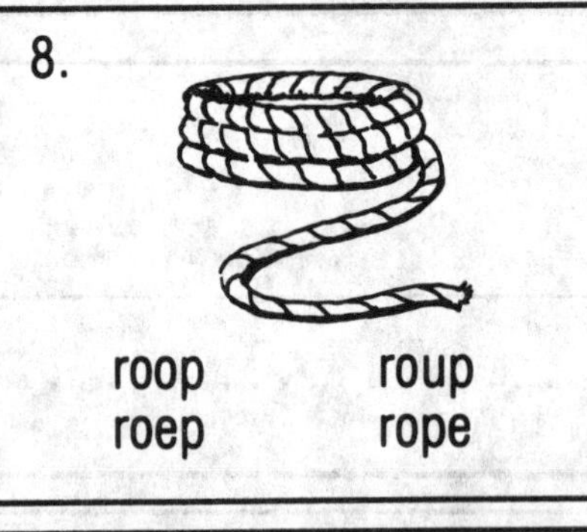

roop roup
roep rope

9.

paper papir
papur papper

10.

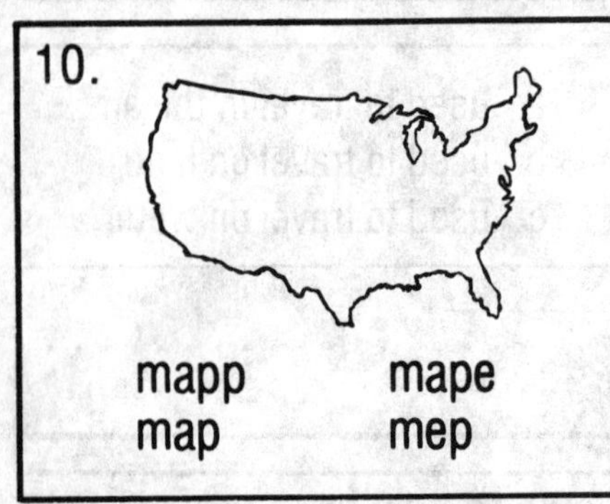

mapp mape
map mep

11.

soup supe
soop suip

12.

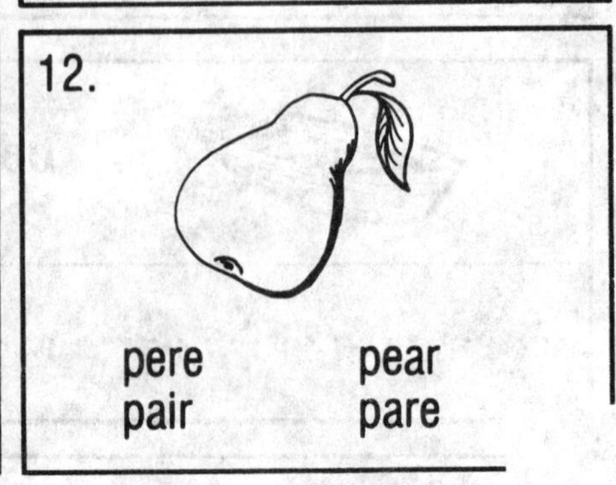

pere pear
pair pare

6 + 2 Squirrels

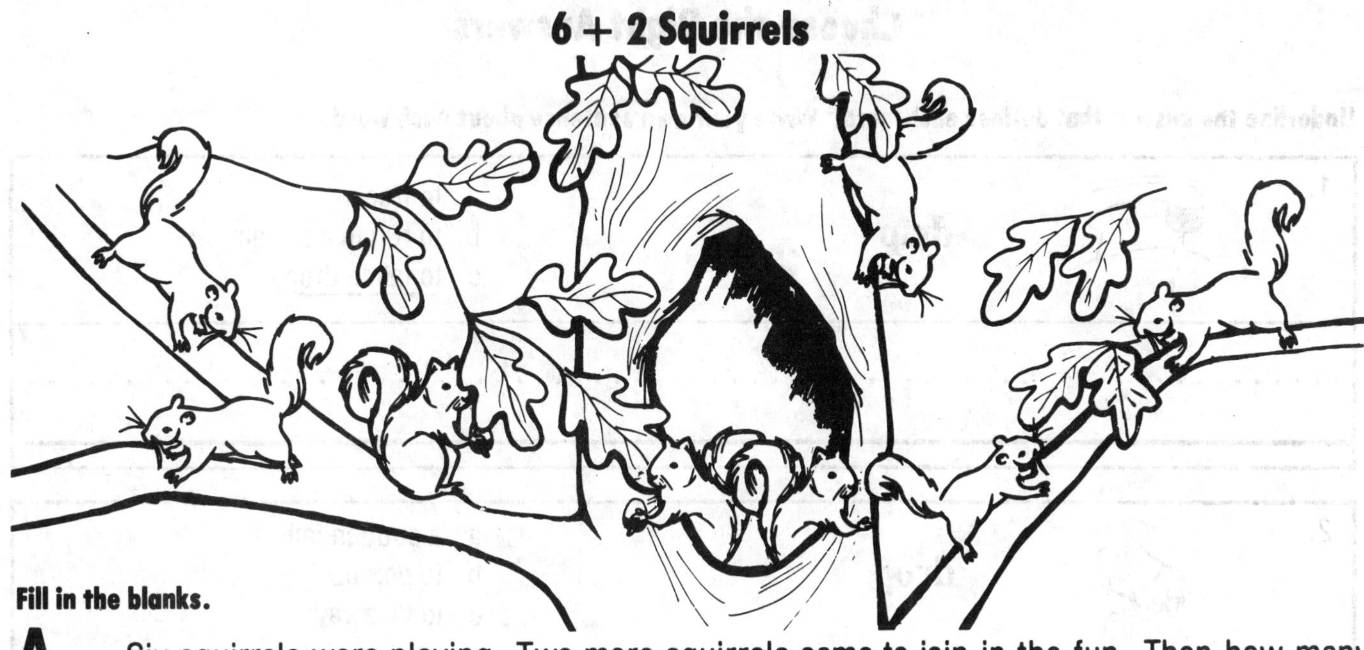

Fill in the blanks.

A. Six squirrels were playing. Two more squirrels came to join in the fun. Then how many squirrels were playing?

$6 + 2 =$ ______

$\begin{array}{r} 6 \\ +2 \\ \hline \end{array}$

six + two = __________

B. Two squirrels were playing. Six more squirrels came to join in the fun. Then how many squirrels were playing?

$2 + 6 =$ ______

$\begin{array}{r} 2 \\ +6 \\ \hline \end{array}$

two + six = __________

C. Eight squirrels were playing in a tree. Two of them jumped to the ground. Then how many squirrels were playing in the tree?

$8 - 2 =$ ______

$\begin{array}{r} 8 \\ -2 \\ \hline \end{array}$

eight − two = __________

D. Eight squirrels were playing in a tree. Six of them jumped to the ground. Then how many squirrels were playing in the tree?

$8 - 6 =$ ______

$\begin{array}{r} 8 \\ -6 \\ \hline \end{array}$

eight − six = __________

Choose the Right Answers

Underline the answer that defines each word. Write your own sentence about each word.

1. **drip**
   a. to freeze
   b. to run in a stream
   c. to fall in drops

2. **drop**
   a. a sudden fall
   b. to pop up
   c. to fly away

3. **paint**
   a. used to clean windows
   b. used to wash walls
   c. used to color a surface

4. **ape**
   a. a large fish
   b. a large cat
   c. a large monkey

5. **pants**
   a. something worn over the arms
   b. something worn over the legs
   c. something worn over the ears

6 + 3 Chicks

Fill in the blanks.

A. Six baby chicks were eating corn with the mother hen. Three more baby chicks were nearby. How many baby chicks were there in all?

6 + 3 = _____

six + three = _________

$$\begin{array}{r} 6 \\ +3 \\ \hline \end{array}$$

B. Three baby chicks were eating corn with the mother hen. Six more baby chicks were standing nearby. How many baby chicks were there in all?

3 + 6 = _____

three + six = _________

$$\begin{array}{r} 3 \\ +6 \\ \hline \end{array}$$

C. Nine baby chicks were eating corn with the mother hen. Six of them stopped eating. Then how many baby chicks were eating with the mother hen?

9 – 6 = _____

nine – six = _________

$$\begin{array}{r} 9 \\ -6 \\ \hline \end{array}$$

D. Nine baby chicks were eating corn with the mother hen. Three of them stopped eating. Then how many baby chicks were eating corn with the mother hen?

9 – 3 = _____

nine – three = _________

$$\begin{array}{r} 9 \\ -3 \\ \hline \end{array}$$

Picture, Word Matching

Pick the word from the box that matches each picture, and write the word in the space. See sample "1."

queen	quake	question	quiet
quart	quartet	quiz	quail
quick	quack	quarter	squid

Can You Choose the Correct Answers?

Underline the answer that defines each word. Write your own sentence about each word.

1. **soap**

   a. used to wash with
   b. used to rinse with
   c. used to dry with

2. **peanut**

   a. a flower
   b. grows on a tree
   c. a nutlike seed, good to eat

3. **rope**

   a. a chain
   b. a thin string
   c. a strong, thick cord

4. **paper**

   a. made from leaves
   b. what you write with
   c. what you write on

5. **map**

   a. a picture of a person
   b. a drawing of the land
   c. a ticket

Recognizing Correctly Spelled Words

Circle the correctly spelled word that matches each picture.
See the example.

EXAMPLE:

graz graiz
grase graze

1.

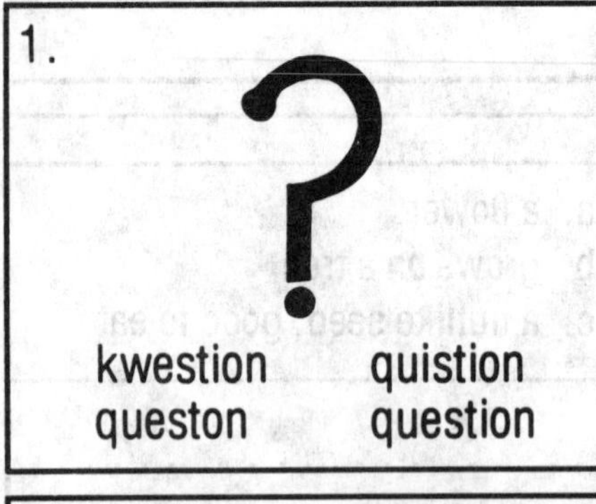

kwestion quistion
queston question

2.

quail queil
kwail quael

3.

qween queen
queene kween

4.

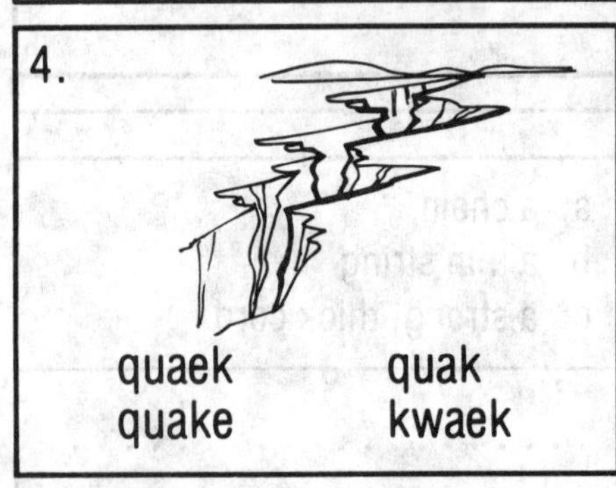

quaek quak
quake kwaek

5.

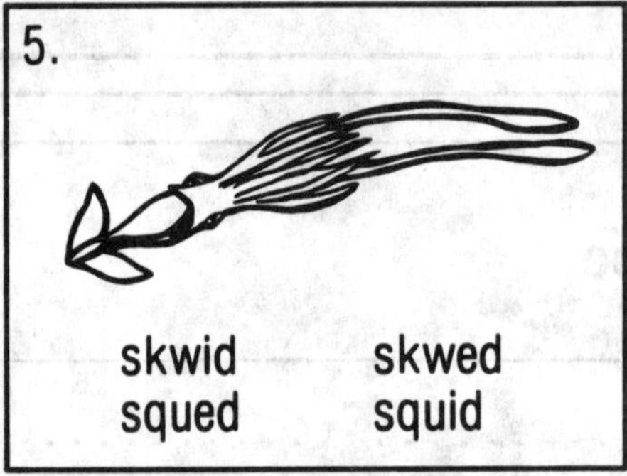

skwid skwed
squed squid

6.

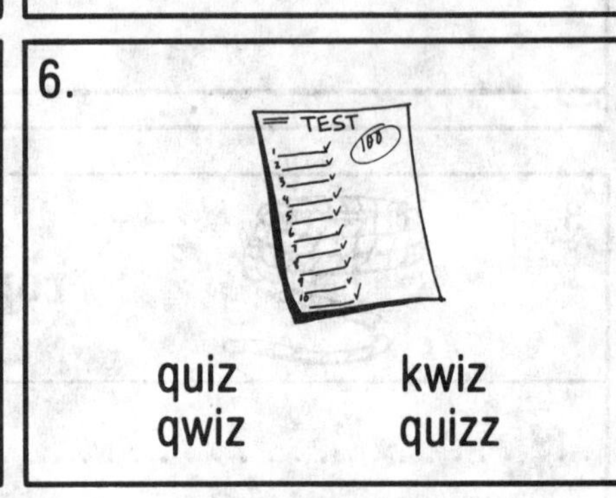

quiz kwiz
qwiz quizz

7.

quick quik
kwick queck

8.

kwartet quartat
quartet quartut

9.

kwarter quartir
querter quarter

10.

kwyet quiit
kwiet quiet

11.

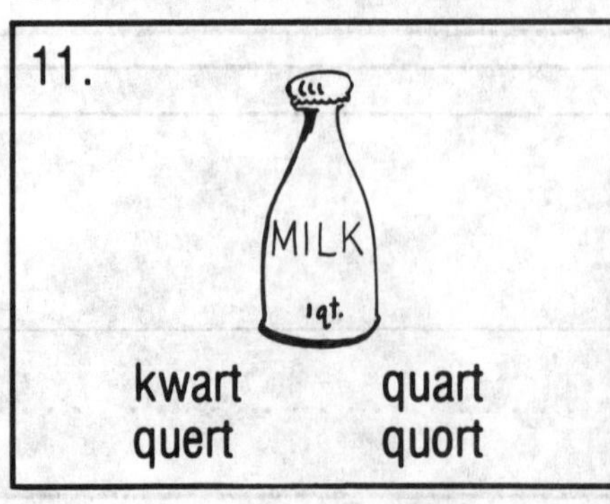

kwart quart
quert quort

12.

quack quac
quak kwack

6+4 Cookies

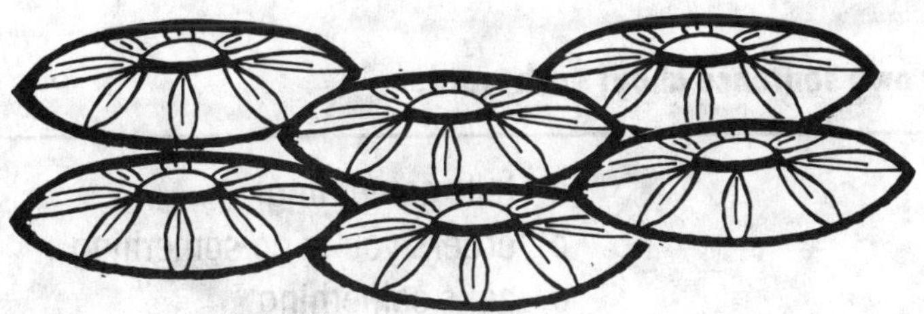

Fill in the blanks.

A. Mother was baking cookies. She baked six cookies in one pan and four cookies in another pan. How many cookies did Mother bake?

$6 + 4 =$ ______

six + four = __________

$$\begin{array}{r} 6 \\ +4 \\ \hline \end{array}$$

B. Susan gave Mother's cookies to her friends at her birthday party. She gave one cookie to each. There were four boys and six girls at the party. How many of Mother's cookies did Susan give to her friends?

$4 + 6 =$ ______

four + six = ______

$$\begin{array}{r} 4 \\ +6 \\ \hline \end{array}$$

C. Mother made ten cookies for the party. Six of the cookies were eaten. How many cookies were left?

$10 - 6 =$ ______

ten − six = __________

$$\begin{array}{r} 10 \\ -6 \\ \hline \end{array}$$

D. Mother made ten cookies for the party. Four of the cookies were chocolate covered. How many of the cookies were not chocolate covered?

$10 - 4 =$ ______

ten − four = __________

$$\begin{array}{r} 10 \\ -4 \\ \hline \end{array}$$

Give the Correct Answers

Underline the answer that defines each word. Write your own sentence about each word.

1. **question**
   a. tells something
   b. orders you to do something
   c. asks something

2. **quail**
   a. a fish
   b. a bird
   c. a cat

3. **queen**
   a. a female ruler
   b. a male ruler
   c. daughter of a king

4. **quake**
   a. to shake
   b. to close up
   c. to join together

5. **squid**
   a. a land animal
   b. a sea animal
   c. an animal that flies

6 + 5 Frogs

Fill in the blanks.

A. Six frogs were swimming in the pond. Five frogs were sunning on the bank. How many frogs were there?

$6 + 5 =$ ______

$\begin{array}{r} 6 \\ +5 \\ \hline \end{array}$

six + five = __________

B. Five frogs were jumping into the water. Six frogs were already in the water. How many frogs were at the pond?

$5 + 6 =$ ______

$\begin{array}{r} 5 \\ +6 \\ \hline \end{array}$

five + six = __________

C. Eleven frogs were swimming in the pond. Six frogs jumped out of the pond. How many frogs were still in the water?

$11 - 6 =$ ______

$\begin{array}{r} 11 \\ -6 \\ \hline \end{array}$

eleven − six = __________

D. Eleven frogs were sitting on the bank. Five of them jumped into the water. How many frogs were left on the bank?

$11 - 5 =$ ______

$\begin{array}{r} 11 \\ -5 \\ \hline \end{array}$

eleven − five = __________

Matching Words with Pictures

Pick the word from the box that matches each picture, and write the word in the space. See sample "1."

ride	tire	cry	hare
tree	pair	burn	draw
rest	dress	crash	rug

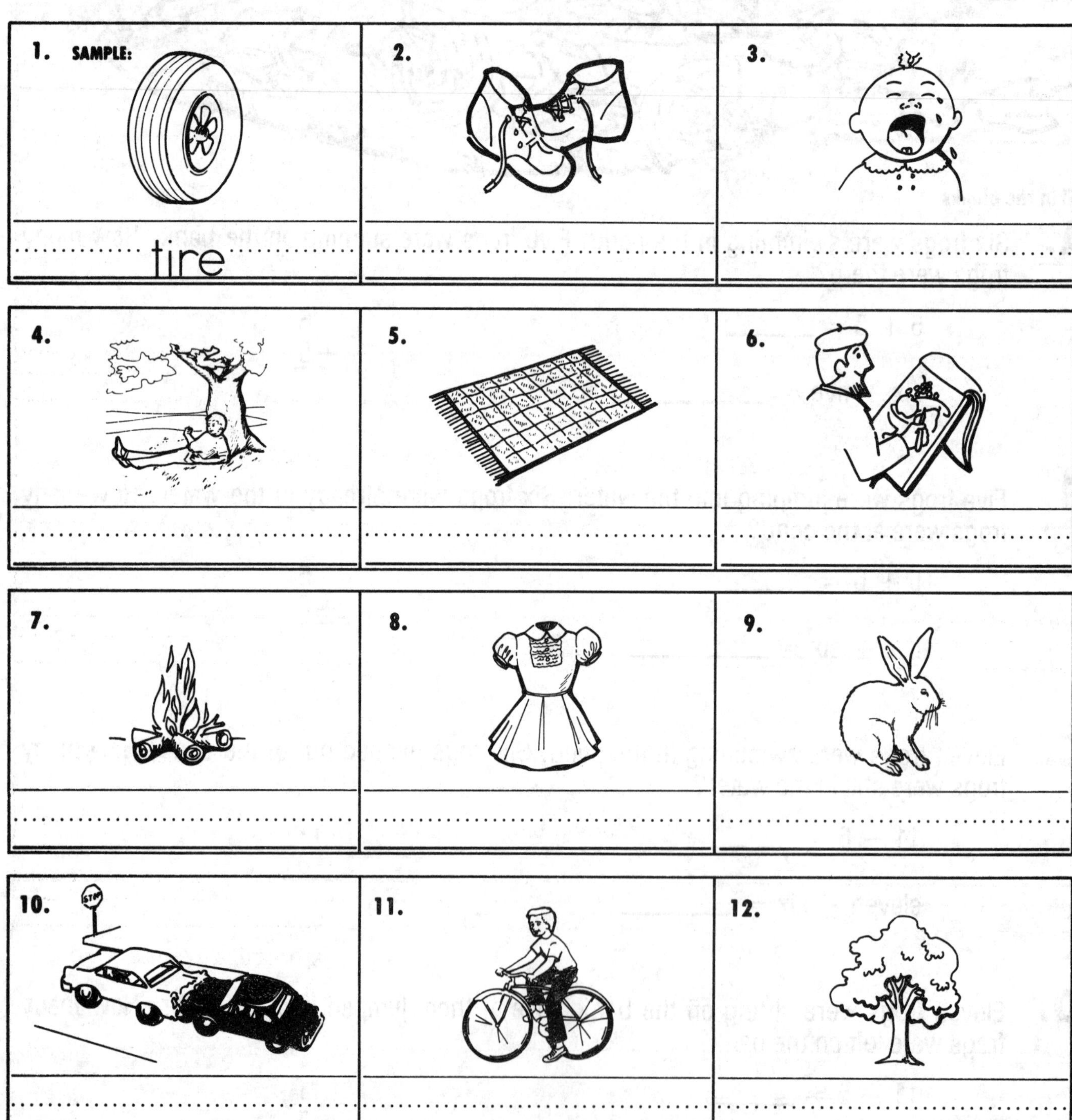

Remember the Meanings

Underline the answer that defines each word. Write your own sentence about each word.

1. **quiz**
   - a. homework
   - b. a short test
   - c. a reward

2. **quick**
   - a. hard to do
   - b. very slow
   - c. very fast

3. **quartet**
   - a. two people
   - b. three people
   - c. four people

4. **quarter**
   - a. five cents
   - b. ten cents
   - c. twenty-five cents

5. **quiet**
   - a. making no noise
   - b. very loud
   - c. making too much noise

Fun with Pictures

Circle the correctly spelled word that matches each picture.
See the example.

EXAMPLE:

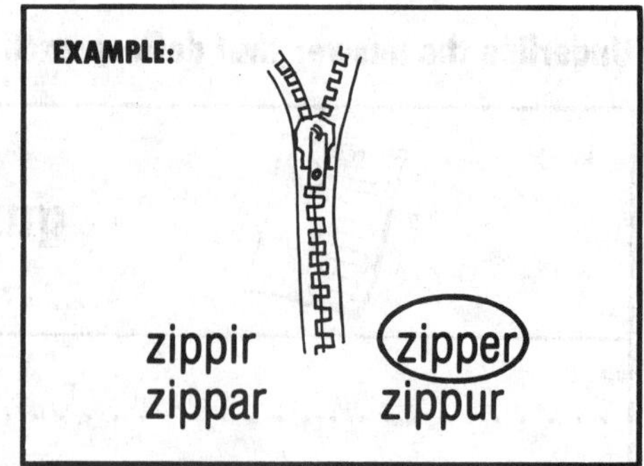

zippir zipper
zippar zippur

1.

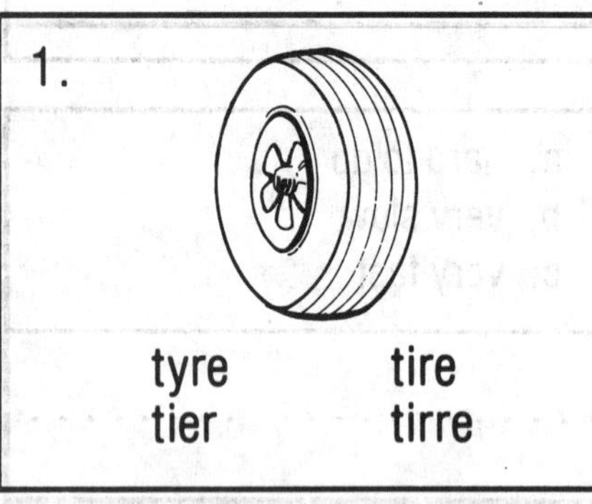

tyre tire
tier tirre

2.

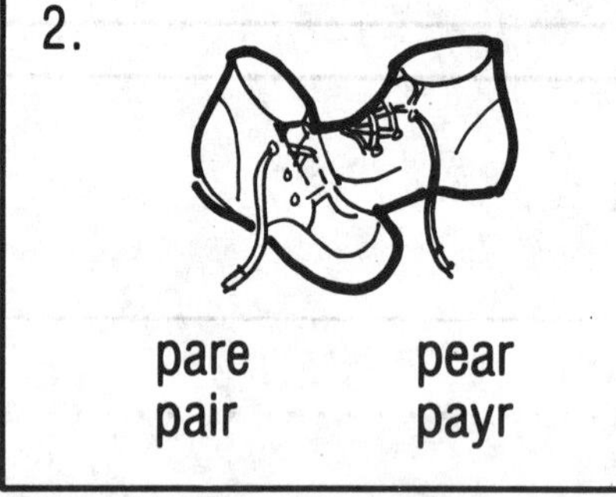

pare pear
pair payr

3.

kri kry
cri cry

4.

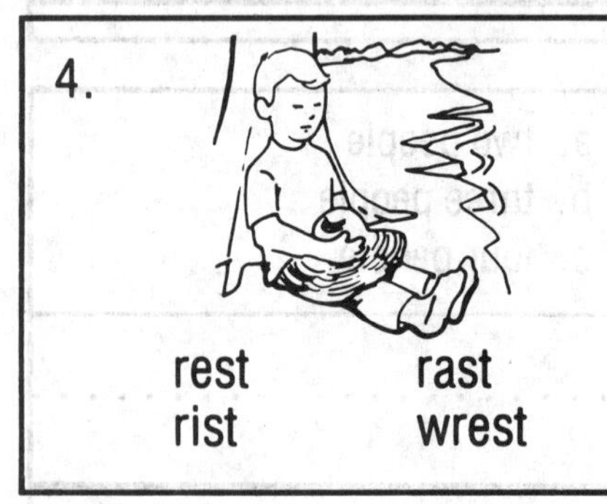

rest rast
rist wrest

5.

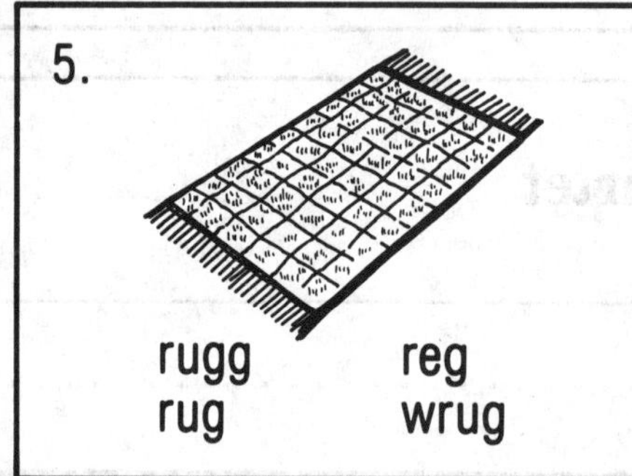

rugg reg
rug wrug

6.

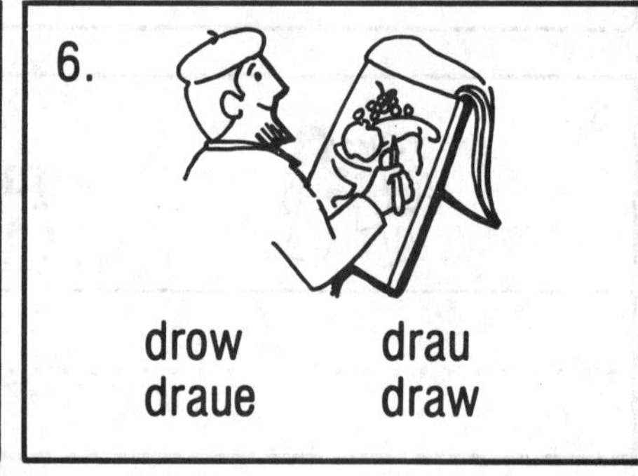

drow drau
draue draw

7.

bern birn
burrn burn

8.

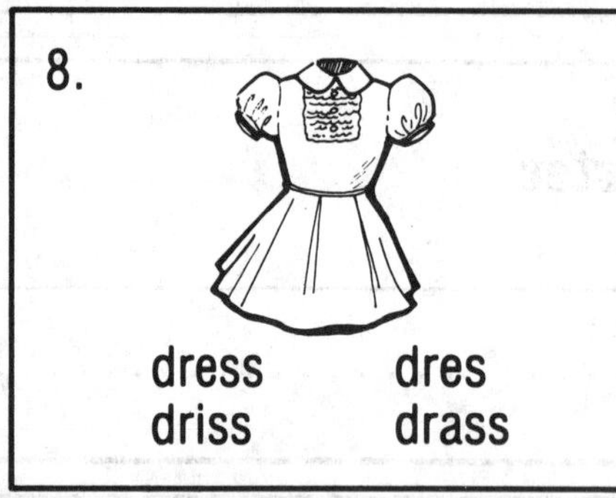

dress dres
driss drass

9.

har hair
hare hayr

10.

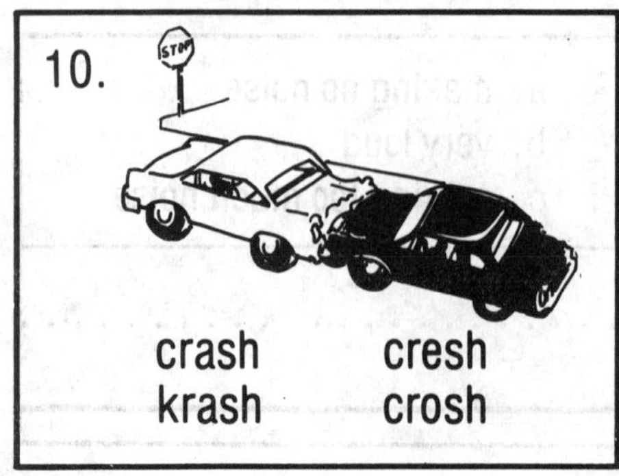

crash cresh
krash crosh

11.

ryde ride
ridd reid

12.

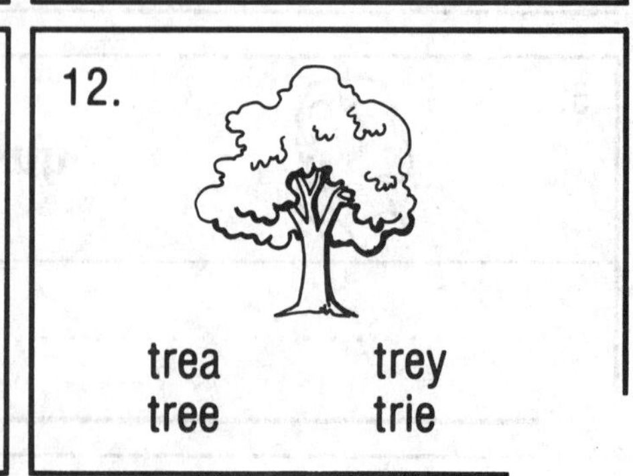

trea trey
tree trie

7 + 2 Kittens

Fill in the blanks.

A. Seven kittens were playing with each other. Two kittens were playing with a ball of yarn. How many kittens were playing?

7 + 2 = ______

$$\begin{array}{r} 7 \\ +2 \\ \hline \end{array}$$

seven + two = __________

B. Two kittens were asleep in a basket. Seven kittens were eating cat food. How many kittens were there?

2 + 7 = ______

$$\begin{array}{r} 2 \\ +7 \\ \hline \end{array}$$

two + seven = __________

C. Nine kittens were eating breakfast. Seven kittens went to sleep. How many kittens were still eating breakfast?

9 − 7 = ______

$$\begin{array}{r} 9 \\ -7 \\ \hline \end{array}$$

nine − seven = __________

D. Nine kittens were running after a mouse. Two kittens stopped running and started playing with a ball of yarn. How many kittens were still running after the mouse?

9 − 2 = ______

$$\begin{array}{r} 9 \\ -2 \\ \hline \end{array}$$

nine − two = __________

Let's Choose the Correct Answers

Underline the answer that defines each word. Write your own sentence about each word.

1. **tire**
   a. the inside of a wheel
   b. the center of a wheel
   c. the rubber on a wheel

2. **pair**
   a. set of two
   b. set of three
   c. set of four

3. **cry**
   a. to look happy
   b. to shed tears
   c. to go to sleep

4. **rest**
   a. to work hard
   b. to make tired
   c. not working

5. **rug**
   a. covers the floor
   b. covers a window
   c. covers a door

7 + 3 Pigs

Fill in the blanks.

A. Seven little pigs were eating corn. Three joined them and began eating corn too. Then how many pigs were eating corn?

7 + 3 = ______

seven + three = __________

$$\begin{array}{r} 7 \\ +3 \\ \hline \end{array}$$

B. Three little pigs were sleeping in the barnyard. Seven little pigs were running and playing. How many pigs were sleeping and playing in the barnyard?

3 + 7 = ______

three + seven = __________

$$\begin{array}{r} 3 \\ +7 \\ \hline \end{array}$$

C. Ten little pigs were running and playing in the barnyard. Seven of the little pigs went to sleep. How many little pigs were still running and playing in the barnyard?

10 − 7 = ______

ten − seven = __________

$$\begin{array}{r} 10 \\ -7 \\ \hline \end{array}$$

D. Ten little pigs were running from their mother. Three of the little pigs stopped and started eating corn. How many little pigs were still running from their mother?

10 − 3 = ______

ten − three = __________

$$\begin{array}{r} 10 \\ -3 \\ \hline \end{array}$$

Select the Proper Words

Pick the word from the box that matches each picture, and write the word in the space. See sample "1."

mask	dust	seal	sea
last	twins	ship	music
asleep	skirt	shine	brush

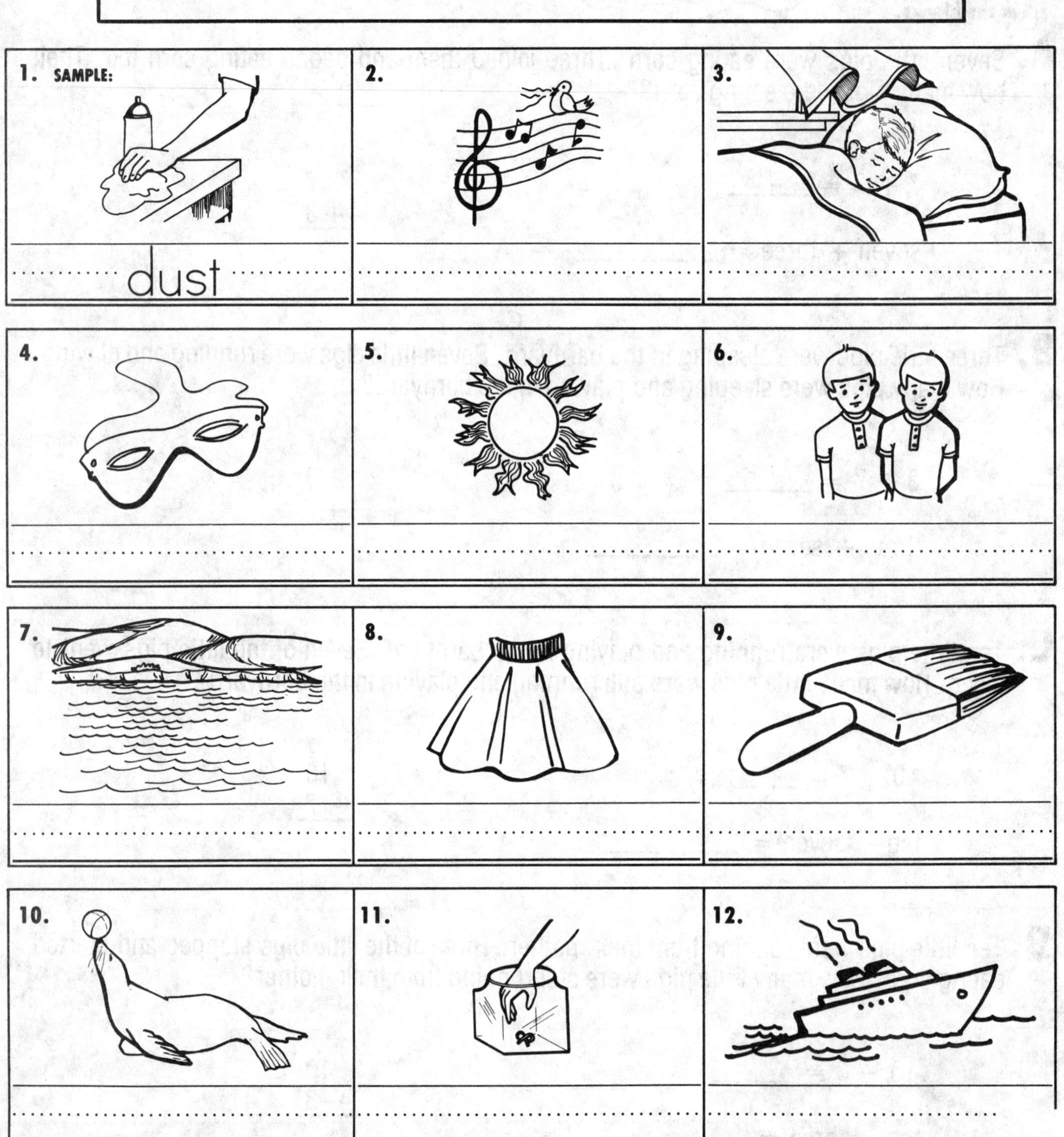

Describe the Words

Underline the answer that defines each word. Write your own sentence about each word.

1. **draw**

a. to paint black
b. <u>to make a picture of</u>
c. to build with wood

2. **burn**

a. to pack with ice
b. to freeze
c. to be on fire

3. **dress**

a. something worn on the head
b. something worn by a girl
c. something worn on the feet

4. **hare**

a. an animal that lives in a shell
b. an animal that swims
c. an animal that runs quickly

5. **crash**

a. to hit hard together
b. to pull apart
c. to move slowly

Match Words and Pictures

**Circle the correctly spelled word that matches each picture.
See the example.**

EXAMPLE:

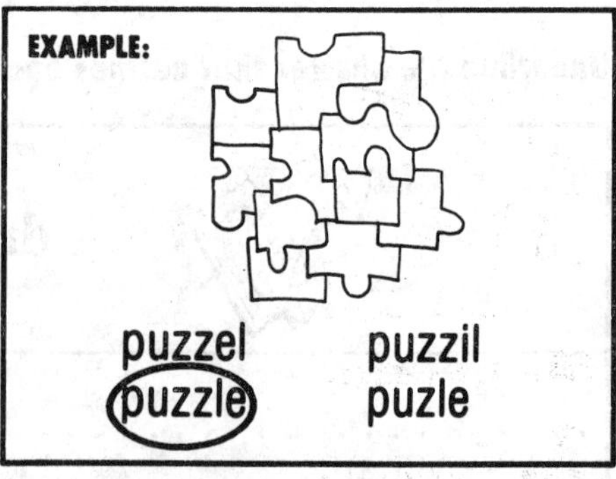

puzzel puzzil
puzzle puzle

1.

duste duzt
dist dust

2.

muzic muzik
music musik

3.

asleep aslep
asleap aslepe

4.

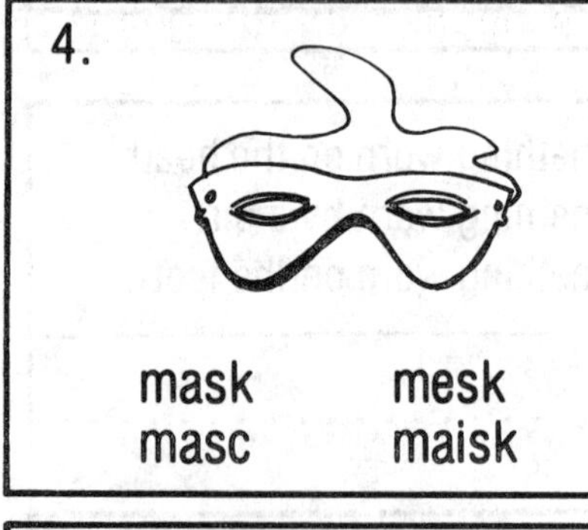

mask mesk
masc maisk

5.

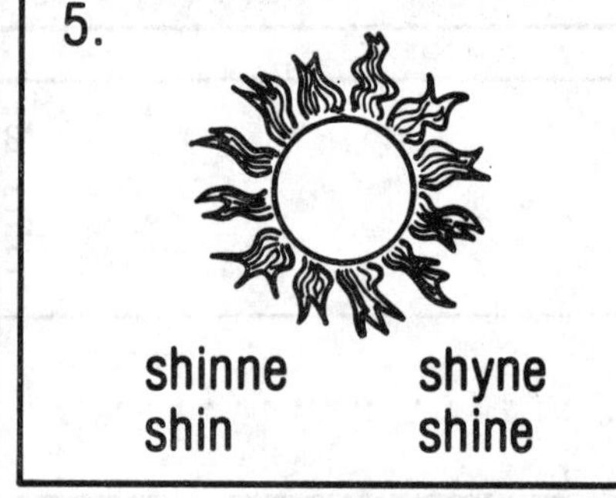

shinne shyne
shin shine

6.

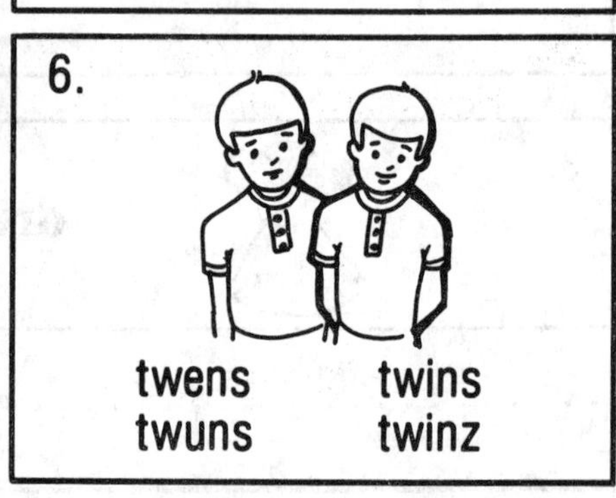

twens twins
twuns twinz

7.

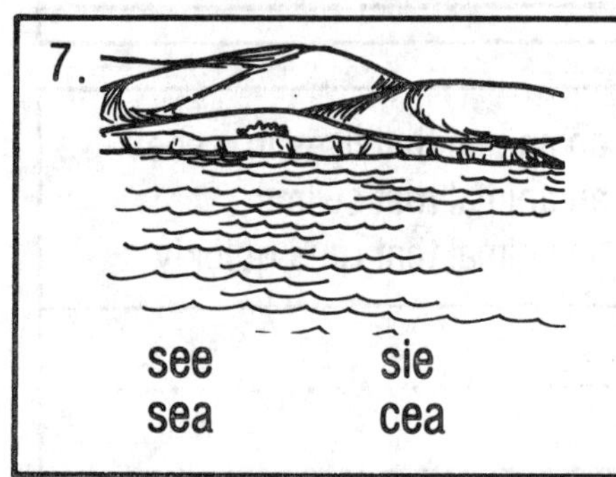

see sie
sea cea

8.

skirt skert
skurt skart

9.

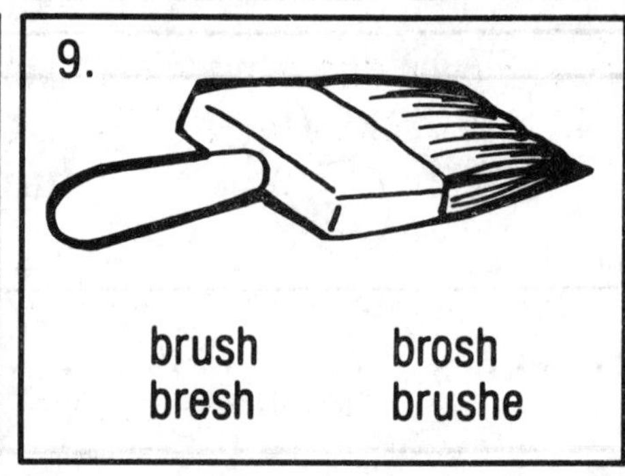

brush brosh
bresh brushe

10.

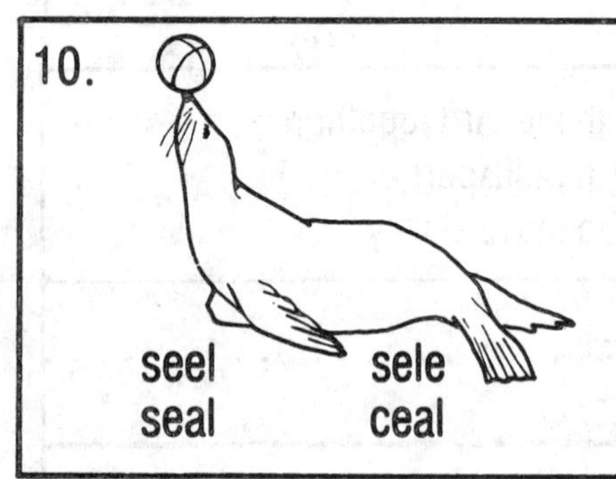

seel sele
seal ceal

11.

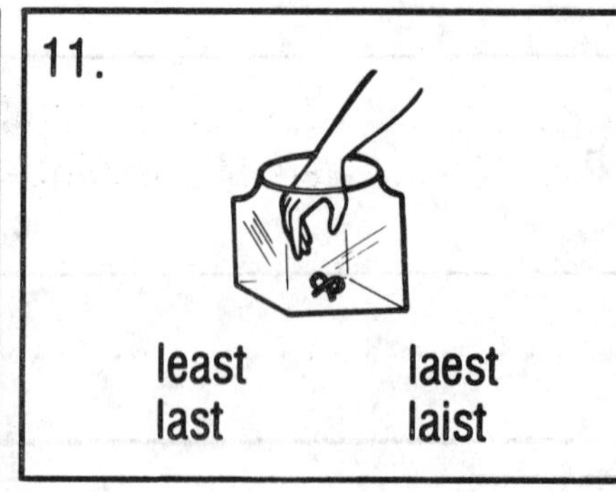

least laest
last laist

12.

shipe shep
shipp ship

7 + 4 Ducks

Fill in the blanks.

A. Seven ducks were swimming near the edge of the pond. Four ducks were wading in the shallow water. How many ducks were in the water?

$7 + 4 =$ ______

$\begin{array}{r} 7 \\ +4 \\ \hline \end{array}$

seven + four = __________

B. Four ducks were on the bank of the pond. Seven ducks were swimming in the pond. How many ducks were in or near the pond?

$4 + 7 =$ ______

$\begin{array}{r} 4 \\ +7 \\ \hline \end{array}$

four + seven = __________

C. Eleven ducks were flying over the pond. Seven of them landed in the water. How many of the ducks were still flying over the pond?

$11 - 7 =$ ______

$\begin{array}{r} 11 \\ -7 \\ \hline \end{array}$

eleven − seven = __________

D. Eleven ducks were wading in the shallow water of the pond. Four of them started swimming in the deep water. How many ducks were still wading in the shallow water?

$11 - 4 =$ ______

$\begin{array}{r} 11 \\ -4 \\ \hline \end{array}$

eleven − four = __________

Can You Remember the Definitions?

Underline the answer that defines each word. Write your own sentence about each word.

1. **dust**
   a. fine dirt
   b. wet dirt
   c. dirt with rocks

2. **music**
   a. loud sound
   b. terrible noise
   c. pleasant sound

3. **asleep**
   a. awake
   b. not awake
   c. working

4. **mask**
   a. covers part of the face
   b. covers the ears
   c. covers the nose

5. **shine**
   a. send out light
   b. make dull
   c. make dark

7 + 5 Monkeys

Fill in the blanks.

A. Seven monkeys were eating bananas. Five monkeys were sleeping. How many monkeys were there?

$7 + 5 =$ ______

seven + five = __________

$$\begin{array}{r} 7 \\ +5 \\ \hline \end{array}$$

B. Five monkeys were playing. Seven monkeys were swinging by their tails from a tree. How many monkeys were there in all?

$5 + 7 =$ ______

five + seven = __________

$$\begin{array}{r} 5 \\ +7 \\ \hline \end{array}$$

C. Twelve monkeys were riding in a wagon. Seven monkeys jumped out of the wagon. How many were still riding in the wagon?

$12 - 7 =$ ______

twelve − seven = __________

$$\begin{array}{r} 12 \\ -7 \\ \hline \end{array}$$

D. Twelve monkeys were eating watermelon. Five of them stopped eating and held their stomachs. How many monkeys were still eating watermelon?

$12 - 5 =$ ______

twelve − five = __________

$$\begin{array}{r} 12 \\ -5 \\ \hline \end{array}$$

Which Pictures Match the Words?

Pick the word from the box that matches each picture, and write the word in the space. See sample "1."

tool	tooth	boot	steam
bottle	fat	team	toes
wet	cut	eat	tail

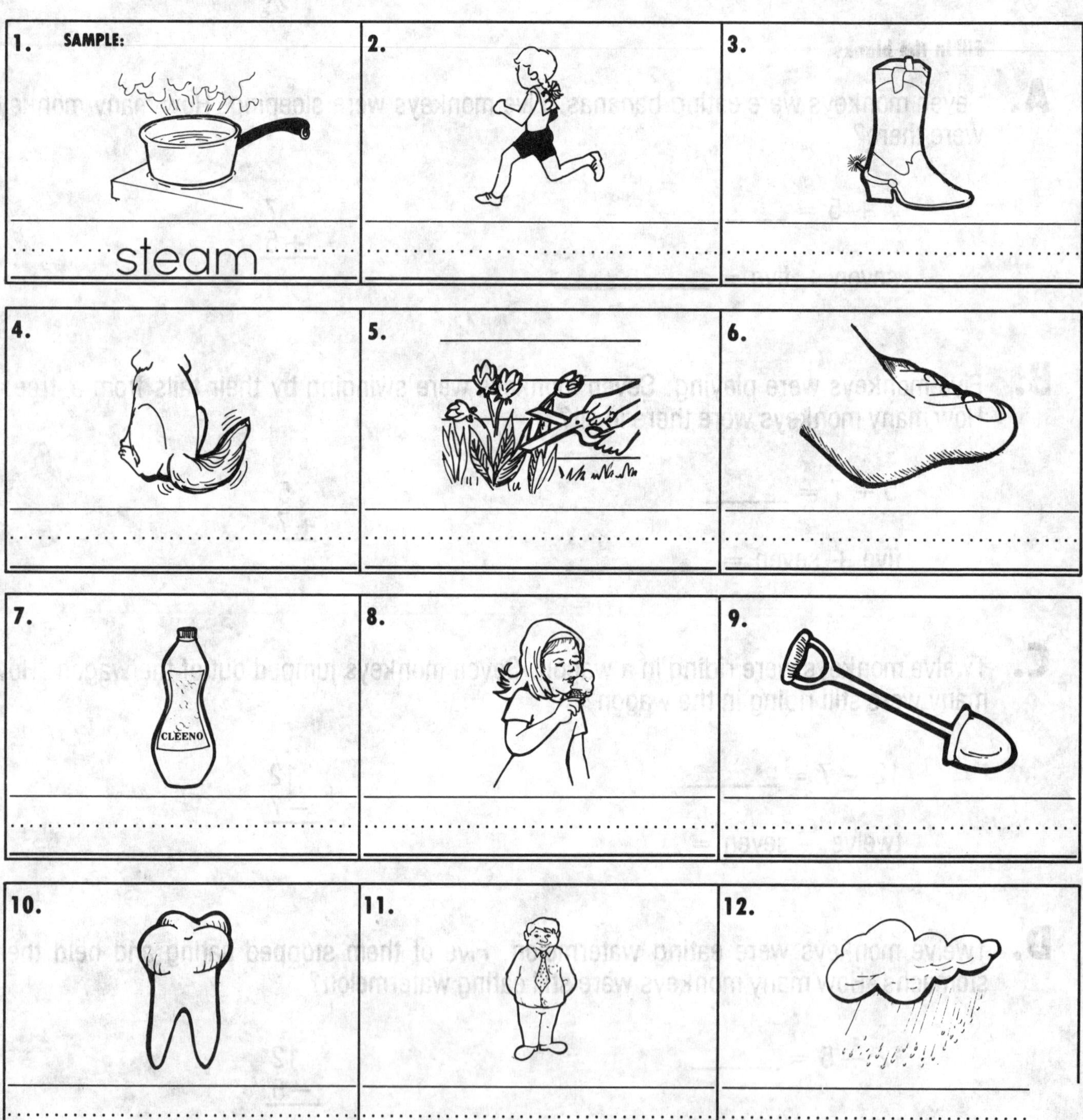

Developing Your Vocabulary

Underline the answer that defines each word. Write your own sentence about each word.

1. **twins**
   a. brothers and sisters
   b. a set of three
   c. <u>two people born at same time, same mother</u>

2. **sea**
   a. sky
   b. water
   c. land

3. **skirt**
   a. worn on the head
   b. worn above the waist
   c. worn below the waist

4. **brush**
   a. a tool for putting on paint
   b. used to wash the face
   c. holds things together

5. **seal**
   a. animal that lives in a cold area
   b. animal that lives in the jungle
   c. animal that lives on the desert

Name the Pictures

Circle the correctly spelled word that matches each picture. See the example.

EXAMPLE:

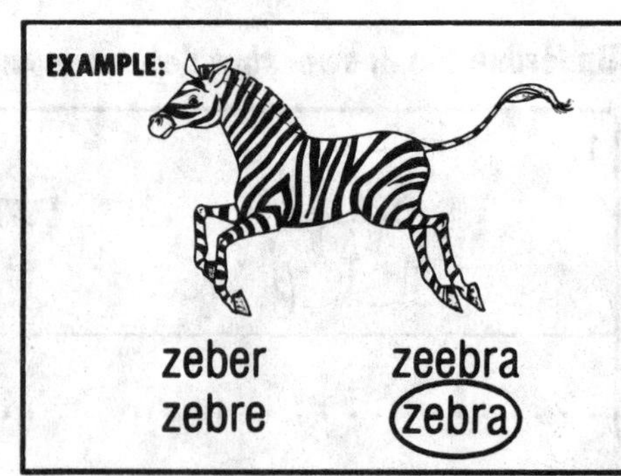

zeber zebre zeebra ~~(zebra)~~

1.  steam, steem, steme, stime	2.  teem, teme, team, teame	3. 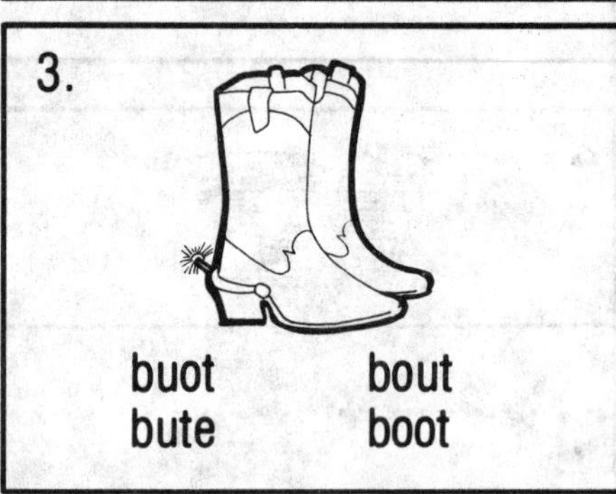 buot, bout, bute, boot
4.  tayl, tail, tael, tale	5. 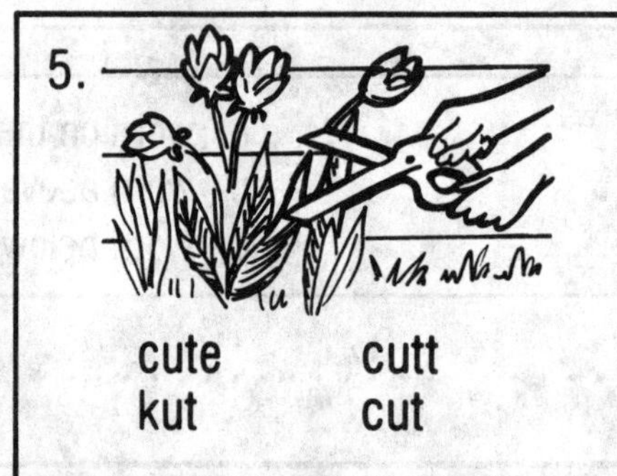 cute, cutt, kut, cut	6. 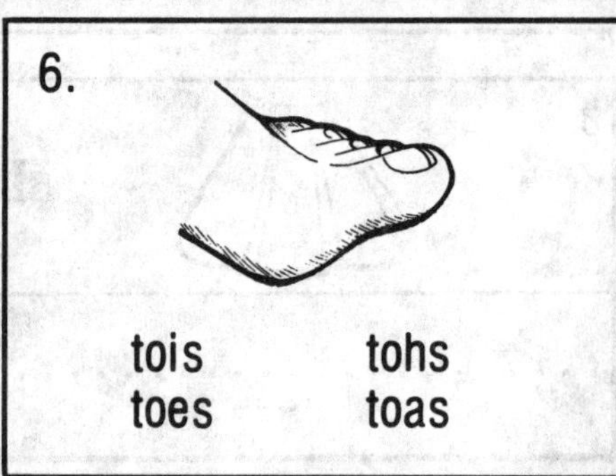 tois, tohs, toes, toas
7.  bottel, bottal, bottil, bottle	8.  eat, aet, eet, et	9. 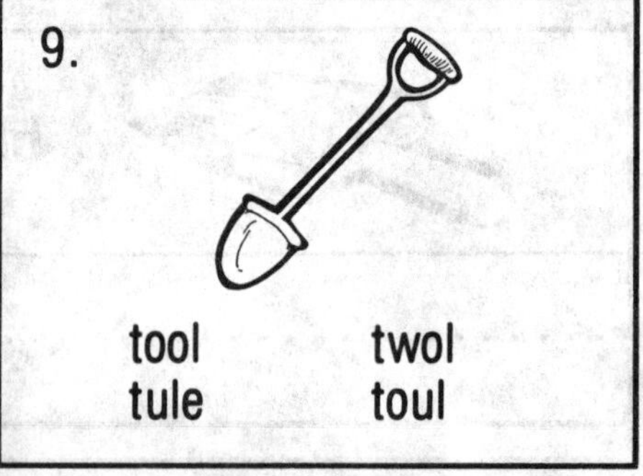 tool, twol, tule, toul
10. 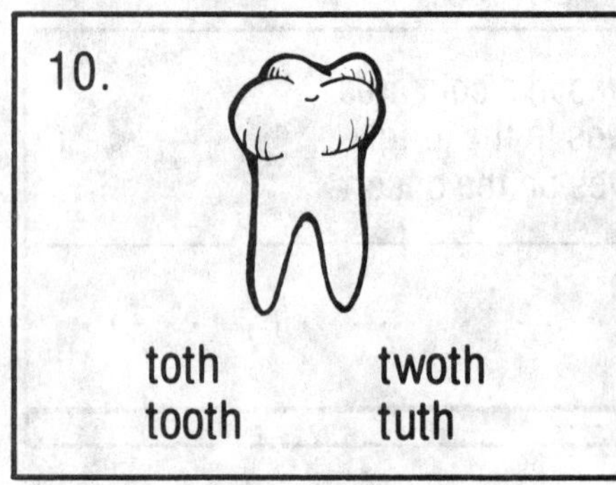 toth, twoth, tooth, tuth	11.  fatt, fat, fate, phat	12. 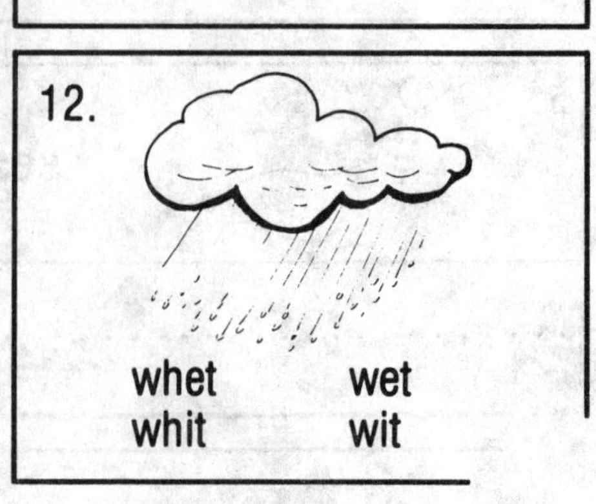 whet, wet, whit, wit

7 + 6 Giraffes

Fill in the blanks.

A. Seven giraffes were eating leaves from high in the trees. Six giraffes were waiting to get to the trees. How many giraffes were there in all?

7 + 6 = ______

$$\begin{array}{r} 7 \\ +6 \\ \hline \end{array}$$

seven + six = __________

B. Six giraffes were spreading their legs to lower their heads to get a drink of water. Seven giraffes were standing straight. How many giraffes were there?

6 + 7 = ______

$$\begin{array}{r} 6 \\ +7 \\ \hline \end{array}$$

six + seven = __________

C. Thirteen giraffes were in a herd. Seven of them were asleep standing up. How many giraffes were not standing?

13 − 7 = ______

$$\begin{array}{r} 13 \\ -7 \\ \hline \end{array}$$

thirteen − seven = __________

D. There were thirteen giraffes in the zoo. Six of the giraffes were calves. How many of the herd were adult giraffes?

13 − 6 = ______

$$\begin{array}{r} 13 \\ -6 \\ \hline \end{array}$$

thirteen − six = __________

Select the Correct Answers

Underline the answer that defines each word. Write your own sentence about each word.

1. **steam**
   a. dirty water
   b. frozen water
   c. mist

2. **team**
   a. working alone
   b. people or animals working together
   c. animals fighting

3. **boot**
   a. covering for the foot
   b. covering for the hand
   c. covering for the head

4. **tail**
   a. the beginning
   b. the middle
   c. the end

5. **cut**
   a. to divide with a knife
   b. to put together
   c. to close

8 + 2 Books

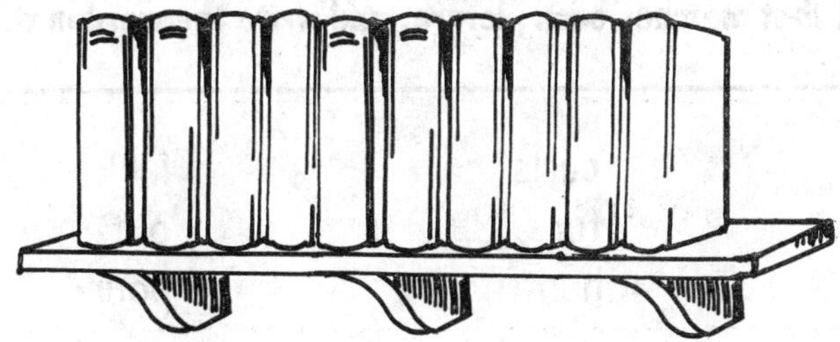

Fill in the blanks.

A. Susan read eight books. Phyllis has read two books. The two students have read how many books in all?

8 + 2 = ______

eight + two = __________

$$\begin{array}{r} 8 \\ +2 \\ \hline \end{array}$$

B. On one shelf at the library, two books have black covers and eight books have red covers. How many books are there on this shelf?

2 + 8 = ______

two + eight = __________

$$\begin{array}{r} 2 \\ +8 \\ \hline \end{array}$$

C. Jerry's goal for reading library books is ten books. He has already read eight. How many more books must Jerry read to reach his goal?

10 − 8 = ______

ten − eight = __________

$$\begin{array}{r} 10 \\ -8 \\ \hline \end{array}$$

D. There were ten books on a shelf. Billie removed two of them. How many books were then left on the shelf?

10 − 2 = ______

ten − two = __________

$$\begin{array}{r} 10 \\ -2 \\ \hline \end{array}$$

Choosing Proper Words

Pick the word from the box that matches each picture, and write the word in the space. See sample "1."

butter	curls	luck	suit
buy	fur	out	study
button	hunt	pour	turtle

What Are the Answers?

Underline the answer that defines each word. Write your own sentence about each word.

1. **toe**
   a. part of the face
   b. one of five end parts of the hand
   c. one of five end parts of the foot

2. **bottle**
   a. a container for bread
   b. a container for meat
   c. a container for liquids

3. **eat**
   a. to chew and swallow food
   b. to make clean
   c. to fix

4. **tool**
   a. something used to play
   b. something used to do work
   c. something used to make music

5. **tooth**
   a. used for hearing
   b. used for chewing
   c. used for seeing

Naming Objects

Circle the correctly spelled word that matches each picture.
See the example.

EXAMPLE:

doze doez
dose dozz

1.

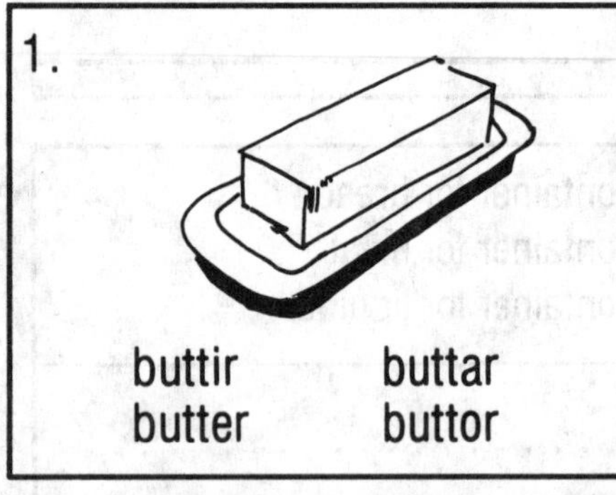

buttir buttar
butter buttor

2.

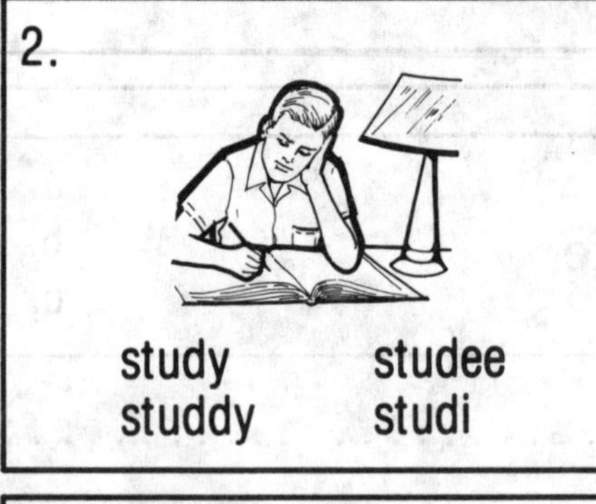

study studee
studdy studi

3.

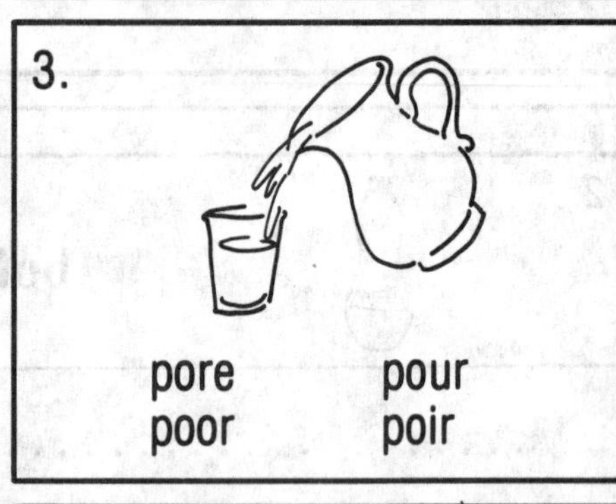

pore pour
poor poir

4.

cerls curls
cirls kurls

5.

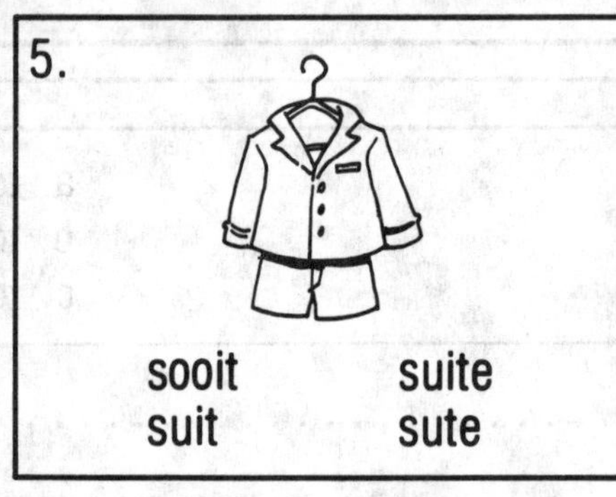

sooit suite
suit sute

6.

turtle turtel
turtil turtal

7.

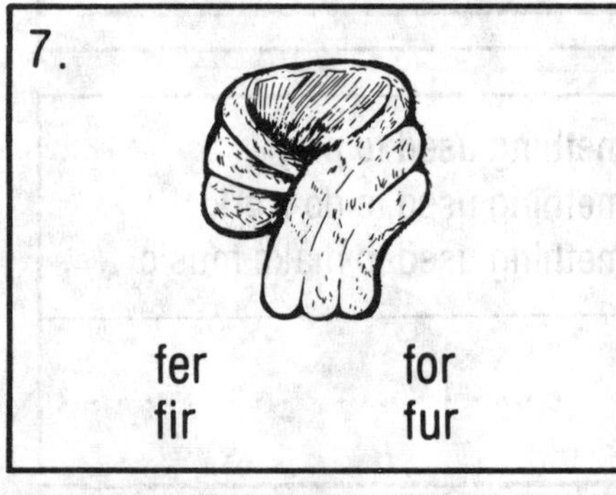

fer for
fir fur

8.

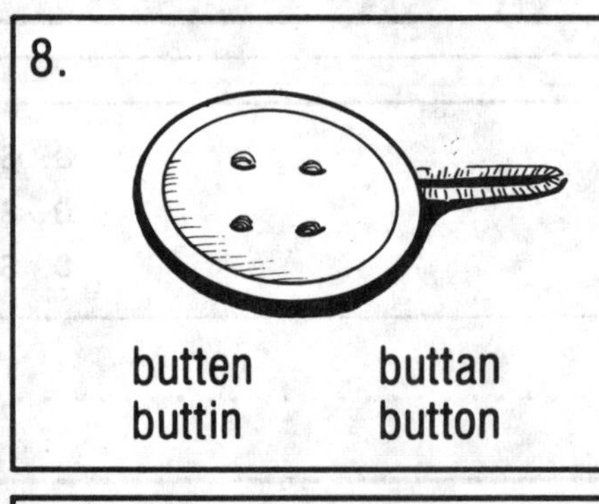

butten buttan
buttin button

9.

hont hent
hunt hunte

10.

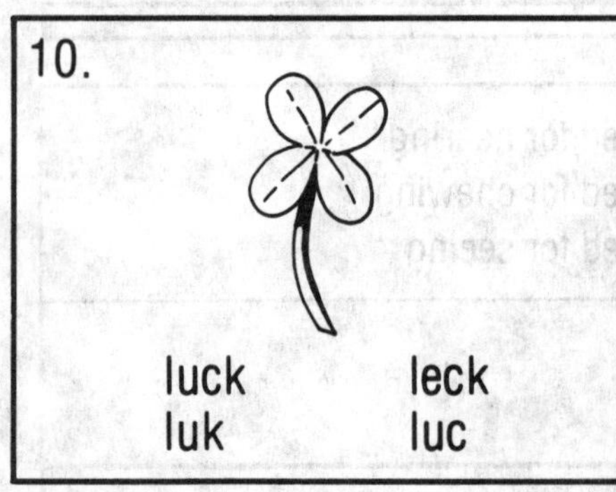

luck leck
luk luc

11.

by biy
buy bye

12.

owet outt
owt out

8+3 Apples

Fill in the blanks.

A Susan had eight apples. Billie had three apples. How many apples did they have in all?

$8 + 3 =$ ______

eight + three = __________

$$\begin{array}{r} 8 \\ +3 \\ \hline \end{array}$$

B Jerry had three apples. He bought eight more apples. Then how many apples did he have?

$3 + 8 =$ ______

three + eight = __________

$$\begin{array}{r} 3 \\ +8 \\ \hline \end{array}$$

C Susan had eleven apples. She sold eight of them. How many apples did she have left?

$11 - 8 =$ ______

eleven − eight = __________

$$\begin{array}{r} 11 \\ -8 \\ \hline \end{array}$$

D Jerry's father gave him eleven apples. He ate three of them. Then how many apples did he have?

$11 - 3 =$ ______

eleven − three = __________

$$\begin{array}{r} 11 \\ -3 \\ \hline \end{array}$$

Give the Descriptions

Underline the answer that defines each word. Write your own sentence about each word.

1. **butter**
   a. something you drink
   b. something you must freeze
   c. a food made from milk

2. **study**
   a. teach
   b. learn
   c. forget

3. **pour**
   a. to cause the flow of
   b. to keep from flowing
   c. to make dirty

4. **curl**
   a. to burn
   b. to make straight
   c. twist into rings

5. **suit**
   a. set of clothes
   b. a hat and coat
   c. a shirt with a tie

8 + 4 Lambs

Fill in the blanks.

A. Here are Farmer Carter's lambs. Eight of them are wearing bells. Tomorrow Farmer Carter plans to put bells on four more. Then how many lambs will have bells on?

$8 + 4 =$ ______

eight + four = __________

$$\begin{array}{r} 8 \\ +4 \\ \hline \end{array}$$

B. Four of Farmer Carter's lambs are black. Eight are white. How many black and white lambs does Farmer Carter have all together?

$4 + 8 =$ ______

four + eight = __________

$$\begin{array}{r} 4 \\ +8 \\ \hline \end{array}$$

C. Twelve lambs were playing. Eight of them went away. How many lambs were still playing?

$12 - 8 =$ ______

twelve − eight = __________

$$\begin{array}{r} 12 \\ -8 \\ \hline \end{array}$$

D. Twelve lambs were drinking water. Four of them started playing. How many lambs were still drinking water?

$12 - 4 =$ ______

twelve − four = __________

$$\begin{array}{r} 12 \\ -4 \\ \hline \end{array}$$

Writing Words in Spaces

Pick the word from the box that matches each picture, and write the word in the space. See sample "1."

slave	cave	vine	weave
serve	waves	dive	leave
save	five	voice	river

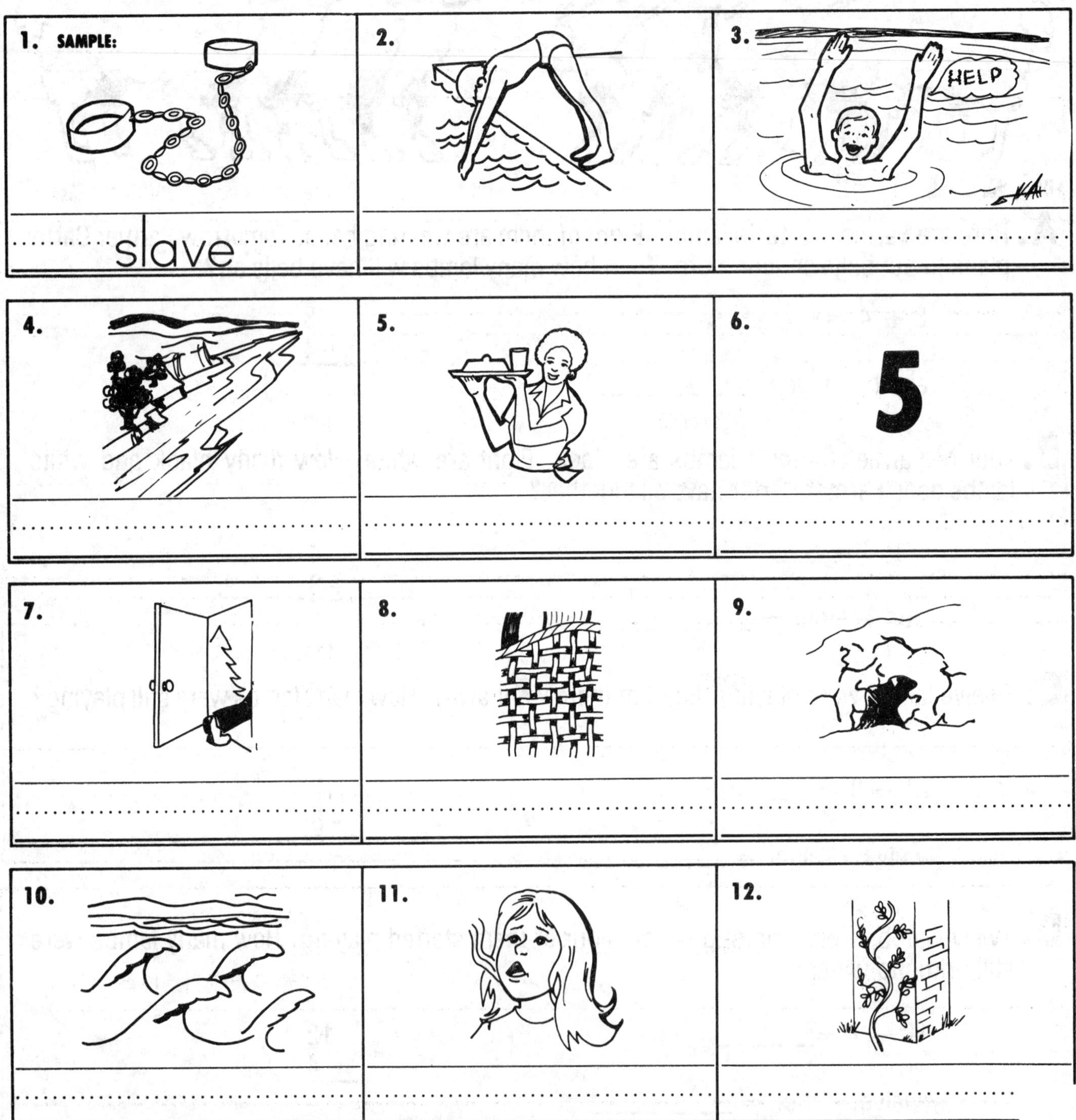

Giving Correct Answers

Underline the answer that defines each word. Write your own sentence about each word.

1.  **turtle**
   a. animal that lives in a shell
   b. animal that lives in a tree
   c. animal that lives in the snow

2.  **fur**
   a. hair on our heads
   b. thick skin
   c. the hair covering of an animal

3. 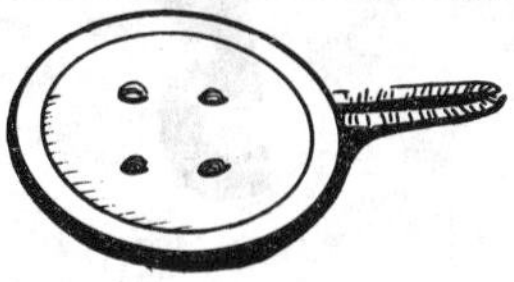 **button**
   a. keeps things apart
   b. holds things together
   c. something that zips

4.  **hunt**
   a. to lose
   b. to look for
   c. to hide

5.  **luck**
   a. happens on purpose
   b. happens by chance
   c. to cause to happen

Identify the Pictures

Circle the correctly spelled word that matches each picture.
See the example.

EXAMPLE:

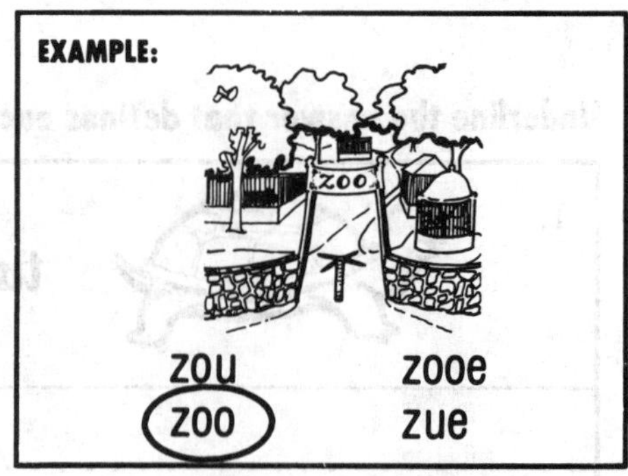

zou zooe
zoo (circled) zue

1.

slaev slaiv
slav slave

2.

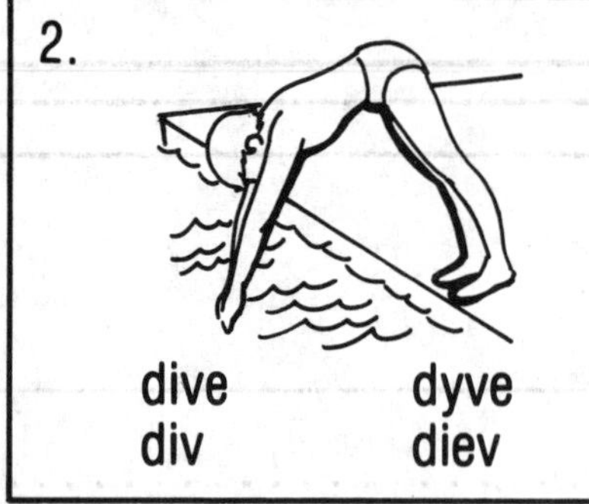

dive dyve
div diev

3.

saeve save
saiv sav

4.

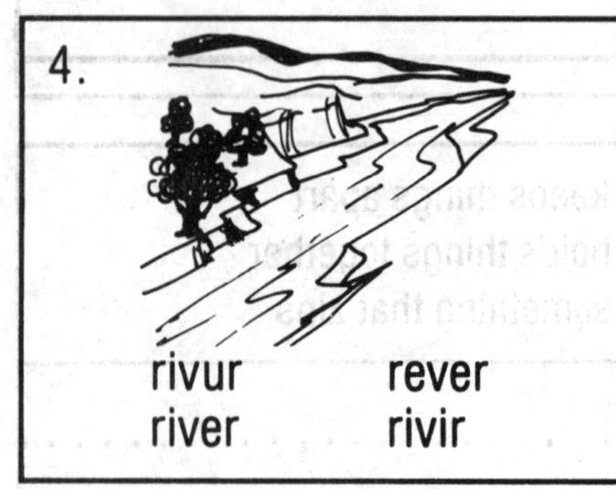

rivur rever
river rivir

5.

serve sirve
surve serv

6.

fiv five
fiev fivie

7.

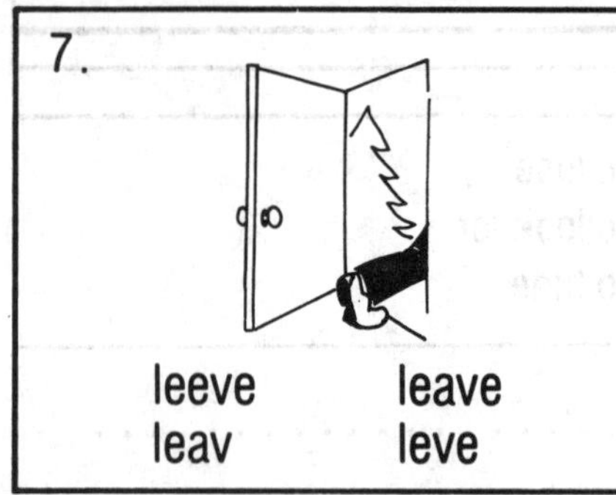

leeve leave
leav leve

8.

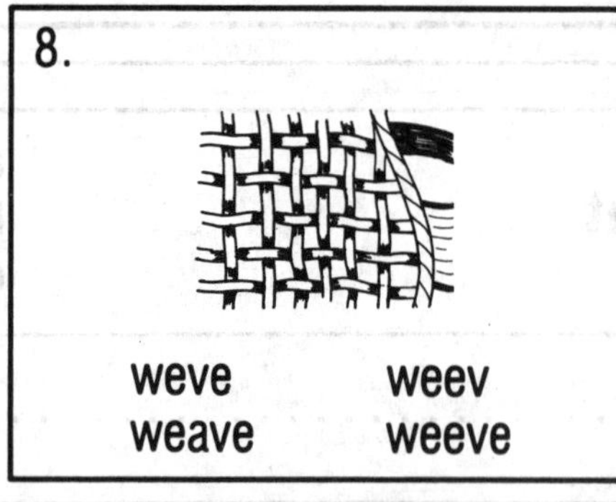

weve weev
weave weeve

9.

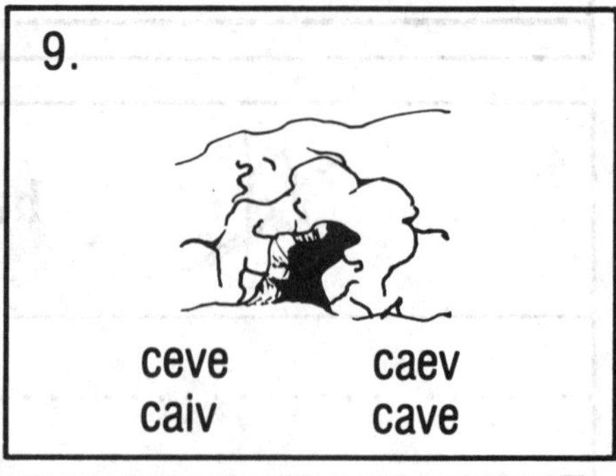

ceve caev
caiv cave

10.

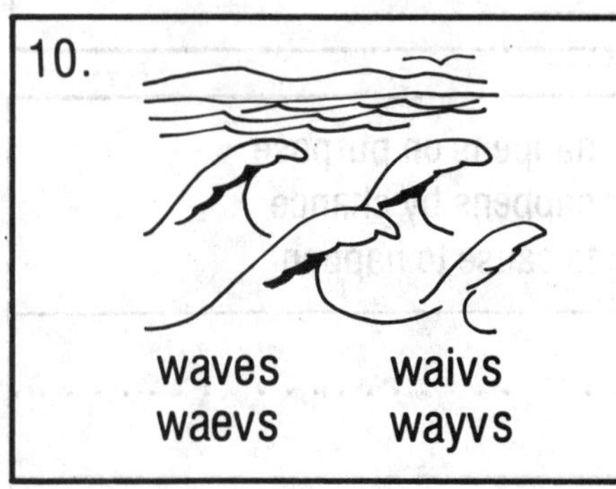

waves waivs
waevs wayvs

11.

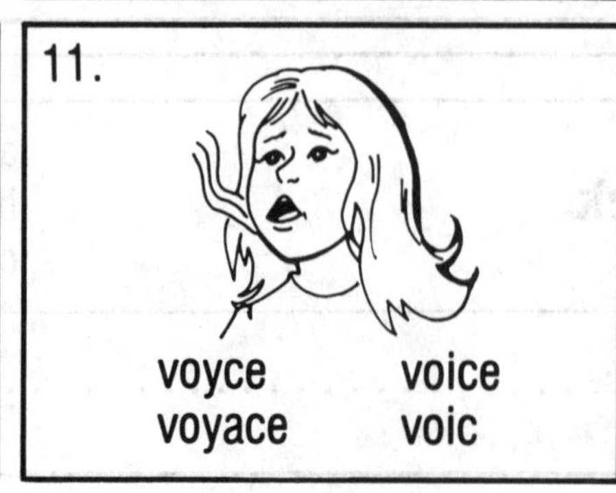

voyce voice
voyace voic

12.

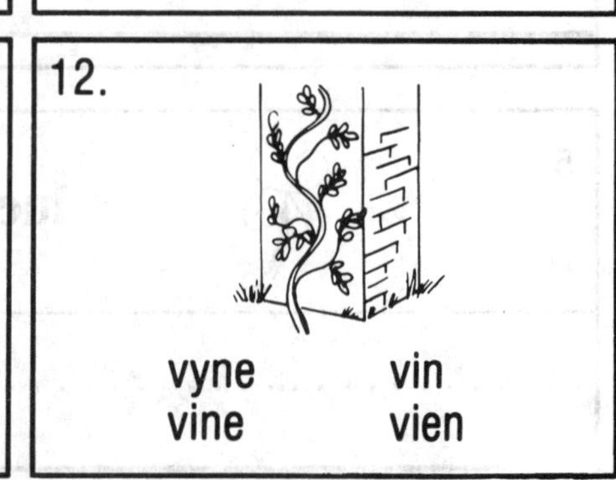

vyne vin
vine vien

8 + 5 Turtles

Fill in the blanks.

A. Yesterday we went to the creek. We saw eight large turtles and five small ones. How many turtles did we see?

$8 + 5 =$ _____

eight + five = ________

$$\begin{array}{r} 8 \\ +5 \\ \hline \end{array}$$

B. Jerry has five pet turtles. Susan has eight. How many pet turtles do they both have?

$5 + 8 =$ _____

five + eight = ________

$$\begin{array}{r} 5 \\ +8 \\ \hline \end{array}$$

C. Thirteen turtles were crawling in the sunshine. Eight of them stopped. How many were still crawling?

$13 - 8 =$ _____

thirteen − eight = ________

$$\begin{array}{r} 13 \\ -8 \\ \hline \end{array}$$

D. Tim had thirteen turtles. He sold five of them. Then how many turtles did he have?

$13 - 5 =$ _____

thirteen − five = ________

$$\begin{array}{r} 13 \\ -5 \\ \hline \end{array}$$

Pick the Correct Answers

Underline the answer that defines each word. Write your own sentence about each word.

1.  **slave**
   a. person owned by another
   b. person who owns another
   c. someone who does not work

2.  **dive**
   a. to jump in headfirst
   b. to jump out
   c. to get wet

3.  **save**
   a. to look for
   b. to hurt
   c. to make safe

4.  **river**
   a. a pond on a farm
   b. a small stream of water
   c. a large stream of water

5.  **serve**
   a. to bring food to guests
   b. to take food from
   c. to throw at

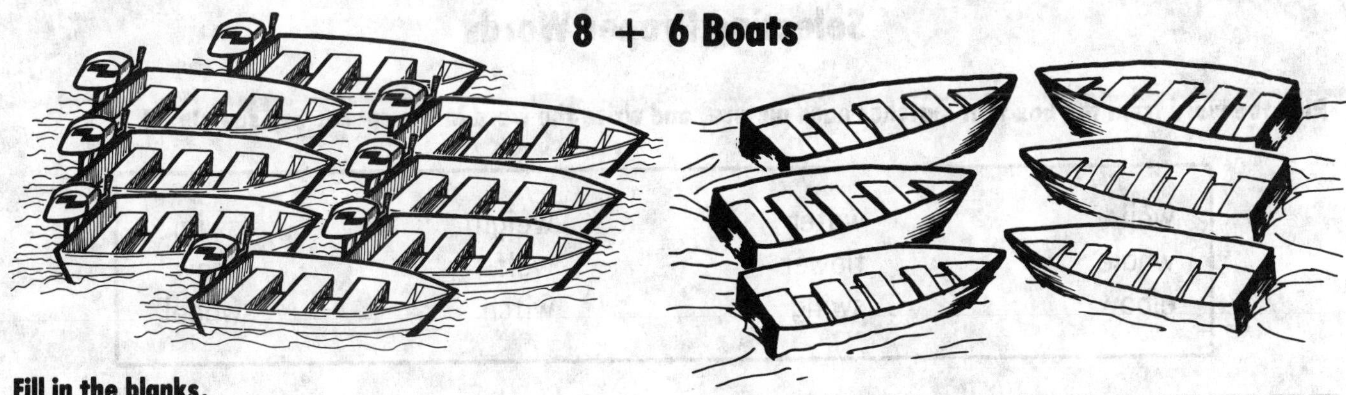

8 + 6 Boats

Fill in the blanks.

A. Sunday we went to the lake. We saw eight boats with motors and six boats without motors. How many boats did we see in all?

8 + 6 = ______

$$\begin{array}{r} 8 \\ +6 \\ \hline \end{array}$$

eight + six = __________

B. Mr. Smith said that he did own six boats. Now he has purchased eight more. How many boats does Mr. Smith now own?

6 + 8 = ______

$$\begin{array}{r} 6 \\ +8 \\ \hline \end{array}$$

six + eight = __________

C. We saw fourteen boats at the lake. Eight of them were sailboats. How many were not sailboats?

14 − 8 = ______

$$\begin{array}{r} 14 \\ -8 \\ \hline \end{array}$$

fourteen − eight = __________

D. Fourteen boats were at the dock. Six of them were racing boats. How many boats were not racing boats?

14 − 6 = ______

$$\begin{array}{r} 14 \\ -6 \\ \hline \end{array}$$

fourteen − six = __________

Selecting Proper Words

Pick the word from the box that matches each picture, and write the word in the space. See sample "1."

well	water	weight	swim
whale	flower	wolf	snow
elbow	swing	witch	wheel

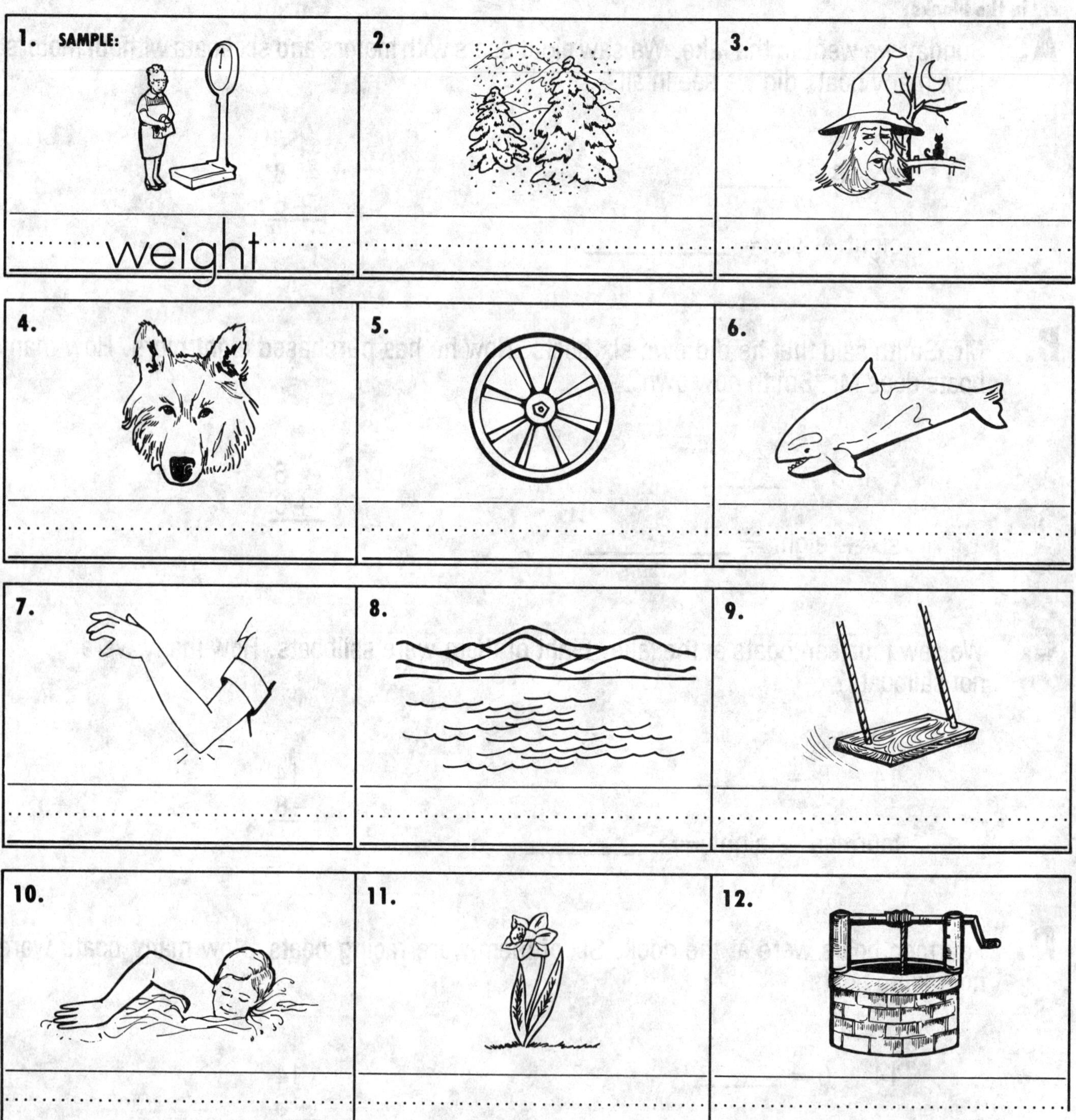

Do You Know the Meanings?

Underline the answer that defines each word. Write your own sentence about each word.

1. 5 **five**
   a. two plus one
   b. three plus one
   c. four plus one

2. **leave**
   a. to come home
   b. to arrive
   c. to go away

3. **weave**
   a. to sew
   b. to form threads into cloth
   c. to press

4. **cave**
   a. opening in top of a mountain
   b. opening in side of a hill
   c. opening in a tree

5. **wave**
   a. a moving ridge of water
   b. water that does not move
   c. running water

Learning Spelling Words

Circle the correctly spelled word that matches each picture. See the example.

EXAMPLE:

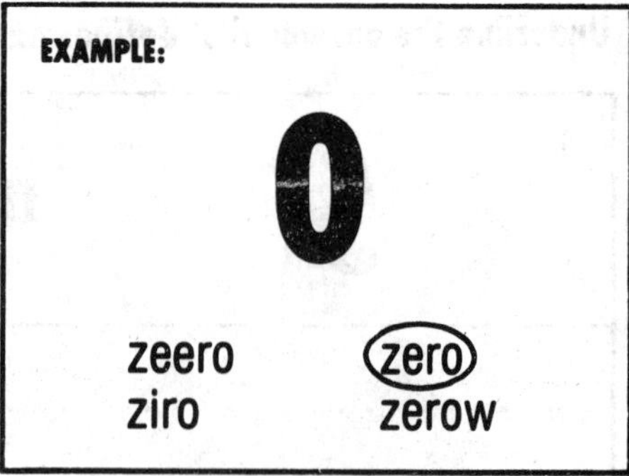

zeero (zero)
ziro zerow

1.

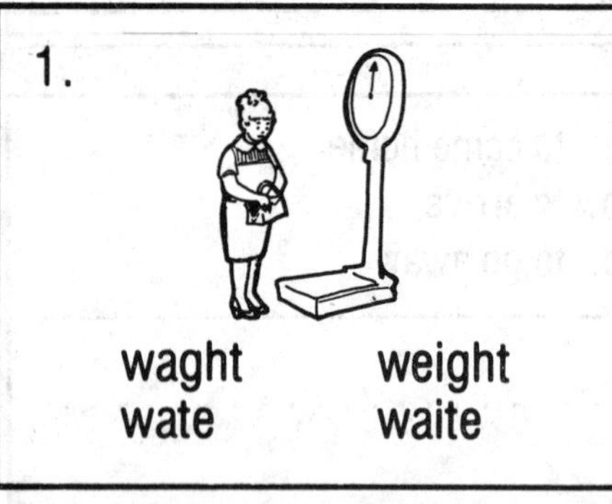

waght weight
wate waite

2.

snou sno
snoe snow

3.

witch wittch
wich whitch

4.

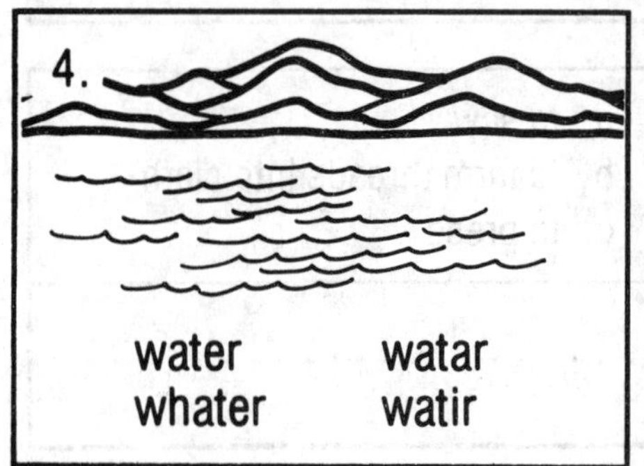

water watar
whater watir

5.

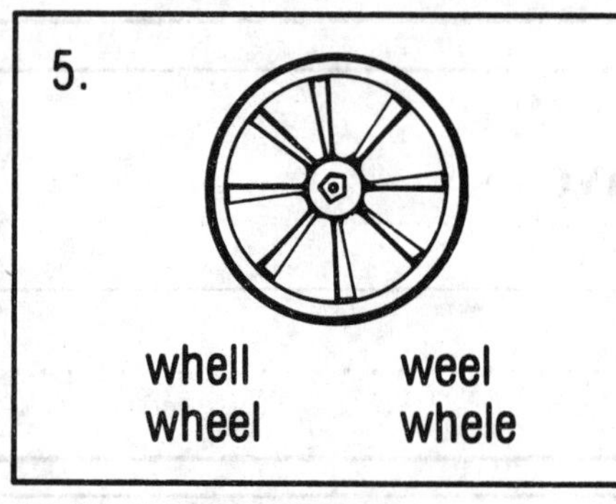

whell weel
wheel whele

6.

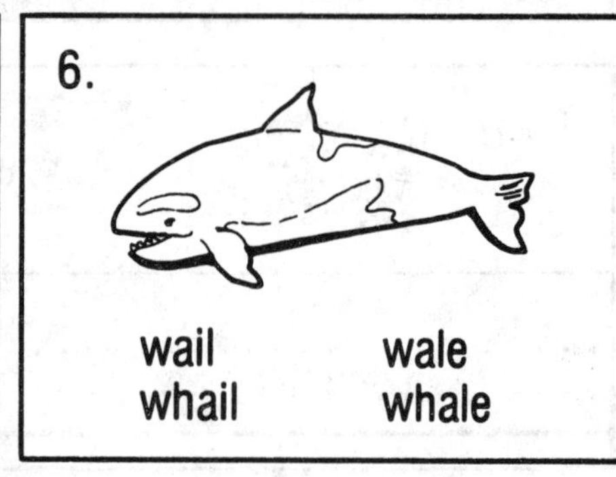

wail wale
whail whale

7.

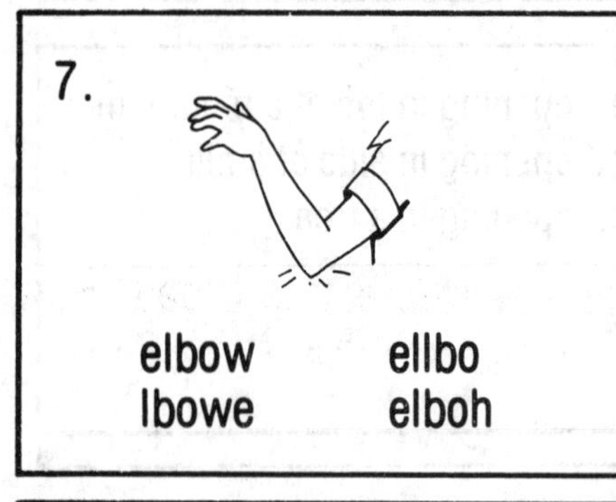

elbow ellbo
lbowe elboh

8.

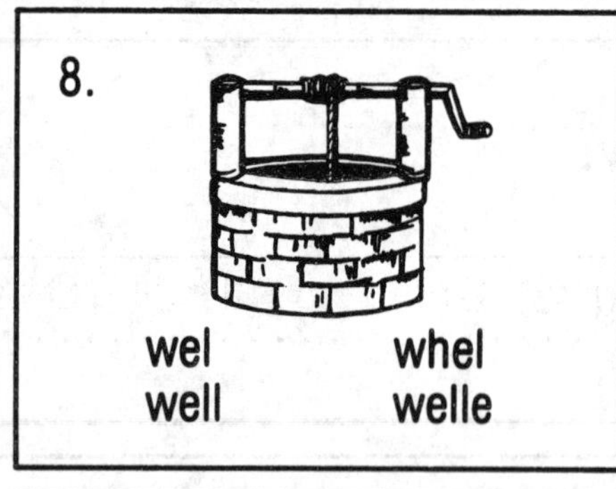

wel whel
well welle

9.

swing sweeng
sweng sweang

10.

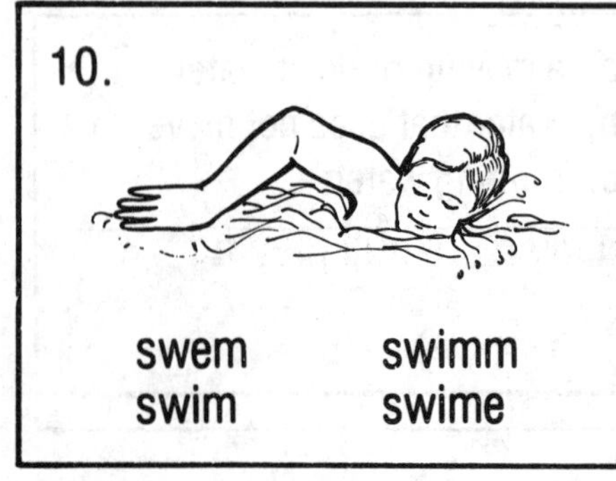

swem swimm
swim swime

11.

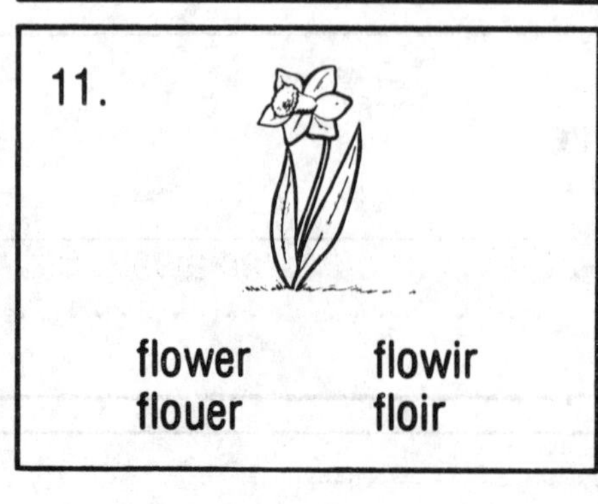

flower flowir
flouer floir

12.

wolef wolf
welf wulf

8 + 7 Mice

Fill in the blanks.

A. Eight white mice were eating cheese. Seven black mice came to eat cheese also. Then how many mice were there?

8 + 7 = ______

$$\begin{array}{r} 8 \\ +7 \\ \hline \end{array}$$

eight + seven = __________

B. Seven mice were playing. Eight more came to play. Then how many mice were playing?

7 + 8 = ______

$$\begin{array}{r} 7 \\ +8 \\ \hline \end{array}$$

seven + eight = __________

C. Fifteen mice were eating grain. Eight stopped eating grain and started eating bread. How many were still eating grain?

15 − 8 = ______

$$\begin{array}{r} 15 \\ -8 \\ \hline \end{array}$$

fifteen − eight = __________

D. Fifteen mice were playing. Seven of them ran away. How many were still playing?

15 − 7 = ______

$$\begin{array}{r} 15 \\ -7 \\ \hline \end{array}$$

fifteen − seven = __________

Can You Select the Right Answers?

Underline the answer that defines each word. Write your own sentence about each word.

1. **weight**
   a. what color
   b. how heavy
   c. how tall

2. **snow**
   a. white flakes of frozen water
   b. large drops of rain
   c. frozen dew

3. **witch**
   a. someone who wears a hat
   b. woman with magical power
   c. a person who likes cats

4. **water**
   a. needed for life
   b. not needed for life
   c. something you eat

5. **wheel**
   a. a flat tire
   b. a square box
   c. round frame that turns

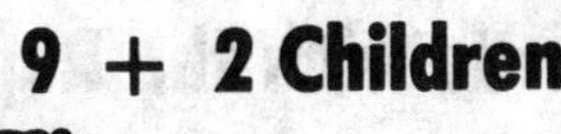

9 + 2 Children

Fill in the blanks.

A. Susan invited nine girls and two boys to her birthday party. How many children were invited to Susan's birthday party?

$9 + 2 =$ ______

nine + two = __________

$$\begin{array}{r} 9 \\ +2 \\ \hline \end{array}$$

B. Two children were playing hopscotch, and nine children were playing ring-around-a-rosy. How many children were playing?

$2 + 9 =$ ______

two + nine = __________

$$\begin{array}{r} 2 \\ +9 \\ \hline \end{array}$$

C. Eleven children were playing. Nine of them went home. Then how many children were playing?

$11 - 9 =$ ______

eleven − nine = __________

$$\begin{array}{r} 11 \\ -9 \\ \hline \end{array}$$

D. Eleven children were playing at Susan's party. Two of them went to sleep. Then how many children were still playing?

$11 - 2 =$ ______

eleven − two = __________

$$\begin{array}{r} 11 \\ -2 \\ \hline \end{array}$$

Match Words with the Right Pictures

Pick the word from the box that matches each picture, and write the word in the space. See sample "1."

ax	wax	fix	exercise
explode	relax	ox	mix
extra	six	box	cowboy

Selecting Correct Answers

Underline the answer that defines each word. Write your own sentence about each word.

1. **whale**
   a. lives on land
   b. lives in the sea
   c. lives in the air

2. **elbow**
   a. joint between upper and lower arm
   b. joint between upper and lower leg
   c. joint in finger

3. **well**
   a. a hole in a tree
   b. having no water
   c. hole in the ground to get water

4. **swing**
   a. move up and down
   b. move back and forth
   c. move in and out

5. **swim**
   a. to move on land
   b. to move in the air
   c. to move in water

Identifying Pictures

Circle the correctly spelled word that matches each picture. See the example.

EXAMPLE:

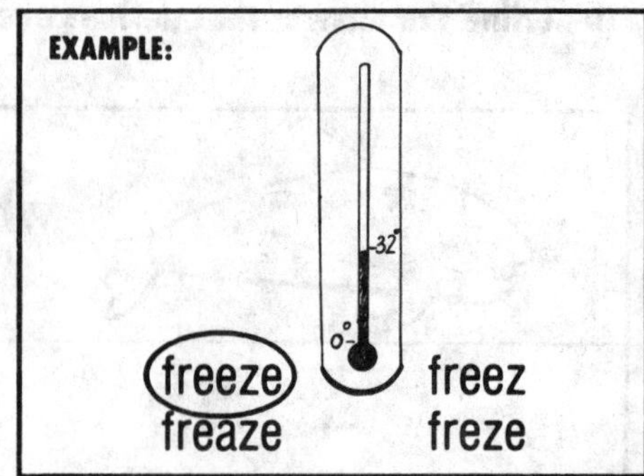

freeze (circled) freez
freaze freze

1.

exercise exercize
exurcise exersize

2.

oks ahx
ox oxe

3.
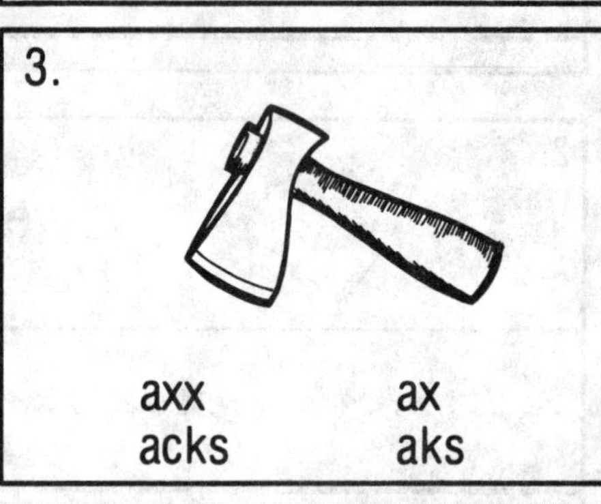

axx ax
acks aks

4.
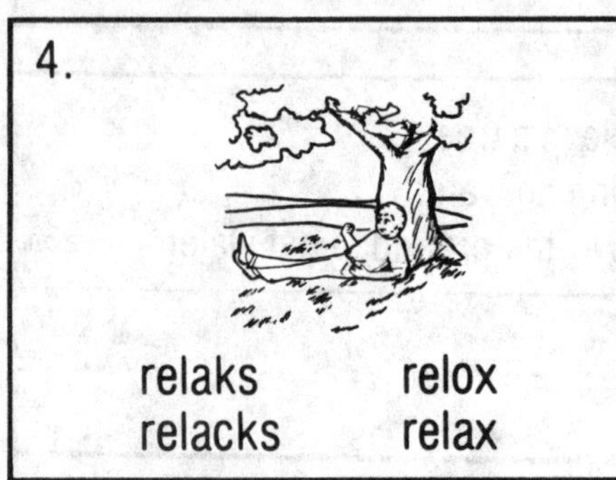

relaks relox
relacks relax

5.
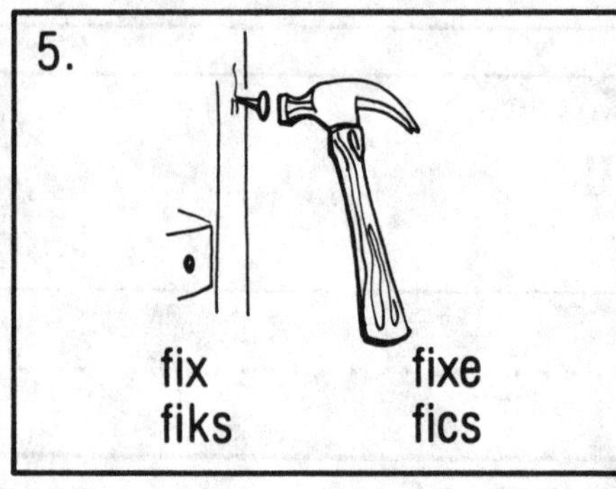

fix fixe
fiks fics

6.
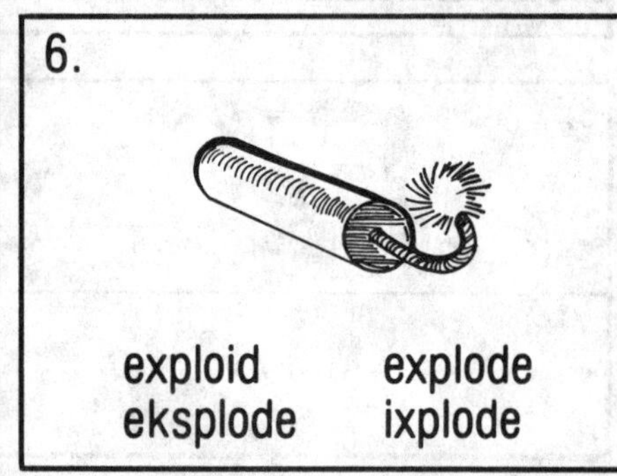

exploid explode
eksplode ixplode

7.

cowboy cowboi
kowboy couboy

8.

mics mix
micks miks

9.
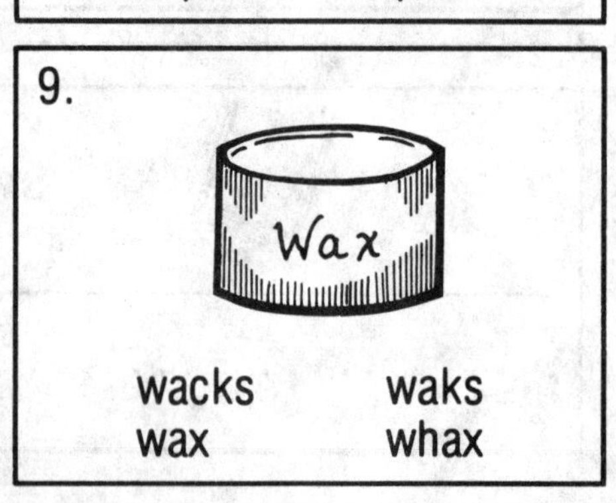

wacks waks
wax whax

10.
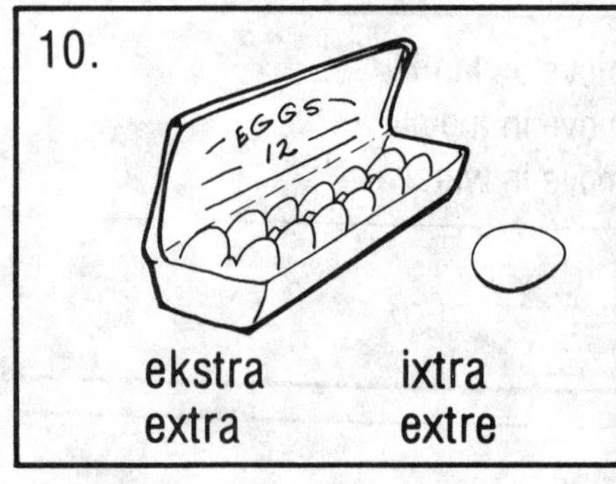

ekstra ixtra
extra extre

11.
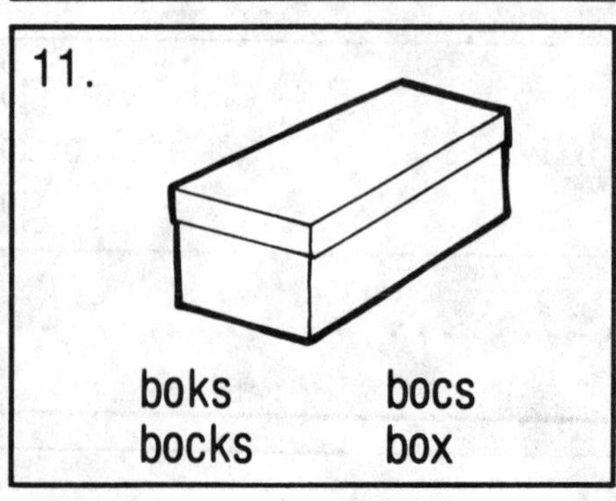

boks bocs
bocks box

12.
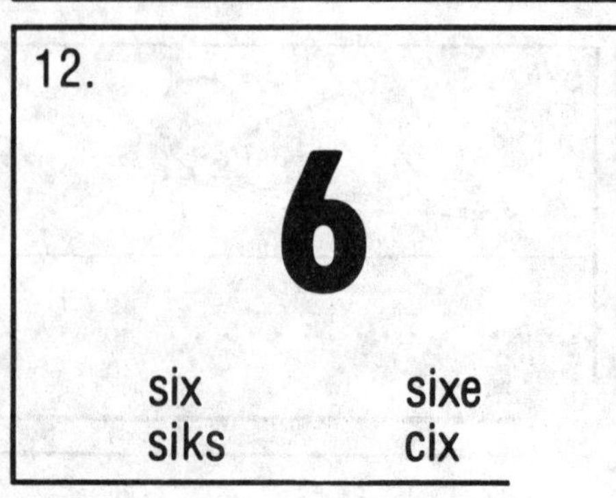

six sixe
siks cix

9 + 3 Bears

Fill in the blanks.

A. Nine bears are playing. Three more are coming to play. Then how many bears will be playing?

$9 + 3 =$ ______

nine + three = __________

$$\begin{array}{r} 9 \\ +3 \\ \hline \end{array}$$

B. Three bears are eating fish. Nine more bears are coming to eat with them. Then how many bears will be eating fish?

$3 + 9 =$ ______

three + nine = __________

$$\begin{array}{r} 3 \\ +9 \\ \hline \end{array}$$

C. Twelve bears were playing on the ground. Three bears waded into water. How many were still playing on the ground?

$12 - 3 =$ ______

twelve − three = __________

$$\begin{array}{r} 12 \\ -3 \\ \hline \end{array}$$

D. Twelve bears were playing. Nine of them went to sleep. Then how many bears were awake?

$12 - 9 =$ ______

twelve − nine = __________

$$\begin{array}{r} 12 \\ -9 \\ \hline \end{array}$$

Selecting the Right Answers

Underline the answer that defines each word. Write your own sentence about each word.

1. **exercise**
   a. being lazy
   b. being active
   c. being unable to work

2. **ox**
   a. a slow, but strong animal
   b. a tiny animal
   c. a pet

3. **ax**
   a. used to peel apples
   b. used to cut grass
   c. used to chop wood

4. **relax**
   a. to work
   b. to play
   c. to rest

5. **fix**
   a. to set right
   b. to make wrong
   c. to make crooked

9 + 4 Flowers

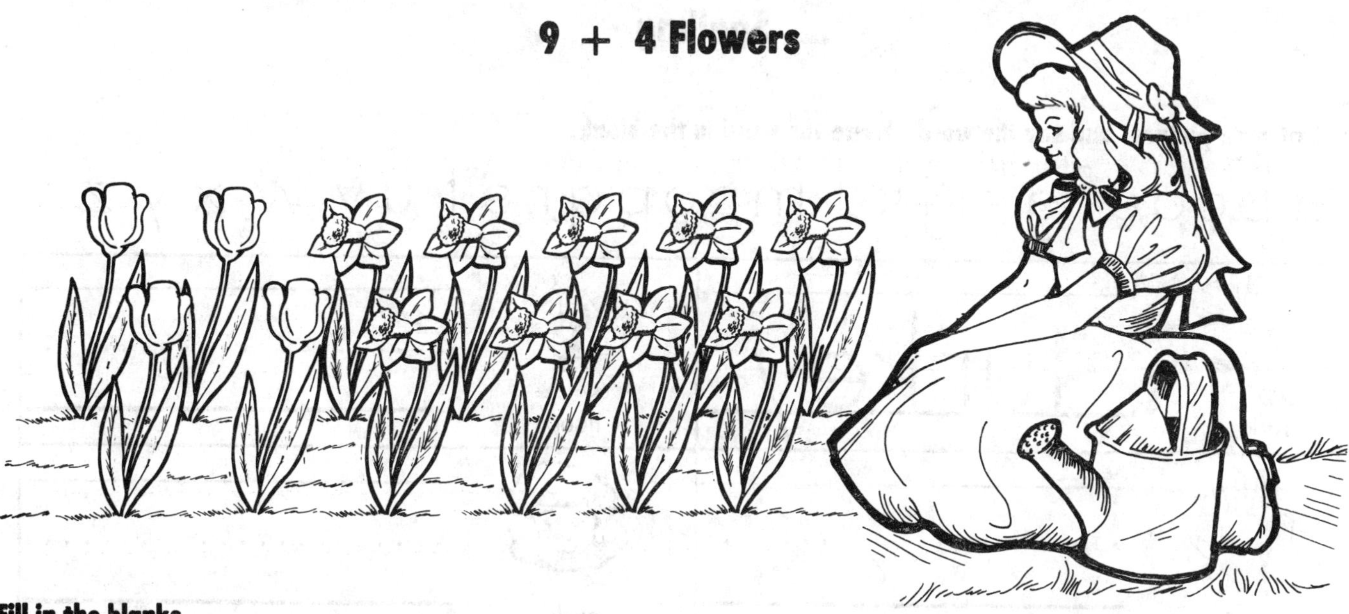

Fill in the blanks.

A. The flowers in Susan's flower garden are beginning to bloom. There are nine daffodils and four tulips blooming. How many flowers are blooming in Susan's garden?

9 + 4 = ______

$$\begin{array}{r} 9 \\ +4 \\ \hline \end{array}$$

nine + four = __________

B. Susan's Rambling Rose has four blooms on one stem and nine blooms on another. How many blooms are there on both stems?

4 + 9 = ______

$$\begin{array}{r} 4 \\ +9 \\ \hline \end{array}$$

four + nine = __________

C. Susan has thirteen roses in bloom. If nine of them are red roses and the others are yellow, how many yellow roses does Susan have in bloom?

13 − 9 = ______

$$\begin{array}{r} 13 \\ -9 \\ \hline \end{array}$$

thirteen − nine = __________

D. Susan has thirteen beautiful gladioli. She sold four of them. Then how many did she have left?

13 − 4 = ______

$$\begin{array}{r} 13 \\ -4 \\ \hline \end{array}$$

thirteen − four = __________

Spelling

Look at each picture, and say the word. Write the word in the blank.

a b c d e f g h i j k l m n o p q r s t u v w x y z

turkey — turkey	hoop
count	curly
camp	going
save	hungry
rose	group
ate	crayon
eight	snort
early	puzzle

Let's Describe the Words

Underline the answer that defines each word. Write your own sentence about each word.

1. **explode**
   a. to make smaller
   b. to make larger
   c. to blow up

2. **cowboy**
   a. works on rice farm
   b. looks after cattle
   c. works in an orchard

3. **mix**
   a. to stir together
   b. to pour water in
   c. to make hard

4. **wax**
   a. used to paint a floor
   b. used to clean a floor
   c. used to protect a floor

5. **extra**
   a. not enough
   b. more than enough
   c. exact amount

Matching Words and Pictures

Look at each picture, and say the word. Write the word in the blank.

a b c d e f g h i j k l m n o p q r s t u v w x y z

hole — hole	feed
whole	out
turn	fun
junk	hard
chicks	nest
mix	clock
silly	police
suit	sneeze

9 + 5 Candy Bars

Fill in the blanks.

A. Susan went to the store. She bought nine chocolate bars of candy and five peanut bars. How many bars of candy did Susan buy?

$9 + 5 =$ ______

nine + five = __________

$$\begin{array}{r} 9 \\ +5 \\ \hline \end{array}$$

B. Billie has five caramel bars of candy, and Jerry has nine chocolate bars. How many bars of candy do they both have?

$5 + 9 =$ ______

five + nine = __________

$$\begin{array}{r} 5 \\ +9 \\ \hline \end{array}$$

C. Mother made fourteen bars of candy. We ate nine bars. How many bars were left?

$14 - 9 =$ ______

fourteen − nine = __________

$$\begin{array}{r} 14 \\ -9 \\ \hline \end{array}$$

D. Jerry had fourteen candy bars. He sold five of them. How many bars did he then have?

$14 - 5 =$ ______

fourteen − five = __________

$$\begin{array}{r} 14 \\ -5 \\ \hline \end{array}$$

Spelling

Look at each picture, and say the word. Write the word in the blank.

a b c d e f g h i j k l m n o p q r s t u v w x y z

corner — corner	hay
sheep	work
rooster	rich
pop	guess
honey	hook
wish	swing
leap	grow
fairy	pool

9 + 6 Oranges

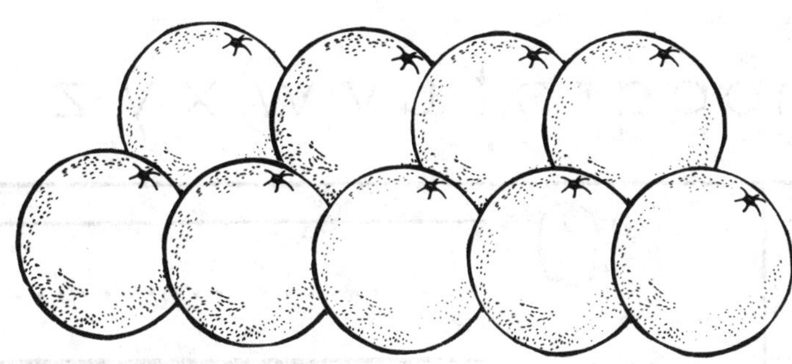

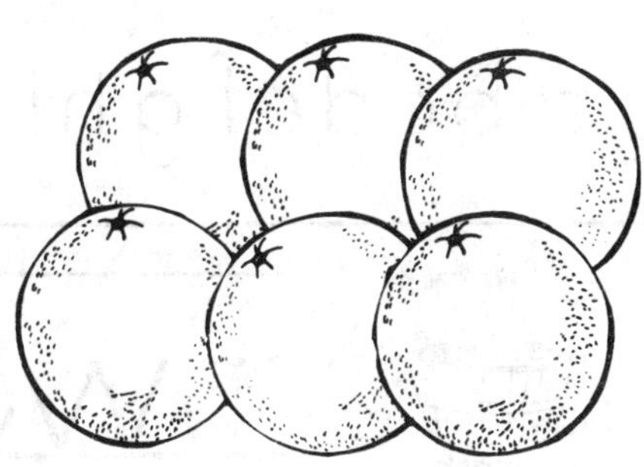

Fill in the blanks.

A. Mother went to the store. She bought nine plain oranges and six navel oranges. How many oranges did Mother buy?

$9 + 6 =$ ______

nine + six = __________

$$\begin{array}{r} 9 \\ +6 \\ \hline \end{array}$$

B. Last week Mother went to the store two times. She bought six oranges the first time and nine oranges the second trip. How many oranges did Mother buy last week?

$6 + 9 =$ ______

six + nine = __________

$$\begin{array}{r} 6 \\ +9 \\ \hline \end{array}$$

C. When we went to breakfast this morning, there were fifteen oranges in a bowl. During breakfast we ate nine of them. How many oranges were left?

$15 - 9 =$ ______

fifteen − nine = __________

$$\begin{array}{r} 15 \\ -9 \\ \hline \end{array}$$

D. Mother had fifteen oranges this morning. She used six of them to make juice. How many oranges did she then have?

$15 - 6 =$ ______

fifteen − six = __________

$$\begin{array}{r} 15 \\ -6 \\ \hline \end{array}$$

Fun in Naming Pictures

Look at each picture, and say the word. Write the word in the blank.

a b c d e f g h i j k l m n o p q r s t u v w x y z

wash — wash	noise
pedal	lazy
honk	waves
itch	howl
cold	fall
hear	story
here	iron
smoke	towel

Our Flag

Read the Pledge of Allegiance and fill in the blanks. Then write the Pledge of Allegiance.

I pledge allegiance to the flag of the United States of America and to the Republic for which it stands, one Nation under God, indivisible with liberty and justice for all.

1. The colors of our flag are red, white and blue.
2. There are ____________ stars on our flag.
3. Each star stands for a ____________.
4. The flag should never touch the ____________.
5. Name some places that a flag may fly over. ____________
6. The flag should fly from ____________ to ____________.

The Pledge of Allegiance

Fun with Stories

Read each story, and underline the correct answers. If you have problems, read the story again.

My Room

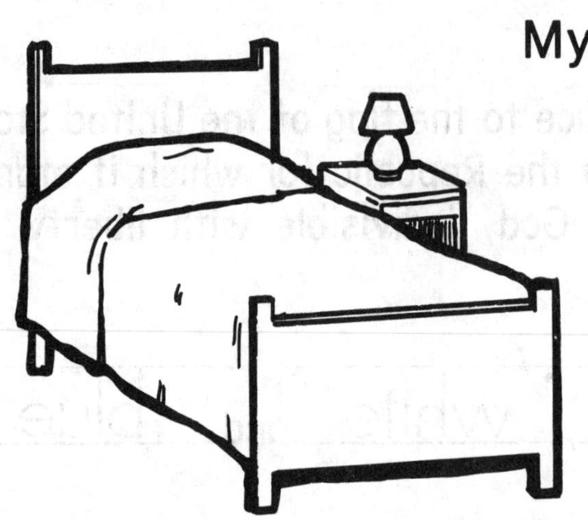

In my room is a bed, a desk, and a bureau. I also have two tables, lamps, and a bookcase.

I take good care of my room. Sometimes my friends and I play there. I like to spend time in my room.

1. Who takes care of my room? (a) Mother (b) me (c) a maid
2. My room has (a) furniture (b) dishes (c) trees.
3. When do I play in my room? (a) never (b) always (c) sometimes
4. Where do I like to go? (a) my room (b) my friend's room (c) outside

Bicycle Riding

Riding a bicycle is fun. However, you should be sure your bicycle is safe. You should also learn to ride well. This takes practice. Your mom or dad will help you.

Stay near home. Stay away from cars. Always be careful. Never ride two on a bicycle.

1. Who will help you practice? (a) your teacher (b) a friend (c) your mom or dad
2. What was the story about? (a) skating (b) bicycle riding (c) gardening
3. When should you be careful? (a) never (b) always (c) seldom
4. You should ride (a) near home (b) in the street (c) in the house.

9 + 7 Butterflies

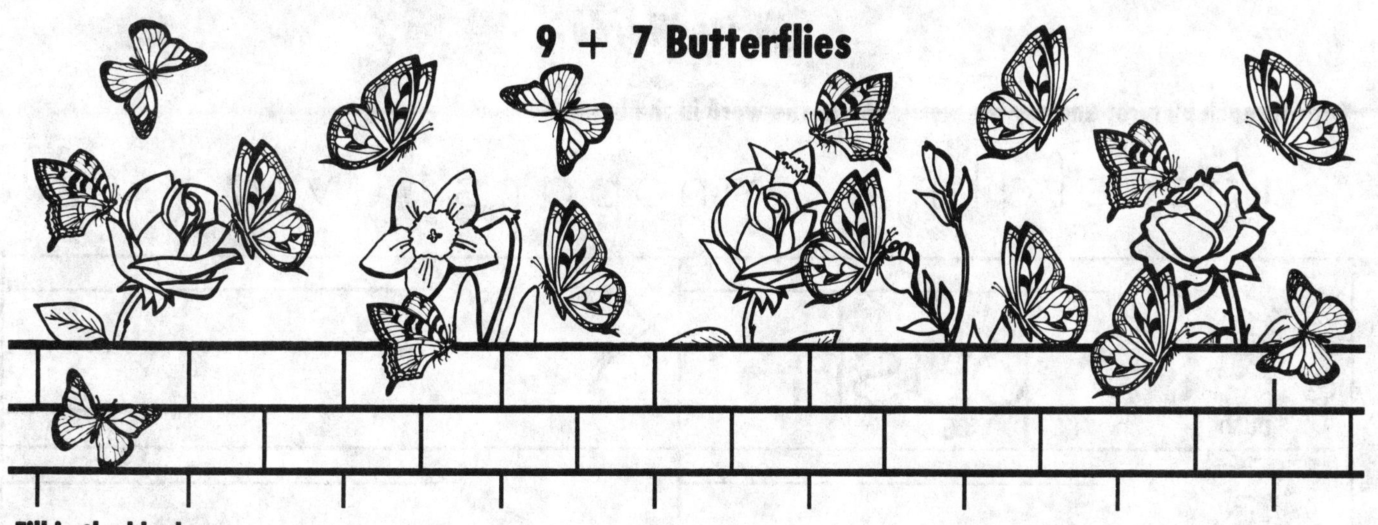

Fill in the blanks.

A. Nine butterflies were in Mother's garden. Seven more came into the garden. Then how many butterflies were in Mother's garden?

9 + 7 = ______

nine + seven = __________

$$\begin{array}{r} 9 \\ +7 \\ \hline \end{array}$$

B. Seven butterflies were near the flowers. Nine butterflies were near the vegetables. How many butterflies were in the garden?

7 + 9 = ______

seven + nine = __________

$$\begin{array}{r} 7 \\ +9 \\ \hline \end{array}$$

C. There were sixteen butterflies in Mother's garden. Nine of them flew away. How many butterflies were still in the garden?

16 – 9 = ______

sixteen – nine = __________

$$\begin{array}{r} 16 \\ -9 \\ \hline \end{array}$$

D. Sixteen butterflies were in Mother's garden. Seven butterflies were red. The others were blue. How many blue butterflies were in Mother's garden?

16 – 7 = ______

sixteen – seven = __________

$$\begin{array}{r} 16 \\ -7 \\ \hline \end{array}$$

Write Words

Look at each picture, and say the word. Write the word in the blank.

a b c d e f g h i j k l m n o p q r s t u v w x y z

push	push	soft	
wind		pencil	
butter		jacket	
cork		inch	
skate		blow	
check		heavy	
pepper		crown	
warm		young	

The Wheat Farmer

Read the story, and answer the questions.

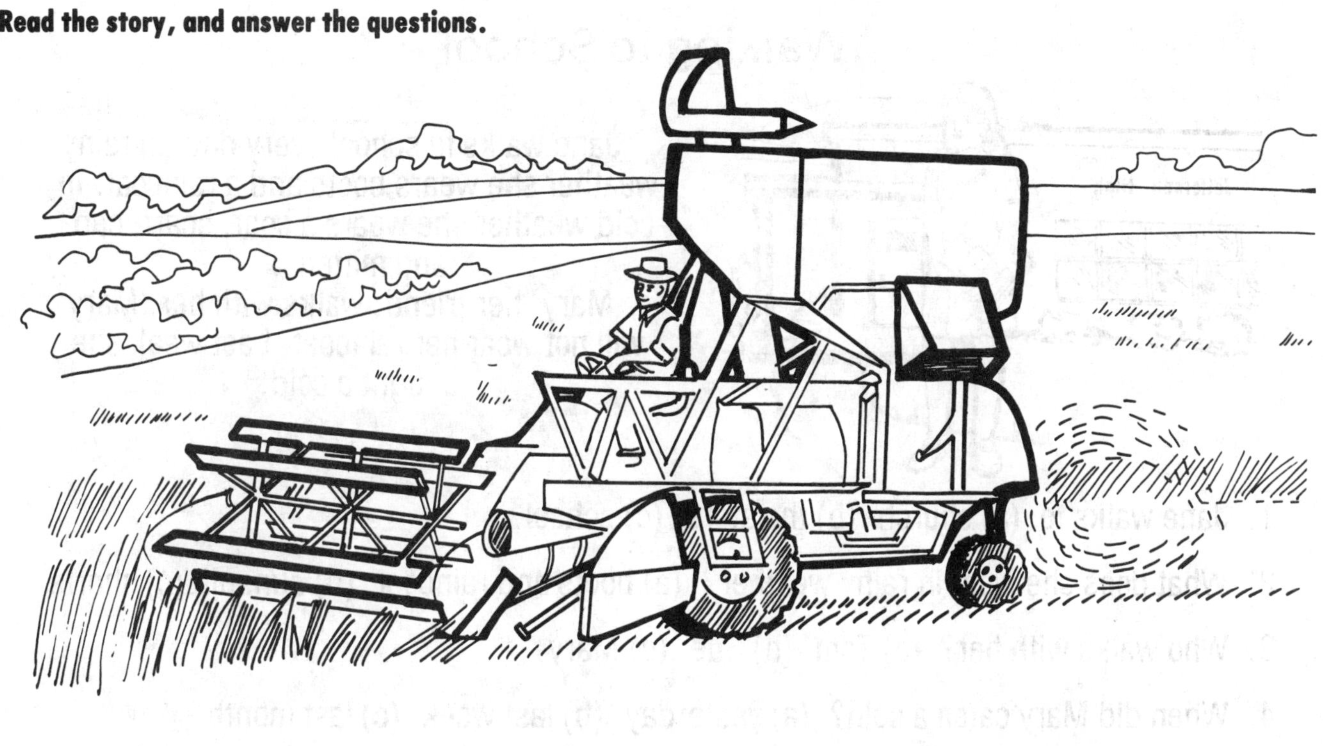

Wheat farmers sow seeds in their fields. Some sow their seeds in the spring. Other farmers sow their seeds in the fall.

At first the wheat looks like long green grass. It turns yellow when it ripens. Then the wheat is cut and threshed. Wheat grains, or seeds, are used to make breads, cakes, cookies, and cereals.

1. Name some things made from wheat. ______________________________
2. At first the color of wheat is ____________.
3. Farmers sow ____________ in their fields.
4. Ripened wheat is not green, but ____________.
5. Farmers can sow seeds in the ____________ and ____________.

Stories

Read each story, and underline the correct answers. If you have problems, read the story again.

Walking to School

Jane walks to school every day. In rainy weather she wears boots and a raincoat. In cold weather she wears a coat, scarf, cap, and mittens.

Mary, her friend, walks with her. Mary will not wear her raincoat. Last week she caught a cold.

1. Jane walks to (a) church (b) the store (c) school.
2. What does she wear in rainy weather? (a) boots and raincoat (b) sunsuit (c) shorts
3. Who walks with her? (a) Tom (b) Sue (c) Mary
4. When did Mary catch a cold? (a) yesterday (b) last week (c) last month

Learning About a Hospital

A hospital provides medical care for people. Most people who stay at a hospital are sick. They need special care and treatment. Well people may also receive care at a hospital.

A hospital never closes. Workers provide care at all hours and on all days.

1. Who usually stays in a hospital? (a) well people (b) sick people (c) animals
2. What does a hospital provide? (a) insurance (b) medical care (c) clothing
3. Where should a sick person go? (a) hospital (b) camping (c) museum
4. When can a person go to the hospital? (a) mornings only (b) evenings only (c) anytime

9 + 8 Marbles

Fill in the blanks.

A. Jerry had nine marbles. He bought eight more. How many marbles did he have then?

9 + 8 = ______

nine + eight = __________

$$\begin{array}{r} 9 \\ +8 \\ \hline \end{array}$$

B. Tommy had eight marbles. He traded a pocketknife for nine more. Then how many marbles did he have?

8 + 9 = ______

eight + nine = __________

$$\begin{array}{r} 8 \\ +9 \\ \hline \end{array}$$

C. Jerry had seventeen marbles. He traded nine of them for a white mouse. How many marbles did he have left?

17 − 9 = ______

seventeen − nine = __________

$$\begin{array}{r} 17 \\ -9 \\ \hline \end{array}$$

D. Susan had seventeen marbles. She gave eight of them to Billie. How many marbles did Susan then have?

17 − 8 = ______

seventeen − eight = __________

$$\begin{array}{r} 17 \\ -8 \\ \hline \end{array}$$

Writing Spelling Words

Look at each picture, and say the word. Write the word in the blank.

a b c d e f g h i j k l m n o p q r s t u v w x y z

 stone	stone	 wipe	
 shake		 dish	
 tower		 hunt	
 next		 prize	
 moo		 learn	
 doctor		 dirty	
 plant		 wink	
 head		 yell	

Neighbors That Help Us

Read each short story, and answer the questions. Use the words from the boxes.

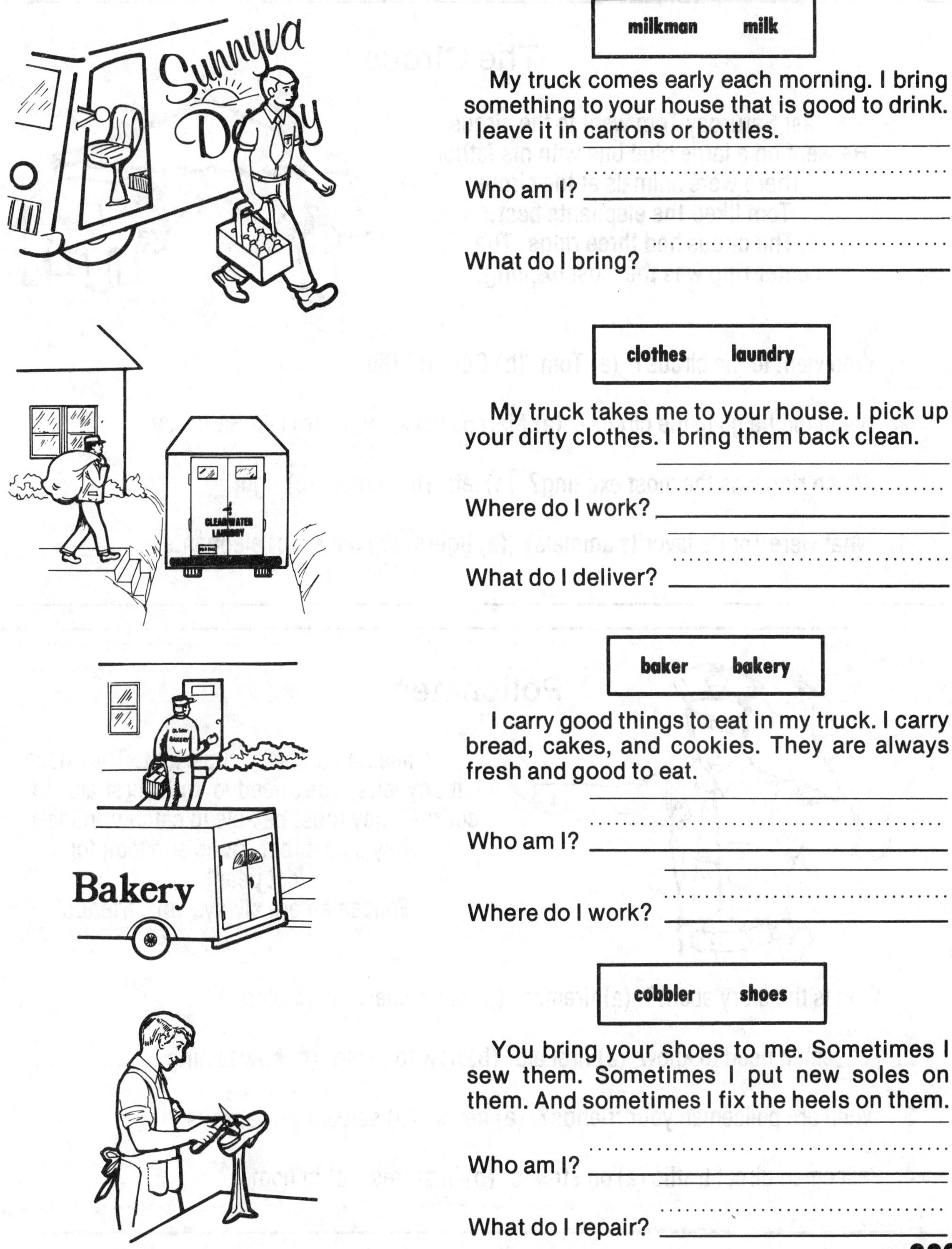

milkman milk

My truck comes early each morning. I bring something to your house that is good to drink. I leave it in cartons or bottles.

Who am I? ______________________

What do I bring? ______________________

clothes laundry

My truck takes me to your house. I pick up your dirty clothes. I bring them back clean.

Where do I work? ______________________

What do I deliver? ______________________

baker bakery

I carry good things to eat in my truck. I carry bread, cakes, and cookies. They are always fresh and good to eat.

Who am I? ______________________

Where do I work? ______________________

cobbler shoes

You bring your shoes to me. Sometimes I sew them. Sometimes I put new soles on them. And sometimes I fix the heels on them.

Who am I? ______________________

What do I repair? ______________________

Story fun

Read each story, and underline the correct answers. If you have problems, read the story again.

The Circus

Last Saturday Tom went to the circus. He went on a large blue bus with his father. There were animals at the circus. Tom liked the elephants best. The circus had three rings. The center ring was the most exciting.

1. Who went to the circus? (a) Tom (b) Sue (c) Bill
2. When did he go to the circus? (a) March (b) August (c) last Saturday
3. Which ring was the most exciting? (a) left (b) center (c) right
4. What were Tom's favorite animals? (a) tigers (b) dogs (c) elephants

Policemen

Policemen are very important. They have many jobs. They need to know first aid. Of course, they must be able to catch criminals. They also direct traffic and look for lost people. Policemen are always your friends.

1. Who is the story about? (a) firemen (b) policemen (c) doctors
2. Policemen need to know (a) first aid (b) how to skate (c) how to sing.
3. When are policemen your friends? (a) never (b) seldom (c) always
4. Policemen direct traffic (a) on streets (b) in stores (c) in homes.

How Is Your Spelling?

Look at each picture, and say the word. Write the word in the blank.

a b c d e f g h i j k l m n o p q r s t u v w x y z

alike — alike	sank
sled	pinch
igloo	make
stamp	spill
hammer	goose
friend	hump
quart	today
spin	yoyo

Friendly Helpers

Do you know these two men? They help us to build our houses. They help to keep our houses in good order.

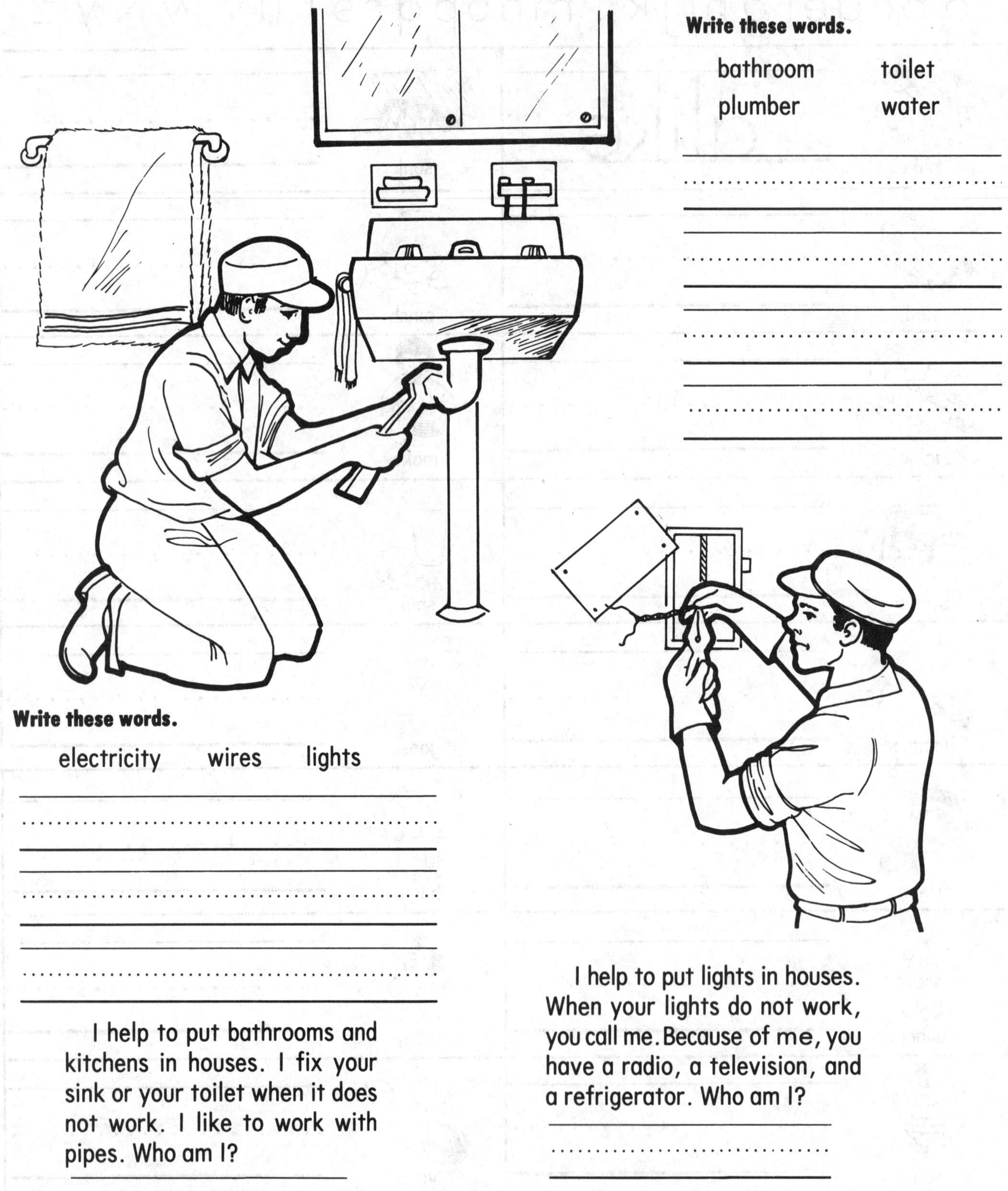

Write these words.

bathroom toilet
plumber water

Write these words.

electricity wires lights

I help to put bathrooms and kitchens in houses. I fix your sink or your toilet when it does not work. I like to work with pipes. Who am I?

I help to put lights in houses. When your lights do not work, you call me. Because of me, you have a radio, a television, and a refrigerator. Who am I?

Stories of Interest

Read each story, and underline the correct answers. If you have problems, read the story again.

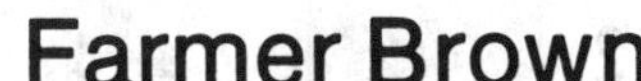

Farmer Brown

Farmer Brown raises wheat. He farms many acres of land. He uses big machines to do the work.

Farmer Brown sells his wheat. Some of it goes to bakeries to make bread.

1. Who is the story about? (a) grocer Tom (b) farmer Brown (c) baker Ben
2. What does he raise? (a) wheat (b) corn (c) rice
3. To do the work, he uses (a) mules (b) people (c) machines.
4. Wheat is used to make (a) milk (b) gas (c) bread.

A Trip to the Zoo

Tomorrow we are going to the zoo. We will see many wild animals. I will feed peanuts to the elephants. My brother will feed fish to the seals. My parents will buy lunch for all of us.

1. Where am I going? (a) to a movie (b) to the zoo (c) to a party
2. When am I going? (a) tomorrow (b) today (c) next week
3. Who is going with me? (a) my friends (b) my class (c) my family
4. What will my brother feed? (a) seals (b) elephants (c) monkeys

Addition and Subtraction Through 9's

A Draw a line under each as you read.

1. 1 + 2 = 3   3 − 1 = 2   2 + 2 = 4   4 − 2 = 2   2 + 3 = 5
   5 − 3 = 2   5 − 2 = 3   3 + 3 = 6   6 − 3 = 3
2. 1 + 5 = 6   1 + 2 = 3   5 + 1 = 6   6 − 1 = 5   2 + 2 = 4
   4 + 3 = 7   7 − 4 = 3   7 − 3 = 4   3 + 4 = 7
3. 8 − 3 = 5   3 + 5 = 8   6 + 1 = 7   1 + 6 = 7   7 − 1 = 6
   7 − 6 = 1   9 − 6 = 3   8 + 6 = 14   14 − 7 = 7

B Complete the number sentences by filling in the blanks.

4. 1 + 2 = ______   3 − 1 = ______   2 + 2 = ______
   4 − 2 = ______   5 − 3 = ______   3 + 6 = ______
   9 − 5 = ______   7 + 8 = ______   7 − 4 = ______
5. 9 + 8 = ______   17 − 9 = ______   16 − 9 = ______
   7 + 9 = ______   8 + 5 = ______   13 − 8 = ______
   12 − 7 = ______   10 − 8 = ______   6 + 5 = ______
6. 15 − 8 = ______   8 − 5 = ______   16 − 9 = ______
   12 − 4 = ______   6 + 6 = ______   7 + 7 = ______
   7 − 2 = ______   12 − 8 = ______   9 + 3 = ______

C Fill in the blanks.

7. ______ Jerry had five Hot Wheels, and his mother bought eight more for him. How many Hot Wheels does Jerry now have?
8. ______ Jane had fourteen ice-cream cones and gave six away. How many ice-cream cones does she have left?
9. ______ Mary spent eight cents for an apple and seven cents for candy. How many cents did she spend?
10. ______ Larry had six apples, and Tom had three apples. How many more apples did Larry have than Tom?

Fun with Spelling

a b c d e f g h i j k l m n o p q r s t u v w x y z

Look at each picture, and say the word. Write the word in the blank.

trick — trick	month
shine	short
dozen	barn
sweep	luck
race	down
monkey	think
pack	barber
eyebrow	jam

Helpful Neighbors

Here is a man who helps us fix our houses. He builds new houses for us to live in. He also makes old houses look pretty. He is called a ______________.

This man uses many tools to repair homes. He must measure many things to build homes too. Name some tools that he might use.

____

____

____

____

____

Here is a man who makes our houses look pretty. He works on the insides and outsides of the houses. This man helps to keep the wood in the houses looking pretty.

This man is called a ______________. He also uses many tools. Name some tools that he might use.

____

____

____

Interesting Stories

Read each story, and underline the correct answers. If you have problems, read the story again.

Maps

Maps give directions. My dad uses maps when we travel. He shows me how to read the maps.

Last summer we visited my grandmother. She lives in another part of the country. We had to use maps to find the way. Then, we had to use a city map to find her house.

1. Maps give (a) the time (b) directions (c) the date.
2. Who helps me read maps? (a) Dad (b) Mom (c) a friend
3. When did we visit Grandmother? (a) last week (b) last winter (c) last summer
4. To find her house, we used (a) a state map (b) a city map (c) an almanac.

Water Systems

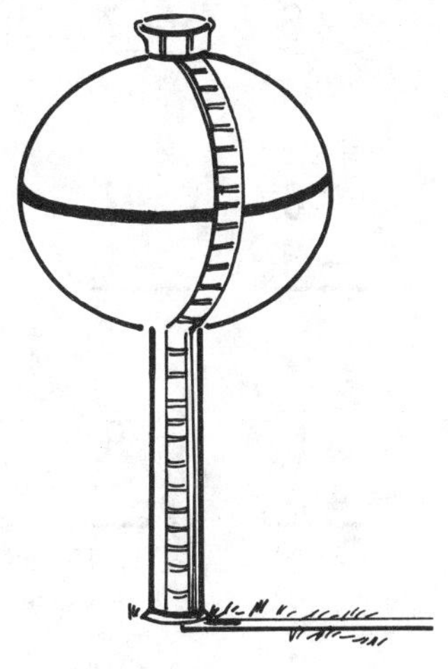

Water is used by everyone. Water systems are very important.

A city water system is very important. It must supply clean safe water to many people. Wells furnish water to people who live in the country. The water must be tested. Unsafe water can cause diseases.

1. Who uses water? (a) city people (b) everyone (c) few people
2. City water systems supply (a) safe water (b) dirty water (c) salt water.
3. In the country water comes from (a) rain (b) melted snow (c) wells.
4. What kind of water can cause diseases? (a) safe (b) salt (c) unsafe

Practicing Addition & Subtraction Through 9's

Solve these problems. Write your answer under each.

A.	8 − 7	8 − 3	7 + 2	7 + 3	8 − 5	9 − 1	8 + 2	8 + 7	3 + 9	7 + 1
B.	9 + 3	7 − 3	8 − 2	9 − 6	9 − 8	9 + 7	7 + 6	8 + 3	9 − 7	7 + 2
C.	8 + 2	7 + 3	8 − 1	9 − 3	7 + 2	8 + 2	8 + 7	9 + 5	9 − 2	9 − 4
D.	9 + 8	8 − 5	9 − 1	9 + 7	8 − 6	9 − 2	8 + 3	7 − 5	9 + 3	9 + 7
E.	8 − 2	8 − 3	7 + 4	9 − 8	9 − 3	7 + 6	8 − 5	9 + 2	8 − 1	9 − 2
F.	7 − 5	8 + 6	9 − 2	9 + 1	8 − 5	8 − 4	7 − 5	9 − 6	8 + 7	9 + 3
G.	8 + 1	8 + 2	9 + 7	9 − 8	8 + 5	7 + 6	9 + 8	8 − 3	7 − 1	9 + 4
H.	8 − 2	7 − 5	9 + 3	9 + 7	8 − 2	9 − 2	7 + 6	9 + 3	9 − 1	7 − 3
I.	9 + 7	8 + 4	9 − 2	9 − 1	9 + 3	8 + 3	9 − 1	8 − 6	8 + 4	8 + 3
J.	9 + 3	8 + 2	7 − 2	9 − 8	9 + 8	7 + 4	8 + 5	9 − 2	8 + 2	

Recognizing Words

Look at each picture, and say the word. Write the word in the blank.

a b c d e f g h i j k l m n o p q r s t u v w x y z

fin — fin	mess
punish	crack
ribbon	lake
animals	fur
tick	zipper
cheese	angry
sniff	up
laugh	button

Doctor and Dentist

Read each statement, and answer the questions.

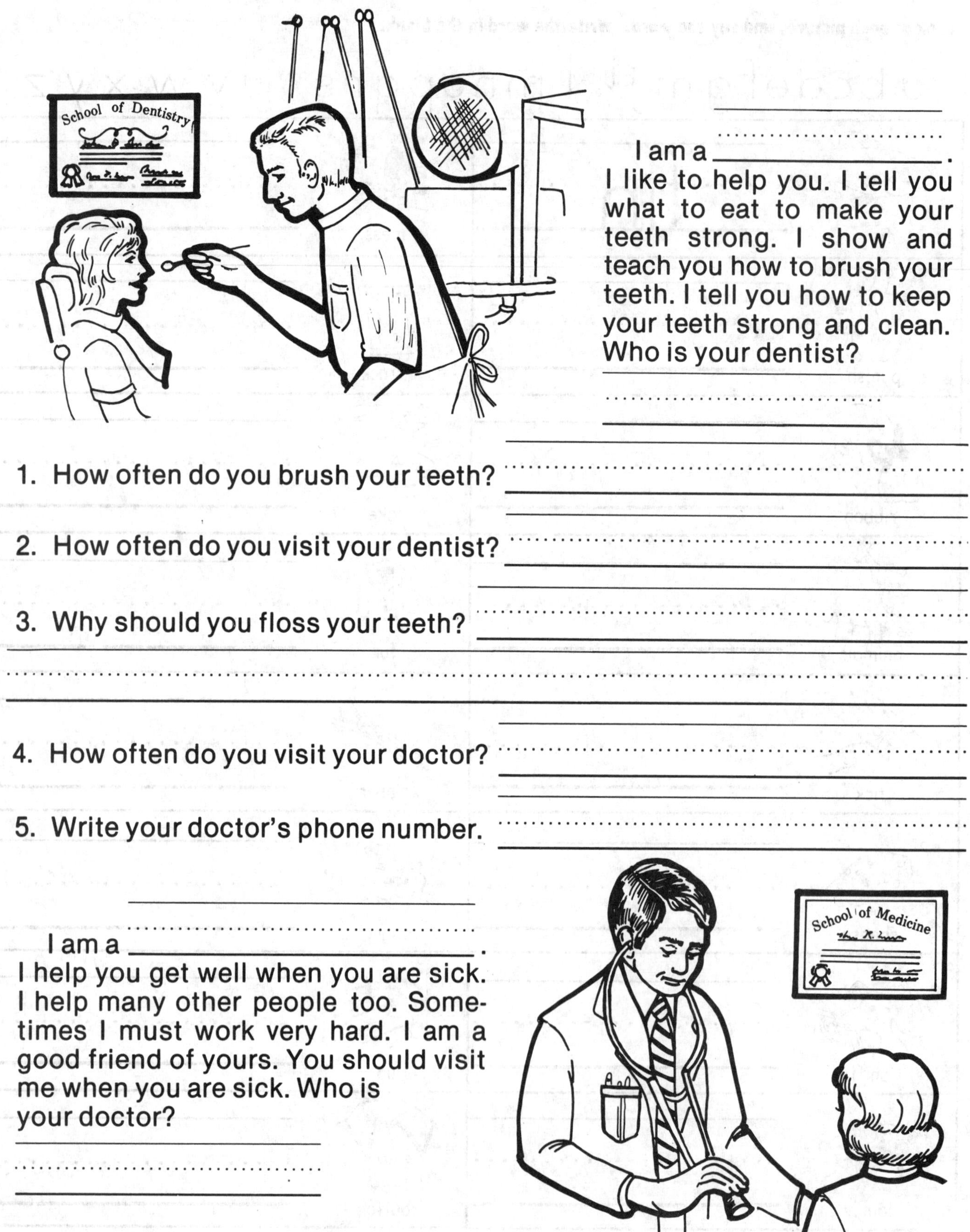

I am a ________________.
I like to help you. I tell you what to eat to make your teeth strong. I show and teach you how to brush your teeth. I tell you how to keep your teeth strong and clean. Who is your dentist?

1. How often do you brush your teeth?
2. How often do you visit your dentist?
3. Why should you floss your teeth?
4. How often do you visit your doctor?
5. Write your doctor's phone number.

I am a ________________.
I help you get well when you are sick. I help many other people too. Sometimes I must work very hard. I am a good friend of yours. You should visit me when you are sick. Who is your doctor?

Enjoyable Stories

Read each story, and underline the correct answers. If you have problems, read the story again.

My School

My school is a large brick building. It is called West School. I am in the second grade.

At school I learn many things each day. It is exciting to learn new things. I also play with my friends. I like school.

1. My school is built out of (a) bricks (b) wood (c) concrete.
2. What do I do at school? (a) sleep (b) cook (c) learn
3. What grade am I in? (a) first (b) second (c) third
4. What is the name of my school? (a) East School (b) West School (c) South School

The Library

The library has books about many different things. My teacher takes us to the library every week.

This week I am going to find a book about horses. My friend John wants a book about dogs. We will take the books home to read.

1. What is in a library? (a) food (b) books (c) radios
2. Who takes us to the library? (a) teacher (b) parents (c) friends
3. How often do we go to the library? (a) every day (b) every week (c) every month
4. Where will we read our books? (a) school (b) store (c) home

Recognizing Spelling Words

Look at each picture, and say the word. Write the word in the blank.

a b c d e f g h i j k l m n o p q r s t u v w x y z

wise — wise	high
mail	low
male	study
slide	note
leave	good-bye
ice cream	buy
his	by
joke	tool

Firemen

Firemen are very important people in your neighborhood. When there is a fire, the firemen know just what to do. They go to work quickly putting out the fire.

Find the name of each tool, and draw a line to match each picture on the left. Write the name of each tool.

1.

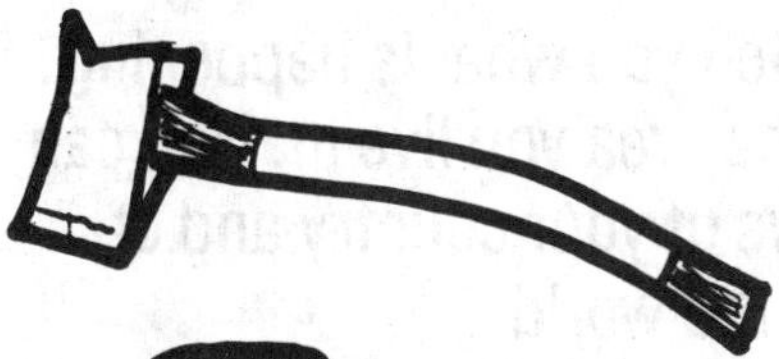

2.

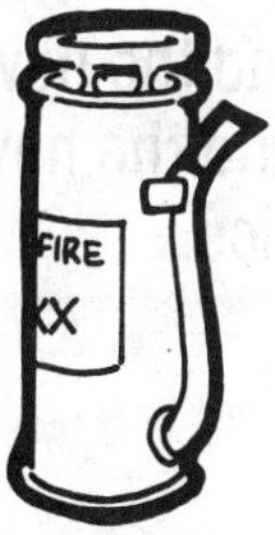

3.

4.

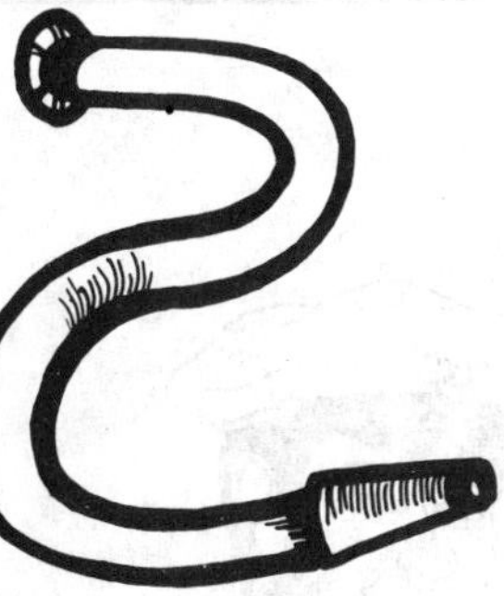

5.

6.

Light

light

Shovel

Fire extinguisher

Rubber Hat and Coat

Ax

Hose

Reading for Fun

Read each story, and underline the correct answers. If you have problems, read the story again.

Newspapers

Newspapers tell you what is happening. They tell about the area you live in. You can also read news of your country and of the world.

Every day my mom and I read the newspaper. She helps me understand the news. Then, I read the comics.

1. What is the story about? (a) magazines (b) books (c) newspapers
2. Who helps me understand the news? (a) my mom (b) a friend (c) my aunt
3. When do I read the paper? (a) weekly (b) every day (c) monthly
4. What else do I read in the paper? (a) sports (b) comics (c) ads

Vince the Bus Driver

My name is Vince. I drive a bus in a large city. I wear a blue and gray uniform.

Many people ride my bus every day. Most of them are going to work.

1. Who is the story about? (a) Bob (b) Vince (c) Vernon
2. What does he do? (a) drives a bus (b) farms (c) teaches
3. Many people ride his bus (a) once a month (b) once a week (c) every day.
4. Where are they going? (a) work (b) school (c) library

Names of Tens

one 10 = 10 = ten
two 10's = 20 = twenty
three 10's = 30 = thirty
four 10's = 40 = forty
five 10's = 50 = fifty

six 10's = 60 = sixty
seven 10's = 70 = seventy
eight 10's = 80 = eighty
nine 10's = 90 = ninety
ten 10's = 100 = hundred

Write the correct number for each row. Then write the name of that number. See the example.

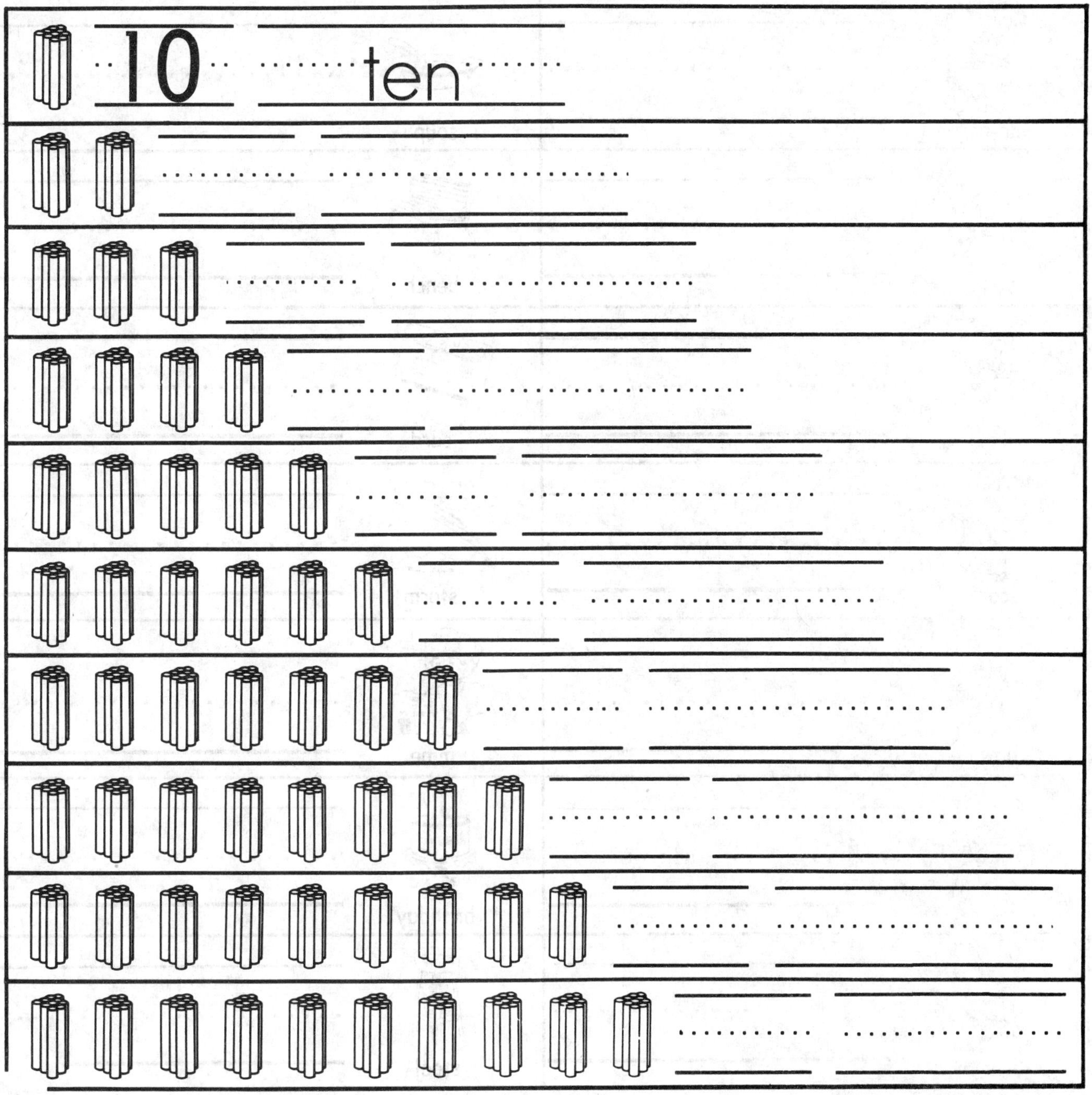

10 ten

Writing Picture Words

a b c d e f g h i j k l m n o p q r s t u v w x y z

Look at each picture, and say the word. Write the word in the blank.

 place	place	 teacher	
 dream		 soup	
 stem		 bench	
 climb		 card	
 scare		 storm	
 bow		 mine	
 rub		 birthday	
 toss		 stool	

Health Review

A **Write three of each of the foods listed below.**

	Fruits	Vegetables	Meats	Cereals
1.				
2.				
3.				

B **True or False**

1. It is important to have plenty of light when you read.
2. A dim light is hard on your eyes.
3. The throat is behind the backbone.
4. The mouth, nose, and throat are the gateways to the body.
5. Loud noises will not injure your ears.
6. Never pick at your ears with anything.
7. Clean hair causes the scalp to itch.
8. You should wash your hair at least once a month.
9. It is not healthy to bite your nails.
10. A hard blow to the ears will not hurt them.

C **Unscramble the following words to name four things found in the mouth.**

1. mugs
2. eteht
3. tstae dbus
4. geunot

Understanding What You Read

Read each story, and underline the correct answers. If you have problems, read the story again.

Bill's Garden

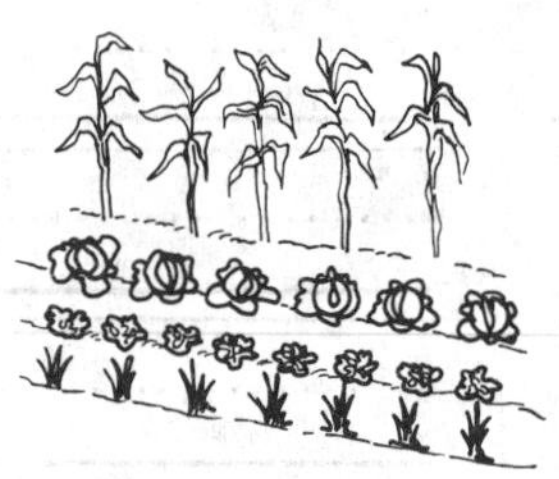

This spring Bill will plant a garden. His dad will help him. First, they will till the ground. Next, they will fertilize it. Then, they will plant the garden.

Bill wants to grow carrots, lettuce, beans, and tomatoes. All the family will eat these vegetables when they are ready.

1. Who is the story about? (a) Bob (b) Bill (c) David
2. What will Bill do? (a) plant a garden (b) paint the fence (c) wash the dog
3. When will Bill plant a garden? (a) summer (b) winter (c) spring
4. Bill will grow (a) vegetables (b) fruits (c) flowers.

Helping Mother

Mother works very hard. We help her because we love her. I help set the table. Then, I help wash the dishes. My big brother takes out the trash. He plays with our little brother. All of us put our toys and clothes away. Mother appreciates our help.

1. Who helps Mother? (a) her children (b) her friends (c) her neighbors
2. Why do they help Mother? (a) Father makes them. (b) nothing else to do (c) love
3. Big brother takes care of the (a) dusting (b) trash (c) cooking.
4. Where do they put their toys and clothes? (a) on a chair (b) on the floor (c) away

Tens

Fill in the blanks with the correct tens. See the examples.

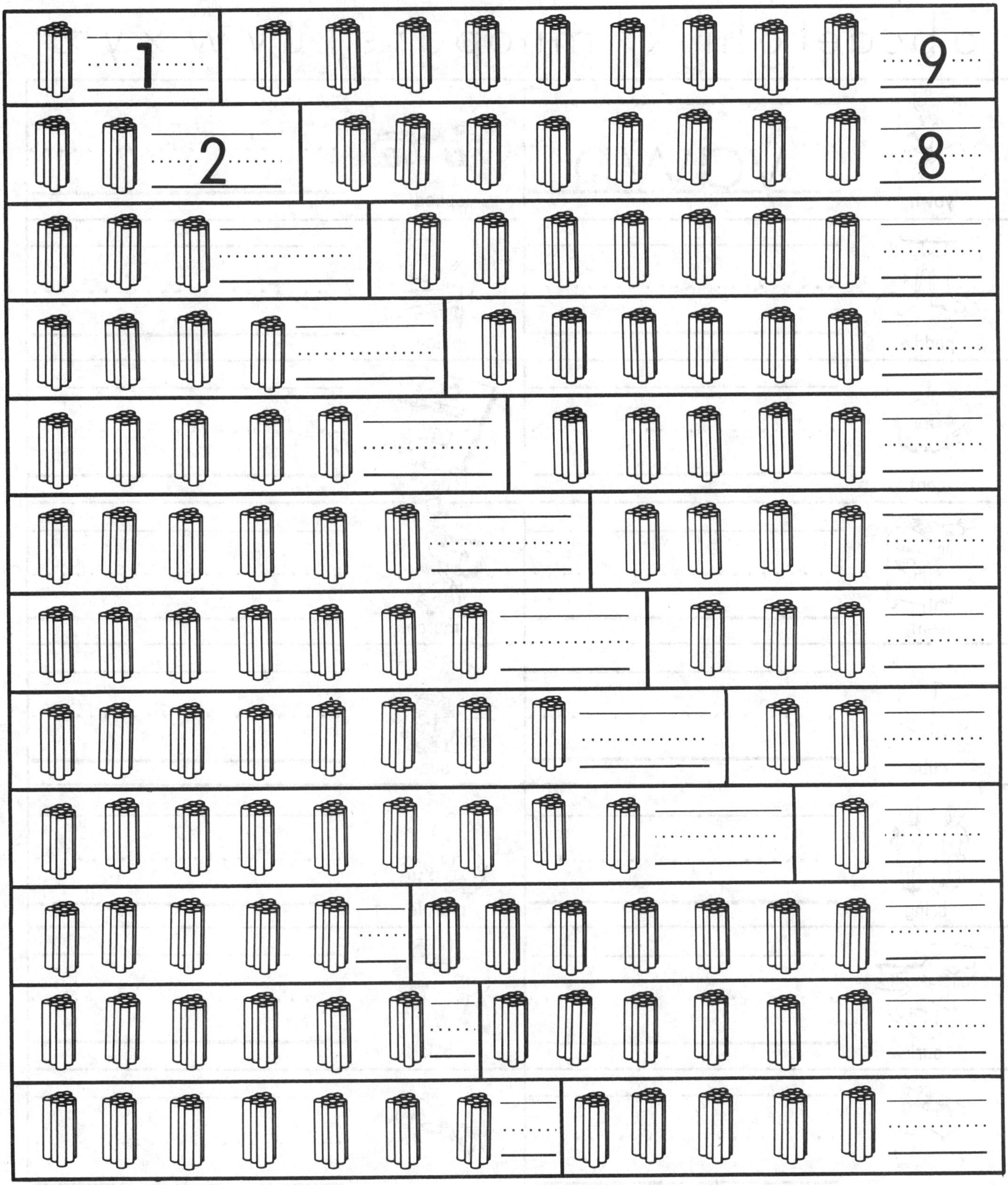

1 9

2 8

Improving Spelling

Look at each picture, and say the word. Write the word in the blank.

a b c d e f g h i j k l m n o p q r s t u v w x y z

yawn	yawn	speed	
puddle		pillow	
cent		day	
sent		march	
cube		pile	
bring		marble	
park		ask	
none		join	

Exercises to Do

Read each story, and underline the correct answers. If you have problems, read the story again.

Fire Drills

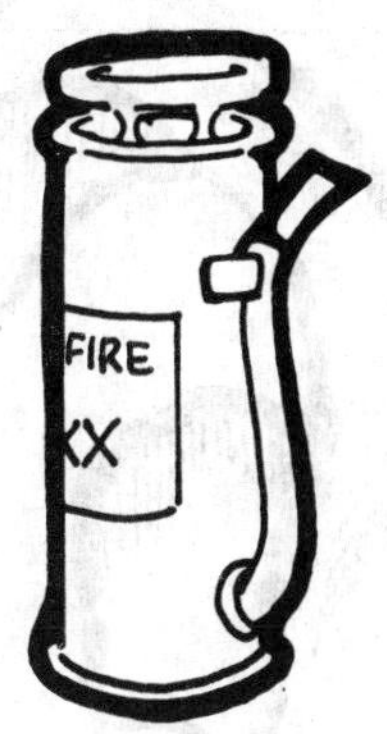

Fire drills are an important safety plan. Everyone should know what to do if a fire occurs.

Fire drills are important at school and at home. Always stay calm during a drill. At school do exactly what your teacher tells you to do. At home work out a plan with your parents.

1. Fire drills are (a) important (b) fun (c) unnecessary.
2. Where should fire drills be held? (a) only at home (b) only at school (c) at home and school
3. Stay calm during (a) meals (b) play (c) a fire drill.
4. At school who will instruct you during a fire drill? (a) friends (b) teacher (c) parents

The Fourth of July Twins

Joe and Joyce are twins. Last Fourth of July they were seven years old. They had a big picnic party in the park. All of their friends came. After the picnic dinner they played games. Then, their parents brought a big cake with candles on it. The cake was decorated in red, white, and blue.

1. Who is the story about? (a) John and Jean (b) Bob and Lisa (c) Joe and Joyce
2. When was their birthday? (a) Memorial Day (b) Thanksgiving Day (c) Fourth of July
3. What kind of party did they have? (a) picnic (b) skating (c) swimming
4. The cake was decorated in (a) red, white, and blue (b) green and yellow (c) pink.

Ears

You should learn all you can about your ears.

A Answer the following questions about your ears.

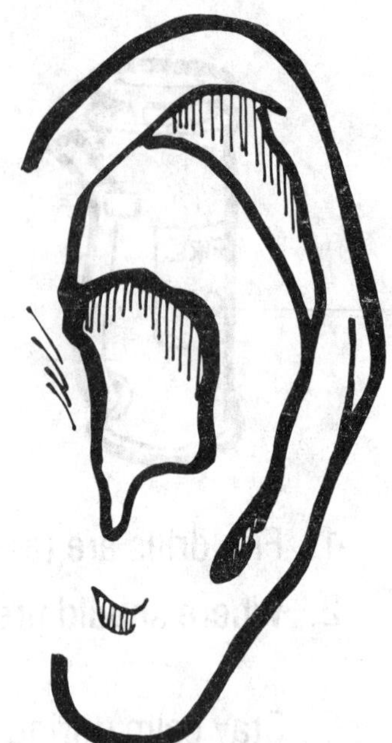

1. We hear sounds that warn us of danger.
   yes ____ no ____

2. Our ears help us to hear the sounds others make.
   yes ____ no ____

3. Our ears help us to hear pleasant sounds such as music, singing, etc.
   yes ____ no ____

B Underline the words that are related to the ear. Write each word.

danger ____

loud ____

fish ____

sing ____

music ____

noise ____

germ ____

sounds ____

whistle ____

whale ____

car ____

laughter ____

wagon ____

hear ____

swim ____

Learning Words

Look at each picture, and say the word. Write the word in the blank.

a b c d e f g h i j k l m n o p q r s t u v w x y z

stop	stop	pal	
drink		under	
with		aim	
feel		salt	
stay		fold	
beg		love	
jelly		her	
row		lay	

More About Ears

A **If the object makes a noise you can hear, draw a line from it to the ear.**

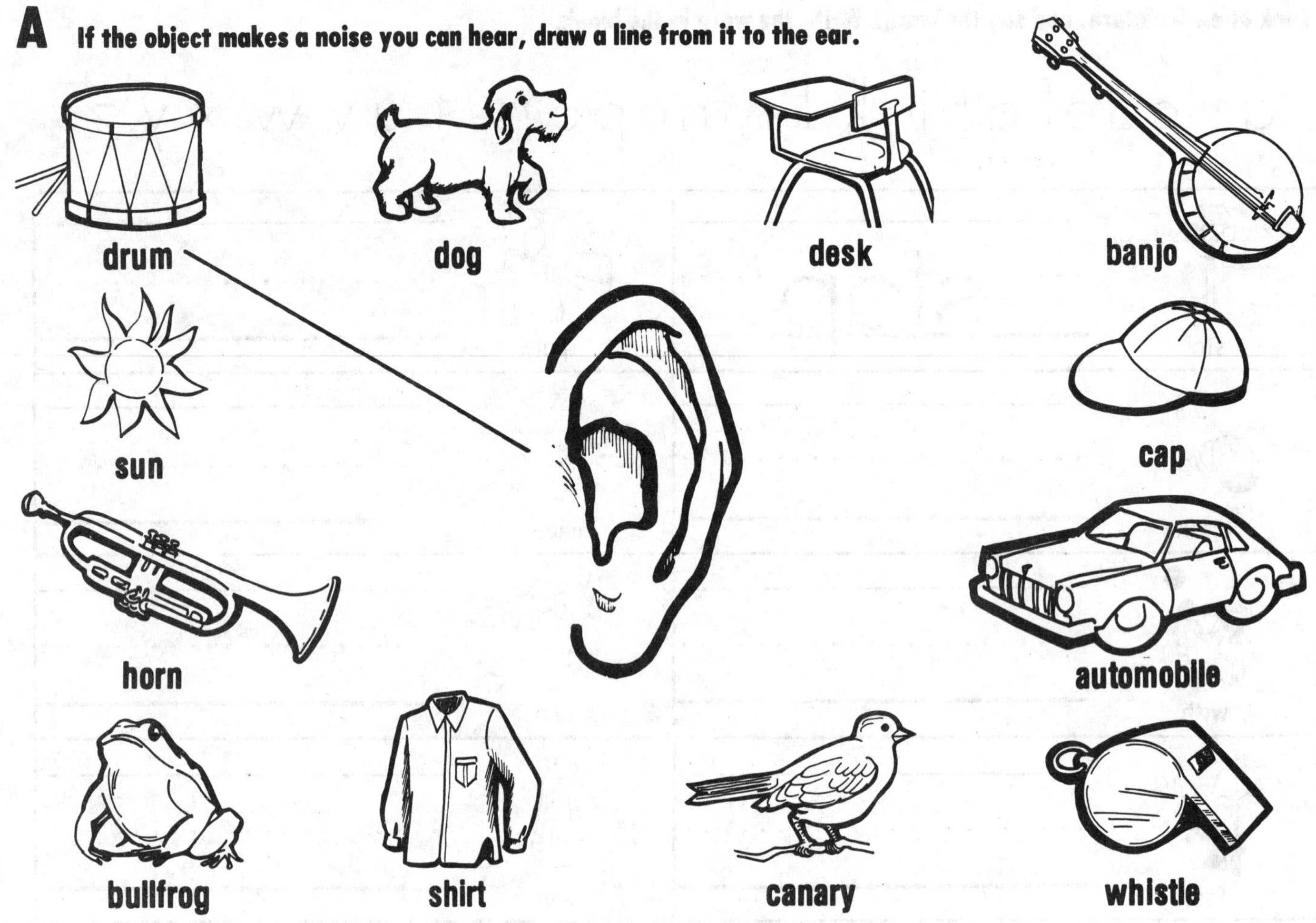

B **Answer these questions about your ears and hearing. Underline the best answers.**

1. Clean your ears with (a) your finger (b) a stick (c) a cotton swab.
2. I should pick my ears with a toothpick. true __ false __
3. When you have an earache, you should (a) take an aspirin (b) go to bed (c) see your doctor.
4. A blow on the ear could (a) feel good (b) cause injury (c) do no harm.
5. Earwax should be removed by (a) an adult (b) yourself (c) your classmate.
6. Our ears furnish us the sense of (a) smell (b) touch (c) hearing.

Enjoying Stories

Read each story, and underline the correct answers. If you have problems, read the story again.

Tom the Mailman

I am Tom the mailman. I deliver the mail in all kinds of weather.

Sometimes I walk through a neighborhood and take the mail to the houses. Other times I drive a vehicle and put the mail in boxes by the street.

1. Who is Tom? (a) a grocer (b) a judge (c) the mailman
2. What does he do? (a) pumps gas (b) delivers mail (c) digs ditches
3. In what kind of weather does he deliver the mail? (a) good weather only (b) all weather (c) rainy weather only
4. When driving, he puts mail in (a) street boxes (b) doors (c) cars.

A Dangerous Job

A fireman's job may be dangerous. He helps put out fires. He also helps rescue people from burning buildings.

Firemen must be strong and healthy. They work different hours. There are always some firemen at work. We need firemen in all communities.

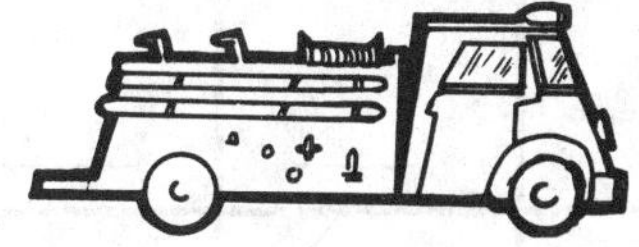

1. Who has a dangerous job? (a) firemen (b) dentists (c) nurses
2. Firemen must be (a) handsome (b) tall (c) strong and healthy.
3. When are firemen at work? (a) mornings (b) always (c) afternoons
4. Firemen are needed in (a) large cities only (b) small towns only (c) all communities.

Completing Each Row

Complete each row by filling in the blanks.

A.	0	1	2	3	4	5	6	7	8
B.	87	___	89	___	91	___	___	94	___
C.	___	1	___	3	___	5	___	7	___
D.	___	___	___	17	18	19	___	___	___
E.	___	58	___	___	61	___	63	___	___
F.	___	___	39	40	41	___	___	___	___
G.	___	___	___	___	4	5	6	___	___
H.	___	___	___	___	97	98	99	___	___
I.	___	___	71	72	73	___	___	___	___

Write the Spelling Words

Look at each picture, and say the word. Write the word in the blank.

a b c d e f g h i j k l m n o p q r s t u v w x y z

pour — pour	pot
poor	snap
drop	juice
map	open
tag	floor
thing	plug
ivy	grass
lasso	tune

Protecting Eyes

Check the ways you can protect your eyes by answering the following questions:

A.	B.
Do you have plenty of light when you study? yes ____ no ____	Do you visit your eye doctor each year? yes ____ no ____
C.	**D.**
Do you avoid games that could injure your eyes? yes ____ no ____	Do you avoid direct glare or harsh light? yes ____ no ____
E.	**F.**
Do you avoid dust and dirt that could cause eye injury? yes ____ no ____	Are you careful not to cause injury to other people's eyes? yes ____ no ____

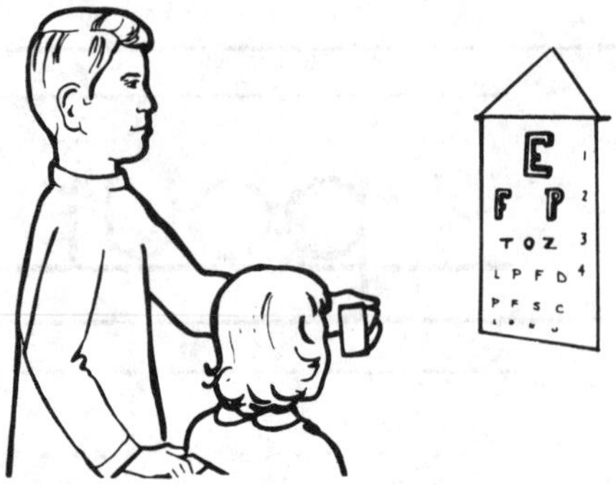

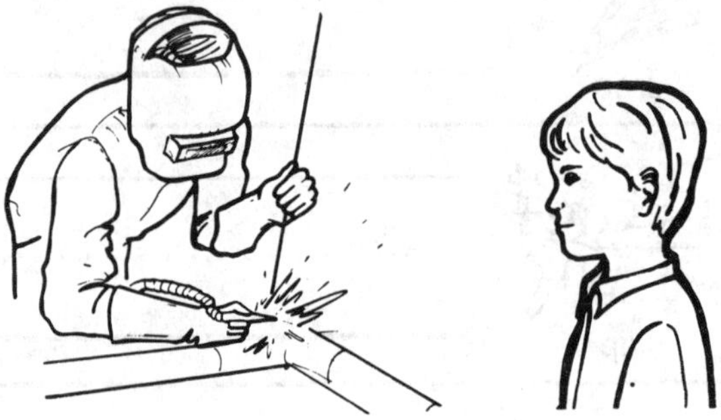

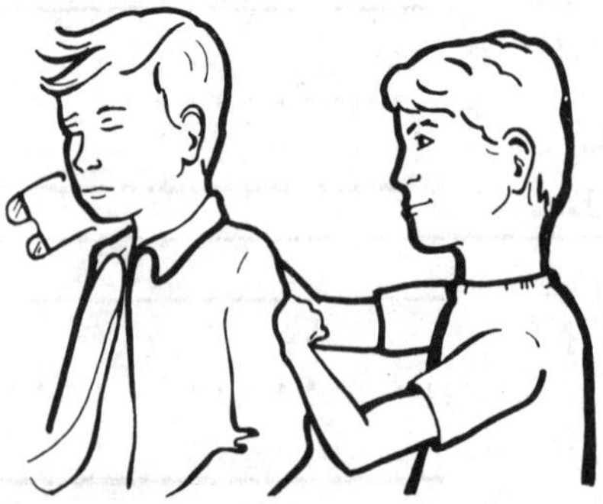

Puzzling Stories

Read each story, and underline the correct answers. If you have problems, read the story again.

Germs

There are germs everywhere. Germs are tiny living things. Some germs can make you sick.

You can fight germs. Take a bath every day. Wash your hands before eating. Wash your hands after using the toilet. Wash all cuts and scratches. You will help keep germs out of your body.

1. Whom can germs make sick? (a) only boys (b) anyone (c) only girls
2. What can you do about germs? (a) fight them (b) ignore them (c) help them
3. Germs are found (a) only in the air (b) only in water (c) everywhere.
4. When should you bathe? (a) daily (b) weekly (c) monthly

Airports

Airplanes take off and land at airports. Most airports are very busy. Many large airports operate all day and all night.

Many people work at airports. Some sell tickets. Some take care of baggage. The pilot and crew get directions at the airport.

1. Who flies a plane? (a) pilot (b) ticket clerk (c) baggage clerk
2. Most airports are (a) dirty (b) busy (c) quiet.
3. When do large airports operate? (a) all the time (b) mornings only (c) evenings only
4. Planes land at (a) schools (b) offices (c) airports.

What Comes Before?

Write the number that comes before the number listed in each box. See example "A."

A. 3 4	7 8	10 11	13 14	14 15
B. ___ 20	___ 25	___ 28	___ 32	___ 36
C. ___ 39	___ 42	___ 45	___ 41	___ 18
D. ___ 12	___ 24	___ 29	___ 33	___ 37
E. ___ 13	___ 19	___ 26	___ 34	___ 43
F. ___ 47	___ 50	___ 17	___ 35	___ 44
G. ___ 53	___ 60	___ 64	___ 22	___ 31
H. ___ 56	___ 38	___ 16	___ 21	___ 62
I. ___ 48	___ 40	___ 23	___ 30	___ 27

Learn to Spell Better

Look at each picture, and say the word. Write the word in the blank.

a b c d e f g h i j k l m n o p q r s t u v w x y z

show — show	jet
heat	bread
string	hurry
circus	hide
go	no
teach	know
carry	X ray
trunk	pole

Understanding Stories

Read each story, and underline the correct answers. If you have problems, read the story again.

A Lady Doctor

Mary Benson is a doctor. She takes care of sick and well people.

Well people get yearly checkups in her office. Dr. Benson takes care of some sick people at their homes. She also takes care of sick people in her office and in the hospital.

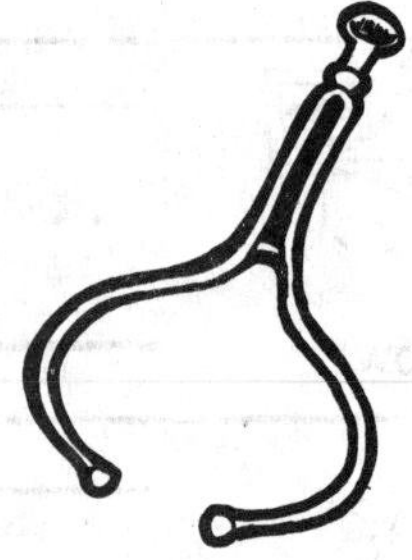

1. Who is the story about? (a) a man doctor (b) a lady doctor (c) a dentist
2. Where does she take care of well people? (a) office (b) home (c) hospital
3. Well people get checkups (a) weekly (b) yearly (c) monthly.
4. In the hospital she takes care of (a) well people (b) tired people (c) sick people.

The Dentist

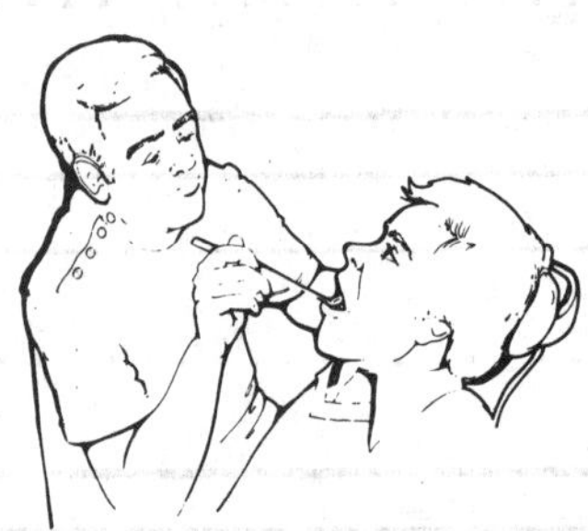

Healthy teeth and gums are important. Visiting the dentist twice a year helps keep them healthy.

In his office the dentist cleans and fixes teeth. He teaches people how to care for their teeth and gums. The dentist is a good friend.

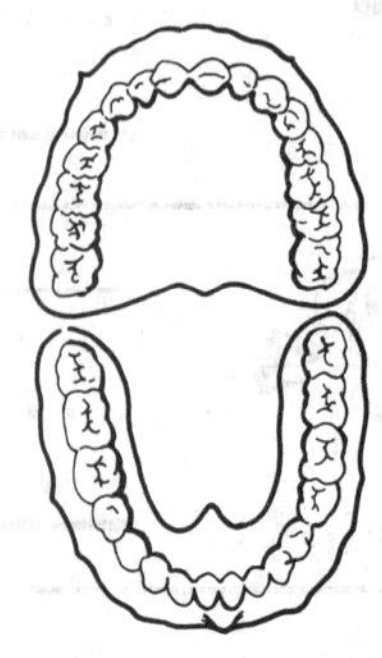

1. Who takes care of teeth and gums? (a) teacher (b) doctor (c) dentist
2. When should you visit the dentist? (a) twice a year (b) monthly (c) every two years
3. Where does the dentist work? (a) the hospital (b) his office (c) the courthouse
4. The dentist is your (a) friend (b) enemy (c) employer.

Keeping Clean

Keeping clean not only makes you look better, but it also helps to keep you healthy.

Underline the correct answers.

1. What are the most important items needed to keep clean?

water	towel	dirt	soap
sports	clothing	shoes	

2. How often should we take baths?

each day	each week
each month	each year

3. How often should we wash our hands?

before each meal	after each meal

4. How many times should we brush our teeth?

after each meal	never
each week	at night only

5. We should wash our faces several times each day.

yes	no

Know the Words

Look at each picture, and say the word. Write the word in the blank.

a b c d e f g h i j k l m n o p q r s t u v w x y z

will	will	game	
gown		near	
them		tall word	
much		large	
wild		kind	
each		want	
keep		nice	
flew		never	

Reading Exercises

Read each story, and underline the correct answers. If you have problems, read the story again.

Nurse Margaret

I am a nurse, and my name is Margaret. I used to work in Dr. Jone's office. Now I work in a very large hospital.

Each day I wear a clean white uniform and cap. I take good care of my sick patients. Nursing is an important job.

1. Who is the story about? (a) Sue (b) Martha (c) Margaret
2. What is she? (a) nurse (b) librarian (c) teacher
3. She now works in a (a) clinic (b) store (c) hospital.
4. She wears a clean uniform (a) once in a while (b) each day (c) each week.

An Orange Cat

Tom has an orange cat named Sam. He is very big. His fur is thick and soft.

Sam likes for me to pet him. He purrs and rubs against my legs. I am always nice to Sam. You know, Sam is always nice to me too.

1. Who owns Sam? (a) Tim (b) Tom (c) Ben
2. What does Sam do when I pet him? (a) purrs and rubs (b) walks away (c) scratches
3. Sam rubs against (a) a tree (b) the ground (c) my legs.
4. When am I nice to Sam? (a) seldom (b) always (c) never

Our Best Foods

Select and write each food that is best for you. Pick its name from the center list. Use each word only once. Circle each word used. See the sample.

1. milk
2. orange
3. vegetables
4. bread
5. meat
6. gum
7. cereal
8. candy
9. sucker
10. apple

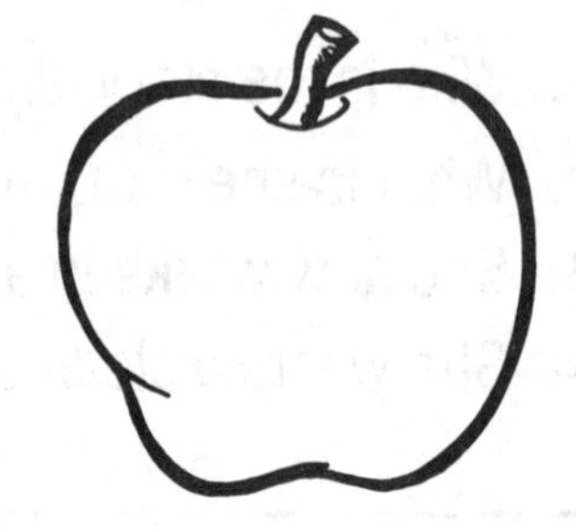

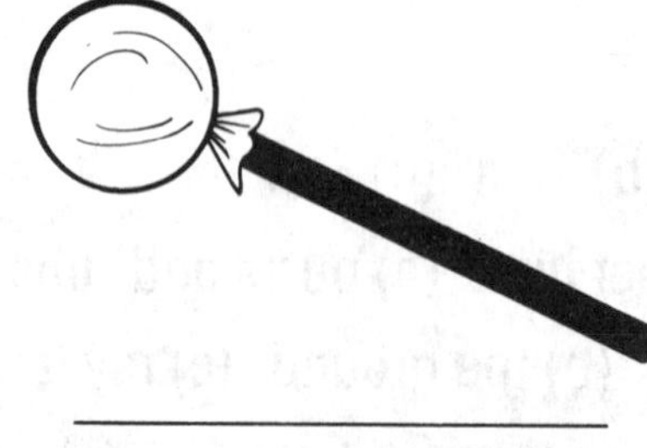

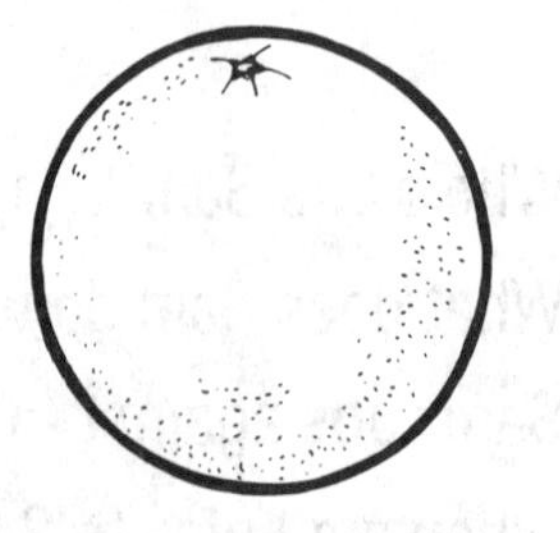

What Comes After?

Write the number that comes after the number listed in each box. See example "A."

A. 3 4	**B.** 7 ___	**C.** 10 ___	**D.** 13 ___	**E.** 14 ___
F. 19 ___	**G.** 24 ___	**H.** 27 ___	**I.** 31 ___	**J.** 35 ___
K. 38 ___	**L.** 41 ___	**M.** 44 ___	**N.** 40 ___	**O.** 17 ___
P. 11 ___	**Q.** 23 ___	**R.** 28 ___	**S.** 32 ___	**T.** 36 ___
U. 12 ___	**V.** 18 ___	**W.** 25 ___	**X.** 33 ___	**Y.** 42 ___
Z. 46 ___	**A.** 49 ___	**B.** 16 ___	**C.** 34 ___	**D.** 43 ___
E. 52 ___	**F.** 59 ___	**G.** 63 ___	**H.** 21 ___	**I.** 30 ___
J. 55 ___	**K.** 37 ___	**L.** 15 ___	**M.** 20 ___	**N.** 61 ___
O. 47 ___	**P.** 39 ___	**Q.** 22 ___	**R.** 29 ___	**S.** 26 ___

Writing Different Words

Look at each picture, and say the word. Write the word in the blank.

a b c d e f g h i j k l m n o p q r s t u v w x y z

cover — cover	gas
rocket	clothes
mountain	wool
chase	grin
throw	frown
shower	bubbles
coffee	write
patch	right

The Many Forms of Water

Water is found in many different forms. Here are some pictures of forms of water. Can you put these words in the correct blanks?

dew	frost	sleet	snow	steam	vapor

1. Visible water that floats in the air is vapor.

2. Water changed into a gas is called ________. ________ cannot be seen.

3. Snow or hail mixed with rain is ________.

4. Ice that forms on blades of grass on a clear night is called ________.

5. Children enjoy playing in the ________.

6. Water that collects on plants and grass early on clear mornings is called ________.

Questions to Answer

Read each story, and underline the correct answers. If you have problems, read the story again.

A Good Diet

Jane and Keith help their mother plan meals. Then, they go to the store with her. They want to eat properly.

Each day they drink milk. They eat a variety of foods. They are sure to include meat, fruits, and vegetables. They also eat breads and cereals.

1. Jane and Keith help their (a) mother (b) father (c) aunt.
2. What do they do? (a) wash clothes (b) vacuum (c) plan meals
3. They go with their mother to the (a) store (b) school (c) park.
4. When do they drink milk? (a) occasionally (b) each day (c) never

Growing

Everything needs three things to grow properly. They are good food, plenty of sleep, and exercise.

All parts of your body grow. Growth will stop after you are an adult.

1. What is the story about? (a) food (b) sleeping (c) growing
2. Who grows? (a) boys only (b) girls only (c) everyone
3. Where do you grow? (a) all over (b) arms only (c) legs only
4. Your growth will stop when you are (a) 12 (b) an adult (c) 32.

Even Numbers to 100

Write the even numbers in the blanks.

1	2	3	4	5	6	7	___	9	___
11	___	13	___	15	___	17	___	19	___
21	___	23	___	25	___	27	___	29	___
31	___	33	___	35	___	37	___	39	___
41	___	43	___	45	___	47	___	49	___
51	___	53	___	55	___	57	___	59	___
61	___	63	___	65	___	67	___	69	___
71	___	73	___	75	___	77	___	79	___
81	___	83	___	85	___	87	___	89	___
91	___	93	___	95	___	97	___	99	___

Knowing and Writing Words

Look at each picture, and say the word. Write the word in the blank.

a b c d e f g h i j k l m n o p q r s t u v w x y z

track	track	phone	
fruit		spool	
geese		pocket	
pirate		suds	
float		garage	
sting		ground	
castle		spell	
blocks		why	

Wealth from the Earth

We get many things from the earth. Some of the earth's treasures are shown.

Draw a line from each picture to the correct name. Write the name in the blank.

diamonds

diamonds

coal

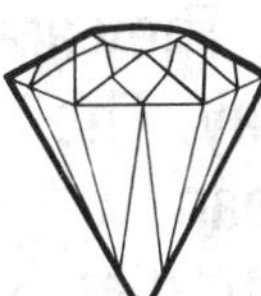

water

lumber

Exercises We Do

Read each story, and underline each correct answer. If you have problems, read the story again.

My Backyard

There are five big trees in my backyard. Three of them are oak trees. Two are maple trees. On an oak branch Dad has hung a swing. My friends come to swing with me.

Mother plants flowers in the backyard. They make the yard pretty.

1. What is in the backyard? (a) trees and flowers (b) garage (c) doghouse
2. Three of the trees are (a) pine trees (b) nut trees (c) oak trees.
3. What does Mother do? (a) plants flowers (b) cuts the grass (c) swings
4. Who comes to swing with me? (a) cousins (b) friends (c) strangers

Dairy Farms

Dairy farms have many cows. They are milked by machines twice a day. The machines are kept very clean.

Milk is an important part of your diet. Aren't you glad there are dairy farms?

1. Milk comes from (a) barns (b) cows (c) machines.
2. Dairy farms cows are milked by (a) hand (b) gravity (c) machines.
3. What is very important to a dairy farm? (a) size (b) cleanliness (c) color of barn
4. When are cows milked? (a) weekly (b) daily (c) twice a day

Odd Numbers to 100

Write the odd numbers in the blanks.

1 2 3 4 5 6 ___ 8 ___ 10

___ 12 ___ 14 ___ 16 ___ 18 ___ 20

___ 22 ___ 24 ___ 26 ___ 28 ___ 30

___ 32 ___ 34 ___ 36 ___ 38 ___ 40

___ 42 ___ 44 ___ 46 ___ 48 ___ 50

___ 52 ___ 54 ___ 56 ___ 58 ___ 60

___ 62 ___ 64 ___ 66 ___ 68 ___ 70

___ 72 ___ 74 ___ 76 ___ 78 ___ 80

___ 82 ___ 84 ___ 86 ___ 88 ___ 90

___ 92 ___ 94 ___ 96 ___ 98 ___ 100

Writing Many Words

Look at each picture, and say the word. Write the word in the blank.

a b c d e f g h i j k l m n o p q r s t u v w x y z

shake	shake	broom	
cling		heart	
enter		whip	
prop		clue	
cloud		echo	
bottle		tablet	
heel		halt	
heal		better	

Reading Stories

Read each story, and underline the correct answers. If you have problems, read the story again.

Staying with a Friend

Julie wants me to spend tonight at her house. We will ask my mother. I hope she says "yes."

I can go! We will have a good time. We will make popcorn. Julie's mom will make hot chocolate for us. We will play games.

1. Who invited me to spend the night? (a) Sarah (b) Ann (c) Julie
2. Where did Julie ask me to spend the night? (a) her house (b) motel (c) her aunt's
3. When did Julie want me to spend the night with her? (a) tonight (b) next week (c) next weekend
4. What will we make? (a) cake (b) popcorn (c) cookies

A Halloween Party

Let's have a Halloween party. It can be in Martha's basement. We'll play games. Bobbing for apples is a good game.

Everyone will wear a costume. I will be a witch. But I think I'll be a nice witch.

1. What kind of party will we have? (a) Valentine's party (b) Halloween party (c) birthday party
2. Where will we have the party? (a) Martha's basement (b) outside (c) at school
3. What will we do? (a) tell ghost stories (b) go trick or treating (c) play games
4. How should we dress? (a) costumes (b) jeans (c) good clothes

The Earth's Different Places

Fill in the blanks with these words:

Canyon	Hills	oceans	Prairies	forests	streams

1. Boys fish in small ______________.

2. Ships travel on ______________

3. ______________ usually make good farming land.

4. The Grand ______________ is deep and wide.

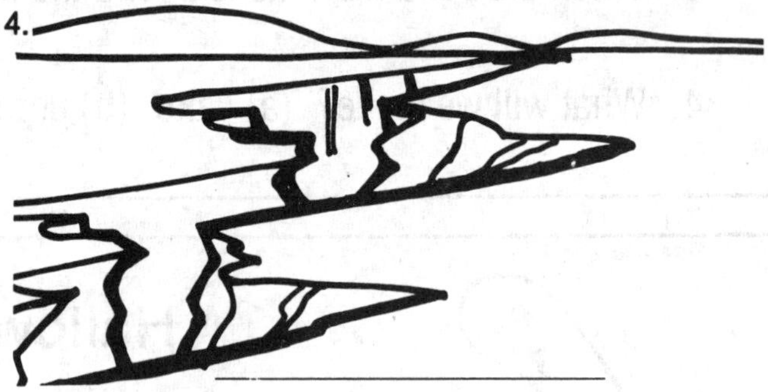

5. ______________ are smaller than mountains.

6. America was once covered with many ______________

What Time Is It?

Write the correct time below each clock.

A.

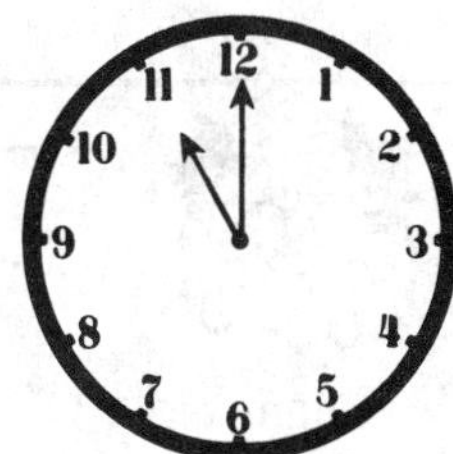

____ o'clock ____ o'clock ____ o'clock ____ o'clock ____ o'clock

B.

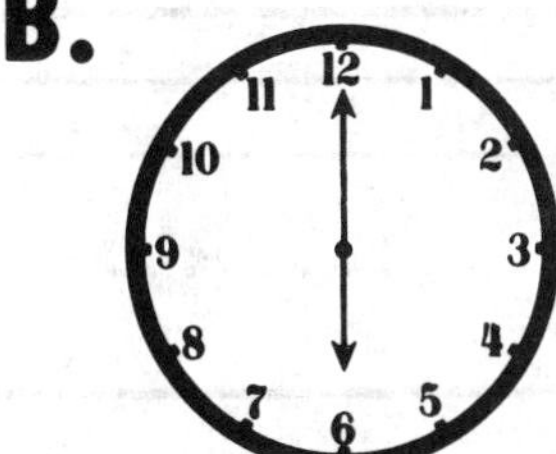

____ o'clock ____ o'clock ____ o'clock ____ o'clock ____ o'clock

C.

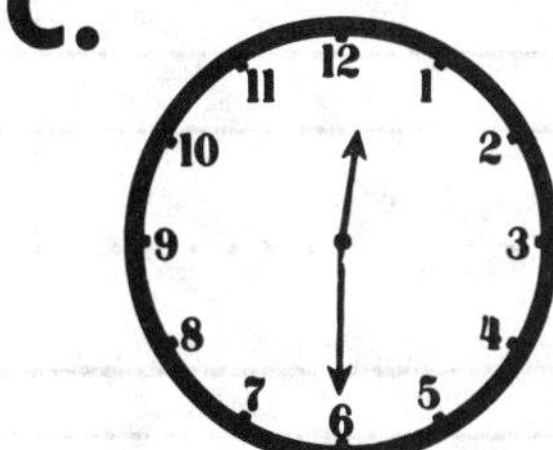
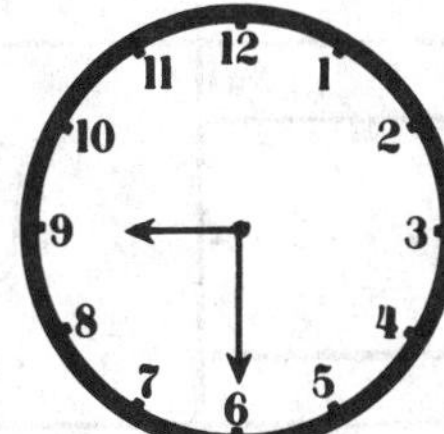

________ ________ ________ ________ ________

D.

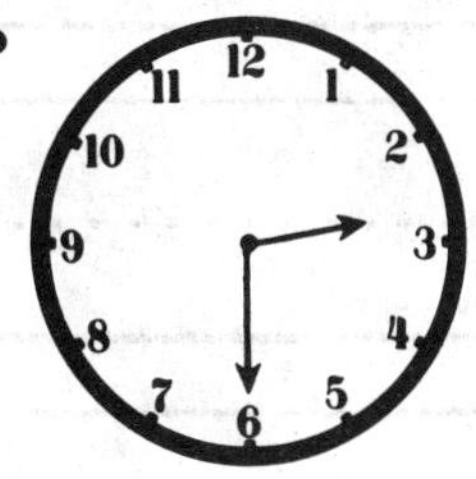

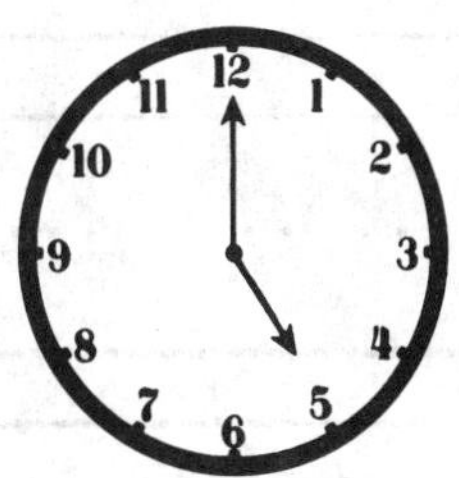
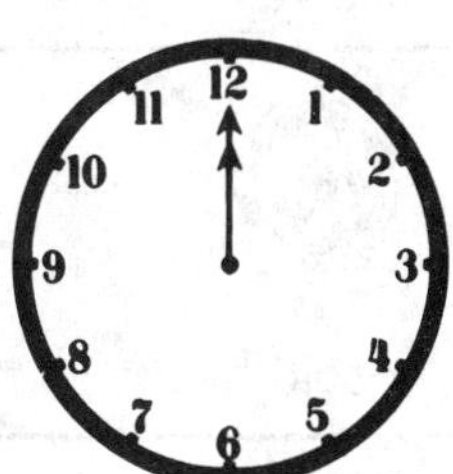

________ ________ ________ ________ ________

Learning to Spell Better

Look at each picture, and say the word. Write the word in the blank.

a b c d e f g h i j k l m n o p q r s t u v w x y z

funny — funny	voice
soon	wheel
this	self
only	gift
fast	straw
give	collar
said	slept
garden	beast

Water on the Earth

All plants and animals need water to live and grow. They will die if they have no water.

Water is found in many places. It is used for many things.

Write what each picture shows about water. Color the pictures.

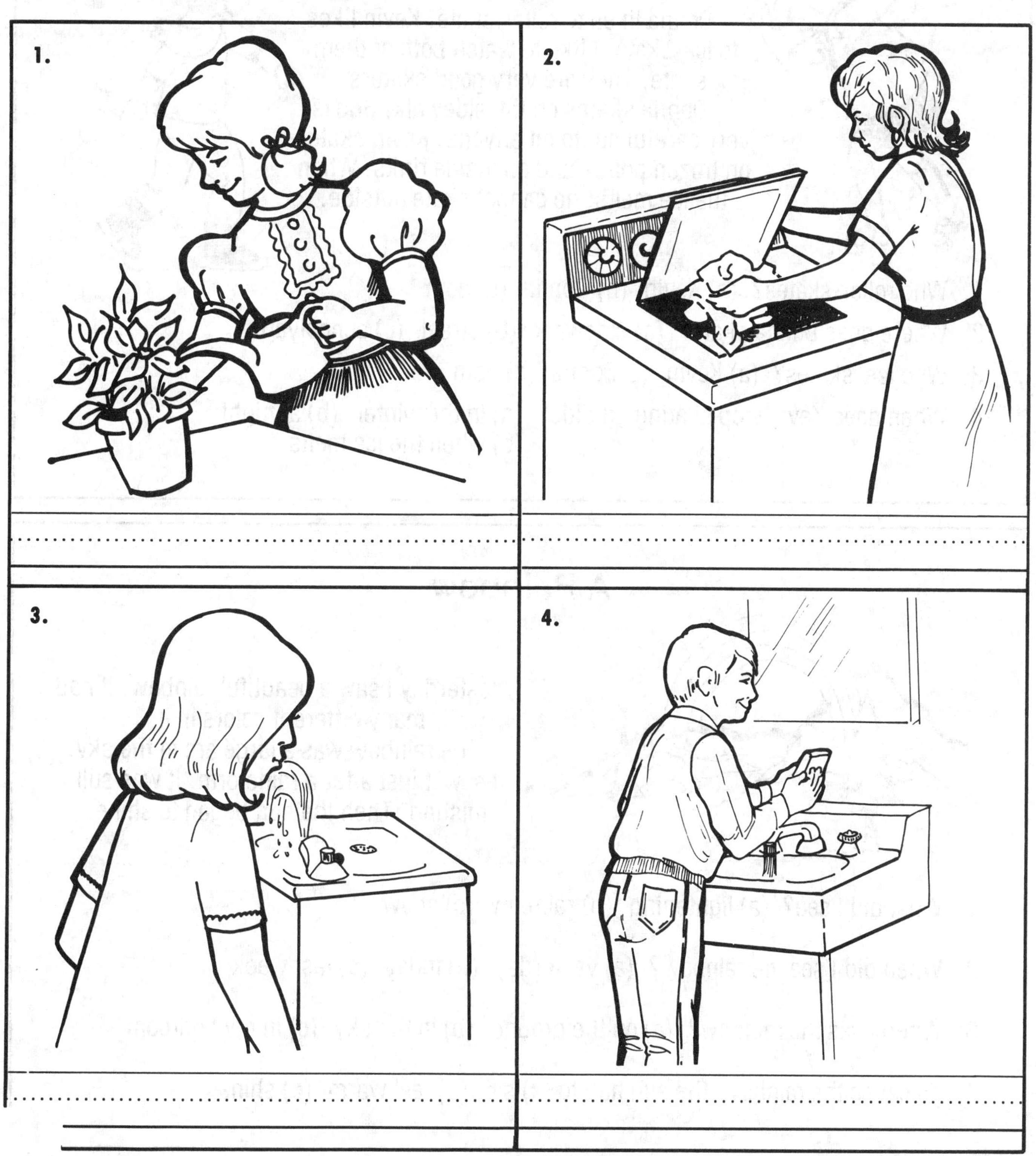

Choosing Correct Answers

Read each story, and underline the correct answers. If you have problems, read the story again.

Skating

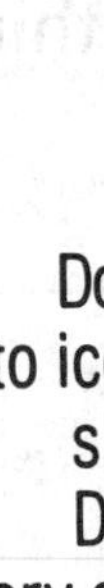

Donna likes to roller-skate. Kevin likes to ice-skate. I like to watch both of them skate. They are very good skaters.

Donna skates on the sidewalk. She is very careful not to hit anyone. Kevin skates on frozen ponds and on inside rinks. When the ice melts, he cannot skate outside.

1. Who roller-skates? (a) Kevin (b) Donna (c) both
2. Where does Donna skate? (a) sidewalk (b) street (c) schoolyard
3. Who ice-skates? (a) Kevin (b)Donna (c) both
4. When does Kevin stop skating outside? (a) in the winter (b) at night (c) when the ice melts

A Rainbow

Yesterday I saw a beautiful rainbow. It had many different colors in it.

The rainbow was a large arc in the sky. I saw it just after a rainstorm. It was still misting. Then the sun began to shine.

1. What did I see? (a) lightening (b) rainbow (c) snow
2. When did I see the rainbow? (a) yesterday (b) today (c) last week
3. Where was the rainbow? (a) on the ground (b) in the sky (c) in my bedroom
4. To cause the rainbow, the sun had to (a) set (b) feel warm (c) shine.

Spelling Fun

Look at each picture, and say the word. Write the word in the blank.

a b c d e f g h i j k l m n o p q r s t u v w x y z

to	to	art	
too		carrot	
two		across	
mash		seat	
round		rail	
hike		farmer	
north		basket	
fist		glass	

Time Problems

A Draw the hands on the clock showing the time given below each.

4:00 o'clock

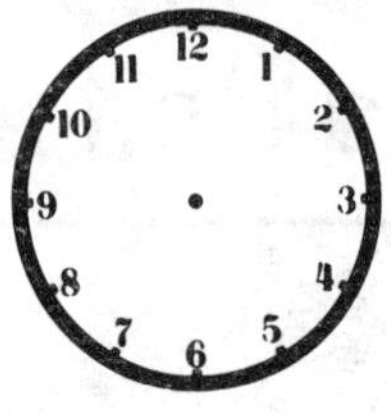

9:30 o'clock

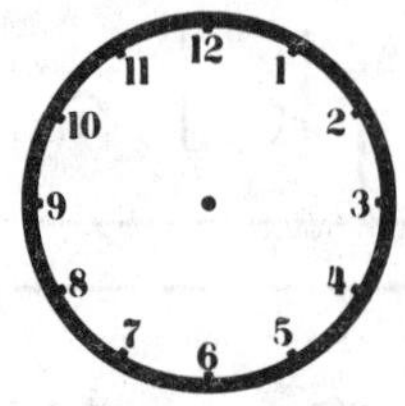

11:00 o'clock

10:30 o'clock

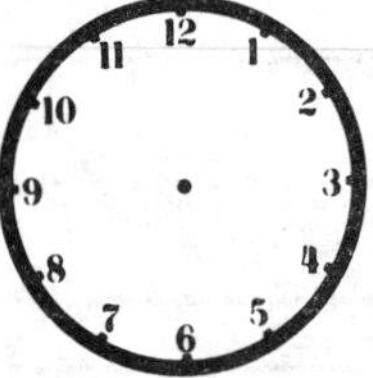

2:00 o'clock

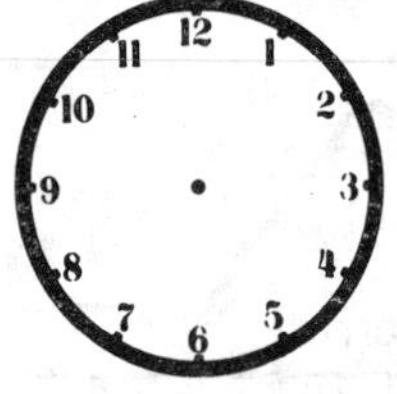

3:30 o'clock

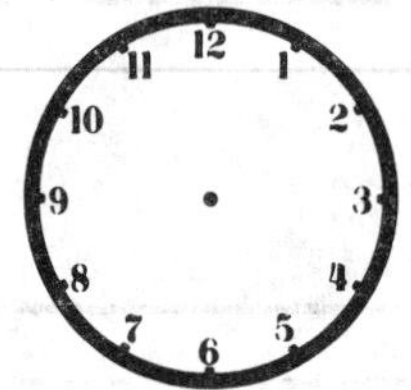

5:00 o'clock

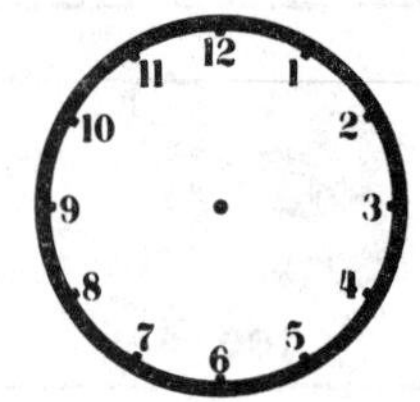

4:30 o'clock

B Write the number of each clock on the blank beside the correct time.

1. 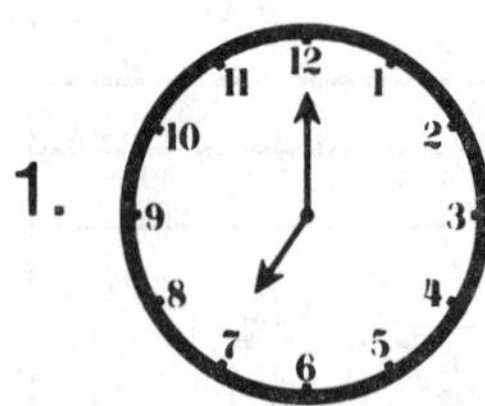

2. 

3. 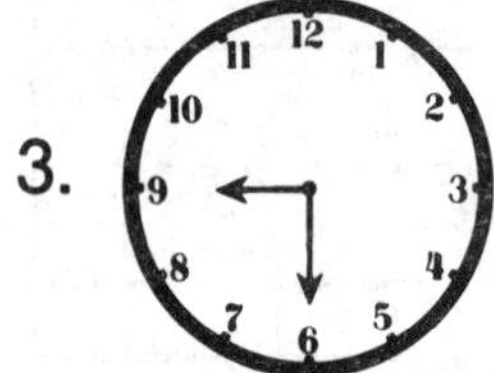

4. 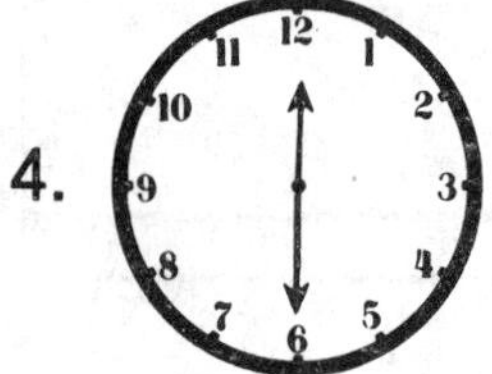

____ 12:30 o'clock

____ 7:00 o'clock

____ 2:00 o'clock

____ 9:30 o'clock

C Draw a line from each clock to the clock with the same time.

1.

a. 

b. 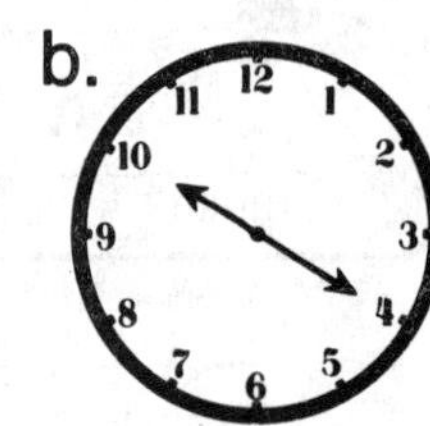

2.

c. 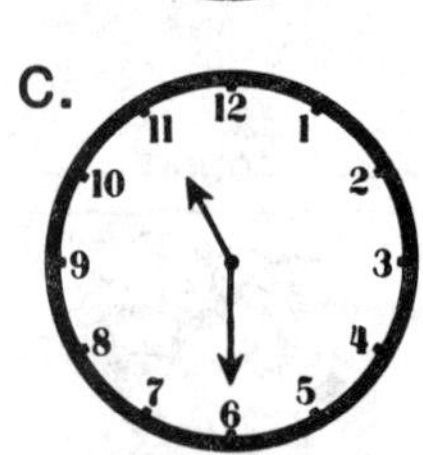

3.

d. 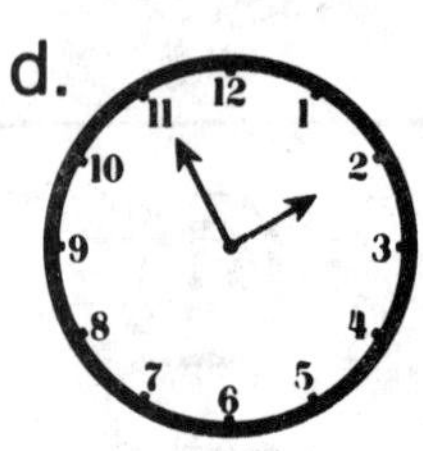

4.

5. 

e. 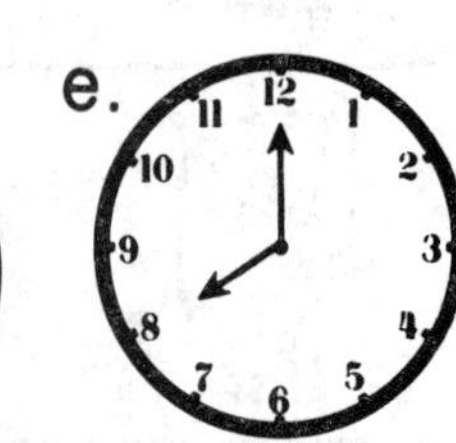

The Earth's Land Parts

desert

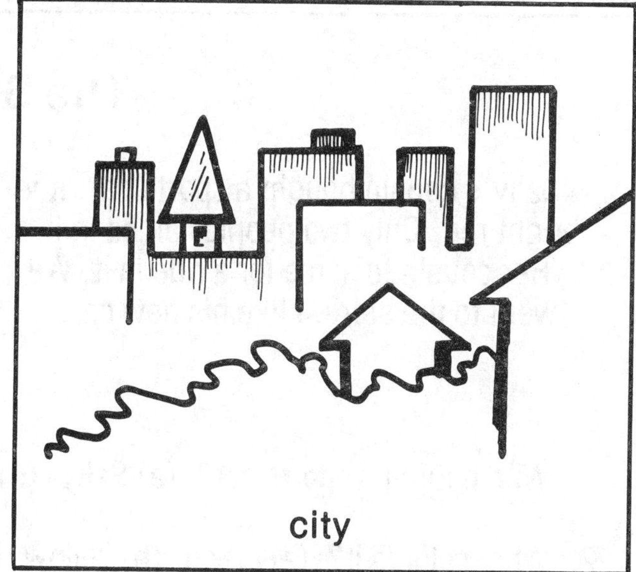
city

Do you live in one of these places? Tell about the place, and color the picture. Write each place.

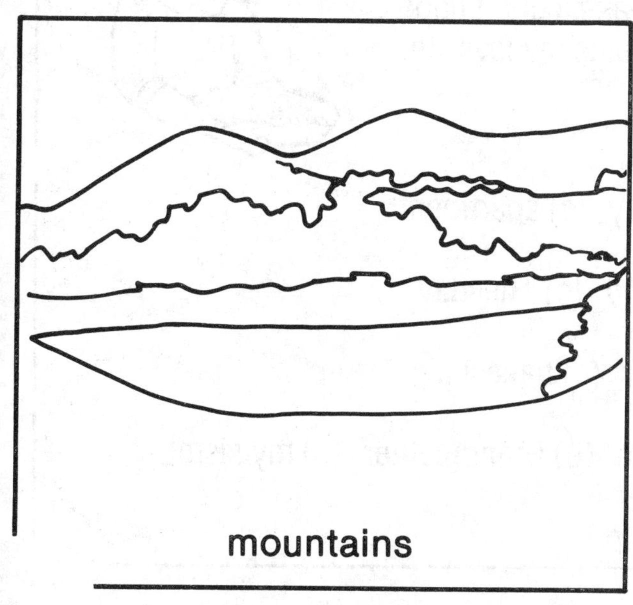
mountains

farm

We Like Stories

Read each story, and underline the correct answers. If you have problems, read the story again.

The Sports Car

Sally's cousin bought a sports car. It is bright red. Only two people can sit in it. Her cousin took me for a ride in it. We went to the store. I like his new car.

1. Who bought a sports car? (a) Sally (b) Sally's cousin (c) Sally's brother
2. What color is it? (a) green (b) yellow (c) red
3. How many people can sit in it? (a) two (b) four (c) one
4. Where did we go? (a) library (b) movies (c) grocery store

A Visit with Grandmother

I like to visit Grandmother. She lives on a farm. I will spend the weekend with her. I am going to learn to bake a pie. I hope we make a cherry pie. That is my favorite.

1. Where does Grandmother live? (a) farm (b) city (c) apartment
2. When will I visit? (a) next summer (b) weekend (c) Tuesday
3. What will I do? (a) milk a cow (b) churn butter (c) bake a pie
4. Who will teach me to bake a pie? (a) Aunt Millie (b) Grandmother (c) my sister

Using Picture Words

Look at each picture, and say the word. Write the word in the blank.

a b c d e f g h i j k l m n o p q r s t u v w x y z

sailor — sailor	weak
cab	father
nurse	could
act	sink
club	lumber
glad	snail
false	away
week	meal

Air Is Everywhere

The following sentences tell about air. Can you put these words in the sentences?

above	caught	inside	moves	pushes	turns

1. Air is caught inside the glass.

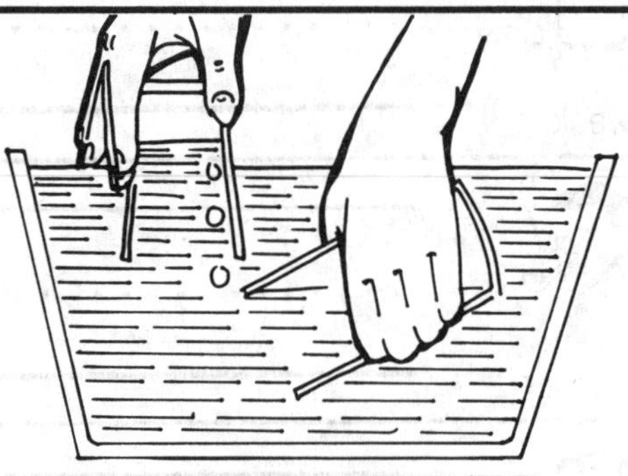

2. Air ______ the sailboat.

3. Air is several miles ______ the earth. It keeps the man from falling too fast.

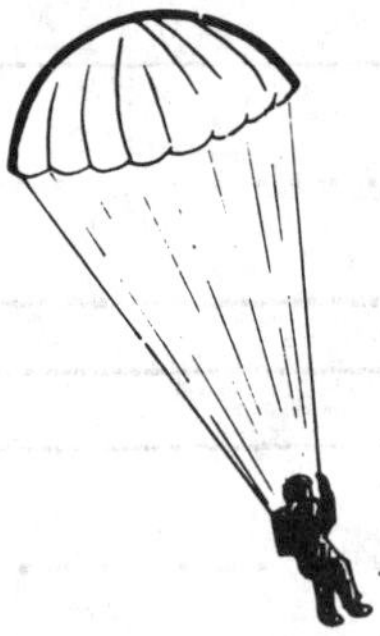

4. Air is ______ the football.

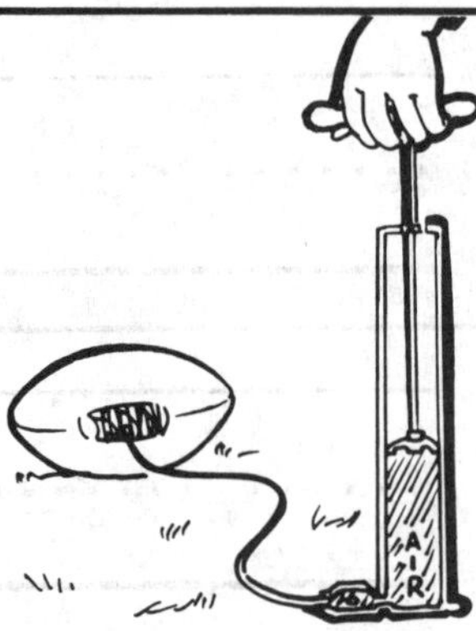

5. Air ______ the windmill that pumps water from the ground.

6. Air ______ into the glass as the liquid is sipped into the mouth.

Using Naming Words

Look at each picture, and say the word. Write the word in the blank.

a b c d e f g h i j k l m n o p q r s t u v w x y z

wood — wood	dance
would	knight
small	night
turtle	sky
droop	glide
flame	pretty
daddy	forest
stare	camel

Objects of Different Colors

Some objects have only one color because they have only one part. Others may have more than one part and more than one color.

Write the name of the objects below in the blanks. Color them the way you think they should be.

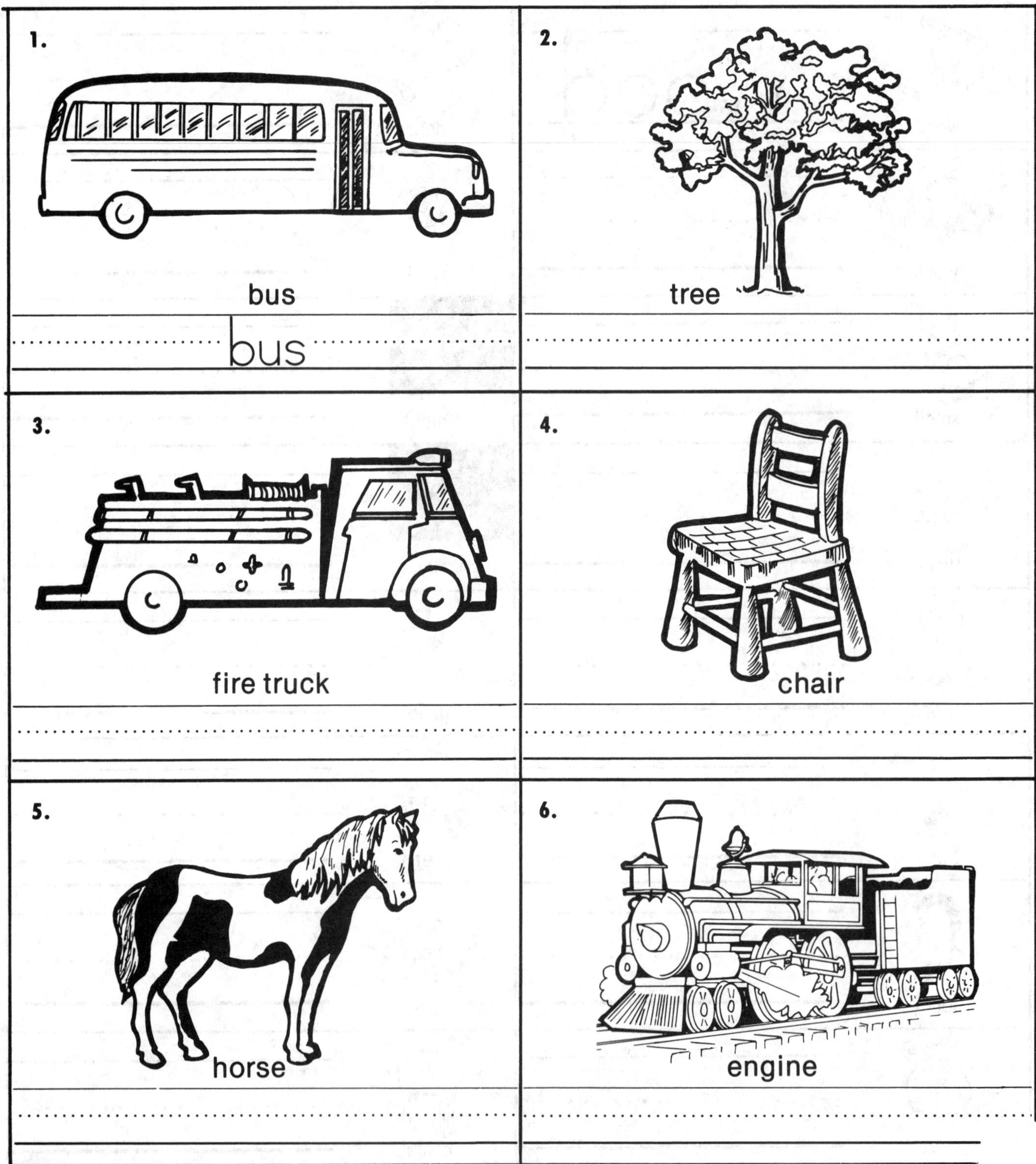

Having Fun with Stories

Read each story, and underline the correct answers. If you have problems, read the story again.

Geese

Wild geese fly south for the winter. In the spring they fly north again. Some go as far north as the Arctic Circle.

Tame geese are raised by farmers. Some of them make good pets.

Geese are smart. They mate for life. Some live as long as 30 years.

1. Which geese fly south for the winter? (a) wild (b) tame (c) white
2. When do they fly north again? (a) winter (b) fall (c) spring
3. How far north do some fly? (a) Wisconsin (b) Arctic Circle (c) Canada
4. How long may geese live? (a) 12 years (b) 30 years (c) 65 years

Teri Fixes Breakfast

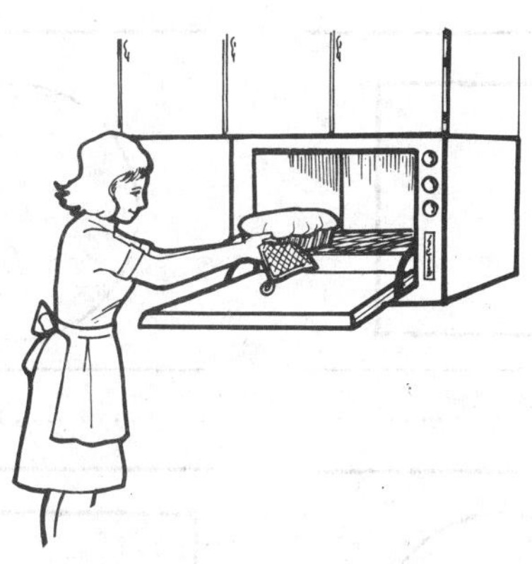

Teri decides to fix her own breakfast for one week. Her mother helps her plan her menus. They decide what Teri should eat each morning. A good breakfast keeps Teri from getting tired during the morning. It gives her energy to work and play. It helps her feel good all day.

1. What is the story about? (a) school (b) fixing breakfast (c) playing
2. How long will Teri fix her breakfast? (a) one week (b) one day (c) one month
3. Who helps Teri decide her menus? (a) Mother (b) teacher (c) friend
4. A good breakfast furnishes (a) sleep (b) exercise (c) energy.

Plane Figures

A triangle has 3 sides.

A square has 4 equal sides and 4 equal angles.

A circle is shaped like a ring.

A rectangle has 4 sides. 2 are usually longer than the other 2.

square triangle rectangle circle

Write the name of each plane figure. See samples.

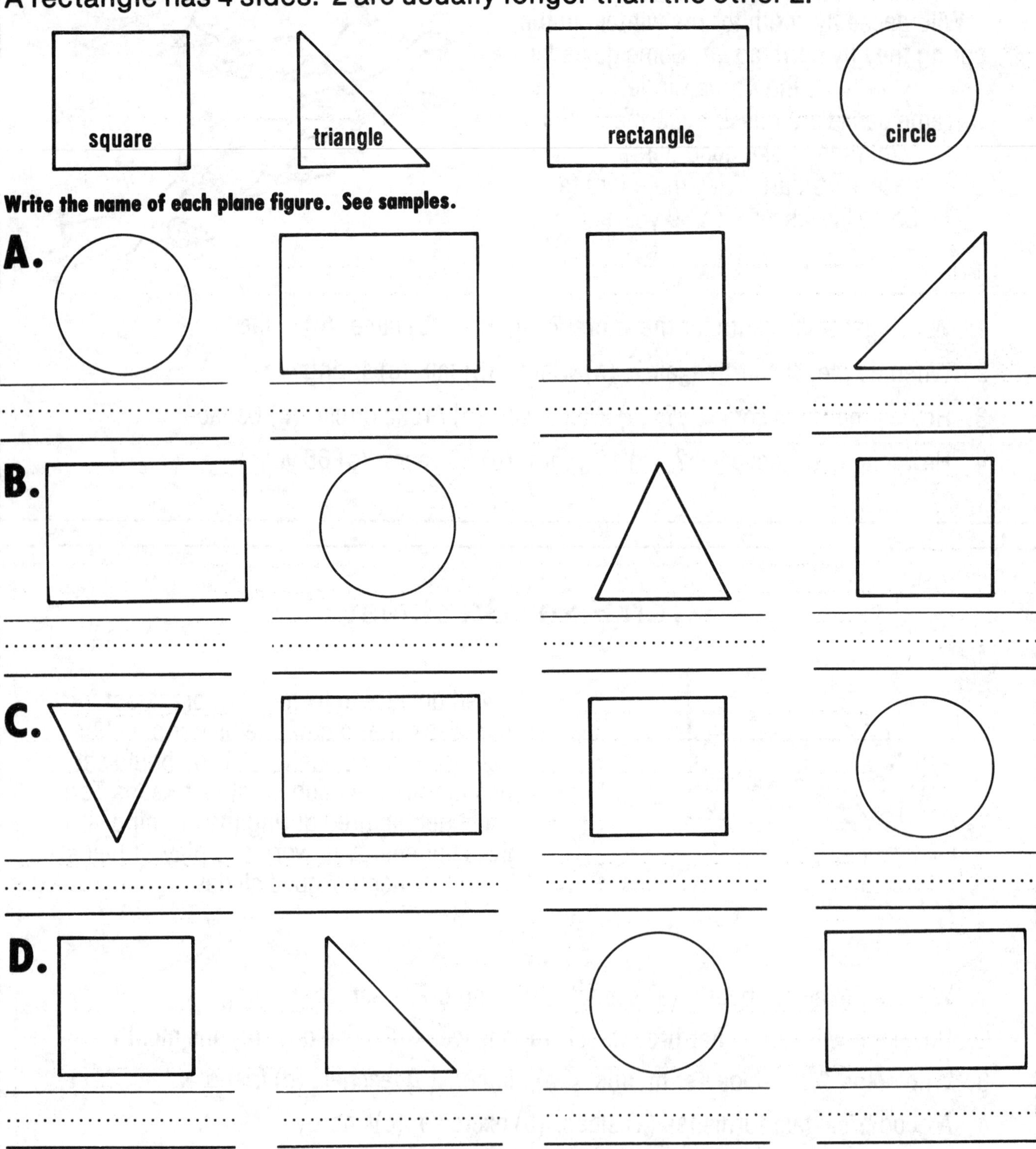

Correctly Spelled Words

Look at each picture, and say the word. Write the word in the blank.

a b c d e f g h i j k l m n o p q r s t u v w x y z

river	river	snake	
pouch		hut	
hollow		rag	
donkey		store	
spot		lips	
cabin		pond	
little		glasses	
oil		glove	

Do You Know?

A **Write the alphabet in lower-case letters.**

B **Alphabetize these words.**

beg

apple

fox

cart

hotel

event

deliver

golf

in

angry

green

C **Write two statements about your home. Don't forget to use capital letters at the beginnings and periods at the ends.**

Reading Comprehension

Read each story, and underline the correct answers. If you have problems, read the story again.

Our Family

Our family works and plays together. Mother takes care of the house. Two days a week she works in a hospital.

Dad goes to his office every day. He also takes care of the yard and paints the house.

My brother and I help both our parents. Then our parents take us many different places. Our family has good times together.

1. Mother works in a (a) school (b) church (c) hospital.
2. Where does Dad work? (a) office (b) factory (c) bakery
3. My brother and I help (a) each other (b) both parents (c) our friends.
4. Where do our parents take us? (a) zoo (b) different places (c) nowhere

The Dictionary

The dictionary is very helpful. It helps me spell words. It also teaches me what words mean.

At home I have my own dictionary. I keep it on my desk. I use it most when I write letters.

1. The dictionary is (a) helpful (b) dull (c) useless.
2. What helps me spell words? (a) magazine (b) dictionary (c) almanac
3. Where do I keep my dictionary? (a) desk (b) bookcase (c) drawer
4. When do I use my dictionary most? (a) reading (b) helping Mother (c) writing letters

Arithmetic Word Problems

Write the correct answers to the problems. See example "A."

A. 1 apple costs 10 ¢. 2 apples cost 20 ¢. 3 apples cost 30 ¢.	**G.** 1 cap costs 50¢. 1 hat costs 75¢. Which costs more? ____
B. 1 chicken costs 30 ¢. 2 chickens cost ____ ¢. 3 chickens cost ____ ¢.	**H.** 1 balloon costs $.05. How much will 5 cost? ____ ¢
C. 1 cone costs 12 ¢. 2 cones cost ____ ¢. 3 cones cost ____ ¢.	**I.** 12 cookies cost 24 ¢. How much does one cost? ____ ¢
D. 1 ball costs 18 ¢. 2 balls cost ____ ¢. 3 balls cost ____ ¢.	**J.** ☐ ☐ ☐ ☐ ☐ Which coin is worth more? ____
E. 1 candy bar costs 7 ¢. 2 candy bars cost ____ ¢. 3 candy bars cost ____ ¢.	**K.** Which is longer? 1 mile ____ 1 foot ____ 1 yard ____ 1 inch ____
F. Mary bought 5 lollipops for a dime. How much did one cost? ____ ¢	**L.** Which weighs more? 1 ounce ____ 1 pound ____ 1 ton ____

The Reindeer

Look at the boxes. Say, spell, and write each word. Read the story, and fill in the blanks. Reread the story if you have trouble.

1. reindeer

2. strong

3. sled

4. snow

5. horse

6. sheep

Reindeer live in the cold country of Lapland. They are very strong, fast-moving animals that love the cold. They find their food under the snow. The people of the North are glad to have reindeer. Our farm animals could not live in this cold country.

In Lapland, reindeer take the place of sheep and cows. Their skins are used to make warm clothes for the people. Their milk is given to babies.

Reindeer also take the place of horses. They are able to pull heavy sleds over the snow.

THINGS TO REMEMBER

1. Reindeer are ____________, fast-moving animals.
2. They live in ____________ places.
3. Their ____________ can be used for clothes.
4. Babies in Lapland drink reindeer ____________.
5. Reindeer can run ____________.
6. Reindeer can pull heavy ____________.

7. farm

8. cold

9. cow

10. food

11. clothes

12. baby

Public Places

You need to show respect for and take care of public places. It is important to keep places clean so other people might enjoy them. There are many public places that people use. Children play in the parks and on the playgrounds. They also visit the zoo and the swimming pools. Many people like to have picnics in the woods. Others like to read in the library and look at things in the museum.

Use one of the six places, and make a sign about each public place. See example "A."

1. playgrounds
2. library
3. zoo
4. woods
5. lake
6. swimming pool
7. museum

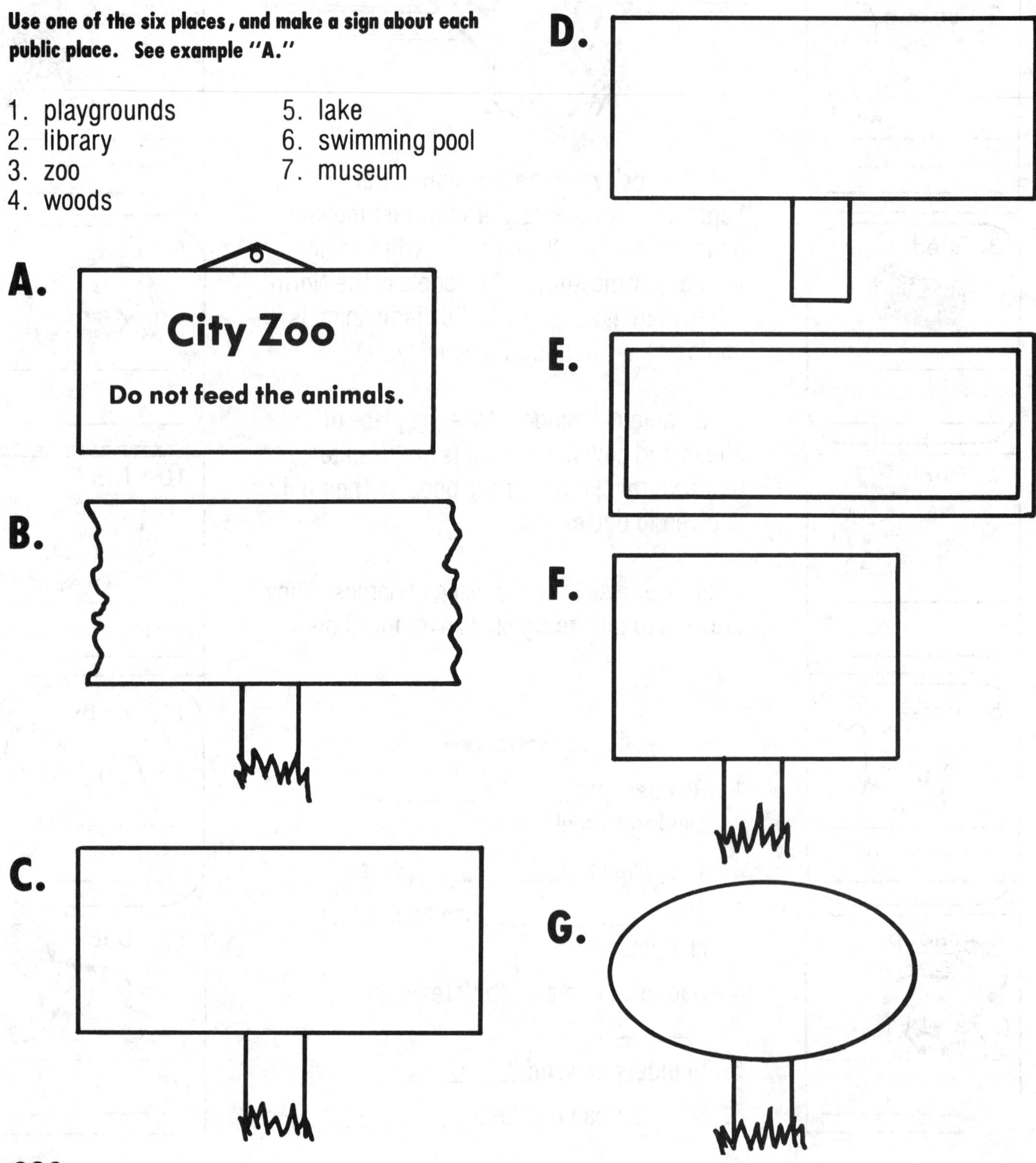

Arithmetic Word Problems

Write the correct answers to the problems. See sample "A."

A.

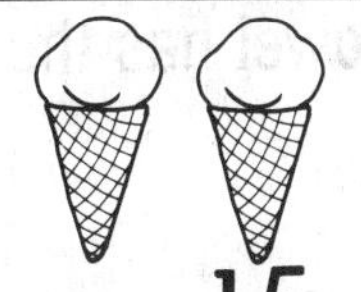

1 costs 15 ¢
2 cost 30 ¢
3 cost 45 ¢
4 cost 60 ¢

B.

1 costs 10 ¢
2 cost ____ ¢
3 cost ____ ¢
4 cost ____ ¢

C.

1 costs ____ ¢
2 cost 12 ¢
3 cost ____ ¢
4 cost ____ ¢

D. Mrs. Brooks asked her pupils to bring fudge to the bake sale. Sally brought 14 pieces, Pam brought 12, and Peggy brought 10. How many pieces of fudge were brought all together? ____

E. Tamee Jo had 45¢. She bought a candy bar for 15¢ and bubble gum for 4¢. How much money did she have left? ____ ¢

F.

1 costs 13 ¢
2 cost ____ ¢
3 cost ____ ¢
4 cost ____ ¢

G.

1 costs ____ ¢
2 cost 50 ¢
3 cost ____ ¢
4 cost ____ ¢

H.

1 costs 35 ¢
2 cost ____ ¢
3 cost ____ ¢
4 cost ____ ¢

I.

1 costs 50 ¢
2 cost ____ ¢
3 cost ____ ¢
4 cost ____ ¢

J. Rhonda jumped rope 10 times, Rita jumped 5 times, and Linda jumped 7 times. How many times did all three girls jump? ____

K. Jimmy has 4 white rabbits, 3 black rabbits, and 5 black-and-white rabbits. How many rabbits does Jimmy have? ____

Vowel Sounds

A **Mark the first long (—) or short (˘) vowel in each of the following words. See samples "1" and "2."**

Vowels are the letters "a," "e," "i," "o," and "u." The long vowel has the sound of its alphabet name.

1. păn
2. cāne
3. bled
4. men
5. mean
6. shake
7. tube
8. wake
9. key
10. note
11. night
12. bread
13. coat
14. tea
15. fix
16. main
17. final
18. funny
19. nap
20. open
21. doctor
22. go
23. five
24. made

B **In each of the following pairs of words, write the word in which you hear the short vowel sound. See samples "1" and "2."**

1. ten	eat	ten	
2. use	us	us	
3. meat	mat		
4. mad	mate		
5. car	case		
6. meet	met		
7. lock	open		
8. pine	pin		
9. trail	tract		
10. plate	cup		
11. dime	dim		
12. note	not		
13. kite	fix		
14. man	main		
15. might	milk		
16. coat	cot		
17. fast	slow		
18. maid	nap		
19. up	tube		
20. yes	no		

C **Underline each vowel, and mark it as a long vowel sound.**

j b f a n u p s c e v d g i h k o q m t w

How Does Jack Feel?

A **Below are four faces. Choose from the word list the correct word that describes each expression, and write it in the blank below each one.**

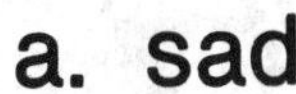

a. sad	b. happy	c. mad	d. sleepy

1. 

2.

3.

4.

________________ ________________ ________________ ________________

B **Match the words that are alike. Draw a line from each word to the word it matches in the word list.**

1. cross	a. tired
2. scared	b. angry
3. sleepy	c. laugh
4. happy	d. afraid
5. smile	e. glad

Counting Money

Write in the correct amount of money.

= 1¢  = 5¢ 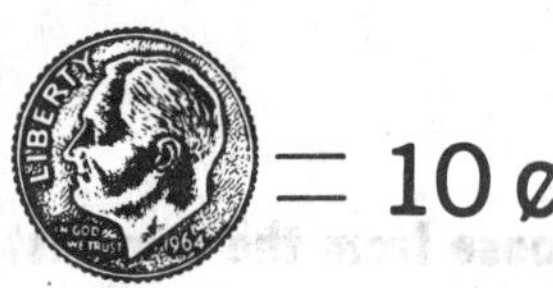 = 10¢ = 25¢

A.  = ___¢  = ___¢  = ___¢

B.  = ___¢ 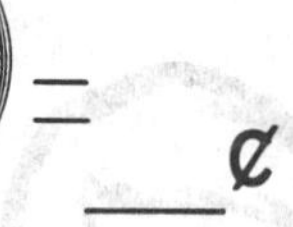 = ___¢  = ___¢

C.  = ___¢ = ___¢  = ___¢

D.  = ___¢ = ___¢  = ___¢

E. 1 nickel + 3 pennies = ___¢ 2 dimes + 4 pennies = ___¢

F. 1 quarter + 2 nickels = ___¢ 3 dimes + 2 nickels = ___¢

G. 3 dimes + 2 quarters = ___¢ 3 nickels + 4 pennies = ___¢

H. 3 quarters + 2 nickels = ___¢ 1 quarter + 3 dimes = ___¢

I. 5 nickels + 3 pennies = ___¢ 2 dimes + 6 pennies = ___¢

J. 3 quarters + 2 dimes = ___¢ 3 nickels + 2 dimes = ___¢

Where You Live

A **Write in the information about you and where you live.**

I live on this street. ____________________

I live in this city. ____________________

I live on the ____________________ side of the street.

I live in this state. ____________________

My name is ____________________.

My address is ____________________.

My zip code is ____________________.

My next-door neighbor is ____________________.

B **Write your name and address on the mailbox.**

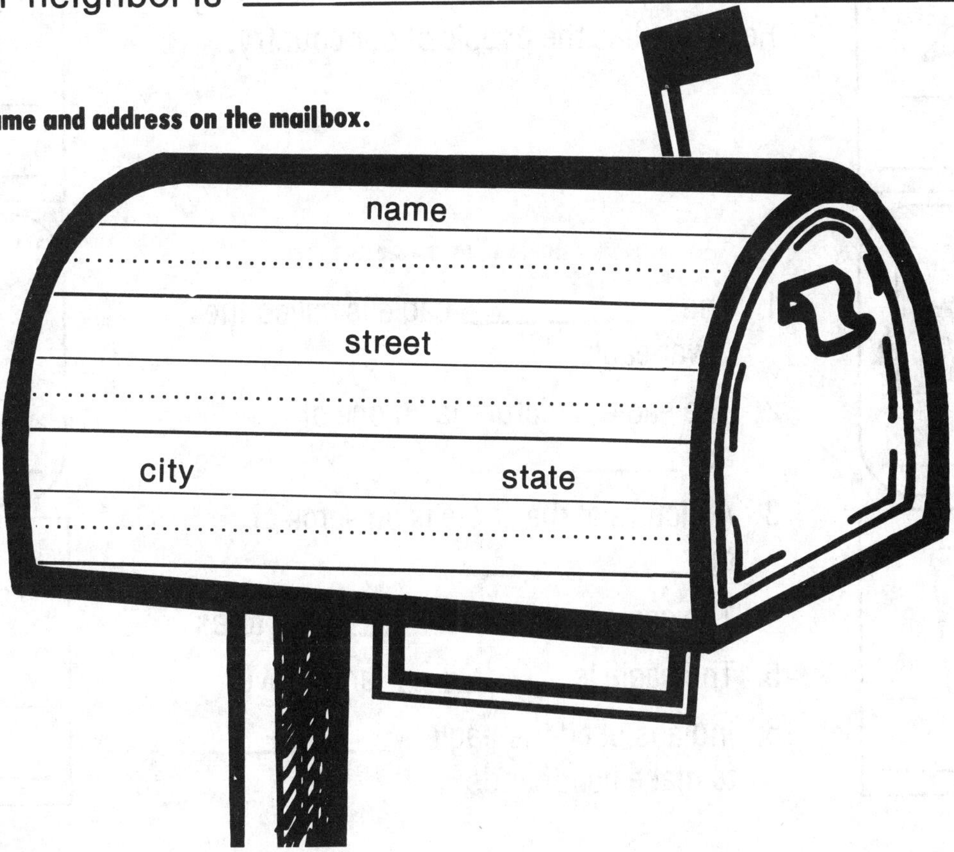

name

street

city state

The Eagle

Look at the boxes. Say, spell, and write each word. Read the story, and fill in the blanks. Reread the story if you have trouble.

Two kinds of eagles live in our country. The bald eagle is the one seen in many pictures. This bird builds his nest in tall trees. His nest is always close to water.

The golden eagle is another eagle. Many people call him the ''war eagle.'' His feathers were once used by the Indians to make headbands for war.

The eagle is a large bird. He is very strong and brave. In our country his picture is on one of our flags and also on some of our money. He is free like the people of our country.

1. Indian

2. eagle

3. water

4. feather

5. picture

6. flag

7. bird

8. trees

9. money

10. nest

11. headband

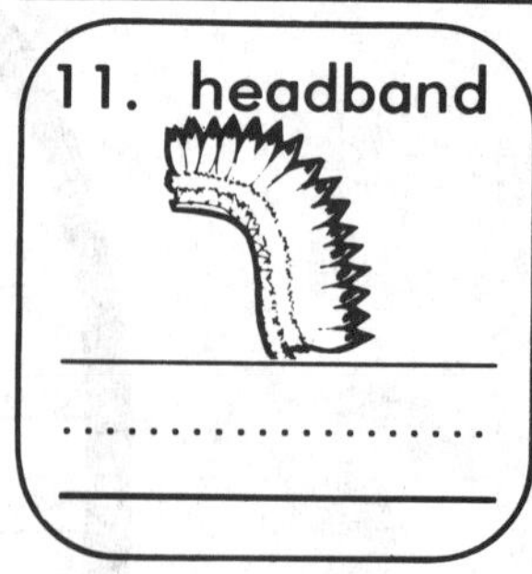

12. tall

THINGS TO REMEMBER

1. The ____________ eagle is called the ''war eagle.''
2. The eagle's picture is on one of our ____________.
3. A picture of the eagle is on some of our ____________.
4. The eagle builds his ________ in trees.
5. The eagle is __________ and brave.
6. Indians used the eagle's ____________ to make headbands.

Two-Letter Vowel Sounds "oo"

Sometimes two vowels work together to make a sound. The sound you hear in "room" is the long sound of "oo." The sound you hear in "book" is the short sound of "oo."

A **Look at the pictures. Write the name of each picture in the blank. Say each name, and listen to the sound of the "oo." If the sound is long, make a long mark over the "o͞o." If the sound is short, draw a curved mark over the "o͝o."**

EXAMPLE:	1.	2.	3.
bo͝ok			
4.	**5.**	**6.**	**7.**

B **Fill in each blank with an "oo" word. Use the words from the pictures. See sample "1."**

1. The moon shines in the sky at night.
2. Cowboys wear ________ instead of shoes.
3. We eat lunch at ________.
4. We have some ________ to eat.
5. We need ________ to build a fire.
6. The tree has long ________.
7. If you brush your teeth, you will have less ________ decay.

Supply Rhyming Words

Underline all the words that rhyme in each box.

A.	B.	C.
1. cat 2. fat 3. ball 4. sat	1. meal 2. bell 3. steal 4. deal	1. boy 2. ring 3. toy 4. joy

D.	E.	F.
1. toe 2. go 3. be 4. so	1. tree 2. shoe 3. me 4. see	1. head 2. bed 3. yellow 4. red

G.	H.	I.
1. bump 2. song 3. thump 4. lump	1. nose 2. finger 3. rose 4. goes	1. town 2. black 3. brown 4. down

J.	K.	L.
1. hay 2. lay 3. stay 4. here	1. book 2. look 3. up 4. took	1. door 2. more 3. roar 4. bear

Money Problems

Write the amount of money in each collection.

Is there enough money in the two collections to buy the toy? Write "yes" or "no." See example "A."

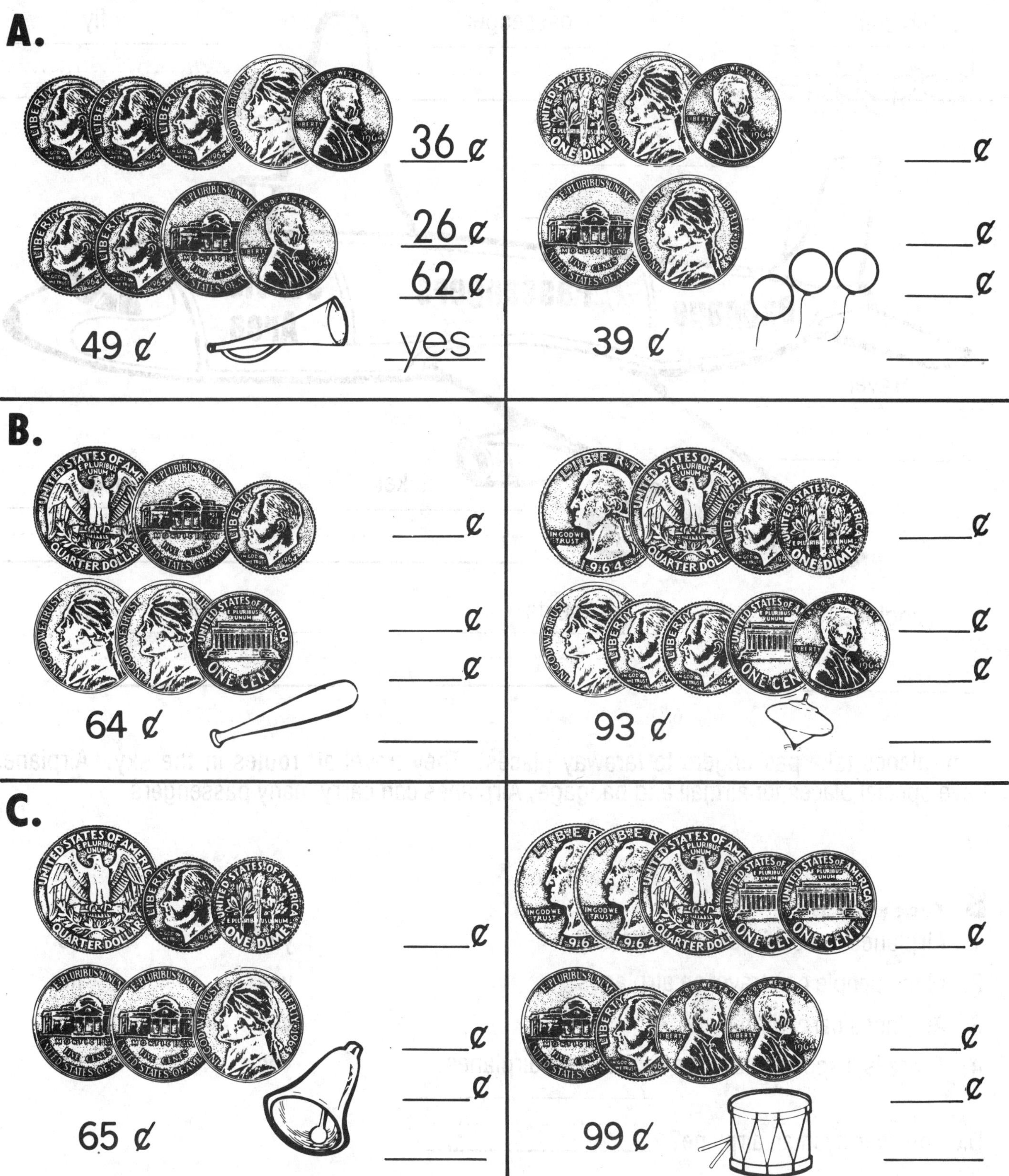

Airplanes

A **Rewrite the words about airplanes.**

baggage

baggage

passenger

fly

pilot

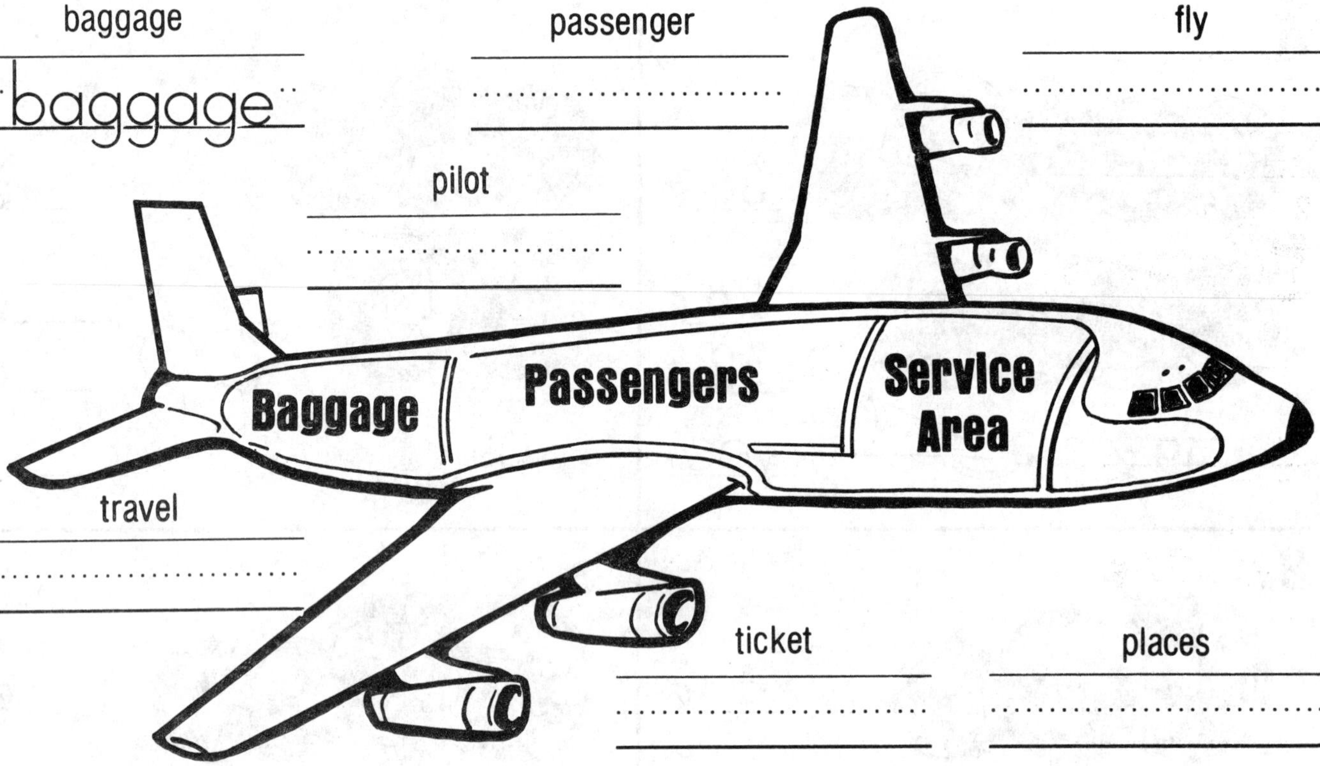

Baggage

Passengers

Service Area

travel

ticket

places

engines

seats

wings

Airplanes take passengers to faraway places. They travel air routes in the sky. Airplanes have special places for airmail and baggage. Airplanes can carry many passengers.

B **Circle yes or no.**

1. Airplanes travel air routes in the sky.	yes	no
2. Many people can travel on airplanes.	yes	no
3. Airplanes carry airmail.	yes	no
4. There is a special place for baggage on airplanes.	yes	no

Did you ever fly in an airplane? __________

What kind? __________

The Snake

Look at the boxes. Say, spell, and write each word. Read the story, and fill in the blanks. Reread the story if you have trouble.

The snake is an interesting animal. It is able to swallow things much bigger than itself. Even a small snake can swallow bird eggs without breaking them.

The snake can move very fast. It has no arms or legs and is able to feel with its tongue.

A snake can grow a new skin. It just slides out of the old coat when the new skin has grown. The snake does this many times in one year.

Most snakes are helpful. They eat bugs and mice. Bugs and mice are harmful to farmers. Only poisonous snakes are not good to have around.

THINGS TO REMEMBER

1. The snake can slide out of its old __________.
2. The snake can move very __________.
3. Snakes eat __________ and bugs.
4. A snake grows many new __________ each year.
5. The snake feels with its __________.
6. A snake can swallow animals __________ than itself.

1. skin

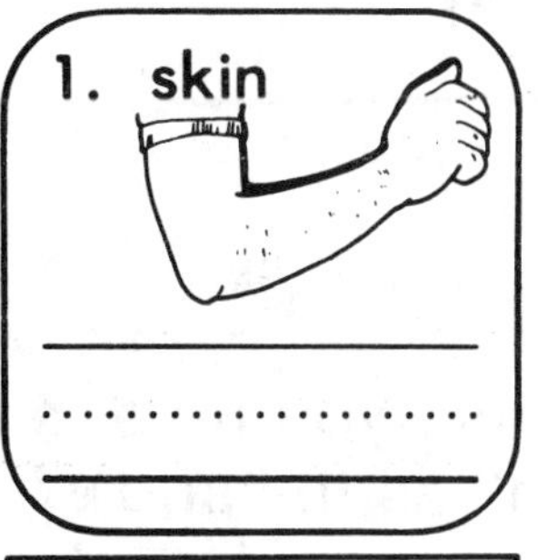

2. snake

3. tongue

4. arms

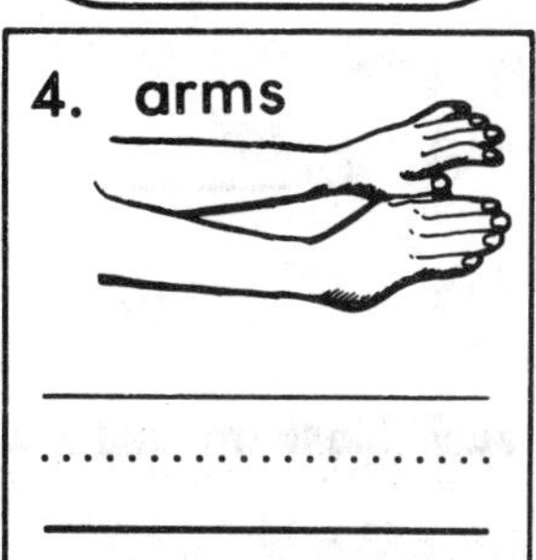

5. eggs

6. bird

7. swallow

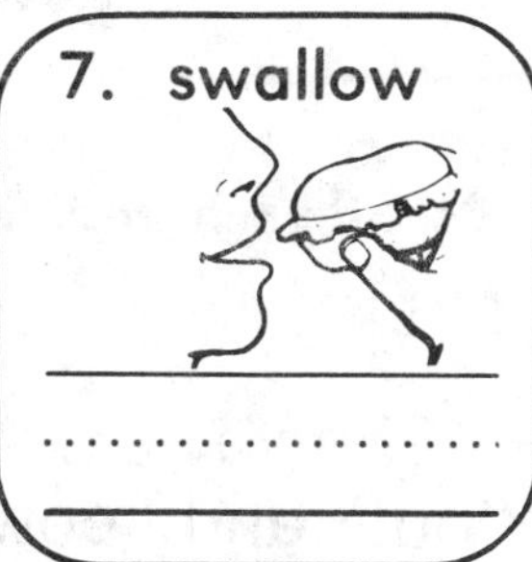

8. legs

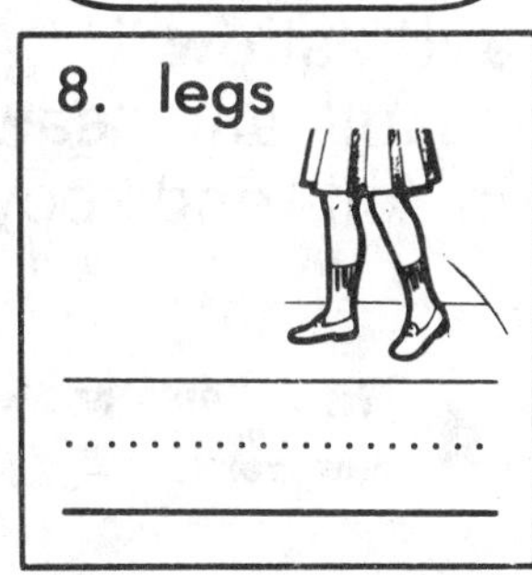

9. animal

10. farmer

11. bugs

12. mice

Vowel Sounds "ou," "ow," "au," "aw," "oi," "oy"

Read the paragraph carefully before completing each of the following sections.

The vowels, "ou" and "ow" work together to make the sound you here in "out" and "cow." Sometimes you hear the long sound of "o" as in "snow" and "show." "Au" and "aw" work together to make the sound you hear in "haul" and "saw." "Oi" and "oy" work together to make the sound you hear in "oil" and "boy."

A **Write "ou" or "ow" in each blank to make a new word.**

1. n_OW_
2. l______d
3. h______
4. cl______d
5. s______th
6. t______n
7. m______th
8. d______n

B **Write "ow" in each blank to make a word that has the "o" sound.**

1. ______n
2. b______l
3. sl______
4. l______
5. r______
6. cr______
7. gr______
8. bl______

C **Write "au" or "aw" in each blank below to make a new word.**

1. l______n
2. dr______
3. c______se
4. y______n
5. j______
6. f______lt
7. l______
8. c______ght

D **Write "oi" or "oy" in each blank to make a new word.**

1. b______l
2. j______
3. t______
4. sp______l
5. b______
6. p______nt
7. j______n
8. s______l

Listening with Eyes

Write in the correct word from the word list.

left	quiet	stop
happy	hurt	hello
love	sad	turn

1. turn

2.

3.

4.

5.

6.

7.

8.

9.

Odd Tens, Counting by 10's to 1,000

Write the odd tens in the blanks.

10	20	30	40	___	60	___	80	___	100
___	120	___	140	___	160	___	180	___	200
___	220	___	240	___	260	___	280	___	300
___	320	___	340	___	360	___	380	___	400
___	420	___	440	___	460	___	480	___	500
___	520	___	540	___	560	___	580	___	600
___	620	___	640	___	660	___	680	___	700
___	720	___	740	___	760	___	780	___	800
___	820	___	840	___	860	___	880	___	900
___	920	___	940	___	960	___	980	___	1,000

Buses

A **Rewrite these words.**

bus — bus

ride

driver

terminal

baggage

Bus Terminal

B **Read the story, and answer each statement yes or no.**

The bus in the picture will take the people on long trips. It travels from city to city. The bus will only stop long enough to let its passengers rest and eat.

There are other kinds of buses. The school bus takes children to school. The city bus takes its passengers along city streets. The church bus takes its passengers to church each Sunday.

1. The church bus takes its passengers along city streets each day. yes no
2. There are different kinds of buses. yes no
3. Some buses travel from city to city. yes no
4. School buses take children to church. yes no

What kinds of buses do you see in your neighborhood? ______

All About Salt

Look at the boxes. Say, spell, and write each word. Read the story, and fill in the blanks. Reread the story if you have trouble.

Salt is clean, white, and beautiful. People cannot live without it. Animals also need salt.

People in some countries get salt from the sea. They dig deep holes in the ground. These holes are filled with sea water. The sun dries up the water, and salt is left on the ground.

Some of our salt comes from salt wells. Salt wells are like deep water wells. Pipes bring the salt to the top.

Most of our salt comes from salt mines under the ground. Sometimes, men have to dig very deep to find the salt.

THINGS TO REMEMBER

1. The color of salt is __________.
2. We get salt from __________ wells.
3. Salt comes from __________ the ground.
4. Salt __________ are under the ground.
5. Men must dig __________ to find salt.
6. People and __________ need salt.

1. salt

2. people

3. top

4. well

5. water

6. pipe

7. hole

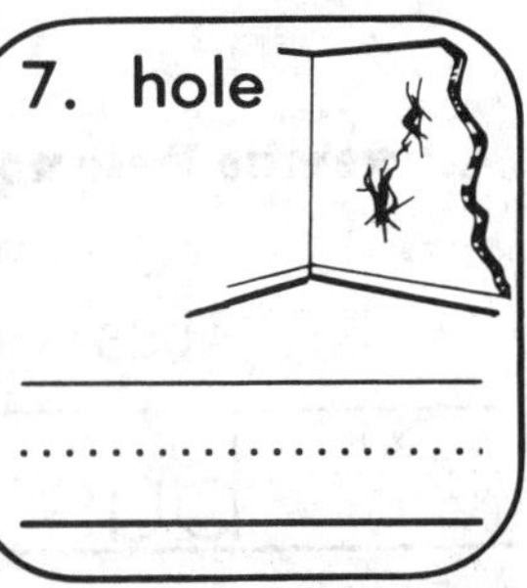

8. sea

9. sun

10. dig

11. ground

12. deep

Recognizing Long Vowels

The long vowel sound says its name. When a vowel is at the end of a word, it is usually long. Sometimes the "y" is a vowel because it sounds like "i."

A **Underline the long vowel in each word. See the sample.**

SAMPLE: sky	4. we	8. go	12. sly
1. me	5. so	9. use	13. be
2. fly	6. light	10. no	14. tray
3. hay	7. fry	11. way	15. wild

B **Complete each sentence by writing the correct word that has a long vowel sound. See sample "1."**

1. The baby will __cry__.	a. cry	b. talk	c. crawl
2. Birds can ________.	a. swim	b. sing	c. fly
3. I can _______ to the picnic.	a. swim	b. crawl	c. go
4. Give the puppy to _______.	a. me	b. us	c. him
5. Look at the clouds in the _______.	a. water	b. sky	c. picture
6. _________ cat is sick.	a. My	b. His	c. Our

A Listening Poster

A **Write the correct word from the word list.**

1. Always sit ___still___ .
2. Never ______________ when someone else is talking.
3. Pay ______________ .
4. Be ______________ .
5. Keep ______________ quiet in your lap.

A. polite
B. attention
C. hands
D. still
E. interrupt

B **Draw a line to the correct picture that tells the helper in each sentence.**

A. are to hear with

B. are to blink

C. help us to hold things

D. help us think

E. help to carry

F. will walk

G. can help one talk

1. heads
2. feet
3. eyes
4. ears
5. lips, teeth, tongue
6. arms
7. thumbs

Counting by 10's to 1,000 (Even 10's)

Write the even tens in the blanks.

10	20	30	40	50	___	70	___	90	___
110	___	130	___	150	___	170	___	190	___
210	___	230	___	250	___	270	___	290	___
310	___	330	___	350	___	370	___	390	___
410	___	430	___	450	___	470	___	490	___
510	___	530	___	550	___	570	___	590	___
610	___	630	___	650	___	670	___	690	___
710	___	730	___	750	___	770	___	790	___
810	___	830	___	850	___	870	___	890	___
910	___	930	___	950	___	970	___	990	___

Traveling by Train

Rewrite these words.

train

tracks

baggage

travel

passenger

engineer

The train in the picture is a passenger train. It takes people on long trips. This train travels from city to city. Sometimes passengers travel all day.

When the train travels to faraway places, the passengers may ride for several days and nights. They eat and sleep on the train.

Read the story, and answer these questions.

1. Have you ever been to a train station? ______ Where? ______
2. Who drives a train? ______
3. Have you ever ridden on a train? ______ Where? ______

Write a short paragraph about a train.

Beagles

Look at the boxes. Say, spell, and write each word. Read the story, and fill in the blanks. Reread the story if you have trouble.

Beagles are popular dogs. They are small dogs with floppy ears, short legs, and big sad eyes. They have smooth, white coats with big black and brown patches.

Beagles are usually thought of as hunting dogs. They like to chase rabbits. Their short legs help them run fast.

Beagles make good pets too. They are very gentle and friendly. They like to run and play with children. Beagles are good watchdogs. Beagles are very popular dogs!

THINGS TO REMEMBER

1. Beagles have __________ ears.
2. Beagles are usually thought of as __________ dogs.
3. Beagles are very __________ and __________.
4. Beagles like to chase __________.
5. __________ like to run and play with children.
6. Beagles are also good __________.

Following Vowels with "R"

Vowels are hard to hear when followed by "r." "Ar" has the sound you hear in "far." "Ir" has the sound you hear in "stir." "Ur" has the sound you hear in "purse." "Er" has the sound you hear in "her." "Or" has the sound you hear in "for."

Put each word under the correct sound in the proper column. Circle each word used. See the samples.

farm	skirt	for	yard	term	turn	curl
every	girl	far	sir	clerk	nurse	dirt
first	church	or	water	purse	fir	barn
whirl	stork	shirt	her	stir	fern	park
cork	germ	curve	north	burn	hammer	
dark	sport	fur	hurt	bark	summer	

"ir" sound	"ar" sound	"er" sound	"ur" sound	"or" sound
shirt	farm	germ	fur	cork

Music for Quiet Time

Write the name of each instrument. Use the words in the box.

piano	bicycle	banjo	calliope	typewriter	clock
telephone	harp	guitar	trumpet	stereo	radio

< Means "Is Less Than"

Write this sign (<) in each blank if the first number is less than the second number. See sample "A."

A. 3 _<_ 4	**B.** 8 ____ 2	**C.** 2 ____ 8
D. 4 ____ 0	**E.** 6 ____ 4	**F.** 4 ____ 6
G. 7 ____ 9	**H.** 0 ____ 7	**I.** 8 ____ 9
J. 1 ____ 4	**K.** 5 ____ 4	**L.** 4 ____ 5
M. 1 ____ 3	**N.** 3 ____ 1	**O.** 0 ____ 1
P. 5 ____ 6	**Q.** 10 ____ 11	**R.** 9 ____ 8
S. 12 ____ 13	**T.** 13 ____ 11	**U.** 18 ____ 20
V. 22 ____ 25	**W.** 31 ____ 28	**X.** 36 ____ 38
Y. 45 ____ 49	**Z.** 39 ____ 41	**A.** 48 ____ 101

The Post Office

A **Rewrite these words.**

postage

postage

zip code

postmaster

stamp

mail

ZIP CODES

U.S. MAIL

There are many mailmen who work at the post office. Some mailmen work during the daytime. Other mailmen work at night.

The mailmen put marks on the letters. Then, they put the letters into mailbags. Soon, a mail truck picks up the mailbags and delivers the mail.

B **Read the story, and draw a box around yes or no.**

1. All the mailmen work at night.	yes	no
2. The letters are put into boxes.	yes	no
3. Some mailmen work at night.	yes	no
4. The mailmen put marks on the letters.	yes	no
5. A mail truck picks up the mailbags.	yes	no
6. There are many men who work at the post office.	yes	no
7. Have you ever been in your neighborhood post office?	yes	no

Pictures in Caves

Look at the boxes. Say, spell, and write each word. Read the story, and fill in the blanks. Reread the story if you have trouble.

Men that lived long ago did not know how to build houses. Many of them lived in caves. The caves were warm and dry.

Cave men did not have stores. They could not buy clothes or food. They hunted wild animals. The cave men used animal skins to make clothes. They ate the meat of these animals.

Many old caves have been found. We know that cave men could not write, but they did draw pictures. These pictures tell stories about their lives. They were drawn on the stone walls in the caves. We have learned many things about cave men from their pictures.

THINGS TO REMEMBER

1. Cave pictures tell __________.
2. Before men knew how to build houses, they lived in __________.
3. They drew the pictures on the __________.
4. Cave men did not have __________.
5. The caves kept the men __________ and __________.
6. Cave men could not __________.

1. cave

2. store

3. skin

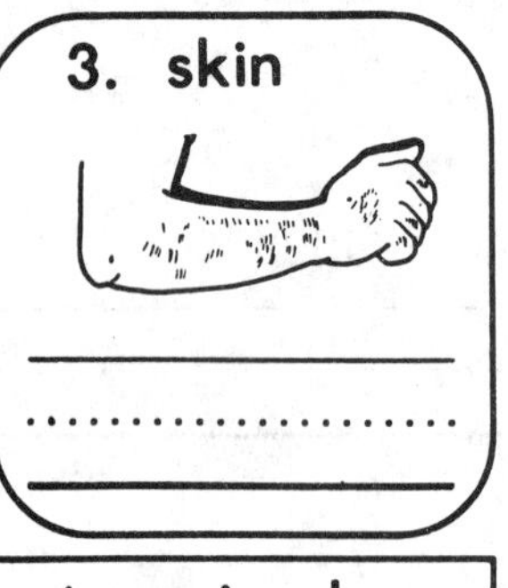

4. animal

5. food

6. clothes

7. stones

8. picture

9. house

10. hunt

11. wall

12. story

Beginning or Final Sounds

In many words you may hear two or more consonants together at the beginning or end of a word. They are called consonant blends.

A **In each of the following, write the beginning sound or blend in column I and the final sound or blend in column II. See sample "1."**

B **In the following words underline the consonants. See samples "1" and "2."**

1. tub
2. bear
3. log
4. moon
5. lion
6. seal
7. bean
8. jug
9. mat
10. book
11. wood
12. deer
13. pail
14. cot
15. pear

Applying What You Know

A **Put an "X" on the picture that is different from the others.**

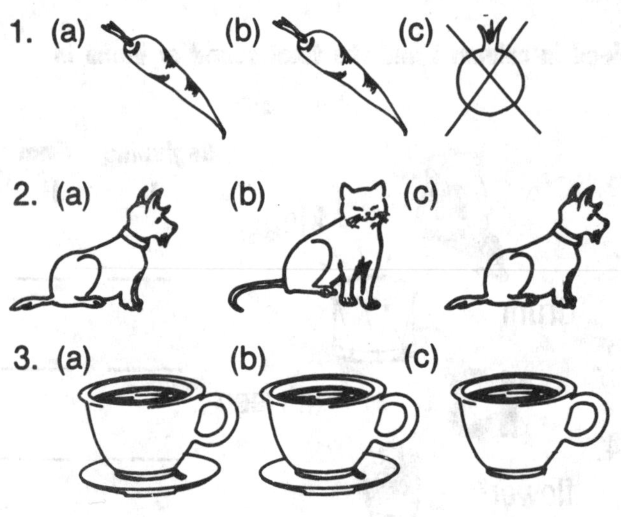

B **Choose the biggest object in each row, and draw a box around it.**

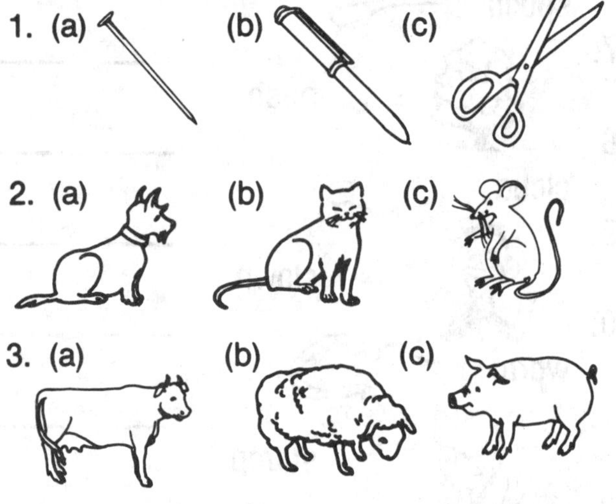

C **Put an "X" on the pictures in each row which can best be classified with the picture in the box on the left.**

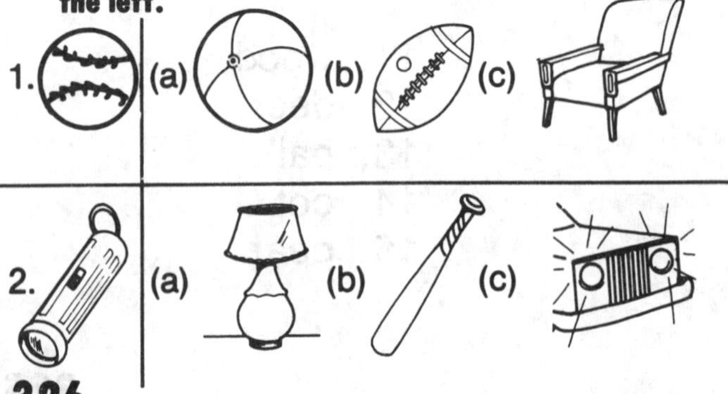

D **Which comes first? Number each set of pictures in the correct order.**

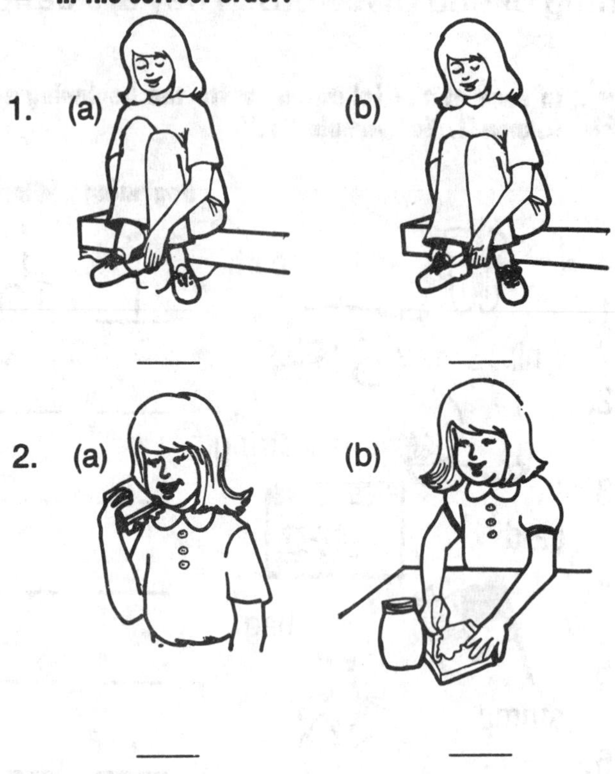

E **Read the poem, and answer the questions. Underline the correct answer for each question.**

Three Guests

I had a little tea party,
This afternoon at three;
'Twas very small,
Three guests in all,
Just I, myself, and me.

Jessica Nelson North

1. What time was the party?
   12 o'clock 3 o'clock
2. What kind of party was it?
   tea birthday
3. Who else was at the party besides I and myself?
   mother me

> Means "Is Greater Than"

Write this sign (>) in each blank if the first number is greater than the second number. See example "A."

A. 4 ___>___ 3	B. 8 ______ 6	C. 5 ______ 7
D. 17 ______ 12	E. 20 ______ 10	F. 15 ______ 14
G. 27 ______ 26	H. 39 ______ 36	I. 88 ______ 87
J. 22 ______ 21	K. 49 ______ 45	L. 16 ______ 19
M. 59 ______ 58	N. 47 ______ 48	O. 35 ______ 30
P. 63 ______ 64	Q. 69 ______ 68	R. 93 ______ 91
S. 81 ______ 80	T. 96 ______ 97	U. 74 ______ 76
V. 73 ______ 70	W. 82 ______ 79	X. 51 ______ 25
Y. 40 ______ 30	Z. 27 ______ 23	A. 22 ______ 29

The Supermarket

The supermarket is a helpful place to shop. It is a big store where we go to buy our food. Most people shop by pushing a basket up and down the aisles. They select the items they need as they go down the aisles.

Make a list of the things you buy at a supermarket. Write those things.

1. ____________________ 6. ____________________

2. ____________________ 7. ____________________

3. ____________________ 8. ____________________

4. ____________________ 9. ____________________

5. ____________________ 10. ____________________

Autumn

Look at the boxes. Say, spell, and write each word. Read the story, and fill in the blanks. Reread the story if you have trouble.

1. leaves

2. cold

3. ground

4. squirrel

5. birds

6. fly

When autumn comes, we know that winter will soon follow. The air gets cool and brisk. Leaves on trees turn red and gold and brown. Frost covers the ground in the mornings.

Animals know that winter is coming too. Squirrels gather nuts and store them for winter. Other animals build winter homes. Many birds fly south to escape the winter cold.

People get ready for winter also. Farmers work hard in the autumn. They must harvest their crops before the cold weather comes. It seems that everyone is busy in the autumn!

7. south

8. frost

9. farmer

10. crop

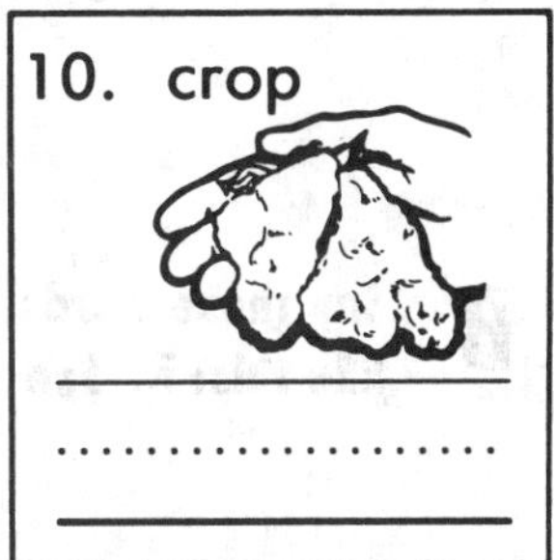

11. nuts

12. home

THINGS TO REMEMBER

1. In the autumn, ___________ covers the ground in the mornings.
2. Squirrels gather _______________ in the autumn.
3. When autumn comes, we know that ___________ will soon follow.
4. Many birds fly ___________ to escape the winter cold.
5. _____________ work hard in the autumn.
6. ___________ turn red and gold and brown in the autumn.

Consonant and Vowel Sounds

A

Finish each word by writing "ch," "sh," "th," or "wh" in the blank. See sample "1."

1. su<u>ch</u>
2. ______ase
3. ______ite
4. ______is
5. ______an
6. rea______
7. wi______
8. tra______
9. ______ade
10. ______ink

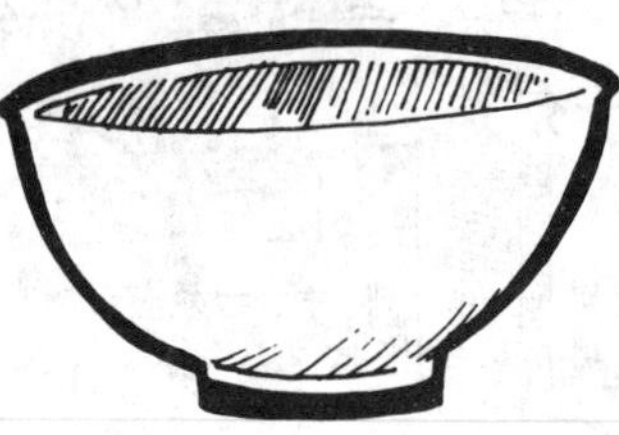

11. ea______
12. di______
13. ______ile
14. ______ine
15. fre______
16. bran______
17. mu______
18. tea______
19. ri______
20. tra______

B

Say these words. Listen to the vowel sounds. Mark each short vowel like this: ă. Mark each long vowel like this: ā. See samples "1" and "2."

1. săng
2. sāy
3. tent
4. thick
5. rock
6. rag
7. pan
8. nut
9. bat
10. his

11. fan
12. on
13. am
14. just
15. hot
16. pin
17. no
18. ran
19. slow
20. we

Repeating Instructions

A Draw a line from each sentence to the correct picture.

1. The cat is playing with a ball.
2. The boy is wearing a hat.
3. The girl is reading.

a. 

b. 

c. 

4. The dog is sleeping.
5. The fox is running.
6. The duck is swimming.

a. 

b. 

c. 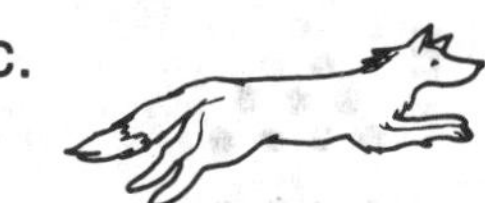

B Underline the rhyming words in each line.

1. ran	run	tan	top
2. pen	rake	cake	book
3. moon	spoon	rug	hook
4. car	bug	fat	jar
5. house	top	fish	mop
6. cat	book	rat	bat
7. car	box	fox	bug
8. fan	two	man	ran
9. boat	goat	cat	dog
10. see	boy	wall	tall

C Read the sentences, and draw a line through the one that does not belong.

1. (a) It is raining.
   (b) The ground is wet.
   (c) I like to read.

2. (a) Sam likes to play baseball.
   (b) Red is a color.
   (c) He has a good bat.

3. (a) The tree is big.
   (b) I like to fly a kite.
   (c) The wind carries the kite into the sky.

4. (a) My cat's name is Fluff.
   (b) This apple is good.
   (c) She has long fur.

5. (a) I like to watch TV.
   (b) It is two o'clock.
   (c) Some of the shows are funny.

6. (a) It is a warm day.
   (b) I would like to go for a swim.
   (c) John drinks milk.

7. (a) A truck is large.
   (b) An airplane flies in the sky.
   (c) It looks like a bird.

8. (a) Jane went to the candy store.
   (b) She bought some gum.
   (c) I like to help mother.

Writing Numerals

Write in the blank the number for each set. See examples "A," "B," and "C."

A. 37	B. 23	C. 60	D. ____
E. ____	F. ____	G. ____	H. ____
I. ____	J. ____	K. ____	L. ____
M. ____	N. ____	O. ____	P. ____
Q. ____	R. ____	S. ____	T. ____
U. ____	V. ____	W. ____	X. ____

Starfish

Look at the boxes. Say, spell, and write each word. Read the story, and fill in the blanks. Reread the story if you have trouble.

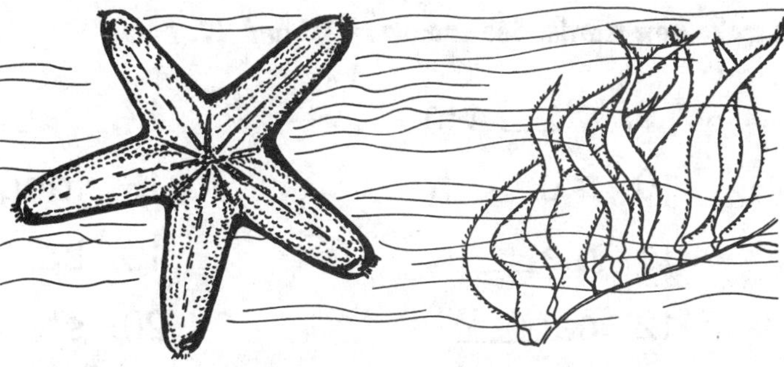

Some people think starfish are fish that look like stars. They are really animals that look like stars and that live in the sea as fish do.

The starfish is an amazing little animal. It has five or more arms. One eye is at the tip of each arm. If one arm is lost, a starfish can grow a new arm. If a starfish is cut in two, a new starfish will grow from each piece!

Starfish have a hard, spiny covering. They are pretty when they are dry. Children often find them on the beach and take them home.

THINGS TO REMEMBER

1. Starfish are really __________ that look like stars.
2. Starfish have a hard, spiny __________.
3. The starfish has __________ or more arms.
4. Starfish live in the __________.
5. At the tip of each arm, the starfish has an __________.
6. If a starfish is cut in two, a new __________ will grow from each piece.

1. five

2. sea

3. pretty

4. dry

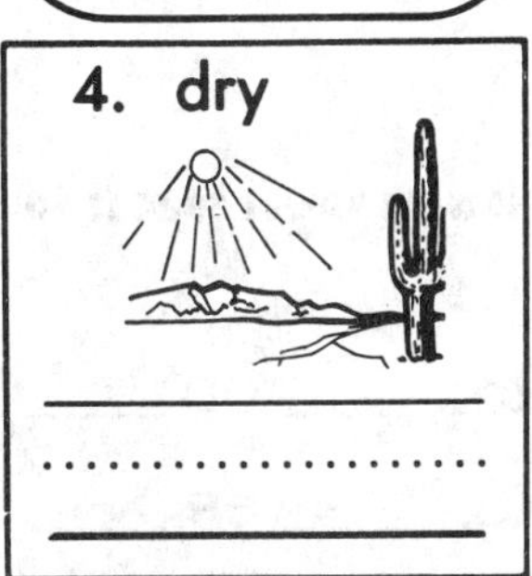

5. eye

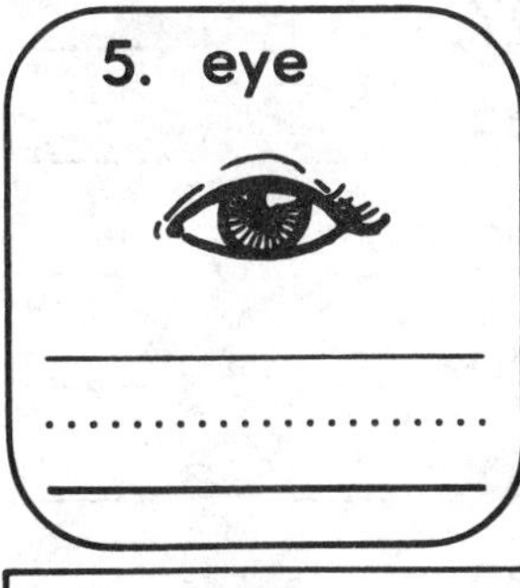

6. star

7. covering

8. fish

9. starfish

10. arm

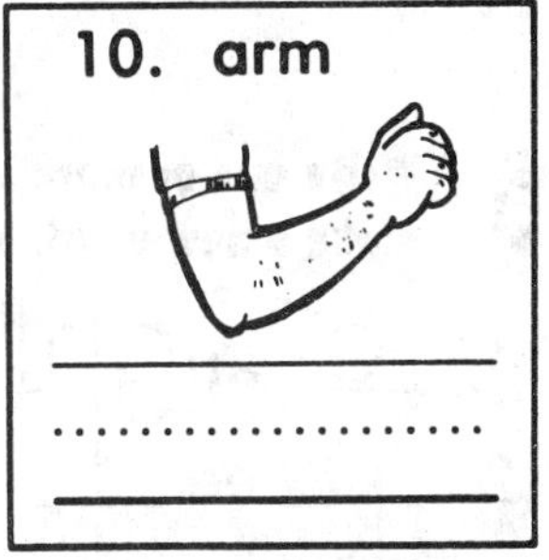

11. beach

12. spiny

Making Words

A **Add the missing letters to make new words. See samples "1" and "2."**

1. Soap
2. fresh
3. cl____ck
4. c____rn
5. cr____
6. pl____nt
7. box____s
8. penn____es
9. cl____wn
10. mu____h
11. pla____e
12. cal____
13. ____ime
14. cak____
15. ou____
16. glasse____
17. sai____
18. longes____
19. ba____h
20. sh____w
21. st____r
22. oi____
23. h____lp
24. th____nk

B **Write one or more initial consonants and one or more final consonants for each of the following vowel sounds to make a new word. See samples "1," "2," and "3."**

1. c au ght
2. p ee t
3. p oo t
4. ____ or ____
5. ____ oi ____
6. ____ e ____
7. ____ a ____
8. ____ u ____
9. ____ ea ____
10. ____ ai ____
11. ____ ir ____
12. ____ i ____
13. ____ o ____
14. ____ oa ____
15. ____ ou ____
16. ____ oe ____
17. ____ e ____
18. ____ ur ____
19. ____ ie ____
20. ____ aw ____
21. ____ ow ____
22. ____ ar ____
23. ____ er ____
24. ____ e ____
25. ____ oo ____
26. ____ ee ____
27. ____ u ____
28. ____ a ____
29. ____ i ____
30. ____ o ____
31. ____ ea ____
32. ____ oa ____
33. ____ oe ____
34. ____ or ____
35. ____ au ____

Selecting Best Answers

A Draw a box around the biggest thing in each line.

1\. a.  b.  c.  d. 

2\. a.  b.  c.  d. 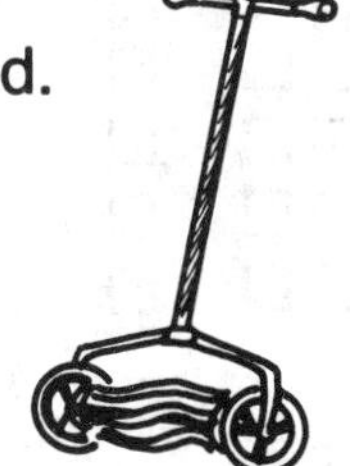

B Underline the true sentence beneath each picture.

1\.

(a) The boy is running.
(b) The boy is eating.
(c) The boy is sleeping.
(d) The boy is sitting.

2\.

(a) There are six birds.
(b) There are two birds.
(c) There are four birds.
(d) There are three birds.

3\.

(a) Mother is resting.
(b) Mother is cooking.
(c) Mother is reading.
(d) Mother is sewing.

C Write a check mark by the correct answer for each question.

1\. When does it snow?
____ (a) in summer
____ (b) in winter
____ (c) only at night

2\. How much are two and two?
____ (a) 5
____ (b) 4
____ (c) 3

3\. What game is played with a bat?
____ (a) baseball
____ (b) football
____ (c) kickball

4\. What day is the first day of the school week?
____ (a) Friday
____ (b) Sunday
____ (c) Monday

Ten + 1, 2, 3, 4, 5

Fill in each blank with the number of items in each set. See examples "A," "E," and "I."

A.	B.	C.	D.
11	____	____	____
E.	**F.**	**G.**	**H.**
15	____	____	____
I.	**J.**	**K.**	**L.**
10	____	____	____
M.	**N.**	**O.**	**P.**
____	____	____	____
Q.	**R.**	**S.**	**T.**
____	____	____	____
U.	**V.**	**W.**	**X.**
____	____	____	____

No Clothes for Animals

Look at the boxes. Say, spell, and write each word. Read the story, and fill in the blanks. Reread the story if you have trouble.

1. feather

2. bird

3. dog

4. hair

5. fluff

6. clothes

Have you ever wondered why animals don't wear clothes as people do? Well, animals have their own kind of clothes. They don't need clothes like people wear.

When birds are cold in the winter, they will fluff their feathers to hold the warm air in. Rabbits, dogs, and other animals just grow more hair to keep them warm in winter.

In summer, birds play in birdbaths to keep cool. Other animals lose the extra hair they had grown for winter. Dogs stick their tongues out when they are hot to let the cool air come into their mouths.

Animals wear their clothes all the time. They are not the kind of clothes that people wear.

THINGS TO REMEMBER

1. Some animals grow more ____________ in winter to keep them warm.
2. Animals have their own kind of ____________.
3. Birds play in ____________ in the summer.
4. A dog sticks its ____________ out when it is hot.
5. Animals do not need clothes like ____________ wear.
6. A bird can fluff its ____________ to keep warm air in.

7. time

8. birdbath

9. tongue

10. winter

11. mouth

12. extra

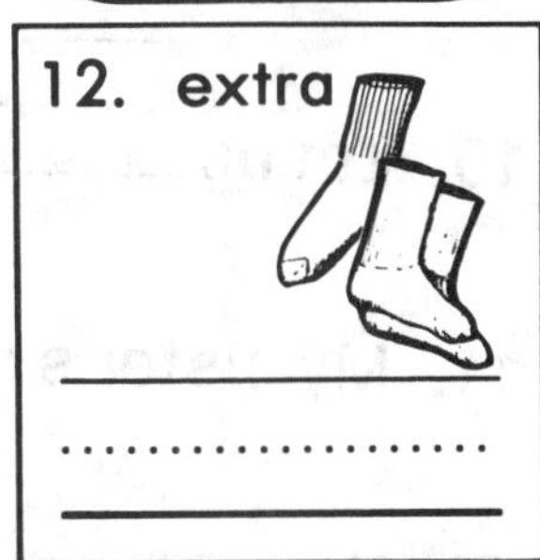

"le" Words

Complete each sentence by selecting the correct "le" word from the box. Fill in each blank. Use each word only once. Circle the word used. See sample "1."

raffle	handle	wrestle	eagle
bundle	candle	Myrtle	pickle
people	purple	settle	able

1. The frying pan has no handle.
2. Our church is having a cake ________.
3. The bald ________ is our national bird.
4. My new dress is ________.
5. I would like to eat a dill ________.
6. He does not want to arm ________ with you.
7. It is getting dark; light the ________.
8. Hand me that ________ of sticks.
9. There is a crowd of ________ at the picnic.
10. Let us ________ our argument at recess.
11. My sister's name is ________.
12. Will you be ________ to come to my party?

Taking Tests

Pretend this is a test your teacher has just passed out. Follow the directions carefully.

A **Draw lines between the words that match.**

1. here
2. cat
3. blue
4. girl
5. run

a. blue
b. girl
c. here
d. run
e. cat

B **Underline the word that matches the picture.**

1. a. ball b. doll
2. a. cat b. dog
3. a. car b. boat
4. a. ring b. bell
5. a. shoes b. socks

C **In each line draw boxes around all the words that begin with the same letter.**

1. play pig baby
2. with is work
3. boy bad girl
4. doll ride run
5. see look sad
6. big bag small

D **Look at the picture, and fill in each blank with the correct number.**

1. Here is ______ girl.
2. She has ______ balloons.
3. There are ______ birds.
4. There are ______ flowers.
5. ____ butterflies can be seen.
6. There are ____ clouds in the sky.

E **Yes or No**

______ 1. Two and two equals five.
______ 2. A frog can run.
______ 3. A doll is a toy.
______ 4. One is more than four.
______ 5. Winter is colder than summer.
______ 6. Pigs can fly.

Ten + 6, 7, 8, 9

Fill in each blank with the number of items in each set. See examples "A," "E," and "I."

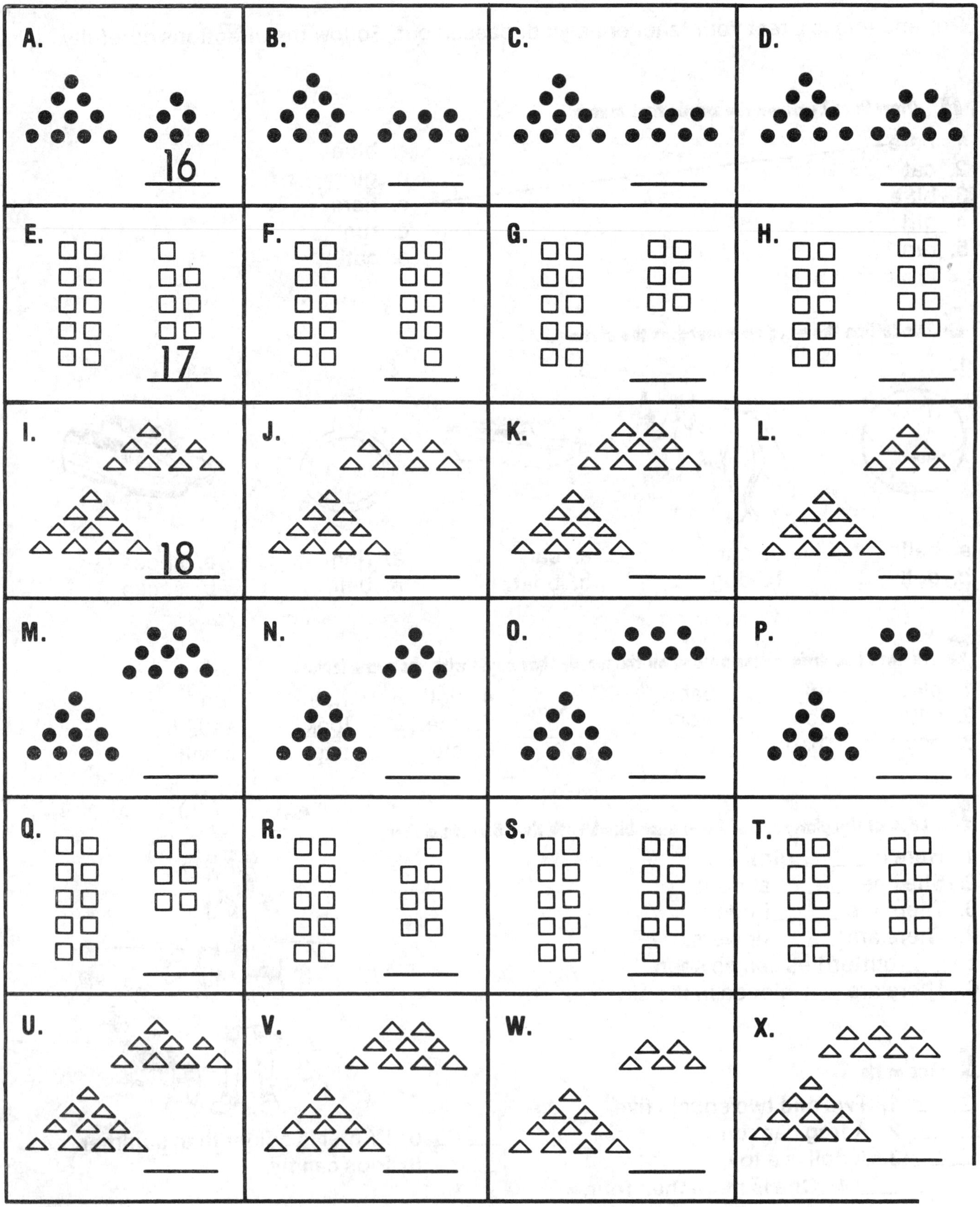

A. 16	B. ____	C. ____	D. ____
E. 17	F. ____	G. ____	H. ____
I. 18	J. ____	K. ____	L. ____
M. ____	N. ____	O. ____	P. ____
Q. ____	R. ____	S. ____	T. ____
U. ____	V. ____	W. ____	X. ____

1. pouch

2. kangaroo

3. tail

4. opossum

5. baby

6. size

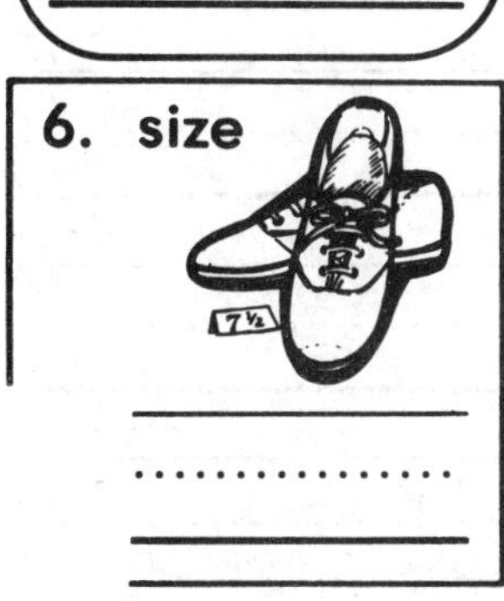

The Opossum

Look at the boxes. Say, spell, and write each word. Read the story, and fill in the blanks. Reread the story if you have trouble.

Have you every "played 'possum"? If you pretended to be asleep, you did. When an opossum is frightened, it rolls over and acts like it is dead.

An opossum is a small animal. It lives in trees. It sometimes hangs by its tail from a tree. The opossum rests in the daytime and hunts its food at night.

The mother opossum has a pouch like a kangaroo. She carries her babies in the pouch. They are very tiny babies at first. They are about the size of bees.

THINGS TO REMEMBER

1. When frightened, an opossum plays __________.
2. An opossum is a __________ animal.
3. It has a __________ like a kangaroo.
4. Opossum babies are about the size of __________.
5. The opossum hunts its food at __________.
6. An opossum can hang by its __________.

"er" and "est" Endings

To add "er" or "est" to a word that already ends in "e," we add only "r" or "st."

A **Add "er" and "est" endings to each word below. See sample "1."**

	"er"	"est"
1. cute	cuter	cutest
2. brave		
3. ripe		
4. pale		
5. nice		

To add "er" or "est" to a word ending in "y", change the "y" to "i" before adding "er" or "est."

B **Add "er" and "est" endings to the words below. See sample "1."**

	"er"	"est"
1. shiny	shinier	shiniest
2. silly		
3. fuzzy		
4. sleepy		
5. curly		

Following Poems

Read each of the poems on the page, and underline the correct answer for each question.

A. Twenty Froggies

Twenty froggies went to school,
Down beside a rushy pool.
Twenty little coats of green,
Twenty vests all white and clean.

George Cooper

1. Where did the froggies go?
   school church
2. How many frogs went?
   ten twenty
3. The frogs' coats were what color?
   black green

B. Three Guests

I had a little tea party,
This afternoon at three;
'Twas very small,
Three guests in all,
Just I, myself, and me.

Jessica Nelson North

1. What time was the party?
   12 o'clock 3 o'clock
2. What kind of party was it?
   tea birthday
3. Who else was at the party besides I and myself?
   mother me

C. The Little Turtle

There was a little turtle.
He lived in a box.
He swam in a puddle.
He climbed on the rocks.

Vachel Lindsay

1. Where did the little turtle live?
   a house a box
2. Where did the little turtle swim?
   in a puddle in a pond
3. What did the turtle climb on?
   a mountain the rocks

D. The Rainbow

Boats sail on the rivers,
And ships sail on the seas;
But clouds that sail across the sky
Are prettier far than these.

Christina Rossetti

1. Where do boats sail?
   lakes rivers
2. Where do ships sail?
   seas lakes
3. Where do clouds sail?
   ocean sky

E. Shore

Play on the seashore
And gather up shells,
Kneel in the damp sands
Digging wells.

Mary Britton Miller

1. What can be gathered at the seashore?
   shells leaves
2. How does the sand feel?
   dry damp
3. What can be dug in the sand?
   wells gold

Twenty + 6, 7, 8, 9

Write in the blank the correct number for each set. See examples "A," "E," and "I."

A. 26	B. ____	C. ____	D. ____
E. 27	F. ____	G. ____	H. ____
I. 28	J. ____	K. ____	L. ____
M. ____	N. ____	O. ____	P. ____
Q. ____	R. ____	S. ____	T. ____
U. ____	V. ____	W. ____	X. ____

The Spider's Web

Look at the boxes. Say, spell, and write each word. Read the story, and fill in the blanks. Reread the story if you have trouble.

1. threads

2. web

3. fly

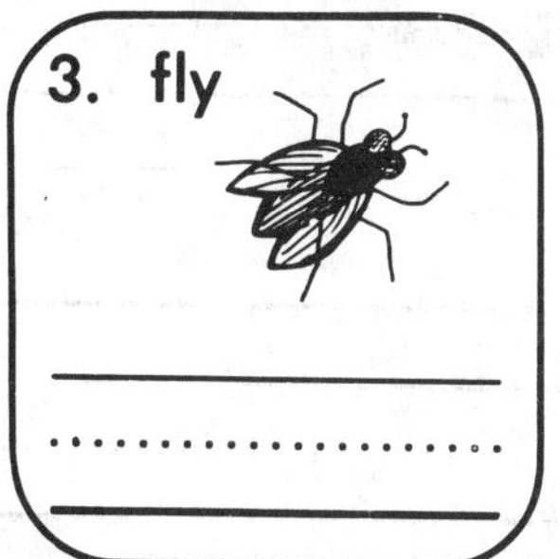

4. spider

5. sticky

6. food

7. run

8. catch

9. spin

10. thin

11. wind

12. meal

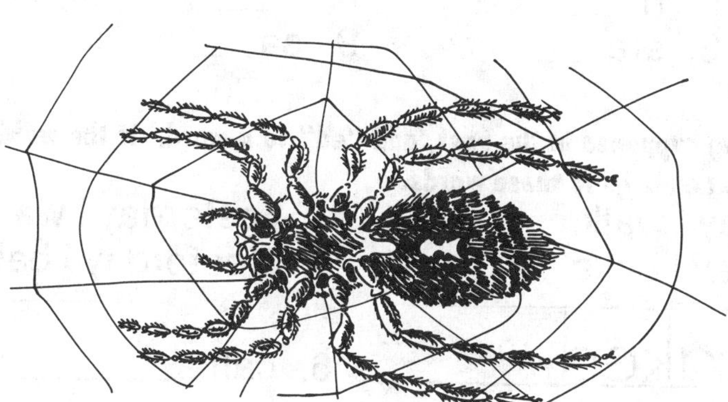

A spider lives in a web. The web is made of thin threads like silk which the spider spins. The threads are very sticky. The spider can run all over its web.

The web is used to catch food. Flies try to go through the web and get caught in the sticky threads. Then the spider winds more threads around the flies. The flies are caught, and the spider has a meal.

THINGS TO REMEMBER

1. The spider lives in a __________.
2. The web is also used to catch __________.
3. The spider spins thin __________.
4. The threads are very __________.
5. __________ often get caught in the __________ threads of the spider's web.
6. After the fly is caught, the __________ winds more __________ around it.

Final Letters and Endings

A **Add the final letter or letters that will complete each word. See sample "1."**

1. me n
2. pi ____
3. tu ____
4. si ____
5. ri ____
6. ste ____
7. ru ____
8. fi ____
9. sa ____
10. ba ____
11. ca ____
12. do ____

B **To show that something happened in the past, add "ed" to a word. If the word already ends in "e," add "d" only. Add past endings to these words.**

Today I walk. Yesterday I walked.
Today I bake. Yesterday I baked.

1. rake raked
2. lock ____
3. stare ____
4. plant ____
5. show ____
6. call ____
7. use ____
8. paint ____
9. rent ____
10. care ____

C **For each of the following words, add "d" or "ed" to form the past tense. See the example "1."**

EXAMPLE:

1. rain rained
2. start ____
3. trade ____
4. pretend ____
5. ransom ____
6. thread ____
7. add ____
8. shave ____
9. part ____
10. tame ____
11. end ____
12. happen ____

Practicing Directions

A **Draw a box around the numbers that are in order.**

1. (a) 5, 4, 3, 1, 2 (b) 8, 6, 7, 5 (c) 1, 2, 3, 4 (d) 6, 5, 3, 1
2. (a) 10, 9, 7, 6 (b) 7, 6, 5, 3 (c) 6, 4, 3, 7 (d) 4, 5, 6, 7
3. (a) 5, 7, 8, 6 (b) 7, 8, 9, 10 (c) 8, 6, 4, 7 (d) 5, 6, 7, 8

B **Draw a line from each picture on the left to the matching picture on the right.**

1. a.
2. b. 
3. c.
4. d. 

C **Complete each sentence by crossing out the wrong answers.**

1. A cat is (an animal, a bug).
2. A ball can (walk, roll).
3. A frog (runs, hops).

D **Complete each sentence by choosing the right word from the list. Write the letter of the word in the blank.**

1. A ______ can fly.
2. A ______ can swim.
3. A ______ can roar.
4. A ______ can sing.

a. girl
b. bird
c. lion
d. duck

E **True or False**

____ 1. Most flowers bloom in the winter.
____ 2. A doctor helps people who are sick.
____ 3. Winter days are long; summer days are short.

F **Color the circles red. Color the squares blue. Color the triangles yellow.**

1. 3. 5.

2. 4. 6.

Recognizing Tens

Circle the correct numeral. See examples "A," "B," and "C."

A.	B.	C.
2 tens and 5 35 52 (25)	7 tens and 7 67 (77) 14	1 ten and 4 5 (14) 41
D. 8 tens and 3 83 38 11	E. 6 tens and 1 17 16 61	F. 2 tens and 4 24 42 14
G. 6 tens and 0 55 60 65	H. 2 tens and 2 22 24 42	I. 1 ten and 0 11 10 16
J. 9 tens and 0 10 81 90	K. 5 tens and 8 85 58 13	L. 4 tens and 6 10 64 46
M. 7 tens and 0 70 80 71	N. 0 tens and 7 7 17 27	O. 6 tens and 3 36 63 19
P. 2 tens and 8 82 28 10	Q. 4 tens and 9 49 13 94	R. 7 tens and 9 79 97 16
S. 8 tens and 0 79 81 80	T. 8 tens and 1 18 81 19	U. 1 ten and 1 21 31 11
V. 9 tens and 5 95 45 54	W. 5 tens and 4 45 54 19	X. 4 tens and 2 42 31 24
Y. 3 tens and 6 63 36 16	Z. 1 ten and 8 18 81 16	A. 3 tens and 9 93 39 12

Beach Hermit

Look at the boxes. Say, spell, and write each word. Read the story, and fill in the blanks. Reread the story if you have trouble.

Crabs live around water. They have four pairs of legs. They have one pair of pincers, or claws. The pincers are used to catch food.

One type of crab is called a hermit crab. It got this name because it does not make its own house. It lives in the empty shells of snails and other sea animals on the beach. It may eat a snail just to get his shell.

The hermit crab backs into the shell. The back part is the softest part of its body. Soon it gets too big for one shell. It moves on to find a bigger one. If it finds a shell with another crab inside, it will usually pull the other crab out and take over his home.

THINGS TO REMEMBER

1. The back part is the ____________ part of the crab's body.
2. It has one pair of pincers, or ________.
3. The hermit crab does not make its own ____________.
4. It eats __________ to get their shells.
5. Crabs have __________ pairs of legs.
6. Crabs live on the __________.

1. crab

2. house

3. beach

4. shell

5. pincers

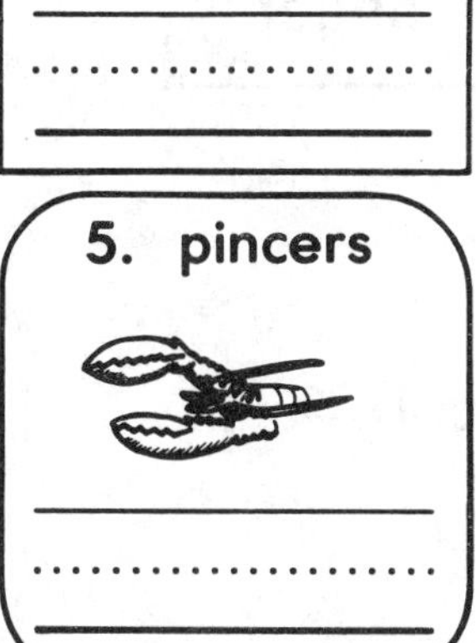

6. snail

7. pull

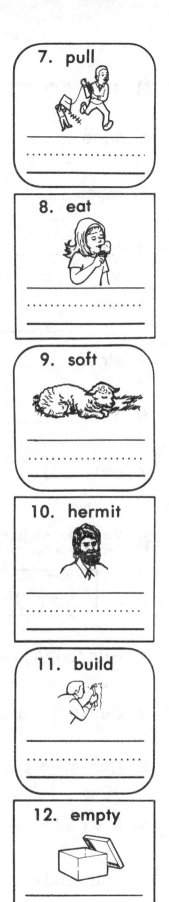

8. eat

9. soft

10. hermit

11. build

12. empty

Making Words and Sentences

A **Add "ly," "y," "er," or "est" to each of the following words to make new words. See example "1."**

1. wind windy
2. quick ______
3. rainy ______
4. hill ______
5. sleep ______
6. stick ______
7. dirty ______
8. friend ______
9. strong ______
10. soft ______
11. fast ______
12. soon ______
13. soap ______
14. late ______

B **Using these words, complete the following sentences. Use each word only one time. Circle the word used. See sample "1."**

quickly	silliest	deepest	curlier	hilly	longer

1. Run to the house quickly!
2. Susan is the ______ girl in our room at school.
3. Billy swims in the ______ part of the pool.
4. Mary's hair is ______ than mine.
5. This land is very ______.
6. Your foot is ______ than mine.

Watching for Clues

A **Read the sentences, and make an "X" on each fruit that answers the riddle. Write the name of each fruit under the sentence.**

1. I am big and round. I am yellow, and I am usually eaten for breakfast.

grapefruit

2. I can be green or purple. I grow in bunches on a vine.

3. I am long and yellow. I grow in bunches hanging upside down.

4. I am sweet and juicy. I am the same color as my name.

5. I am yellow and very sour. I am used to make a good refresh-ing drink.

6. I am red or yellow. I am crunchy and very good for you. I am round and have a core.

B **Read each sentence. Fill in the blank with the correct letter.**

1. Bill wants to help people who are sick. He wants to be a ______.
2. Jim wants to wear a uniform, protect people, and help those in trouble. He wants to be a ______.
3. Jill wants to help children learn to read and write. She wants to be a ______.
4. Bob wants to operate a big truck and haul freight. He wants to be a ______.
5. Sue wants to help people who are riding on a plane. She wants to be a ______.
6. Jane wants to take care of people in the hospital. She wants to be a ______.
7. Joe wants to be a star kicker in a game. He wants to be a ______.
8. Ellen wants to preside over the courtroom. She wants to be a ______.

A. B. C. D. E. F. G. H.

Total Coins

What is the value of each set of coins? Write your answers in the blanks.

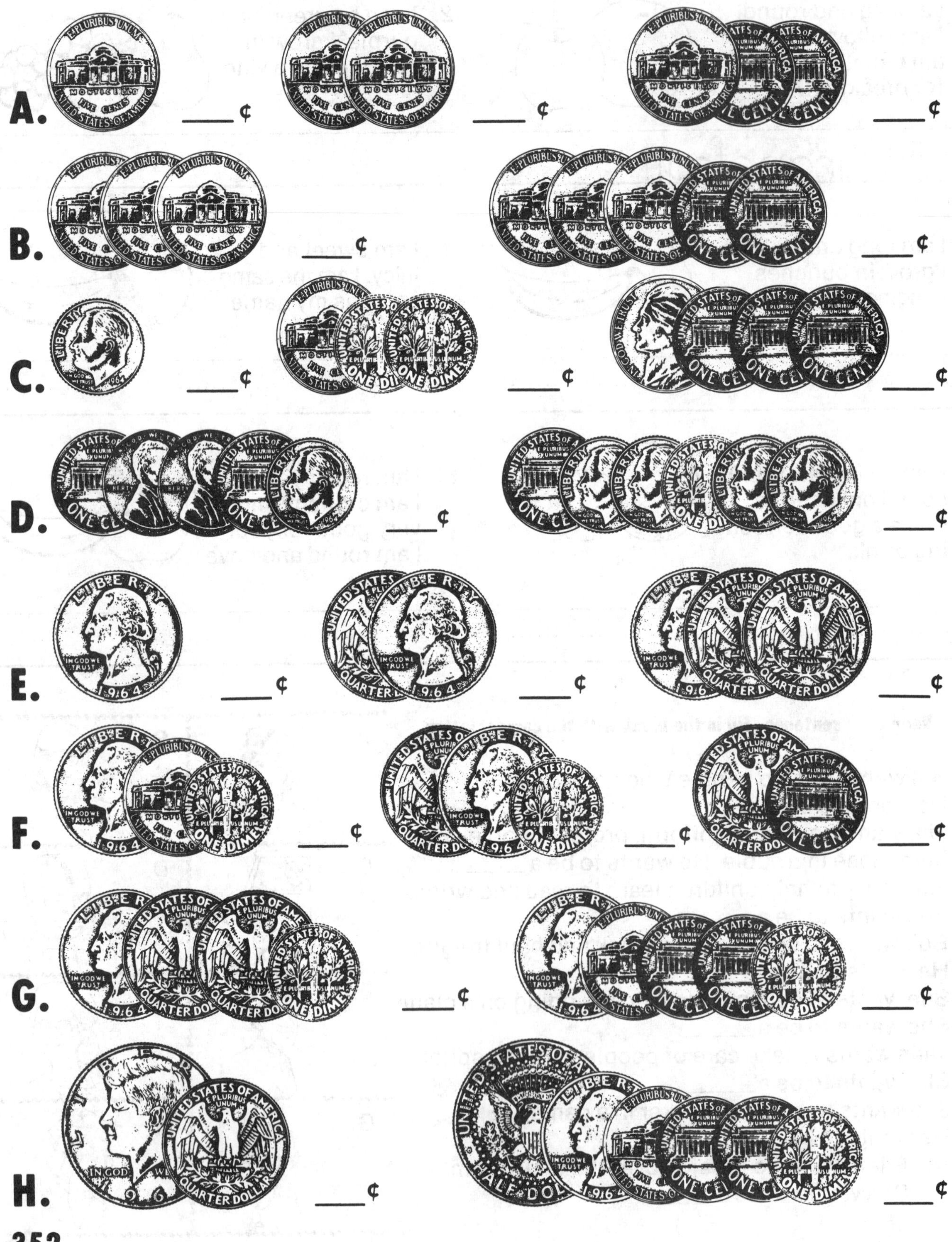

The Sand Dollar

Look at the boxes. Say, spell, and write each word. Read the story, and fill in the blanks. Reread the story if you have trouble.

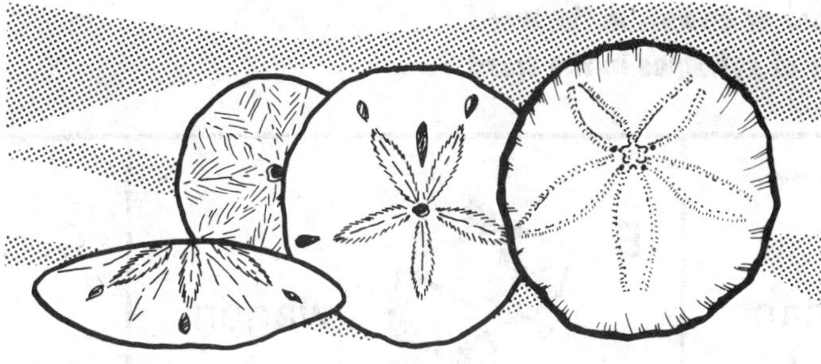

Where does the sand dollar get its name? It gets its name from the silver dollar because it looks like one.

The sand dollar is round. It is covered with little hairs. It lives in the sand at the bottom of the sea.

The sand dollar has holes on both sides of it. If it needs to move, it sticks its feet out the holes.

Sand dollars wash up out of the water when they die. Their skeletons are found on the seashore.

THINGS TO REMEMBER

1. The sand dollar is __________.
2. It looks like a __________ dollar.
3. It has __________ on both sides.
4. It sticks its _________ through the holes.
5. The sand dollar is covered with little __________.
6. Only its ________________ is found on the seashore.

1. sand

2. sea

3. silver dollar

4. bottom

5. holes

6. hair

7. little

8. seashore

9. round

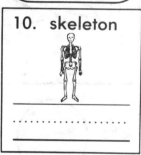

10. skeleton

11. feet

12. move

Dividing Words (Closed Syllables)

Look at each picture, and whisper the word.
First Line: Write the number of vowel sounds in the word.
Second Line: Write the number of vowels in the word.
Third Line: Write the number of syllables in the word.

A. man 1 1 1	B. wagon ___ ___ ___	C. teapot ___ ___ ___
D. kite ___ ___ ___	E. feather ___ ___ ___	F. sheep ___ ___ ___
G. airplane ___ ___ ___	H. popcorn ___ ___ ___	I. book ___ ___ ___
J. orange ___ ___ ___	K. horse ___ ___ ___	L. playground ___ ___ ___
M. ship ___ ___ ___	N. bicycle ___ ___ ___	O. grasshopper ___ ___ ___
P. groceries ___ ___ ___	Q. mitten ___ ___ ___	R. policeman ___ ___ ___

Differences (Big)

A Make an "X" on each big thing.

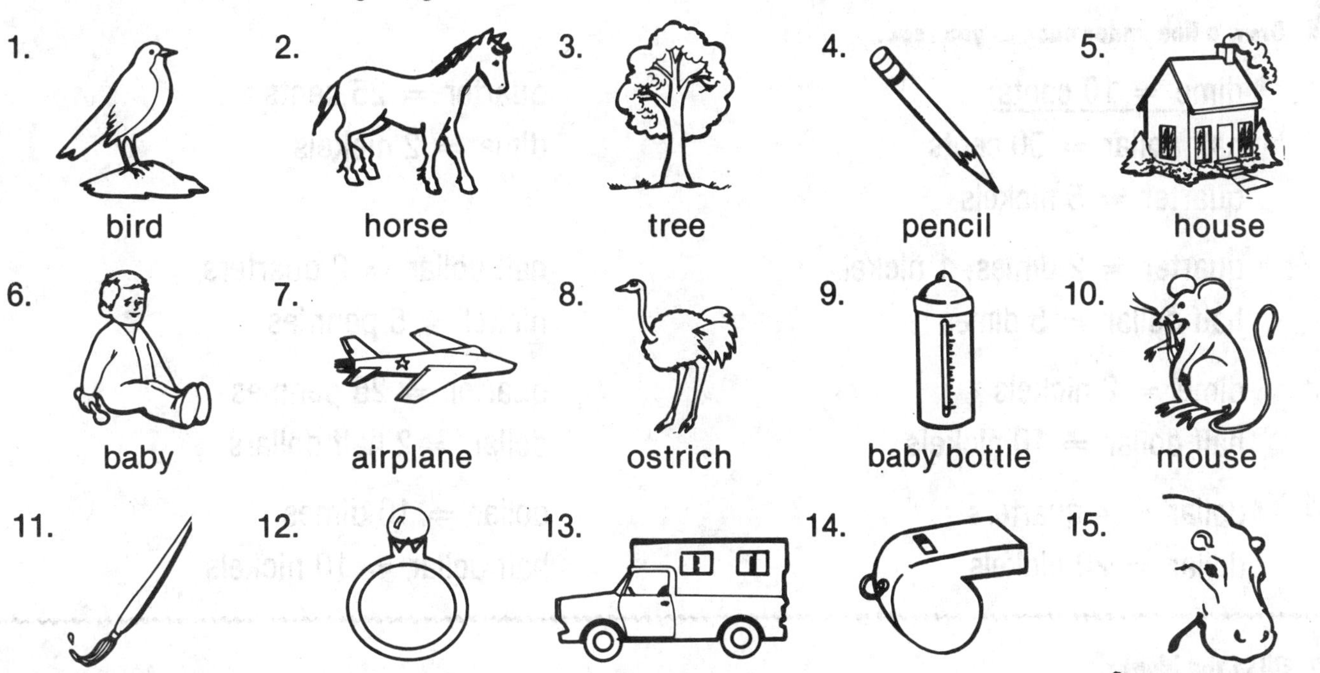

B Underline the biggest object in each box.

1. a. b. c. 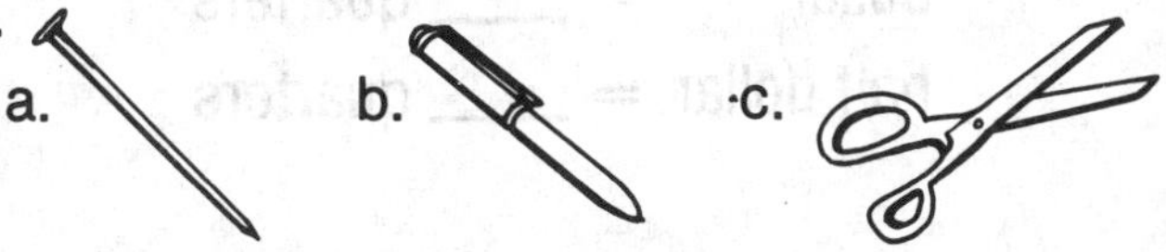
2. a. b. c. 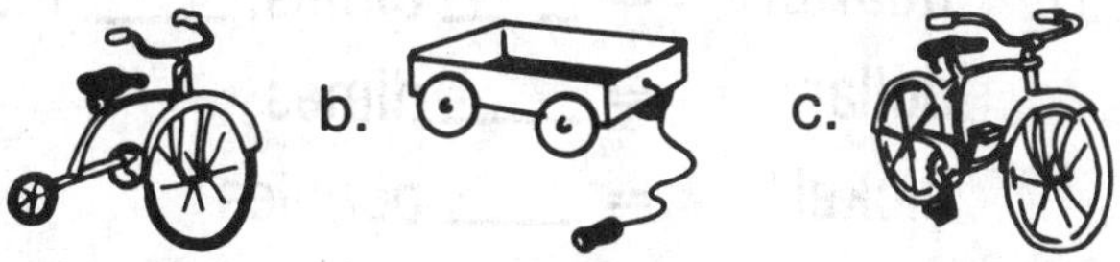
3. a. b. c. 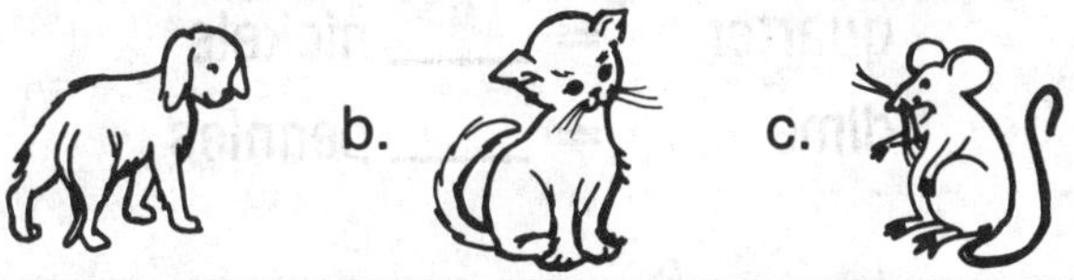
4. a. b. c. 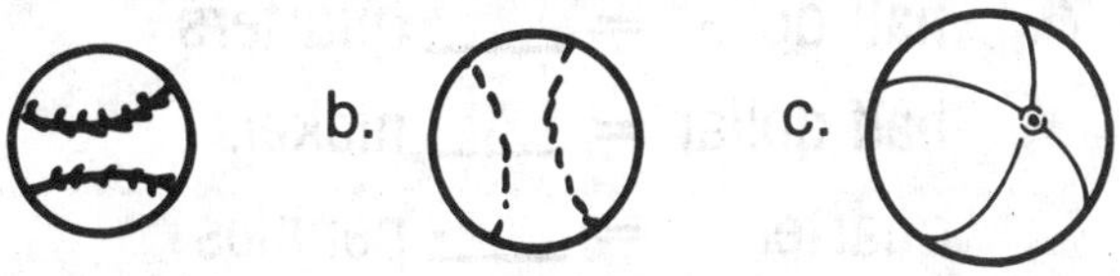
5. a. b. c. 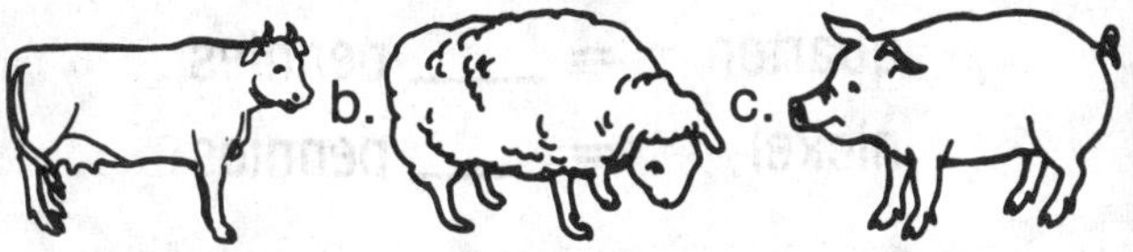
6. a. b. c. 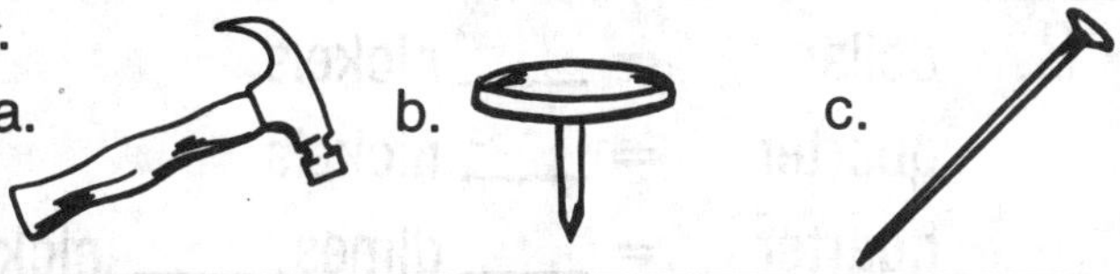
7. a. b. c. 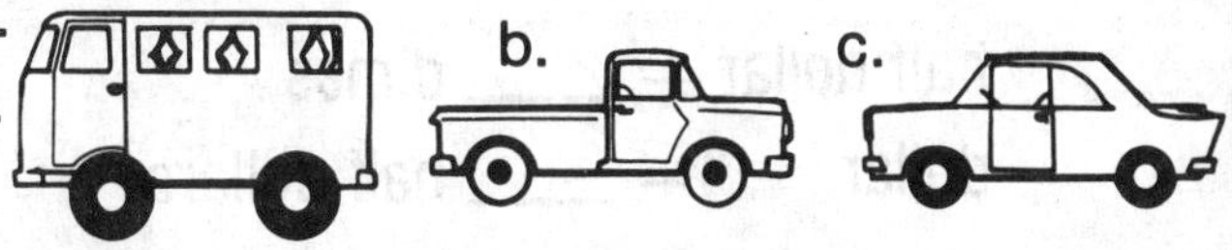
8. a. b. c. 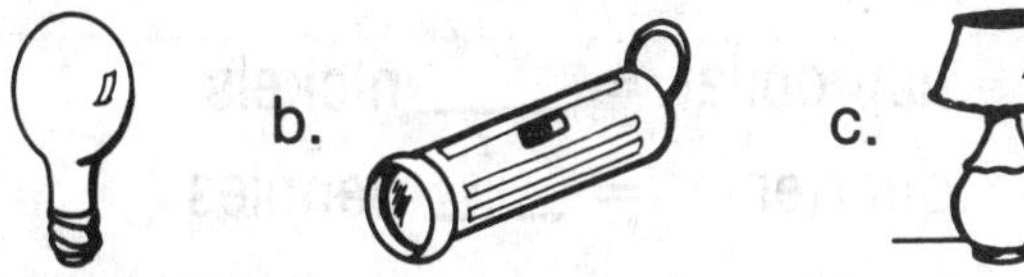
9. a. b. c. 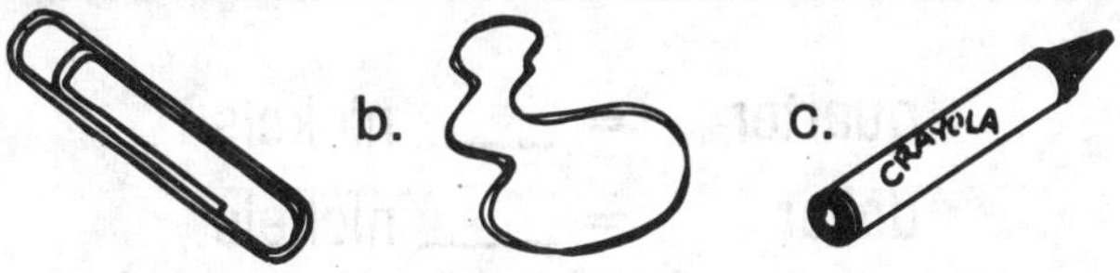 CRAYOLA
10. a. b. c.

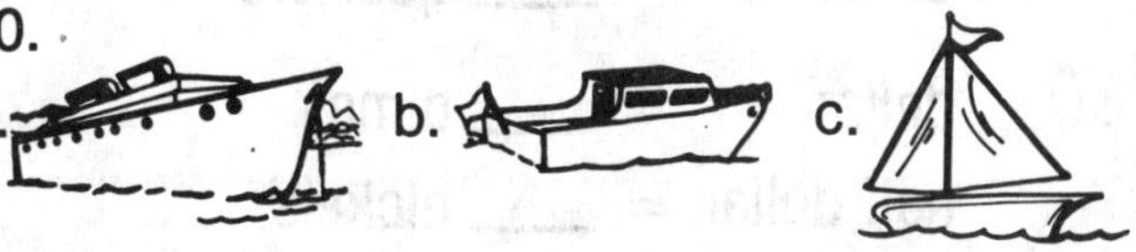

Counting Money (Coins)

A **Draw a line under each as you read.**

1. dime = 10 cents
   half dollar = 50 cents
   quarter = 5 nickels
   quarter = 25 cents
   dime = 2 nickels
2. quarter = 2 dimes, 1 nickel
   half dollar = 5 dimes
   half dollar = 2 quarters
   nickel = 5 pennies
3. dime = 2 nickels
   half dollar = 10 nickels
   quarter = 25 pennies
   dollar = 2 half dollars
4. dollar = 4 quarters
   dollar = 20 nickels
   dollar = 10 dimes
   half dollar = 10 nickels

B **Fill in the blanks.**

5. dime = ____ nickels
   half dollar = ____ quarters
   half dollar = ____ nickels
   quarter = ____ nickels
   half dollar = ____ dimes
6. quarter = ____ dimes, ____ nickel
   dollar = ____ dimes
   nickel = ____ pennies
   dollar = ____ quarters
   half dollar = ____ quarters
7. half dollar = ____ quarters
   half dollar = ____ nickels
   quarter = ____ pennies
   quarter = ____ nickels
   dime = ____ pennies
8. dollar = ____ nickels
   quarter = ____ nickels
   quarter = ____ dimes, ____ nickel
   quarter = ____ pennies
   nickel = ____ pennies
9. half dollar = ____ nickels
   quarter = ____ pennies
   dollar = ____ quarters
   half dollar = ____ dimes
   dollar = ____ half dollars
10. dollar = ____ dimes
    half dollar = ____ nickels
    quarter = ____ nickels
    dollar = ____ nickels

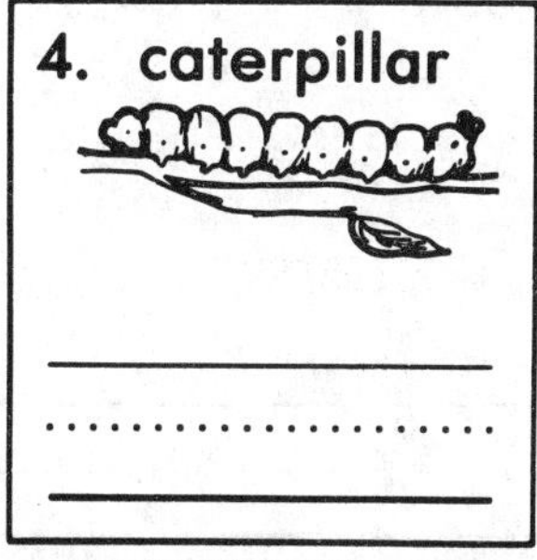

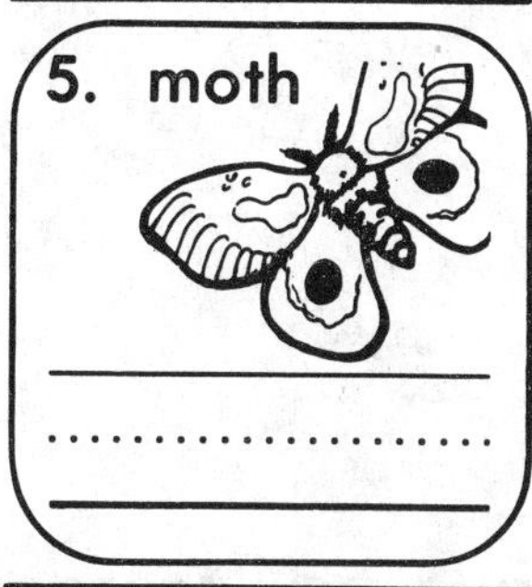

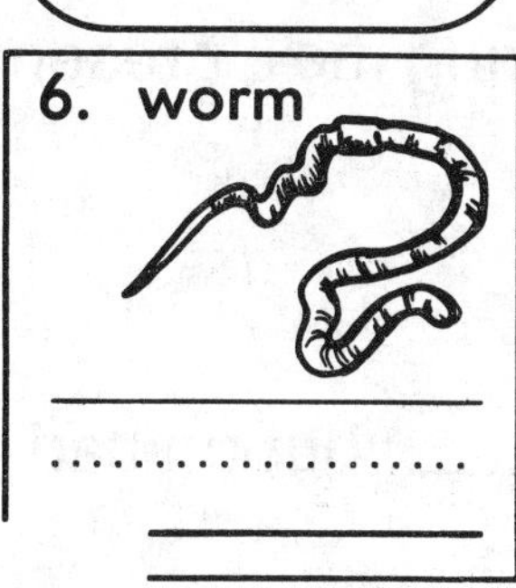

Caterpillars

Look at the boxes. Say, spell, and write each word. Read the story, and fill in the blanks. Reread the story if you have trouble.

Caterpillars are small crawling animals. They look like worms. They are really a stage of insects' lives. Many of them will be moths or butterflies some day.

In the spring, tent caterpillars live in trees. They eat the leaves. Many of them live together in a silk tent. They make the silk in their bodies.

The caterpillars grow inside their tent house. They are safe there. Spiders and birds can't eat them. The silk tent is very strong. The caterpillars stay there until they are grown.

THINGS TO REMEMBER

1. Caterpillars look like __________.
2. __________ caterpillars live in trees.
3. The silk tent is very __________.
4. They live together until they are __________.
5. The silk is made in the caterpillars' __________.
6. Caterpillars eat __________.

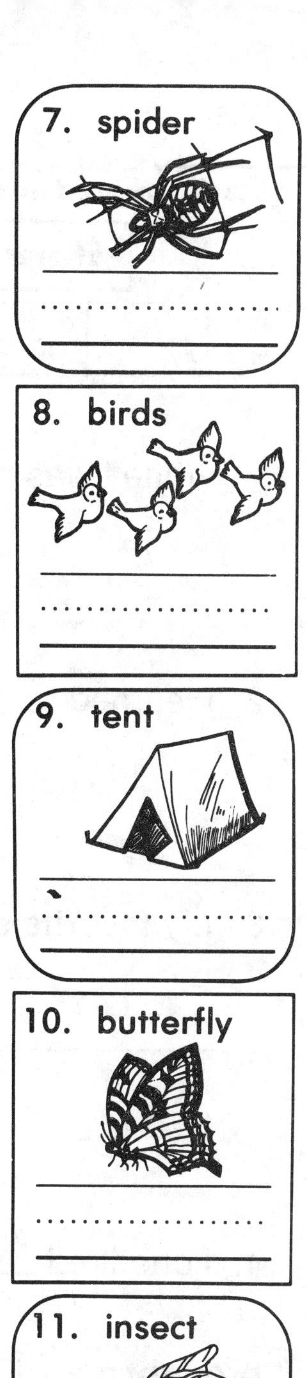

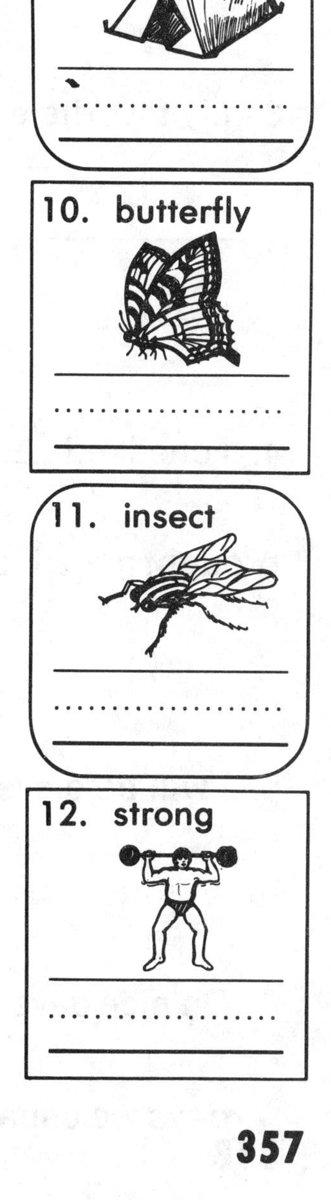

Using Compound Words

Use the compound words to fill in the blanks. Use the words above each sentence.

afternoon	**basketball**	**shoelace**

1. My shoelace on my tennis shoe broke this ________________ while I was playing ________________.

cookbook	**butterscotch**

2. I learned to bake ________________ cookies from my favorite ____________.

football	**softball**

3. My favorite sport in the fall is ________________ but in the summer I like ________________.

postman	**today**

4. I checked ________________ to see if the ________________ brought me a letter.

birthday	**mailman**

5. I will be eleven years old on my next ____________ will bring me a present.

inside	**playground**

6. On nice days at recess time, we play on the ________________; but on bad days we usually play games ________________ the room.

Classifications

Put an "X" on each picture in each row which can best be classified with the picture in the little box at the beginning.

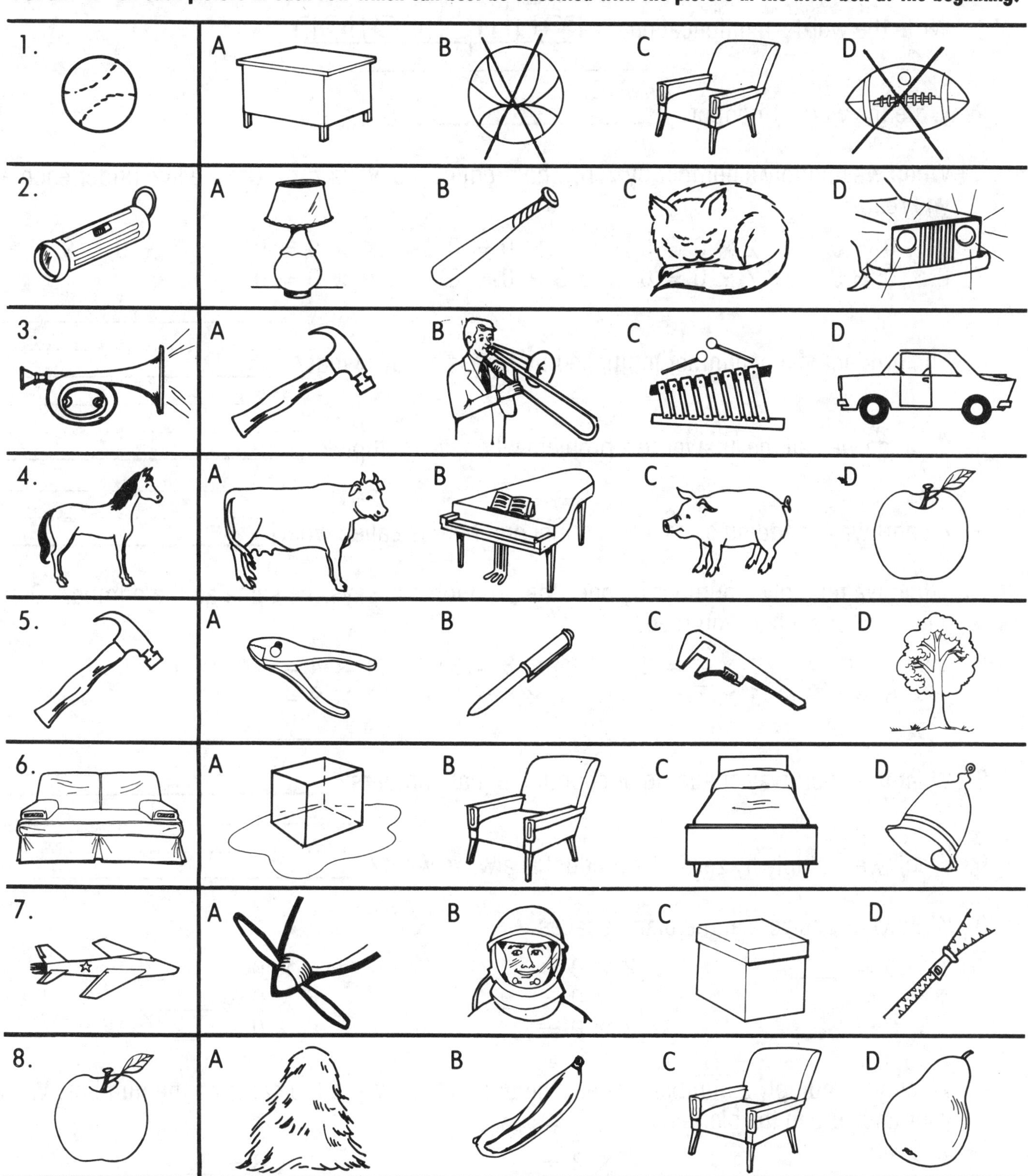

Multiplication Properties of 0 and 1

Complete these exercises.

1. Write the word "multiplication." multiplication ______________

2. Write the word "product." ______________

3. When we multiply a number by zero, the product is always zero. Draw a line under each as you read.

   1 × 0 = 0   2 × 0 = 0   3 × 0 = 0   4 × 0 = 0   5 × 0 = 0
   6 × 0 = 0   7 × 0 = 0   8 × 0 = 0   9 × 0 = 0

4. The product of any number multiplied by zero is always what? ______________

5. What do we call the answer to a problem when we multiply? ______________

6. A short way of adding or counting equal numbers is called what? ______________

7. When we multiply a number by one, the product is always the same as the number. Draw a line under each as you read.

   1 × 1 = 1   1 × 2 = 2   1 × 3 = 3   1 × 4 = 4   1 × 5 = 5
   1 × 6 = 6   1 × 7 = 7   1 × 8 = 8   1 × 9 = 9

8. What is a short way of adding or counting equal numbers? ______________

9. When we multiply by zero, the product is always what? ______________

10. Write your answers in the blank spaces.

    1 × 0 = ____   2 × 0 = ____   3 × 0 = ____
    4 × 0 = ____   5 × 0 = ____   6 × 0 = ____
    7 × 0 = ____   8 × 0 = ____   9 × 0 = ____

11. When you multiply a number by one, the product is always the same as the number. Write your answers in the blanks.

    1 × 1 = ____   1 × 2 = ____   1 × 3 = ____
    1 × 4 = ____   1 × 5 = ____   1 × 6 = ____
    1 × 7 = ____   1 × 8 = ____   1 × 9 = ____

Wolves

Look at the boxes. Say, spell, and write each word. Read the story, and fill in the blanks. Reread the story if you have trouble.

Wolves are wild animals that look like large dogs. Most wolves weigh over one hundred pounds. They can travel for hours at about twenty miles per hour.

Wolves may be black, brown, white, gray, or red. They have long sharp teeth and long bushy tails.

Wolves live in holes or among large rocks. Their homes are called dens. Wolves usually live in wilderness areas. Some wolves live in cold areas like Alaska. Some live on prairies. The small wolves that live on the prairies in our country are called coyotes.

Wolves sometimes kill farm animals. Because of this, many wolves have been killed. Today the wolf is in danger of dying out.

THINGS TO REMEMBER

1. A wolf looks like a large __________.
2. A wolf's home is called a __________.
3. __________ are small wolves that live on prairies in our country.
4. Most wolves weigh over __________ __________ pounds.
5. Wolves usually live in __________ areas.
6. Wolves have long bushy __________.

1. dog

2. wolf

3. teeth

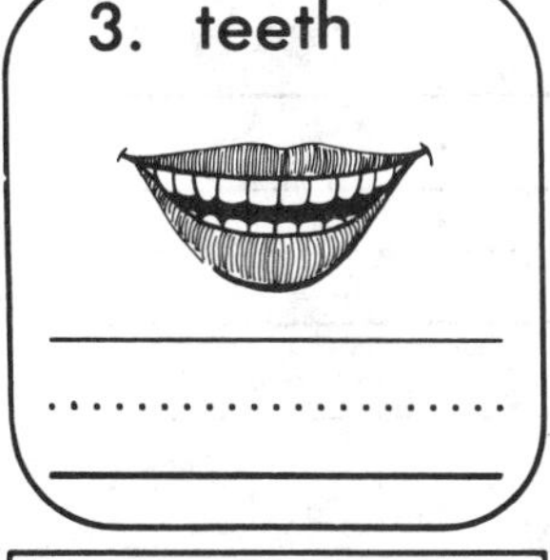

4. long

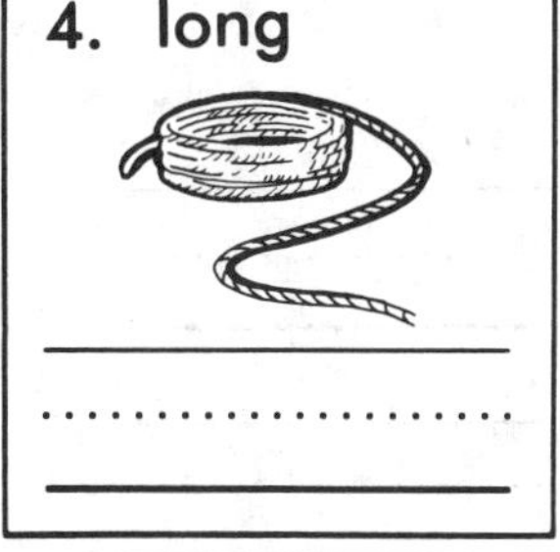

5. weight

6. rocks

7. hole

8. bushy

9. den

10. wilderness

11. prairies

12. coyote

Root Words

When several words may be formed from one word, we call this word a root word.

EXAMPLE: The root word of rests, rested, resting, restful, restless, and unrest is rest.

A Build some words from the root words listed below.

1. buy	buyer buying	6. cover	
2. flat		7. part	
3. long		8. care	
4. happy		9. cold	
5. own		10. free	

B Write the root word of each word below. See sample "1."

1. uncover	cover	8. below	
2. discovery		9. harden	
3. settlers		10. covering	
4. careless		11. freely	
5. asleep		12. lovely	
6. carefree		13. dislike	
7. freedom		14. kindness	

Milk and Other Liquids

To have a good, balanced diet you need liquids to go with your food. Liquids satisfy thirst. Liquids provide many of the vitamins the body needs to work each day.

One of the most important liquids is milk. Did you know that you can get the nourishment of milk through ways other than drinking it? You can eat ice cream and cheese. Milk is a good source of vitamin D.

Another very important liquid is water. You need it to live.

Other liquids come from fruit juices. Juices provide a variety of vitamins we need. Fruit juice is also one way of drinking water, since it contains some water.

A **Milk and milk products are important to all of us. Name these milk products.**

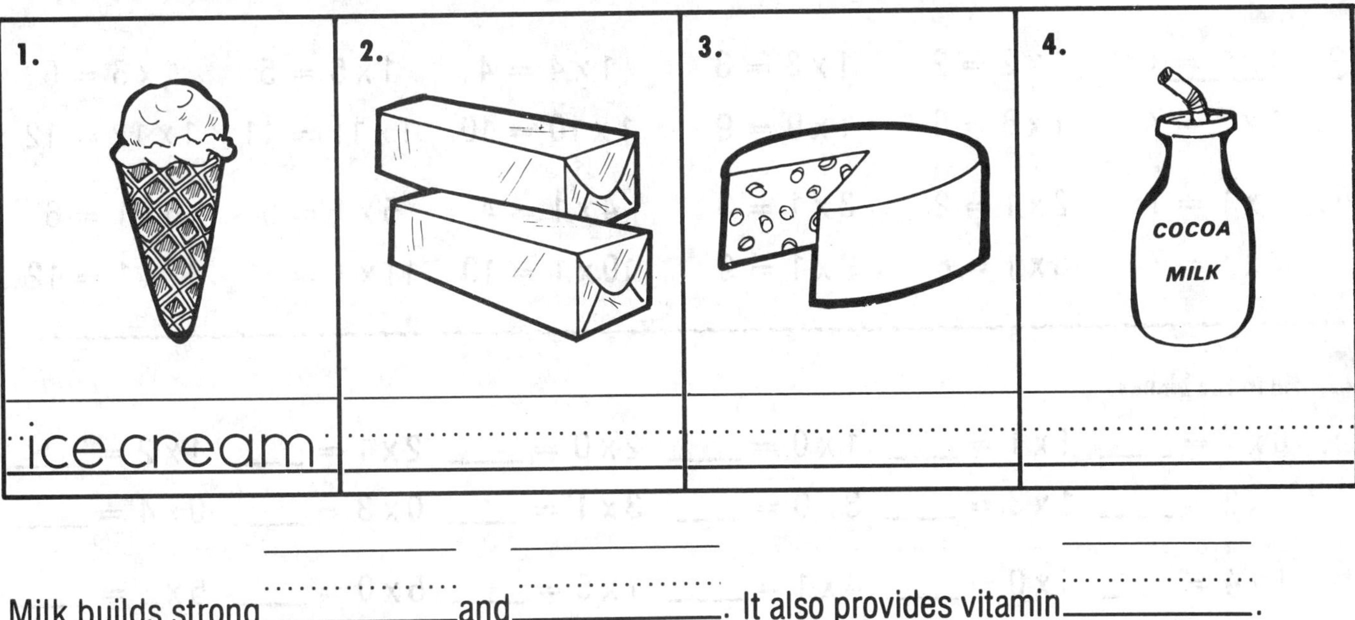

Milk builds strong __________ and __________. It also provides vitamin __________.

Fruit juices are good to have with our foods. Fruit juice also makes a good snack drink. Fruit juice is naturally sweet and good for us.

B **Write the names of these fruits from which we get juice.**

1.	2.	3.	4.
__________	__________	__________	__________

Practicing Multiplication Properties of 0 and 1

A **When a number is multiplied by zero, the product is always zero. Draw a line under each problem as you read.**

1.	1 x 0 = 0	2 x 0 = 0	3 x 0 = 0	4 x 0 = 0	5 x 0 = 0	6 x 0 = 0
	7 x 0 = 0	8 x 0 = 0	9 x 0 = 0	10 x 0 = 0	11 x 0 = 0	12 x 0 = 0
2.	0 x 1 = 0	0 x 2 = 0	0 x 3 = 0	0 x 4 = 0	0 x 5 = 0	0 x 6 = 0
	0 x 7 = 0	0 x 8 = 0	0 x 9 = 0	0 x 10 = 0	0 x 11 = 0	0 x 12 = 0

B **When a number is multiplied by one, the product is always that number. Draw a line under each problem as you read.**

3.	1 x 1 = 1	1 x 2 = 2	1 x 3 = 3	1 x 4 = 4	1 x 5 = 5	1 x 6 = 6
	1 x 7 = 7	1 x 8 = 8	1 x 9 = 9	1 x 10 = 10	1 x 11 = 11	1 x 12 = 12
4.	1 x 1 = 1	2 x 1 = 2	3 x 1 = 3	4 x 1 = 4	5 x 1 = 5	6 x 1 = 6
	7 x 1 = 7	8 x 1 = 8	9 x 1 = 9	10 x 1 = 10	11 x 1 = 11	12 x 1 = 12

C **Fill in the blanks.**

5.	0 x 1 = ____	1 x 1 = ____	1 x 0 = ____	2 x 0 = ____	2 x 1 = ____	1 x 2 = ____
	0 x 2 = ____	1 x 3 = ____	3 x 0 = ____	3 x 1 = ____	0 x 3 = ____	0 x 4 = ____
6.	1 x 4 = ____	4 x 0 = ____	4 x 1 = ____	1 x 5 = ____	5 x 0 = ____	5 x 1 = ____
	0 x 5 = ____	0 x 6 = ____	1 x 6 = ____	6 x 0 = ____	6 x 1 = ____	7 x 0 = ____
7.	1 x 7 = ____	7 x 1 = ____	0 x 7 = ____	8 x 1 = ____	8 x 0 = ____	1 x 8 = ____
	0 x 8 = ____	9 x 1 = ____	0 x 9 = ____	1 x 9 = ____	1 x 1 = ____	0 x 1 = ____
8.	1 x 6 = ____	0 x 6 = ____	1 x 5 = ____	0 x 5 = ____	1 x 4 = ____	0 x 4 = ____
	0 x 3 = ____	0 x 2 = ____	2 x 1 = ____	1 x 0 = ____	0 x 2 = ____	9 x 1 = ____
9.	1 x 8 = ____	0 x 8 = ____	9 x 1 = ____	3 x 1 = ____	6 x 0 = ____	0 x 6 = ____
	5 x 0 = ____	7 x 0 = ____	6 x 1 = ____	5 x 1 = ____	4 x 1 = ____	3 x 1 = ____
10.	2 x 1 = ____	1 x 1 = ____	9 x 0 = ____	8 x 0 = ____	7 x 0 = ____	6 x 0 = ____
	5 x 0 = ____	4 x 0 = ____	3 x 0 = ____	2 x 0 = ____	1 x 0 = ____	9 x 1 = ____

Sea Shells

Look at the boxes. Say, spell, and write each word. Read the story, and fill in the blanks. Reread the story if you have trouble.

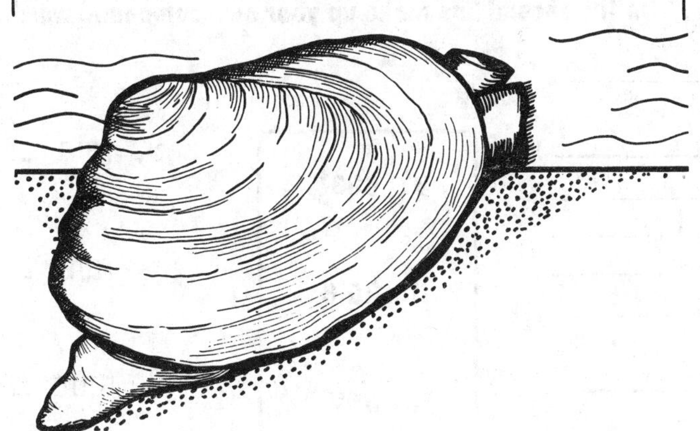

Many sea animals live in shells. They are called mollusks. Oysters, clams, mussels, snails, and slugs are mollusks. Some of them are eaten for food.

Shells are many different shapes and sizes. Some of them are round like balls. Others are long and pointed. Snails carry their shells on their backs.

Some animals can go in and out of their shells. Mussels, clams, and oysters have shells that open and close like traps.

You can find empty sea shells on the beach. The animals no longer live in them. Most of these shells are very colorful and shiny.

THINGS TO REMEMBER

1. You can find empty shells on the ____________.
2. A __________ carries its shell on its back.
3. Shells are different shapes and __________.
4. Some shells are ________ like balls.
5. Some mollusks are eaten for ________.
6. Most shells are __________ and shiny.

1. trap

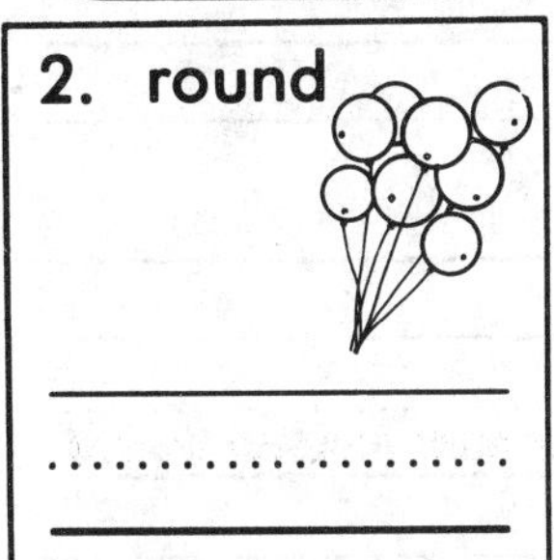

2. round

3. pointed

4. empty

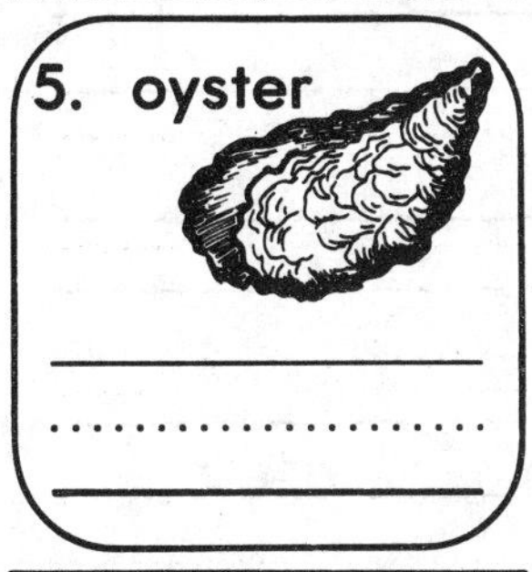

5. oyster

6. shine

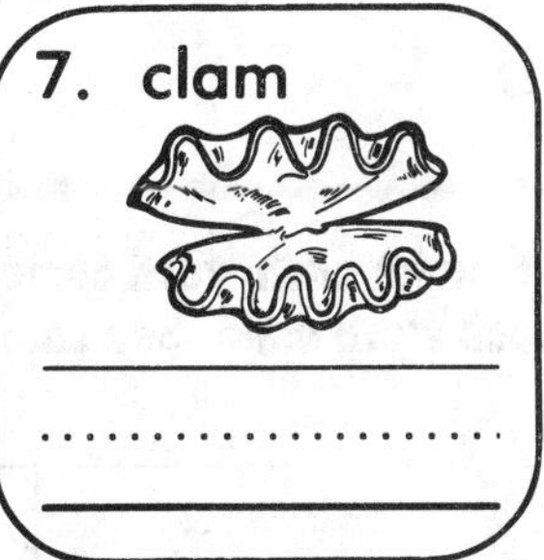

7. clam

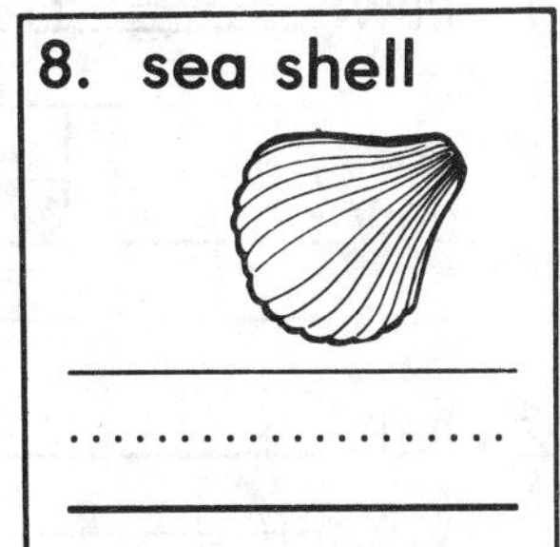

8. sea shell

9. beach

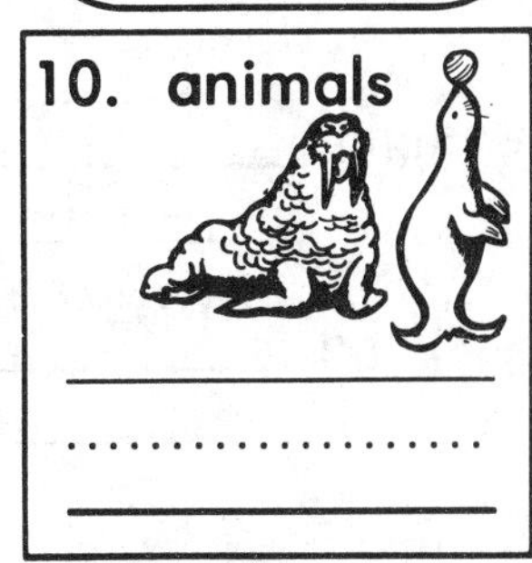

10. animals

11. snail

12. ball

Compound Words to Write

To make each word compound, choose a word from the center box, and write it in the blank. Cross out the letter of each word used. See sample "1." On the second line make up your own compound word. See sample "2."

1. cow boy
   cow bird
2. hat
   hat
3. milk
   milk
4. hand
   hand
5. up
   up
6. wind
   wind
7. dust
   dust

a. coat
b. hole
~~c.~~ boy
d. tie
e. some
f. time
g. box
h. ride
i. man
j. be
k. top
l. bag
m. mill
n. set

8. rain
   rain
9. mud
   mud
10. hill
    hill
11. neck
    neck
12. hay
    hay
13. may
    may
14. meal
    meal

Protein Foods

Do you know what protein is? Your body is made up of cells that have to be fed and cared for. This is the job of protein. Protein helps keep you healthy by taking care of your cells.

Protein foods are fun foods to eat. They give you plenty of energy to work and play. Protein foods are fish, meat, poultry, nuts, dried peas and beans, and peanut butter.

Here are some pictures of protein foods. Can you name them?

poultry

1. From what animal do we get bacon and ham? __________

2. From what animal do we get a beef steak? __________

3. Name two poultry animals. __________ and __________

4. The meat mutton comes from what animal? __________

Here are some protein foods. Write them.

PEANUT BUTTER

1. __________

2. __________

3. __________

4. __________

5. __________

Honey

Look at the boxes. Say, spell, and write each word. Read the story, and fill in the blanks. Reread the story if you have trouble.

1. bee

2. thick

3. flowers

4. king

5. honey

6. sweet

What does a bee usually remind you of? It reminds some people of honey. Honey is the sweet, thick syrup made by bees from flowers. Many people raise honeybees just to get this sweet food.

Honey is good to eat. It is also a good energy food. About 280 million pounds of honey are produced each year in the United States.

In ancient times people did not have so much honey. In fact, honey was once thought of as a food for kings. Only in the homes of very rich people could you find a jar of honey on the table.

THINGS TO REMEMBER

1. Honey is made by bees from ________.
2. Honey was once thought of as a food for __________.
3. Honey is a good __________ food.
4. Many people raise _______________ to get honey.
5. About 280 million pounds of ______ are produced each year in the United States.
6. In __________ times people did not have as much honey as we do today.

7. pound

8. table

9. rich

10. jar

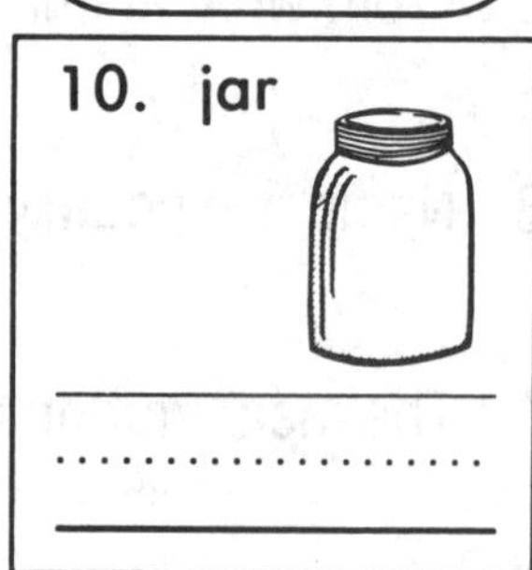

11. food

12. eat

Forming New Words

A **Study each word carefully, and underline the root word. See samples "A" and "B."**

A. <u>retire</u>ment
B. <u>relation</u>ship
C. itemize
D. otherwise
E. braver
F. importance
G. harden
H. tallest
I. smaller
J. lovely
K. tallest
L. handsome
M. greenish
N. wonderful
O. American
P. stupidity
Q. careless
R. clearing
S. invention
T. automatic

B **Fill in the blanks with the root words at the right to form new words. Circle each word used. See sample "1."**

1. hard ly
2. ______ ize
3. ______ ance
4. ______ some
5. ______ ment
6. ______ ful
7. ______ ion
8. ______ ive
9. ______ ship
10. ______ ness
11. ______ ing
12. ______ ish

lone	wood
act	hope
soon	cold
joy	guide
Europe	read
kind	alphabet
comfort	perfect
(hard)	improve
friend	care
humid	self

Our Grain Foods

Foods made from grains such as wheat, oats, and rice make us grow. They help build and keep bones and muscles strong. Grain foods also help teeth grow.

Some of the foods made from grains are cereal, bread, pastries, yeast, and hominy.

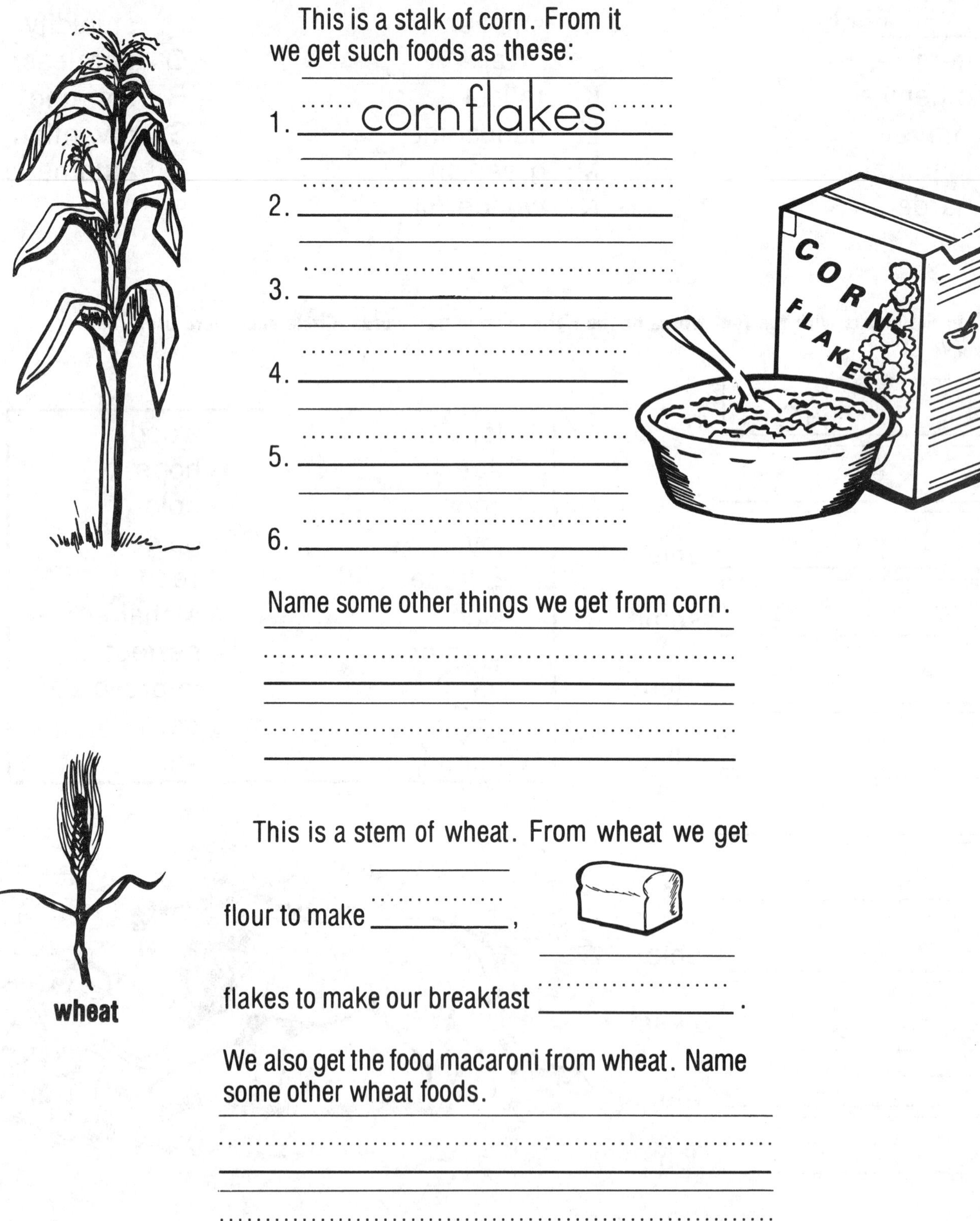

This is a stalk of corn. From it we get such foods as these:

1. cornflakes
2. __________
3. __________
4. __________
5. __________
6. __________

Name some other things we get from corn.

____

____

wheat

This is a stem of wheat. From wheat we get

flour to make __________,

flakes to make our breakfast __________.

We also get the food macaroni from wheat. Name some other wheat foods.

____

____

The Friendly Squirrel

Look at the boxes. Say, spell, and write each word. Read the story, and fill in the blanks. Reread the story if you have trouble.

Squirrels are active little animals with large black eyes and long bushy tails. They can run fast. They can climb trees and jump from branch to branch.

You will often see gray squirrels in the park. Squirrels are friendly animals. They make friends very quickly.

Gray squirrels are not afraid of people. If you put food out for them, they will eat it. Never feed them from your hand. They may bite you. They are tiny animals, but they have sharp teeth. If you give food to squirrels, put it on the ground!

THINGS TO REMEMBER

1. The squirrel is a __________ animal.
2. It has __________ teeth.
3. Never feed a squirrel from your ______.
4. You will often see the gray squirrel in the __________.
5. The squirrel makes __________ fast.
6. If you feed him from your hand, he may __________ you.

1. squirrel

2. bushy

3. park

4. climb

5. jump

6. branch

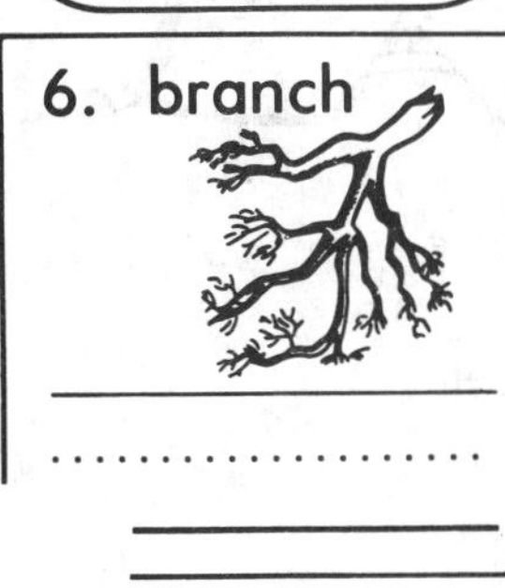

7. friend

8. feed

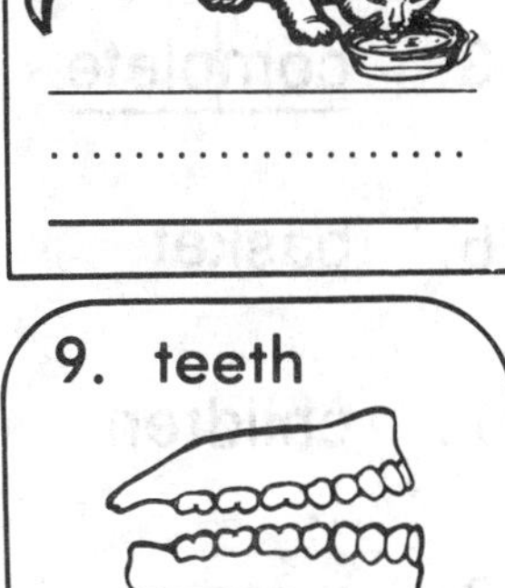

9. teeth

10. sharp

11. hand

12. bite

Count Syllables

A closed syllable is the part of the word that ends in a consonant.

Draw a line under each word containing a closed first syllable. Divide each word by drawing a slash line between the syllables. The first three are samples.

1. price|less
2. nar|row

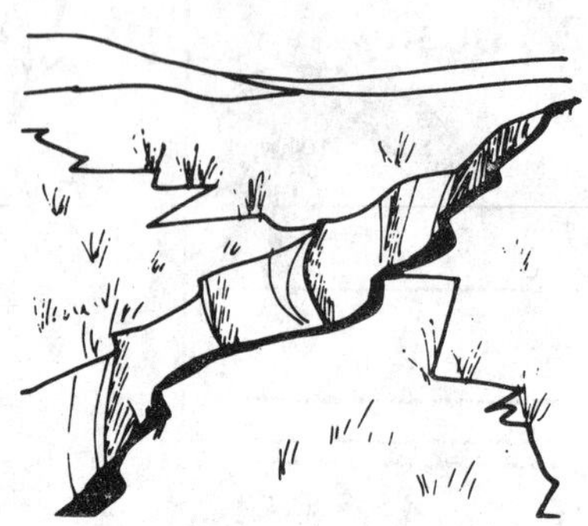

3. com|plete
4. averted

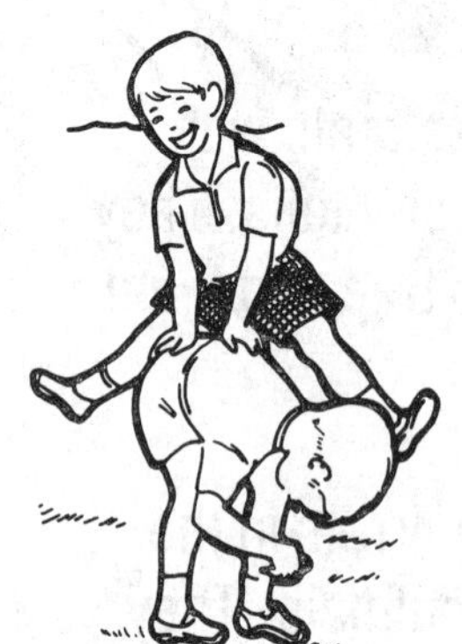

5. basket
6. target
7. children
8. discharge
9. dictate
10. exported
11. restless
12. please

13. purple
14. servant

15. displaying
16. address
17. nearest
18. circus
19. combine
20. account
21. across
22. unlikely

23. disgrace
24. uncertain
25. carpenter
26. comfort

27. swimming
28. alight
29. telephone
30. trapeze

Fruits to Grow On

Did you know that we have food to grow on? We do, and that food is fruit! Fruit contains all the things we need to grow straight and tall and to stay healthy. Fruit tastes good too.

Fruit makes a good dessert for our meals. Fruit is also a good snack food.

A **Here is a list of fruits that are good to eat. Match them with the pictures. Write your answers in the boxes beside the pictures.**

A apple
B bananas
C cherries
D orange
E pear
F lemon
G grapes
H strawberries
I pineapple

B **Complete each sentence.**

1. Fruits are good for you to ____________ .
2. Fruit makes a good ____________ for our meals.
3. It helps you grow ____________ and ____________ .
4. My favorite fruits are ____________ .
5. Other fruits that are good for us are ____________ .

Storks

Look at the boxes. Say, spell, and write each word. Read the story, and fill in the blanks. Reread the story if you have trouble.

Storks are considered good luck birds. People are happy to see them return each spring. They always come back to the same nests. Each time, they make their nests a little bigger. They usually build them on roofs.

They are big beautiful white birds. They have shiny, black wings. They have long red bills and long red legs. Storks get their name from their stiff-legged walk.

Storks can't sing. They have no voices. They make sounds with their wings. They can rattle their bills too.

Storks are good parents. They take loving care of their babies. That is why we have the story that a stork brings the new baby into the home.

1. stork
2. stiff-legged
3. feather

4. wings

5. legs

6. bill

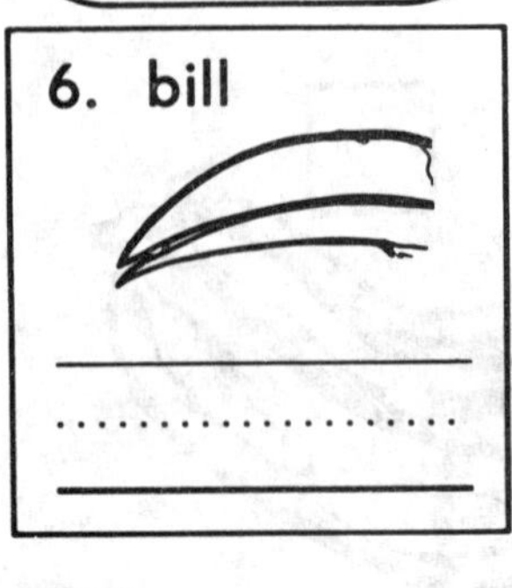

7. shiny

8. nest

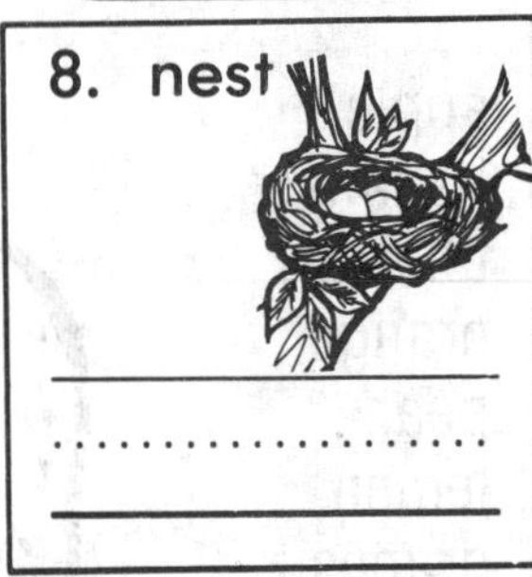

9. roof

10. rattle
11. babies

12. sing

THINGS TO REMEMBER

1. Storks are white __________.
2. They have red bills and long red ______.
3. Storks have no __________.
4. They always come back to the same __________.
5. Storks take good care of their __________.
6. Storks are considered __________ __________ birds.

Syllabication

Divide each of the following words into syllables by drawing a line between the syllables. See the sample.

1. com|plete
2. admit
3. define
4. defense
5. unlikely
6. unreal
7. postman
8. sudden
9. beforehand
10. carpenter
11. misprint
12. distrust
13. mountain
14. accepted
15. remember
16. adoption
17. turnpike
18. unfasten
19. uncertain
20. depart
21. joyful
22. nearest
23. better
24. telegraph
25. uncommon
26. elephant
27. detergent
28. monument
29. occasion
30. sweeter
31. refund
32. fairness
33. expensive
34. dislocation
35. defrost
36. celebrate

Vegetables to Grow On

Vegetables make up an important part of your diet. You should have at least one serving of vegetables a day.

Green, yellow, and leafy vegetables and tomatoes help supply your body with vitamins A, B, and C. These vegetables also supply your body with calcium and iron. Calcium helps your bones stay strong. Iron keeps your blood healthy.

Other vegetables like potatoes, celery, beets, and corn help supply your body with carbohydrates and minerals. Carbohydrates give you much energy to work and play. Minerals help your body grow straight and stay strong.

Without vegetables your body would not grow very well.

Write the names of these vegetables.

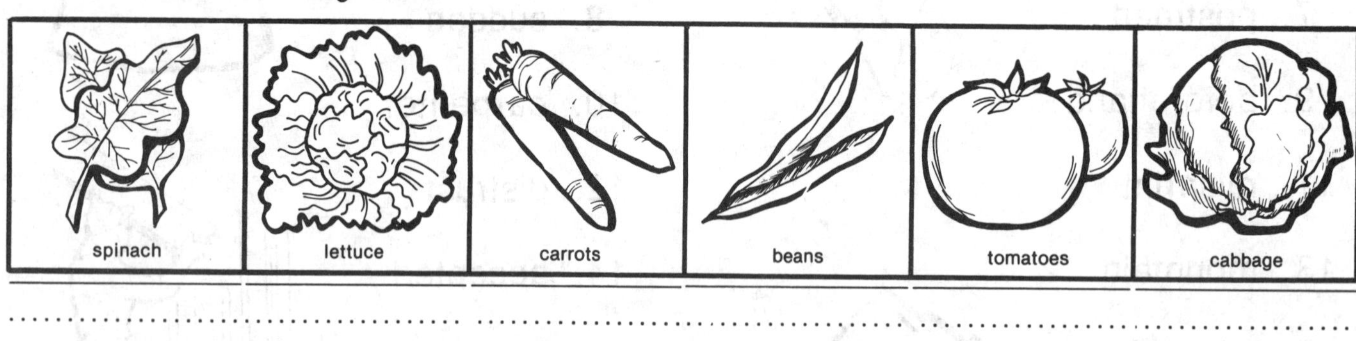

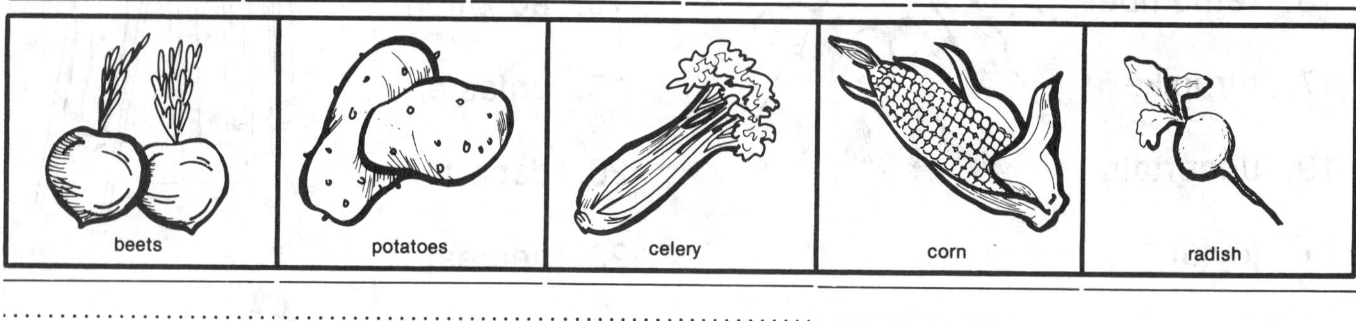

Complete these sentences.

1. Vegetables, like potatoes, supply my body with ____________ and ____________.
2. Carbohydrates give me ____________.
3. Vegetables, like carrots, supply my body with vitamins ______, ______, and ______.
4. ____________ keeps my blood healthy.
5. ____________ keeps my bones strong.

The Eskimo Dog

Look at the boxes. Say, spell, and write each word. Read the story, and fill in the blanks. Reread the story if you have trouble.

1. dog

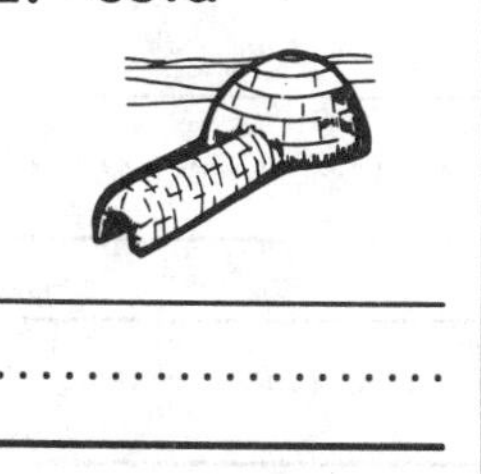

2. cold

3. snow

4. howl

5. head

6. tail

The Eskimo dog likes cold weather. Cold weather does not hurt him. He has long thick hair to keep him warm. He also has large hairy feet to keep him from sinking into the snow.

The Eskimo dog has great courage. He can defend himself well. He can also endure great hardships. The Eskimo dog must be able to do these things. Life is not easy in the cold places where he lives.

Eskimo dogs are very useful dogs. They are trained to pull long sleds. They can travel 20 to 40 miles a day. These dogs are also used to hunt seals and bears.

THINGS TO REMEMBER

1. The Eskimo dog has great __________.
2. He has long thick __________ to keep him warm.
3. Eskimo dogs are trained to pull long __________.
4. The Eskimo dog has large hairy __________ to keep him from sinking into the snow.
5. Eskimo dogs are used to hunt __________ and __________.
6. The Eskimo dog likes __________ weather.

7. hair

8. sled

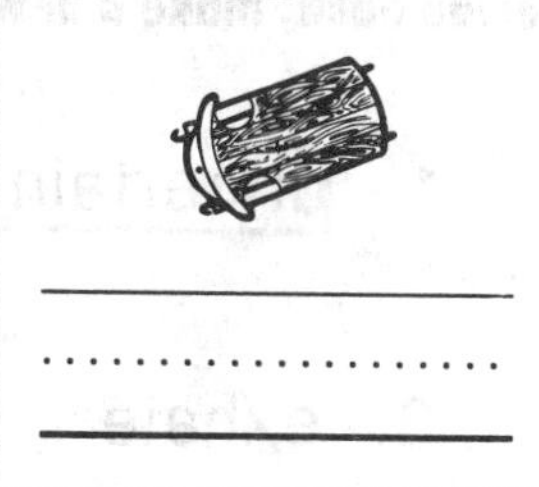

9. feet

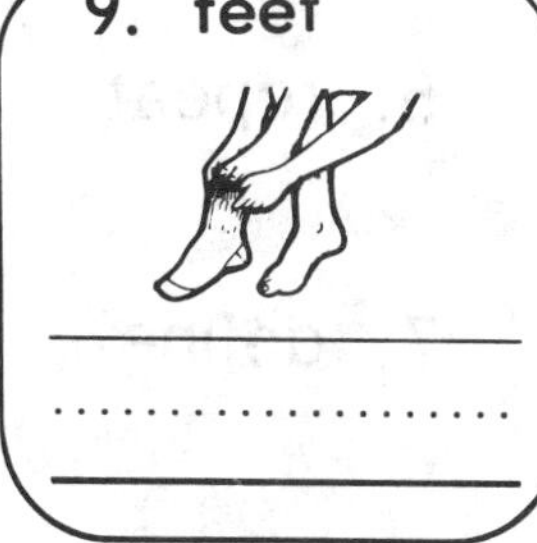

10. Eskimo

11. travel

12. bear

What Is a Prefix?

A syllable is sometimes added to the beginning of a root word and called a prefix. A prefix changes the meaning of the word.

EXAMPLE: The prefix "re" means "again" (remake), "pre" means "before" (prepay), and "un" means "not" (unfed).

In the following underline each root word, and draw a box around each prefix. (See example "1.") On the blank beside each, make a new word using the same prefix.

1. uncertain uncommon
2. except ________
3. exhale ________
4. excuse ________
5. repeat ________
6. invite ________
7. define ________
8. disappear ________
9. subtract ________
10. dispose ________
11. deface ________
12. recall ________
13. involve ________
14. apart ________
15. decode ________
16. demerit ________
17. unhappy ________
18. dislike ________
19. discard ________
20. rejoin ________
21. enforce ________
22. avert ________
23. return ________
24. prepare ________

Healthy Ways

Look at the words. Write the correct words in the blanks. Circle each word after use.

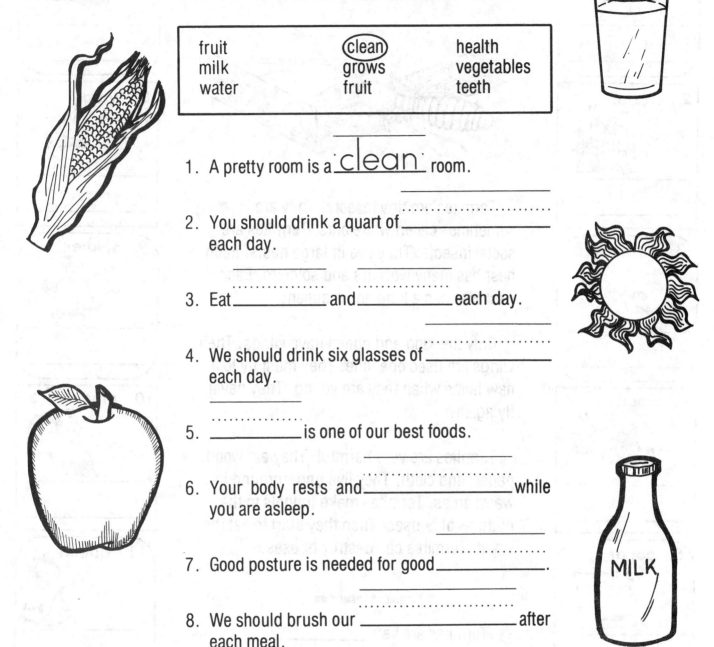

fruit	clean	health
milk	grows	vegetables
water	fruit	teeth

1. A pretty room is a clean room.
2. You should drink a quart of ____________ each day.
3. Eat ____________ and ____________ each day.
4. We should drink six glasses of ____________ each day.
5. ____________ is one of our best foods.
6. Your body rests and ____________ while you are asleep.
7. Good posture is needed for good ____________.
8. We should brush our ____________ after each meal.

MORE GOOD MANNERS

Before you begin to eat, help pass the dishes at the table to see that everyone present is served. Be careful not to express your special dislike to any food. Eat soup slowly and quietly from the side of your spoon. Bring your food to your mouth; don't meet it halfway. Don't duck down to meet it coming up. Be willing to try a little of any food once. If you must leave before the others have finished eating, always ask to be excused. Take small bites, and chew your food well. Always eat leisurely at mealtime. Practice good manners at home.

The Little Termite

Look at the boxes. Say, spell, and write each word. Read the story, and fill in the blanks. Reread the story if you have trouble.

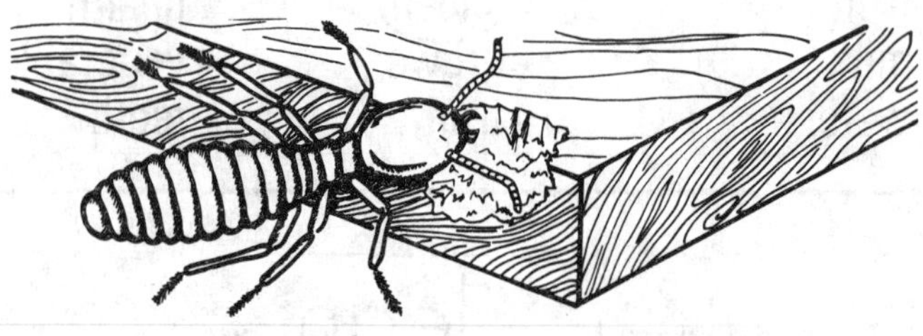

Termites are tiny insects. They are sometimes called white ants. Termites are social insects. They live in large nests. Each nest has many workers and soldiers. Each nest also has a king and a queen.

Only the king and queen have wings. Their wings are used one time. They must fly to a new home when they are young. They never fly again.

Termites are very harmful. They eat wood, paper, and cloth. They live underground in warm areas. Termites make tunnels to the bottoms of houses. Then they start to eat the wood. Termites can destroy houses.

THINGS TO REMEMBER

1. Termites are very __________.
2. They eat __________, paper, and cloth.
3. Termites are tiny __________.
4. They are sometimes called white __________.
5. They live underground in __________ areas.
6. Each nest has a king and a __________.

1. insect

2. worker

3. ant

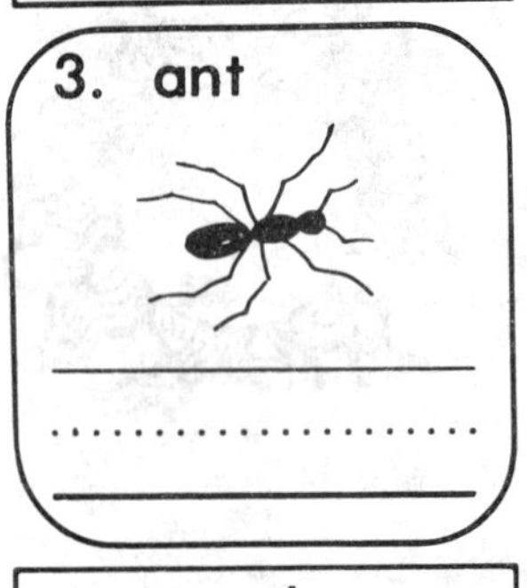

4. wood

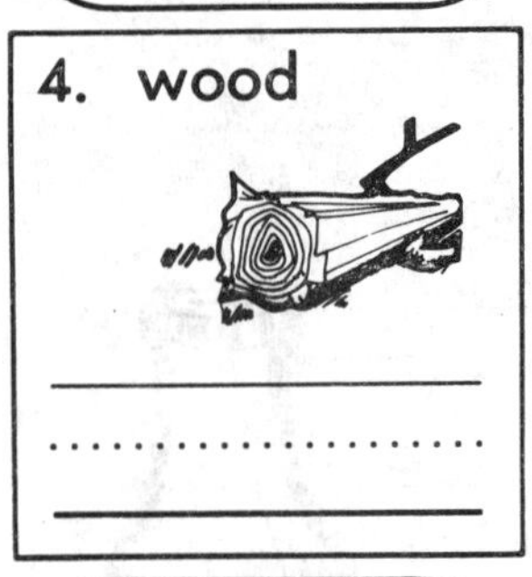

5. paper

6. cloth

7. nest

8. wings

9. soldier

10. king

11. queen

12. tunnel

What Is a Suffix?

A suffix is a syllable that is sometimes added to the end of a word or word part to change the meaning. EXAMPLES: applying, bitterness, comical, likely

Underline each word or word part, and draw a box around each suffix. (See example "1.") On the blank beside each word, make a new word using the suffix.

1. harder	softer	2. drying	
3. longest		4. colonize	
5. disturbance		6. useful	
7. handsome		8. tiresome	
9. shorter		10. boring	
11. childless		12. modernize	
13. uppermost		14. frightful	
15. upward		16. goodness	
17. securely		18. appearance	
19. funniest		20. shyly	
21. kingdom		22. treatment	
23. courageous		24. greater	
25. respectable		26. appendicitis	
27. overactive		28. hilly	
29. ridiculous		30. itemize	

Eat Fresh Fruits

Write the name of each fruit. Choose the name from the box. Use each name only once. Circle each name after using.

a.

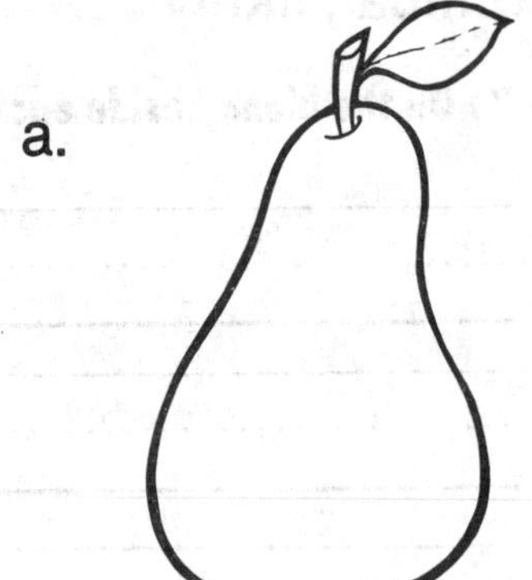

pear

e.

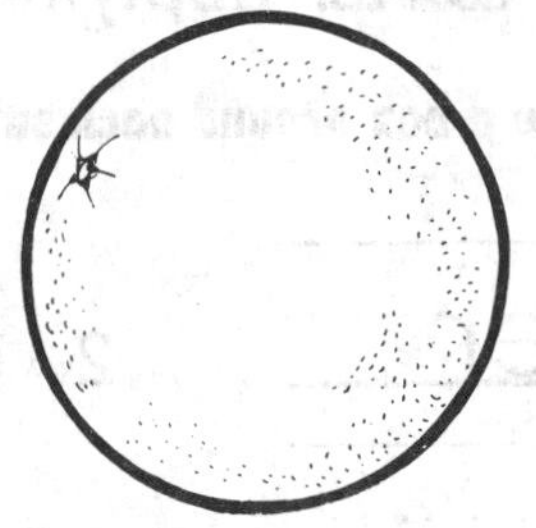

g.

b.

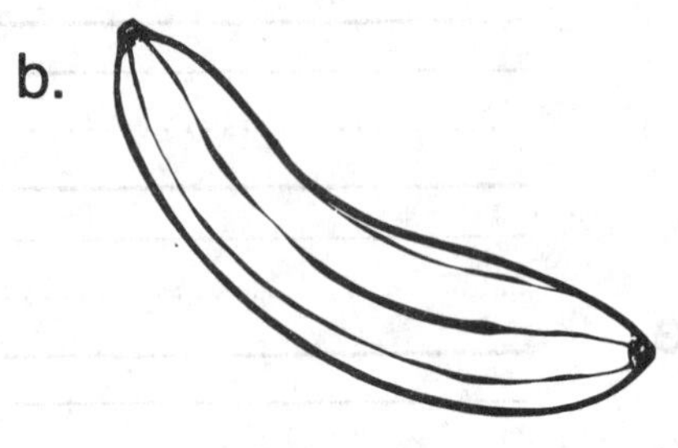

1. strawberries
2. banana
3. pineapple
4. peach
5. grapes
6. cherries
7. orange
8. apple
9. plums
10. pear

h.

c.

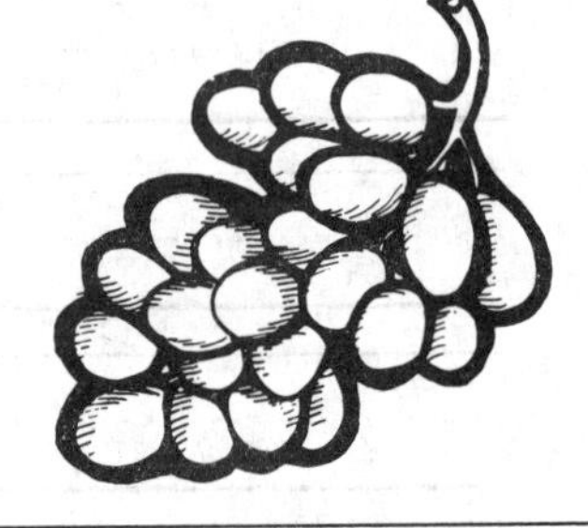

i.

d.

f.

j.

All About Lizards

Look at the boxes. Say, spell, and write each word. Read the story, and fill in the blanks. Reread the story if you have trouble.

Lizards are reptiles. They have scaly skin and long tails. They are too small to fight. They protect themselves by playing tricks.

One lizard's tail comes off when something takes hold of it. The lizard then gets away. Another type of lizard can blow itself up. It looks three times as big as it really is.

Lizards have different ways of moving around. Some jump through trees. They are called flying dragons. Some walk on feet; others do not. Some can walk on ceilings. Others walk upright on their two back feet!

THINGS TO REMEMBER

1. Lizards have ___________ skin.
2. One lizard's ___________ comes off.
3. Some lizards walk on _________.
4. Some walk on their _________ back feet.
5. Lizards protect themselves by playing ___________.
6. Some jump through ___________.

1. lizard

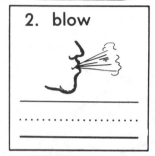

2. blow

3. scaly

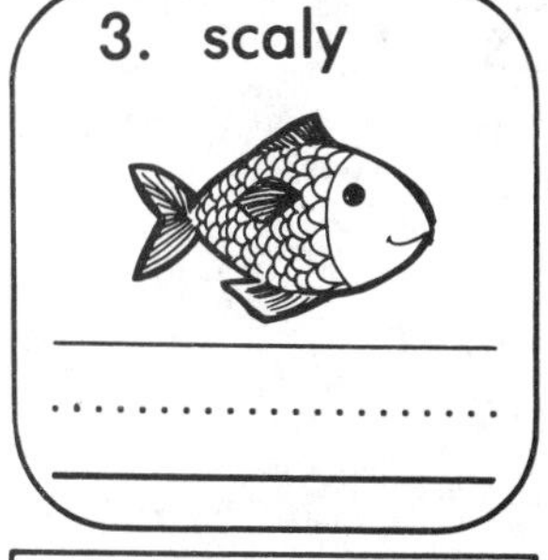

4. tail

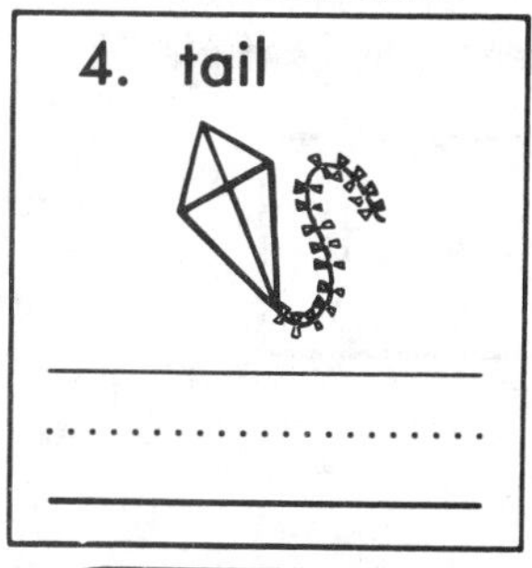

5. reptile

6. walk

7. fight

8. upright

9. feet

10 jump

11. tree

12. dragon

Adding Prefixes and Suffixes

A **In each sentence add a prefix from the box to the root to form a word that makes sense. See sample "1."**

dis	un	ex	re	mis	in	ac	a

1. Our scout troop __dis__ covered a deserted mine.
2. My father is very ________ happy with my poor grades.
3. I want to ________ change this blue shirt for a red one.
4. Please do not ________ peat this story; it is a secret.
5. The pilot ________ judged the airstrip and crashed.

B **In each sentence add a suffix from the box to the word part to form a word that makes sense. See sample "1."**

less	ness	tion	ful	en	ly	able	ward

1. The dog was very faith __ful__ to his master.
2. The natives were rest ________ because of the tiger.
3. It is very like ________ that rain will come today.
4. Pets need love and kind ________.
5. Our vacation was most enjoy ________.

Vegetables

Vegetables help us to grow and to stay healthy. Some vegetables grow above the ground. Other vegetables grow under the ground.

Write the name of each vegetable. Color the vegetables. Underline each vegetable that grows under the ground.

Frogs

Look at the boxes. Say, spell, and write each word. Read the story, and fill in the blanks. Reread the story if you have trouble.

1. frog

2. sticky

3. land

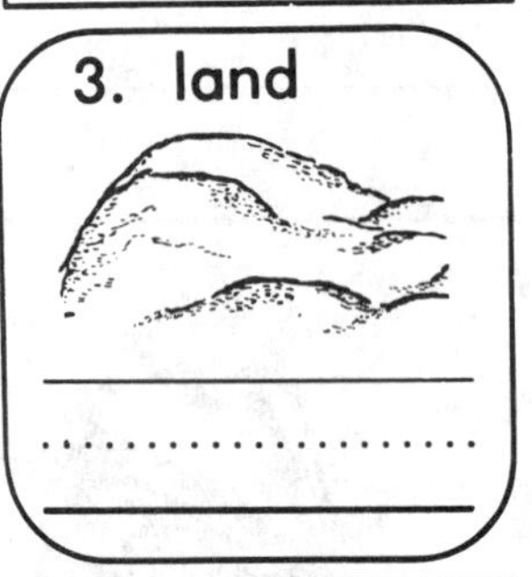

4. bulging

5. swim

6. jump

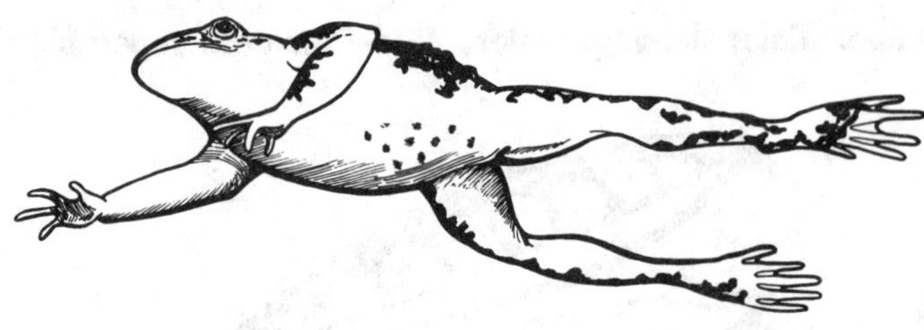

Did you know there are about 2,000 different kinds of frogs living today? Well, there are! There are bullfrogs and grass frogs and wood frogs — all kinds of frogs! Most frogs are alike in many ways.

Frogs have bulging eyes and make low croaking noises. They have long back legs that help them jump on the ground and swim in the water. Frogs are lucky. They can live in water or on land. Frogs also have long sticky tongues. Frogs can shoot out their tongues and catch insects. Frogs help people by eating many insects. They also eat minnows, earthworms, and spiders.

Frogs have many enemies. Snakes and birds eat frogs. Fish eat frogs. Even people eat frogs. In some places people like frogs' legs very much.

THINGS TO REMEMBER

1. Frogs help people by eating many ___________.
2. Frogs can live in ___________ or on ___________.
3. There are about ___________ different kinds of frogs living today.
4. Frogs have long sticky ___________.
5. They have long back legs that help them _________ on the ground and _________ in the water.
6. Frogs have many ___________.

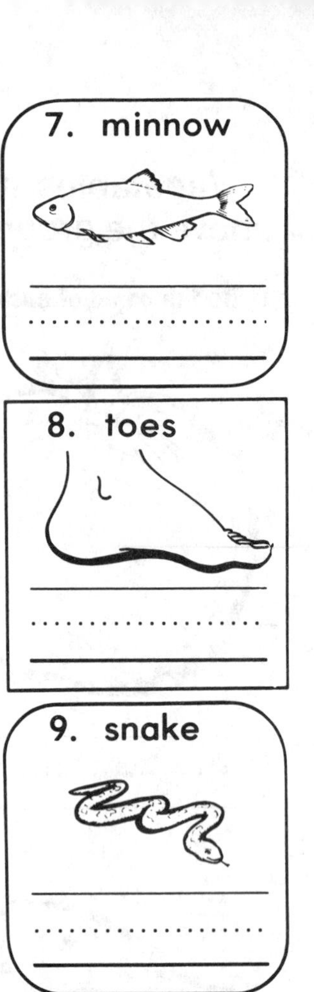

7. minnow

8. toes

9. snake

10. spiders

11. tongue

12. earthworm

Matching Synonyms

In the following, match group "A" to "B" and group "C" to "D." Draw a line through each word in the "B" and "D" lists as they are used. See sample "1."

	A	B
o	1. present	a. moist
____	2. timid	b. silent
____	3. shy	c. wealthy
____	4. damp	d. sack
____	5. below	e. coat
____	6. dashed	f. yell
____	7. quiet	g. closed
____	8. remain	h. end
____	9. near	i. stone
____	10. rich	j. high
____	11. large	k. odd
____	12. shut	l. bashful
____	13. bag	m. big
____	14. rock	n. fast
____	15. jacket	~~o. gift~~
____	16. sad	p. glad
____	17. happy	q. raced
____	18. shout	r. jump
____	19. queer	s. forest
____	20. finish	t. shy
____	21. leap	u. unhappy
____	22. quick	v. stay
____	23. tall	w. under
____	24. woods	x. close

	C	D
h	1. also	a. sleep
____	2. noise	b. mannerly
____	3. cross	c. questioned
____	4. shouted	d. start
____	5. woman	e. limb
____	6. merry	f. visitor
____	7. circle	g. several
____	8. build	~~h. too~~
____	9. nap	i. lake
____	10. begin	j. speak
____	11. guest	k. silly
____	12. invite	l. excellent
____	13. branch	m. scared
____	14. place	n. ring
____	15. afraid	o. insect
____	16. foolish	p. lady
____	17. asked	q. spot
____	18. some	r. gay
____	19. talk	s. angry
____	20. idea	t. plan
____	21. pond	u. called
____	22. polite	v. sound
____	23. fine	w. ask
____	24. bug	x. make

A Good Breakfast

Write the names of the foods. Circle the ones that are good breakfast foods. Select the words from the box.

tomato	cereal	corn	bread	eggs	celery
cake	soup	milk	carrots	oranges	ice cream

1. cereal

2.

3.

4.

5.

6.

7.

8.

9.

10.

11.

12.

Salmon

Look at the boxes. Say, spell, and write each word. Read the story, and fill in the blanks. Reread the story if you have trouble.

1. salmon

2. eggs

3. story

4. flows

5. ocean

6. stream

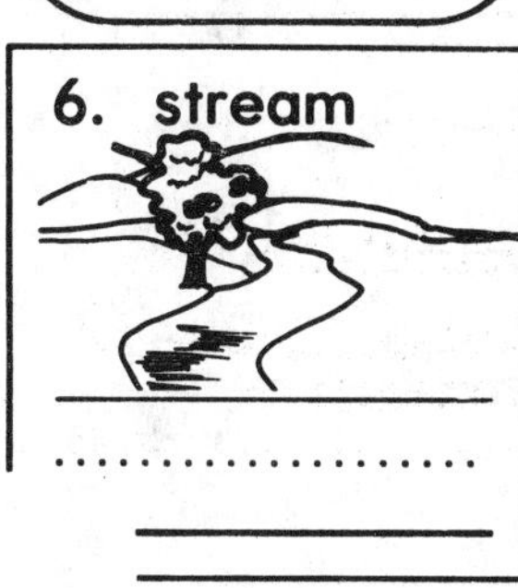

7. city

8. food

9. thin

10. factory

11. float

12. tired

The salmon, a very important food fish, has a strange life story. Salmon are born in small streams. In a few months they start downstream toward the ocean. Many never reach the ocean. They are eaten by other fish or die in areas where cities and factories have polluted the water. Those that do reach the ocean find plenty of food and live there for years.

At some time in salmon life, something causes the fish to start back toward the freshwater streams. Some may even return to the same areas where they were hatched. There they lay their eggs. Then, thin and tired, they float downstream to die.

THINGS TO REMEMBER

1. Salmon are born in small __________.
2. The salmon is a very important __________ fish.
3. Some salmon return to the same areas where they were __________.
4. There they lay their __________.
5. The salmon that reach the __________ find plenty of __________ there.
6. After laying their eggs, salmon float downstream to __________.

Greater Than or Less Than

The sign for greater than is ($>$). The sign for less than is ($<$).

Use $>$ or $<$ to make each sentence true. See example "A."

A.	6 + 7	$<$	7 + 7	O.	6 + 3	____	5 + 2
B.	3 + 6	____	4 + 4	P.	5 + 6	____	5 + 4
C.	9 + 1	____	6 + 10	Q.	8 + 8	____	5 + 7
D.	4 + 7	____	5 + 5	R.	9 + 5	____	10 + 3
E.	3 + 5	____	3 + 6	S.	9 + 7	____	4 + 6
F.	6 + 6	____	3 + 8	T.	7 + 8	____	9 + 9
G.	10 + 3	____	8 + 4	U.	6 + 8	____	7 + 5
H.	5 + 5	____	3 + 8	V.	10 + 5	____	4 + 10
I.	4 + 9	____	9 + 3	W.	8 + 4	____	3 + 7
J.	8 + 6	____	10 + 2	X.	10 + 8	____	9 + 10
K.	5 + 9	____	7 + 6	Y.	6 + 5	____	10 + 4
L.	8 + 7	____	7 + 4	Z.	9 + 6	____	10 + 7
M.	10 + 5	____	2 + 10	A.	9 + 8	____	10 + 6
N.	9 + 6	____	8 + 8	B.	9 + 10	____	5 + 8

Matching Antonyms

A **Antonyms are words that do not mean the same thing. They are opposite in meaning. Fill in each blank with the correct word. See sample "1."**

1. Mary cried at the show when the little girl died in the movie. (laughed, cried)

2. I wore my coat to school today, because it was __________ outside. (chilly, warm)

3. At the beginning of the play, the curtain is __________. (raised, lowered)

4. The owl is thought to be a very __________ bird. (foolish, wise)

5. We are usually __________ when we are sleeping. (loud, quiet)

B **Put the letter for each word in the blank beside its antonym. Circle the word used. See sample "1."**

I

g	1. laugh	a. gentle
____	2. break	b. awake
____	3. different	c. fix
____	4. yes	d. timid
____	5. tame	e. good
____	6. asleep	f. alike
____	7. midnight	g. cry
____	8. gruff	h. no
____	9. wicked	i. noon
____	10. brave	j. wild

II

f	1. pull	a. slow
____	2. forget	b. later
____	3. safe	c. quiet
____	4. fast	d. small
____	5. light	e. straight
____	6. sooner	f. push
____	7. crooked	g. poor
____	8. noisy	h. dangerous
____	9. rich	i. dark
____	10. large	j. remember

Health and Safety Quiz

Write the number of the correct picture that fits each description. See the sample.

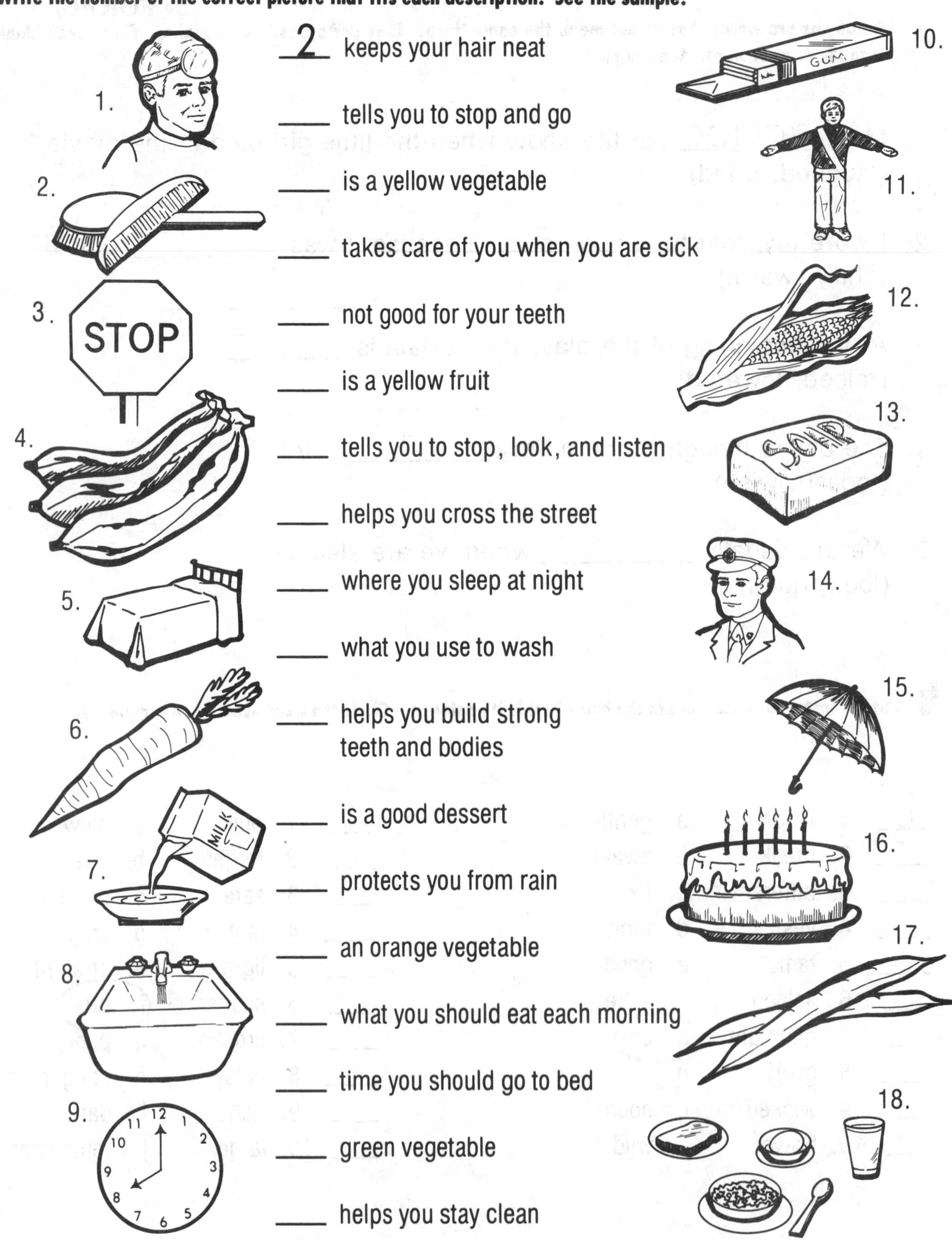

1. – 18. (pictures)

__2__ keeps your hair neat

____ tells you to stop and go

____ is a yellow vegetable

____ takes care of you when you are sick

____ not good for your teeth

____ is a yellow fruit

____ tells you to stop, look, and listen

____ helps you cross the street

____ where you sleep at night

____ what you use to wash

____ helps you build strong teeth and bodies

____ is a good dessert

____ protects you from rain

____ an orange vegetable

____ what you should eat each morning

____ time you should go to bed

____ green vegetable

____ helps you stay clean

Baby Animals

JUST FOR FUN

Vocabulary Study ● Draw a line under each correct answer.

1. A need is something you	(a) must have	(b) want	(c) should have.
2. When you protect something, you	(a) hurt it	(b) watch over it	(c) use it.
3. ''Some'' means	(a) ''all''	(b) ''none''	(c) ''not all.''
4. Another name for ''babies'' is	(a) ''young''	(b) ''parents''	(c) ''old.''

Some baby animals come from eggs. Others come from their mothers' bodies.

Many baby animals cannot take care of themselves. They need their mothers. They need their fathers. The mothers and fathers take care of their young. The parents feed the babies. They protect them. The babies stay with their parents until they can help themselves. The parents teach them.

Some baby animals never see their parents. These babies know how to find food. They can care for themselves.

Baby animals usually look like their parents. They are often cute and playful.

Answer these questions about the story:

1. Baby animals need their	(a) brothers	(b) mothers	(c) fathers.
2. Baby animals come from	(a) eggs	(b) mothers' bodies	(c) fathers' bodies.
3. Parents	(a) feed babies	(b) protect babies	(c) teach babies.
4. Baby animals usually look like	(a) parents	(b) puppies	(c) mice.
5. Baby animals are often	(a) cute	(b) mean	(c) playful.

Identify each picture.

____

____

3.

____

4.

____

5.

____

6.

____

7.

____

8.

____

Writing Digits

Write digits from number words. See sample "A."

	NUMBER WORDS	DIGITS
A.	eleven	11
B.	twenty-five	
C.	sixteen	
D.	thirty-seven	
E.	fourteen	
F.	thirty-one	
G.	eighteen	
H.	twenty-four	
I.	twelve	
J.	twenty-two	
K.	nineteen	
L.	twenty-eight	

	NUMBER WORDS	DIGITS
M.	seventeen	
N.	twenty-three	
O.	fifteen	
P.	thirty-three	
Q.	thirteen	
R.	forty-six	
S.	fifty-seven	
T.	thirty-five	
U.	twenty-six	
V.	thirty-two	
W.	forty-nine	
X.	fifty-five	

Food

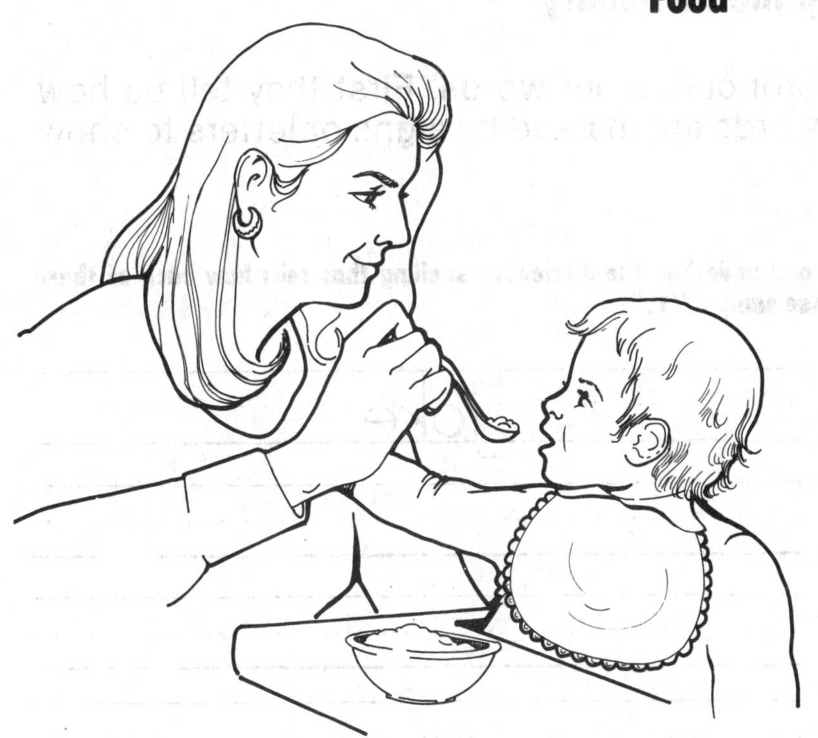

Food is our most basic need. No one can live for long without something to eat. Many people in the world are hungry because there is not enough food for them to eat. These people are not healthy. They often suffer from disease. Some even die from hunger.

A **Fill in the blanks using the words from the box.**

disease	hungry	healthy	food

1. Our most basic need is ______________.
2. ______________ people often suffer from ______________.
3. People who eat enough of the right foods have ______________ bodies.

B **True or False**

T F 1. Everyone must eat food to live.
T F 2. Everyone in the world has enough food to eat.
T F 3. Hungry people are healthy.
T F 4. Some people die from hunger.
T F 5. The child in the picture on the right side of this sheet is healthy and happy.

Using the Dictionary

Dictionaries help us learn to pronounce our words. First they tell us how the words are spelled. Then the words are marked by signs or letters to show how they are pronounced.

Look the following words up in the dictionary, and underline the dictionary spelling that tells how each of these words should be pronounced. Write each word. See sample "1."

1. joke — (a) gŏk (b) jōk — joke
2. writer — (a) rīt′ẽr (b) wrīt ẽr
3. car — (a) kār (b) kär
4. climb — (a) klīm (b) klĭm
5. juice — (a) jo͝os (b) jo͞os
6. plain — (a) plăn (b) plān
7. baby — (a) bā bī (b) bā bĭ
8. come — (a) kūm (b) kŭm
9. high — (a) hĭg (b) hī
10. fancy — (a) făn sĭ (b) făncy
11. meat — (a) māt (b) mēt
12. edge — (a) ĕj (b) ēj
13. pillow — (a) pĭl lo͞o (b) pĭl lō

Planning Our Breakfast Menu

Look at the pictures, and draw circles around those foods we eat for breakfast. Write the numbers of the correct terms in the blanks.

Dogs

Vocabulary Study ● Draw a line under each correct answer. **JUST FOR FUN**

1.	A puppy is a	(a) baby dog	(b) boy dog	(c) girl dog.
2.	The opposite of "wild" is	(a) "tame"	(b) "not tame"	(c) "mean."
3.	"Some" means	(a) "all"	(b) "none"	(c) "not all."
4.	Another word for "follow" is	(a) "ahead"	(b) "obey"	(c) "go before."

Dogs are found all over the world. Some are wild. Most dogs are not wild. They make very good pets.

Dogs are very smart. They can be trained to do tricks. They can be trained to follow orders.

Dogs are very loyal. Pets are usually faithful to their owners. Wild dogs often help each other.

A dog's nose is very important. With it he finds foods. He finds his way around. He knows a friend.

If you want a dog to be friendly, you must pet it as a puppy. The dog has been called "man's best friend."

Answer these questions about the story:

1.	Dogs are found	(a) only in cold places	(b) only in hot places	(c) all over the world.
2.	Dogs are	(a) smart	(b) stupid	(c) hard to train.
3.	Dogs are loyal to	(a) everyone	(b) no one	(c) their owners.
4.	Dogs have a very good sense of	(a) smell	(b) sight	(c) touch.
5.	Dogs are called	(a) "kings of beasts"	(b) "man's best friends"	(c) "man's worst friends."

Draw a line from each picture to the correct word.

1. 2. 3.

boy
bell
box
baby
bear
boat

4.

5.

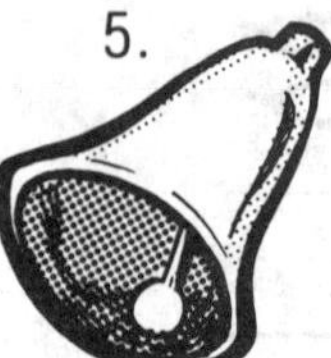

6.

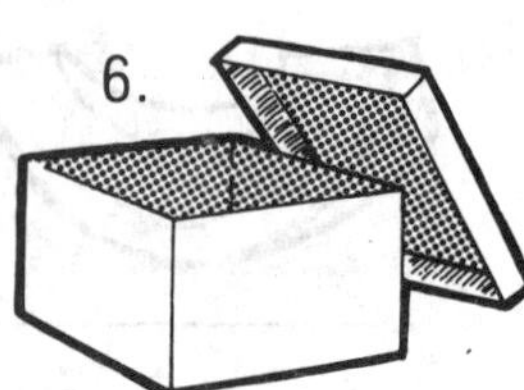

Small and Large Numbers

Circle the smallest number in each box. See sample "A."

A.	15	8	(3)	22	19	(7)	(9)	11	18
B.	24	17	21	32	22	12	11	6	14
C.	13	23	16	11	17	13	20	16	12
D.	51	50	56	30	39	37	36	39	34
E.	12	13	11	6	10	7	18	81	80
F.	75	82	60	89	90	92	64	69	66
G.	42	40	49	51	62	49	10	98	99
H.	10	14	9	17	19	24	21	20	12

Circle the largest number in each box. See sample "A."

A.	31	13	(34)	90	(92)	91	40	46	(49)
B.	75	70	73	28	30	82	82	79	83
C.	46	50	49	69	62	65	57	52	56
D.	84	89	90	10	26	12	92	93	91
E.	13	9	5	12	10	2	45	40	35
F.	50	49	38	79	89	86	31	24	19
G.	80	86	81	20	19	10	40	39	38
H.	75	43	82	3	7	11	14	17	21

Milk

Milk is nature's most nearly perfect food. It has more of the nutrients our bodies need than any other food. Milk contains much calcium which is necessary for strong bones and teeth.

A Write "yes" or "no" after each sentence.

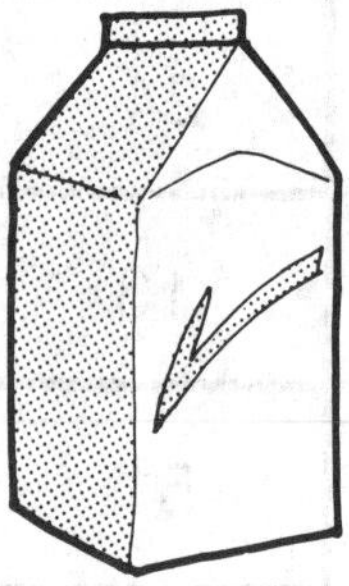

1. Milk has all of the nutrients your body needs. ______________
2. You can have strong bones and teeth without drinking milk. ______________
3. Milk is necessary for a healthy body. ______________

Foods made from milk are called dairy products. These include butter, cheese, and ice cream.

B Draw a box around each picture that is a dairy product, and write its name in the blank.

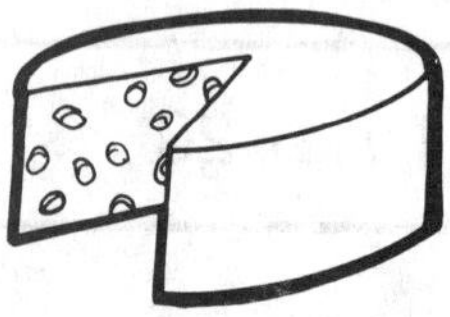

A. 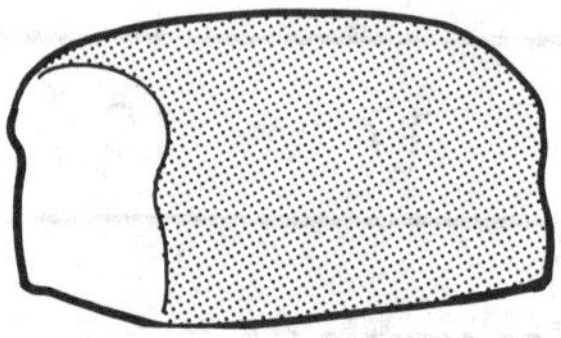 ______________ B. 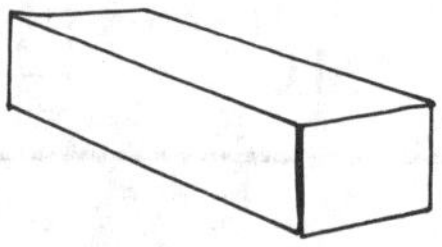 ______________ C. ______________

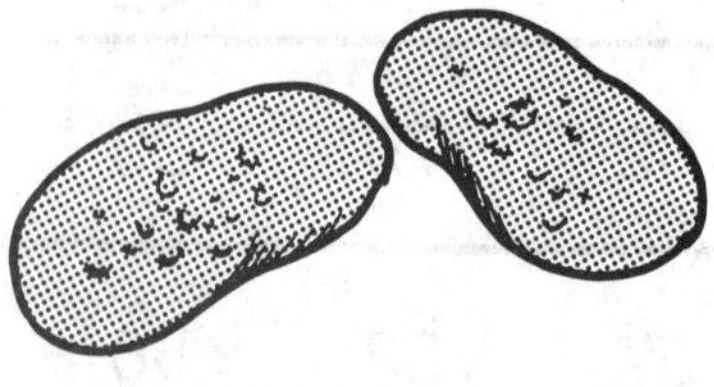

D.  ______________ E. 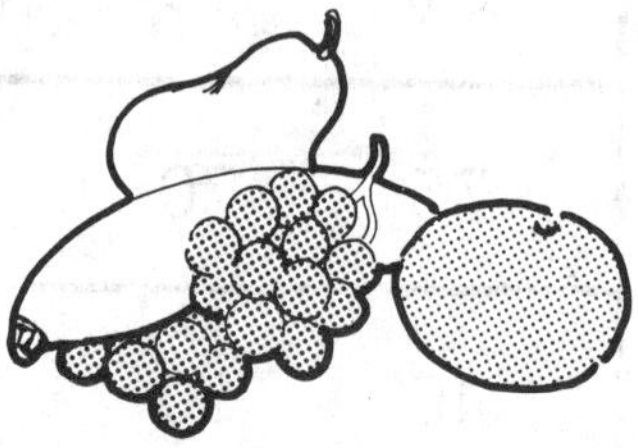 ______________ F. ______________

C Draw a line from each picture to its name. Put an "X" over the drink that does not contain milk.

1.

hot chocolate
shake
soda pop
milk

2.

3.

4.

Vowel Rules

1. A vowel within a word or syllable is usually short.
2. Usually, when there are two vowels within a word or syllable, the first one is long; and the second one is silent.
3. A vowel at the end of a word or syllable is usually long.

A **In the following rows underline each word that has the same vowel sound as the object pictured. See the samples.**

1.	2.	3.	4.	5.	6.
hope	rush	fence	mind	sail	leg
wrote	such	sew	village	happy	mend
trouble	huge	real	ice	race	meal
boil	shoe	else	mile	fast	teeth
oil	true	beat	winter	father	week
young	suit	deep	sister	wag	lead
bone	uncle	lazy	inch	gather	tent
float	dug	tear	hidden	large	leak

B **Mark the first vowel in each word below as either a short (◡) or a long (—) sound. See the samples.**

0. rĭch
1. fāke
2. tălent
3. bit
4. pride
5. pig
6. back
7. solve
8. lunch
9. rose
10. sap
11. funny
12. men
13. cup
14. five
15. nap
16. cape
17. tender
18. pine
19. kite
20. transport
21. drink
22. rock
23. nest
24. feet
25. doctor
26. cane
27. shake
28. night
29. glue
30. go
31. melon

Fruits

Finish each sentence. Answer each question. Color the pictures.

1. I am an ____________.

   I grow on ____________.

   What color am I? ____________

2. I am a bunch of ____________.

   I grow on a ____________ .

   What color am I? ____________

3. I am an ____________.

   People drink my juice at ____________.

   What color am I? ____________

4. I am a ____________.

   People ____________ me to eat me.

   What color am I? ____________

5. I am a ____________.

   When I am ripe, I turn ____________.

   Before I turn red, I am ____________.

Working Dogs

JUST FOR FUN

Vocabulary Study ● Draw a line under each correct answer.

1. "Train" means (a) "teach" (b) "learn" (c) "help."
2. The opposite of "heavy" is (a) "strong" (b) "light" (c) "big."
3. A herd has (a) one member (b) two members (c) many members.
4. "Lead" means (a) "to follow" (b) "to guide" (c) "to go behind."

Dogs make good pets. Some dogs are also good workers.

In the cold Arctic, dogs are trained to pull sleds. These dogs work in teams. They pull heavy loads for long distances.

Sheep dogs watch over animals. They are found wherever people farm. They keep the herd together. They take animals from one place to another. They protect animals from danger.

Guard dogs are usually big. They are willing to fight. Most have strong jaws. They are loyal to their masters.

Guide dogs lead the blind. They are trained when they are young.

Dogs are important animals. They help many people.

Answer these questions about the story:

1. Sled dogs live (a) in the Arctic (b) in mountains (c) in the desert.
2. Sheep dogs work (a) on farms (b) in cities (c) in schools.
3. Guard dogs are usually (a) small (b) big (c) strong.
4. Guide dogs lead the (a) deaf (b) blind (c) sick.
5. Dogs are (a) pets (b) workers (c) helpers.

Draw a line from each picture to the correct word.

1.

3.

2.

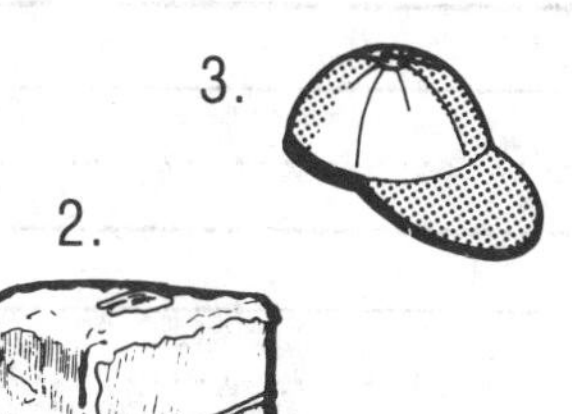

cow
cake
cap
cat
car
coat

4.

5.

6.

Batting Lineup

1. Cobb **rf**
2. Ward **cf**
3. Chance **1b**
4. Baker **3b**
5. Ruth **lf**
6. Collins **2b**
7. Banks **ss**
8. Kelly **c**
9. Waddell **p**
10. Aaron **dh***

*In American League the designated hitter bats for the pitcher.

Using the above information, answer these questions.

A. Who bats sixth? Collins

B. Who is listed in the eighth place?

C. Who bats last in the National League?

D. Who bats in the seventh place?

E. Who is the third batter?

F. Who bats first?

G. Who bats fourth?

H. Who bats ninth in the American League?

I. Who bats second?

J. Who bats fifth?

Grain

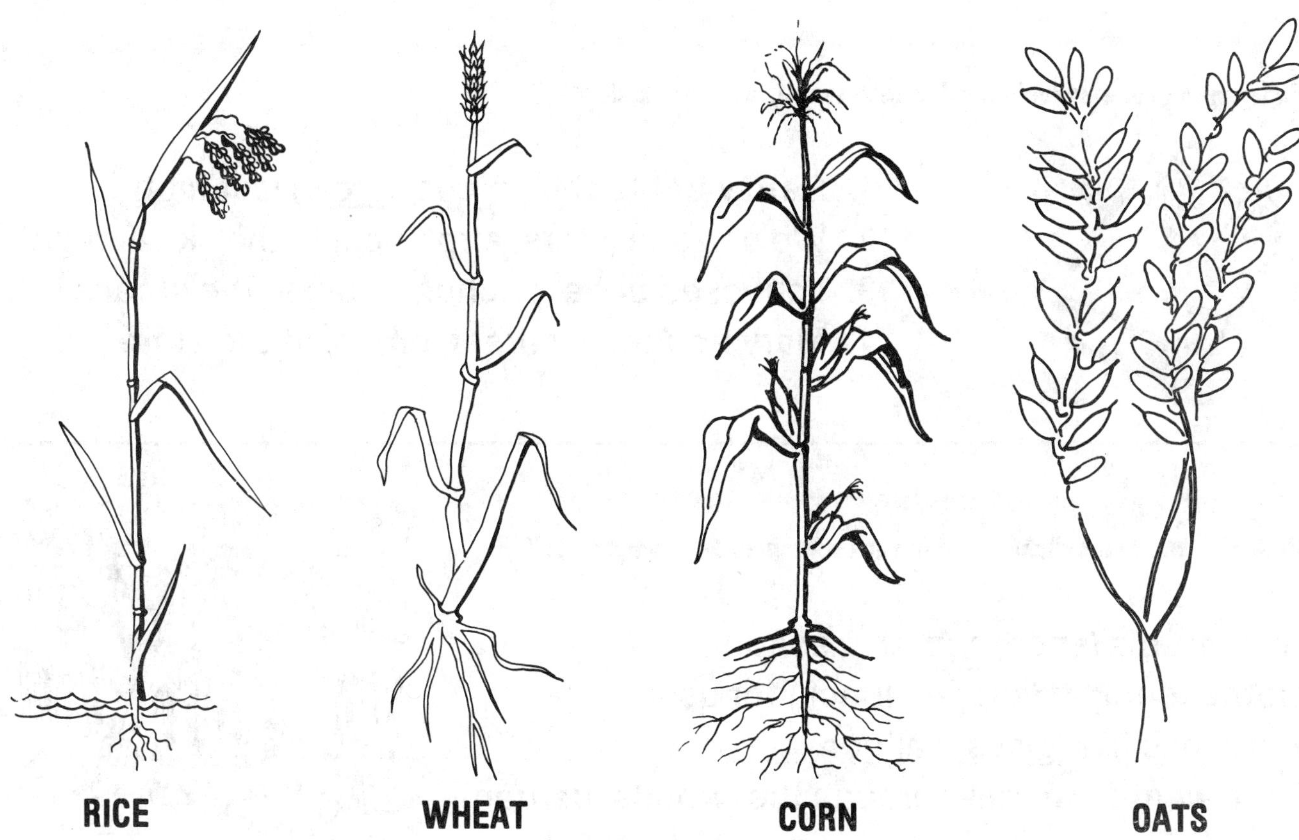

A Put the letter of the correct answer in each blank.

1. Grain is small, dried ______C______.
2. Wheat seed is ground into __________.
3. ______________________ is made from flour.
4. Cornflakes and oatmeal are ______________.
5. __________ is the main food of some countries.

A.	Bread
B.	cereals
C.	seeds
D.	Rice
E.	flour

B Put the letter of the correct word in each blank.

1. ______ and ______ are breakfast breads.
2. Hamburgers and hot dogs are eaten with ______.
3. Sandwiches are made from ______.
4. ______are good with dinner meals.
5. ______ is made from corn which has been ground.

A.	Corn bread	C.	Biscuits	E.	toast
B.	loaf bread	D.	buns	F.	Hot rolls

Sentence Completion

A **Underline the one-syllable word in each sentence. See sample "1."**

1. Beth went to the (circus, show) last night.
2. We can see (stars, airplanes) in the sky at night.
3. I checked out a (pitcher, book) at the library.
4. Mary bought a (carpet, dress) at the store.

B **Underline the two-syllable word in each sentence. See sample "1."**

1. Tom left his (shoe, paper) at school.
2. Mother cooked (supper, lunch) for us.
3. Jim broke the (glass, balloon).
4. Alice wanted to walk through the (woods, garden).

C **Underline the three-syllable word in each sentence. See sample "1."**

1. The (pears, tomatoes) are ready to pick.
2. The (painter, carpenter) is working on our house.
3. Jane and I saw a/an (lion, elephant) at the zoo.
4. The art teacher drew a picture of a/an (octopus, tree).

D **Choose the correct word for each sentence. Draw a line under it. See sample "1."**

1. Flowers have pretty (carpet, blossoms).
2. Linda read a (dress, letter) to her grandmother.
3. Susan put the letter in the (sandbox, mailbox).
4. The stars twinkle in the (sky, sun) at night.
5. We saw a (giraffe, star) at the zoo.

Mr. Health Food

Fruits, vegetables, meats, and bread make us healthy. Write the name of each picture. Choose words from the box.

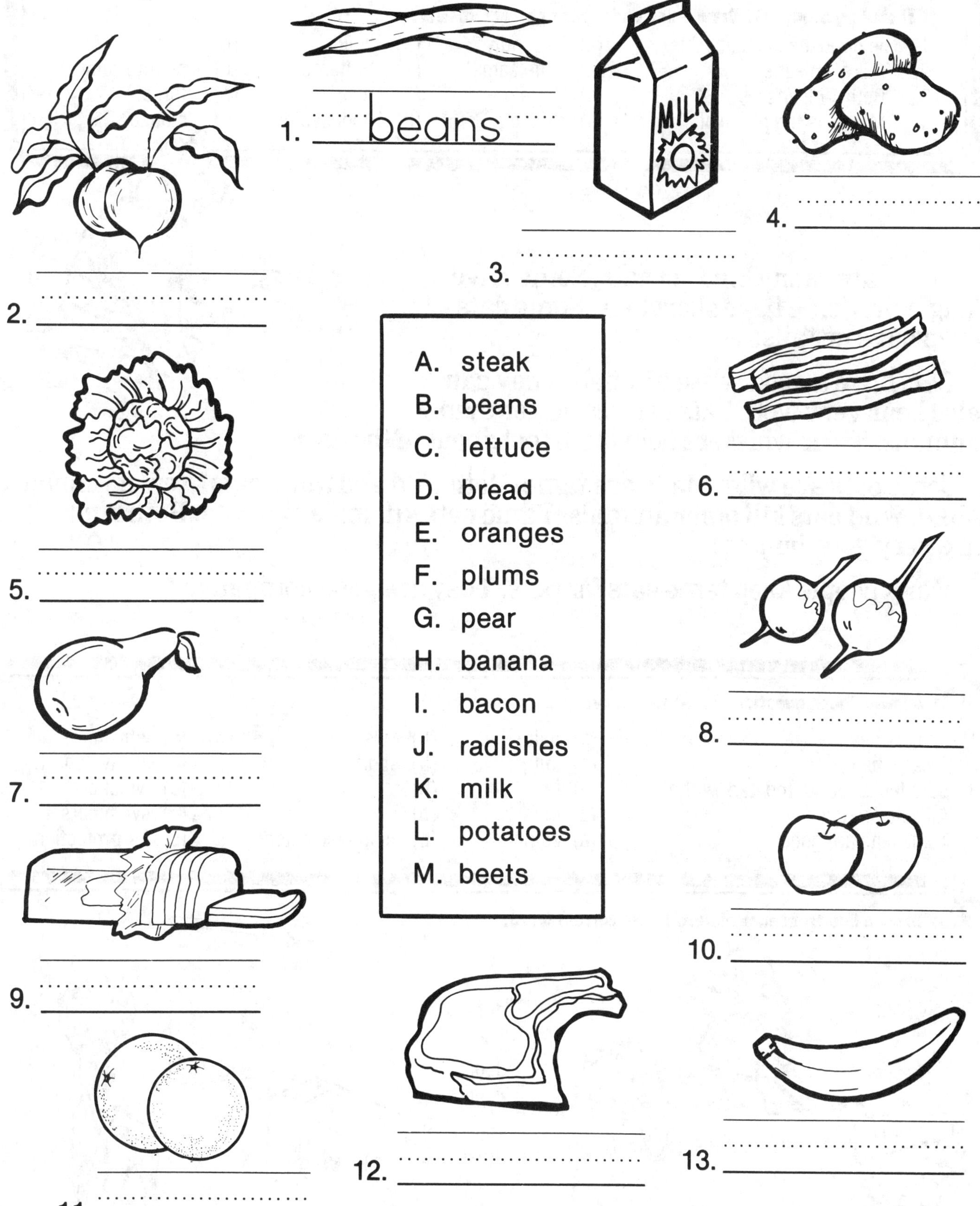

Cats

JUST FOR FUN

Vocabulary Study ● Draw a line under each correct answer.

	(a)	(b)	(c)
1. The opposite of "tame" is	"friendly"	"wild"	"happy."
2. "Alike" means	"the same"	"different"	"not the same."
3. "Both" means	"one"	"two"	"three."
4. "Mice" is the plural of	"mices"	"mouses"	"mouse."

There are many kinds of cats. Some have long hair. Some have short hair. Some cats even have no tails.

Cats have a good sense of smell. They can also hear very well. Cats can see better than humans. Their whiskers help them feel about in the dark.

Some cats are wild. Many are tame. Both wild and tame cats are very much alike. Wild cats kill other animals. Tame cats kill mice and rats. Both kinds are very good hunters.

Many people keep tame cats for pets. They are good company.

* **Answer these questions about the story:**

	(a)	(b)	(c)
1. All cats have	hair	tails	whiskers.
2. A cat's hair is	long	short	always short.
3. Cats feel about in the dark with their	feet	tails	whiskers.
4. All cats are good	pets	hunters	swimmers.
5. Tame cats are good	as pets	as mouse catchers	for protection.

Draw a line from each picture to the correct word.

duck
doll
door
desk
deer
dress

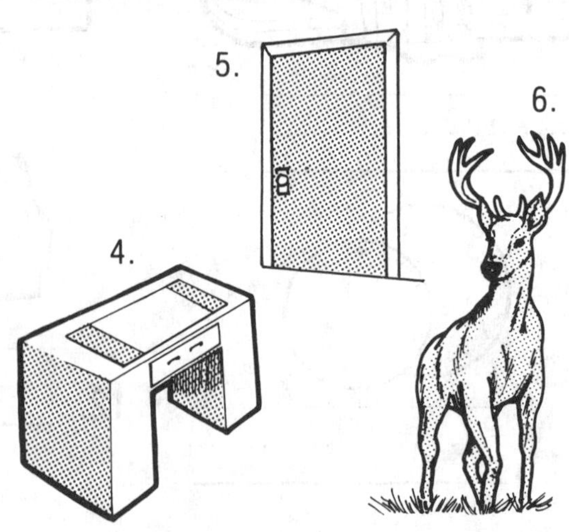

Equivalent Sets

Match the sets that are equivalent. Sets are equivalent if they have the same number of members. See sample "1."

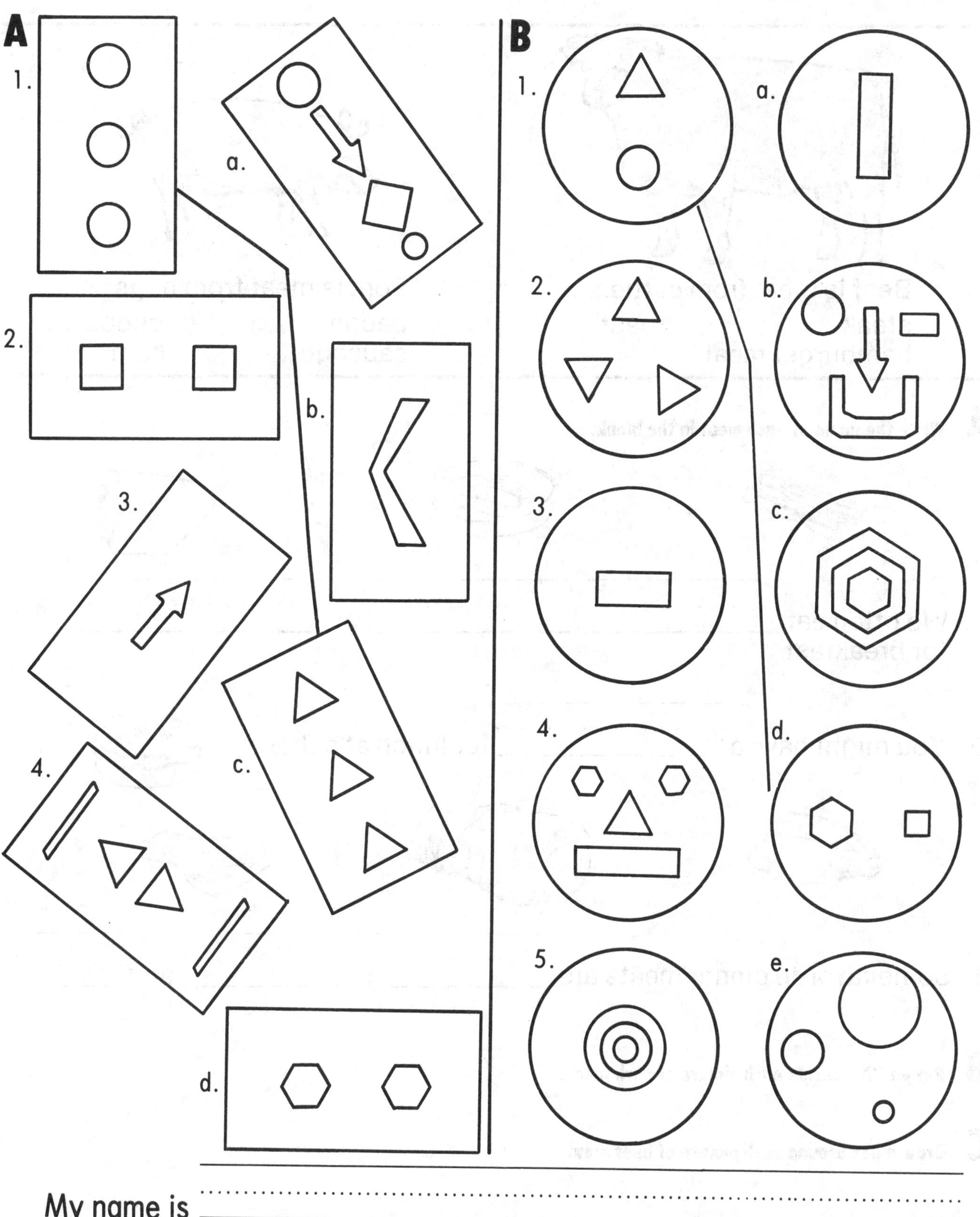

My name is ________________________________.

Beef, Pork

Meat is an energy food which is rich in protein and many other nutrients. Most of the meat we eat is beef or pork.

Beef is meat from cattle.

steak roast

hamburger meat

Pork is meat from hogs.

bacon chops

sausage ham

A **Write the name of each meat in the blank.**

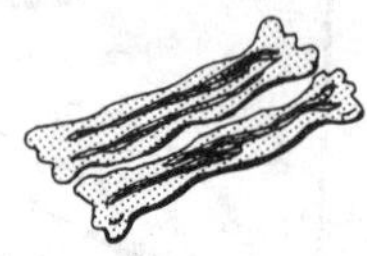

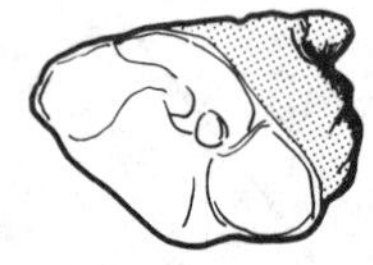

1. We often eat ______________, ______________, or ______________ for breakfast.

2. You might have a ______________ for lunch at school.

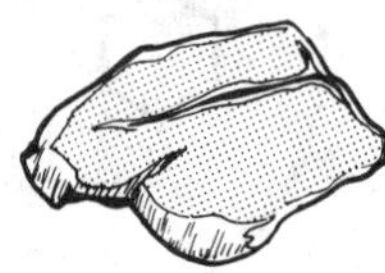

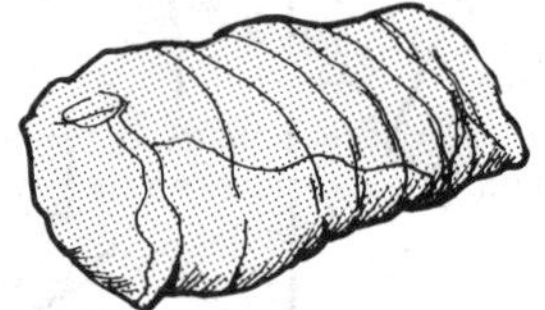

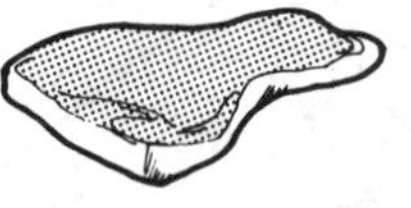

3. Some favorite dinner meats are ______________, ______________, and ________.

B **Put an "X" beside each picture of pork meat.**

C **Draw a box around each picture of beef meat.**

Everyday Helpers

There are many things that help to make us clean, healthy, and safe. Write the letters of the correct terms in the blanks.

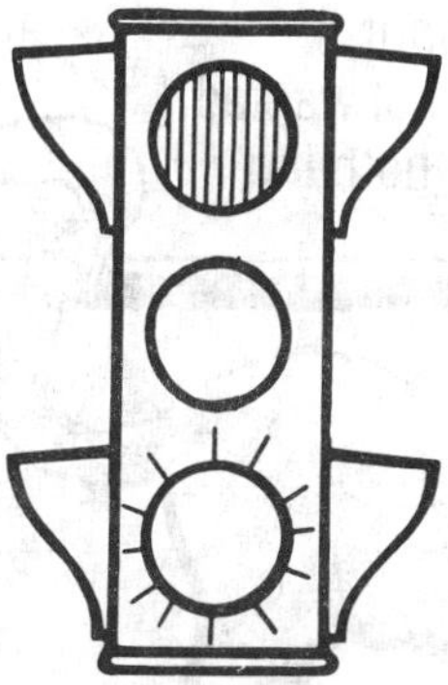

1. G
2.
3.
4.
5.
6.
7.
8.
9.
10.
11.

A. patrol boy
B. policeman
C. signs
D. soap and towel
E. milk
F. toothbrush
toothpaste
G. traffic light
H. meat
I. brush and comb
J. fruit
K. vegetables

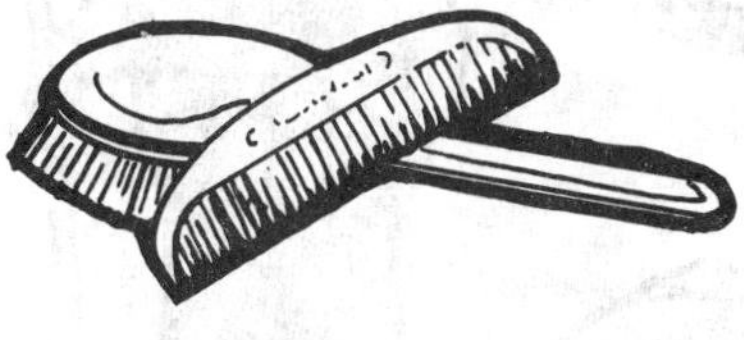

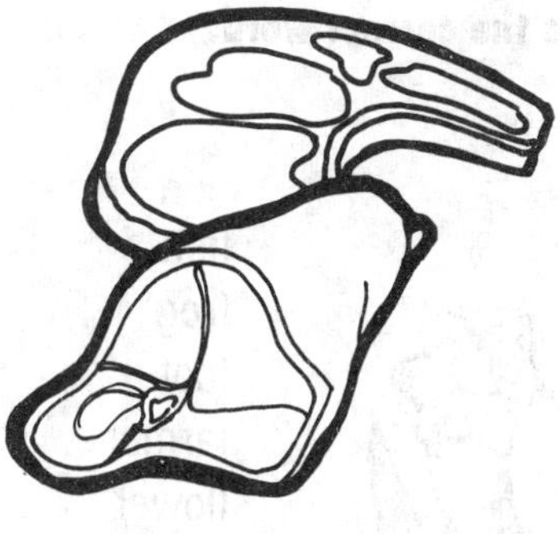

Working Cats

JUST FOR FUN

Vocabulary Study ● Draw a line under each correct answer.

1. The opposite of "teach" is	(a) "show"	(b) "learn"	(c) "tell."
2. A pest is something you	(a) like	(b) do not like	(c) want.
3. "Unwanted" means	(a) "needed"	(b) "liked"	(c) "not wanted."
4. "Nothing" is made up of	(a) "no thing"	(b) "not hing"	(c) "noth ing."

Cats are very important to people. Cats kill mice and rats.

Cats do not have to be taught to catch mice. They are born knowing how to do it.

Rats and mice are unwanted pests. They eat crops. They eat things in our houses. They carry germs. The germs make people very sick.

Cats are kept on farms. They are kept in cities. They are kept in stores. They are kept on ships. Cats are kept wherever there are rats and mice. Nothing gets rid of these pests as good as cats.

Answer these questions about the story:

1. Cats kill	(a) mice	(b) rats	(c) dogs.
2. Rats and mice	(a) eat crops	(b) carry germs	(c) are pests.
3. Germs make people	(a) happy	(b) sick	(c) feel good.
4. Cats are kept	(a) in stores	(b) on farms	(c) on ships.
5. Cats are	(a) important	(b) not important	(c) pests.

Draw a line from each picture to the correct word.

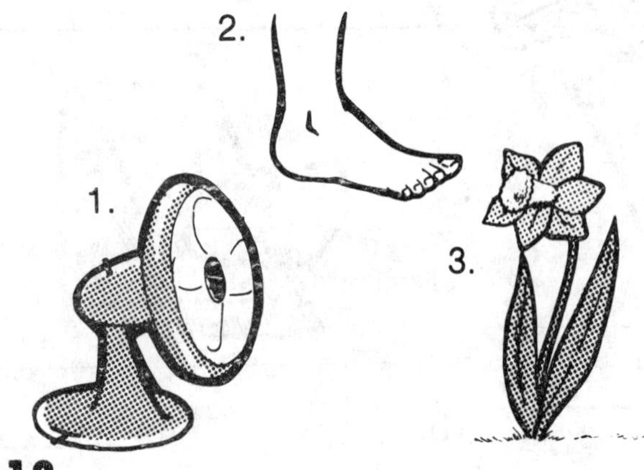

fish
frog
foot
farmer
flower
fan

Fowl, Fish

A **Write the name of each fowl in the blank.**

B **Draw a line under each correct answer.**

1. Fowl are also called (poultry, pork).
2. Fowl are in the (fruit, meat) group.
3. Fowl are covered with (feathers, fur).
4. Fowl provide us with (milk, eggs).
5. Fowl are raised (on farms, in gardens).

C **Put a "T" beside the picture of the fowl usually eaten on Thanksgiving.**

D **Put a "P" beside the fowl you might eat on a picnic.**

E **Put a "W" beside the two fowl that can swim in water.**

F **Write the name of each fish in the blank.**

tuna	perch	catfish	trout

G **Draw a line under each correct answer.**

1. Fish are in the (fruit, meat) group.
2. Fish live (in water, in cages).
3. Fish have many small (bones, seeds).
4. Fish are covered with (scales, hair).
5. Fish swim by using (legs, fins).

H **Put an "F" beside the two pictures of freshwater fish.**

I **Put an "S" beside the two pictures of saltwater fish.**

J **Put a check mark beside the name of each fish that you have eaten.**

Halves

Draw a line between the two correct points in each drawing that will divide it into halves. See sample "A."

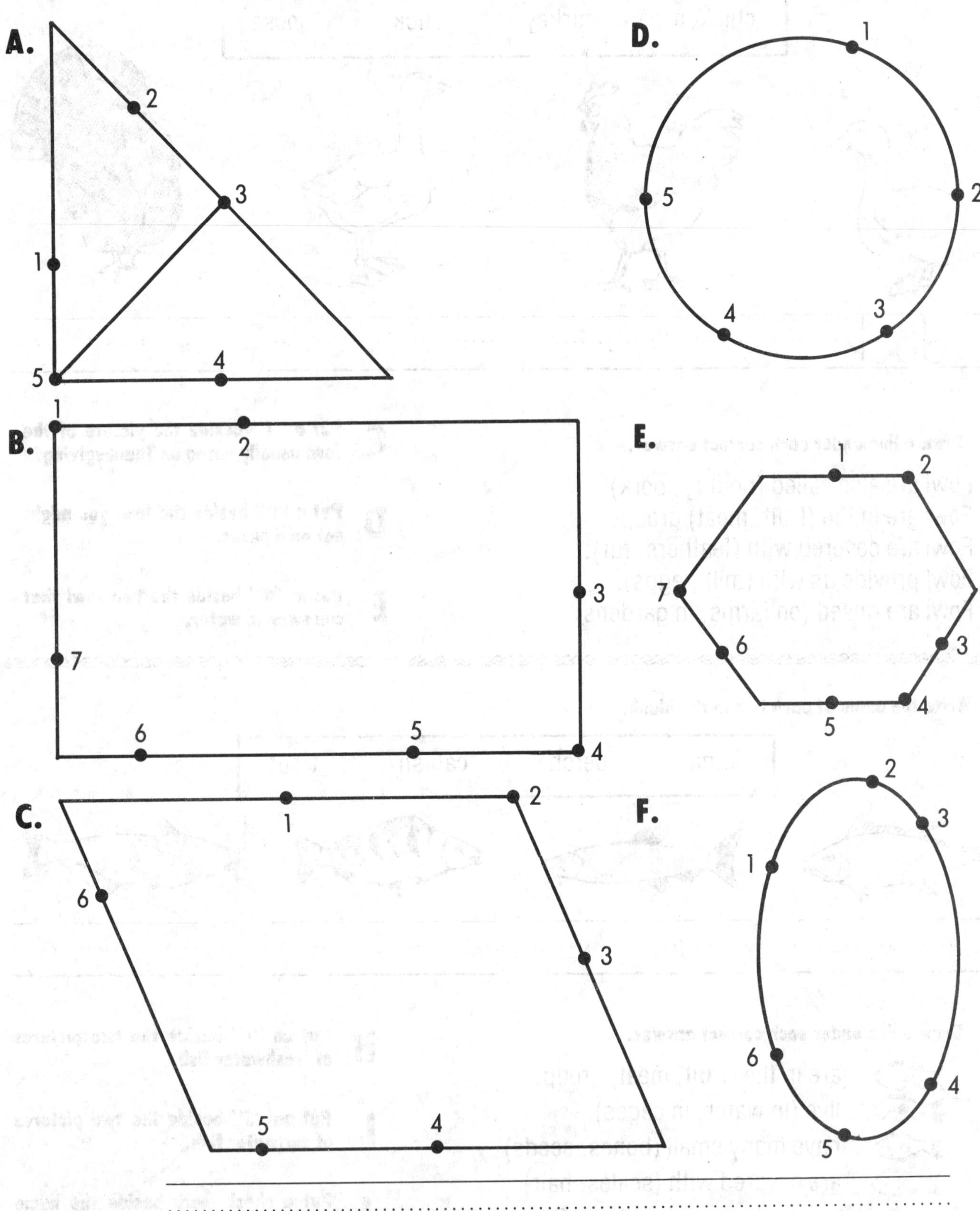

My name is ______________________________.

Eating a Good Breakfast

Write the names of the foods that make a good breakfast. Put hands on the clock to show what time you eat breakfast every morning.

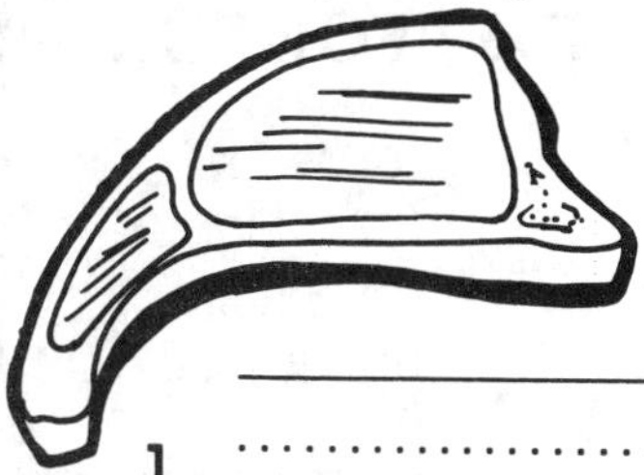

1. ______________________

2. ______________________

3. ______________________

MILK

4. ______________________

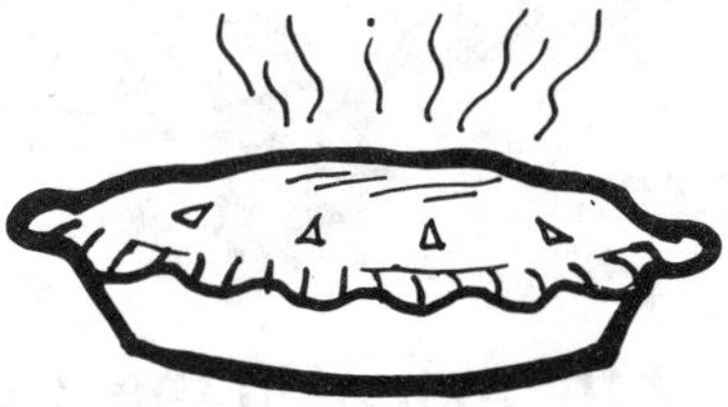

5. ______________________

CHOCOLATE CHIPS

6. ______________________

GUM

7. ______________________

Cola

12 1 2 3 4 5 6 7 8 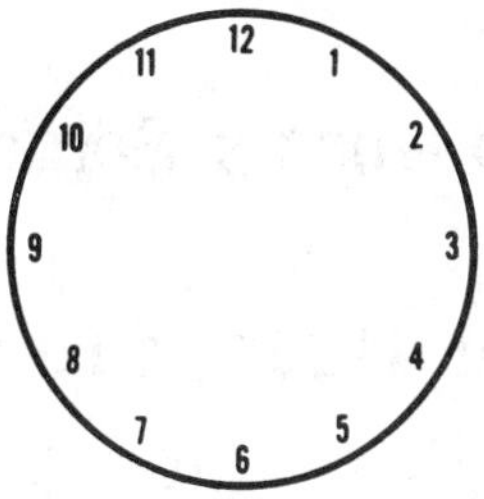 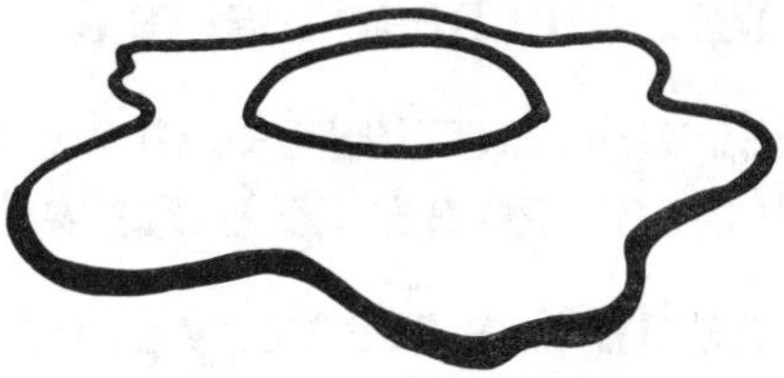 9 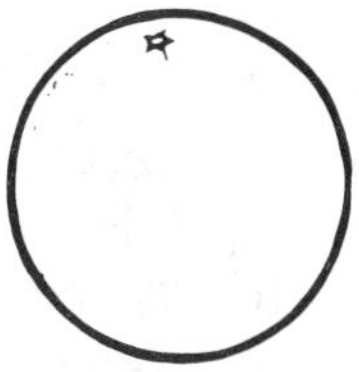 10 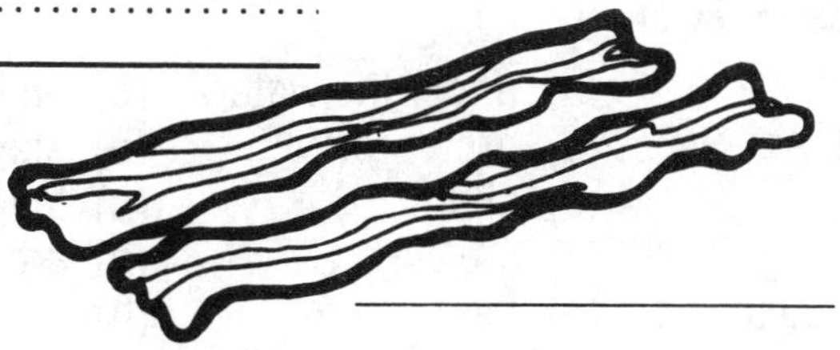 11

8. ______________________

9. ______________________

10. ______________________

11. ______________________

12. ______________________

CEREAL

13. ______________________

14. ______________________

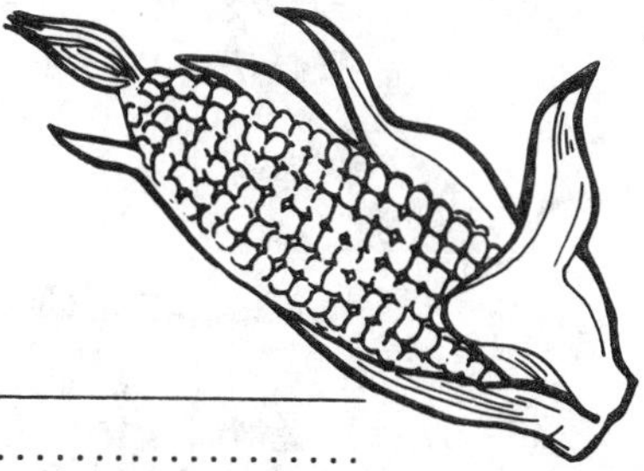

15. ______________________

Turtles

Vocabulary Study ● Draw a line under each correct answer. **JUST FOR FUN**

1. Where you live is your	(a) home	(b) school	(c) work.
2. The opposite of "long" is	(a) "tall"	(b) "short"	(c) "high."
3. "Also" means	(a) "too"	(b) "not"	(c) "none."
4. A person without food has	(a) plenty of food	(b) some food	(c) no food.

A turtle is an animal that lives in a shell. The shell is its home. As the turtle grows, its shell grows too.

There are many kinds of turtles. Many of them live in the water. Many live on land.

A turtle has four legs and a tail. It has a long neck. The turtle can pull its legs, tail, and head inside its shell.

Most land turtles eat insects and worms. Some also eat leaves and berries. Turtles can go a long time without food.

Some turtles are very good to eat. Have you ever eaten turtle soup?

Answer these questions about the story:

1. A turtle's home is	(a) under the water	(b) on land	(c) its shell.
2. As the turtle grows, its shell	(a) grows too	(b) stays the same	(c) gets smaller.
3. The turtle's neck is	(a) short	(b) long	(c) thin.
4. All turtles	(a) are alike	(b) are not alike	(c) live on land.
5. Turtles can go a long time without	(a) food	(b) breathing	(c) sleeping.

Draw a line from each picture to the correct word.

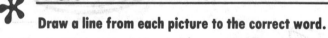

5.

giraffe
goat

girl
ghost

goose
guitar

Fruits

Fruits provide many nutrients needed for a healthy body. You should eat some fruits each day. Also, we can take the liquid from some fruits and make juice to drink.

Match each fruit with its correct name from the box. Then draw a line under the name of each fruit listed in the center that we also can drink as a juice. See the example.

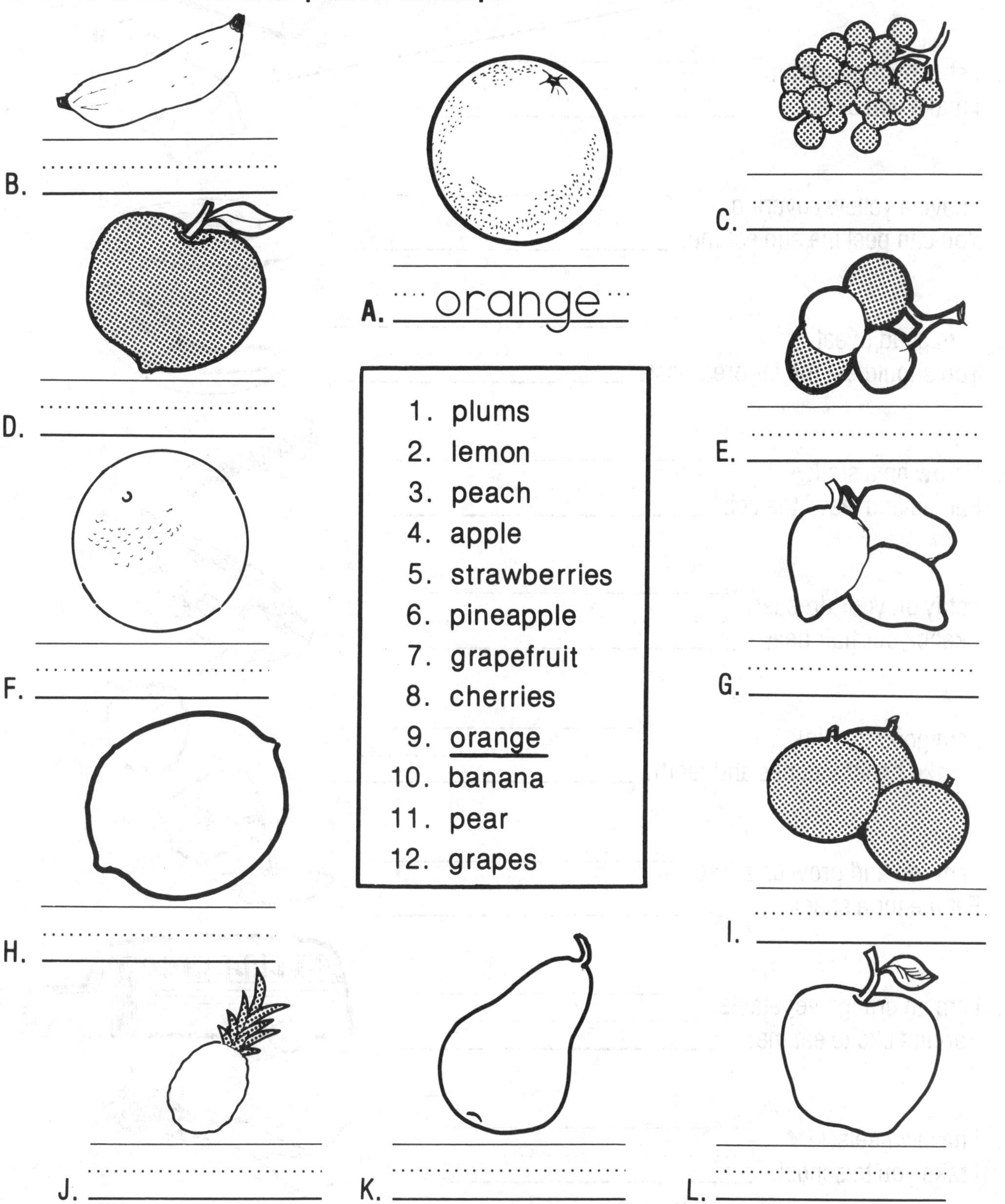

1. plums
2. lemon
3. peach
4. apple
5. strawberries
6. pineapple
7. grapefruit
8. cherries
9. orange
10. banana
11. pear
12. grapes

What Am I?

Draw a line from each riddle to the picture that fits it. Write its name. See sample "1."

1. I am in your bedroom. You sleep on me. bed
2. I stay by the bathtub. I make you clean.
3. I have a yellow covering. You can peel me and eat me.
4. I am good to eat. You should eat me for breakfast.
5. I grow on a stalk. Eat me and leave the cob.
6. I stay on your dresser. I keep your hair neat.
7. I am good to drink. I make healthy bones and teeth.
8. I am red and grow on a tree. Eat me for a snack.
9. I am an orange vegetable. Rabbits like to eat me.
10. I have wheels. I take you to school.

SOAP

MILK

Rabbits

Vocabulary Study ● Draw a line under each correct answer. **JUST FOR FUN**

1. "Long" means	(a) "not short"	(b) "short"	(c) "tiny."
2. The opposite of "soft" is	(a) "hard"	(b) "easy"	(c) "big."
3. A blind animal	(a) can see	(b) cannot see	(c) cannot hear.
4. A word that sounds like "hare" is	(a) "her"	(b) "here"	(c) "hair."

Rabbits have long ears. They have big eyes. They have short tails. They have thick, soft fur.

Rabbits can run quickly. Their hind legs are longer than their front legs. When moving about slowly, rabbits hop.

Rabbits have a good sense of smell. They can also hear very well. Both senses help rabbits hunt for food. Rabbits eat vegetables.

Rabbits are often mistaken for hares. Baby rabbits are born blind and without fur. Baby hares are not.

Many people have rabbits for pets. Some raise them for food. Others raise them for their fur.

Answer these questions about the story:

1. Rabbits have	(a) long ears	(b) soft fur	(c) short tails.
2. Rabbits	(a) hop	(b) crawl	(c) walk.
3. Rabbits eat	(a) meat	(b) wood	(c) vegetables.
4. Rabbits are mistaken for	(a) mice	(b) hares	(c) cats.
5. Rabbits are kept for	(a) food	(b) fur	(c) pets.

Draw a line from each picture to the correct word.

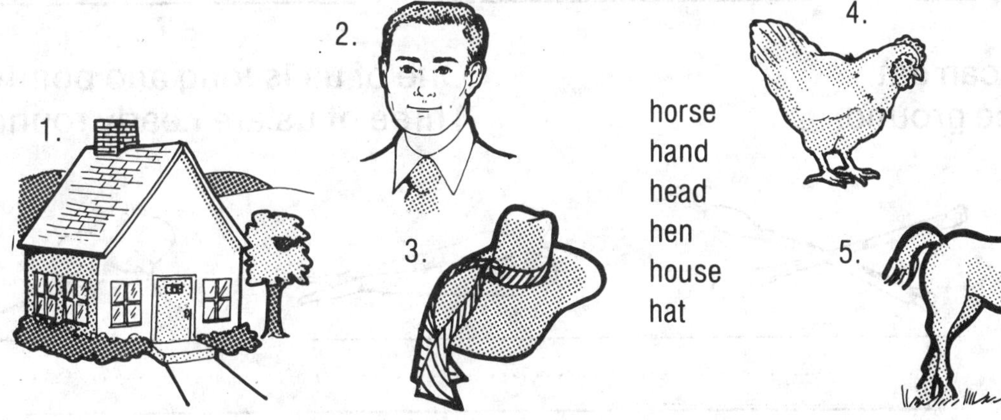

Vegetables

There are many different foods in the vegetable group. Eating a variety of vegetables each day will help you have a healthy body.

Name the vegetables by answering the riddles.

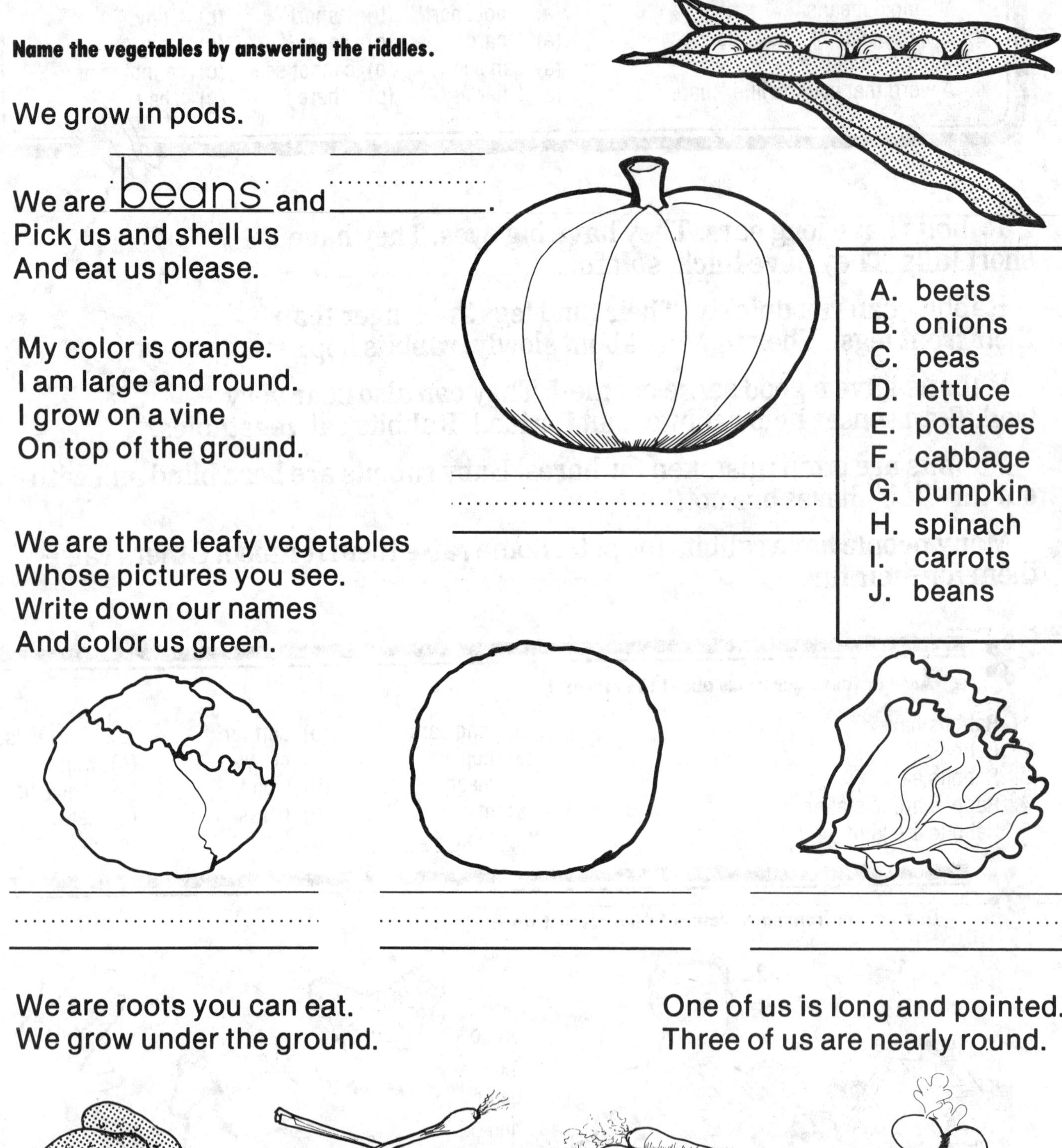

We grow in pods.

We are beans and __________.
Pick us and shell us
And eat us please.

My color is orange.
I am large and round.
I grow on a vine
On top of the ground.

____

A. beets
B. onions
C. peas
D. lettuce
E. potatoes
F. cabbage
G. pumpkin
H. spinach
I. carrots
J. beans

We are three leafy vegetables
Whose pictures you see.
Write down our names
And color us green.

__________ __________ __________

We are roots you can eat.
We grow under the ground.

One of us is long and pointed.
Three of us are nearly round.

__________ __________ __________ __________

Health and Safety

Match the picture of each helper with the term that describes the helper. Write the term.

1. bus driver

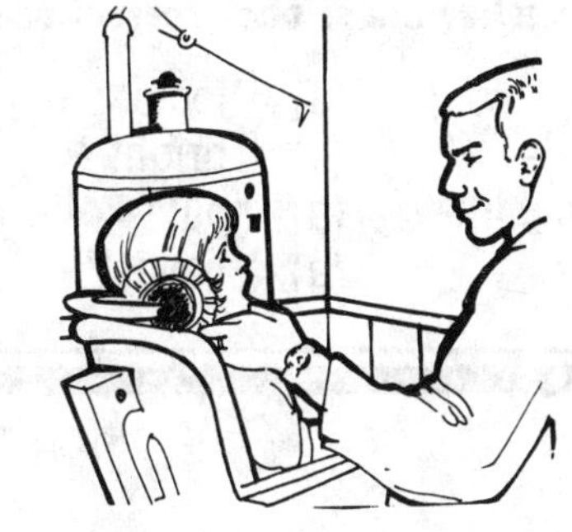

2. ______________

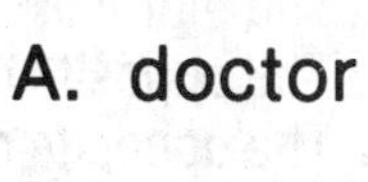

A. doctor
B. nurse
C. bus driver
D. fireman
E. housewife
F. policeman
G. milkman
H. garbageman
I. dentist
J. school patrol

3. ______________

4. ______________

5. ______________

6. ______________

7. ______________

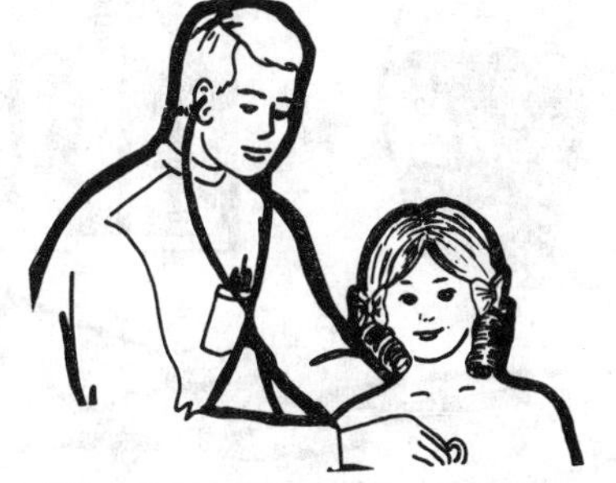

8. ______________

9. ______________

10. ______________

Ducks

Vocabulary Study ● Draw a line under each correct answer. **JUST FOR FUN**

1. The plural of ''foot'' is	(a) ''foots''	(b) ''feet''	(c) ''feets.''
2. The opposite of ''dull'' is	(a) ''bright''	(b) ''ugly''	(c) ''plain.''
3. The opposite of ''in'' is	(a) ''out''	(b) ''into''	(c) ''within.''
4. ''Often'' is the same as	(a) ''never''	(b) ''always''	(c) ''many times.''

Ducks are water birds. They have webbed feet. The feet help them to swim. Ducks are very good swimmers.

Male ducks are called drakes. They are very colorful. The female ducks are dull. They are also smaller than the males.

Ducks feed in or near the water. They eat plants.

When they are scared, ducks fly away. They are strong fliers. Ducks often fly in a V-form.

Ducks like to be with other ducks. They live together in large flocks.

Ducks are often hunted. Their meat is very good.

Answer these questions about the story:

1. Ducks have	(a) tiny feet	(b) webbed feet	(c) no feet.
2. Ducks are good	(a) swimmers	(b) fliers	(c) runners.
3. Male ducks are	(a) smaller	(b) duller	(c) drakes.
4. Ducks often fly in	(a) a V-form	(b) an X-form	(c) a Y-form.
5. A group of ducks is a	(a) herd	(b) flock	(c) crowd.

Draw a line from each picture to the correct word.

jar
jeep
jet
jelly
jail
jump

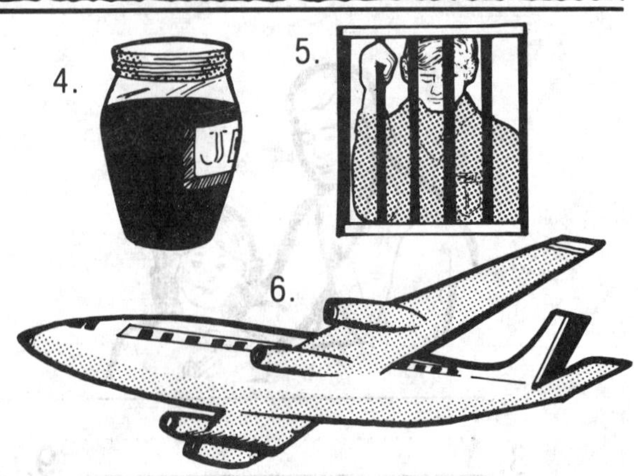

Sweets

A **Check the yes box if the picture is a sweet food. Check no if it is not.**

1. ☐ yes ☐ no	2. ☐ yes ☐ no	3. ☐ yes ☐ no
4. ☐ yes ☐ no	5. ☐ yes ☐ no	6. ☐ yes ☐ no
7. ☐ yes ☐ no	8. ☐ yes ☐ no	9. ☐ yes ☐ no

B **Draw a line from each beginning to the correct ending of each sentence.**

1. Sweets contain much	energy.
2. Sweets are usually eaten for	tooth decay.
3. Sweets are a quick source of	sugar.
4. Too many sweets can cause	dessert.

C **Put an "X" beside the pictures of sweets that you usually eat for snacks.**

Breakfast

Write the names of the foods. Draw circles around the foods that make a good breakfast.

1. soda

2.

3.

4.

5.

6.

7.

8.

9.

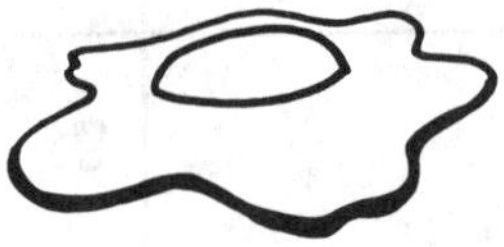

10.

11.

12.

13.

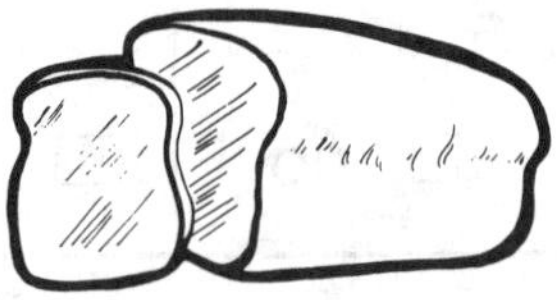

14.

15.

16.

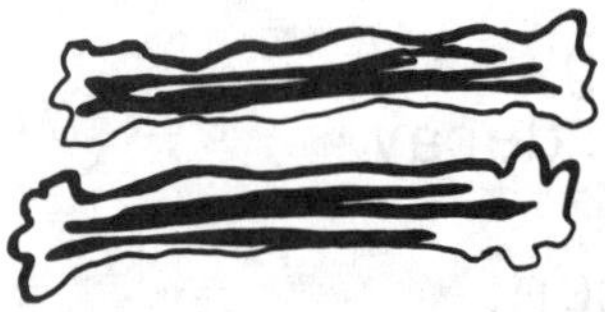

17.

18.

19.

Capitalization

ABCDEFGHIJKLMNOPQRSTUVWXYZ
a b c d e f g h i j k l m n o p q r s t u v w x y z

Rewrite each sentence, and capitalize the words that should be capitalized. See the example. Capitalize the first word of a sentence, proper nouns, the word "I," the days of the week, the months of the year, and the 50 states.

1. the man drives a truck.
2. his name is george.
3. he lives in texas.
4. he will be here tuesday.
5. i saw him in march.
6. georgia is a pretty state.
7. that book is mine.
8. that is mr. allen.
9. today is monday.
10. i'll see you in new york.
11. turn on the light.
12. my mom is coming.

1. The man drives a truck.
2.
3.
4.
5.
6.
7.
8.
9.
10.
11.
12.

Geese

Vocabulary Study ● Draw a line under each correct answer. **JUST FOR FUN**

1. The opposite of ''soft'' is (a) ''hard'' (b) ''easy'' (c) ''silky.''
2. You hear with your (a) eyes (b) ears (c) nose.
3. ''Stuff'' means (a) ''to put into'' (b) ''take out'' (c) ''let out.''
4. ''Geese'' is the plural of (a) ''geeses'' (b) ''gooses'' (c) ''goose.''

Geese are birds. Some geese are tame. Some are wild.

Tame geese are raised on farms. They give us meat and eggs. Their feathers are also used to stuff pillows. The feathers are very soft.

The most common geese are the Canada geese. They live in the United States and Canada. Canada geese fly in groups called flocks. They are heard long before they are seen. They are hunted for their meat.

Geese like to be with other geese. They eat together. They fly together. They live as one big family.

Answer these questions about the story:

1. All geese are (a) tame (b) wild (c) birds.
2. Tame geese live (a) on farms (b) in woods (c) in mountains.
3. Geese are (a) noisy (b) very quiet (c) silent birds.
4. A group of geese is a (a) herd (b) flock (c) den.
5. Geese give us (a) meat (b) eggs (c) feathers.

Draw a line from each picture to the correct word.

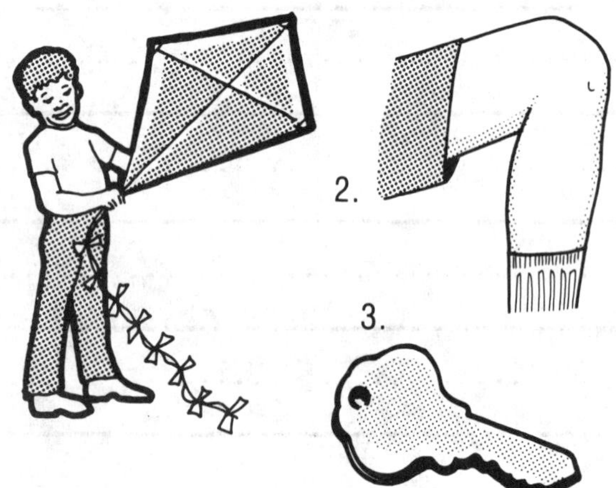

key
kite
knife
knee
king
kangaroo

Nuts

A **Name each nut by writing the letter of its name in the blank.**

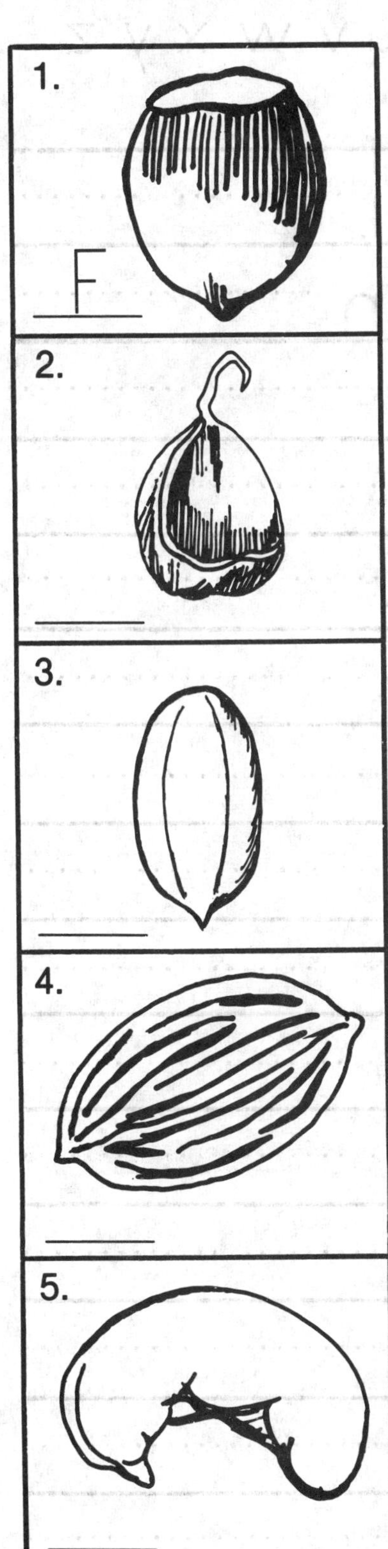

A. walnuts
B. coconut
C. pecan
D. butternut
E. hickory nut
F. hazelnut
G. Brazil nut
H. chestnut
I. cashew
J. almond

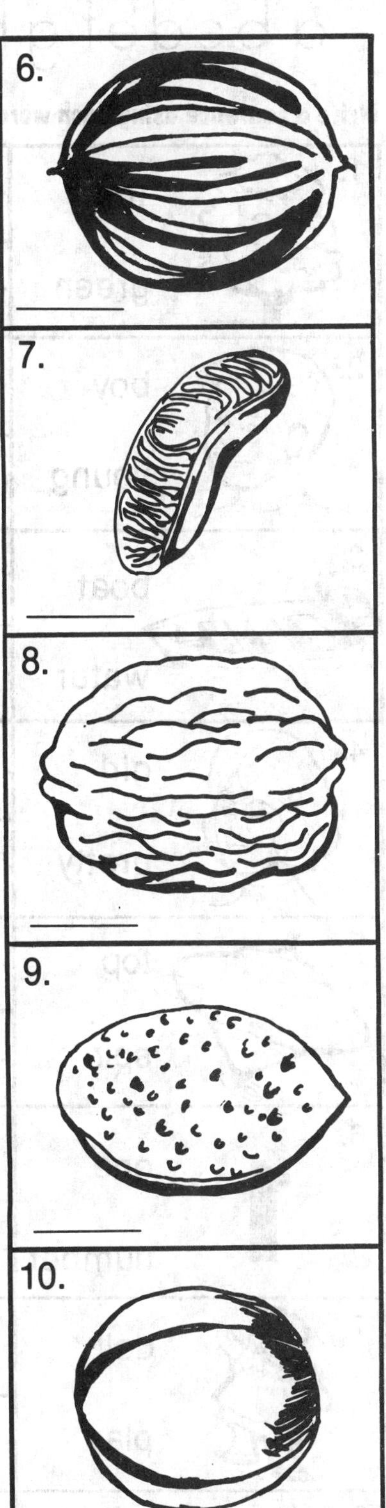

B **Draw a line from each beginning to the correct ending of each sentence.**

1. Nuts have hard	small.
2. Nuts grow on	protein.
3. Nuts are many	shells.
4. Most nuts are	trees.
5. Nuts are rich in	sizes.

Writing Sentences

ABCDEFGHIJKLMNOPQRSTUVWXYZ
abcdefghijklmnopqrstuvwxyz

Write a sentence using each word in the box. See example "1."

1. tree	The tree is tall.
green	Grass is green.
2. boy	
young	
3. boat	
water	
4. girl	
pretty	
5. top	
spin	
6. 1 one	
number	
7. doll	
play	
8. bear	
big	

Turkeys

JUST FOR FUN

Vocabulary Study ● Draw a line under each correct answer.

1. The opposite of ''early'' is	(a) ''soon''	(b) ''first''	(c) ''late.''
2. ''Hard'' means	(a) ''difficult''	(b) ''easy''	(c) ''simple.''
3. ''Hunt'' is the same as	(a) ''lose''	(b) ''look for''	(c) ''find.''
4. ''Roost'' means	(a) ''rest''	(b) ''eat''	(c) ''fly.''

Wild turkeys are game birds. People like to hunt turkeys. Turkeys are very hard to catch.

Turkeys like to live in the woods. They roost in trees.

Turkeys eat grain and seeds. They also eat large insects. Turkeys eat early in the morning. They eat late in the evening.

Turkeys are nervous birds. They move about all the time. They would rather walk than fly. They will fly when they are scared.

Not all turkeys are wild. Some are raised on farms. Turkeys are good to eat.

Answer these questions about the story:

1. Turkeys live	(a) in the woods	(b) in mountains	(c) in water.
2. Turkeys eat	(a) in the morning	(b) in the evening	(c) at night.
3. Instead of flying, turkeys	(a) crawl	(b) swim	(c) walk.
4. Turkeys are good	(a) to eat	(b) as pets	(c) for protection.
5. Turkeys are	(a) game birds	(b) nervous	(c) hard to catch.

Draw a line from each picture to the correct word.

1.

3.

2.

lion
lamb
light
leaf
ladder
lock

4.

5.

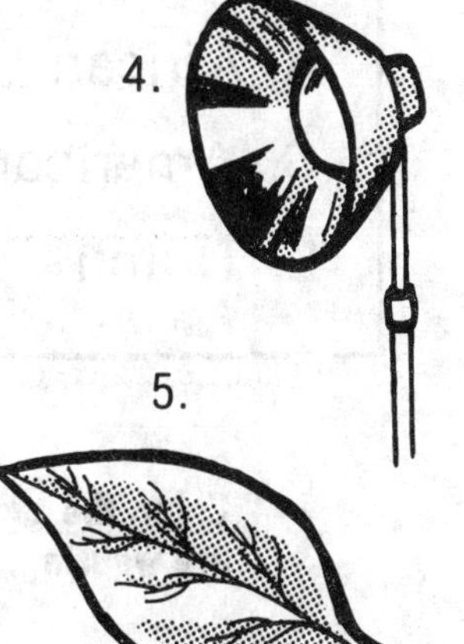

6.

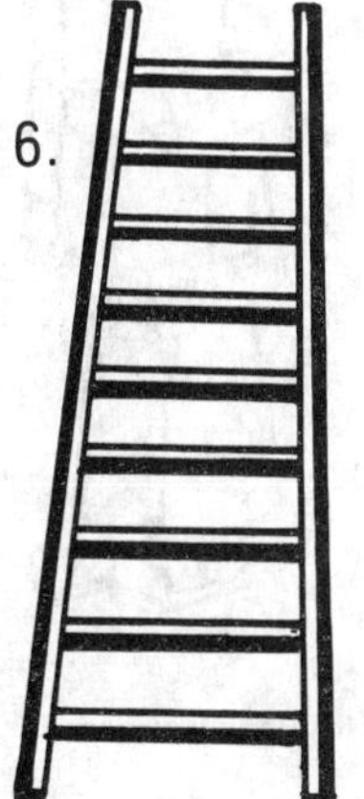

Clothing

1. B

4. ____

A True or False

T F 1. Clothing is one of our basic needs.

T F 2. Clothes are worn to protect the body.

T F 3. All people wear the same kind of clothes.

T F 4. Clothing can be made from many different materials.

T F 5. Clothing can be worn on the head, body, and feet.

T F 6. Heavy clothing is needed in warm climates.

T F 7. Some people wear clothes made of skins.

T F 8. In most countries boys and girls wear different clothes.

2. ____

5. ____

3. ____

B Identify the children on this worksheet by putting the correct letter under each picture.

A. African	B. Eskimo
C. American	D. Mexican
E. Dutch	F. Japanese

6. ____

C Color the clothes the children on this worksheet are wearing.

Forming Sentences

ABCDEFGHIJKLMNOPQRSTUVWXYZ
abcdefghijklmnopqrstuvwxyz

Write a sentence using each word in the box. See example "1."

1. 5	five	I have five cents.
	add	Add the numbers.
2.	pony	
	ride	
3.	cow	
	milk	
4.	ride	
	fun	
5.	nest	
	eggs	
6.	look	
	up	
7.	farm	
	grow	
8.	baby	
	small	

Bears

Vocabulary Study ● Draw a line under each correct answer. **JUST FOR FUN**

1. ''Thick'' means (a) ''not thin'' (b) ''thin'' (c) ''small.''
2. Someone who is strong has (a) weak legs (b) no power (c) power.
3. The opposite of ''asleep'' is (a) ''awake'' (b) ''quiet'' (c) ''noisy.''
4. When you move, you (a) stand still (b) do not stand still (c) are lazy.

There are many kinds of bears. They are big animals. They have thick coats of fur. They are very strong.

Bears look clumsy. However, they move fast. They are good swimmers too.

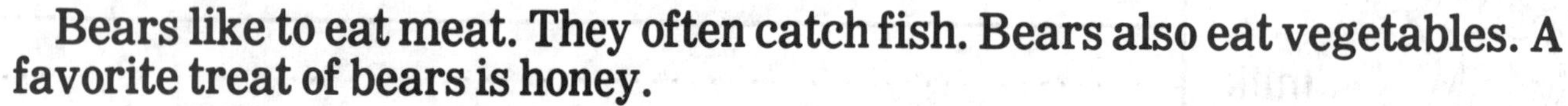

Bears like to eat meat. They often catch fish. Bears also eat vegetables. A favorite treat of bears is honey.

Bears usually come out at night. They hunt by smelling.

Bears sleep in the winter. They do not come out of their homes. They do not have to eat all winter. In the spring, bears wake up. They are very hungry.

Answer these questions about the story:

1. Bears are (a) big (b) strong (c) covered with fur.
2. Bears move (a) slowly (b) quickly (c) very slowly.
3. Bears eat (a) meat (b) vegetables (c) honey.
4. Bears hunt (a) at night (b) in the daytime (c) in the afternoon.
5. In winter, bears (a) hunt (b) eat (c) sleep.

Draw a line from each picture to the correct word.

1. 

2. 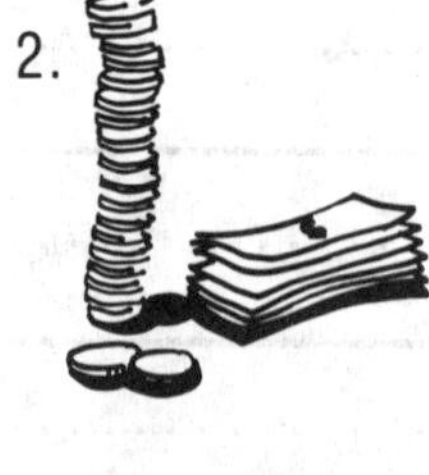

3. 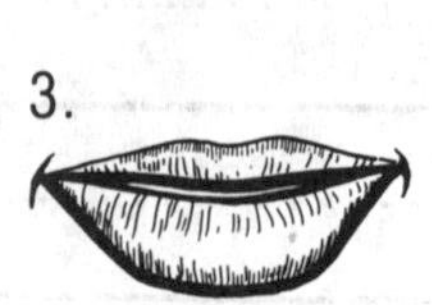

mouse
monkey
man
mouth
moon
money

4. 

5. 

6. 

Clothes We Wear

Complete each riddle by writing the correct word in each blank. The picture clues will help you.

1. coat
2. caps
3. boots
4. gloves
5. dresses
6. hats
7. suits
8. pants
9. jacket
10. shirt
11. sweater
12. blouse
13. gown
14. skirt
15. pajamas
16. raincoats

1. A girl might wear a blouse and ________.
   A boy would wear ________ and a ________.

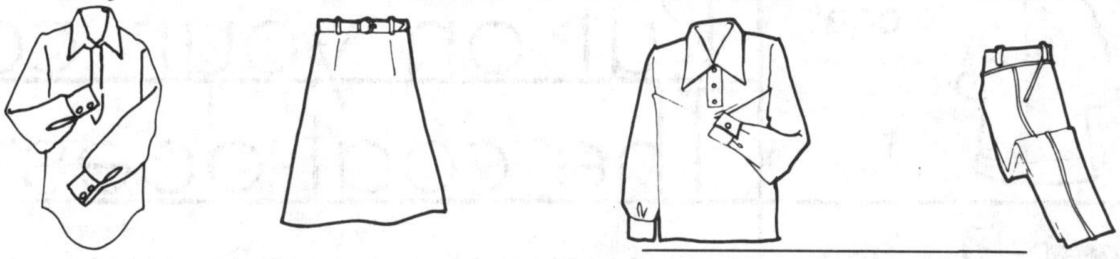

2. On Sundays we wear ________ and ________.
   For rainy days we need ________ and ________.

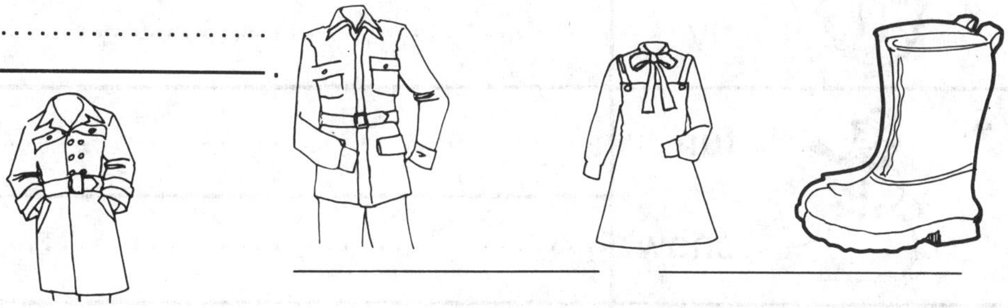

3. You may wear a ________ or ________ to school.
   Wear a ________ and some ________ when the weather is cool.

4. We wear ________ and ________ on our heads.
   A ________ or ________ is worn to bed.

Creating Sentences

ABCDEFGHIJKLMNOPQRSTUVWXYZ
a b c d e f g h i j k l m n o p q r s t u v w x y z

Write a sentence using each word in the box. See example "1."

1. coat fit	Put on your coat. The coat does not fit.
2. flag wave	
3. bird fly	
4. fun snow	
5. 9 nine more	
6. barn hay	
7. shoes fit	
8. car drive	

Horses

Vocabulary Study ● Draw a line under each correct answer. **JUST FOR FUN**

	(a)	(b)	(c)
1. The opposite of "pull" is	(a) "throw"	(b) "push"	(c) "hold."
2. "Pleasure" is another word for	(a) "a good time"	(b) "a bad time"	(c) "fun."
3. "Travel" means	(a) "to move about"	(b) "to be still"	(c) "to live."
4. "Beautiful" means	(a) "not pretty"	(b) "ugly"	(c) "very pretty."

Horses come in many sizes. They come in many colors. Whatever their size or color, people like horses.

Some horses are used for working. Some are used for racing. Most horses are used for pleasure. They are fun to ride. Would you like to ride on a horse?

Horses can run very fast. They can run for long distances. Long ago, horses were used to bring the mail. Horses were also used to pull wagons. People traveled on horseback.

Horses are beautiful animals. There are many kinds of horses. The best are Arabian horses.

Answer these questions about the story:

	(a)	(b)	(c)
1. Horses are used for	(a) working	(b) racing	(c) pleasure.
2. Horses can run	(a) long distances	(b) short distances	(c) fast.
3. Long ago, horses were used to	(a) cross rivers	(b) bring the mail	(c) travel.
4. Horses were used to pull	(a) cars	(b) trains	(c) wagons.
5. The best horse is the	(a) Arabian	(b) Shetland pony	(c) wild horse.

Draw a line from each picture to the correct word.

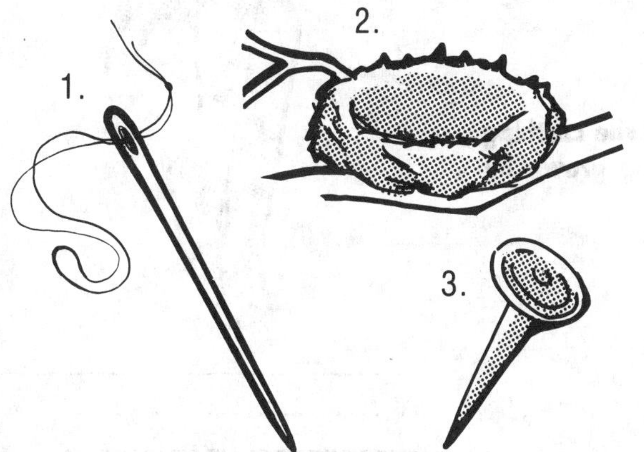

nest
nurse
needle
nine
nail
nut

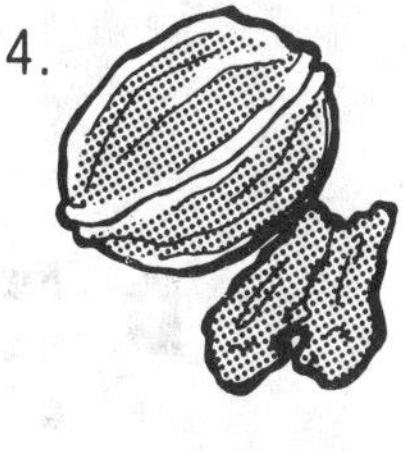

6. 9

What Clothes Are Made Of

1.

D

A **Match the clothing with the material from which it was made by putting the correct letter in each blank.**

4.

A. leather
B. synthetic material
C. furs and hides
D. grass and leaves
E. rubber
F. cotton cloth

2.

5.

B **Draw a box around the clothing that would be worn in the coldest climate.**

C **Put an "X" beside the clothing that would be waterproof.**

3.

6.

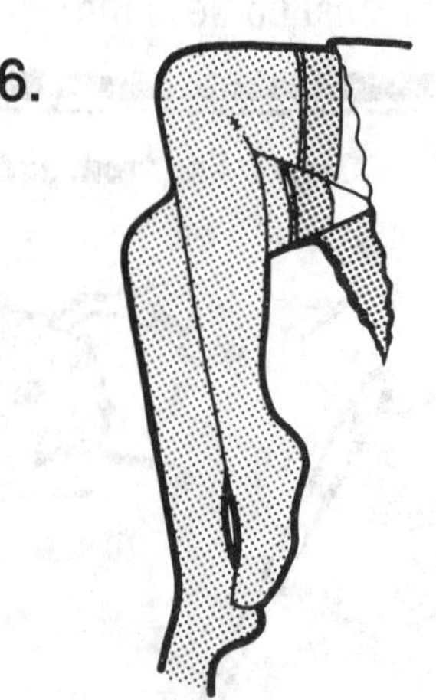

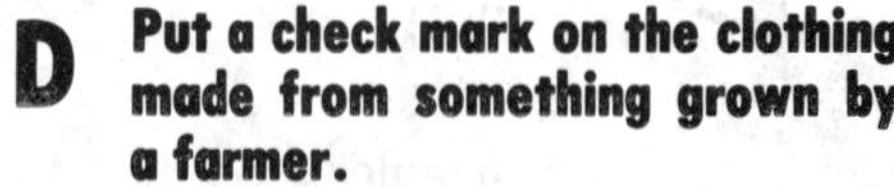

D **Put a check mark on the clothing made from something grown by a farmer.**

Composing Sentences

ABCDEFGHIJKLMNOPQRSTUVWXYZ
a b c d e f g h i j k l m n o p q r s t u v w x y z

Write a sentence using each word in the box. See example "1."

1.	milk	Drink your milk.
	drink	Water is good to drink.
2.	pig	
	bacon	
3.	that	
	this	
4.	love	
	sick	
5.	over	
	fence	
6.	jump	
	rope	
7.	time	
	clock	
8.	walk	
	girl	

Cows

Vocabulary Study ● **Draw a line under each correct answer.** **JUST FOR FUN**

1. The opposite of "fat" is	(a) "skinny"	(b) "big"	(c) "thick."
2. "Ahead" means	(a) "behind"	(b) "after"	(c) "before."
3. Another word for "curious" is	(a) "nosy"	(b) "uninterested"	(c) "careless."
4. "Gentle" means	(a) "calm"	(b) "mean"	(c) "wild."

Cows are gentle animals. Some like warm weather. Others like cold weather.

Some cows give us milk. Dairy cows have long legs. They are not fat.

Some cows give us meat. The meat is called beef. Beef cattle have short stocky legs. Their bodies are big and thick.

Cows move about in herds. Each herd has a "boss" cow. The "boss" cow is the leader of the herd. She always walks ahead of the herd.

Cows are curious animals. They like to watch people.

Answer these questions about the story:

1. Dairy cows	(a) give milk	(b) are fat	(c) have long legs.
2. Beef cattle	(a) are fat	(b) have short legs	(c) give milk.
3. Meat from a cow is called	(a) beef	(b) pork	(c) chicken.
4. The leader of the herd is the	(a) king	(b) queen	(c) "boss" cow.
5. Cows are	(a) mean	(b) gentle	(c) curious.

Draw a line from each picture to the correct word.

puppy
pie
pencil
pear
pan
pony

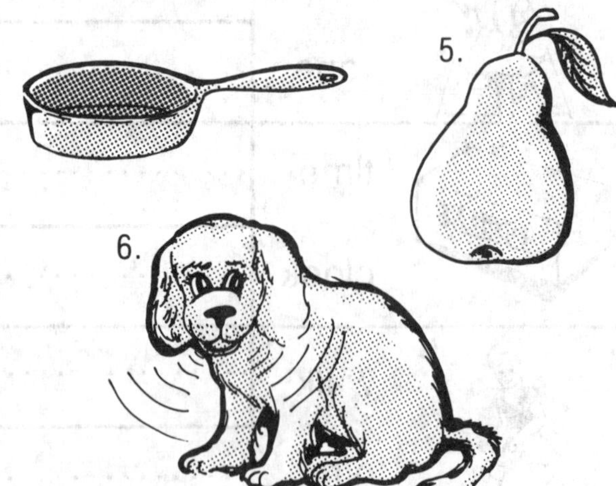

Fibers for Thread

Fibers are threadlike parts of material which can be made into thread. Some fibers come from plants and animals. Other fibers are man-made. For example, men make rayon from wood pulp and nylon from a mixture of several different things.

A **Write the correct word in each blank to tell where each fiber originates.**

wool
cotton
rayon
silk
flax
nylon

B **Put an "A" beside the fibers which come from animals.**

C **Put a "P" beside the fibers which come from plants.**

D **Put an "M" beside the fibers which are man-made.**

Developing Sentences

ABCDEFGHIJKLMNOPQRSTUVWXYZ
abcdefghijklmnopqrstuvwxyz

Write a sentence using each word in the box. See example "1."

1.	store	I went to the store.
	food	The food was good.
2.	little	
	zoo	
3.	house	
	home	
4.	help	
	wash	
5.	give	
	gift	
6.	chair	
	sit	
7.	swim	
	fish	
8.	ball	
	play	

Sheep

Vocabulary Study ● Draw a line under each correct answer. **JUST FOR FUN**

1. A ranch is a	(a) farm	(b) town	(c) city.
2. The plural of "sheep" is	(a) "sheep"	(b) "sheeps"	(c) "sheepes."
3. Weather can be	(a) cold	(b) warm	(c) hot.
4. "Mow" means	(a) "cut"	(b) "grow"	(c) "make."

There are many kinds of sheep. Some are wild. They live in the mountains.

Many sheep are raised on ranches. They can live in very cold climates. Their coats of wool keep them warm.

The sheep are raised for their coats of wool. When the weather is warm, the rancher cuts the wool from the sheep. When the weather turns cold, the sheep grow new coats. The wool is used to make clothes and blankets.

Sheep live on grasses and leaves. Some people let them mow their lawns. The sheep are gentle animals.

Answer these questions about the story:

1. Wild sheep live in the	(a) mountains	(b) forests	(c) deserts.
2. Sheep are often raised	(a) in cities	(b) on ranches	(c) in towns.
3. The sheep's coat is	(a) fur	(b) tough skin	(c) wool.
4. Wool is used	(a) for food	(b) for clothes	(c) for blankets.
5. Sheep eat	(a) grass	(b) meat	(c) fruit.

Draw a line from each picture to the correct word.

queen question quarter quail quilt

1. 2. 3. 4. 5.

How Thread Is Made

Thread is long thin string made by spinning different fibers. To make thread, strands of cotton, silk, linen, wool, and man-made fibers are twisted tightly together. Many different devices have been used to make thread. Some of these devices are described below.

SPINDLE: This is a smooth stick about a foot long. A small bowl made the spindle turn like a top. A notch in one end caught the thread.

SPINNING WHEEL: A spindle was fastened to a wooden support. It was turned by a belt connected to a large wheel. The spinner used a foot pedal to turn the wheel. It made one thread at a time.

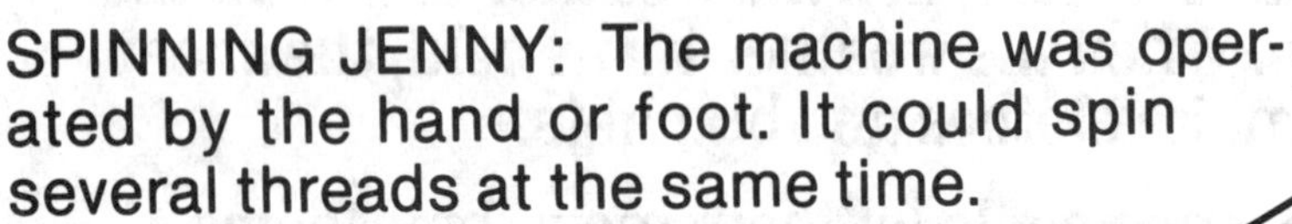

SPINNING JENNY: The machine was operated by the hand or foot. It could spin several threads at the same time.

SPINNING MULE: This machine had 48 spindles. It made thread better and faster than earlier devices.

SPINNING MACHINE: This large modern machine can twist the fibers into thread.

Answer the following:

1. What is the oldest device used for spinning thread? ______________________

2. What is the newest method of making thread? ______________________

3. Which device was used by colonial women? ______________________

Constructing Sentences

ABCDEFGHIJKLMNOPQRSTUVWXYZ
abcdefghijklmnopqrstuvwxyz

Write a sentence using each word in the box. See sample "1."

1. candy	The candy was sweet.
sugar	Pass the sugar.
2. may	
ask	
3. train	
fast	
4. wagon	
ride	
5. uncle	
man	
6. some	
more	
7. book	
read	
8. mother	
woman	

Goats

JUST FOR FUN

Vocabulary Study ● Draw a line under each correct answer.

1. ''Both'' means	(a) ''one''	(b) ''two''	(c) ''three.''
2. ''Almost'' means	(a) ''not all''	(b) ''all''	(c) ''everything.''
3. The opposite of ''close'' is	(a) ''near''	(b) ''by''	(c) ''far.''
4. ''Alike'' means	(a) ''the same as''	(b) ''not like''	(c) ''not the same.''

Some goats are wild. Some are raised on ranches. Both kinds are very much alike.

Male goats are called bucks. Female goats are called nannies. Baby goats are called kids.

Goats are restless animals. They are very curious about everything.

Goats will eat almost anything. They live best on leaves and grasses.

Goats are closely related to sheep. Goats give us milk and meat. Their hair is used to make cloth.

Male goats have beards. They like to butt each others' heads. Goats are fun to watch.

Answer these questions about the story:

1. Wild goats and ranch goats are	(a) very different	(b) not alike	(c) much alike.
2. Baby goats are called	(a) bucks	(b) nannies	(c) kids.
3. Goats are closely related to	(a) cows	(b) sheep	(c) horses.
4. Goats give us	(a) meat	(b) milk	(c) cloth.
5. Goats are	(a) curious	(b) restless	(c) lazy.

Draw a line from each picture to the correct word.

rat
rain
rabbit
rope
rake
rug

Cloth from Thread

Cloth is fabric for clothing which is made by weaving different kinds of thread. The thread is made from man-made or natural fibers.

A **Use the underlined words from above to fill in the blanks.**

1. fibers 2. ________ 3. ________

Frames or machines called looms are used to weave thread into cloth. Lengthwise threads are called warp. Crosswise threads are called woof. Cloth is made by weaving the two kinds of thread together.

B **Use the underlined words from above to fill in the blanks.**

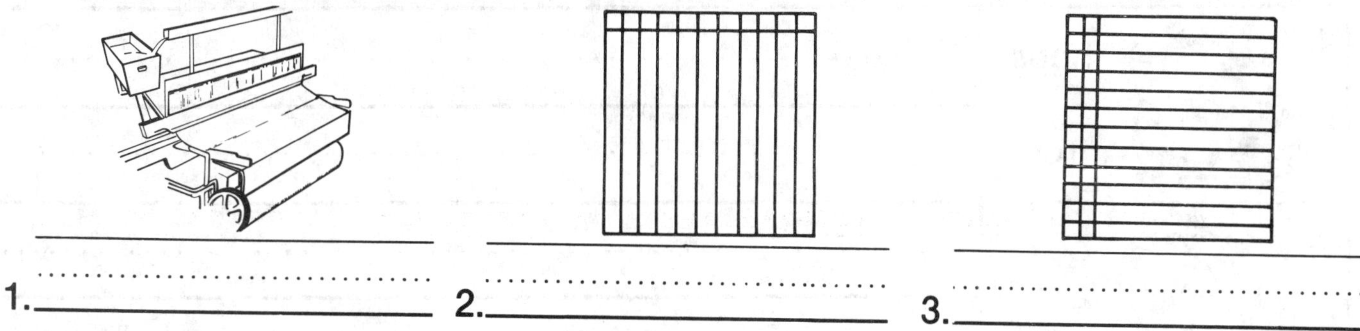

1. ________ 2. ________ 3. ________

Cloth can be made plain or very colorful.

1. Some cloth is dyed a solid color.
2. Machines are used to print designs on some materials.
3. Designs are woven into some fabrics by using colored thread.

C **Write the number of the sentence above which describes each fabric below.**

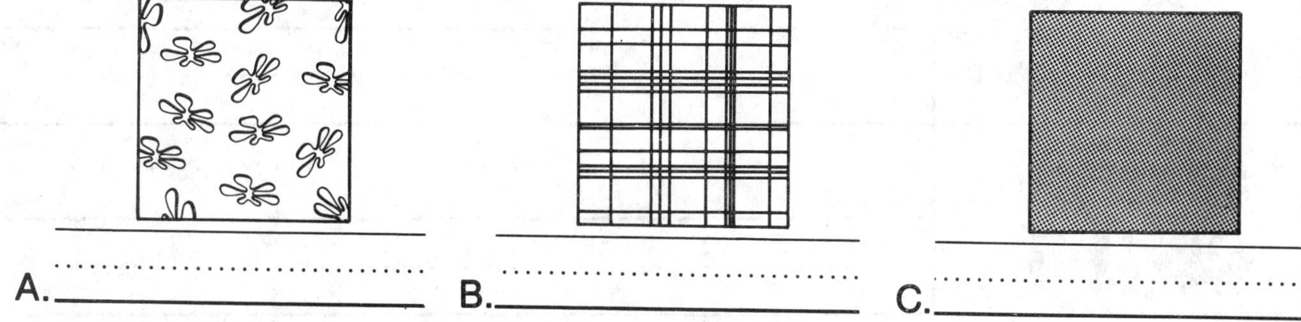

A. ________ B. ________ C. ________

Building Sentences

ABCDEFGHIJKLMNOPQRSTUVWXYZ
abcdefghijklmnopqrstuvwxyz

Write a sentence using each word in the box. See sample "1."

1. 2	two	I have two cookies.
	and	Bob and Bill are twins.
2.	bed	
	sleep	
3.	write	
	desk	
4.	hops	
	frog	
5.	box	
	wrap	
6.	cat	
	fast	
7.	lady	
	dance	
8.	hay	
	fork	

Pigs

Vocabulary Study ● **Draw a line under each correct answer.** **JUST FOR FUN**

1. "Too" means	(a) "some"	(b) "no"	(c) "also."
2. "Plenty" means	(a) "enough"	(b) "not much"	(c) "too much."
3. "Snout" is another name for	(a) "mouth"	(b) "nose"	(c) "eyes."
4. The opposite of "true" is	(a) "right"	(b) "correct"	(c) "false."

Most pigs live on farms. They are raised for their meat. The meat is called pork.

There are many kinds of pigs. All male pigs are called boars. Females are called sows.

Pigs eat corn and other grains. They need plenty of water.

Pigs are easily known by their snouts. Their bodies are covered with stiff hair.

Many people think pigs are dirty. They think pigs eat too much. These things are not true. Pigs eat only enough to fill themselves. They are not dirty animals. They roll in the mud only to cool themselves. Pigs like clean homes too.

Answer these questions about the story:

1. Most pigs live	(a) in the wild	(b) in cities	(c) on farms.
2. Meat from pigs is called	(a) pork	(b) beef	(c) poultry.
3. Female pigs are called	(a) boars	(b) sows	(c) piglets.
4. Pigs are covered with	(a) soft fur	(b) soft hair	(c) stiff hair.
5. Pigs eat	(a) corn	(b) grains	(c) meat.

*

Draw a line from each picture to the correct word.

1.

2.

3.

sun
star
ship
snake
sheep
shoe

4. 5. 6.

Clothes from Cloth

A **Draw a line from each word to the phrase which best describes it.**

1. cloth
2. clothes
3. cotton
4. wool
5. silk

a. a heavy fabric worn in cold weather
b. a smooth, shiny fabric used for fancy clothes
c. fabric woven from thread
d. a lightweight fabric worn in warm weather
e. garments worn on the body

B **Write the name of the fabric from the list above which would be used to make the clothes below.**

1.  ____________ 2.  ____________ 3. ____________

C **Write "yes" under each picture which is something made from cloth. Write "no" if it is not.**

1.  ____________ 2.  ____________ 3. ____________

4.  ____________ 5. 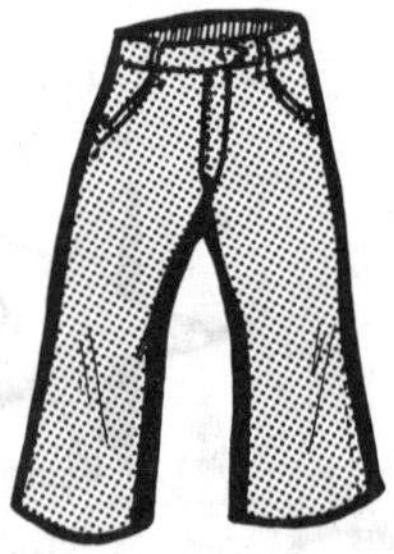 ____________ 6.  ____________ 7. ____________

Double Letters

ABCDEFGHIJKLMNOPQRSTUVWXYZ
a b c d e f g h i j k l m n o p q r s t u v w x y z

Rewrite each word.

buzz	buzz	ribbon	ribbon
cheer		eggs	
penny		valley	
hurry		address	
coffee		cattle	
comma		dipper	
flipper		account	
glass		planning	
fuzz		beggar	
sparrow		speed	
bless		goose	
supper		different	
street		muddy	
follow		puppy	
cellar		lesson	
cool		caller	

Chickens

Vocabulary Study ● **Draw a line under each correct answer.**

JUST FOR FUN

1. ''Hatch'' means (a) ''come from'' (b) ''break'' (c) ''die.''
2. ''Warm'' means (a) ''very cold'' (b) ''very hot'' (c) ''not too hot.''
3. When you grow, you get (a) shorter (b) smaller (c) bigger.
4. The opposite of ''stay'' is (a) ''go'' (b) ''stop'' (c) ''be.''

Chickens are birds. They are important to people. Chickens give us meat and eggs.

Chickens hatch from eggs. Baby chickens are called chicks. It takes 21 days for eggs to hatch.

Baby chicks must stay warm. They do not need to be taught anything. They know how to scratch for food. They grow very quickly.

Some chicks are hatched without the mother hen. The eggs are kept warm under lights. These chicks act the same as those with a mother hen.

*

Answer these questions about the story:

1. Chickens give us (a) eggs (b) meat (c) milk.
2. Baby chickens are called (a) hens (b) roosters (c) chicks.
3. Chicks must stay (a) warm (b) cool (c) in the dark.
4. Chicks need to be taught (a) everything (b) some things (c) nothing.
5. Without a hen, eggs are kept (a) under a light (b) on ice (c) in water.

Draw a line from each picture to the correct word.

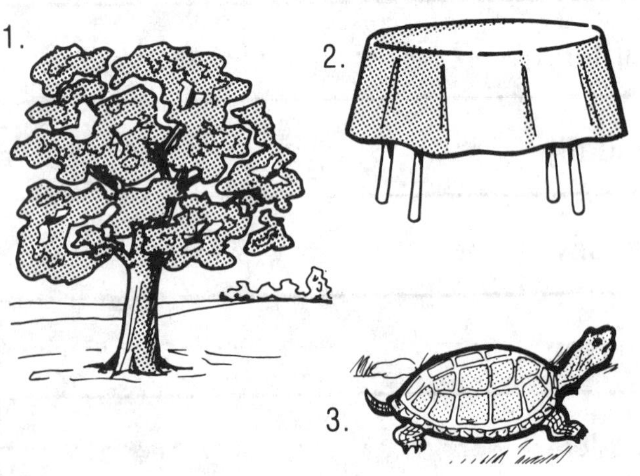

1. 2. 3.

tree
train
turtle
truck
tie
table

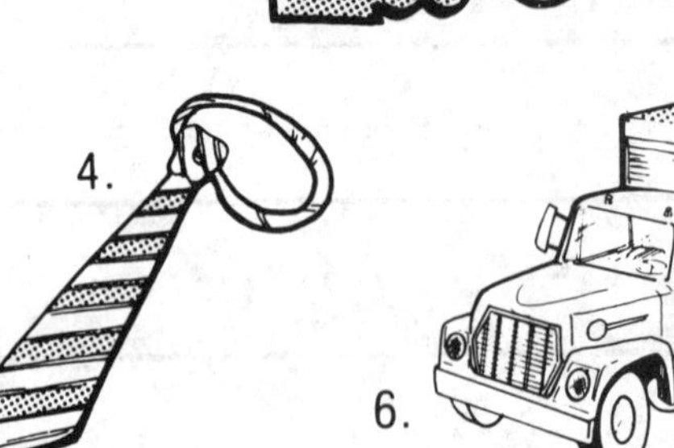

4. 5. 6.

Clothes for You

A **What clothes you wear depends a great deal upon the weather. Match the clothes to the season by putting the correct letter in each blank.**

A. spring
B. summer
C. fall
D. winter

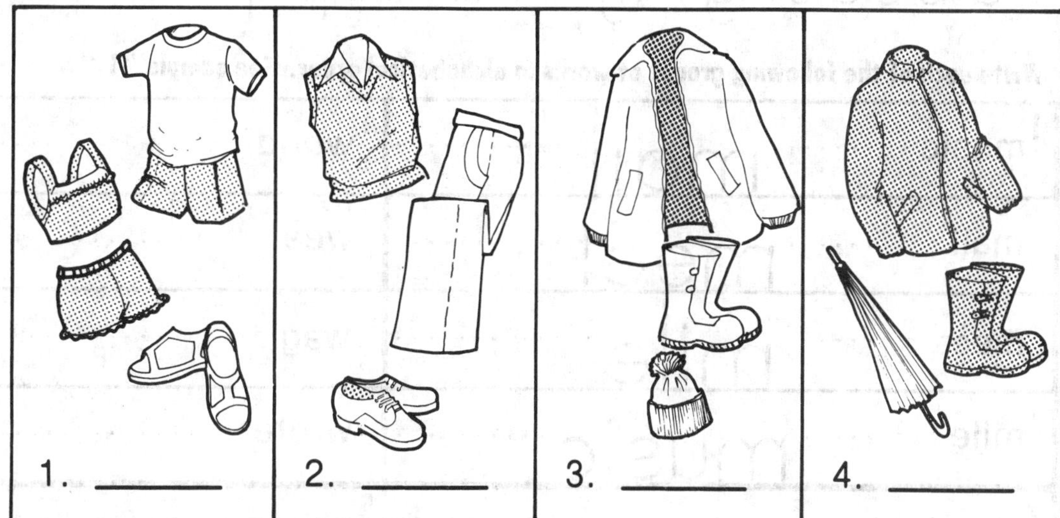

1. **Draw a line under the name of your favorite season of the year.**
2. **Put a check mark in the box showing clothes you would wear while building a snowman.**

B **Where you are and what you are doing also make a difference in the clothes you wear. Match each picture with the correct letter telling where each would be worn.**

A. school
B. church
C. home
D. playground

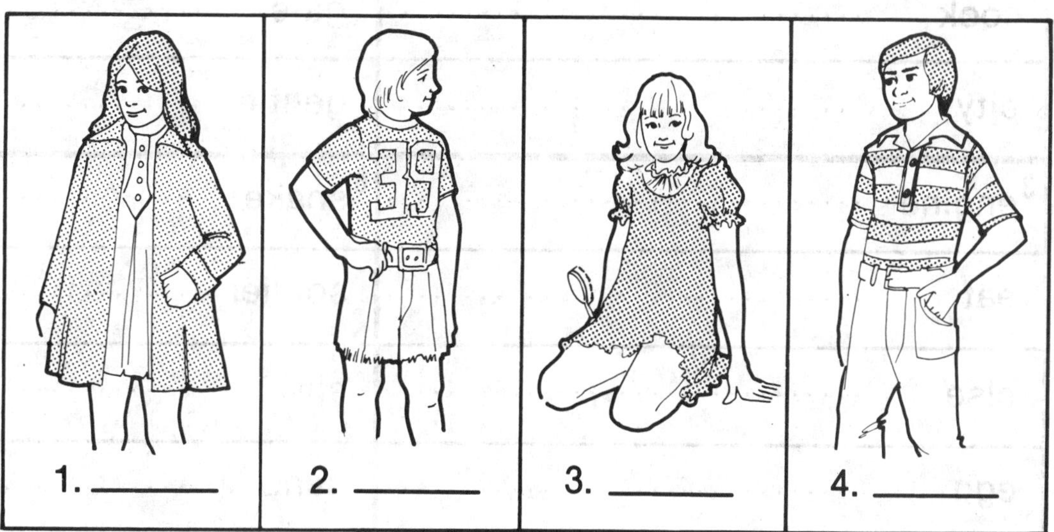

1. **Draw a line under the name of the place you would go on Sunday dressed in your nicest clothes.**
2. **Put a check mark in the box showing clothes you might put on after taking a bath at night.**

Alphabetical Order

ABCDEFGHIJKLMNOPQRSTUVWXYZ
a b c d e f g h i j k l m n o p q r s t u v w x y z

Write each of the following groups of words in alphabetical order. See sample "1."

1	
music	mail
mail	meet
meet	mile
mile	music

2	
cloud	
curl	
cab	
cent	
cook	
city	

3	
engine	
eat	
else	
egg	
echo	
eight	

4	
world	
wee	
wag	
wrote	

5	
goose	
girl	
grade	
guess	
gate	
gentle	

6	
snake	
soldier	
silk	
sand	
sea	
shape	

Map Directions

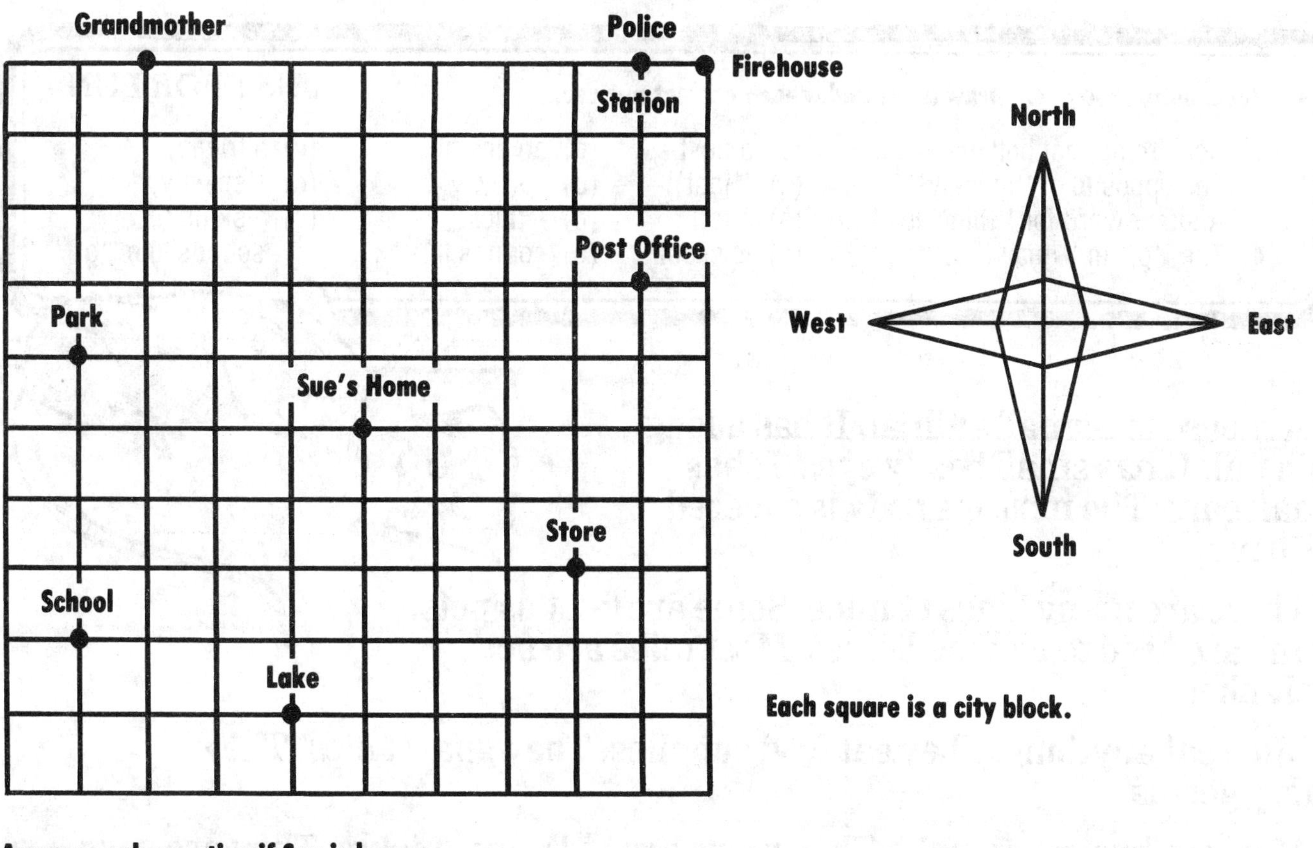

Answer each question if Sue is home:

1. How far does Sue walk to school?
2. How many blocks east and how many blocks north is the firehouse?
3. If Sue goes three blocks west and five blocks north, where will she be?
4. What place is four blocks east and two blocks north?
5. Sue walked to and from the Post Office. How many blocks did she walk?
6. What directions will she go to get to the lake?
7. How many blocks east and south must she travel to go to the store?
8. Give the directions for going to the police station from the lake.

Mice

Vocabulary Study ● Draw a line under each correct answer.

JUST FOR FUN

1. Something that bothers you is	(a) a pest	(b) an enemy	(c) a friend.
2. The opposite of "quickly" is	(a) "fast"	(b) "slowly"	(c) "speedy."
3. Another word for "thin" is	(a) "fat"	(b) "thick"	(c) "skinny."
4. The "g" in "gnaw"	(a) is silent	(b) sounds like "j"	(c) sounds like "g."

A mouse is a small animal. It has a long thin tail. It has small beady eyes. It has small ears. The mouse's body is covered with fur.

There are many kinds of mice. Some are kept as pets. Some are used to test medicines. Most mice are not well-liked.

Mice eat anything. They eat food supplies. They gnaw holes. They carry germs.

Mice are busiest at night. They move around very quickly. They are very nervous. They make squeaking noises.

Mice are found all over the world. Everywhere they are pests.

Answer these questions about the story:

1. Mice are	(a) small	(b) covered with fur	(c) big.
2. Most mice are	(a) well-liked	(b) not well-liked	(c) friendly.
3. Mice eat	(a) meat only	(b) cheese only	(c) anything.
4. Mice are busiest	(a) in the morning	(b) during the day	(c) at night.
5. Mice are found	(a) only in hot places	(b) only in cold places	(c) everywhere.

Identify each picture.

1. 

2. 

3. 

4. 

5. 

van	violin	vine	vase	vest

Leather

Leather is animal skins from which the hair has been removed. The skins go through a treatment called tanning before being made into clothing. Here are several pictures of things you wear which can be made of leather.

A **Write the correct name for each piece of clothing in each blank. Then draw a line from each picture to the part of the body where it would be worn. See the example.**

belt	cap	boots	jacket	gloves	shoes

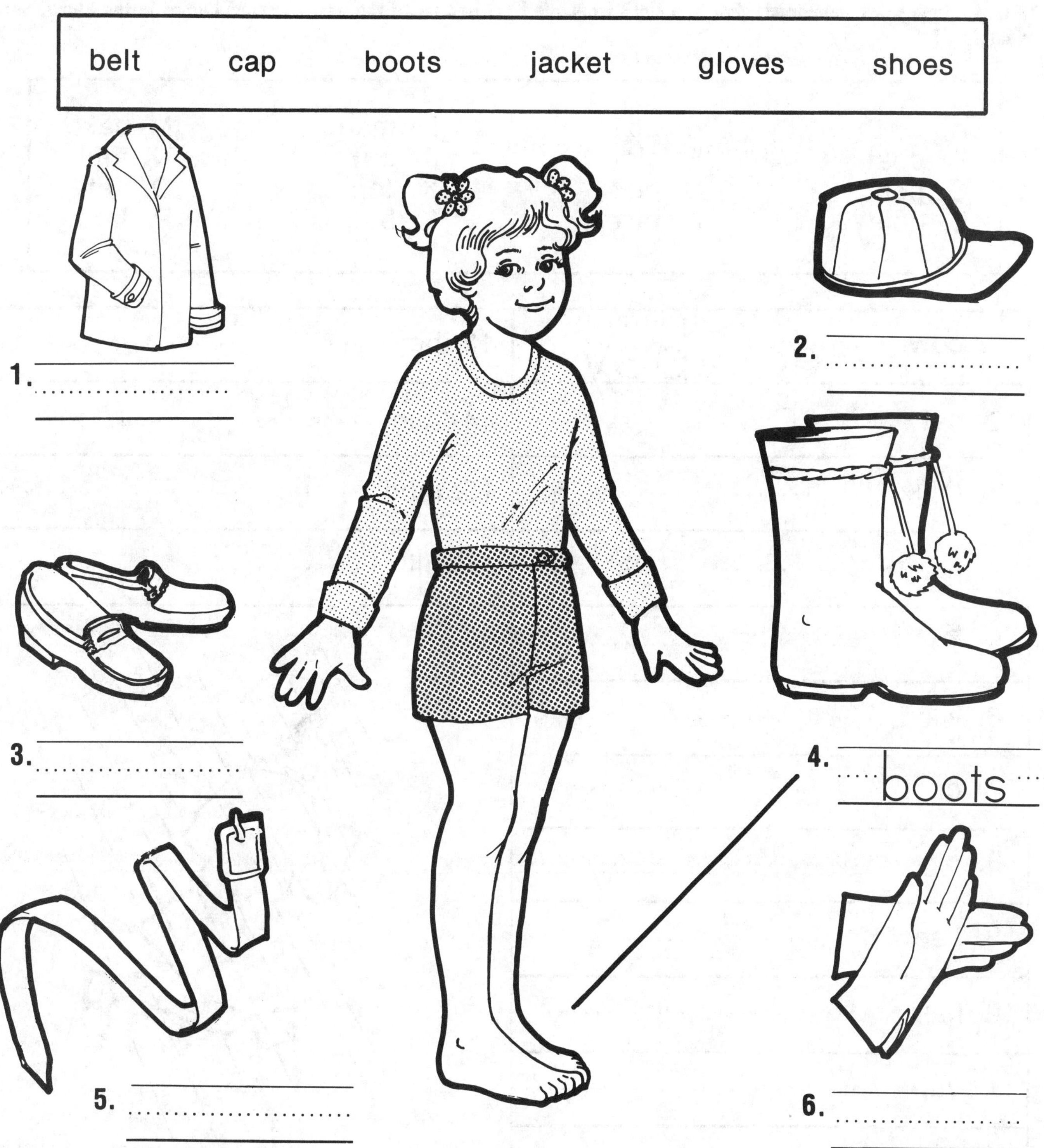

B **Color each picture on this page which is like something you own that is made of leather.**

Write Compound Words

ABCDEFGHIJKLMNOPQRSTUVWXYZ
abcdefghijklmnopqrstuvwxyz

To make each word compound, choose a word from the box; and write the new compound word in the blank. See example "1."

A. cloth	E. boy	I. man	M. cake
B. coat	F. side	J. cut	N. mill
C. pen	G. box	K. top	O. set
D. hole	H. hive	L. bag	P. line

1. cow ...... cowboy	13. be ....
2. hat	14. rain ....
3. milk	15. mud ....
4. hand	16. hill ....
5. up	
6. wind	
7. dust	
8. pig	
9. bee	
10. hair	
11. cup	
12. pipe	

Snakes

Vocabulary Study ● Draw a line under each correct answer. **JUST FOR FUN**

	(a)	(b)	(c)
1. The opposite of "open" is	(a) "not closed"	(b) "closed"	(c) "wide."
2. "None" means	(a) "some"	(b) "all"	(c) "not one."
3. The opposite of "dangerous" is	(a) "safe"	(b) "not safe"	(c) "fear."
4. "Whole" means	(a) "part of"	(b) "most of"	(c) "all."

There are many kinds of snakes. Some are dangerous. Some are not.

Snakes crawl about on the ground. They have no legs. Snakes move about slowly. Some can move very quickly.

All snakes can swim. Some can stay underwater for hours.

Snakes live on other animals. Most eat worms, insects, frogs, fish, and other snakes. The food is caught in the mouth. It is swallowed whole.

Snakes always have their eyes open. They do not have eyelids like us.

Do not play with snakes. Some snakes will hurt you.

Answer these questions about the story:

	(a)	(b)	(c)
1. Snakes get about by	(a) walking	(b) crawling	(c) flying.
2. All snakes	(a) can swim	(b) cannot swim	(c) are fast.
3. Snakes eat	(a) meat	(b) fruit	(c) vegetables.
4. A snake's eyes are	(a) never open	(b) closed	(c) never closed.
5. Snakes catch food	(a) with their mouths	(b) with their tails	(c) with their bodies.

*

Draw a line from each picture to the correct word.

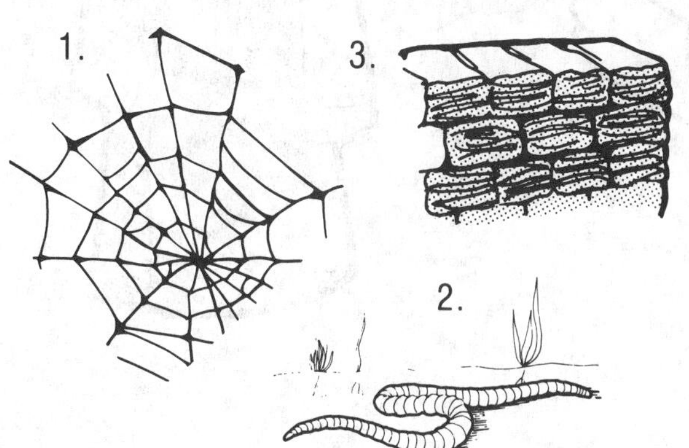

well
whale
wing
worm
web
wall

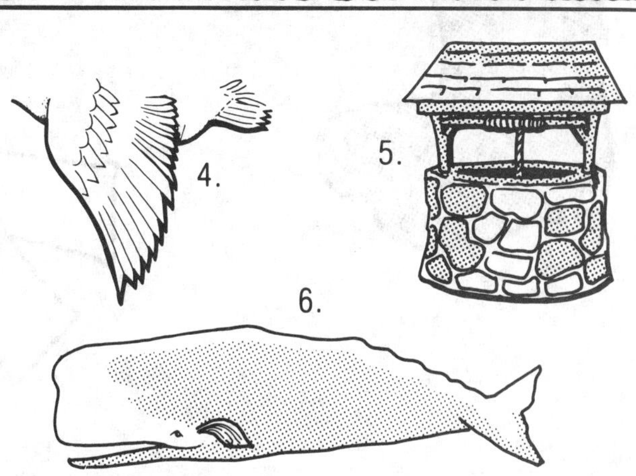

Rubber

Rubber is a stretchy, waterproof material. Natural rubber comes from the juice of the rubber trees which grow in the warm countries of the Far East. Men can also make rubber from chemicals. Clothing made from rubber is most often for special rather than everyday use.

Tell which clothes made of rubber would be needed by each person by putting the correct letter in each blank.

A.

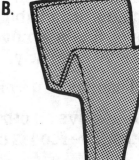

F.

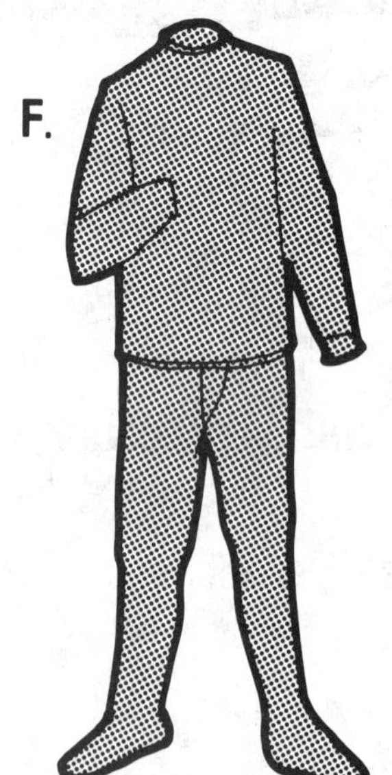

B.

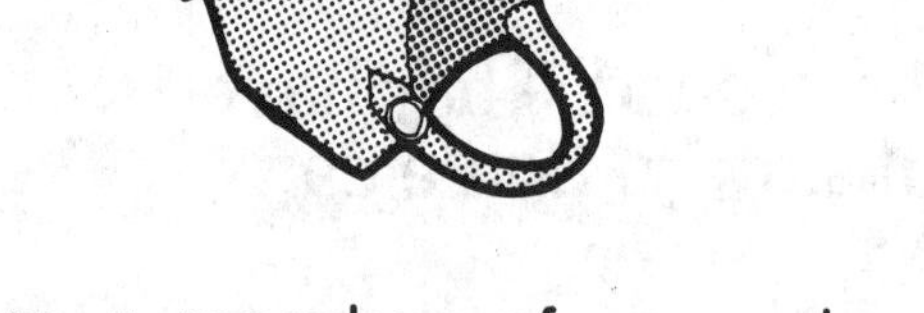

1. I am a member of an underwater search crew. What should I wear?
   ______

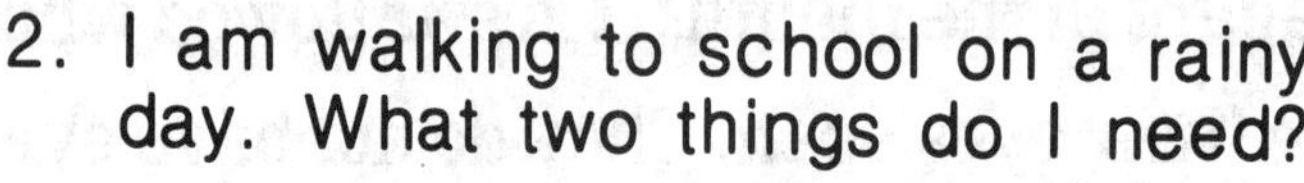

2. I am walking to school on a rainy day. What two things do I need?
   ______ ______

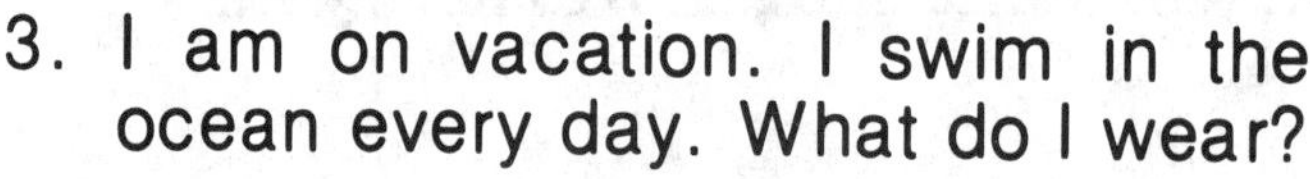

3. I am on vacation. I swim in the ocean every day. What do I wear?
   ______

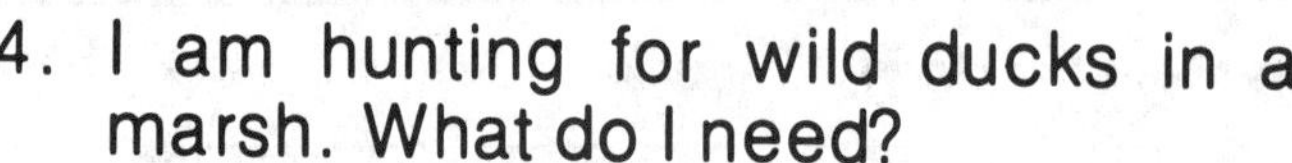

4. I am hunting for wild ducks in a marsh. What do I need?
   ______

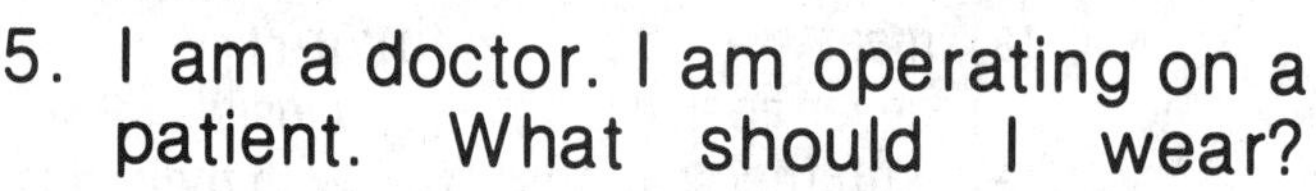

5. I am a doctor. I am operating on a patient. What should I wear?
   ______

C.

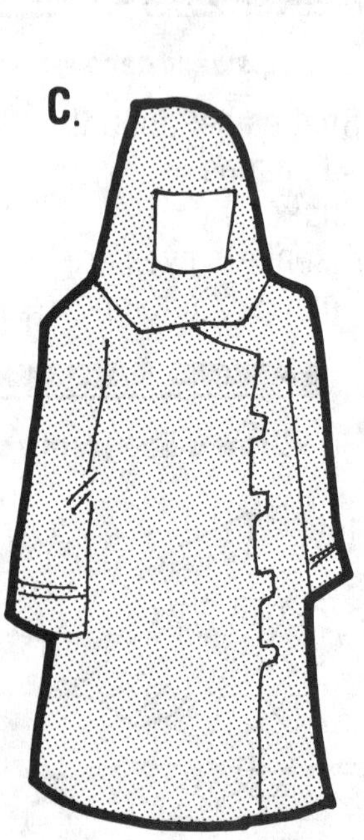

E.

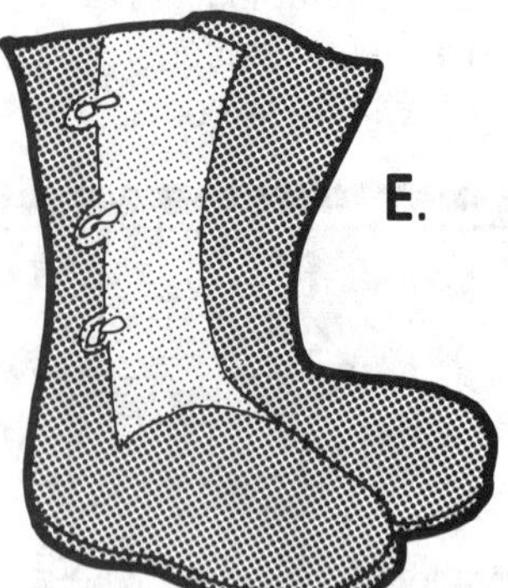

D.

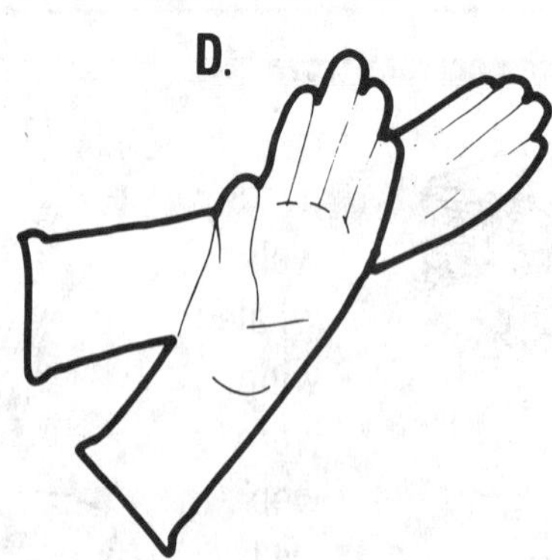

Vowels — Upper Case

A **Words contain vowels — "A, E, I, O, U." Words that start sentences and words that tell exact names use large or upper-case letters. Copy each letter several times.**

A ....
E ....
I ....
O ....
U ....

B **Each word begins with an upper-case vowel. Copy each word in the space. Underline each upper-case vowel.**

1. Apple ...... Apple	12. Union ....
2. One	13. Each ....
3. Iris	14. Until ....
4. Alone	15. Unit ....
5. Europe	16. Organ ....
6. Ant	17. Oil ....
7. Andy	18. Enough ....
8. Open	19. Add ....
9. Under	20. Itch ....
10. East	21. Over ....
11. Enter	22. Igloo ....

Lizards

Vocabulary Study ● Draw a line under each correct answer. **JUST FOR FUN**

1. "Underground" means	(a) "in the ground"	(b) "on the ground"	(c) "over the ground."
2. "Able" means	(a) "can"	(b) "cannot"	(c) "will."
3. The opposite of "bright" is	(a) "shiny"	(b) "dull"	(c) "light."
4. "New" means	(a) "old"	(b) "used"	(c) "not old."

There are many kinds of lizards. Some are small. Some are large.

Some lizards live on land. Their homes may be in trees or on rocks. Their homes may be underground.

Other lizards live in the water. All lizards, however, are able to swim. All like warm weather.

Many lizards are brightly colored. Some can even change their colors.

Never try to catch a lizard by holding its tail. The tail will break off. The lizard will not be hurt. It will just grow a new one.

Answer these questions about the story:

1. Lizards are	(a) small	(b) large	(c) all the same size.
2. Land lizards make homes	(a) in trees	(b) on rocks	(c) underground.
3. All lizards are able to	(a) swim	(b) change colors	(c) fly.
4. Lizards like	(a) cold weather	(b) cool weather	(c) warm weather.
5. When a lizards loses its tail, it	(a) dies	(b) gets sick	(c) grows a new one.

Identify each picture.

1. 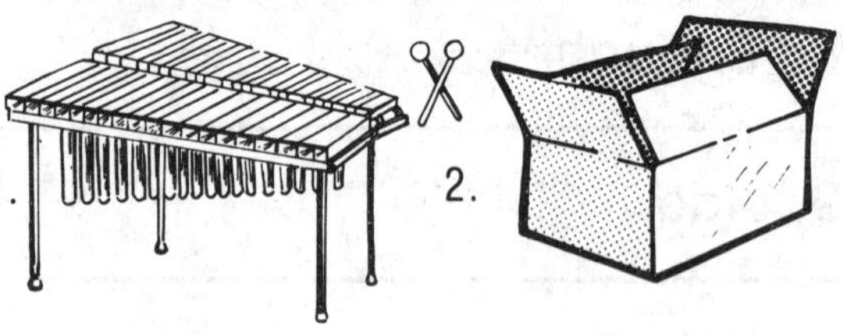 2. 3.  4. 

__________ __________ __________ __________

X ray	fox	xylophone	box

Special Holidays

A Fill in the blanks.

1. My favorite holiday is ______________________.
2. On Thanksgiving my mother cooks ______________________.
3. On Christmas our favorite dessert is ______________________.
4. It's fun to have a picnic on the Fourth of ______________________.

B Underline the correct answers.

At our (hous, house) we have a big Thanksgiving celebration. My grandparents (come, com) to see us. My aunts and (uncles, uncls) also come. Mother cooks a (larg, large) turkey. Grandmother (maks, makes) pies. Grandfather tells us (funny, funnie) stories. We are thankful we (hav, have) so much.

Christmas is (such, suche) fun. We put up a (big, bigg) tree. Everyone (helpes, helps) decorate it. We (wrap, wrapp) our gifts and put them under the tree. We give (som, some) food to another family. They do not have as (muche, much) as we do. Sharing makes us (happie, happy).

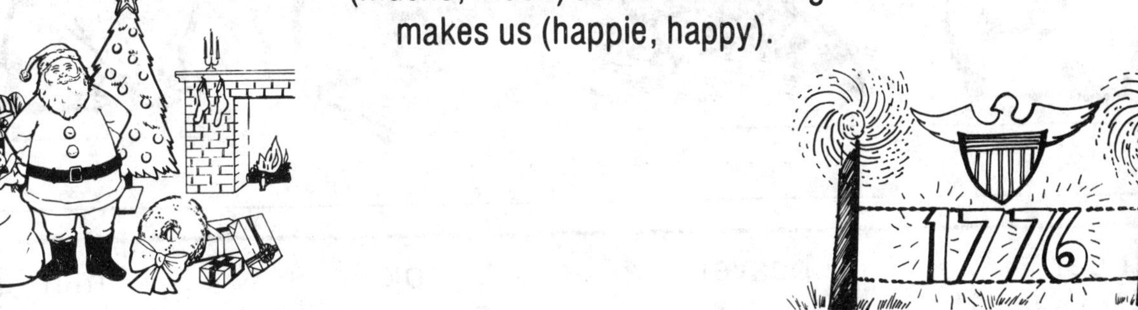

Furs

A Draw a line from each word to its definition.

1. fur
2. trapper
3. mink
4. Alaska
5. pelt
6. parka

a. an animal important for fur
b. the hairy covering of animals
c. a state important for its fur
d. a person who captures the animals
e. a heavy fur coat with a hood
f. the hide of the skinned animal

B True or False

T F 1. Fur is one of the earliest forms of clothing worn by man.
T F 2. There are only a few fur-bearing animals in the world.
T F 3. Fur clothing is necessary in warm climates.
T F 4. Fur trading was important in early America.
T F 5. Fur coats can cost thousands of dollars.

C Write the name of each fur-bearing animal under its picture.

bear	beaver	fox	mink
muskrat	rabbit	raccoon	seal

Vowels — Lower Case

A **Words contain vowels — "a, e, i, o, u." Words that do not begin sentences or words that are not exact names all use small or lower-case letters. Copy each letter several times.**

a ....
e ....
i ....
o ....
u ....

B **Each word contains one or more lower-case vowels. Copy each in the space. Underline each vowel.**

1. across ... across ...	12. know ....
2. feed	13. dirty ....
3. cabin	14. yard ....
4. grass	15. cloud ....
5. lazy	16. saw ....
6. make	17. cold ....
7. fruit	18. hear ....
8. tool	19. low ....
9. rubber	20. tooth ....
10. forest	21. circus ....
11. sick	22. grin ....

Alligators

Vocabulary Study ● Draw a line under each correct answer. **JUST FOR FUN**

1.	The opposite of "dark" is	(a) "not light"	(b) "light"	(c) "shade."
2.	The number after "eleven" is	(a) "ten"	(b) "twelve"	(c) "nine."
3.	"Cute" means	(a) "mean"	(b) "ugly"	(c) "pretty."
4.	When you take money for a thing, you	(a) give it away	(b) buy it	(c) sell it.

Alligators are very strong animals. They are dark brown or black. Big alligators are about twelve feet long.

Alligators always live near water. They like to bathe in the warm sun. Then they cool off in the water.

The alligators' homes are caves. They dig caves in the ground in or near water. Female alligators build other nests on land. Here they lay their eggs. Baby alligators head for the water after they are born.

Baby alligators are often sold as pets. They are cute when they are small. When they get big, they are dangerous.

Answer these questions about the story:

1.	Alligators are	(a) strong	(b) weak	(c) big.
2.	Alligators always live near	(a) sand	(b) water	(c) mountains.
3.	An alligator's home is a	(a) cave	(b) den	(c) tree.
4.	Alligators lay eggs	(a) in the water	(b) on land	(c) in a cave.
5.	Big alligators are	(a) cute	(b) dangerous	(c) harmless.

Complete each sentence with a word from the box.

yes	yell
you	yellow
your	yo-yo
young	yarn
year	yak
yard	yet

1. A __________ is an animal.
2. Don't come __________.
3. I am __________ friend.
4. The color is __________.
5. He is too __________.
6. Cats like __________.
7. Who are __________?
8. The answer is __________.
9. Stay in the __________.
10. We've been here one __________.
11. Don't __________ at me.
12. I want a __________.

Synthetics

Synthetics are man-made materials produced by a chemical process. Several elements like coal, air, and water are combined with petroleum, gas, or limestone to make synthetics. Many synthetic fabrics are stronger and longer lasting than natural fibers. Also, synthetics are usually less expensive. Many of the clothes you wear are made of synthetic materials.

A **Each box contains clothing made of synthetic material. Write the correct name for each piece of clothing in each blank.**

tennis shoes
pajamas
scarf
tank top
jacket
bathing suit
pants
stockings

B **In this list below, mark out the name of each material that is not synthetic.**

rayon
cotton
nylon
wool
Orlon
Dacron
silk
fur

Consonants — Upper Case

All letters in the alphabet except "A, E, I, O," and "U" are consonants. Words that begin sentences and words that tell exact names all use upper-case letters. Copy each letter several times.

B	C
D	F
G	H
J	K
L	M
N	P
Q	R
S	T
V	W
X	Y
Z	
B	C
D	F
H	M
N	R
S	T

Lions

Vocabulary Study ● **Draw a line under each correct answer.** **JUST FOR FUN**

1. When you share, you	(a) keep all	(b) keep part	(c) keep none.
2. "Most" means	(a) "all"	(b) "none"	(c) "almost all."
3. A lion talks by	(a) roaring	(b) growling	(c) barking.
4. The opposite of "like" is	(a) "love"	(b) "dislike"	(c) "need."

The "king of the beasts" is the lion. He is big and strong. His roar scares all the other animals.

The lion is a member of the cat family. He is often found in Africa. The lion likes to live in small groups. He likes the open country.

The lion usually hunts at night. He eats meat. The female really does most of the hunting. She kills the food and shares it with her mate.

The male lion has a big mane of hair around his neck. The female does not. Both have short yellowish hair.

A female lion is called a lioness. Her babies are called cubs.

Answer these questions about the story:

1. The lion is a member of the	(a) dog family	(b) cat family	(c) cow family.
2. Lions usually hunt	(a) at night	(b) in the morning	(c) in the daytime.
3. The lion's hair is	(a) short	(b) long	(c) yellowish.
4. Which lion has a big mane of hair?	(a) female	(b) male	(c) both
5. Baby lions are called	(a) puppies	(b) kittens	(c) cubs.

Identify each picture.

1. 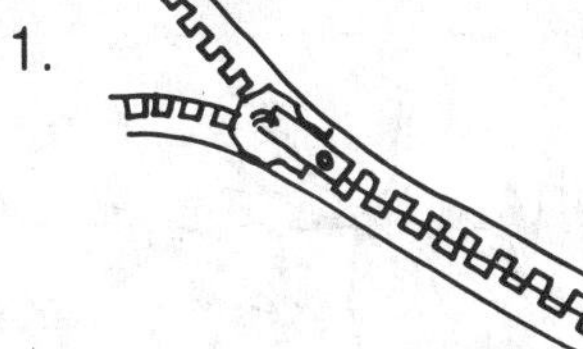

2. 

3. 

4. 

zebra zoo zipper zero

Shelter

One of our basic needs is for shelter. Shelters provide protection from different things that can harm people.

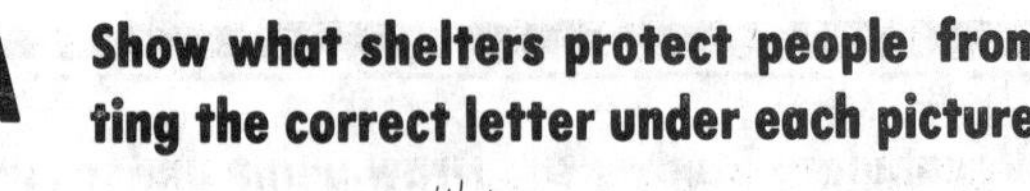

A **Show what shelters protect people from by putting the correct letter under each picture.**

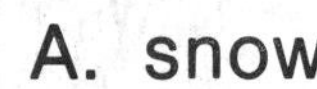

A. snow
B. animals
C. wind
D. enemies
E. sun
F. rain

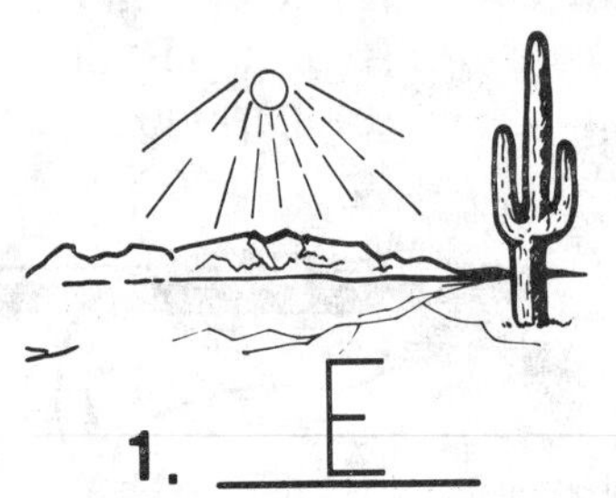

1. E

2. ______

3. ______

4. ______

5. ______

6. ______

B **Many different shelters have been used by man. Put the letter of the correct name under each picture of a shelter.**

A. igloo
B. castle
C. tent
D. tree house
E. log cabin
F. wigwam

1. ___

2. ___

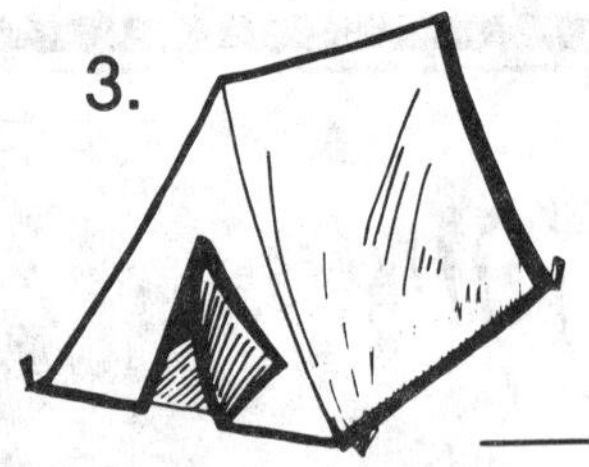

3. ___

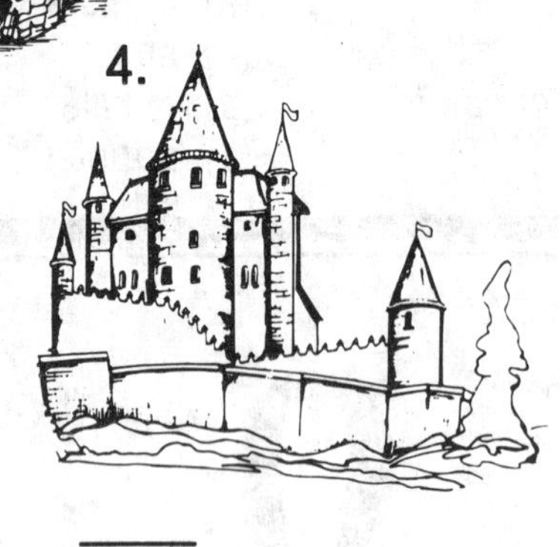

4. ___

5. ___

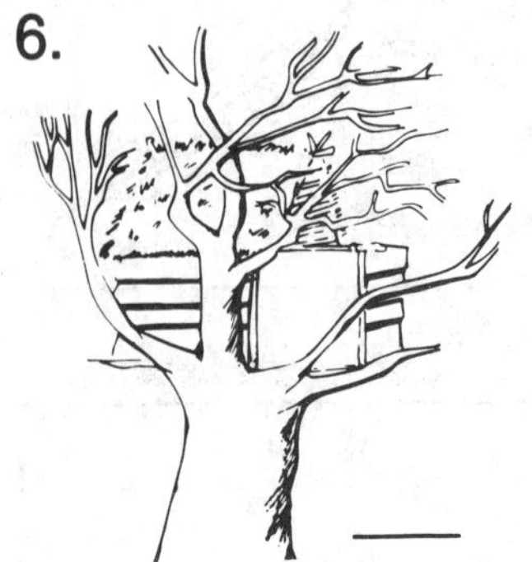

6. ___

C **Tell who used each shelter by putting the right number on the picture.**

1. nomad
2. tribal man
3. Indian
4. pioneer
5. nobleman
6. Eskimo

Hobbies

A **Fill in the blanks with the correct words.**

(is or are)

1. Hobbies ________ fun.

   A good hobby ________ coin collecting.

(to or two)

2. I am going ________ see Jim's stamp collection.

   He has ________ albums of foreign stamps.

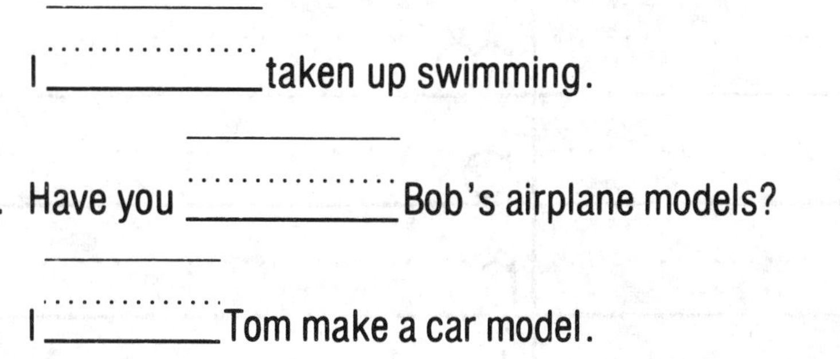

(has or have)

3. Mary ________ taken up skating as her hobby.

   I ________ taken up swimming.

(saw or seen)

4. Have you ________ Bob's airplane models?

   I ________ Tom make a car model.

(go or went)

5. Jane likes to ________ fishing with her dad.

   Lask week they ________ to Lake Charles.

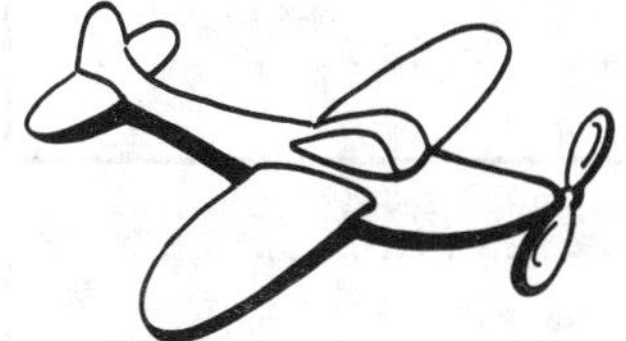

(has or have)

6. Joe and Bill ________ started playing on a softball team.

   Sue ________ gone to watch each game.

(did or done)

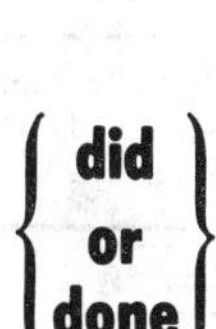

7. Sally ________ take painting lessons.

   Laura has ________ something different.

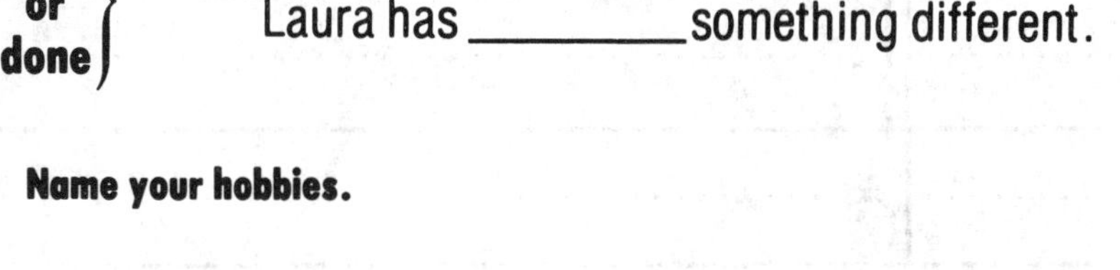

B **Name your hobbies.**

Consonants — Lower Case

All letters in the alphabet except "a, e, i, o," and "u" are consonants. Words that do not begin sentences and words that are not exact names all use lower-case letters. Copy each letter several times.

b	c
d	f
g	h
j	k
l	m
n	p
q	r
s	t
v	w
x	y
z	m
p	d
r	h
s	n
k	b
t	c

Tigers

Vocabulary Study ● **Draw a line under each correct answer.** **JUST FOR FUN**

1. "Belong" means (a) "to be part of" (b) "to want" (c) "to have."
2. A jungle is a/an (a) animal (b) person (c) place.
3. When you look for a thing, you (a) hunt it (b) find it (c) see it.
4. "Roam" means (a) "to be still" (b) "to move around" (c) "to sleep."

Tigers belong to the cat family. They are quick. They are strong. They are beautiful animals.

Most tigers live in Asia. They roam the jungles. Tigers are good swimmers. They are also good tree climbers.

Tigers rest during the day. At night they hunt. Tigers eat meat.

Tigers are easily recognized. They are rust-colored with black stripes. People often hunt tigers for their fur coats.

Tigers are very popular animals at the zoo. Have you ever seen a tiger?

Answer these questions about the story:

1. Tigers belong to the (a) cat family (b) dog family (c) horse family.
2. Tigers live in the (a) mountains (b) jungles (c) deserts.
3. Tigers hunt (a) at night (b) in the daytime (c) in the morning.
4. Tigers have (a) stripes (b) spots (c) solid coats.
5. Tigers are hunted (a) for food (b) for fur (c) for teeth.

Write the name of each picture.

1.  ____________
2.  ____________
3.  ____________
4. 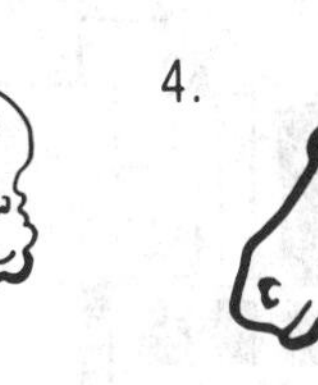 ____________
5.  ____________
6.  ____________
7.  ____________
8.  ____________

Building Materials

Many different materials have been used in the building of shelters.

A **Draw a line from the shelter to the material from which it was made. Show where shelters from these materials were found by putting the correct letter in each blank.**

______	1. igloo	cloth	A. African desert
______	2. cabin	bark	B. North Pole
______	3. tent	stone	C. Medieval Europe
______	4. wigwam	snow	D. United States wilderness
______	5. castle	logs	E. North American woodlands

B **Below are pictures of the three most common building materials used in the United States. Write the name of the correct material under each.**

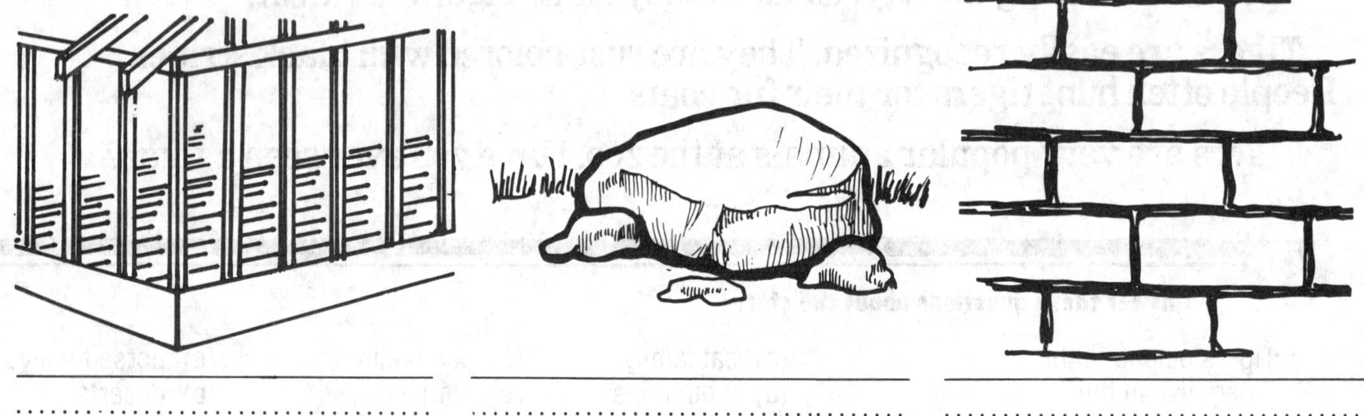

C **Put an "X" on the building found in the city. Put a "C" beside the building that might be in the country.**

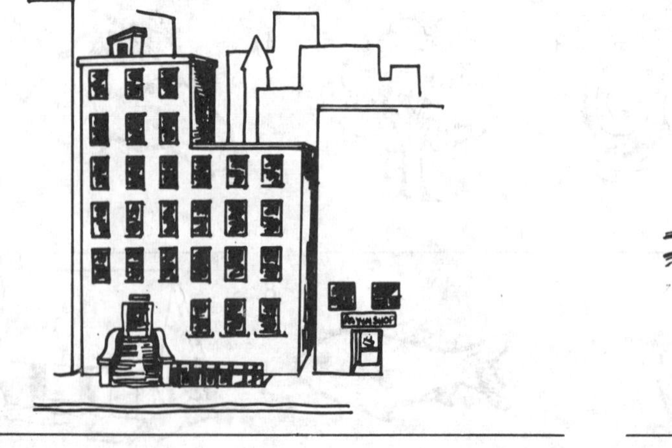

Root Words

ABCDEFGHIJKLMNOPQRSTUVWXYZ
abcdefghijklmnopqrstuvwxyz

When several words may be formed from one word, we call this word a root word.

EXAMPLE: The root word of "rests," "rested," "resting," "restful," "restless," and "unrest" is "rest."

Write the root word of each word. See example "1."

1. uncover ..... cover	15. kindness ....
2. discover	16. depart ....
3. running	17. unlock ....
4. homeward	18. freedom ....
5. sleepy	19. thankful ....
6. careful	20. slowly ....
7. freedom	21. harmful ....
8. nightly	22. deepest ....
9. harden	23. going ....
10. eastern	24. wonderful ....
11. freely	
12. lovely	
13. dislike	
14. joyful	

Leopards

Vocabulary Study ● Draw a line under each correct answer. JUST FOR FUN

1. Yellow is a (a) light color (b) dark color (c) shade of blue.
2. To fear something is to (a) like it (b) be afraid of it (c) hear it.
3. A sound is something you (a) see (b) feel (c) hear.
4. The opposite of "without" is (a) "with" (b) "not have" (c) "less."

Leopards are beautiful animals. Most leopards have yellow fur with black spots. There are some leopards which are all black.

Leopards belong to the cat family. People fear leopards more than any other cat.

Leopards are very strong animals. They are smart hunters. They usually hunt at night. They can move about without making a sound. Leopards eat meat.

Leopards are good swimmers. They are also good tree climbers. They usually attack from trees.

Leopards are hunted by people. Their fur is used to make coats.

Answer these questions about the story:

1. Leopards have (a) stripes (b) spots (c) checks.
2. Leopards belong to the (a) cat family (b) dog family (c) horse family.
3. Leopards usually hunt (a) at night (b) in the morning (c) during the day.
4. Leopards move about (a) clumsily (b) noisily (c) without noise.
5. Leopards are hunted for (a) meat (b) teeth (c) fur.

Underline the words which begin with capital letters.

1. Arnold
2. cat
3. Liz
4. Tommy
5. is
6. Sam
7. home
8. Kathy
9. see
10. Jim
11. you
12. Randy
13. Debbie
14. Gene
15. pretty
16. come
17. Susan
18. Ben
19. Henry
20. water
21. Frank
22. Craig
23. man
24. Brad

Homes

A True or False

T F 1. The place where you live is your home.
T F 2. All homes look just alike.
T F 3. Every home has many rooms in it.
T F 4. One building can be the home of several families.
T F 5. Some families rent homes instead of buying them.
T F 6. All homes have large yards to play in.
T F 7. Many different materials are used in building homes.

B Tell which home each family described below would live in by putting the correct letter in each blank.

1. My father, mother, brother, and I live in a small town. My father is a schoolteacher.

   ______

2. My mother and I live in a building with three other families. My mother works in a factory.

   ______

3. Our family of five lives in the country with my grandparents. My father is a farmer.

   ______

4. My father is a doctor. There are six people in my family. We live in a suburb.

   ______

A.

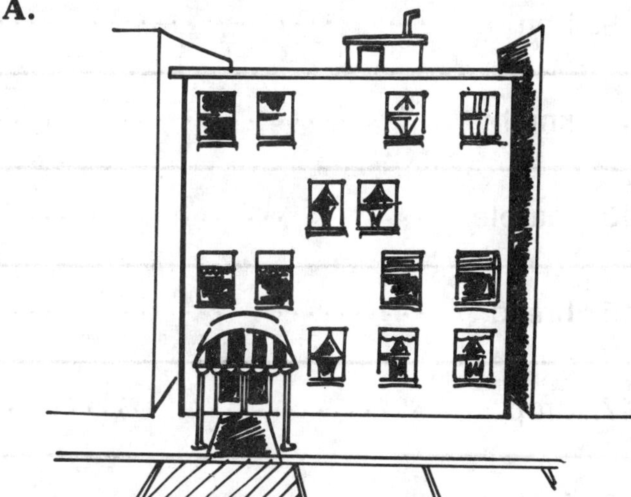

B.

D.

C.

Writing Letters — Lower Case

Rewrite each word. On the last two lines rewrite the lower-case alphabet.

1. chair ····· chair ·········	2. improve ························
3. apple ························	4. learn ························
5. early ························	6. paper ························
7. glove ························	8. shovel ························
9. iron ························	10. kitchen ························
11. knight ························	12. pencil ························
13. marble ························	14. monkey ························
15. bread ························	16. bicycle ························
17. drop ························	18. tractor ························
19. finger ························	20. dragon ························
21. hammer ························	22. cradle ························
23. jacket ························	24. feather ························
25. never ························	26. pedal ························

a b c d e f g h i j k l m n o p q r s t u v w x y z

27. ··

28. ··

Elephants

Vocabulary Study ● Draw a line under each correct answer. **JUST FOR FUN**

1. "Largest" means	(a) "smallest"	(b) "tiniest"	(c) "biggest."
2. The opposite of "warm" is	(a) "hot"	(b) "cool"	(c) "very cold."
3. When you like something, you	(a) hate it	(b) enjoy it	(c) do not enjoy it.
4. "Peaceful" means	(a) "quiet"	(b) "mad"	(c) "noisy."

The elephant is the largest animal on land. There are two kinds of elephants. One is the African elephant. The other is the Asian elephant. The African elephant is the larger one.

Elephants live in herds. They eat grasses. Elephants like warm weather.

The elephant has a long nose called a trunk. The trunk is very useful. It is used to pick up things. It carries water to the elephant's mouth. It carries food to the mouth.

Elephants are big, but they are peaceful animals. They are often seen in zoos and circuses.

Answer these questions about the story:

1. Elephants are the largest animals	(a) ever	(b) in water	(c) on land.
2. Elephants live	(a) alone	(b) in pairs	(c) in herds.
3. Elephants eat	(a) grasses	(b) meat	(c) fish.
4. An elephant's nose is called	(a) a trunk	(b) a horn	(c) a hose.
5. Elephants are	(a) mean	(b) peaceful	(c) noisy.

Draw a line from each picture to the correct word. What is the sound of the "a" in each word?

cake
flag
cat
snake
hat
train

Writing Letters — Mixed

Rewrite each word. On the last lines write the matching lower-case letter beside the upper-case letter. The first three are examples.

1. Camel .... Camel	2. Across .... Across
3. Basket .... Basket	4. Sight ....
5. Empty	6. Yard ....
7. Glass	8. Heavy ....
9. Igloo	10. Jelly ....
11. King	12. March ....
13. Nurse	14. Race ....
15. Shirt	16. Life ....
17. Down	18. Open ....
19. Foot	20. Push ....
21. Wheel	22. Thumb ....
23. Goose	24. Knee ....

25. A ..... B ..... C ..... D ..... E ..... F ..... G .....

H ..... I ..... J ..... K ..... L ..... M ..... N .....

O ..... P ..... Q ..... R ..... S ..... T ..... U .....

V ..... W ..... X ..... Y ..... Z .....

Monkeys

Vocabulary Study ● **Draw a line under each correct answer.**

JUST FOR FUN

1. Most of something is (a) all of it (b) nearly all of it (c) none of it.
2. If you watch something, you (a) listen to it (b) smell it (c) look at it.
3. "Can" means (a) "able" (b) "not able" (c) "may."
4. A forest has (a) much water (b) no trees (c) many trees.

Of all animals monkeys look the most like humans. They have hands with fingers. They have feet with toes. Their faces are made like humans' faces. They can walk on two legs.

There are many kinds of monkeys. Most live in forests. They usually live in large families.

Some monkeys live in trees. Some live on the ground.

Almost all monkeys eat fruits. Some also eat grasses. Others may eat insects.

Many people like to watch monkeys. Monkeys are very popular at the zoo.

Answer these questions about the story:

1. Monkeys look much like (a) humans (b) cats (c) dogs.
2. Most monkeys live (a) in water (b) on mountains (c) in forests.
3. Monkeys usually live (a) alone (b) in pairs (c) in families.
4. Monkeys eat (a) fruits (b) meat (c) wood.
5. Monkeys are kept at the (a) park (b) zoo (c) school.

Draw a line from each picture to the correct word. What is the sound of the "e" in each word?

1. 

2. 3. 

bed
egg
seal
leaf
fence
teeth

4. 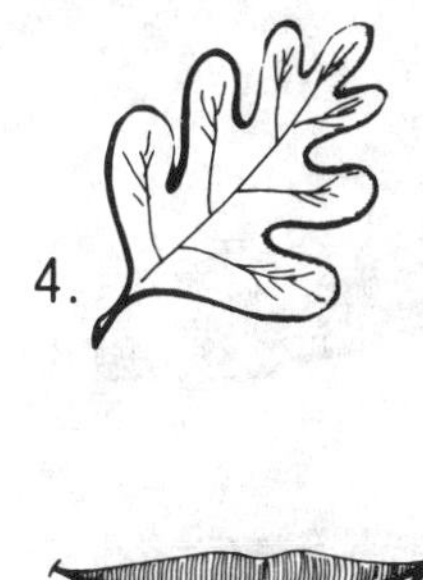

5. 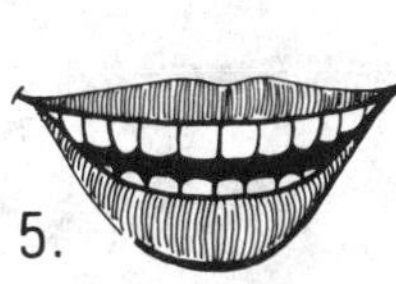

6. 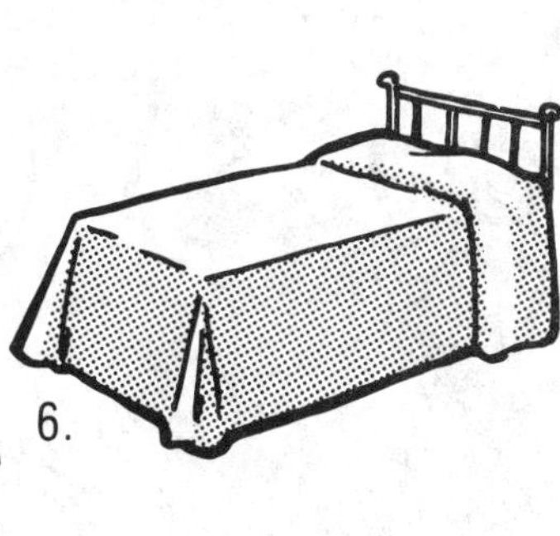

Zebras

JUST FOR FUN

Vocabulary Study ● Draw a line under each correct answer.

1. The opposite of ''leader'' is	(a) ''head''	(b) ''follower''	(c) ''ruler.''
2. ''Far'' means	(a) ''near''	(b) ''close by''	(c) ''away.''
3. Someone you fear is	(a) an enemy	(b) a friend	(c) a fellow.
4. ''Often'' means	(a) ''many times''	(b) ''seldom''	(c) ''never.''

A zebra looks much like a horse. It has a white body with black and brown stripes.

Zebras live in Africa. They move about in large groups. These large groups are called herds. Each herd has a leader.

Zebras live in open country. They eat grasses. The herds never live far from water.

Lions are the zebras' enemies. When lions come near, the zebras run away. Zebras are fast runners.

Sometimes zebras are tamed. They are often seen in circuses. Zebras can also be seen in zoos.

Answer these questions about the story:

1. Zebras look much like	(a) horses	(b) lions	(c) giraffes.
2. A group of zebras is a	(a) flock	(b) herd	(c) school.
3. Zebras eat	(a) meat	(b) fish	(c) grasses.
4. The zebra's enemy is the	(a) lion	(b) horse	(c) snake.
5. Zebras are often seen in	(a) parks	(b) zoos	(c) circuses.

Draw a line from each picture to the correct word. What is the sound of the "i" in each word?

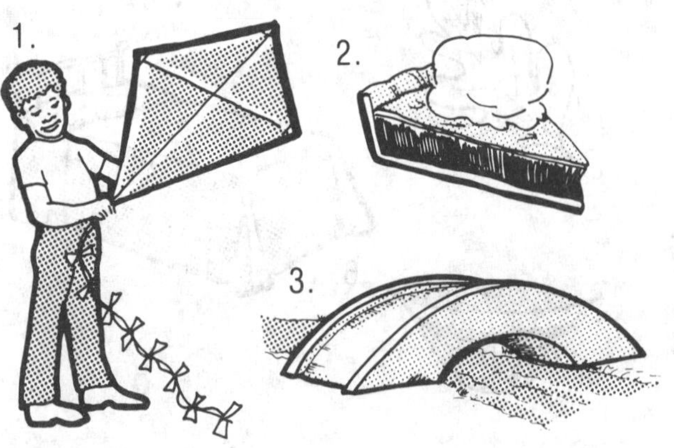

pig
fire
kite
fish
pie
bridge

Writing Synonyms

ABCDEFGHIJKLMNOPQRSTUVWXYZ
a b c d e f g h i j k l m n o p q r s t u v w x y z

Words that have similar meanings are called synonyms. Choose a word from the box, and write it next to the word that has a similar meaning. See the example.

gift	yell	stone	high
shy	stay	close	closed
glad	too	fast	raced
forest	sack	jump	coat
wealthy	bashful	moist	silent
under	end	big	unhappy

1. present .... gift	13. bag ....
2. timid	14. rock ....
3. shy	15. jacket ....
4. damp	16. sad ....
5. below	17. happy ....
6. dashed	18. shout ....
7. quiet	19. finish ....
8. remain	20. leap ....
9. near	21. quick ....
10. rich	22. tall ....
11. large	23. woods ....
12. shut	24. also ....

Deer

Vocabulary Study ● **Draw a line under each correct answer.** **JUST FOR FUN**

1. The plural of "deer" is	(a) "deers"	(b) "deeres"	(c) "deer."
2. "Quiet" is another word for	(a) "loud"	(b) "noisy"	(c) "silent."
3. "Across" means	(a) "under"	(b) "over"	(c) "into."
4. The opposite of "near" is	(a) "close"	(b) "far"	(c) "here."

Deer are beautiful animals. Male deer are called bucks. Female deer are does. Baby deer are fawns.

Fawns have white spots on their fur. The spots protect the fawns.

When danger is near, the fawn stays quiet. The mother deer runs away. She makes noise. She can run very quickly. She jumps over logs and across brooks. The danger follows the mother deer. The fawn is safe.

Deer like the taste of salt. That is why deer at the zoo like to lick people's hands. Have deer ever licked your hands?

Answer these questions about the story:

1. Male deer are called	(a) bucks	(b) does	(c) fawns.
2. Baby deer are called	(a) fawns	(b) ponies	(c) calves.
3. The fawns have fur with	(a) brown spots	(b) stripes	(c) white spots.
4. When danger comes, mother deer	(a) run away	(b) fight	(c) kick.
5. Deer like the taste of	(a) sugar	(b) pepper	(c) salt.

Draw a line from each picture to the correct word. What is the sound of the "o" in each word?

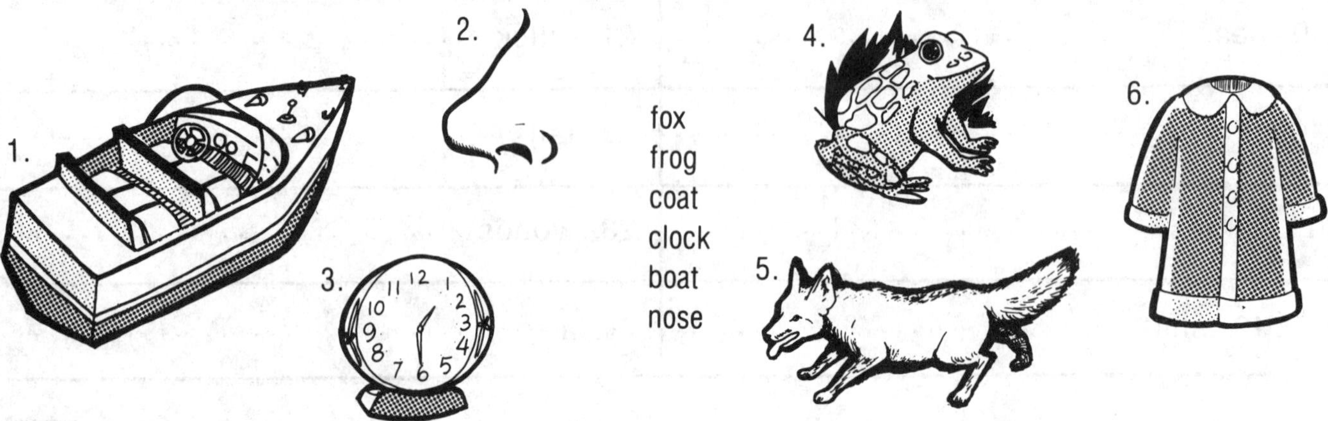

Proper Names

A **Proper names are sometimes hard to say, spell, and write. They always begin with an upper-case letter. Write each word listed in the box. See sample "1."**

Dan	Europe	Jan	Jim	Thurmond	Lassie	Oregon	San Francisco
Memphis	Buffalo	Wanda	Loretta	Elizabeth	Washington	Wyoming	Dorothy
Connie	Kathy	Derek	Kim	New York	Utah	Lester	Atlanta
Billy	Gracie	Milwaukee	Dallas	Chevrolet	Vicki		
Fred	Bobby	Cleveland	Mississippi	Elvis	Paul		

1. Buffalo	13.	25.
2.	14.	26.
3.	15.	27.
4.	16.	28.
5.	17.	29.
6.	18.	30.
7.	19.	31.
8.	20.	32.
9.	21.	33.
10.	22.	34.
11.	23.	35.
12.	24.	36.

B **Write other proper names.**

	3.	6.
1.	4.	7.
2.	5.	8.

Giraffes

Vocabulary Study ● Draw a line under each correct answer. **JUST FOR FUN**

1. The opposite of "tall" is	(a) "long"	(b) "thin"	(c) "short."
2. "Seldom" means	(a) "often"	(b) "not often"	(c) "never."
3. "Away" means	(a) "here"	(b) "not here"	(c) "near."
4. "Quick" is another word for	(a) "fast"	(b) "slow"	(c) "even."

The giraffe is the tallest animal in the world. It has very long thin legs. It has a very long neck.

Being so tall, the giraffe can see everything. It can see its enemies, the lion and the leopard. When danger is near, the giraffe runs. Seldom does the giraffe fight.

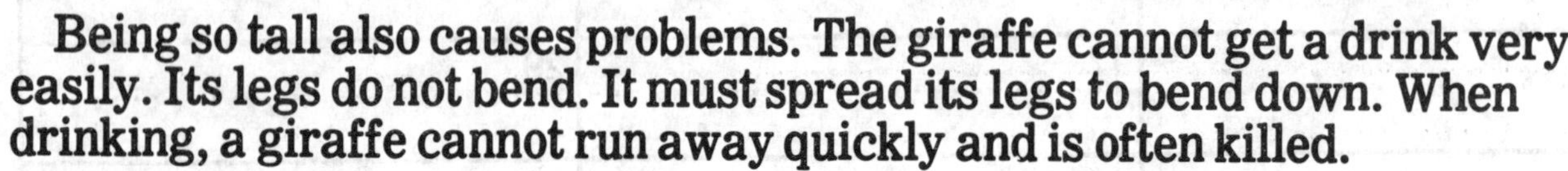

Being so tall also causes problems. The giraffe cannot get a drink very easily. Its legs do not bend. It must spread its legs to bend down. When drinking, a giraffe cannot run away quickly and is often killed.

The giraffe is a beautiful animal. Have you ever seen a giraffe?

Answer these questions about the story:

1. The giraffe is	(a) tall	(b) short	(c) fat.
2. The giraffe has	(a) a long neck	(b) long legs	(c) long ears.
3. When in danger, the giraffe	(a) runs away	(b) attacks	(c) bites.
4. The giraffe's legs	(a) are short	(b) bend easily	(c) do not bend.
5. The giraffe has trouble	(a) drinking	(b) eating	(c) sleeping.

Draw a line from each picture to the correct word. What is the sound of the "u" in each word?

1. 2.

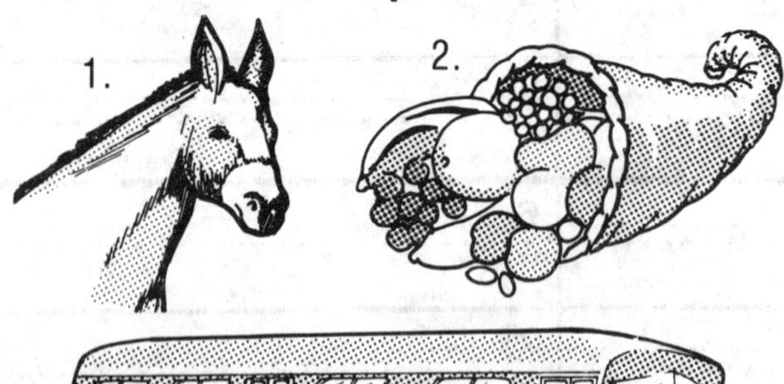

truck
bus
puppy
mule
fruit
bug

3.

4. 5. 6.

Writing Opposites

ABCDEFGHIJKLMNOPQRSTUVWXYZ
abcdefghijklmnopqrstuvwxyz

Beside each word in "List A," write the word that is its opposite from "List B." See example "1."

List A		List B
1. old	new	open
2. first		bottom
3. slow		wild
4. shut		fast
5. happy		cry
6. good		last
7. laugh		hot
8. tame		✓ new
9. top		good
10. wicked		bad
11. tall		fix
12. pull		short
13. break		gentle
14. gruff		sad
15. up		push
16. cold		down

A Trip to the Zoo

JUST FOR FUN

Vocabulary Study ● Draw a line under each correct answer.

1. If something is fun, it makes you	(a) sad	(b) cry	(c) happy.
2. The opposite of "clean" is	(a) "dirty"	(b) "pretty"	(c) "nice."
3. "All" means	(a) "whole"	(b) "part"	(c) "some."
4. "Only" means	(a) "too"	(b) "more"	(c) "nothing else."

Animals from all over the world are kept in a zoo. People visit a zoo. They look at the animals.

The zookeeper takes care of the animals. He feeds the animals. He cleans their cages.

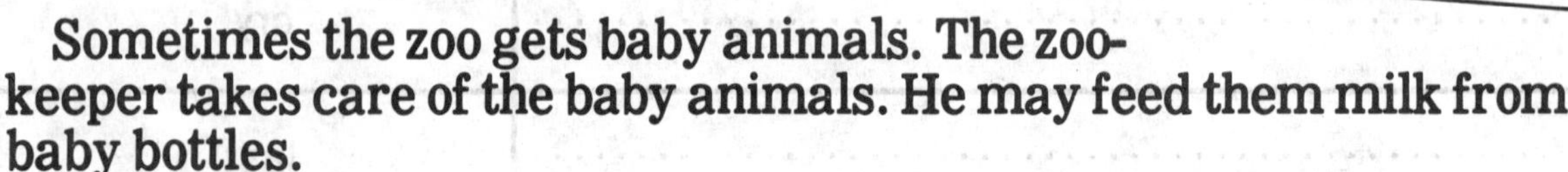

Sometimes the zoo gets baby animals. The zookeeper takes care of the baby animals. He may feed them milk from baby bottles.

The zookeeper takes sick animals to the zoo doctor. He and the doctor, nurse the sick animals.

The zookeeper takes care of big animals. He takes care of little animals. The zookeeper makes the zoo a nice place to visit. Have you ever been to a zoo?

Answer these questions about the story:

1. A zoo is a park for	(a) plants	(b) animals	(c) birds only.
2. Inside the zoo are	(a) pictures	(b) all kinds of animals	(c) books.
3. A person who takes care of the animals is the	(a) zookeeper	(b) teacher	(c) trainer.
4. Sick animals are taken	(a) home	(b) to the zoo doctor	(c) to their cages.
5. Animals in a zoo come from	(a) Africa only	(b) all over the world	(c) America only.

Underline the correct definitions.

1. may....	(a) let	(b) cannot	7. here...	(a) there	(b) not there
2. down...	(a) up	(b) not up	8. best...	(a) bad	(b) very good
3. make...	(a) break	(b) put together	9. dark...	(a) without light	(b) with light
4. leave...	(a) go	(b) come	10. now...	(a) this time	(b) soon
5. buy....	(a) sell	(b) pay for	11. off....	(a) on	(b) not on
6. kind...	(a) mean	(b) nice	12. new....	(a) not old	(b) old

Writing Adjectives

Adjectives are words used to describe things — a tall tree, a red rose, the roaring jet. Write the correct adjective listed that fits each sentence.

white	red	little	yellow	old
happy	big	black	tall	beautiful
dirty	pretty	small	short	fat
cold	hot	new	tired	slim

1. Tim lives in a ____________ house.
2. My friend has a ____________ bicycle.
3. Joe saw a ____________ mouse.
4. Sally is a ____________ girl.
5. The ____________ building burned.
6. Tom lives in a ____________ house.
7. Mary has a ____________ puppy.
8. The ____________ eagle flew away.
9. Sam bought a ____________ kite.
10. My ____________ turtle eats much.
11. The ____________ girl stood up.
12. Mother washed the ____________ dishes.
13. Father mowed the ____________ grass.
14. Alice wore a ____________ dress.
15. Jim bought a ____________ shirt.

Animals on the Farm

Vocabulary Study ● Draw a line under each correct answer. JUST FOR FUN

1. Another word for "job" is	(a) "work"	(b) "play"	(c) "rest."
2. The opposite of "good" is	(a) "bad"	(b) "nice"	(c) "best."
3. A farm is a	(a) person	(b) animal	(c) place.
4. When you protect something, you	(a) hurt it	(b) guard it	(c) own it.

Farms are the homes for many animals. Some farms keep only one kind of animal. Others keep many kinds. Each animal on the farm has a job to do.

Many farms raise cows. Cows give us milk. They also give us meat. Their meat is called beef.

Pigs are also raised on a farm. They give us meat. Their meat is called pork. Pigs are also called hogs.

Most farms have chickens. They give us meat and eggs.

Dogs work on the farm. They drive the cows home. They guard the farm. They make good pets.

Cats keep the farm free from rats and mice. They are also good pets.

Answer these questions about the story:

1. Cows give us	(a) meat	(b) milk	(c) eggs.
2. Pig meat is called	(a) beef	(b) pork	(c) poultry.
3. Chickens give us	(a) meat	(b) milk	(c) eggs.
4. Dogs are used	(a) to drive cows	(b) to guard farms	(c) as pets.
5. Cats catch	(a) bugs	(b) mice	(c) rats.

Identify each picture.

1.  __________

2.  __________

3.  __________

4.  __________

5.  __________

6.  __________

7.  __________

8.  __________

Words That Sound the Same

ABCDEFGHIJKLMNOPQRSTUVWXYZ
a b c d e f g h i j k l m n o p q r s t u v w x y z

Beside each word in "List A," write a word from "List B" that sounds the same. See example "1."

List A	List B
1. dear .... deer	hour
2. here	cent
3. two	flour
4. bear	meat
5. eight	road
6. flower	knew
7. one	✓ deer
8. rode	ate
9. maid	bare
10. meet	sail
11. new	hear
12. our	made
13. sale	write
14. right	won
15. sent	to

Interesting Cities

A **Study the spelling words. Then fill in the blanks with the words.**

visit
city
will
learn
ever

Have you ______ been to Washington, D.C.? This ______ is the capital of the United States. You can ______ many famous places. You can ______ the history of our nation. You ______ like Washington.

---

made
map
is
river
means
other

Detroit, Michigan, ______ called "Motor City." Many cars are ______ here. Many ______ things are also made here. The French word "Detroit" ______ "strait." Look at a ______ of the city. You will see the ______ that is a strait.

B **Write the names of cities you have visited.**

1. ______
2. ______
3. ______
4. ______
5. ______
6. ______

A Trip to the Farm

Vocabulary Study ● Draw a line under each correct answer. **JUST FOR FUN**

1. The opposite of ''far'' is	(a) ''there''	(b) ''away''	(c) ''near.''
2. ''Stored'' means	(a) ''kept''	(b) ''thrown away''	(c) ''wasted.''
3. The opposite of ''country'' is	(a) ''farm''	(b) ''city''	(c) ''outdoors.''
4. A chore is a	(a) job	(b) game	(c) hobby.

On the farm are many kinds of animals. The farmer has to take care of his animals every day. He feeds them. He waters them. He cleans their homes.

There are many buildings on a farm. The house looks like one in the city. Not far from the house is a barn. Animals are kept in the barn. Some farms have silos. A silo is a tall round building. Grain is stored in the silo. There are many sheds on the farm. The sheds protect the farm machinery.

Every person on the farm has chores. People on a farm must work together. They work hard.

Answer these questions about the story:

1. The farmer cares for his animals by	(a) feeding them	(b) watering them	(c) cleaning their homes.
2. Houses on the farm	(a) are small	(b) are different	(c) are like city houses.
3. Animals live in the	(a) house	(b) barn	(c) silo.
4. Grain is stored in the	(a) barn	(b) silo	(c) shed.
5. People on a farm	(a) never work	(b) seldom work	(c) work hard.

Put each set of letters in alphabetical order.

1. b, a, c ______	7. p, m, n ______	13. c, u, y ______	19. h, l, c ______
2. x, z, y ______	8. d, f, e ______	14. p, s, e ______	20. s, u, z ______
3. o, q, p ______	9. u, w, v ______	15. i, w, d ______	21. e, a, r ______
4. k, j, l ______	10. l, t, c ______	16. g, a, n ______	22. m, i, l ______
5. a, z, f ______	11. g, i, h ______	17. o, e, i ______	23. s, v, b ______
6. s, r, t ______	12. r, j, b ______	18. q, x, t ______	24. z, g, n ______

Writing an Outline

An outline is a writer's plan and gives the main ideas of a story. Copy each sentence,

1. Choose a title for your story.

Choose a title for your story.

2. What is the story about?

3. Who are the main players?

4. Where does it take place?

5. How does the story start?

6. Is the plot interesting?

7. How does the story end?

8. Does it have a theme?

9. Did you check for mistakes?

The Pet Hospital

JUST FOR FUN

Vocabulary Study ● Draw a line under each correct answer.

1. The opposite of "very large" is (a) "very small" (b) "big" (c) "huge."
2. "Checked" means (a) "looked at" (b) "found" (c) "helped."
3. Another word for "stay" is (a) "leave" (b) "go" (c) "remain."
4. The opposite of "well" is (a) "sick" (b) "better" (c) "good."

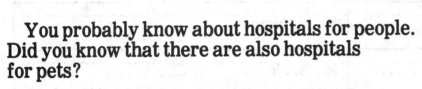

You probably know about hospitals for people. Did you know that there are also hospitals for pets?

Unless the animal is very large, the owner must bring the animal to the hospital. There the animal is checked by a pet doctor. The pet doctor is called a veterinarian, or vet.

At the hospital there are many rooms. There are rooms for checking the pet, for operating, and for making X rays. There are even rooms where animals stay until they get well.

Many kinds of pets go to the pet hospital. They are given very good care.

Answer these questions about the story:

1. A pet doctor is called a (a) veterinarian (b) vet (c) dentist.
2. The animal is usually brought to the hospital by (a) the owner (b) the doctor (c) the police.
3. The hospital has rooms for (a) checking the pet (b) operating (c) X rays.
4. At the hospital the animal (a) always stays (b) never stays (c) sometimes stays.
5. A pet hospital treats (a) only dogs (b) only cats (c) all kinds of animals.

Write each small letter as a capital letter.

1. a ____	8. h ____	15. o ____	22. v ____
2. b ____	9. i ____	16. p ____	23. w ____
3. c ____	10. j ____	17. q ____	24. x ____
4. d ____	11. k ____	18. r ____	25. y ____
5. e ____	12. l ____	19. s ____	26. z ____
6. f ____	13. m ____	20. t ____	
7. g ____	14. n ____	21. u ____	

Writing Contractions

ABCDEFGHIJKLMNOPQRSTUVWXYZ
abcdefghijklmnopqrstuvwxyz

A contraction is formed by putting two words together and leaving out one or more letters. An apostrophe is used in place of the missing letters. **EXAMPLE:** The contraction for "does not" is "doesn't."

Write the contraction for each word.

1. cannot ..... can't	17. was not ....
2. that is	18. are not ....
3. you will	19. he would ....
4. she will	20. could not ....
5. I am	21. it is ....
6. is not	22. did not ....
7. there is	23. I will ....
8. let us	24. there is ....
9. you would	25. were not ....
10. has not	26. it will ....
11. did not	27. we have ....
12. here is	28. he will ....
13. do not	29. would not ....
14. we are	30. have not ....
15. they will	31. you are ....
16. will not	32. is not ....

Having a Pet

JUST FOR FUN

Vocabulary Study ● Draw a line under each correct answer.

1. The opposite of "better" is	(a) "good"	(b) "best"	(c) "worse."
2. A bird is an animal that	(a) flies	(b) hops	(c) swims.
3. When you care for something, you	(a) hurt it	(b) look after it	(c) harm it.
4. When you are happy, you	(a) cry	(b) frown	(c) smile.

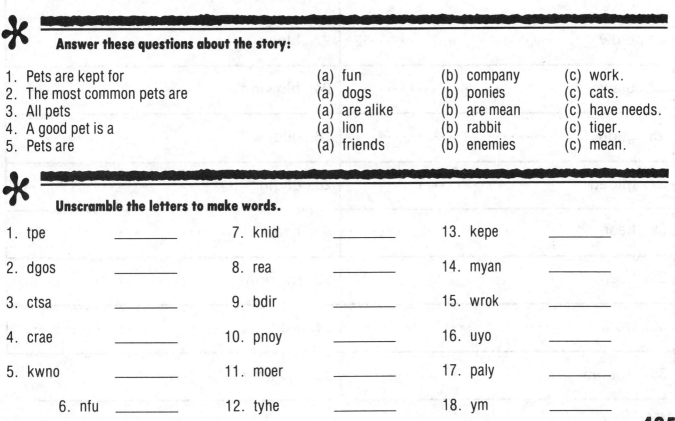

Many people have pets. Pets do not have to work. They are kept for fun.

The most common pets are cats and dogs. There are many other kinds of pets. Birds and fish are pets. Rabbits, hamsters, and guinea pigs are pets. Lambs and ponies are also pets.

People should know how to care for pets. Pets have special needs. The more people know about their pets, the better they can take care of them.

Pets are friends. They keep people company. They make people smile. People should always be good to their pets.

Answer these questions about the story:

1. Pets are kept for	(a) fun	(b) company	(c) work.
2. The most common pets are	(a) dogs	(b) ponies	(c) cats.
3. All pets	(a) are alike	(b) are mean	(c) have needs.
4. A good pet is a	(a) lion	(b) rabbit	(c) tiger.
5. Pets are	(a) friends	(b) enemies	(c) mean.

Unscramble the letters to make words.

1. tpe ________	7. knid ________	13. kepe ________
2. dgos ________	8. rea ________	14. myan ________
3. ctsa ________	9. bdir ________	15. wrok ________
4. crae ________	10. pnoy ________	16. uyo ________
5. kwno ________	11. moer ________	17. paly ________
6. nfu ________	12. tyhe ________	18. ym ________

Spelling in Writing

Write each word. Turn your paper over, and make up a sentence using each word.

1. spell ..... spell	2. spells .....
3. spelled	4. spelling .....
5. act	6. acts .....
7. acted	8. acting .....
9. join	10. joins .....
11. joined	12. joining .....
13. love	14. loves .....
15. loved	16. loving .....
17. check	18. checks .....
19. checked	20. checking .....
21. blow	22. blows .....
23. blew	24. blowing .....
25. glide	26. glides .....
27. glided	28. gliding .....
29. hear	30. hears .....
31. heard	32. hearing .....
33. work	34. works .....
35. worked	36. working .....

Ants

Vocabulary Study ● Draw a line under each correct answer. **JUST FOR FUN**

1. "Together" means	(a) "with one another"	(b) "alone"	(c) "apart."
2. The opposite of "under" is	(a) "below"	(b) "over"	(c) "bottom."
3. "Almost" means	(a) "none"	(b) "all"	(c) "not all."
4. A tunnel is a	(a) hallway	(b) house	(c) room.

Ants are insects. They live together. They work together. Sometimes thousands of ants live in the same home.

There are many kinds of ants. These ants make their homes. Some ants live in anthills. Some live under rocks. Some live under wood. Some live in trees. Some live in the ground. Inside every nest, ants build long tunnels.

Ants can live almost anywhere in the world. Some live in cold weather. Some live in hot weather. Some ants do not like the sun and come out only at night.

Answer these questions about the story:

1. Ants live and work	(a) alone	(b) together	(c) in pairs.
2. Ants live	(a) only in trees	(b) only in the ground	(c) almost anywhere.
3. Ants that do not like the sun	(a) never come out	(b) come out at night	(c) come out in the winter.
4. Inside each ant nest are	(a) tunnels	(b) large rooms	(c) windows.
5. Ants are	(a) insects	(b) birds	(c) fish.

Draw a line to connect the words that rhyme.

1. wet	no	7. dish	fish	13. red	fell
2. go	live	8. say	many	14. bell	to
3. boy	toy	9. any	run	15. sad	bed
4. soon	noon	10. fun	day	16. do	hide
5. look	let	11. we	how	17. ride	bad
6. give	cook	12. cow	see	18. best	test

Good Health Habits

Good health comes from practicing good health habits.

Fill in the blanks using the words in the box. Use each word only once. Circle each word used. See example "1."

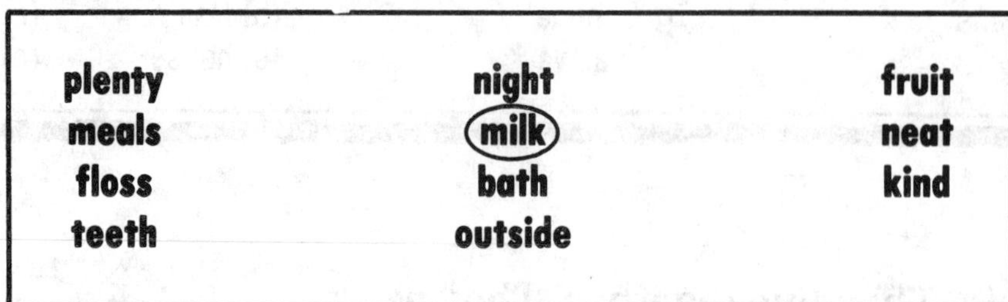

plenty	night	fruit
meals	milk	neat
floss	bath	kind
teeth	outside	

1. Drink at least three glasses of milk each day.
2. Get ____________ of exercise each day.
3. Keep your hair clean and ____________.
4. Eat well-balanced ____________ each day.
5. Eat fresh ____________ each day.
6. Play ____________ when possible.
7. ____________ your teeth daily.
8. Take a ____________ each day.
9. Brush your ____________ after each meal.
10. Be ____________ and helpful.
11. Get plenty of rest each ____________.

Worms

Vocabulary Study ● Draw a line under each correct answer. **JUST FOR FUN**

1. The opposite of "above" is (a) "up" (b) "over" (c) "below."
2. "Moist" means (a) "wet" (b) "dry" (c) "cold."
3. A burrow is a (a) tunnel (b) big room (c) open room.
4. "Soil" is another word for (a) "air" (b) "water" (c) "dirt."

Have you ever seen a worm? Worms are everywhere. The most common worms are the earthworms.

Earthworms live in the ground. They come out above the ground after a heavy rain. They breathe air through their skin. The skin must always be moist.

Earthworms have no legs or feet. They wriggle to get about.

Earthworms make burrows in the soil. The burrows let air and water into the soil. Earthworms make the soil better.

Many people dig in the soil to find earthworms. They sell the worms. The worms are used for fishing bait.

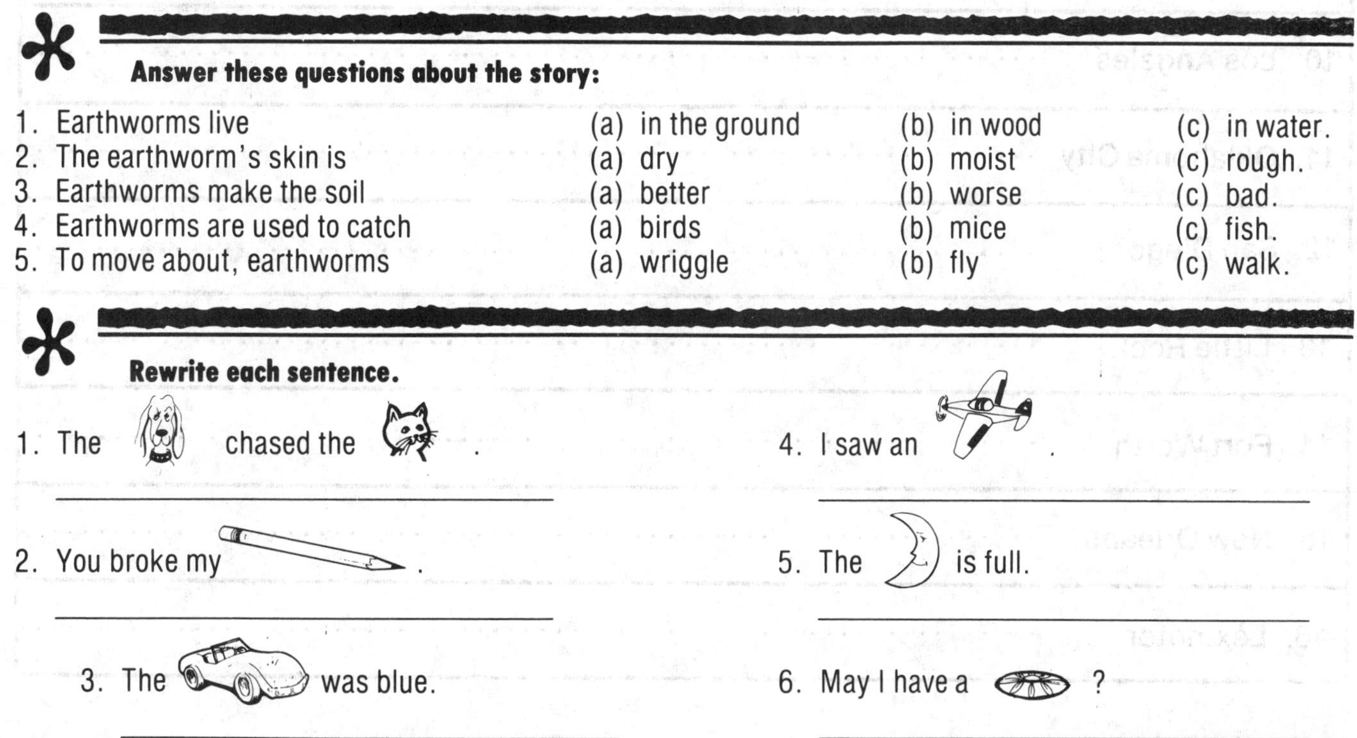

Answer these questions about the story:

1. Earthworms live (a) in the ground (b) in wood (c) in water.
2. The earthworm's skin is (a) dry (b) moist (c) rough.
3. Earthworms make the soil (a) better (b) worse (c) bad.
4. Earthworms are used to catch (a) birds (b) mice (c) fish.
5. To move about, earthworms (a) wriggle (b) fly (c) walk.

Rewrite each sentence.

1. The [dog] chased the [cat] .
2. You broke my [pencil] .
3. The [car] was blue.
4. I saw an [airplane] .
5. The [moon] is full.
6. May I have a [cookie] ?

Writing Cities

The name of a city should always begin with an upper-case letter. Write each city.

1. Atlanta .... Atlanta
2. Miami ....
3. Chicago ....
4. Phoenix ....
5. Dallas ....
6. Reno ....
7. Memphis ....
8. Buffalo ....
9. New York ....
10. Los Angeles ....
11. Oklahoma City ....
12. San Diego ....
13. Little Rock ....
14. Fort Worth ....
15. New Orleans ....
16. Lexington ....
17. Seattle ....
18. Madison ....
19. Pittsburg ....
20. St. Louis ....
21. Denver ....
22. Omaha ....
23. Salem ....
24. Boston ....

Frogs

Vocabulary Study ● Draw a line under each correct answer. JUST FOR FUN

1. A friend	(a) helps us	(b) hurts us	(c) does not help us.
2. The opposite of "smooth" is	(a) "soft"	(b) "rough"	(c) "even."
3. "Young" means	(a) "not new"	(b) "old"	(c) "not old."
4. The front of something is at the	(a) beginning	(b) middle	(c) end.

Frogs are our friends. They eat many insects.

There are many kinds of frogs. They all have smooth skins. They have large heads with big eyes.

Very young frogs live in the water. Older frogs live on land and in the water.

The frog's tongue is hooked to the front of its mouth. It catches insects with its tongue. The food is swallowed whole. If the food is large, the frog pushes it in with its front feet.

Frogs get around by hopping. They are often mistaken for toads. Toads are fatter than frogs.

Answer these questions about the story:

1. Frogs eat	(a) insects	(b) grass	(c) frogs.
2. Very young frogs live	(a) on land	(b) in trees	(c) in water.
3. A frog's tongue is hooked	(a) to the back of its mouth	(b) on the side of its mouth	(c) to the front of its mouth.
4. Frogs get around by	(a) crawling	(b) hopping	(c) flying.
5. Frogs are often mistaken for	(a) toads	(b) fish	(c) snakes.

Write the name of each picture.

1. 

2. 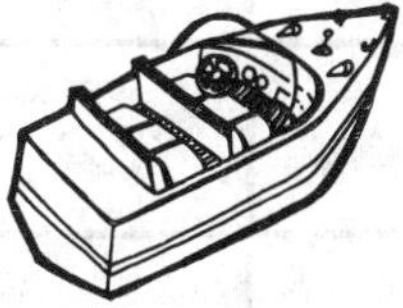

3. 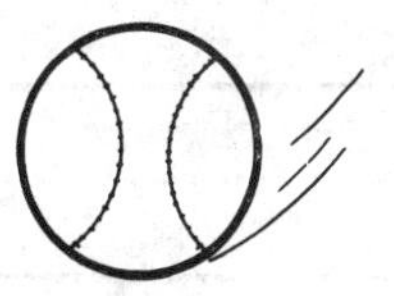

4. 

5. 

6. 

7. 

8. 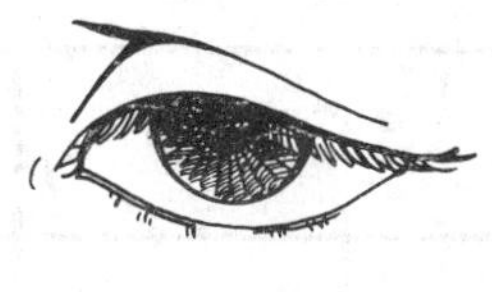

"er" and "est" Endings

ABCDEFGHIJKLMNOPQRSTUVWXYZ
a b c d e f g h i j k l m n o p q r s t u v w x y z

To add "er" or "est" to a word that already ends in "e," add only "r" or "st." To add "er" or "est" to a word ending in "y," change the "y" to "i" before adding "er" or "est."

Add "er" and "est" endings to each word. See the examples.

1. cute	cuter	cutest
2. brave		
3. ripe		
4. pale		
5. nice		
6. close		
7. late		
8. fine		
9. shiny		
10. silly		
11. fuzzy		
12. sleepy		
13. furry		
14. salty		
15. curly		

Salamanders

Vocabulary Study ● **Draw a line under each correct answer.** **JUST FOR FUN**

	(a)	(b)	(c)
1. "Moist" means	(a) "dry"	(b) "wet"	(c) "hot."
2. The opposite of "cool" is	(a) "cold"	(b) "very hot"	(c) "warm."
3. Another word for "catch" is	(a) "trap"	(b) "let go"	(c) "free."
4. When something hurts, it causes	(a) pain	(b) happiness	(c) a smile.

Salamanders are small animals. They have long tails. Their skins are soft and moist and feel cool when you touch them.

There are many kinds of salamanders. Most live in brooks or ponds. They move about quickly.

Salamanders breathe through their skins. That is why their skins must always be moist. Salamanders spend much time in the water.

Salamanders are shy. They come out of hiding at night. Sometimes they come out on rainy days.

Salamanders eat insects and worms. They catch their food with their tongues.

Many people keep salamanders as pets. Salamanders do not hurt anyone.

Answer these questions about the story:

	(a)	(b)	(c)
1. A salamander's skin is	(a) rough	(b) soft	(c) moist.
2. Salamanders live in	(a) oceans	(b) ponds	(c) rivers.
3. Salamanders breathe through their	(a) noses	(b) mouths	(c) skins.
4. Salamanders come out	(a) at night	(b) on hot days	(c) on rainy days.
5. Salamanders are	(a) shy	(b) harmless	(c) dangerous.

Draw a line from each picture to the correct word. Do you hear the long "a" sound in each word?

1.

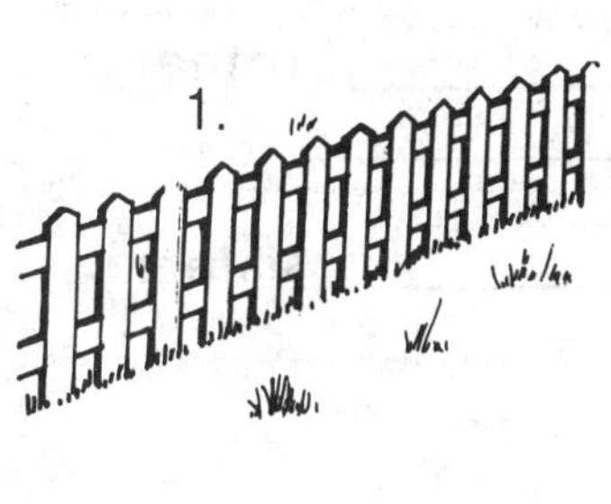

2.

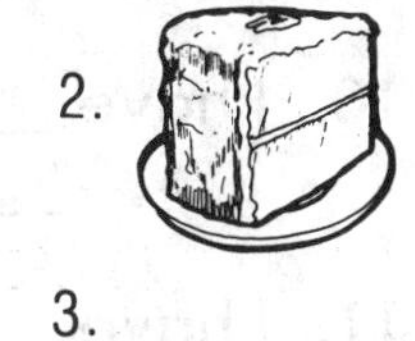

3.

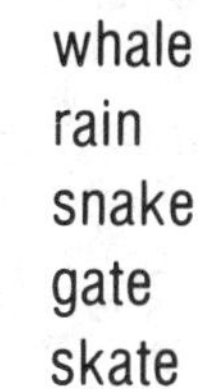

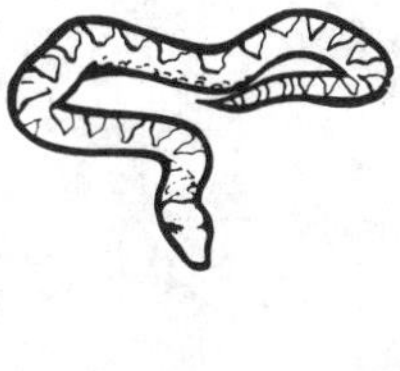

cake
whale
rain
snake
gate
skate

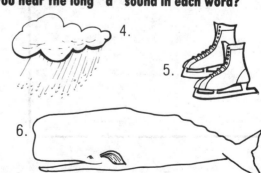

4.

5.

6.

Things About Me

Fill in the blanks. **(Write your full name.)**

1. My name is ____________________.

2. I live at ____________________.

3. The names of my city and state are ____________________.

(Draw a picture of your house.)

4. My zip code number is ____________.

5. My telephone number is ____________.

6. My dad is a/an ____________.

7. He works at ____________.

8. My mother is a/an ____________.

(Draw a picture of your dad.)

(Draw a picture of your mother.)

9. She works at ____________.

10. I have ____________ brothers.

11. I have ____________ sisters.

Writing States

The names of states should always begin with upper-case letters. Write each state.

1. Kansas ····· Kansas ········	17. Hawaii ········
2. Texas ········	18. Alaska ········
3. Georgia ········	19. Ohio ········
4. Missouri ········	20. Wisconsin ········
5. Nebraska ········	21. Florida ········
6. New York ········	22. Indiana ········
7. Colorado ········	23. Oregon ········
8. Louisiana ········	24. Arizona ········
9. Minnesota ········	25. New Jersey ········
10. Kentucky ········	26. Maine ········
11. Wyoming ········	27. Arkansas ········

12. Mississippi ········

13. California ········

14. Pennsylvania ········

15. Massachusetts ········

16. South Dakota ········

Snails

Vocabulary Study ● Draw a line under each correct answer. **JUST FOR FUN**

1. The plural of "foot" is (a) "foot" (b) "foots" (c) "feet."
2. The opposite of "on" is (a) "off" (b) "onto" (c) "at."
3. In spring, the weather gets (a) warmer (b) colder (c) cooler.
4. When you are hungry, you want to (a) sleep (b) eat (c) work.

Snails are very lucky. They carry their homes on their backs. Wherever they go, they are at home.

Each snail has only one foot. The foot moves the snail around. It helps the snail hold onto rocks. The foot also lets water in and out of the shell.

Some snails live in the water. Water snails have two horns. The eyes are at the bottom of the horns.

Other snails live on the land. Land snails have four horns. Their eyes are at the top of the horns.

In winter most snails dig holes in the ground. They sleep all winter. In spring they wake up. The first thing they do is eat. They are very hungry.

* **Answer these questions about the story:**

1. A snail's home is a (a) shell (b) cave (c) tree.
2. Snails have (a) one foot (b) two feet (c) no feet.
3. Water snails have (a) two horns (b) four horns (c) six horns.
4. In winter most snails (a) eat (b) sleep (c) build a home.
5. Snails live (a) in water (b) on land (c) on the desert.

Draw a line from each picture to the correct word. Do you hear the long "e" sound in each word?

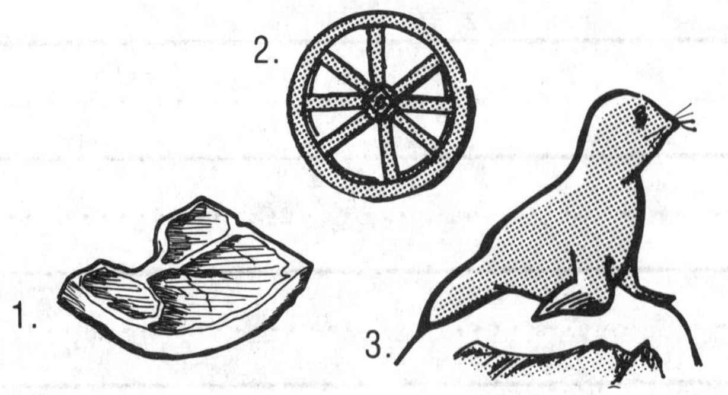

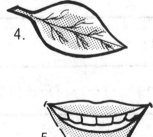

peach
teeth
meat
wheel
seal
leaf

4.

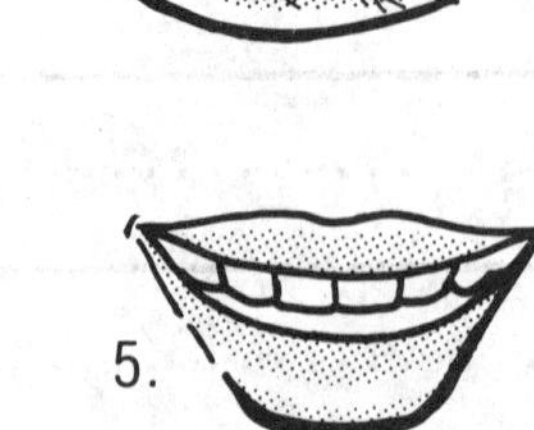

The Prefix

ABCDEFGHIJKLMNOPQRSTUVWXYZ
abcdefghijklmnopqrstuvwxyz

A prefix is added to the beginning of a word to change the meaning of the word.

EXAMPLE: The prefix "re" means "again" (remade), "pre" means "before" (prepay), and "un" means "not" (unfed).

Underline each root word, and draw a box around each prefix. Write a new word using the same prefix. See sample "1."

1. return .... refer	15. dispose ....
2. exhale	16. disappear ....
3. repeat	17. apart ....
4. define	18. disapprove ....
5. subtract	19. dislike ....
6. deface	20. rejoin ....
7. decode	21. prepare ....
8. unhappy	22. alight ....
9. discard	23. renew ....

10. enforce ....

11. uncertain ....

12. demerit ....

13. mistreat ....

14. recall ....

....

Spiders

Vocabulary Study ● Draw a line under each correct answer. **JUST FOR FUN**

	(a)	(b)	(c)
1. The number after "seven" is	(a) "six"	(b) "eight"	(c) "nine."
2. Another word for "guard" is	(a) "protect"	(b) "hurt"	(c) "break."
3. "Enough" means	(a) "too much"	(b) "none"	(c) "plenty."
4. "Leave" means	(a) "stay here"	(b) "go away"	(c) "come."

A spider is not an insect. It has eight legs. An insect has six legs.

There are many kinds of spiders. They live all over the world. Some spiders will not hurt you. There are some which are dangerous.

Most spiders spin webs. The webs are strong. The webs are often used to catch insects. Spiders eat many kinds of insects.

The female spider is usually larger than the male. She is a good mother. She guards her eggs. She feeds her young. When the young are old enough to get their own food, they leave the nest. Each spider likes to have its own home.

*

Answer these questions about the story:

	(a)	(b)	(c)
1. A spider has	(a) four legs	(b) six legs	(c) eight legs.
2. An insect has	(a) four legs	(b) six legs	(c) eight legs.
3. Spiders eat	(a) insects	(b) plants	(c) animals.
4. Female spiders are usually	(a) larger	(b) smaller	(c) weaker.
5. Spiders like to live	(a) in pairs	(b) in groups	(c) alone.

Draw a line from each picture to the correct word. Do you hear the long "i" sound in each word?

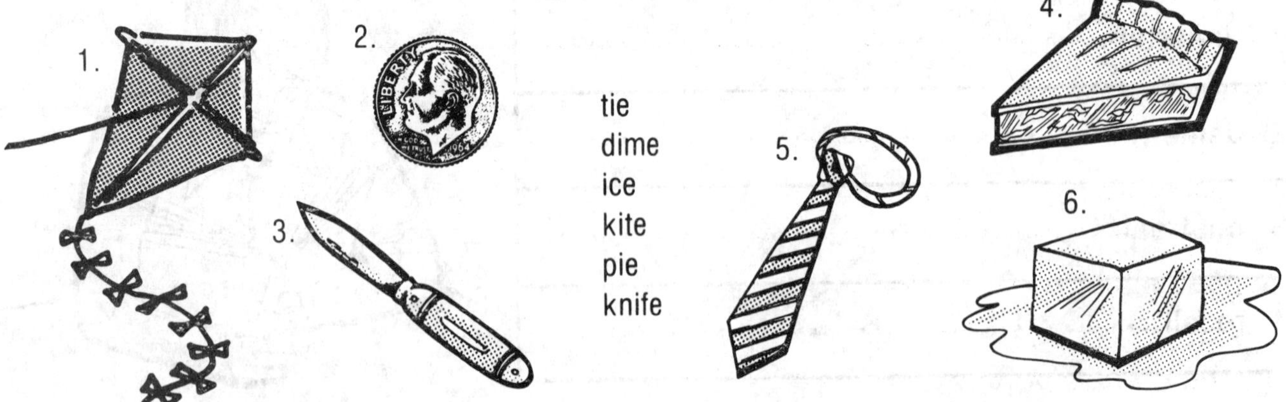

tie
dime
ice
kite
pie
knife

The Suffix

ABCDEFGHIJKLMNOPQRSTUVWXYZ
a b c d e f g h i j k l m n o p q r s t u v w x y z

A suffix is added to the end of a word to change the meaning of the word.

EXAMPLES: applying, bitterness, comical, likely

Underline each word, and draw a box around each suffix. Write a new word using the suffix. See example "1."

1. harder .... softer	15. useful ....
2. longest	16. kingdom ....
3. disturbance	17. drying ....
4. handsome	18. frightful ....
5. childless	19. goodness ....
6. shorter	20. overactive ....
7. uppermost	21. shyly ....
8. upward	22. treatment ....
9. securely	23. greater ....

10. tiresome ....

11. courageous ....

12. respectable ....

13. appearance ....

14. modernize ....

Bees

Vocabulary Study ● Draw a line under each correct answer. **JUST FOR FUN**

	(a)	(b)	(c)
1. In winter the weather is	(a) warm	(b) hot	(c) cold.
2. Honey is	(a) sweet	(b) sour	(c) bitter.
3. "Steal" means	(a) "to give"	(b) "to take"	(c) "to want."
4. If you have enough, you	(a) need more	(b) need less	(c) need no more.

Bees are insects. They live together in a colony. There may be thousands of bees in a colony. Bees like living together. They could not live by themselves.

There are many kinds of bees. Some live in hollow trees. Others may live between the walls of houses. Most bees live in hives.

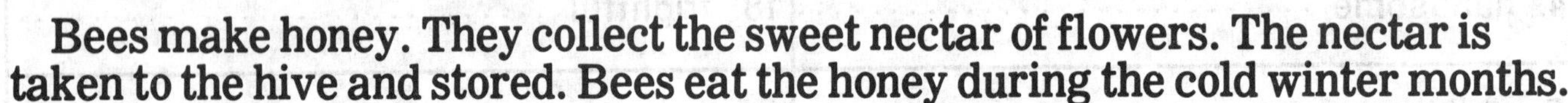

Bees make honey. They collect the sweet nectar of flowers. The nectar is taken to the hive and stored. Bees eat the honey during the cold winter months.

Many animals steal the bees' honey. People often raise bees for their honey. They are careful not to take too much so the bees will have enough to eat.

Answer these questions about the story:

	(a)	(b)	(c)
1. Bees living together are called a	(a) colony	(b) group	(c) city.
2. Bees cannot live	(a) alone	(b) in small colonies	(c) in large colonies.
3. Most bees live in	(a) water	(b) the ground	(c) hives.
4. Bees make	(a) honey	(b) silk	(c) webs.
5. Nectar comes from	(a) leaves	(b) flowers	(c) sugar.

Draw a line from each picture to the correct word. Do you hear the long "o" sound?

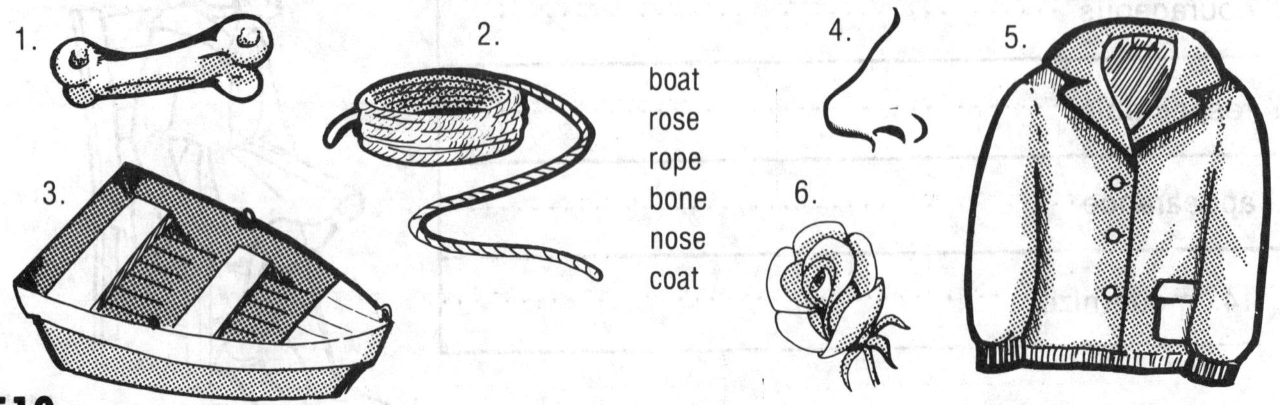

1. 2. 3. 4. 5. 6.

boat
rose
rope
bone
nose
coat

Writing Letters

Write the letter to invite your friends to your birthday party.
Be sure to check with a manuscript chart as you rewrite the letter.

month day year

Dear ,

Would you please come to my birthday party next Saturday afternoon at three o'clock at my house? Bring your bathing suit.

Yours truly,

your name

Fireflies

JUST FOR FUN

Vocabulary Study ● Draw a line under each correct answer.

1. If something is tiny, it is	(a) big	(b) small	(c) tall.
2. "Glow" means	(a) "shine"	(b) "fly"	(c) "call."
3. Another word for "begin" is	(a) "end"	(b) "finish"	(c) "start."
4. "Finally" means	(a) "first"	(b) "second"	(c) "last."

Have you ever looked into a dark sky and seen a tiny light? The light was probably a firefly. A firefly is a tiny insect. It glows in the dark.

Fireflies begin life as glowworms. Glowworms eat all the time. They go through many stages. Finally they become fireflies.

A firefly never eats. It doesn't live a long time. It just flies around. It can turn its light on and off.

Many people catch fireflies. They put them in tiny cages. The cages look pretty.

Have you ever caught fireflies? They won't hurt you.

Answer these questions about the story:

1. A firefly is a	(a) worm	(b) tiny insect	(c) spider.
2. Glowworms	(a) never eat	(b) always eat	(c) become fireflies.
3. A firefly	(a) cannot fly	(b) likes to eat	(c) never eats.
4. A firefly's light	(a) is always on	(b) turns on and off	(c) is always off.
5. Fireflies will	(a) not hurt you	(b) hurt you	(c) bite you.

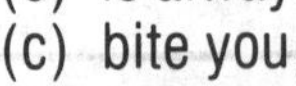

Draw a line from each picture to the correct word. Do you hear the long "u" sound in each word?

mule
ruler
fruit
suit
flute
glue

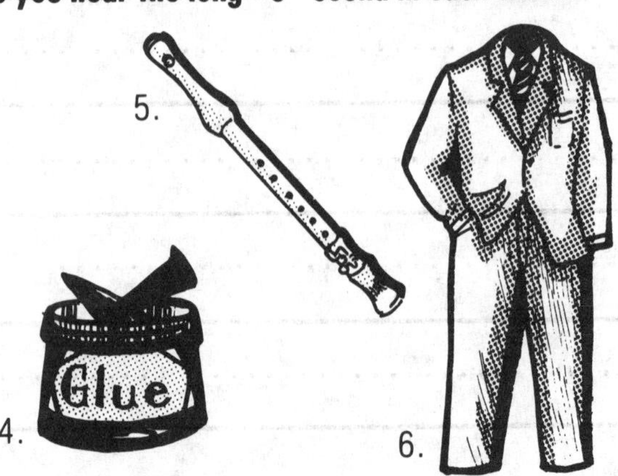

Writing Directions (to you)

Giving directions means to tell, show the way, give information, or direct someone. Write the directions.

1. Turn left at the next corner.

Turn left at the next corner.

2. The fire station is by the school.

3. Cut along the dotted lines.

4. Put the tools in the box.

5. That road goes to the farm.

6. The key unlocks this door.

7. The third bus stops here.

8. Do the problems on this page.

9. The library is closed today.

Fleas

Vocabulary Study ● Draw a line under each correct answer. **JUST FOR FUN**

	(a)	(b)	(c)
1. Another word for "jump" is	(a) "walk"	(b) "crawl"	(c) "leap."
2. A hoop is a	(a) ring	(b) box	(c) can.
3. "Watch" means	(a) "to see"	(b) "to hear"	(c) "to feel."
4. The opposite of "teach" is	(a) "show"	(b) "learn"	(c) "tell."

The flea is the best jumper in the world. It can leap eight inches into the air. That may not sound like very much, but the flea is very, very tiny.

Some people like fleas. They have flea circuses. The fleas are taught to do tricks. They jump through hoops. People pay to watch them.

Most people, however, do not like fleas. The fleas ride on dogs and cats. They even ride on people. Their bites hurt. They are very hard to get rid of. Soap and water help get rid of fleas. The fleas hate to take a bath.

Answer these questions about the story:

	(a)	(b)	(c)
1. The flea is known as the best	(a) jumper	(b) swimmer	(c) flier.
2. Fleas are very	(a) big	(b) tiny	(c) friendly.
3. In flea circuses, fleas	(a) work	(b) do tricks	(c) are sold.
4. Most people	(a) like fleas	(b) want fleas	(c) do not like fleas.
5. Fleas ride on	(a) dogs	(b) cats	(c) people.

Draw a line from each picture to the correct word. Do you hear the short "a" sound in each word?

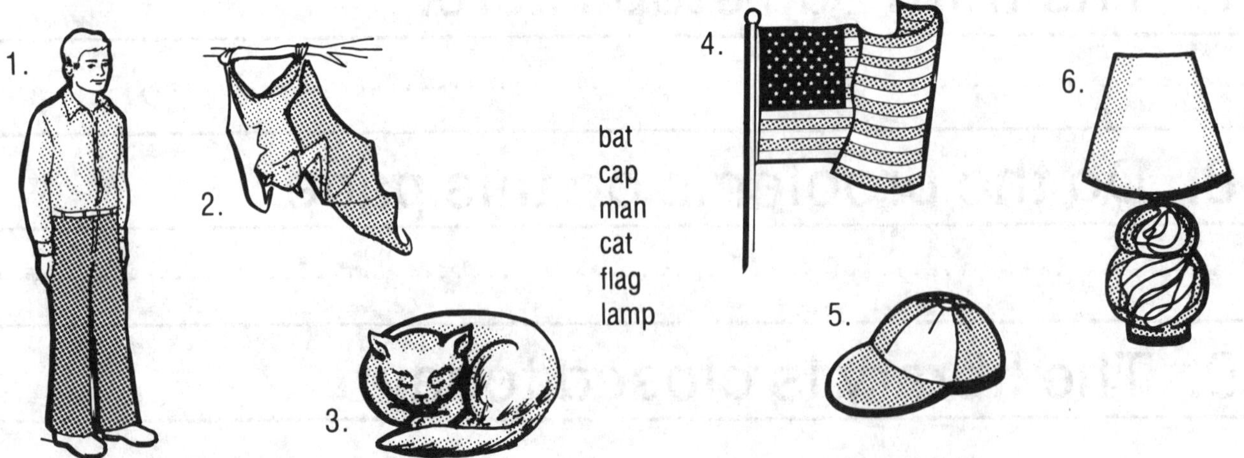

Writing Directions (from you)

Asking directions means getting information or directions from someone. Write the questions.

1. Where is the post office?

2. What time did you arrive?

3. When does the next show start?

4. How do you swim?

5. Can you show me the house?

6. Is your bicycle like mine?

7. Does she live next to Alice?

8. Which coat belongs to you?

Butterflies

JUST FOR FUN

Vocabulary Study ● Draw a line under each correct answer.

1. The opposite of ''day'' is	(a) ''night''	(b) ''morning''	(c) ''noon.''
2. When someone rests, he	(a) works	(b) plays	(c) does nothing.
3. ''None'' means	(a) ''some''	(b) ''not any''	(c) ''much.''
4. A week has	(a) two days	(b) four days	(c) seven days.

There are many kinds of butterflies. They live all over the world. Butterflies can live anywhere as long as there are plants.

Butterflies fly in the daytime. Sometimes they stop to rest. When resting, butterflies hold their wings straight up.

Butterflies sip the sweet nectar of flowers. They eat nothing else.

Butterflies begin life as eggs. From the eggs hatch caterpillars. Caterpillars grow very quickly. Soon they change into butterflies.

Butterflies do not live very long. They are strong fliers, but their wings are thin and easily broken.

Answer these questions about the story:

1. Butterflies always live near	(a) plants	(b) rivers	(c) people.
2. Butterflies fly during the	(a) night	(b) daytime	(c) evening.
3. When resting, the wings are held	(a) straight up	(b) down	(c) flat.
4. Butterflies eat	(a) insects	(b) leaves	(c) nectar.
5. Butterflies are	(a) strong fliers	(b) poor fliers	(c) weak.

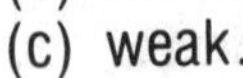

Draw a line from each picture to the correct word. Do you hear the short "e" sound?

1.

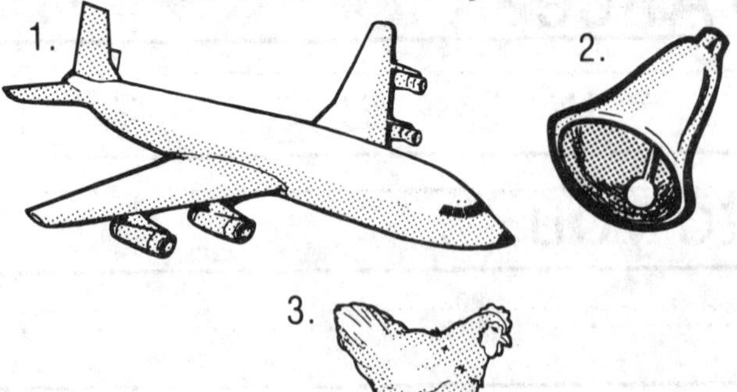

2.

3.

desk
bed
nest
bell
hen
jet

4.

5.

6.

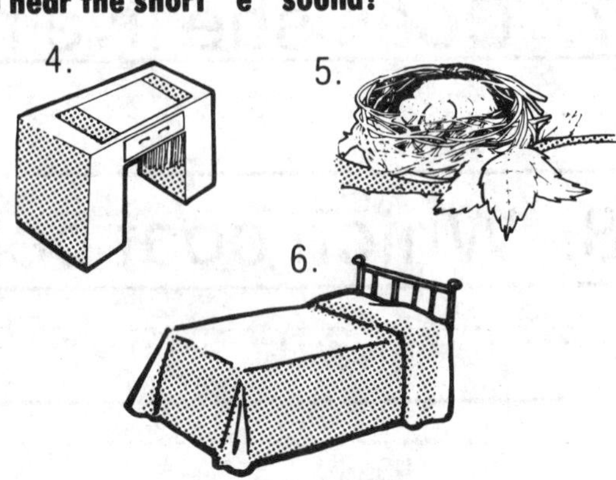

Writing Stories

A story has a title, a beginning, a plot, and an ending. Write the story. Be sure to check with a manuscript chart as you rewrite the sentences.

The Wild Pony

Derek, the rancher's son, found a wild colt caught in quicksand. He threw a rope over his neck and pulled him free. Years later, lost in the mountains and freezing, Derek was saved by the same wild colt, now grown.

The Monarch Butterfly

JUST FOR FUN

Vocabulary Study ● Draw a line under each correct answer.

1. The opposite of ''spring'' is	(a) ''summer''	(b) ''autumn''	(c) ''winter.''
2. A group has	(a) no members	(b) one member	(c) many members.
3. ''Soon'' means	(a) ''not long in time''	(b) ''maybe''	(c) ''never.''
4. ''Good'' is the same as	(a) ''bad''	(b) ''pleasant''	(c) ''unpleasant.''

There are many butterflies in the United States. One of the best known is the monarch butterfly.

The monarch butterfly is sometimes called the "king" of the butterflies.

The monarch is one of the biggest butterflies. It is a strong flier. It also flies very fast.

In autumn, monarch butterflies fly south. They fly for many miles. In spring, monarch butterflies fly north. The butterflies fly in large groups.

Birds do not like to eat monarch butterflies. The butterflies do not taste good.

*

Answer these questions about the story:

1. The monarch butterfly is often called the	(a) ''king''	(b) ''weakest''	(c) ''smallest.''
2. The monarch flies	(a) slowly	(b) very fast	(c) lazily.
3. In autumn the monarch flies	(a) east	(b) north	(c) south.
4. Monarchs fly	(a) alone	(b) in pairs	(c) in large groups.
5. Birds	(a) eat monarchs	(b) do not eat monarchs	(c) chase monarchs.

Draw a line from each picture to the correct word. Do you hear the short "i" sound?

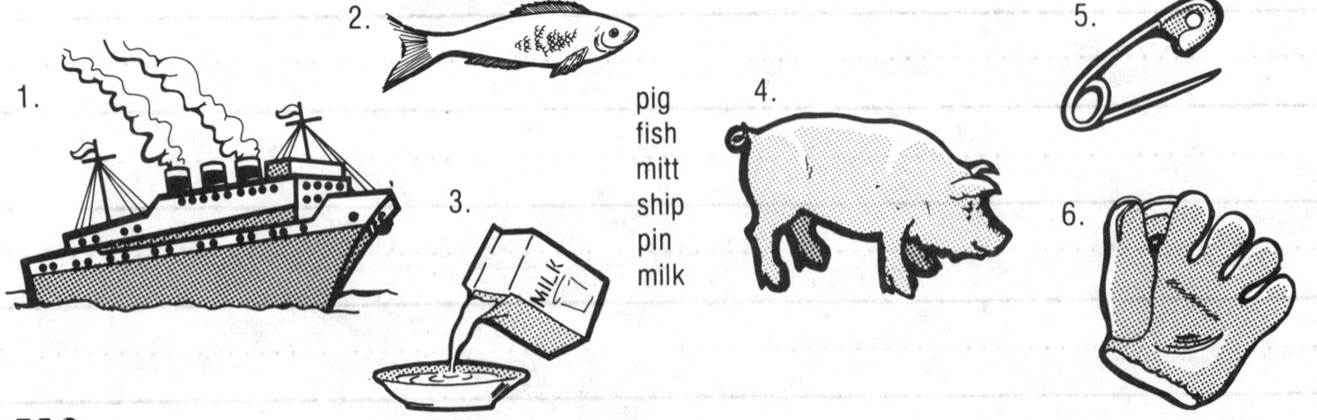

Writing Poems

Poems are fun. Write these well-known poems on the lines below.

Little Boy Blue, come blow your horn,
the sheep's in the meadow, the cow's in the corn;
But where is the little boy tending the sheep?
He's under the haystack fast asleep.

As I went to Bonner,
I met a pig without a wig,
upon my word and honor.

Fish

Vocabulary Study ● Draw a line under each correct answer. **JUST FOR FUN**

1. The plural of "fish" is	(a) "fishs"	(b) "fish"	(c) "fishes."
2. The opposite of "live" is	(a) "die"	(b) "move"	(c) "not move."
3. Water is	(a) wet	(b) dry	(c) thick.
4. The opposite of "whole" is	(a) "all"	(b) "part"	(c) "everything."

Not all animals in water are fish. Fish, however, cannot live without water. Fish may live in the oceans. They may live in rivers. They may live in lakes and ponds.

Most fish are covered with scales. They breathe through their gills. Fish take their air from the water.

Fish push through the water by moving their tails from side to side. They have fins in the place of arms and legs.

Some fish eat plants. Others eat smaller fish. Their food is swallowed whole.

Fish come in many sizes and colors. Some fish are good to eat.

Answer these questions about the story:

1. All animals in the water	(a) look like fish	(b) are fish	(c) are not fish.
2. Fish are covered with	(a) fur	(b) scales	(c) spines.
3. Fish have	(a) arms	(b) legs	(c) fins.
4. Fish eat	(a) plants	(b) other fish	(c) rocks.
5. Fish could not live without	(a) water	(b) land	(c) sand.

Draw a line from each picture to the correct word. Do you hear the short "o" sound in each word?

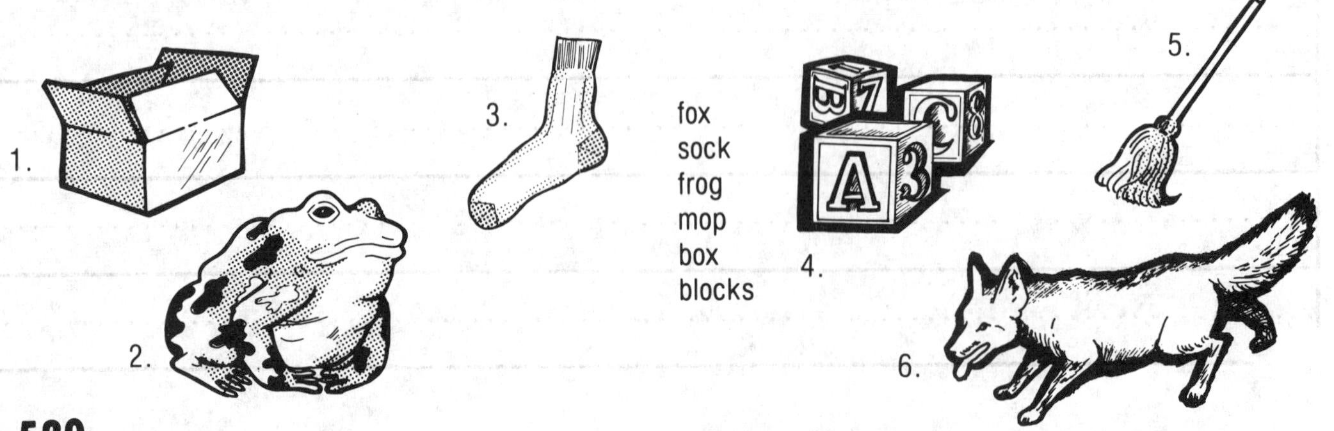

My Family Tree

Ask your parents to help you fill in your family tree.

Fill in the blanks.

1. I like to ______________________.
2. My favorite food is ____________.
3. My favorite color is ____________.
4. My mom is a good ____________.
5. My dad takes me ____________.
6. I have ________ sister(s).

   Their (Her) name(s) are (is) ______________________ ______________________.
7. I have ________ brother(s).

   Their (His) name(s) are (is) ______________________.

Paste a picture of yourself.

(Write your name.)

Paste a picture of your mother.

(mother's name)

Paste a picture of your father.

(father's name)

picture of grandmother

(grandmother's name)

picture of grandfather

(grandfather's name)

picture of grandmother

(grandmother's name)

picture of grandfather

(grandfather's name)

Writing Bulletins

A bulletin is a simple note that contains a message. Write the bulletin.

1. There will be no talking in line.

There will be no talking in line.

2. Lunch will be served at 11:30 a.m.

3. Take out only what you can eat.

4. Sit at your assigned table.

5. Ask your teacher for second helpings.

6. Speak quietly in the lunchroom.

7. Put your tray and scraps in the corner.

8. When finished, leave quietly.

The Octopus

Vocabulary Study ● Draw a line under each correct answer. JUST FOR FUN

1. "Ugly" means (a) "pretty" (b) "nice" (c) "not pretty."
2. The ocean is made of (a) water (b) air (c) land.
3. Where you live is your (a) home (b) school (c) job.
4. Round things are (a) square (b) curved (c) flat.

The octopus is an ugly animal. It is always ready to attack.

The octopus lives in the ocean. Its home is a dark cave in the rocks.

The octopus has a soft, round body. It has eight long arms.

The octopus walks forward. It swims backward.

There are many kinds of octopuses. Most of them are not very large. The giant octopuses are very big. They are dangerous.

The octopus likes to eat crabs. Many people like to eat the octopus. Would you like to eat one?

Answer these questions about the story:

1. The octopus lives in (a) rivers (b) lakes (c) the ocean.
2. The octopus' home is (a) among seaweed (b) a dark cave (c) in sand.
3. An octopus has (a) 2 arms (b) 6 arms (c) 8 arms.
4. Octopuses like to eat (a) crabs (b) fish (c) people.
5. Octopuses swim (a) forward (b) sideways (c) backward.

Draw a line from each picture to the correct word. Do you hear the short "u" sound in each word?

Reading Your Writing

Manuscript writing must be neat enough to be read by you or someone else. Write the word for each number listed. See the examples.

1. one	18.
2. two	19.
3.	20.
4.	21.
5.	22.
6.	23.
7.	24.
8.	25.
9.	26.
10.	27. twenty-seven
11.	28.
12.	29.
13. thirteen	30.
14.	31.
15.	32. thirty-two
16.	33.
17.	34.

Goldfish

JUST FOR FUN

Vocabulary Study ● Draw a line under each correct answer.

1. "Easy" means	(a) "hard"	(b) "not hard"	(c) "very hard."
2. Twelve months make a	(a) day	(b) week	(c) year.
3. "Not" means	(a) "no"	(b) "always"	(c) "usually."
4. A fin is like	(a) an arm	(b) a nose	(c) an ear.

Millions of goldfish are sold each year. They make very good pets. They are easy to take care of. They take up a small amount of space. They are fun to watch.

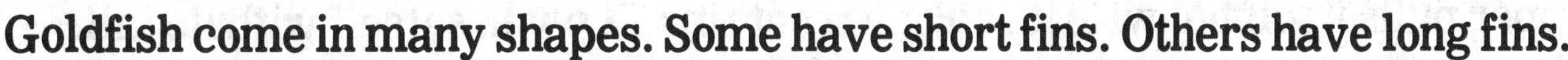

Goldfish come in many shapes. Some have short fins. Others have long fins.

Some goldfish are not gold. They may be white, red, blue, or black. Some goldfish are even speckled.

Goldfish breathe with gills. They get air from the water.

Goldfish are always opening and closing their mouths. Watch them. They are interesting animals.

Answer these questions about the story:

1. Goldfish are good	(a) pets	(b) to eat	(c) for protection.
2. The color of goldfish	(a) is always gold	(b) is not always gold	(c) is always black.
3. Goldfish breathe with	(a) gills	(b) lungs	(c) noses.
4. Goldfish always open and close their	(a) eyes	(b) ears	(c) mouths.
5. Goldfish are	(a) small	(b) easy to keep	(c) interesting.

Draw a line to connect words with the same vowel sounds.

1. red	eat	7. make	fox	13. pet	let
2. so	sat	8. cut	rest	14. nose	me
3. cat	bed	9. bike	lake	15. man	fruit
4. tree	hive	10. desk	ride	16. suit	hat
5. hide	know	11. box	sit	17. fish	toe
6. rule	cube	12. pit	up	18. we	pin

The Mudskipper

Vocabulary Study ● **Draw a line under each correct answer.** **JUST FOR FUN**

1. "Much" means (a) "many" (b) "few" (c) "little."
2. Water and dirt make (a) sand (b) mud (c) rocks.
3. When you jump up and down, you (a) crawl (b) walk (c) hop.
4. What you like best is your (a) favorite (b) least favorite (c) worst.

Can you imagine a fish that climbs trees? The mudskipper is one that does. Wouldn't it be fun to watch a mudskipper?

The mudskipper spends much time in the water. It also spends much time out of the water. The mudskipper pulls itself out with its strong front fins. It pushes itself with its tail.

The mudskipper likes to hop about on the mud. That is where it gets its name. It chases insects. Insects are its favorite food.

Answer these questions about the story:

1. A mudskipper is a (a) fish (b) frog (c) insect.
2. The mudskipper spends time (a) in water (b) out of water (c) on the mud.
3. The mudskipper pulls itself about (a) with its fins (b) with its tail (c) with wings.
4. The mudskipper likes to chase (a) frogs (b) insects (c) other mudskippers.
5. The mudskipper eats (a) fish (b) insects (c) plants.

Complete each sentence with the best word from the box.

drive	chased	fly	crawl	walked	hop	rolled	ran	galloped	swim

1. The horses ________________.
2. Frogs ______________.
3. The birds will ______________ away.
4. Fish ____________.
5. The man ______________ to the store.
6. The dog ______________ the cat.
7. Alex will ____________ the car.
8. The boy ____________ home.
9. Ants ______________.
10. The ball ______________ under the house.

Creative Writing

Answer the following questions. Use complete sentences beginning with capital letters and ending with periods.

1. Pretend you are an astronaut who has been to the moon.
   A. What do you like most about your job?

   B. Who would you like to take to the moon with you?

   Why?

2. Pretend you are grass in a backyard.
   A. How does it feel to be walked on?

   B. What would you like to be instead of grass?

   Why?

3. Pretend you are a duck.
   A. What do you like most about being a duck?

   B. Where do you like to swim?

   Why?

Using a Comma

The comma (,) is a punctuation mark in our language. One of the ways it is used is to separate words or phrases in series inside a sentence.

EXAMPLES: Our flag is red, white, and blue.
I went outside, up to the roof, and down the fire escape.

A Place commas correctly in these sentences.

1. John, Mary, and I went to town.
2. The farmer's cow his horse and his pig all went through the fence.
3. Bill's spelling reading and arithmetic books were lost.
4. I have green red and black pens.
5. She drove to the airport to town and to the office.
6. It's cold wet and windy in February.
7. My notebook paper and pencils are all gone.
8. The old dog the black cat and I ran to the barn.
9. The plants bushes and trees were all covered with snow.
10. He looked through my closet under the bed and in the kitchen.
11. We had eggs bacon toast and coffee for breakfast.
12. The Christmas tree was decorated with red balls gold tinsel and blue lights.

B Write four sentences of your own, using words in a series. Be sure to use the comma rule above.

1. ....

2. ....

3. ....

4. ....

Swordfish

Vocabulary Study ● Draw a line under each correct answer. **JUST FOR FUN**

1. Fish often travel in a	(a) school	(b) group	(c) flock.
2. The opposite of "hard" is	(a) "mild"	(b) "easy"	(c) "simple."
3. When things grow, they get	(a) smaller	(b) shorter	(c) bigger.
4. The edge of something is the	(a) top	(b) bottom	(c) side.

The swordfish is a fish. It lives in the ocean.

The swordfish got its name from its nose. The nose is long and sharp. It has sharp edges. It looks like a sword.

The swordfish uses its nose to catch food. The fish swims into a school of small fish. It hits the small fish with its sharp nose. Then it eats the fish.

A swordfish is hard to catch. It cuts nets with its nose. The nose is very strong. It can break a wooden boat.

A baby swordfish has no sword. It has teeth. As it grows, it loses its teeth. It grows a sword.

Answer these questions about the story:

1. A swordfish lives in	(a) rivers	(b) lakes	(c) the ocean.
2. A swordfish is named for its	(a) nose	(b) eyes	(c) fins.
3. A swordfish's nose is	(a) long	(b) strong	(c) sharp.
4. A swordfish eats	(a) plants	(b) fish	(c) wood.
5. Baby swordfish have	(a) teeth	(b) swords	(c) no teeth.

Write the beginning sound of each word.

1. fish ____	7. toy ____	13. desk ____	19. bike ____
2. eat ____	8. see ____	14. bird ____	20. room ____
3. hat ____	9. bus ____	15. open ____	21. boy ____
4. now ____	10. me ____	16. lion ____	22. pull ____
5. zoo ____	11. each ____	17. game ____	23. rain ____
6. away ____	12. girl ____	18. man ____	24. just ____

Words That Rhyme

When the last parts of words sound the same, the words are said to rhyme. Poets use rhyme to write their poems and verses. The last part of rhyming words may look the same,

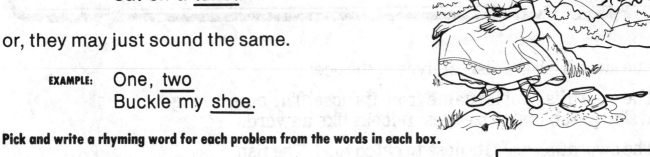

EXAMPLE: Little Miss Muffet
Sat on a tuffet.

or, they may just sound the same.

EXAMPLE: One, two
Buckle my shoe.

Pick and write a rhyming word for each problem from the words in each box.

1. Hickory, dickory, dock!
   ____
   The mouse ran up the ____________!
2. There was an old woman who lived in a shoe;
   ____
   She had so many children, she didn't know what to ________.
3. Little Boy Blue, come blow your horn,
   ____
   The sheep's in the meadow, the cow's in the __________!
4. Little Jack Horner
   ____
   Sat in a __________.
5. He stuck in his thumb
   ____
   and pulled out a ___________.
6. Humpty Dumpty sat on a wall;
   ____
   Humpty Dumpty had a great _________.
7. As I was going to St. Ives,
   ____
   I met a man who had seven _________.
8. There once was a frog
   ____
   who lived in a _________.

cheese wall	1.	chair clock
wear cook	2.	do live
yard corn	3.	barn kitchen
corner chair	4.	bucket puddle
rock bush	5.	plum cherry
line time	6.	pencil fall
wives dollars	7.	cats sacks
pond drawer	8.	log rug

The Remora

Vocabulary Study ● Draw a line under each correct answer. **JUST FOR FUN**

1. "Sometimes" means	(a) "all the time"	(b) "not all the time"	(c) "never."
2. The ocean is made up of	(a) water	(b) sky	(c) land.
3. If two things are alike, they are	(a) the same	(b) not the same	(c) different.
4. Something is free when it	(a) costs nothing	(b) costs a little	(c) costs too much.

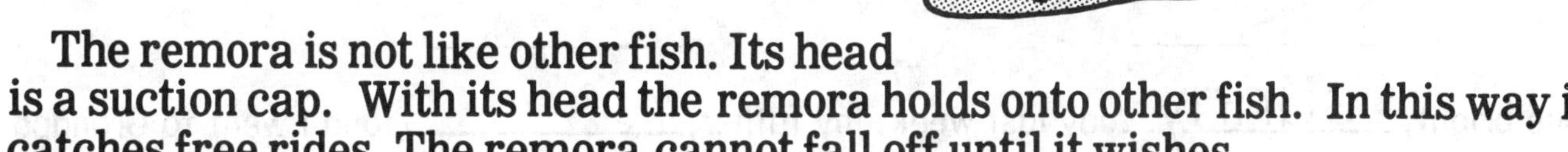

The remora lives in the ocean. It is a fish.

The remora is not like other fish. Its head is a suction cap. With its head the remora holds onto other fish. In this way it catches free rides. The remora cannot fall off until it wishes.

The ride often gets the remora a free meal. The remora eats the leftovers of the bigger fish.

Fishermen sometimes use the remora to fish. They tie a line around the remora's tail. When the remora hooks onto a fish, the fishermen pull it in. The remora is also used to catch turtles.

Answer these questions about the story:

1. The remora lives	(a) in trees	(b) in the ocean	(c) on land.
2. The remora is a	(a) fish	(b) bird	(c) worm.
3. The remora holds onto fish with its	(a) teeth	(b) fins	(c) head.
4. The remora uses other fish for	(a) free rides	(b) free meals	(c) food.
5. The remora is often used for	(a) fishing	(b) pets	(c) food.

Write the ending sound of each word.

1. wet ____	7. he ____	13. eat ____	19. did ____
2. no ____	8. red ____	14. me ____	20. hot ____
3. up ____	9. yes ____	15. car ____	21. box ____
4. man ____	10. cat ____	16. him ____	22. stop ____
5. rub ____	11. pie ____	17. off ____	23. tree ____
6. day ____	12. you ____	18. dog ____	24. call ____

Finish a Story

Fill in the blanks in this story by using the words in the box. Use each word only once. Circle each word as it is used.

present	**sunny**	**name**	**happy**
house	**cookies**	**delicious**	**puppy**
beautiful	**mother**	**go**	

My First Puppy

One bright, sunny day last week, my father, ____________, and I went to Grandpa and Grandma's ____________ in the country. It was a ____________ day for a drive! When we got there, we found that Grandma had baked us some ____________. They were ____________! We visited for a while, and when we got ready to ____________, Grandpa gave me a new puppy as a ____________. My puppy needed a ____________, so I named him Frank, the same as Grandpa. I think it made Grandpa ____________ that I named the ____________ after him.

The Puffer Fish

Vocabulary Study ● Draw a line under each correct answer. JUST FOR FUN

1. The opposite of "slow" is (a) "fast" (b) "little by little" (c) "not fast."
2. "Near" means (a) "far away" (b) "close" (c) "there."
3. A sudden change happens (a) quickly (b) slowly (c) not very fast.
4. "Single" means (a) "together" (b) "alone" (c) "with someone."

The puffer fish is a small fish. It is a slow swimmer. For this reason the puffer fish has to protect itself from other fish.

When a big fish comes near, the puffer fish swallows air and water. It gets bigger and bigger. The sudden change scares the big fish. It leaves the puffer fish alone.

If the big fish is not scared away, it gets another surprise. The body of the puffer fish is covered with sharp spines. The spines hurt the big fish.

Sometimes the puffer fish swallows too much air and water. When this happens, the puffer fish pops.

Answer these questions about the story:

1. The puffer fish is a (a) slow swimmer (b) fast swimmer (c) small fish.
2. The puffer fish swallows (a) air (b) water (c) big fish.
3. Swallowing water makes it (a) smaller (b) bigger (c) sick.
4. The puffer fish is covered with (a) thick skin (b) smooth skin (c) sharp spines.
5. Too much water makes the fish (a) pop (b) too big (c) float.

Rewrite each word correctly.

1. awll ________	7. yu ________	13. burd ________
2. hiz ________	8. eny ________	14. thim ________
3. giv ________	9. gro ________	15. tre ________
4. fli ________	10. kold ________	16. neer ________
5. boi ________	11. buk ________	17. kno ________
6. bigg ________	12. opin ________	18. trane ________

Rhyming Words

Words that sound the same except for their beginning sounds are rhyming words, such as "did" and "lid," "rhyming" and "climbing."

A **Draw lines connecting the rhyming words in these exercises. See example "1."**

1. frog lace
   pace peace
   less duck

2. junk clue
   shoe moo
   luck mouse

3. mouse now
   why then
   loose house

4. loose shape
   ship moose
   shoes lose

5. flag flap
   brag map
   flop flip

6. sunny sunshine
   pencil funny
   Monday money

B **Make up words that rhyme with the words below. See example "1."**

1. game same frame name lame
2. ball mall
3. rough gruff
4. house louse
5. see me
6. why sigh

Seals

Vocabulary Study ● Draw a line under each correct answer. JUST FOR FUN

1. The opposite of "cold" is	(a) "icy"	(b) "cool"	(c) "hot."
2. Dinner is something you	(a) eat	(b) wear	(c) build.
3. An enemy is someone you	(a) like	(b) do not like	(c) love.
4. "And" means	(a) "or"	(b) "also"	(c) "not."

There are many kinds of seals. Most live in the Arctic. Seals have thick bodies. They are covered with fur. Seals like cold weather.

On land, seals are clumsy. They come out of the water to rest. They have their young on the land.

Young seals must be taught to swim. Female seals are good mothers.

Seals are more at home in the water. There they are not clumsy. Their flippers and tails help them swim. The water has the seals' dinner. Seals eat fish.

Seals have many enemies. People and polar bears kill many seals.

Answer these questions about the story:

1. Most seals live	(a) in cold places	(b) in hot places	(c) in warm places.
2. Seals come on land to	(a) eat	(b) rest	(c) have young.
3. Seals are at home	(a) in the water	(b) on land	(c) everywhere.
4. Seals eat	(a) bears	(b) water plants	(c) fish.
5. The seal's enemies are	(a) people	(b) polar bears	(c) other seals.

Draw a line to connect words with the same vowel sounds.

1. at	try	7. ten	pen	13. car	he
2. cup	rain	8. sea	ring	14. three	boat
3. you	too	9. mud	free	15. wet	star
4. old	bat	10. dish	tie	16. plane	cube
5. pie	sun	11. log	rub	17. rose	get
6. cake	boat	12. time	box	18. tube	made

To, Too, Two

Three entirely different words that sound exactly alike are "to," "too," and "two." "To" is used with many other words to help them show action.

EXAMPLES: to touch   to jump
to run   to go

"Too" is used to show an excess of something or to say "also."

EXAMPLES: That ball costs too much.   I want to go too.
Three balls are too many.   He likes you too.

"Two" is the word for the number "2."

EXAMPLES: two hamburgers
two fingers

Put "to," "too," or "two" in each of the blanks.

A. It's too hot to go today.

B. I have _______ pencils _______ write with.

C. _______ people eating one candy bar would be one person _______ many.

D. "_______ be or not _______ be, that is the question."

E. Dad wants _______ eat _______.

F. I told you _______ stop it!

G. There are _______ doughnuts left.

H. "You are _______ little _______ help me," said the lion.

Whales

Vocabulary Study ● **Draw a line under each correct answer.** **JUST FOR FUN**

1. The opposite of "top" is (a) "up" (b) "bottom" (c) "over."
2. "Trap" is another word for (a) "catch" (b) "wait" (c) "hunt."
3. If two things are the same, they are (a) different (b) almost alike (c) just alike.
4. "Huge" means (a) "very big" (b) "very small" (c) "tiny."

The biggest animal in the world is the whale. It lives in the ocean. It has smooth skin. Its head is very large. Its eyes and ears are very small.

The whale looks like a fish. It is not a fish. The whale is a mammal.

The whale cannot breathe under the water. It must come to the top of the water to get air. If it does not come to the top, it will drown.

There are many kinds of whales. Not all are the same size.

The largest whale is the blue whale. It has no teeth. It traps tiny plants in its huge mouth.

Answer these questions about the story:

1. The whale is the (a) smallest animal (b) biggest animal (c) second largest animal.
2. The whale lives (a) in the ocean (b) in rivers (c) on land.
3. The whale is a (a) bird (b) fish (c) mammal.
4. All whales are (a) not the same size (b) the same size (c) blue.
5. The blue whale eats (a) plants (b) fish (c) other whales.

Connect the words that rhyme.

1. she	sun	7. soon	say	13. then	song
2. fun	tree	8. fall	tall	14. show	grow
3. that	too	9. rest	noon	15. long	dish
4. horn	hat	10. fast	last	16. fish	when
5. zoo	corn	11. do	nest	17. game	came
6. nine	mine	12. day	to	18. thing	ring

Get-Well Notes

When one of your friends or someone you know is sick or in the hospital, you might like to send him or her a short get-well note or card. Get-well notes let your friends know you are thinking of them and wishing they will soon be well again.

A **Write a get-well note by filling in the blanks.**

____

Dear ______________,

I am sorry to hear you are sick with ______________. How long ______________ ______________? All your friends at school ______________.

We know ______________.

Hurry and ______________!

Your friend,

____

B **Write a get-well card of your own. Pretend you are sick, and write a note that you would like to receive.**

Birds

Vocabulary Study ● Draw a line under each correct answer. **JUST FOR FUN**

1. Someone you like is	(a) a friend	(b) an enemy	(c) a pal.
2. Something that is fast	(a) moves slowly	(b) moves quickly	(c) doesn't move.
3. The opposite of ''bottom'' is	(a) ''top''	(b) ''below''	(c) ''under.''
4. ''Common'' means	(a) ''unusual''	(b) ''not often seen''	(c) ''often seen.''

Birds are very common animals. They live everywhere in the world except the bottom of the ocean.

Birds are different from other animals. They have feathers. No other animals do.

All birds have wings, but not all birds can fly. Birds that can fly are very fast. Some birds fly faster than others. Some birds can even swim.

Male birds are usually prettier than females. The males have brighter colors than the females.

Some birds are used for food. Some give us eggs. Birds also help us by eating insects. Birds are our friends.

Answer these questions about the story:

1. Birds live	(a) only in cold places	(b) only in warm places	(c) almost everywhere.
2. Birds are different because they have	(a) fur	(b) feathers	(c) scales.
3. Most birds	(a) can fly	(b) cannot fly	(c) swim.
4. The color of male birds is usually	(a) dull	(b) bright	(c) black.
5. Birds are	(a) our friends	(b) our enemies	(c) dangerous.

Underline the words that begin with a "k" sound.

1. cat
2. cent
3. coat
4. change
5. cut
6. child
7. choose
8. call
9. camp
10. center
11. cold
12. come
13. carry
14. care
15. church
16. color
17. cap
18. chick
19. chase
20. cow
21. car
22. cheer
23. can
24. cents

Words That Are Opposites

Words that have directly opposite meanings are called antonyms.

Match each word with its antonym in the box by writing the antonym in the proper blank. Circle the word used. See example "1."

1. light heavy
2. up ______
3. white ______
4. crooked ______
5. smooth ______
6. tight ______
7. shiny ______
8. bad ______
9. hard ______
10. warm ______
11. hot ______
12. fat ______
13. early ______
14. under ______
15. play ______
16. nothing ______
17. few ______
18. short ______
19. pretty ______
20. same ______
21. small ______
22. talk ______

Antonyms

cool	soft	cold	loose
black	down	work	long
listen	skinny	ugly	opposite
dull	straight	over	many
large	good	(heavy)	rough
everything	late		

Cardinals

Vocabulary Study ● Draw a line under each correct answer. **JUST FOR FUN**

1. "Happy" means	(a) "sad"	(b) "not sad"	(c) "joyless."
2. Another word for "near" is	(a) "close"	(b) "away"	(c) "far."
3. The opposite of "dull" is	(a) "dark"	(b) "bright"	(c) "not bright."
4. Your mother and father are your	(a) sisters	(b) brothers	(c) parents.

The cardinal sings a happy, lively song. It says, "Cheer, cheer, cheer!"

Cardinals are friendly. They like to live near people. They often build their nests near houses. The nests are usually in bushes a few feet from the ground.

The male cardinal is bright red. The female cardinal is dull gray.

Cardinals are good parents. The males help the females. They are good fathers and husbands.

Cardinals are active birds. They are seen all year-round. Have you ever seen a cardinal?

Answer these questions about the story:

1. The cardinal's song says	(a) "Caw!"	(b) "Cheer!"	(c) "Eek!"
2. Cardinals live	(a) near people	(b) away from people	(c) alone.
3. Male cardinals are	(a) dull gray	(b) blue	(c) bright red.
4. Cardinals are seen	(a) only in the summer	(b) only in the winter	(c) year-round.
5. Cardinals are	(a) active	(b) lazy	(c) friendly.

Complete each sentence.

1. I like ________________.
2. Ted is my ________________.
3. ________________ lives here.
4. The ________________ is closed.
5. It ________________ today.
6. He went to ________________.
7. We will ride the ________________.
8. The bird flew ________________.
9. The ________________ was sad.
10. She lives on a ________________.

Do You Know?

Write the correct answers in the blanks.

THANK YOU IT WAS SO OF YOU

SORRY TO HEAR YOU'RE NOT FEELING WELL

1. When do you write a thank-you letter?

2. When do you write a get-well note?

3. Write the antonyms of these words.

long ______ clean ______

good ______ out ______

late ______ left ______

sad ______ down ______

4. Use "to," "too," and "two" in these sentences.

A. I am going ______ the dentist.

School of Dentistry

B. He will fill ______ cavities.

C. Mom is going ______.

5. Write the seven days of the week.

6. Name two words that rhyme with "king."

7. Write two words that rhyme with "mare."

Robins

JUST FOR FUN

Vocabulary Study • Draw a line under each correct answer.

1. A city is a	(a) small town	(b) big town	(c) small country.
2. The opposite of "early" is	(a) "late"	(b) "soon"	(c) "never."
3. The first part of the day is	(a) morning	(b) noon	(c) afternoon.
4. The past tense of "feed" is	(a) "feeds"	(b) "feeded"	(c) "fed."

Robins are friendly birds. They build their homes near people. Many robins live in cities.

Robins are songbirds. They start singing early in the morning. Have you ever heard a robin sing?

Robins like to use mud to build their nests. They make many trips to get enough material for their nests. The nests are lined with grasses.

Robins like to eat worms. They also eat fruits and insects.

Baby robins are well cared for by their parents. They are fed worms.

Answer these questions about the story:

1. Robins are	(a) friendly	(b) mean	(c) pests.
2. In the morning, robins like to	(a) sleep	(b) sing	(c) rest.
3. To build nests, robins use	(a) wood	(b) flowers	(c) mud.
4. Robins' favorite food is	(a) worms	(b) fruit	(c) insects.
5. Robins make	(a) good parents	(b) bad parents	(c) poor parents.

*

Underline the words which come first in alphabetical order.

1. he	to	7. am	cut	13. pan	is	19. wish	good
2. it	big	8. you	hill	14. by	has	20. ask	on
3. go	see	9. new	we	15. not	the	21. him	live
4. all	zoo	10. far	red	16. use	pull	22. girl	so
5. up	man	11. eat	was	17. doll	walk	23. top	my
6. old	book	12. rain	do	18. bell	for	24. eye	now

Rocks Are Part of the Earth

Rocks are found under the soil and in mountains. We use rocks for many things. What are some of their uses?

A **Write each use.**

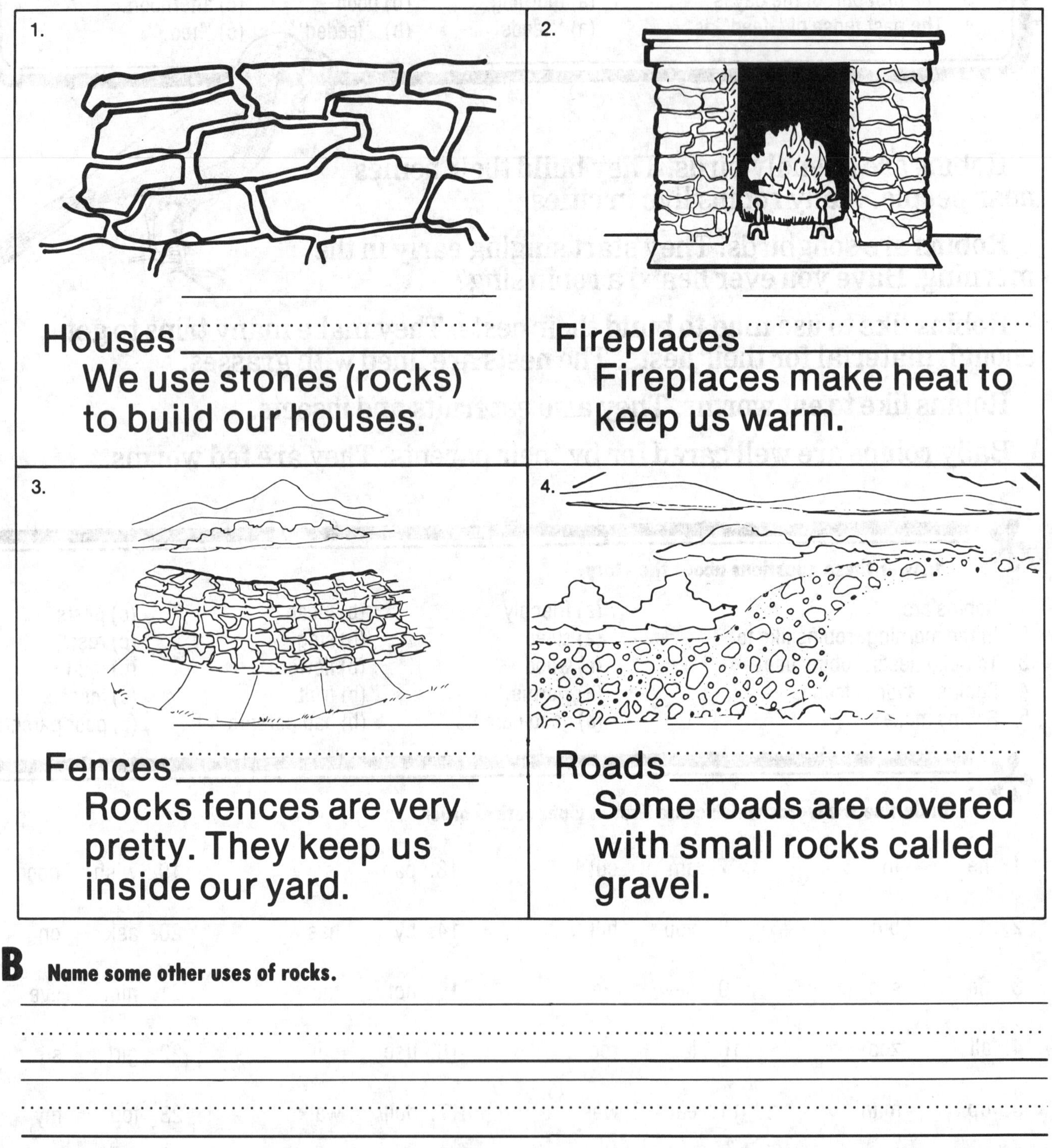

1. Houses
We use stones (rocks) to build our houses.

2. Fireplaces
Fireplaces make heat to keep us warm.

3. Fences
Rocks fences are very pretty. They keep us inside our yard.

4. Roads
Some roads are covered with small rocks called gravel.

B **Name some other uses of rocks.**

The Sandpiper

Vocabulary Study ● Draw a line under each correct answer. **JUST FOR FUN**

1. The opposite of "many" is (a) "none" (b) "few" (c) "very much."
2. "Quick" means (a) "slow" (b) "easy" (c) "fast."
3. A shore is at the (a) edge (b) middle (c) bottom.
4. Gravel is made up of (a) rocks (b) dirt (c) wood.

Sandpipers are small birds. There are many kinds of sandpipers.

Sandpipers have very small feet. They can run very quickly. Sandpipers run along the beaches of the ocean. They are also found on the shores of rivers, lakes, and ponds.

Sandpipers lay their eggs in nests on gravel beaches. Sometimes they use the nests of robins.

Sandpipers like warm weather. They are good swimmers. Sandpipers can even swim underwater. They often get away from danger by diving under the water.

Answer these questions about the story:

1. Sandpipers are (a) small birds (b) big birds (c) fish.
2. Sandpipers move about (a) very slowly (b) slowly (c) quickly.
3. Sandpipers live (a) in trees (b) near water (c) on deserts.
4. Sandpipers like (a) cold weather (b) warm weather (c) hot weather.
5. To get away, sandpipers often (a) dive (b) fly (c) run.

Complete each word with a vowel. (Remember: "a," "e," "i," "o," and "u" are vowels.)

1. b____rd	6. l____ke	11. fl____g	16. w____ter
2. f____rm	7. f____sh	12. st____ry	17. sl____d
3. sh____p	8. r____se	13. sw____n	18. g____me
4. h____rse	9. n____st	14. dr____m	19. w____rk
5. w____rm	10. s____ng	15. l____nd	20. g____te

Owls

JUST FOR FUN

Vocabulary Study ● Draw a line under each correct answer.

1. The front is the opposite of the	(a) side	(b) back	(c) top.
2. Your favorite is the one you like	(a) best	(b) least	(c) last.
3. "Hunt" means	(a) "to find"	(b) "to look for"	(c) "to lose."
4. A noise is a	(a) place	(b) person	(c) sound.

An owl is a bird. It is different from other birds. An owl has two eyes in front of its head. Other birds have eyes at the sides of their heads.

Most owls sleep in the daytime. They rest on high branches in tall trees. That is why we do not see many owls.

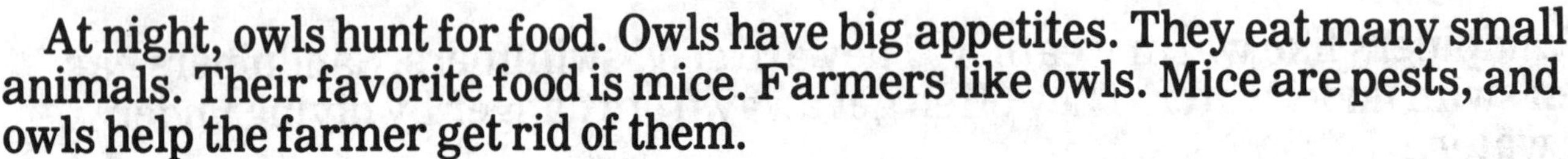

At night, owls hunt for food. Owls have big appetites. They eat many small animals. Their favorite food is mice. Farmers like owls. Mice are pests, and owls help the farmer get rid of them.

An owl makes a noise that sounds like "whoo, whoo!" Have you ever heard an owl?

Answer these questions about the story:

1. An owl is a	(a) bird	(b) mouse	(c) fish.
2. An owl sleeps during the	(a) night	(b) daytime	(c) morning.
3. An owl sleeps	(a) on the ground	(b) in a tree	(c) in a house.
4. At night an owl	(a) sleeps	(b) rests	(c) hunts.
5. An owl's favorite food is	(a) ants	(b) fish	(c) mice.

Add a consonant to make each word.

1. ____ird	7. ____ame	13. ____ive	19. ____ome
2. ____oon	8. ____old	14. ____ish	20. ____all
3. ____arm	9. ____ull	15. ____ong	21. ____amp
4. ____ake	10. ____ide	16. ____ade	22. ____ood
5. ____ose	11. ____op	17. ____ine	23. ____eek
6. ____oat	12. ____eep	18. ____one	24. ____ight

Water

Water is one of the most important elements in the world to us. It is necessary, and it can also be used for fun.

Name the uses for water shown in each picture. Then complete the sentences.

1.

brush teeth

It would be hard to use toothpaste or soap without water. ________

Water helps keep us ________.

2.

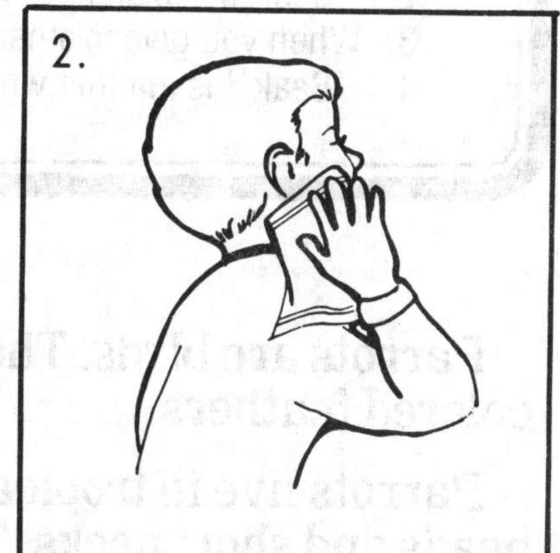

____

3.

____

Did you know that your body weight is almost two-thirds water? We keep water in our bodies by ________ ________.

4.

____

5.

____

Keeping clean is something important to remember at ________ ________ and at ________.

6.

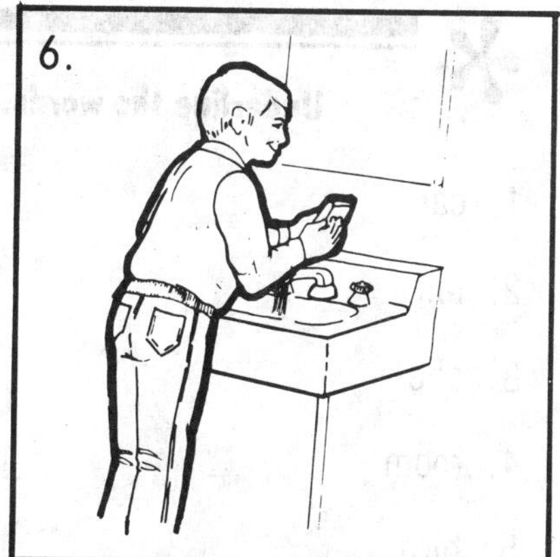

____

Parrots

Vocabulary Study ● **Draw a line under each correct answer.** **JUST FOR FUN**

	(a)	(b)	(c)
1. A pair is	(a) one	(b) two	(c) three.
2. "Search" is another word for	(a) "lose"	(b) "find"	(c) "look for."
3. When you give to others, you	(a) share	(b) take	(c) are mean.
4. "Beak" is another word for	(a) "mouth"	(b) "eye"	(c) "ear."

Parrots are birds. They have brightly colored feathers.

Parrots live in tropical forests. They have round heads and short necks. They have short legs and strong wings.

Parrots usually fly in pairs. Sometimes they fly in groups called flocks. They search for food. When they find food, they call other birds. Parrots share their food. They eat fruits.

Parrots have big beaks. The beaks are used like extra hands.

Parrots are best known because they say words. They repeat things they hear.

Answer these questions about the story:

	(a)	(b)	(c)
1. Parrots are	(a) birds	(b) fish	(c) cats.
2. Parrots usually fly	(a) alone	(b) in pairs	(c) in groups.
3. A group of parrots is a	(a) herd	(b) flock	(c) family.
4. Parrots eat	(a) fruits	(b) meat	(c) wood.
5. Parrots are known for their	(a) bright feathers	(b) talking	(c) black feathers.

Underline the words.

1. car	7. dog	13. frgso	19. book
2. teh	8. see	14. call	20. fish
3. she	9. cta	15. wrko	21. rfie
4. room	10. live	16. water	22. house
5. bird	11. you	17. come	23. bsu
6. npe	12. rtee	18. boat	24. boy

How to Protect Yourself in Bad Weather

Have you ever been caught in the rain, in the snow, or just an extra cold day without enough clothes on? It is not very much fun, is it? Being caught in bad weather can sometimes cause you to catch cold.

A **The boy at the right is dressed properly for a rainy day. Name the things that he is wearing that protect him.**

1. ____________________
2. ____________________
3. ____________________
4. ____________________

B **Here are some pictures of things that can help keep you warm when it is cold or snowy. Write the names of these clothes. Then complete the sentences.**

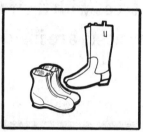

A. ______________ B. ______________ C. ______________ D. ______________

1. A scarf helps keep your ____________ warm.
2. Boots keep your feet ____________ and ____________.
3. ____________ or ____________ keep your hands warm.
4. An ____________ protects your whole body from the rain.
5. If you don't have a hat, ________________ help.

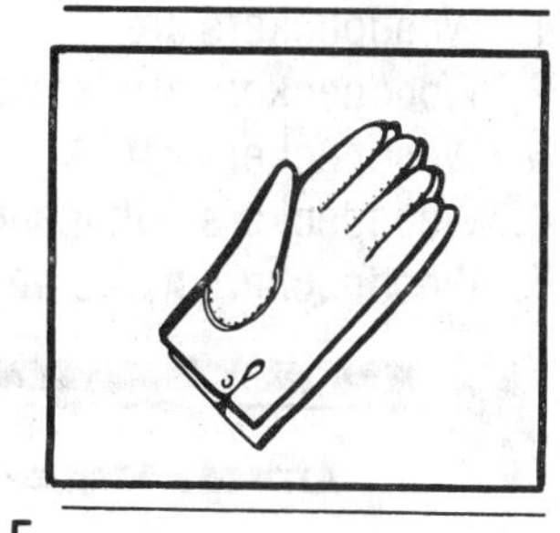

E. ______________

F. ______________

Woodpeckers

JUST FOR FUN

Vocabulary Study ● Draw a line under each correct answer.

1. "Their" means (a) "belong to me" (b) "belong to you" (c) "belong to them."
2. Another word for "strong" is (a) "weak" (b) "powerless" (c) "powerful."
3. A bird's beak is its (a) mouth (b) feet (c) wings.
4. The opposite of "inside" is (a) "within" (b) "outside" (c) "inner."

Have you ever heard a woodpecker? Woodpeckers are noisy birds. They are found only where there are trees.

Woodpeckers are made for climbing. They hop up trees. Their feet have strong claws. They lean on their stiff tail feathers.

Woodpeckers have hard beaks. They dig into trees. Inside the trees are insects. Insects are the woodpeckers' favorite food. Woodpeckers pull the insects out of trees with their long tongues.

Baby woodpeckers are also noisy. Their nests are inside trees. Woodpeckers are good parents.

Answer these questions about the story:

1. Woodpeckers are (a) quiet birds (b) silent birds (c) noisy birds.
2. Woodpeckers are found near (a) water (b) trees (c) cities.
3. Woodpeckers eat (a) wood (b) insects (c) plants.
4. Woodpeckers pull insects out of (a) the ground (b) the water (c) trees.
5. Woodpeckers make nests (a) inside trees (b) underground (c) on the ground.

Arrange each set of letters to make a word.

1. rea __________
2. ohw __________
3. nru __________
4. hto __________
5. lbal __________
6. hsa __________
7. lwil __________
8. ohme __________
9. htsi __________
10. tere __________
11. dmae __________
12. ofot __________
13. neo __________
14. rty __________
15. cloo __________
16. brid __________
17. dfoo __________
18. ti __________

Hands — the Tattletales

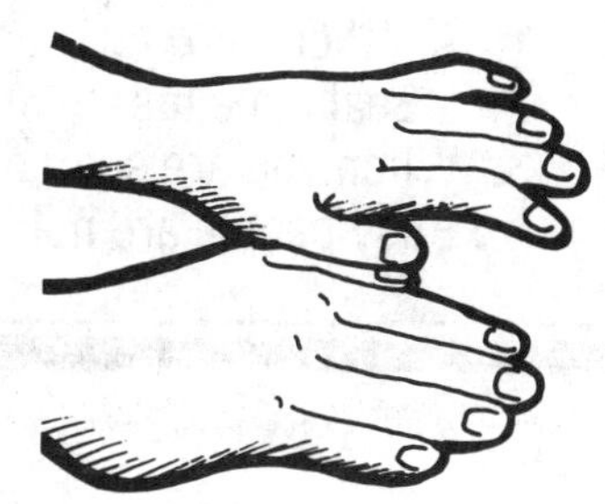

Did you know that parts of your body are tattletales? They are your hands. Your hands tell other people how much you care about yourself.

If you go around with dirty hands and dirty unshaped fingernails, it tells people you do not care much for yourself.

Clean hands and fingernails show people you care how you look. Besides, it is nicer to shake hands with a person who has clean hands.

A **Here are two hands. Write "dirty" or "clean" under the correct picture.**

A. ______________________ B. ______________________

B **Here are five rules for hand care. The words are scrambled. Unscramble them, read them carefully, and remember to follow them.**

1. bite your don't nails. ______________________

2. hands your wash you eat before. ______________________

3. keep your mouth out of your fingers. ______________________

4. after the bathroom you go your hands wash to. soap of plenty use. ______________________

5. nails keep your clean. ______________________

The Hummingbird

Vocabulary Study ● Draw a line under each correct answer. **JUST FOR FUN**

1. Another word for ''tiny'' is (a) ''big'' (b) ''large'' (c) ''small.''
2. ''Beat'' means (a) ''to hold'' (b) ''to hit'' (c) ''to be still.''
3. When you are scared, you are (a) afraid (b) not afraid (c) brave.
4. Busy people are not (a) working (b) doing anything (c) lazy.

The hummingbird is the smallest of all birds. Its name comes from a sound that it makes. The hummingbird beats its wings so fast that it makes a humming noise.

The hummingbird feeds on honey. It gets the honey from flowers. It may be a tiny bird, but it is always hungry.

The hummingbird is not afraid of anything. It has a very bad temper. It attacks animals. It may even attack a person.

The hummingbird's nest is very small. The nest is usually built in a fruit tree. The eggs are the size of jelly beans.

The hummingbird is a fast flier. It is always busy.

Answer these questions about the story:

1. Of all birds the hummingbird is the (a) largest (b) smallest (c) slowest.
2. The humming noise is made by the bird's (a) wings (b) beak (c) feet.
3. The hummingbird eats (a) insects (b) worms (c) honey.
4. The eggs are the size of (a) jelly beans (b) apples (c) oranges.
5. A hummingbird flies (a) slowly (b) not too slowly (c) fast.

Draw a line to connect words with the same vowel sounds.

1. same	game	7. road	lock	13. gate	step
2. cute	hen	8. fell	bone	14. five	for
3. hot	not	9. six	nice	15. bat	snake
4. jet	pin	10. pot	tell	16. desk	cap
5. pig	tune	11. ate	lip	17. more	wheel
6. run	nut	12. ice	pay	18. meat	fire

Telephone Manners

Read the story carefully, and answer the questions.

When you pick up the receiver, speak as you would like to be spoken to. Try to sound interested. The voice with a smile wins. Make it pleasant, and you have won a friend.

Be sure you have the right number when you dial. Identify your voice at once. The telephone company suggests that you do not give up too quickly if no one answers your call. It takes at least five or six rings to get out of the shower or to run in from the garden. If you should get a wrong number, apologize with a brief and courteous ''I'm sorry.''

The one who places the call should decide when it is time to stop talking. However, if he doesn't, you may bring it to a close by saying ''May I call you back later? I really must go now.'' Take messages for absent persons. Write down the number and the name of the person calling. Place the message where it can be found. Hang up gently. Slamming the receiver is very discourteous.

absent	**apologize**	**found**	**slamming**
smile	**speak**	**stop**	**voice**

1. When answering a call, identify your ____________ immediately.

2. The voice with a ____________ wins.

3. On the telephone you should ____________ as you would like to be spoken to.

4. If you should get the wrong number, ____________ immediately.

5. The one who places the call should decide when to ____________ talking.

6. ____________ the receiver is very discourteous.

7. Take messages for ____________ persons.

8. Place the message where it can be ____________.

Bird Homes

Vocabulary Study ● Draw a line under each correct answer. **JUST FOR FUN**

1. "Many" means	(a) "one"	(b) "two"	(c) "a large number."
2. The opposite of "top" is	(a) "bottom"	(b) "side"	(c) "up."
3. To care for something is to	(a) need it	(b) watch over it	(c) hate it.
4. "Soon" means	(a) "not long away"	(b) "today"	(c) "never."

A bird's home is called a nest. No one teaches a bird how to build a nest. It just knows how.

There are many kinds of birds. There are many kinds of nests. Some nests are open at the top. Some are made of grass. Some are made of mud. Still others are made of sticks and stones.

Most birds build their homes in trees. Some birds build nests on the ground. Some build nests under the ground.

Wherever nests are built, mother birds take good care of their baby birds. They feed them. They protect them. They teach them to fly. Soon the baby birds will build their own nests.

Answer these questions about the story:

1. A bird's home is a	(a) house	(b) nest	(c) hive.
2. Nests are made of	(a) grass	(b) mud	(c) sticks.
3. Most birds build nests	(a) in trees	(b) on the ground	(c) on the water.
4. Mother birds are	(a) good mothers	(b) bad mothers	(c) mean mothers.
5. Nests are built	(a) in trees	(b) on the ground	(c) under the ground.

Draw a line to connect the words that rhyme.

1. at	top	7. me	grow	13. make	live
2. ten	ran	8. slow	she	14. give	take
3. can	sat	9. try	fry	15. rose	fill
4. all	pen	10. hand	hay	16. best	rest
5. egg	ball	11. they	sand	17. never	nose
6. pop	leg	12. door	poor	18. will	ever

Table Manners

Read the story carefully, and answer the questions.

When you go to the table, be sure your hands are clean. Sit with your knees together and with both feet on the floor, not on the rounds of the chairs. Keep your elbows off the table. Eat slowly and quietly. Avoid talking with your mouth full. Take small mouthfuls so that you may talk without giving offense. Keep your lips closed when chewing. Never use your knife to carry food to your mouth. Can you imagine a person talking, using gestures with his hands while a fork is in his hand? How shocking it would be to read in the daily news the headline "Student Stabbed with Fork at Lunch as Another Student Drives His Point Home." Do not sit too close to the table. Be a good comfortable distance, and do not "hover" over the table. On the other hand, don't sit too far from the table.

elbows	**floor**	**mouth**	**talk**

1. Sit at a table with both feet on the ________________.
2. Do not put your ________________ on the table.
3. Do not talk with your ________________ full.
4. Take small bites so you may ________________ without giving offense.
5. Keep your ________________ closed while chewing.
6. Don't use your knife to carry food to your ________________.

Bird Talk

Vocabulary Study ● **Draw a line under each correct answer.** JUST FOR FUN

1. Another word for "sound" is	(a) "noise"	(b) "quiet"	(c) "silent."
2. "Probably" means	(a) "never"	(b) "too late"	(c) "a chance of."
3. The opposite of "guess" is	(a) "know"	(b) "not sure"	(c) "think."
4. A guess is something you	(a) know	(b) are not sure of	(c) trust.

Birds do not talk the way we do. They make many sounds. To birds these sounds mean something.

Some sounds tell where food is. Some calls are warnings. They tell other birds to stay away. Some calls warn of danger. Some calls mean anger. Some calls show fear.

We do not really know what the calls mean. We think that singing is a sign of happiness. Sharp calls probably mean anger or fear. Only birds of the same kind know the calls. We can only guess. What do you think they mean?

Answer these questions about the story:

1. Birds	(a) talk	(b) make sounds	(c) make no sounds.
2. Calls tell other birds of	(a) food	(b) anger	(c) fear.
3. Singing is probably a sign of	(a) happiness	(b) danger	(c) sadness.
4. A sharp call may mean	(a) anger	(b) fear	(c) happiness.
5. Birds are understood by	(a) humans	(b) animals	(c) other birds.

Arrange each set of words into a sentence.

1. here I live ______
2. away he ran ______
3. she pretty is ______
4. home is at Dave ______
5. dog barked the ______
6. like you I ______
7. you friend my are ______
8. saw bird I a ______

Your Dentist

Fill in the blanks using the words in the box. Use each word only once. Circle each word used.

sugar	**healthy**	**friend**	**twice**
afraid	**doctor**	**women**	**pretty**
dentist	**soft**	**milk**	

1. You should visit your ______________ twice per year.

2. Your dentist is your __________.

3. Brush your teeth at least __________ per day.

4. Use a __________ toothbrush.

5. You should drink __________ daily for healthy teeth.

6. __________ helps form plaque on your teeth.

7. Dentists help to keep your teeth __________.

8. Healthy teeth are also __________ teeth.

9. You should not be __________ of your dentist.

10. There are men and ________ dentists.

11. Dentists are a kind of __________.

Animal Homes

Vocabulary Study ● **Draw a line under each correct answer.** JUST FOR FUN

1. An enemy is someone you (a) like (b) fear (c) want to see.
2. The opposite of ''down'' is (a) ''under'' (b) ''bottom'' (c) ''up.''
3. Snow is always (a) hot (b) warm (c) cold.
4. ''Little'' means (a) ''not much'' (b) ''much'' (c) ''plenty.''

Animals make their homes in many different places. They live where they can find food and water. They live where the weather suits their needs. They live where they can hide from enemies.

Some animals live in trees. They may come down for food and water. Some never come down.

Some animals live in or near the water. Some must always stay in the water. Some live in and out of the water.

Some animals live in the snow. They like the cold. They have heavy fur coats.

Some animals live in the desert. They like the hot weather. They need little water.

Animals often live near people. Some do not live near people.

Answer these questions about the story:

1. Animals live where they can find (a) food (b) water (c) safety.
2. Animals in the snow have (a) heavy fur coats (b) no fur (c) feathers.
3. Desert animals need little (a) food (b) sun (c) water.
4. Every animal has (a) his own home (b) the same home (c) his own needs.
5. Animals may live (a) in trees (b) in water (c) near people.

Put each set of words in alphabetical order.

1. go ______ in ______	4. toy ______ day ______	7. get ______ we ______	10. one ______ is ______
2. car ______ bat ______	5. hill ______ cow ______	8. dog ______ are ______	11. who ______ ball ______
3. you ______ boy ______	6. big ______ run ______	9. now ______ she ______	12. no ______ yes ______

Health Puzzle

Read each sentence carefully, and write the correct answer word in the puzzle. The first one has been done for you.

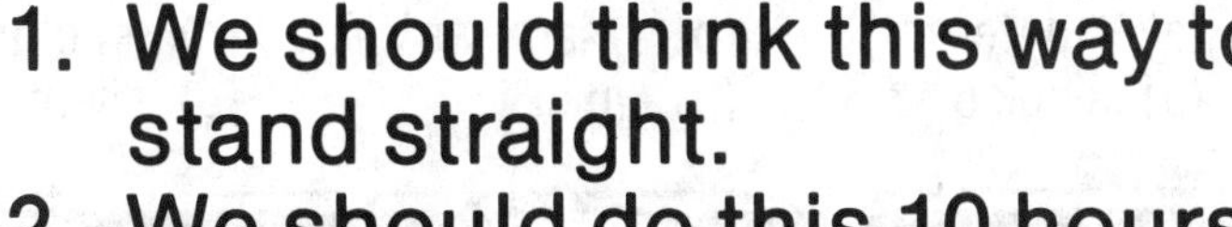

1. We should think this way to stand straight.
2. We should do this 10 hours every night.
3. We should drink a quart of this each day.
4. We should brush our teeth after each of these.
5. We should drink six glasses of this each day.
6. We should always wash these before we eat.
7. We should eat this each morning.

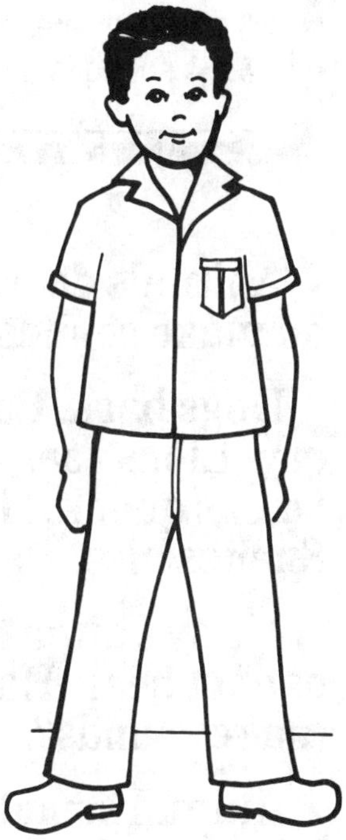

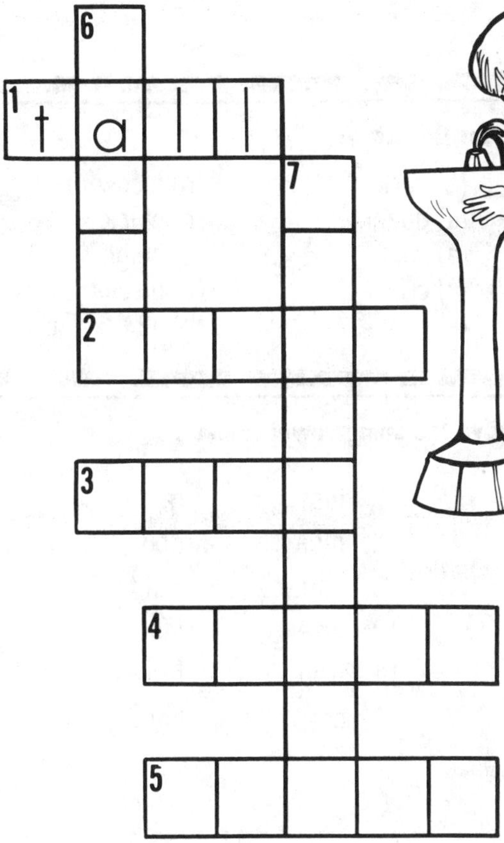

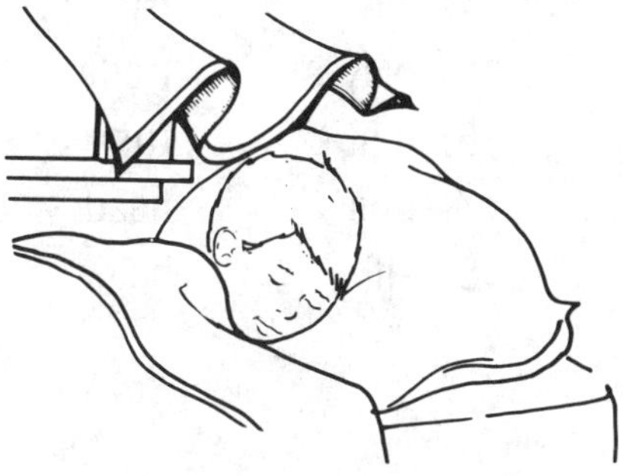

Animal Talk

Vocabulary Study ● Draw a line under each correct answer. JUST FOR FUN

	(a)	(b)	(c)
1. "Mice" is the plural of	(a) "meese"	(b) "mices"	(c) "mouse."
2. "Cannot" is made up of	(a) "can not"	(b) "ca nnot"	(c) "cann ot."
3. "Like" means	(a) "different"	(b) "same as"	(c) "not the same."
4. A sound is	(a) a noise	(b) quiet	(c) silent.

Animals do not talk like we do. Some do make sounds.

Dogs bark. Cats meow. Birds sing or cry. Lions roar. Pigs oink. Turkeys gobble. Ducks quack. Horses neigh. Cows moo. Chickens cluck. Mice squeak. Snakes hiss.

Many animals make no sounds at all. Still others make sounds which we cannot hear. Have you ever heard turtles, fish, spiders, or worms make sounds?

Animal sounds mean something to other animals. Cats understand cats. Horses understand horses. People try to guess what the sounds mean. Only the animals know.

Answer these questions about the story:

	(a)	(b)	(c)
1. Dogs	(a) bark	(b) meow	(c) sing.
2. Turkeys	(a) quack	(b) cluck	(c) gobble.
3. Cows	(a) moo	(b) neigh	(c) roar.
4. An earthworm	(a) cries	(b) hisses	(c) makes no sound.
5. Mice understand	(a) people	(b) other mice	(c) horses.

Connect the words which have the same vowel sounds.

1. sing	eat	7. just	rain	13. kinds	it
2. them	mine	8. nice	dog	14. old	try
3. hurt	ring	9. name	right	15. play	trade
4. leave	hate	10. week	fear	16. tent	rush
5. kite	pen	11. frog	fun	17. bus	head
6. made	dirt	12. car	hat	18. sit	hold

Nutritious Foods

These paragraphs tell about some nutritious foods. Fill in the blanks after reading each paragraph.

Eggs are used in many foods we eat. They are good to eat for breakfast. Eggs help to make us healthy.

When do you eat eggs? ______________________

Fowl is good to eat. It is a kind of meat. There are many kinds of fowl.

1. What is a fowl? ______________________
2. Name some kinds of fowl. ______________________

Some foods are made from grain. These foods help to build our bones and muscles. They also help to make our teeth strong. Breads and cereals are made from grains. We should eat some grain at every meal.

1. When do you eat grain foods? ______________________
2. Name some grains. ______________________

Meats are good for us. We should eat plenty of meat. There are many kinds of meat.

Name some different kinds of meat. ______________________

A Trip to the Bakery

JUST FOR FUN

Vocabulary Study • Draw a line under each correct answer.

1. Things that are the same are	(a) just alike	(b) not alike	(c) almost alike.
2. ''Mix'' means	(a) ''to break apart''	(b) ''to put together''	(c) ''to part.''
3. The opposite of ''cool'' is	(a) ''freeze''	(b) ''warm''	(c) ''cold.''
4. All the food a girl eats is her	(a) diet	(b) lunch	(c) dinner.

The bakery is a place where breads are made. The person who bakes the breads is called a baker.

Big machines measure and mix the bread dough. All loaves must be the same size. All loaves must weigh the same.

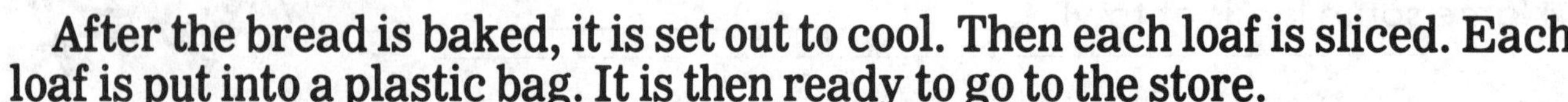

After the bread is baked, it is set out to cool. Then each loaf is sliced. Each loaf is put into a plastic bag. It is then ready to go to the store.

The bakery makes many different kinds of breads. There are loaves of breads. There are buns for hot dogs and hamburgers. There are rolls for dinner. The bakery also makes cookies, pies, and cakes. Bread is an important part of our diets.

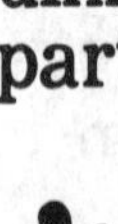

Answer these questions about the story:

1. A bakery is a place for making	(a) breads	(b) candy	(c) ice cream.
2. A person who bakes the bread is a	(a) cook	(b) baker	(c) butcher.
3. The dough is mixed	(a) by hand	(b) by machine	(c) by the baker.
4. Bread is wrapped in	(a) paper bags	(b) boxes	(c) plastic bags.
5. Which of the following is a bread?	(a) buns	(b) rolls	(c) cakes

Rewrite each sentence.

1. Fido is my .

4. The flew away.

2. This is my .

5. I caught a  .

3. The  rang.

6. The  is late.

Kinds of Foods

We should eat many different kinds of foods. Many foods help to make our bodies strong. Eating many different foods is called eating a variety. Each day we should eat some of these foods: fruits, vegetables; meats, eggs, or cheese; breads and cereals; starches. Also, we should drink liquids.

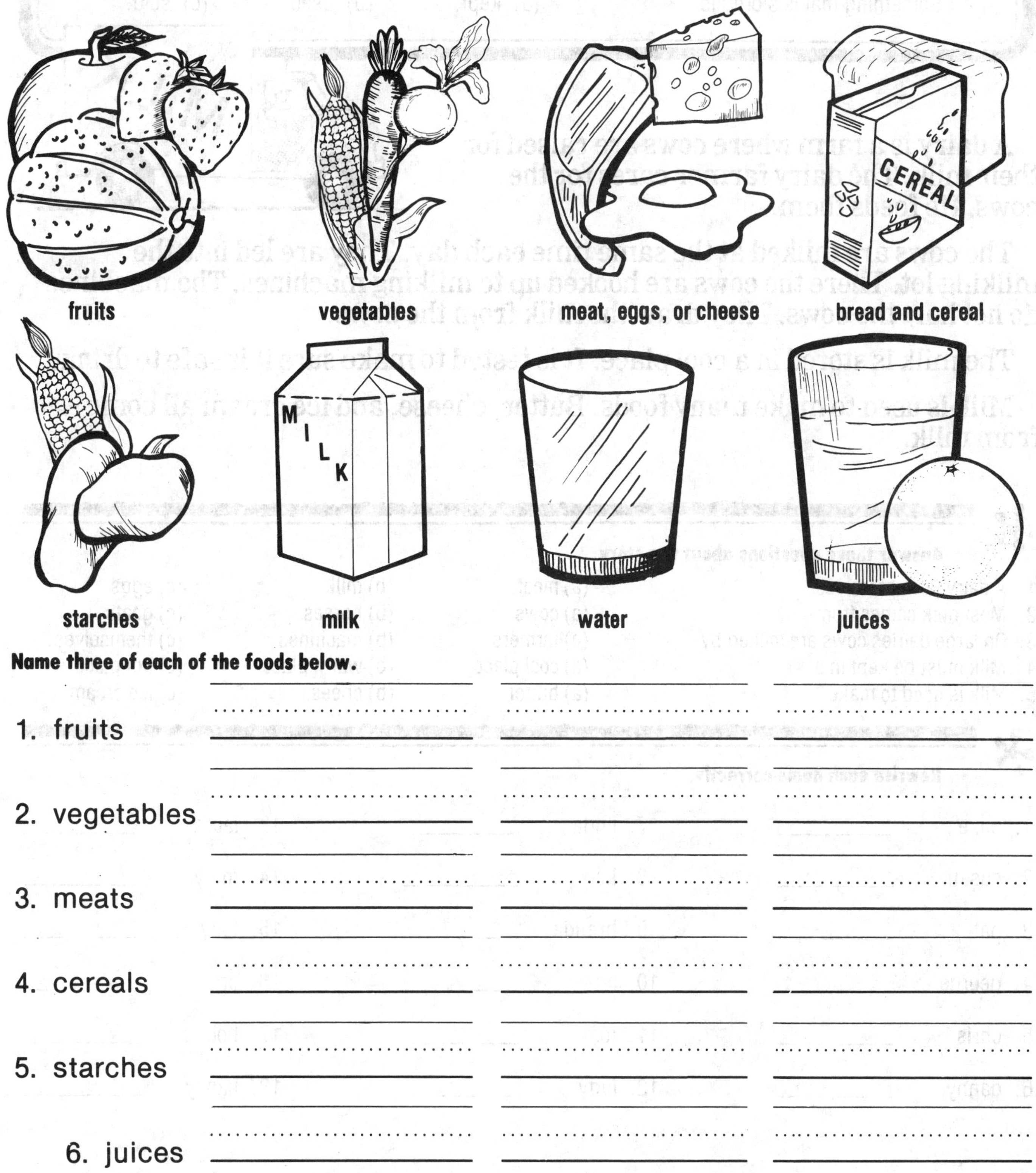

Name three of each of the foods below.

1. fruits
2. vegetables
3. meats
4. cereals
5. starches
6. juices

A Trip to the Dairy

Vocabulary Study ● **Draw a line under each correct answer.**

JUST FOR FUN

	(a)	(b)	(c)
1. Things that do not hurt you are	(a) not safe	(b) safe	(c) dangerous.
2. A farmer is a	(a) person	(b) place	(c) thing.
3. "Each" means	(a) "some"	(b) "none"	(c) "every"
4. Something that is stored is	(a) kept	(b) used	(c) sold.

A dairy is a farm where cows are raised for their milk. The dairy farmer cares for the cows. He feeds them.

The cows are milked at the same time each day. They are led into the milking lot. There the cows are hooked up to milking machines. The machines do not hurt the cows. They draw the milk from the cows.

The milk is stored in a cool place. It is tested to make sure it is safe to drink.

Milk is used to make many foods. Butter, cheese, and ice cream all come from milk.

Answer these questions about the story:

	(a)	(b)	(c)
1. A dairy farm produces	(a) meat	(b) milk	(c) eggs.
2. Most milk comes from	(a) cows	(b) horses	(c) goats.
3. On large dairies cows are milked by	(a) farmers	(b) machines	(c) themselves.
4. Milk must be kept in a	(a) cool place	(b) warm place	(c) hot place.
5. Milk is used to make	(a) butter	(b) cheese	(c) ice cream.

Rewrite each name correctly.

1. mike	________	7. linda	________	13. laura	________
2. susan	________	8. ken	________	14. mary	________
3. pat	________	9. brenda	________	15. tony	________
4. george	________	10. adam	________	16. eric	________
5. chris	________	11. tom	________	17. bob	________
6. danny	________	12. judy	________	18. nancy	________

Fresh Air and Sunshine

We breathe fresh air into our lungs. Our bodies need fresh air to grow. Our skin needs air to stay fresh and glowing.

We also need plenty of sunshine. Sunshine helps us to stay healthy. It gives us vitamin D.

A Unscramble the word at the end of each sentence, and write it in the blank.

1. Plenty of sunshine helps us to stay __________. (tlyhaeh)
2. We get vitamin D from the __________. (eihunssn)
3. Our skin needs fresh air to stay fresh and __________. (gnilogw)
4. We breathe fresh air into our __________. (gnuls)

B Read the sentences, and fill in the blanks. Then fill in the puzzle with the correct words.

1. We breathe fresh air into our __________.
2. Fresh __________ helps us to grow.
3. Our skin needs __________ air.
4. __________ gives us vitamin D.

A Trip to the Airport

Vocabulary Study ● Draw a line under each correct answer.

JUST FOR FUN

1. The opposite of "filled" is	(a) "empty"	(b) "more"	(c) "plenty."
2. "Wait" means	(a) "to go"	(b) "to stay"	(c) "to leave."
3. Another word for "talk" is	(a) "quiet"	(b) "walk"	(c) "tell."
4. A road for airplanes is a	(a) track	(b) highway	(c) runway.

An airport is filled with airplanes. Some airplanes are waiting to land. Some are waiting to take off.

An important person at the airport is the controller. The controller talks to the pilot by radio. He tells the pilot when to land. He tells him when to take off.

When a plane lands, it is checked. Its tires are checked. Its engines are checked. It is refueled. Some passengers get off. New ones get on.

The plane then goes out to the runway. It waits its turn to take off.

Answer these questions about the story:

1. An airport is where planes	(a) land	(b) take off	(c) are built.
2. The controller talks to the	(a) passengers	(b) pilot	(c) workers.
3. The pilot talks on a	(a) radio	(b) telephone	(c) television.
4. A plane lands on a	(a) runway	(b) road	(c) street.
5. People who ride on planes are	(a) pilots	(b) controllers	(c) passengers.

Complete each sentence. Then draw a line from each word to the correct picture.

1. I have four wheels. I drive on a road. I am a __________.

2. I have many cars. I ride on a track. I am a __________.

3. I go to many places. I fly in the air. I am an __________.

4. I can sail far away. I ride on the water. I am a __________.

5. I take children to school. I am yellow. I am a __________.

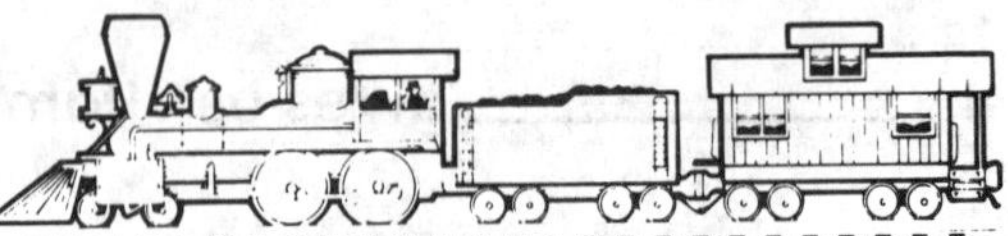

Clean Hair

You should keep your hair clean and neat. Clean hair makes healthy hair. Use shampoo and plenty of warm water to make your hair clean and shiny.

You should wash your hair at least two times per week. Sometimes you may have to wash it more often.

Dirty hair looks dull. It makes the scalp itch.

A Answer these questions.

1. How often do you wash your hair? __________

2. Name four things you should use to keep your hair clean and neat. __________

3. Do all people have the same hair color? __________

4. What is the color of your hair, your mother's hair, your father's hair? __________

5. How often should you wash your hair? __________

6. Is dirty hair healthy hair? __________

7. Does dirty hair look shiny and clean? __________

8. Does clean hair make the scalp itch? __________

B Unscramble the words to write two health sentences.

1. hair makes hair healthy clean

____

2. shampoo clean your to hair plenty use of water and warm

____

A Trip to the Orchard

Vocabulary Study ● Draw a line under each correct answer. **JUST FOR FUN**

1. A market is a	(a) farm	(b) store	(c) city.
2. The opposite of "different" is	(a) "same"	(b) "change"	(c) "new."
3. "Ruin" means	(a) "help"	(b) "save"	(c) "kill."
4. A row is a	(a) line	(b) circle	(c) box.

Have you ever visited an orchard? An orchard is a farm. Fruit trees grow in an orchard. Apples, pears, peaches, apricots, plums, and cherries grow in an orchard.

Some orchards are small. They are grown for the owner's use.

Other orchards are very large. They are grown for markets.

An orchard may grow only one kind of fruit. It may grow many kinds of different fruits. Trees in an orchard are set in rows.

It is hard work to take care of an orchard. Many insects can kill trees or ruin crops. Most farmers spray their trees for insects.

Weather is important in an orchard. It can also ruin a crop.

Answer these questions about the story:

1. An orchard is a	(a) fruit farm	(b) animal farm	(c) rice farm.
2. Fruits in an orchard are	(a) apples	(b) cherries	(c) pears.
3. Orchards are sprayed for	(a) worms	(b) insects	(c) animals.
4. Many crops are ruined by	(a) weather	(b) insects	(c) farmers.
5. Orchards are cared for by	(a) farmers	(b) cowboys	(c) no one.

Rewrite each word correctly.

1. yur ________	6. hert ________	11. thay ________	16. opin ________
2. hous ________	7. sho ________	12. bist ________	17. blak ________
3. wolk ________	8. offe ________	13. lik ________	18. ovir ________
4. gurl ________	9. mak ________	14. haz ________	19. yooz ________
5. toi ________	10. kame ________	15. noze ________	20. whu ________

Gateways to the Body

Read the short story, and write the body parts.

The nose, mouth, and throat are sometimes called "gateways" to the body. Food is ground and chewed in the mouth by the teeth. It is moved around in the mouth and mixed with saliva. The food is then passed down a tube called the esophagus into the stomach.

Much of the air that is breathed enters the body through two openings of the nose. From the nose the air passage turns down toward the throat. There the air enters the windpipe which leads to the lungs.

Write the parts of the drawing.

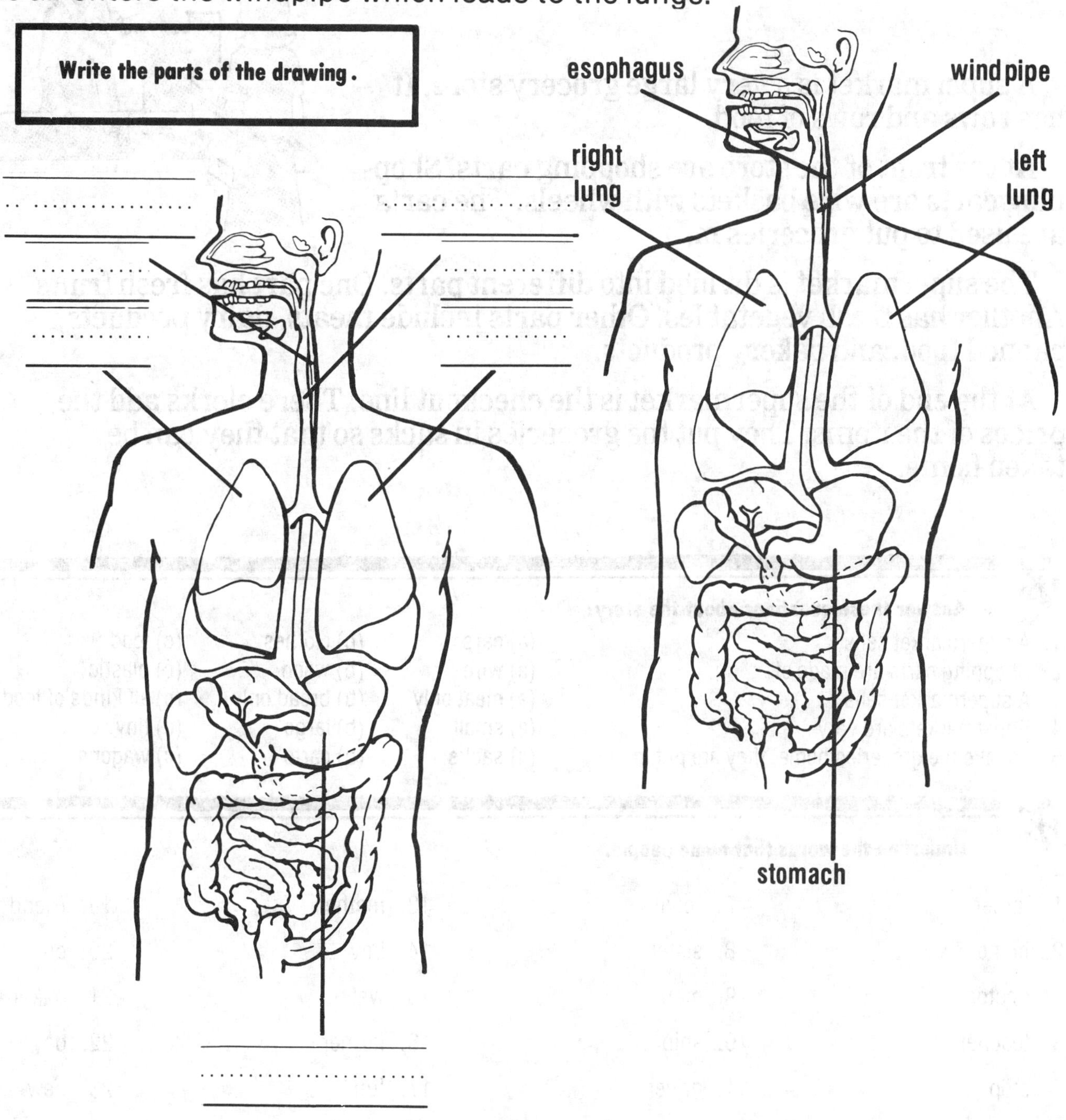

A Trip to the Supermarket

JUST FOR FUN

Vocabulary Study ● Draw a line under each correct answer.

1. If something is large, it is	(a) tiny	(b) small	(c) big.
2. Groceries are	(a) food	(b) clothes	(c) houses.
3. Fresh things are	(a) used	(b) old	(c) new.
4. The price is how much something	(a) weighs	(b) costs	(c) is used.

A supermarket is a very large grocery store. It has rows and rows of food.

At the front of the store are shopping carts. Shopping carts are wire baskets with wheels. The carts are used to put groceries in.

The supermarket is divided into different parts. One part has fresh fruits. Another has fresh vegetables. Other parts include meats, dairy products, canned food, and bakery products.

At the end of the supermarket is the checkout line. There clerks add the prices of the items. They put the groceries in sacks so that they can be taken home.

Answer these questions about the story:

1. A supermarket sells	(a) cars	(b) clothes	(c) food.
2. Shopping carts are made of	(a) wire	(b) wood	(c) plastic.
3. A supermarket sells	(a) meat only	(b) bread only	(c) all kinds of food.
4. Supermarkets are very	(a) small	(b) large	(c) tiny.
5. To take the groceries home, they are put in	(a) sacks	(b) carts	(c) wagons.

Underline the words that name people.

1. father	7. room	13. mother	19. friend
2. home	8. sister	14. boy	20. on
3. doctor	9. man	15. walk	21. baker
4. teacher	10. ship	16. farmer	22. day
5. stop	11. driver	17. fun	23. new
6. woman	12. bird	18. person	24. girl

Making Bread

Read the story, and write the words under the pictures.

Many people help us make our bread. The farmer is a very important person. He takes his wheat to be made into flour. The place where he takes his wheat is known as a mill. Men who work at the mills are called millers. At the mill, the flour is made into white flour or whole-wheat flour to be used later to make bread.

After the flour leaves the mill, it goes to the baker. He adds yeast, salt, shortening, and milk to the flour to make bread. Bakers make several loaves of bread each day. Sometimes your mother may even bake bread at home. This is called homemade bread.

Put the pictures in order by numbering them. Start with the first thing that is done to make bread. Write in each blank "farmer," "miller," "baker," or "mother."

A Trip to a Ranch

Vocabulary Study ● **Draw a line under each correct answer.** JUST FOR FUN

1. The opposite of "big" is	(a) "large"	(b) "huge"	(c) "small."
2. Free from danger means that you are	(a) safe	(b) not safe	(c) dangerous.
3. Cattle are	(a) cows	(b) horses	(c) sheep.
4. The plural of "ranch" is	(a) "ranchs"	(b) "ranches"	(c) "ranchies."

A ranch is a big farm. Cattle and sheep are raised on a ranch.

On a cattle ranch cowboys look after the cattle. They make sure that the cattle are safe. They make sure that the cattle are healthy.

Each calf is branded. The brand is the mark of the ranch.

Cowboys live in the bunkhouse. Sometimes they camp out on the range.

The rancher and his family live in a ranch house. The rancher owns the ranch. He buys and sells the cattle.

There are many ranches in Texas. Most ranches are in the West.

Answer these questions about the story:

1. A ranch is a	(a) person	(b) small farm	(c) big farm.
2. Ranches raise	(a) cattle	(b) cotton	(c) rice.
3. The mark of the ranch is the	(a) brand	(b) X	(c) sign.
4. The owner of the ranch is the	(a) cowboy	(b) rancher	(c) farmer.
5. Most ranches are in the	(a) South	(b) North	(c) West.

Underline the words that name places.

1. farm	7. ranch	13. box	19. table
2. man	8. country	14. city	20. town
3. home	9. mother	15. word	21. bakery
4. cow	10. hospital	16. office	22. car
5. school	11. bus	17. airport	23. dairy
6. ear	12. road	18. nurse	24. day

A Good Citizen

A good citizen is a kind and thoughtful person.

A Write the words that tell how a good citizen needs to be.

polite ______ clean ______ thoughtful ______

selfish ______ cross ______ respectful ______

honest ______ kind ______ unselfish ______

helpful ______ truthful ______ friendly ______

A good citizen does not think of only himself.
He does good deeds for others.

B Write the things that you think a good citizen would do.

always be first ______ respect the flag ______

work well ______ be lazy ______

never be late ______ play safely ______

talk while others talk ______ listen well ______

get along with others ______ never be on time ______

think of others ______ take from others ______

tear up things ______ obey rules ______

The Police Officer

Vocabulary Study ● **Draw a line under each correct answer.** **JUST FOR FUN**

1. The opposite of "lost" is	(a) "found"	(b) "looking for"	(c) "gone."
2. If you obey the rules, you	(a) follow them	(b) break them	(c) make them.
3. If you are on duty, you are	(a) at home	(b) at work	(c) at school.
4. "Protect" means	(a) "to see"	(b) "to watch over"	(c) "to hurt."

A police officer is an officer of the law. He has many duties. He helps people in trouble. He directs traffic. He keeps order at a parade. He helps lost children find their parents. He is always there to help. He sees that people obey the laws.

Some police officers ride in cars. Some ride in helicopters. Some ride motorcycles. Some ride horses. Many police officers walk when on duty.

Most police officers wear blue uniforms. There are always police officers on duty. Day and night police officers protect us.

Answer these questions about the story:

1. A police officer helps	(a) lost children	(b) parents	(c) people in trouble.
2. An officer sees that people	(a) obey laws	(b) break laws	(c) change laws.
3. A police officer rides	(a) in a car	(b) in a helicopter	(c) on a horse.
4. Most officers' uniforms are	(a) red	(b) blue	(c) green.
5. Police officers work	(a) only at night	(b) only in the daytime	(c) day and night.

Unscramble each set of letters to make a word.

1. oyu ________	7. ym ________	13. kys ________
2. gbi ________	8. erte ________	14. cra ________
3. adn ________	9. ese ________	15. lkta ________
4. oobk ________	10. gdo ________	16. nmae ________
5. pu ________	11. omeh ________	17. eta ________
6. npe ________	12. biek ________	18. foto ________

Family Helpers Test

A **Answer the following questions. Use the words from the box. Circle each word used.**

1. Who helps us when we are sick? ______ doctor ______
2. Who grinds grain into flour? ____________________
3. Who puts out fires? ____________________
4. Who delivers milk to our houses? ____________________
5. Who grows wheat to make bread? ____________________
6. Who helps us take care of our teeth? ____________________
7. Who helps us keep our house looking pretty? ____________________

fireman
doctor
painter
dentist
milkman
farmer
miller

B **Complete the following statements by filling in the blanks. Use the words from the box. Circle each word used.**

1. An ____________ fixes our lights, televisions, and radios.
2. A ____________ puts bathrooms and kitchens in houses.
3. A person who fixes our shoes is known as a ____________.
4. We can buy bread and cookies at a ____________.
5. The colors of our flag are ________, ________, and ________.
6. The milkman works for a ____________.
7. A home is made up of a ____________.

electrician
blue
bakery
red
family
dairy
white
cobbler
plumber

The Fire Fighter

Vocabulary Study ● Draw a line under each correct answer. **JUST FOR FUN**

1. A person who rushes is (a) in a hurry (b) slow (c) happy.
2. If something is heavy, it (a) is easy to carry (b) is hard to carry (c) flies.
3. "Always" means (a) "some of the time" (b) "never" (c) "all of the time."
4. If something is dangerous, it is (a) easy (b) not safe (c) safe.

A fire fighter has a very dangerous job. Whenever a fire starts, the fire fighter rushes to put it out.

The fire fighter wears special clothes. He wears heavy rubber boots. The clothes and boots protect the fire fighter from heat and water. The fire fighter always wears a hat.

The fire fighter must always be ready to fight a fire. When on duty, he lives at the fire station. He eats and sleeps there. When the alarm bell rings, the fire fighter hurries to the truck. He helps save many lives.

Answer these questions about the story:

1. A fire fighter's job is (a) fun (b) dangerous (c) easy work.
2. A fire fighter (a) saves lives (b) sets fires (c) builds fires.
3. A fire fighter always wears (a) warm clothes (b) special clothes (c) red clothes.
4. When on duty, a fire fighter lives (a) at home (b) at the fire station (c) on the truck.
5. Fire fighters ride (a) in cars (b) in airplanes (c) on trucks.

Add "s" to each word.

1. fire ________
2. truck ________
3. hat ________
4. bell ________
5. home ________
6. tree ________
7. coat ________
8. flag ________
9. shoe ________
10. boot ________
11. name ________
12. car ________
13. word ________
14. desk ________
15. train ________
16. bird ________
17. apple ________
18. gate ________

A Good Citizenship Test

Answer each statement yes or no. Circle the answer.

1. A good citizen pushes people in line. YES NO
2. Boys and girls should work and play. YES NO
3. Some citizens are women. YES NO
4. Some citizens are men. YES NO
5. Good citizens obey helpful rules. YES NO
6. A good citizen is polite. YES NO
7. Children should always be selfish. YES NO
8. People should respect the flag. YES NO
9. Boys and girls are citizens. YES NO
10. Children should share their toys. YES NO
11. Honest citizens tell the truth. YES NO
12. Good citizens are good neighbors. YES NO
13. A bad citizen is not kind to others. YES NO
14. Citizenship Day is every day. YES NO
15. Boys and girls should play all the time. YES NO
16. A good citizen is nice to the neighbors. YES NO
17. Boys and girls should get into fights. YES NO
18. Good citizens should try to get along with others. YES NO
19. Boys and girls should work all the time. YES NO
20. A good citizen knows the Pledge of Allegiance. YES NO

The Doctor

Vocabulary Study ● **Draw a line under each correct answer.** JUST FOR FUN

1. A sick person is	(a) not well	(b) well	(c) healthy.
2. "Listen" means	(a) "to talk"	(b) "to hear"	(c) "to help."
3. "Stay" means	(a) "to change"	(b) "to keep the same"	(c) "to move."
4. Something that is right is	(a) bad	(b) wrong	(c) good.

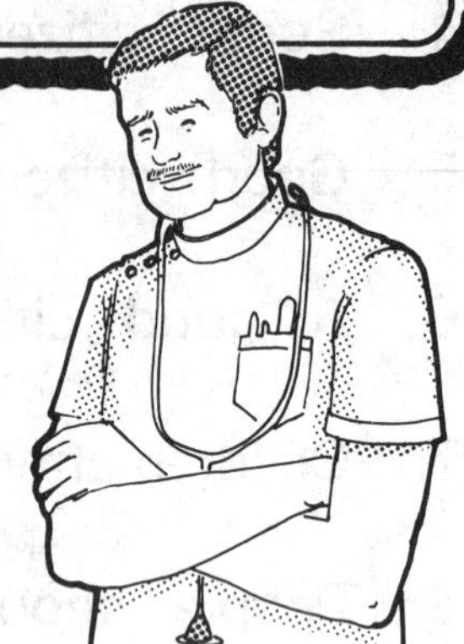

A doctor is a person. He helps sick people. He tells people how to keep from getting sick.

The doctor listens to his patient. He wants to find out what is wrong. Then he checks the patient. He listens to the heart. He checks the lungs. He takes the person's temperature. He checks the eyes and ears. He looks at the throat.

If a person is very sick, the doctor sends him to the hospital. The doctor visits him in the hospital.

The doctor tells people how to stay healthy. He tells them to eat the right foods. He wants them to exercise. He tells them to rest.

The doctor is a friend. He wants to help people.

Answer these questions about the story:

1. A doctor is a	(a) person	(b) place	(c) thing.
2. A person who sees the doctor is a	(a) patient	(b) nurse	(c) customer.
3. The doctor checks the	(a) heart	(b) lungs	(c) throat.
4. Very sick people go	(a) home	(b) to the hospital	(c) to school.
5. To stay healthy, people should	(a) eat right	(b) exercise	(c) rest.

Draw a line to connect the words that sound alike.

1. son	four	7. know	road	13. by	buy
2. to	sun	8. new	blew	14. write	deer
3. for	two	9. rode	no	15. here	right
4. ate	see	10. red	knew	16. week	weak
5. sea	bee	11. blue	meat	17. dear	hear
6. be	eight	12. meet	read	18. it's	its

Who Got Them?

When you want to know something, you ask questions. Most questions begin with "who," "what," "where," "when," "why," or "how."

A Use the picture to answer the following questions about "The Case of the Missing Cookies."

1. What happened? ______________________________

2. Where were they? ______________________________

3. When were they taken? ______________________________

4. How many were taken? ______________________________

5. Who got them? ______________________________

B Use your imagination to make up and answer questions about something that happened to you today.

1. Who ______________? ______________________________

2. What ______________? ______________________________

3. Where ______________? ______________________________

The Sea Horse

Vocabulary Study ● Draw a line under each correct answer. JUST FOR FUN

1. If something is tiny, it is (a) big (b) small (c) long.
2. "Hide" means (a) "to keep out of sight" (b) "to see" (c) "to find."
3. If something is changed, it is (a) the same (b) not the same (c) good as new.
4. "Cannot" means (a) "able" (b) "not able" (c) "to do."

The sea horse is a tiny fish. It does not look like a fish. Its head looks like that of a horse. Its tail is long. The sea horse uses its tail to hang onto plants.

The sea horse has no teeth. It sucks in tiny pieces of food that float by.

Big fish like to eat sea horses. Sea horses hide in seaweed so that the big fish cannot see them. Some sea horses can even change color. The tiny sea horses are helpless against the big fish. They cannot fight.

Answer these questions about the story:

1. The sea horse is a (a) horse (b) tiny fish (c) big fish.
2. The sea horse's head looks like that of a (a) horse (b) fish (c) plant.
3. The sea horse uses its tail (a) to swim (b) to eat (c) to hang onto plants.
4. For protection the sea horse (a) bites (b) swims away (c) hides.
5. Sea horses cannot (a) fight (b) swim (c) eat.

Unscramble each set of letters to make a word.

1. nsu ________
2. hta ________
3. nads ________
4. ew ________
5. oolk ________
6. geg ________
7. esy ________
8. ybo ________
9. psto ________
10. nra ________
11. lkmi ________
12. yee ________
13. sbu ________
14. nrai ________
15. rlgi ________
16. tca ________
17. albl ________
18. xbo ________

Stars

Stars are huge shining balls like the sun. They go together and make pictures in the sky. These pictures are called constellations.

Draw lines to connect the stars and make the pictures.

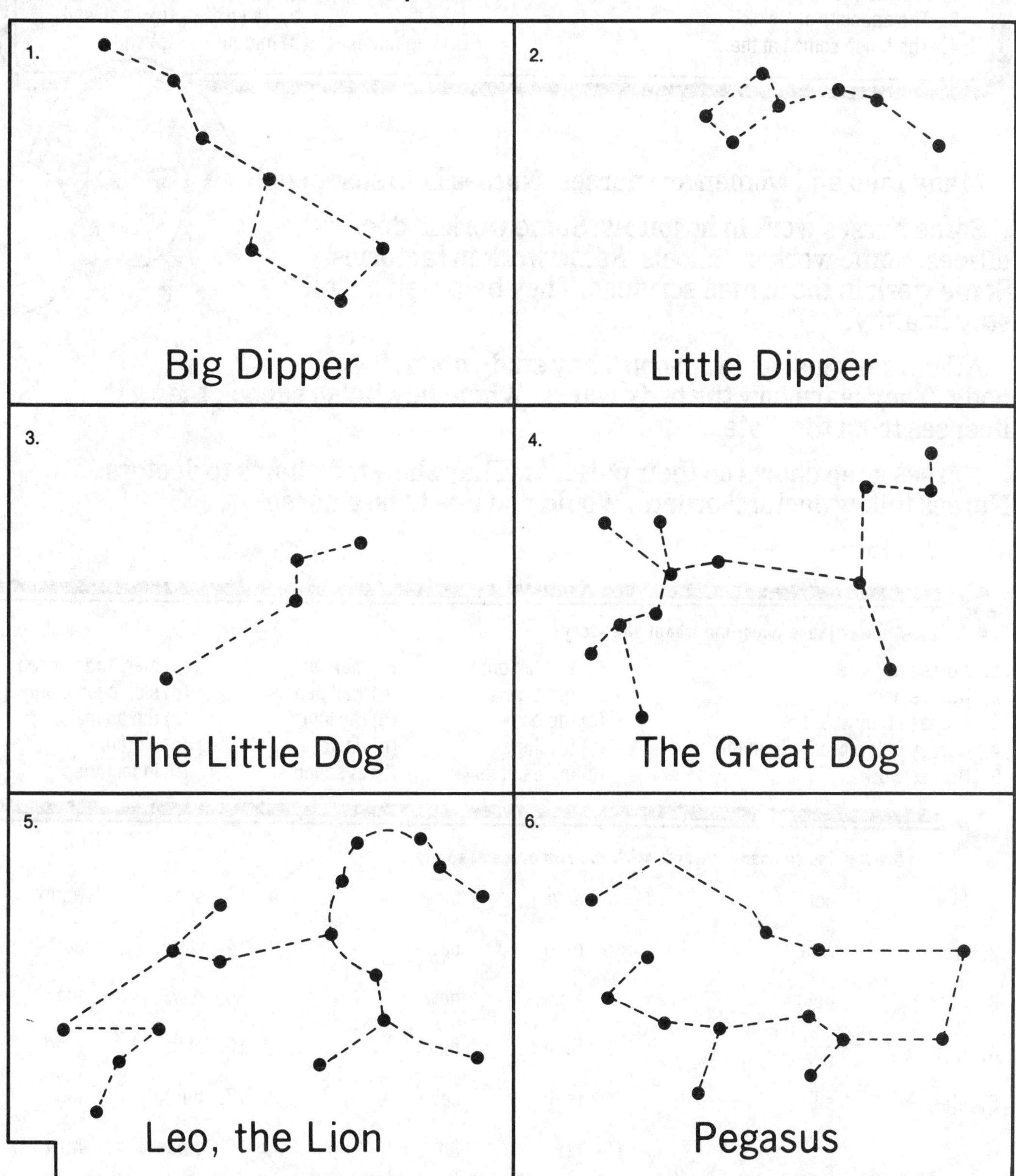

Nurses

JUST FOR FUN

Vocabulary Study ● Draw a line under each correct answer.

1. The plural of "man" is	(a) "mans"	(b) "man"	(c) "men."
2. A place where the sick are cared for is the	(a) hospital	(b) office	(c) factory.
3. The opposite of "sick" is	(a) "ill"	(b) "well"	(c) "not well."
4. The finish comes at the	(a) beginning	(b) middle	(c) end.

Many men and women are nurses. Nurses help sick people.

Some nurses work in hospitals. Some work in doctors' offices. Some work in schools. Some work in factories. Some work in the armed services. They help well people stay healthy.

All nurses must go to school. They study about the body. They learn how the body works. When they finish school, they get licenses from the state.

Nurses keep charts on their patients. They show the charts to doctors. Nurses follow doctors' orders. Would you like to be a nurse?

Answer these questions about the story:

1. Nurses are	(a) women only	(b) men only	(c) men and women.
2. Nurses help	(a) the sick	(b) well people	(c) sick people only.
3. Nurses study about	(a) the body	(b) the land	(c) the animals.
4. Nurses follow orders from the	(a) teachers	(b) doctors	(c) workers.
5. Nurses work	(a) in hospitals	(b) in schools	(c) in factories.

Draw a line to connect words with the same vowel sounds.

1. like	cat	7. save	blow	13. see	hand
2. way	ride	8. men	bet	14. vine	eat
3. at	hold	9. know	new	15. row	toe
4. goat	hay	10. blue	teeth	16. man	kind
5. she	sit	11. feet	cave	17. nurse	face
6. hit	he	12. rat	fat	18. place	hurt

Types of Flying Things

Some of these things fly in the air. Write the names of the pictures in the blanks. Draw circles around the ones that fly. Color them with bright colors.

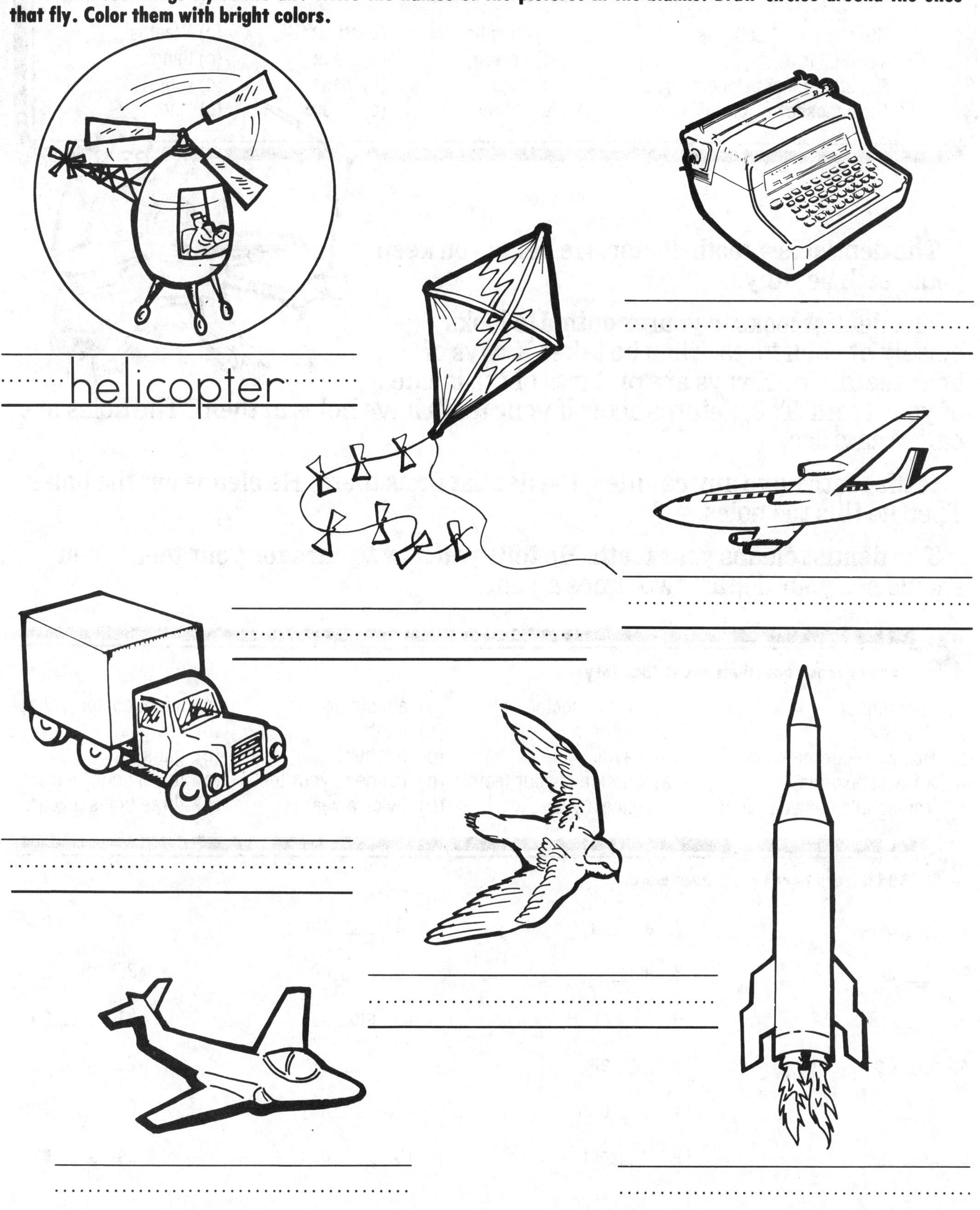

The Dentist

Vocabulary Study ● Draw a line under each correct answer. **JUST FOR FUN**

1. The plural of "tooth" is	(a) "tooths"	(b) "teeth"	(c) "teeths."
2. A dentist is a	(a) person	(b) place	(c) thing.
3. Something that belongs to you is	(a) hers	(b) theirs	(c) yours.
4. The opposite of "clean" is	(a) "dirty"	(b) "pure"	(c) "neat."

The dentist is a tooth doctor. He helps you keep your teeth healthy.

The dentist looks in your mouth. He looks closely at each tooth. Then he takes X rays of your teeth. The X rays are pictures of the insides of your teeth. The pictures show if your teeth have holes in them. The holes are called cavities.

If the teeth have any cavities, the dentist fixes them. He cleans out the holes. Then he fills the holes.

The dentist cleans your teeth. He tells you how to care for your teeth. You should see your dentist two times a year.

Answer these questions about the story:

1. The dentist is	(a) an eye doctor	(b) a tooth doctor	(c) a foot doctor.
2. X rays are	(a) pictures	(b) teeth	(c) cavities.
3. Holes in your teeth are	(a) cavities	(b) ditches	(c) gaps.
4. X rays show the	(a) outside of your teeth	(b) inside of your teeth	(c) top of your teeth.
5. You should see your dentist	(a) once a year	(b) twice a year	(c) three times a year.

Add letters to complete each word.

1. ____oor	7. a____ay	13. ____ain	19. ____ff
2. ____or	8. lio____	14. ____ith	20. gi____e
3. a____	9. ____ot	15. sto____	21. ____ere
4. b____g	10. ____alk	16. ____ow	22. goo____
5. o____e	11. ____ush	17. ____ite	23. ____ome
6. bo____	12. ____our	18. ____ook	24. ____est

Colors

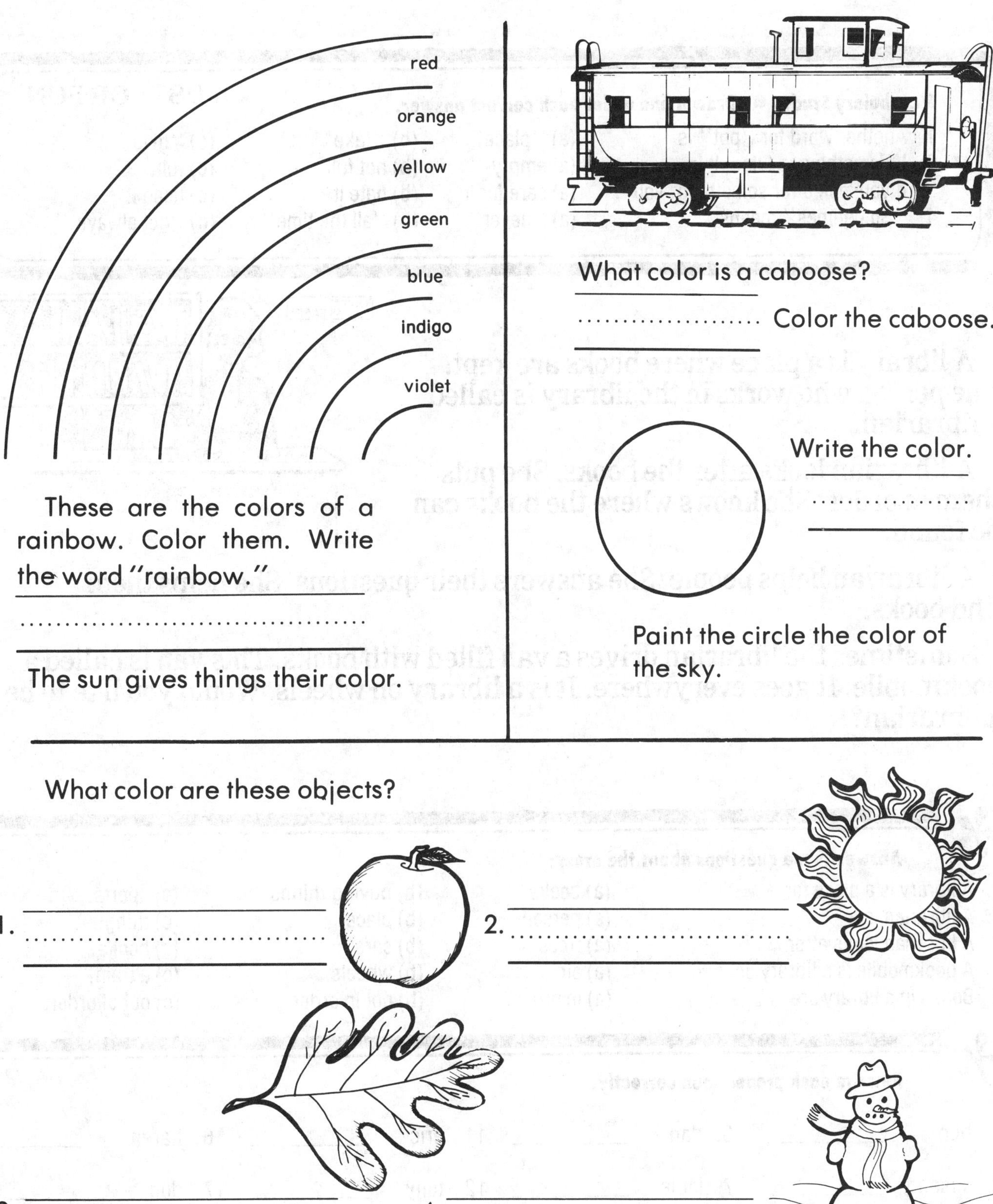

These are the colors of a rainbow. Color them. Write the word "rainbow."

The sun gives things their color.

What color is a caboose?

Color the caboose.

Write the color.

Paint the circle the color of the sky.

What color are these objects?

1.

2.

3.

4.

What color do you like best?

The Librarian

Vocabulary Study ● Draw a line under each correct answer. JUST FOR FUN

1. Another word for "put" is (a) "place" (b) "take" (c) "give."
2. If something is filled, it is (a) empty (b) not full (c) full.
3. If you look after something, you (a) care for it (b) hate it (c) need it.
4. "Sometimes" means (a) "never" (b) "all the time" (c) "not always."

A library is a place where books are kept. The person who works in the library is called a librarian.

A librarian looks after the books. She puts them in order. She knows where the books can be found.

A librarian helps people. She answers their questions. She helps them find books.

Sometimes the librarian drives a van filled with books. This van is called a bookmobile. It goes everywhere. It is a library on wheels. Would you like to be a librarian?

Answer these questions about the story:

1. A library is a place for (a) books (b) buying things (c) sports.
2. A librarian is a (a) person (b) place (c) thing.
3. A librarian looks after (a) trees (b) cars (c) books.
4. A bookmobile is a library on (a) air (b) wheels (c) a train.
5. Books in a library are (a) in order (b) not in order (c) out of order.

*

Rewrite each proper noun correctly.

1. bob ________	6. dan ________	11. eric ________	16. karen ________
2. susan ________	7. louie ________	12. tony ________	17. donna ________
3. cindy ________	8. ken ________	13. pam ________	18. liz ________
4. joe ________	9. alex ________	14. ron ________	19. dave ________
5. larry ________	10. mark ________	15. doug ________	20. nancy ______

Different Sounds We Hear

Draw a line from each picture to its name. Write it.

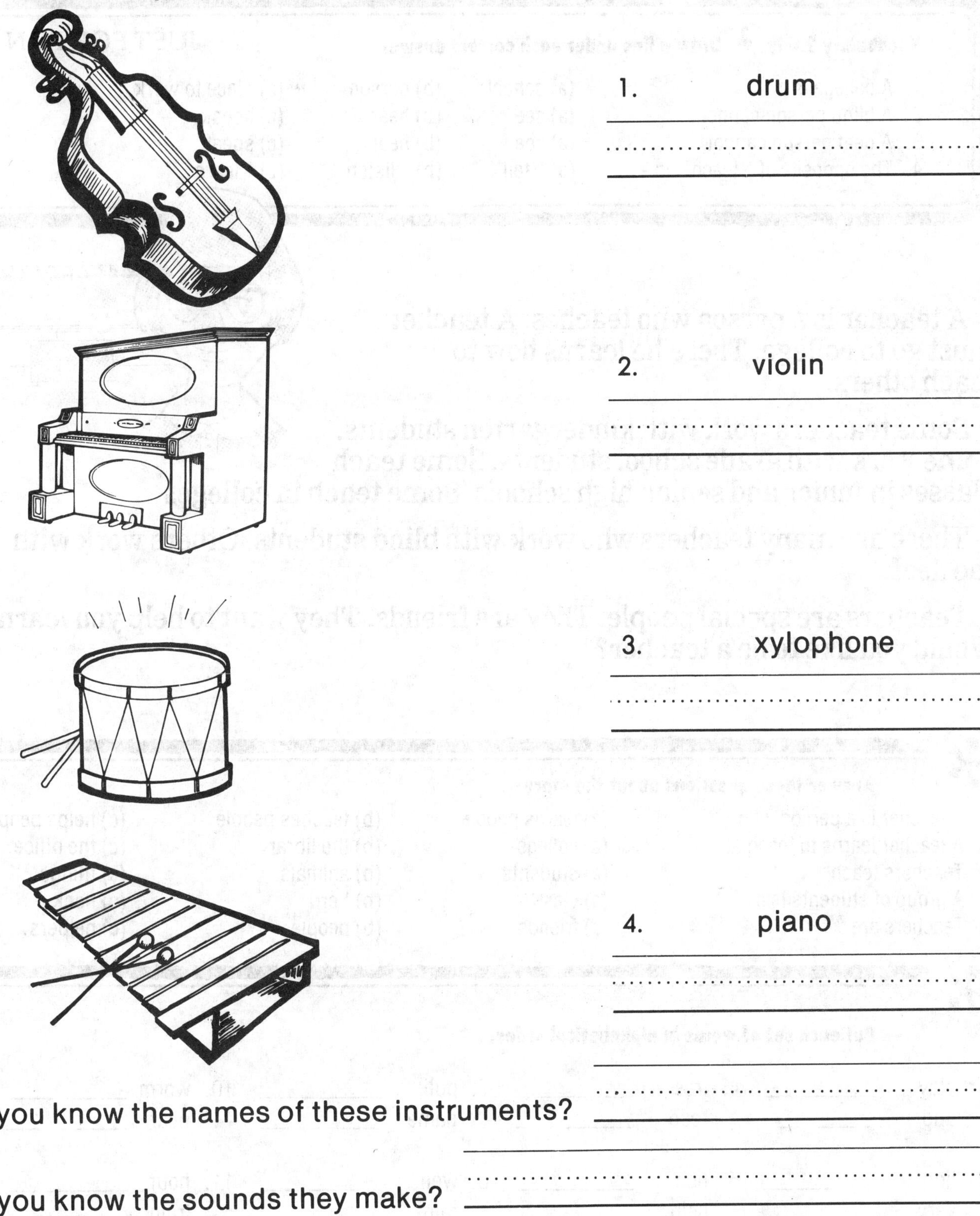

1. drum

2. violin

3. xylophone

4. piano

Do you know the names of these instruments?

Do you know the sounds they make?

Can you play a musical instrument?

The Teacher

Vocabulary Study ● **Draw a line under each correct answer.** JUST FOR FUN

1. A college is a (a) school (b) person (c) place to work.
2. A blind person cannot (a) see (b) hear (c) speak.
3. A deaf person cannot (a) see (b) hear (c) speak.
4. The opposite of ''teach'' is (a) ''tell'' (b) ''listen'' (c) ''learn.''

A teacher is a person who teaches. A teacher must go to college. There he learns how to teach others.

Some teachers work with kindergarten students. Some work with grade school students. Some teach classes in junior and senior high schools. Some teach in colleges.

There are many teachers who work with blind students. Others work with the deaf.

Teachers are special people. They are friends. They want to help you learn. Would you like to be a teacher?

Answer these questions about the story:

1. A teacher is a person who (a) learns people (b) teaches people (c) helps people.
2. A teacher learns to teach at (a) college (b) the library (c) the office.
3. Teachers teach (a) students (b) animals (c) things.
4. A group of students is a (a) class (b) herd (c) flock.
5. Teachers are (a) friends (b) people (c) helpers.

Put each set of words in alphabetical order.

1. play ____ and ____
2. lion ____ very ____
3. home ____ bird ____
4. tree ____ rose ____
5. fish ____ help ____
6. shoe ____ wood ____
7. pull ____ game ____
8. well ____ rain ____
9. fun ____ each ____
10. worm ____ near ____
11. hour ____ train ____
12. pole ____ soon ____

Machines with Wheels

Some machines have wheels on them. The wheels make them work faster. Count the wheels on each machine. Write the number under the picture. Color the wheels black.

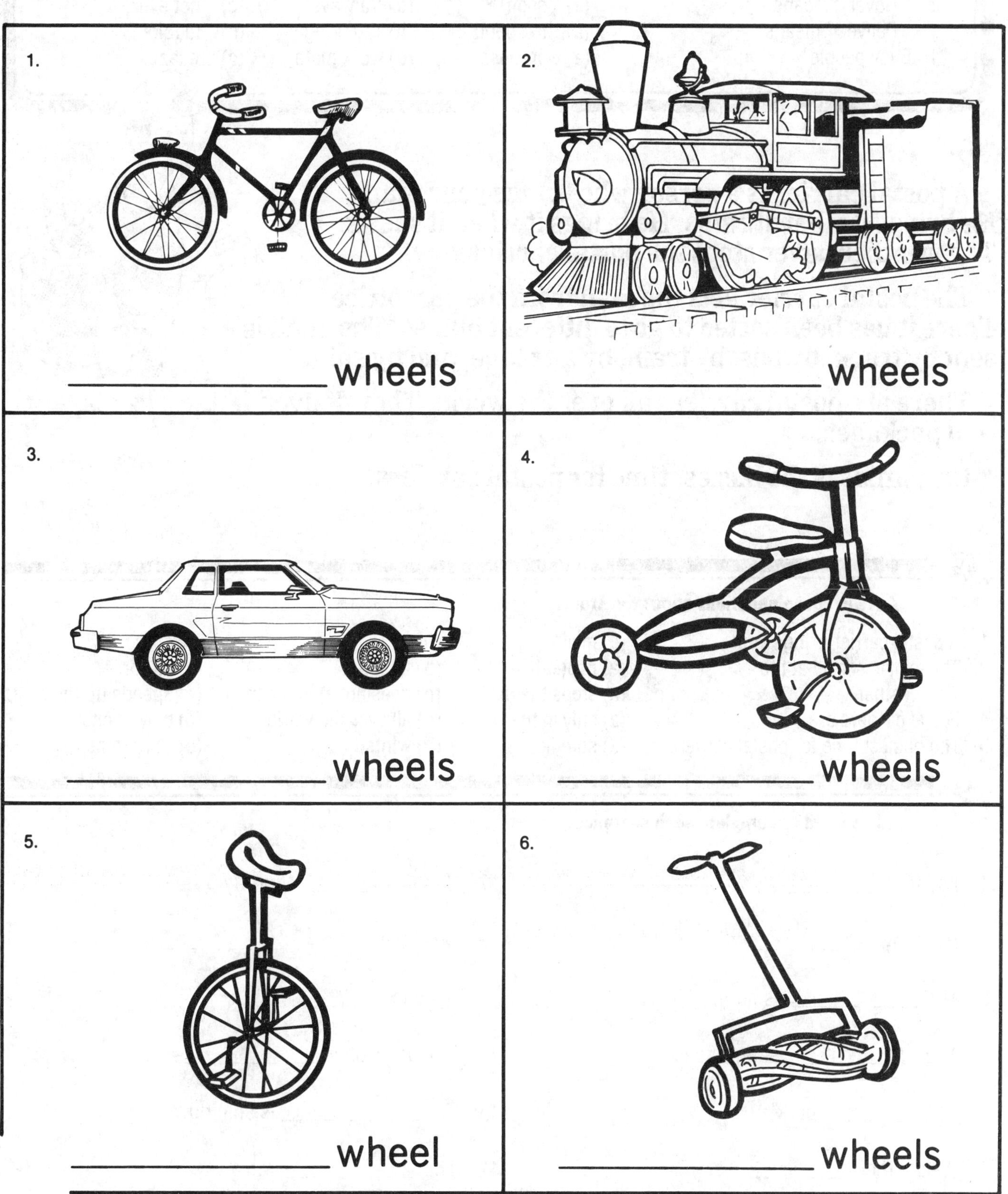

The Postal Carrier

Vocabulary Study ● **Draw a line under each correct answer.** **JUST FOR FUN**

1. Letters and packages are called	(a) mail	(b) male	(c) postal carriers.
2. ''Never'' means	(a) ''soon''	(b) ''always''	(c) ''not ever.''
3. ''Deliver'' means	(a) ''to spend''	(b) ''to bring''	(c) ''to take.''
4. Busy people	(a) work less	(b) work more	(c) are lazy.

A postal carrier is a person who brings your mail. He brings it when it rains. He brings it when it snows. The weather never stops the postal carrier.

The postal carrier gets the mail from the post office. There it has been sorted to go to different places. The mail is sent by truck, by bus, by train, by airplane, and by ship.

There are postal carriers all over the world. They deliver letters, cards, and packages.

Christmas is the busiest time for postal carriers.

Answer these questions about the story:

1. A postal carrier brings your	(a) mail	(b) milk	(c) groceries.
2. The mail is sorted at the	(a) post office	(b) factory	(c) airport.
3. The weather	(a) stops the mail	(b) does not stop the mail	(c) speeds up the mail.
4. Postal carriers are	(a) only in the U.S.	(b) all over the world	(c) only in cities.
5. The busiest time for postal carriers is	(a) summer	(b) winter	(c) Christmas.

Add a word to complete each sentence.

1. I go to ____________.
2. He is my ____________.
3. The ____________ is here.
4. The ____________ sang a song.
5. ____________ bark.
6. We ate the ____________.
7. Susan ____________ pretty.
8. Mrs. Davis is my ____________.
9. I like to ____________.
10. The boy looked ____________.
11. The ____________ is shining.
12. The ____________ ran away.

Inventions We Use

New machines made by man are called inventions. Do you know an inventor? These machines were invented. What are they? Write their names.

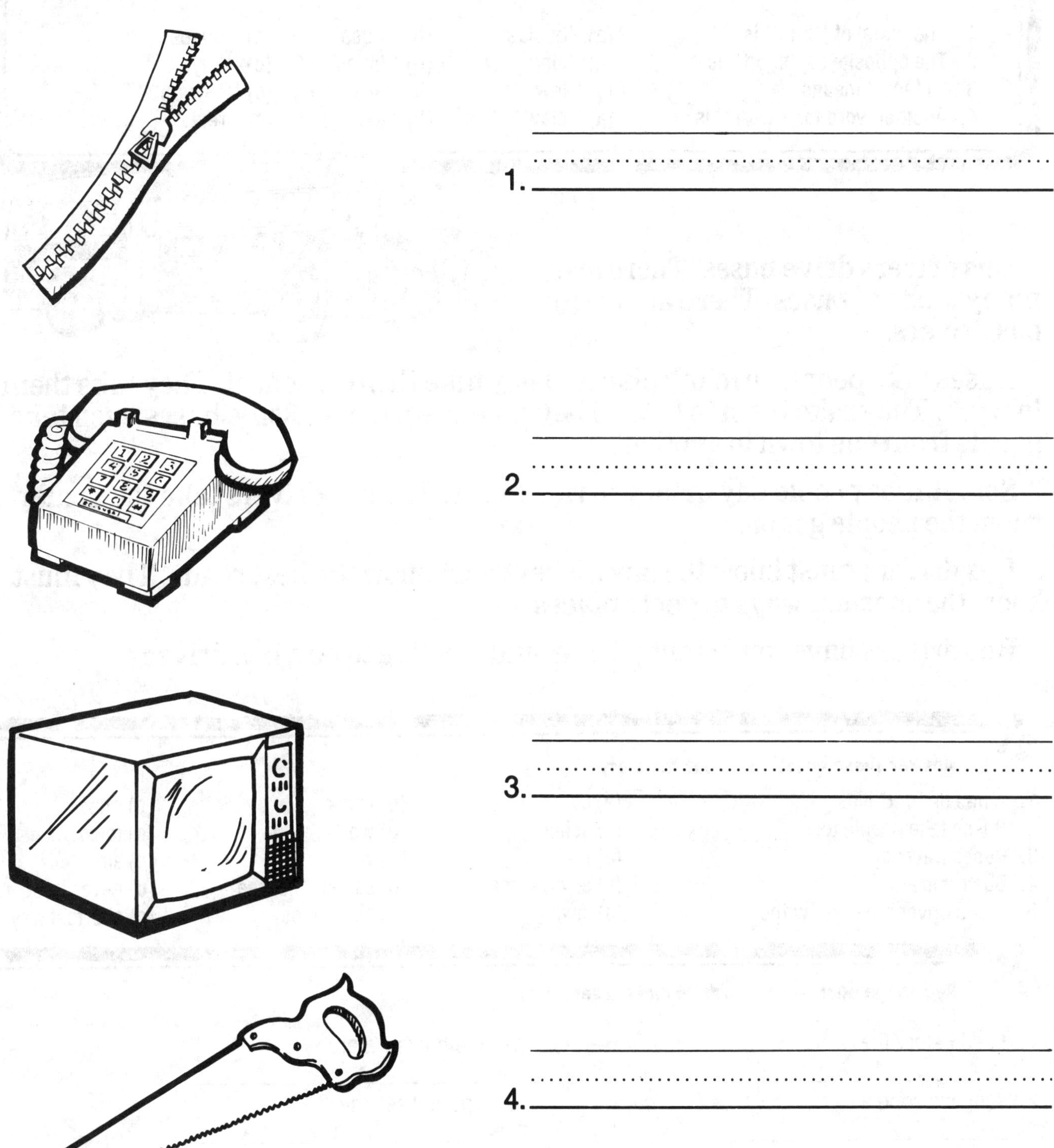

Bus Drivers

Vocabulary Study ● Draw a line under each correct answer. JUST FOR FUN

1. The plural of "bus" is	(a) "busies"	(b) "buss"	(c) "buses."
2. The opposite of "short" is	(a) "long"	(b) "little"	(c) "tiny."
3. "Many" means	(a) "few"	(b) "one"	(c) "several."
4. Another word for "work" is	(a) "play"	(b) "job"	(c) "rest."

Bus drivers drive buses. There are many kinds of buses. There are many bus drivers.

Buses take people to many places. They take them to school. They take them to work. They take them to town. They take them home. Some buses even take people from one town to another.

Sometimes people pay money to ride buses. The bus drivers take the money when the people get on.

Bus drivers must know the laws. They must know the best roads. They must know the shortest ways to get to places.

Bus drivers have important jobs. Would you like to be a bus driver?

Answer these questions about the story:

1. A bus driver drives a	(a) car	(b) truck	(c) bus.
2. Buses take people to	(a) school	(b) work	(c) town.
3. Buses travel on	(a) roads	(b) water	(c) air.
4. Bus rides are	(a) always free	(b) sometimes free	(c) never free.
5. A bus driver must know the	(a) laws	(b) best roads	(c) shortest ways.

Rearrange each set of words to make a sentence.

1. liked I story the ____________________
2. sang we song a ____________________
3. sky blue the is ____________________
4. here Carl is ____________________
5. the hot is water ____________________
6. I puppy see the ____________________
7. here come ____________________
8. made Ann cake the ____________________

Electricity in Your Home

Electricity runs our machines. It makes our work easier. Name the electrical appliances. Draw a line from each machine to the object it makes for us.

1. __r________________

a.

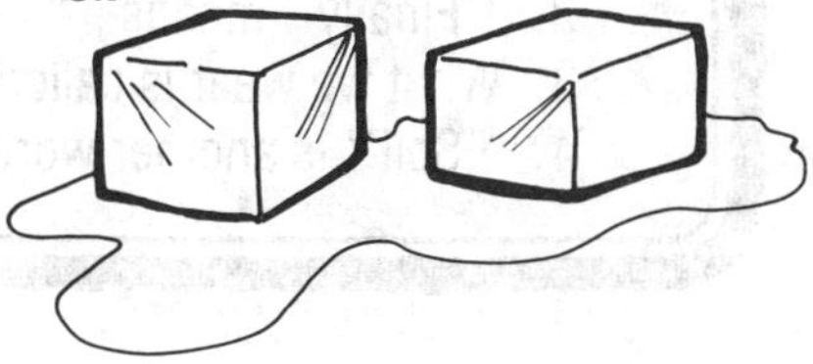

2.  __r________________

b.

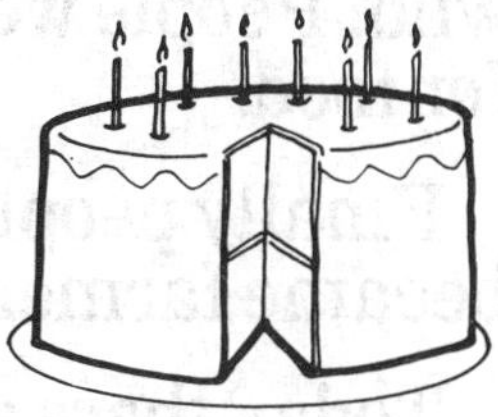

3.  __i________________

c.

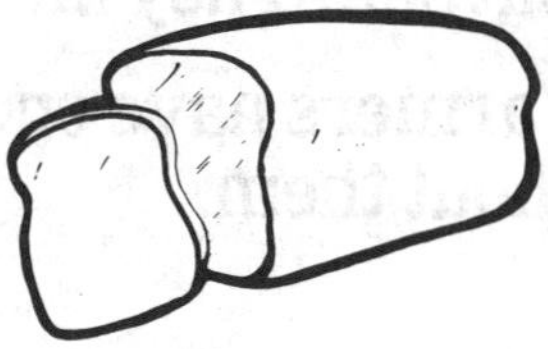

4.  __t________________

d.

5.  __m________________

e.

The Farmer

JUST FOR FUN

Vocabulary Study ● Draw a line under each correct answer.

1. The opposite of "there" is	(a) "away"	(b) "here"	(c) "far."
2. "Finally" means	(a) "first"	(b) "start"	(c) "last."
3. What we wear is called	(a) clothes	(b) food	(c) houses.
4. "Soil" is another word for	(a) "sky"	(b) "water"	(c) "land."

Long ago there were no farmers. Everything grew wild. People were always moving. They were looking for food.

Finally people learned how to grow food. They became farmers.

Today there are still farmers. They produce the food we eat. They grow the materials for our clothes and houses.

Farmers work hard. They do more than work the land. They take care of animals. They take care of machines. They sell their products. They know about soil. They know about weather.

Farmers have one of the most important jobs in the world. We could not live without them.

Answer these questions about the story:

1. Long ago people moved around to look for	(a) food	(b) more land	(c) the sun.
2. Farmers take care of	(a) animals	(b) machines	(c) the land.
3. Farmers must know about	(a) the soil	(b) the land	(c) the weather.
4. A farmer is a	(a) person	(b) place	(c) thing.
5. A farmer's job is	(a) important	(b) not important	(c) silly.

Connect the words that rhyme.

1. word	door	7. air	pear	13. they	run
2. long	sky	8. tax	land	14. must	dust
3. floor	bird	9. look	wax	15. sun	hay
4. fly	song	10. hand	tall	16. still	give
5. keep	sleep	11. beg	leg	17. grow	so
6. burn	turn	12. wall	book	18. live	hill

Birds We See

Birds are fun to watch. Most birds help us by eating harmful insects. Most birds are pretty. They sing for us. Some birds can talk and do tricks. Birds eat worms, berries, seeds, and bugs. What are these birds eating?

Use the words from the box.

The Airplane Pilot

Vocabulary Study ● Draw a line under each correct answer. **JUST FOR FUN**

1. The opposite of "small" is	(a) "tiny"	(b) "large"	(c) "smaller."
2. The first is at the	(a) beginning	(b) middle	(c) end.
3. The finish is at the	(a) beginning	(b) middle	(c) end.
4. "Well" means	(a) "bad"	(b) "good"	(c) "wrong."

The person who flies an airplane is called a pilot. The airplane pilot has a very important job.

A pilot must go to flight school. There he learns all about airplanes. He learns about weather and maps.

At first the pilot must fly with a teacher. He must practice so that he can fly well.

When he learns to fly small planes, the pilot may go to another school. There he can learn to fly bigger planes.

A pilot must take many tests before finishing school. He must show his teachers how well he can fly. Have you ever wanted to be an airplane pilot?

Answer these questions about the story:

1. A person who flies an airplane is a	(a) pilot	(b) driver	(c) sailor.
2. A pilot learns to fly	(a) in school	(b) on TV	(c) by reading books.
3. At first a pilot flies	(a) alone	(b) with a teacher	(c) with a group.
4. Pilots first fly	(a) small planes	(b) big planes	(c) model planes.
5. In flight school, pilots learn about	(a) weather	(b) maps	(c) airplanes.

Underline the best definitions.

1. follow	(a) go first	(b) go after	6. zero.....	(a) none	(b) one
2. both	(a) one	(b) two	7. right	(a) correct	(b) wrong
3. wash.....	(a) make clean	(b) make dirty	8. pick.....	(a) give	(b) choose
4. want	(a) need	(b) wish for	9. near	(a) close	(b) far
5. hour	(a) 30 minutes	(b) 60 minutes	10. jump	(a) hop	(b) run

Machines Around Us

scissors	tractor	shovel	bicycle
truck	ladder	airplane	crane
typewriter	hammer		

These are machines. Color the machines that you have used. Write the names. Use the words from the box.

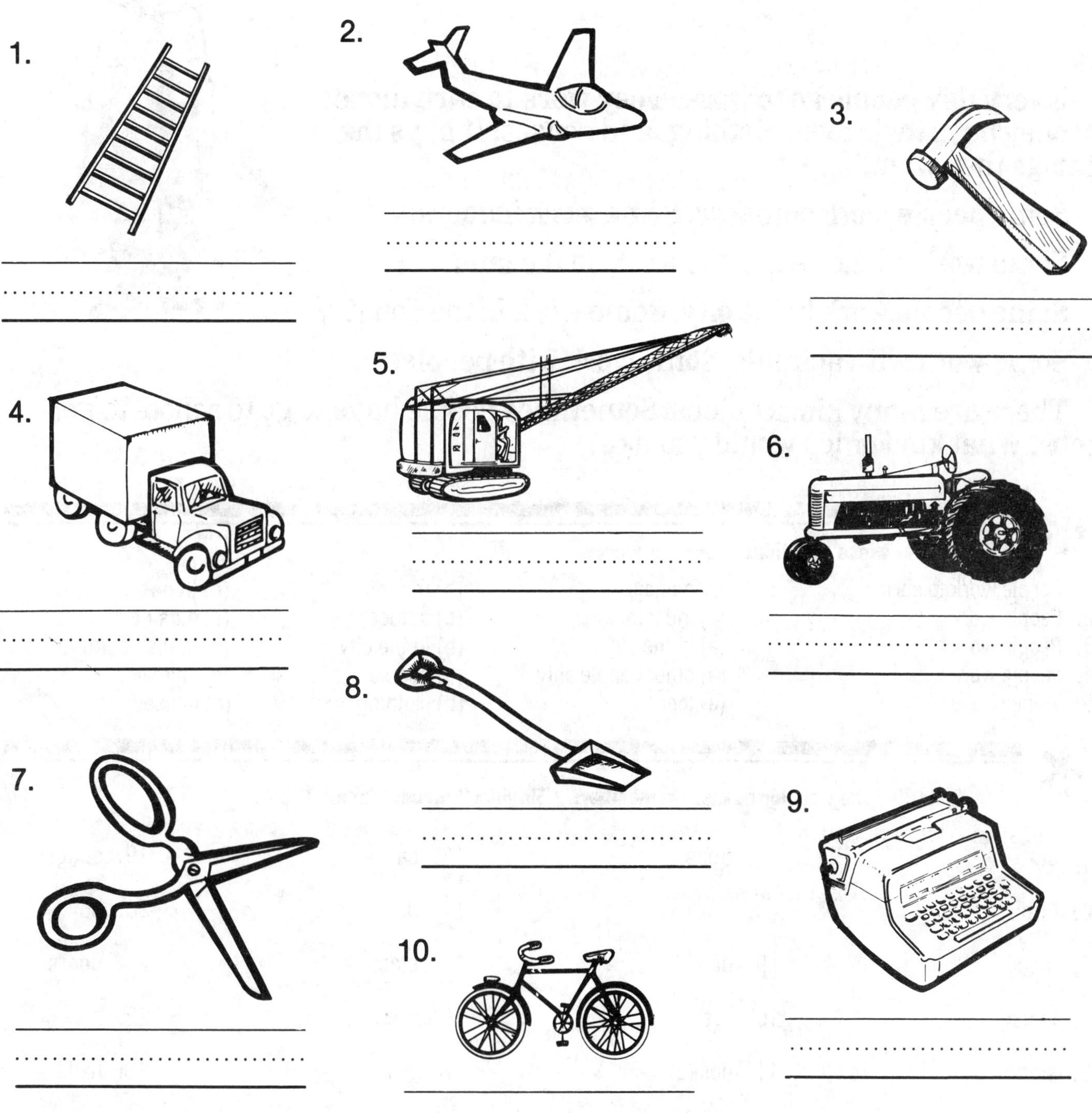

People at Work

Vocabulary Study ● **Draw a line under each correct answer.** JUST FOR FUN

1. The opposite of "buy" is (a) "sell" (b) "use" (c) "have."
2. "Outdoors" is the same as (a) "indoors" (b) "inside" (c) "outside."
3. A place where you learn is a (a) school (b) home (c) job.
4. The opposite of "city" is (a) "town" (b) "water" (c) "country."

Every day people go to work. They work to earn money. Money buys their food, clothing, and houses. It buys the things they want.

Some people work outdoors. Some work indoors.

Some work on the sea. Some work on the land.

Some people work in the city. Some work in the country.

Some work with animals. Some work with people.

There are many kinds of jobs. Sometimes people have to go to school to get jobs. What kind of job would you like?

Answer these questions about the story:

1. People work to earn (a) money (b) friends (c) things.
2. People work (a) indoors (b) outdoors (c) outside only.
3. People work (a) in the city only (b) in the city (c) in the country.
4. People work with (a) other people only (b) people (c) animals.
5. Money buys (a) food (b) clothing (c) houses.

Underline the singular nouns. (Remember: "Singular" means "one.")

1. car
2. birds
3. man
4. house
5. steps
6. table
7. trees
8. truck
9. dog
10. eyes
11. desks
12. school
13. cat
14. book
15. stars
16. train
17. girl
18. noses
19. songs
20. boy
21. doors
22. bike
23. halls
24. farm

The Moon

On some nights the moon looks like a big pale ball in the sky. On other nights it looks like just a slim slice hanging in the sky.

The changes in the shape of the moon from night to night are called phases. They are made because the moon goes around the earth. One phase is the new moon. The new moon cannot be seen. The other phases of the moon can be seen.

Below are the pictures of the phases of the moon. Trace them and write their names.

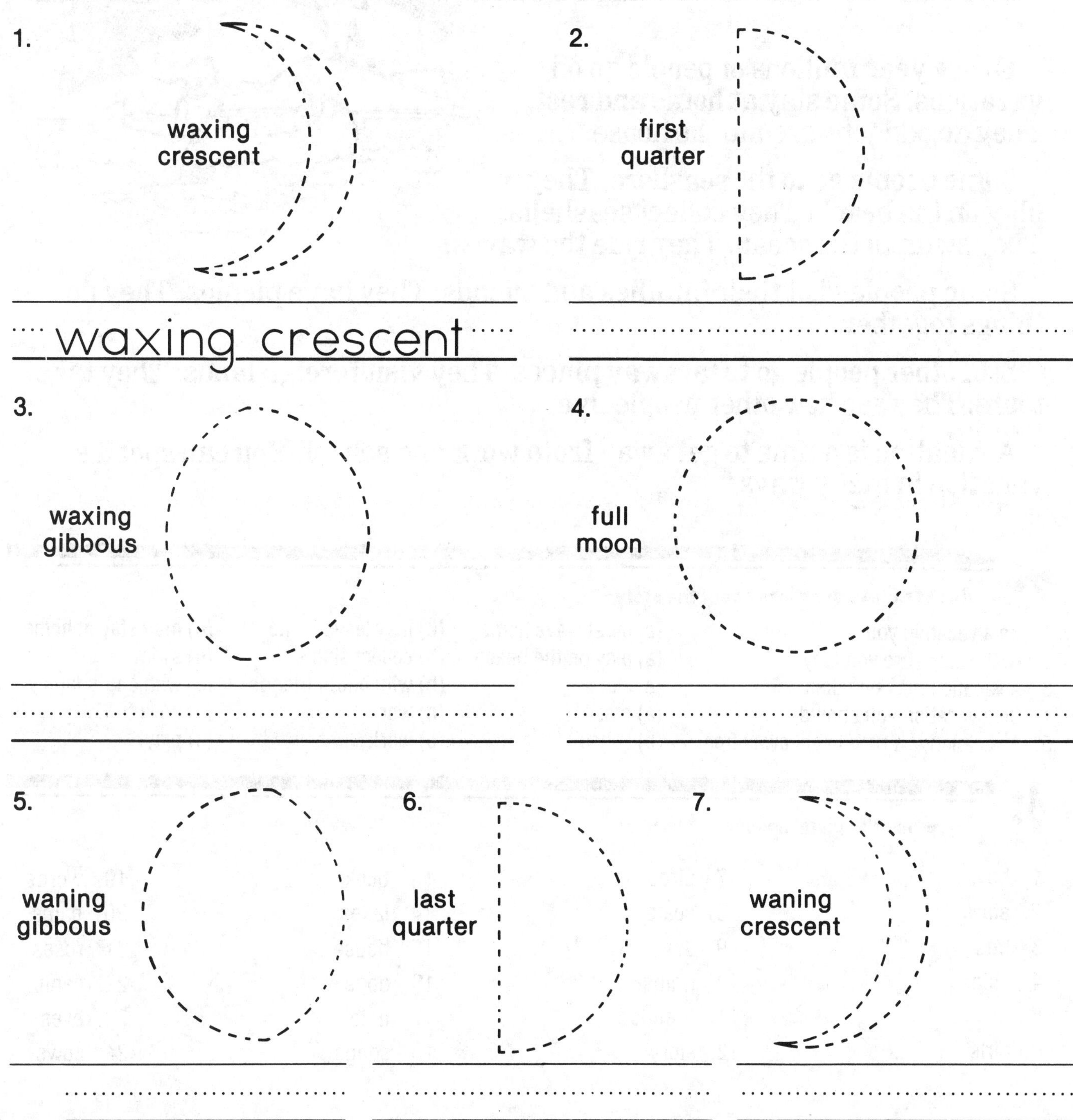

Going on Vacation

Vocabulary Study ● Draw a line under each correct answer. **JUST FOR FUN**

1. The opposite of "rest" is	(a) "sleep"	(b) "play"	(c) "work."
2. A beach is	(a) in the water	(b) by the water	(c) underwater.
3. "Collect" means	(a) "bring together"	(b) "break"	(c) "buy."
4. A tour is a	(a) trip	(b) bus	(c) job.

Every year millions of people go on vacations. Some stay at home and rest. They do odd jobs around the house.

Some people go to the seashore. They play on the beach. They collect seashells. They swim in the ocean. They ride the waves.

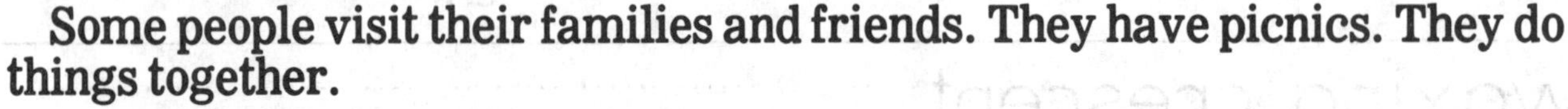

Some people visit their families and friends. They have picnics. They do things together.

Still other people go to faraway places. They visit foreign lands. They take tours. They see how other people live.

A vacation is a time to get away from work and school. You can spend a vacation in many ways.

Answer these questions about the story:

1. On a vacation you	(a) must leave home	(b) may leave home	(c) may stay at home.
2. At the seashore you may	(a) play on the beach	(b) collect shells	(c) swim.
3. A vacation may be taken	(a) alone	(b) with one's friends	(c) with one's family.
4. On a vacation you should	(a) rest	(b) work	(c) have fun.
5. A vacation is a time to get away from	(a) school	(b) work	(c) play.

Underline the plural nouns.

1. boys	7. birds	13. book	19. words
2. stars	8. coats	14. lakes	20. name
3. bus	9. day	15. house	21. roses
4. ships	10. trains	16. dogs	22. camp
5. toy	11. friends	17. gate	23. eyes
6. girls	12. story	18. songs	24. cows

Choosing Breakfast

A Answer the following.

1. Is a good breakfast important? ______

2. Do you eat a good breakfast? ______

3. What did you eat for breakfast this morning? ______

B What should you eat for breakfast? Answer the following to be sure.

1. ______ or fruit juice

2. enriched ______ or enriched bread

3. butter or ______

4. protein food such as meat, ______, or cheese

5. ______

C Plan two good breakfast menus.

1. ______

2. ______

D Yes or No

1. Is a banana on cereal part of a good breakfast? ______

2. Is a soft drink part of a good breakfast? ______

3. Should you always have some milk for breakfast? ______

4. Is an egg on buttered toast part of a good breakfast? ______

5. Should you drink coffee? ______

The Sun

Read the story, and write in the missing words.

The sun does many things for us. It makes plants grow. It makes light for us to see by. It gives us energy to play. It keeps us warm. We could not live without the sun.

Color the pictures, and complete the words under them.

The sun. . .

1. makes ______________ grow.	2. gives us ______________.
3. makes ______________ to see.	4. keeps us ______________.

Christmas

Vocabulary Study • Draw a line under each correct answer. **JUST FOR FUN**

1. Another word for "present" is a	(a) "gift"	(b) "letter"	(c) "card."
2. "Before" means	(a) "ahead"	(b) "after"	(c) "during."
3. An evergreen tree is	(a) never green	(b) not green	(c) always green.
4. The opposite of "under" is	(a) "below"	(b) "over"	(c) "down."

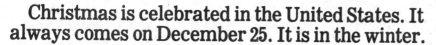

Christmas is celebrated in the United States. It always comes on December 25. It is in the winter.

At Christmas, lights shine on trees. Candles burn in the windows. Houses are decorated with evergreens. Cards are sent to friends. Presents are bought and wrapped. They are put under Christmas trees.

Christmas Eve is the day before Christmas. Many families and friends get together. They give each other presents. People also get together on Christmas Day.

Christians celebrate Christmas. To them Christmas means the birth of Christ.

Answer these questions about the story:

1. Christmas always comes on	(a) December 25	(b) January 1	(c) July 4.
2. Under the Christmas trees are	(a) candles	(b) presents	(c) cards.
3. Christmas Eve comes on the day	(a) before Christmas	(b) of Christmas	(c) after Christmas.
4. Christmas comes in the	(a) summer	(b) fall	(c) winter.
5. Christmas is a time for	(a) friends	(b) family	(c) everyone.

*

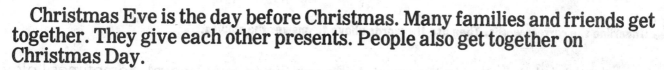

Fill in the blanks with "I" or "me."

1. __________ like school.
2. Give __________ an apple.
3. __________ know the story.
4. Will you talk to __________?
5. Wait for __________.
6. __________ read the book.
7. The puppy came to __________.
8. He sat by __________.
9. __________ will show you the way.
10. __________ made this for you.
11. __________ am busy.
12. Tell __________ your name.

Vacations

A Answer the following.

1. Does your family take vacations? __________ where? __________

2. Have you been on your vacations? __________

B Write the words in alphabetical order.

1. mountains __________
2. camping __________
3. beach __________
4. ranch __________

C Underline the correct words. Then use the words above to answer the riddles.

1. I can (build, bild) castles in the sand. I can see the (waves, wavs). Sometimes I play in the waves.

Where am I? __________

2. We stayed in a (tentt, tent). We cooked over an open (fire, fure).

What were we doing? __________

3. We stayed in a (long, longe) building. We rode horses. We ate with the (cowbuys, cowboys).

We were at a __________.

4. This place has cool nights and (warme, warm) days. I can hike. I can (fish, fishe) in cold streams.

Where am I? __________

What We See Around Us

Follow the directions.

Color the candle yellow.
Put a circle around the spoon.
Color the bird's nest brown.
Put a box around the book.
Color the bird blue.
Draw a line over the table.
Color the tree green.

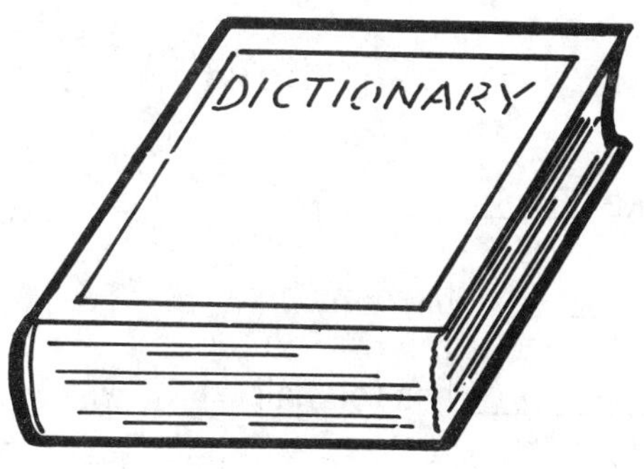

Easter

JUST FOR FUN

Vocabulary Study ● **Draw a line under each correct answer.**

1. "Again" means (a) "never" (b) "sometimes" (c) "one more time."
2. The opposite of "new" is (a) "old" (b) "fresh" (c) "young."
3. "Dye" means (a) "to color" (b) "to break" (c) "to cook."
4. "Joyful" means (a) "sad" (b) "unhappy" (c) "happy."

Easter comes every spring. It is a happy time. Birds sing. Flowers bloom. The grass is green. Easter means that winter is over.

People celebrate Easter. Easter means that the earth is born again.

Many people dye eggs for Easter. The eggs mean new life. Sometimes the eggs are hung on trees.

For Christians, Easter is a joyful time. Christians celebrate Christ's being raised from the dead.

Answer these questions about the story:

1. Easter comes in the (a) winter (b) spring (c) summer.
2. Easter means that winter is (a) here (b) coming (c) over.
3. Eggs mean (a) new life (b) sadness (c) death.
4. At Easter (a) flowers bloom (b) birds sing (c) grass is green.
5. Easter is a time of (a) happiness (b) joy (c) sadness.

Fill in the blanks with "she" or "her."

1. __________ lives next door.
2. Do you know __________?
3. __________ is my sister.
4. I told __________ a story.
5. Ask __________ to come in.
6. __________ took my pencil.
7. I like __________.
8. __________ fixed my bike.
9. __________ has red hair.
10. Will you help __________?
11. __________ has money.
12. Ken will call __________.

Plants

Plants are very interesting. There are many different kinds of plants. They have different sizes, shapes, and colors. Some plants have flowers. Some have stickers. Some have leaves.

Some plants grow in wet places. Others grow in dry places.

Write two words to describe each one. Use the words in the box.

bark	flowers
dry place	stickers
berries	leaves
shade	wet place

1\. 

____

____

2\.

____

____

3\. 

____

____

4\.

____

____

5\. 

____

____

Halloween

Vocabulary Study ● Draw a line under each correct answer. **JUST FOR FUN**

1. If you believe something, you think it is	(a) true	(b) false	(c) wrong.
2. The opposite of "last" is	(a) "end"	(b) "middle"	(c) "first."
3. A costume is something you	(a) drink	(b) eat	(c) wear.
4. A mask covers the	(a) face	(b) foot	(c) hand.

Halloween is an old holiday. Long ago people believed that witches and ghosts came out on Halloween. They thought witches rode through the sky on brooms and carried black cats with them. There are still people who believe this.

Halloween is always the last day in October. On Halloween many people dress up in costumes. They go from door to door. They ask for treats. If they do not get treats from a person, they play a joke on him.

On Halloween you will see many pumpkins with candles in them. You will see many people with masks. Do you think you will see any real ghosts?

Answer these questions about the story:

1. Halloween is a night for	(a) witches	(b) ghosts	(c) black cats.
2. Witches fly on	(a) brooms	(b) rugs	(c) cats.
3. On Halloween, people dress up in	(a) costumes	(b) black clothes	(c) sheets.
4. If people do not get treats from a person, they	(a) go away	(b) play a joke on him	(c) come back again.
5. Halloween is the last day in	(a) December	(b) June	(c) October.

Write "he" or "him" in the blanks.

1. __________ is my brother.
2. Do you know __________?
3. Chris waved at __________.
4. __________ lives here.
5. Give __________ the book.
6. __________ will wait for you.
7. Ask __________ to help us.
8. __________ knew the story.
9. __________ caught a fish.
10. Show __________ the picture.
11. I told __________.
12. __________ rides a bus.

Pets

1. Do you have pets? ____________________

2. Name your pets. ____________________

(If you do not have pets, name some pets you know.)

Underline the correct words, and answer the questions.

(This, Thes) is my dog, Sam. Do you have a dog? ____________

What is (his, her) name?

My (granddmother, grandmother) has a fluffy kitten.

Do you know a kitten or cat? ________ Name it. ________

Some people (kepe, keep) goats for pets.

Have you ever tasted goat's milk? ________ Did you like it? ________

A pony makes a good pet.

Would you (have, hav) a pony if you live in the city? ________

Where should you live to keep a pony? ________

What is a good name for a pony? ________

Name some small pets that are easy to keep.

Gerbils and hamsters are very (smal, small). They do not require (much, muche) care.

Do you have one? ________ Which one? ________

If you could have (eny, any) pet you want, what would you choose? ________

What would you name it? ________

Different Sounds

Draw a line from the animals or objects to their sounds.

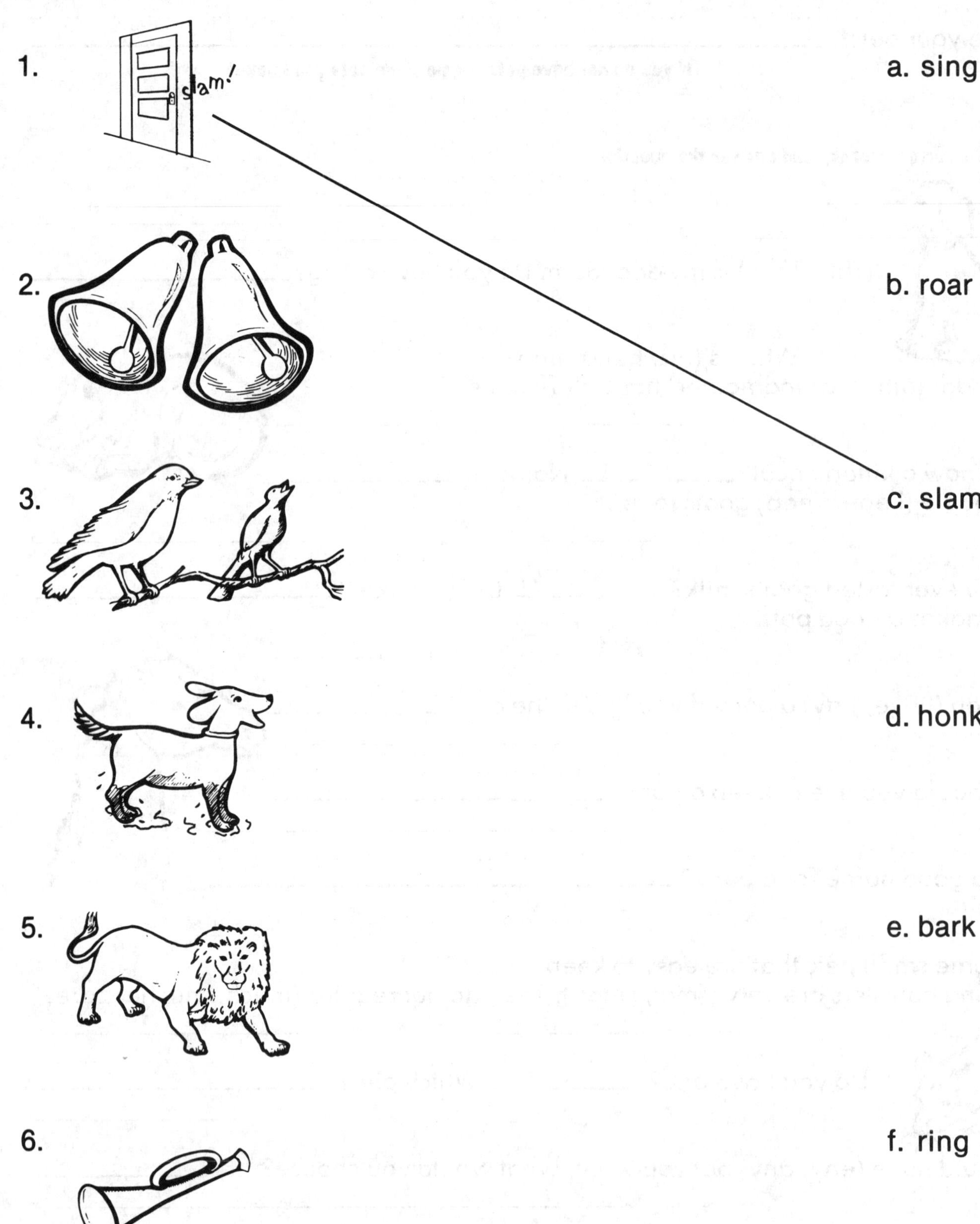

Thanksgiving

Vocabulary Study ● Draw a line under each correct answer. **JUST FOR FUN**

1. The opposite of "good" is (a) "bad" (b) "nice" (c) "best."
2. "Together" means (a) "apart" (b) "with one another" (c) "each."
3. Another word for "share" is (a) "give" (b) "take" (c) "want."
4. The opposite of "remember" is (a) "think" (b) "know" (c) "forget."

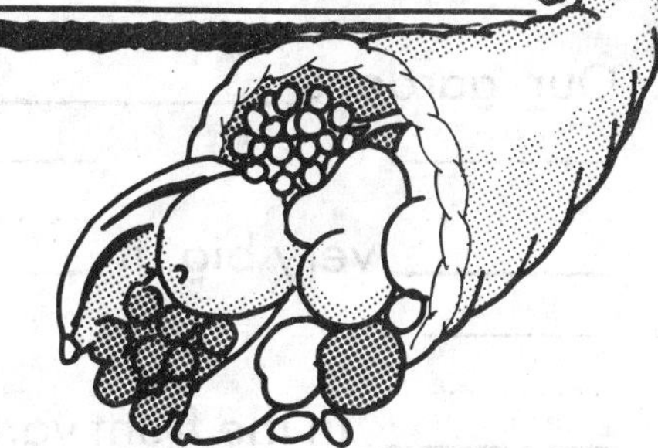

The first Thanksgiving was celebrated long ago. The pilgrims and the Indians celebrated it together. They ate turkey and deer meat. They gave thanks for a good harvest. They gave thanks for friends.

Today we celebrate Thanksgiving. Many families get together. Friends visit each other. We give thanks for all we have had through the year. Most people celebrate with a big turkey dinner.

Thanksgiving always comes in November. It is a time to remember our good fortunes. It is a time to share with others.

Answer these questions about the story:

1. The first Thanksgiving was celebrated by (a) pilgrims (b) Indians (c) French.
2. They gave thanks for (a) a good harvest (b) friends (c) money.
3. At Thanksgiving most people eat (a) chicken (b) pork (c) turkey.
4. Thanksgiving always comes in (a) May (b) October (c) November.
5. Thanksgiving is a time for (a) family (b) friends (c) sharing.

Write "my" or "mine" in the blanks.

1. This is __________ pencil.
2. That is __________.
3. __________ mother is here.
4. The blue one is __________.
5. She is __________ aunt.
6. Do you like __________ coat?
7. Which one is __________?
8. I want __________ book.
9. Is that __________?
10. __________ house is next door.
11. Where is __________ hat?
12. I lost __________.

Gardening

A Fill in the blanks with the correct words.

1. has or have
2. is or are
3. did or done
4. saw or seen

1. Dad ___has___ a vegetable garden. Mom __________ a flower garden. My brother and I __________ both.

2. Our gardens __________ behind the garage. Dad's garden __________ very big. It __________ in the back yard. Mom's garden __________ in the front yard.

3. We __________ all of the work in our gardens. It was __________ in the spring.

4. Have you __________ the flowers blooming? We __________ tiny tomatoes in Dad's garden.

B Answer the following.

1. Do you have a garden? __________

2. If you could plant anything you wanted, what would you plant? __________

3. Why? __________

C Let's plant a garden. Underline the correct words.

(First, Furst) we must till the earth. Dad will (hep, help) us. That (is, are) a hard job. Next, we (muste, must) spread fertilizer. Now, it is (time, tyme) to plant seeds. We must not forget (to, too) water our garden. Look how fast the plants (grow, growe). Soon, we will have food for (hour, our) family.

Objects Around Us That Give Light

Most of our light comes from the sun. Other light comes from man-made materials and from nature.

Choose the correct words to fill in the blanks from this list: firefly, flashlight, lightning, mirror, moon, sun.

1. Do you have a ________________?
2. The __________ is our source of light.
3. ______________ gives light in a storm.
4. The ______________ gives off flashes of light when it flies at night.
5. A ______________ reflects light.
6. Light from the __________ is reflected also.

What Is a Color?

Vocabulary Study ● **Draw a line under each correct answer.** **JUST FOR FUN**

1. The opposite of "light" is (a) "shiny" (b) "dark" (c) "bright."
2. Fires are (a) hot (b) warm (c) cold.
3. "Mix" means (a) "to put together" (b) "to take apart" (c) "to divide."
4. "Without" means (a) "with" (b) "not with" (c) "out."

Without light we could not see. Light may come from fires. It may come from lamps. Most light comes from the sun. Light makes colors.

There are three main colors. They are red, yellow, and blue. All colors together make black. When all colors are gone, we have white.

Mixing colors makes new colors. Blue and yellow make green. Red and blue make purple. Yellow and red make orange.

Some things have only one color. Some things have many colors. Colors make life more exciting. What is your favorite color?

Answer these questions about the story:

1. Most light comes from (a) fires (b) lamps (c) the sun.
2. All colors together make (a) white (b) black (c) blue.
3. Blue and yellow make (a) green (b) purple (c) red.
4. Yellow and red make (a) purple (b) orange (c) blue.
5. When all colors are gone, we have (a) brown (b) white (c) black.

Draw a line to connect words with the same vowel sounds.

1. find	and	7. hill	fly	13. beat	wet
2. land	five	8. jar	car	14. yes	green
3. fed	truck	9. sky	web	15. true	clock
4. the	sell	10. read	fill	16. rock	you
5. luck	glue	11. well	race	17. say	may
6. fruit	be	12. case	need	18. nut	puppy

Question Time

Draw a line from column 1 to the correct words in column 2. See sample "1." Circle the words used.

Column 1	Column 2
1. You should share with	Pledge of Allegiance.
2. Honest citizens tell the	airmail.
3. A good citizen knows the	others.
4. Citizenship Day is	books.
5. Airplanes carry passengers and	city to city.
6. School buses take children to	not kind to others.
7. Some buses travel from	letters.
8. The mailmen put marks on the	baggage.
9. A mail truck picks up the	"Quiet Please."
10. Most people push a basket in the	truth.
11. The sign in the library reads	a bookmobile.
12. The traveling library is called	school.
13. A bad citizen is	mailbags.
14. Airplanes have special places for	supermarket.
15. The supermarket is	every day.
16. The library has many	a helpful shop.

Friends

A Answer the following.

1. My best friend is ______________.
2. We like to play ______________.
3. My friend's favorite food is ______________.
4. My friend's favorite color is ______________.
5. Are you nice to your friend? ______________
6. Do you have other friends? ______________
7. Name three other friends. ______________
8. Do you think friends are important? ______________

B Draw one line under each word that ends with silent "e." Draw a circle around each word that has two sounds or syllables. Draw a box around each word that has the long "a" vowel sound.

I have many nice friends. My best friend is Tom. We play together. Sometimes we rake leaves for our dads. Our moms bake cookies for us. They taste so good.

Do you work and play with your friends? What do you like to do?

C Underline the correct spellings.

1. freind	friend	freend
2. bridge	brigde	brige
3. allmost	almust	almost
4. woodcutter	wodcutter	woodcuter

Why We Wear Shoes

JUST FOR FUN

Vocabulary Study • Draw a line under each correct answer.

1. The opposite of "rough" is	(a) "hard"	(b) "smooth"	(c) "hot."
2. "Clean" means	(a) "dirty"	(b) "not dirty"	(c) "soiled."
3. When you protect something, you keep it	(a) safe	(b) unsafe	(c) hidden.
4. The surface is at the	(a) bottom	(b) middle	(c) top.

Shoes are worn on the feet. They keep the feet clean. They protect the feet from rough surfaces. They protect them from water. They protect them from hot surfaces. They protect them from the cold.

There are many kinds of shoes. There are shoes for work and play. There are shoes for hunting and sports.

The first shoes were probably sandals. They were made of grasses. Then people learned to make shoes from animal skins.

Long ago all shoes were made by hand. Today they are made by machines.

Answer these questions about the story:

1. Shoes are worn on the	(a) head	(b) hands	(c) feet.
2. Shoes protect the feet from	(a) rough surfaces	(b) heat	(c) cold.
3. Shoes are used for	(a) work	(b) hunting	(c) play.
4. The first shoes were made of	(a) grasses	(b) hides	(c) wood.
5. Shoes today are made by	(a) hand	(b) machines	(c) doctors.

Complete each sentence.

1. We ____________ football.
2. Eat your ____________.
3. She read us a ____________.
4. The bus is ____________.
5. The ____________ cried.
6. ____________ the door.
7. The ____________ flew away.
8. Let's ____________ a song.
9. Did you ____________ that?
10. The ____________ rang.
11. The ____________ meowed.
12. ____________ is my friend.

The Bookmobile

Read the story, and answer the questions.

Some schools in the country are small. They do not have a library. These country schools can get good books for the children to read. The library visits these schools.

The library is in a big bus called a bookmobile. It travels to these little country schools. The librarian parks the bookmobile in the schoolyard. The children can go in and pick out books to read.

1. Have you ever seen a bookmobile? ______________ where? ______________________

2. What kind of schools does the bookmobile visit? ______________________________

3. What is the bookmobile? ____

4. Look at the bookmobile in the picture. Color it.

Why We Wear Coats

Vocabulary Study ● Draw a line under each correct answer. **JUST FOR FUN**

1. Winter months are usually	(a) hot	(b) warm	(c) cold.
2. The opposite of "light" is	(a) "heavy"	(b) "thin"	(c) "fine."
3. A lining is on the	(a) top	(b) outside	(c) inside.
4. The opposite of "dry" is	(a) "wet"	(b) "not wet"	(c) "dried."

Coats protect us from the weather. Coats are usually worn in cold weather. They protect us from the cold winds of winter. They keep us warm in the snow.

Coats may be light or heavy. Light coats are thin. Light coats are worn on days that are cool. Heavy coats are thick. Heavy coats are worn on days that are cold.

Coats are made of many materials. Most winter coats are made of wool.

Some coats are worn in the rain. Many raincoats are made of plastic. They keep us dry.

Answer these questions about the story:

1. Coats are usually worn in	(a) warm weather	(b) hot weather	(c) cold weather.
2. Light coats are	(a) thick	(b) thin	(c) worn on cool days.
3. Heavy coats are	(a) thick	(b) thin	(c) made of wool.
4. Raincoats are often made of	(a) plastic	(b) wool	(c) leather.
5. Coats protect us from the	(a) cold	(b) rain	(c) sun.

Rearrange each set of words to make a sentence.

1. penny a I found ____________________
2. down sit ____________________
3. I horses like ____________________
4. followed he me ____________________
5. me for wait ____________________
6. am ready I to go ____________________
7. come may you in ____________________
8. man the smiled ____________________

The Library

Read the story, and answer the questions.

The library has many different books for people to read. There are tables and chairs where people may sit to read. The sign in the library says, "Quiet Please." People must walk and talk quietly in the library. Being quiet helps the people who are reading.

1. Have you visited your neighborhood library? ______________________________

2. What kinds of books do you enjoy reading at the library? ______________________________

3. Have you ever checked out books at the library? ______________________________

4. Do you take good care of library books? ______________________________

5. Color the picture at the top of this page.

Why We Wear Hats

Vocabulary Study ● **Draw a line under each correct answer.** JUST FOR FUN

	(a)	(b)	(c)
1. The opposite of "pretty" is	(a) "nice"	(b) "beautiful"	(c) "ugly."
2. Weather may be	(a) hot	(b) cold	(c) rainy.
3. "Dry" means	(a) "wet"	(b) "not wet"	(c) "cold."
4. Straw is made of	(a) grass	(b) leather	(c) cloth.

Hats are coverings for the head. There are many kinds of hats. Some are worn for protection. Others are worn to look pretty.

Hats are made from many kinds of materials. The weather often helps us decide which material would be best. Straw hats are usually worn on sunny days. They protect the face from the sun. Wool or heavy hats are worn on cold days. They protect the head from the wind and cold. Plastic hats are worn on rainy days. They keep the head dry.

Hats are fun to wear. Do you wear hats?

Answer these questions about the story:

	(a)	(b)	(c)
1. Hats are worn on the	(a) hands	(b) feet	(c) head.
2. Hats in hot weather are often made of	(a) straw	(b) wool	(c) plastic.
3. Hats in cold weather are often made of	(a) straw	(b) wool	(c) plastic.
4. Hats in rainy weather are often made of	(a) straw	(b) wool	(c) plastic.
5. Hats are worn	(a) for protection	(b) to look pretty	(c) for fun.

Place periods where needed.

1. He is Mr. G. H. Adams.
2. Look at this.
3. I knew that
4. Mrs Sims is here
5. Kim looks happy
6. His name is R J Brown
7. Ben asked Dr Jones
8. I like you
9. Mr Roberts called
10. We watched the show
11. It's true
12. This is Ms Fields

Flying a Kite

Vocabulary Study ● **Draw a line under each correct answer.** **JUST FOR FUN**

1. The opposite of "high" is	(a) "low"	(b) "up"	(c) "higher."
2. A breeze is a	(a) light	(b) wind	(c) star.
3. The opposite of "push" is	(a) "pull"	(b) "hold"	(c) "shove."
4. "Beautiful" means	(a) "not pretty"	(b) "ugly"	(c) "very pretty."

A kite flies. It is pushed along by a breeze. It is held by a string. The longer the string, the higher the kite can fly.

Some kites are small. Some are large. All kites are very light in weight. Most are made of paper. Most kites need tails.

A kite's tail holds one end of the kite down. The breeze can then push the other end up.

Some kites are very beautiful. People in China and Japan like to make kites. Their kites are the most beautiful in the world.

Answer these questions about the story:

1. A kite is a	(a) person	(b) place	(c) thing.
2. All kites are	(a) light	(b) small	(c) large.
3. Most kites are made of	(a) iron	(b) paper	(c) grass.
4. The kite is pushed along by a	(a) tail	(b) breeze	(c) string.
5. The most beautiful kites come from	(a) India	(b) China	(c) Japan.

Punctuate the following sentences.

1. Where are you going?
2. She lives in Ohio.
3. Who is he
4. Do you like it
5. I did my homework
6. What did you say
7. Sam rode his bike
8. When is the party
9. Which desk is yours
10. I'm hungry
11. How old are you
12. Will you do it

Watching the Sky

JUST FOR FUN

Vocabulary Study ● Draw a line under each correct answer.

1. The opposite of "heat" is (a) "hot" (b) "cold" (c) "warm."
2. The opposite of "day" is (a) "morning" (b) "noon" (c) "night."
3. "Shine" means (a) "no light" (b) "give light" (c) "darkness."
4. The opposite of "bright" is (a) "dull" (b) "very light" (c) "shiny."

Look at the sky in the daytime. What you probably see is the sun. The sun is a star. It gives us heat and light.

What you cannot see is the moon and other stars. They are there. The sun's light is very bright. The sun keeps you from seeing the moon and stars.

At night the sun is on the other side of the earth. At night you can see the moon. The moon does not shine. It reflects the light of the sun.

At night you can see the other stars. The stars have names.

Look at the sky. What do you see?

Answer these questions about the story:

1. The sun is a (a) moon (b) planet (c) star.
2. The sun gives us (a) heat (b) light (c) darkness.
3. In the daytime other stars are hidden by (a) clouds (b) the moon (c) the sun.
4. At night you can see the (a) moon (b) sun (c) stars.
5. The moon (a) shines (b) does not shine (c) reflects the sun.

***Unscramble each set of letters to make a word.**

1. satr __________
2. nsu __________
3. yuo __________
4. em __________
5. oto __________
6. ese __________
7. ksy __________
8. lkoo __________
9. rnai __________
10. dloc __________
11. wndi __________
12. hto __________
13. mono __________
14. nswo __________
15. wdor __________
16. lnei __________
17. hoess __________
18. tcoa __________

My Room

A Answer the following.

1. Draw a picture of your room.
2. Do you have a room of your own? ____________
3. If not, with whom do you share a room? ____________
4. Do you have your own bed? ____________
5. What other furniture is in your room? ____________
6. Do you help keep your room neat and clean? ____________

(my room)

B Underline the correct answers.

1. I like to spend (time, tyme) in my room.
2. Sometimes I (read, reade).
3. Sometimes I just like to be (alon, alone).
4. Sometimes I play with my (toies, toys).
5. I help take (care, car) of my room.
6. My friends like my room (too, two).

C Underline the correct spellings.

1. soape	saop	soap
2. horse	hors	hurse
3. aple	apple	aplee
4. theng	thing	thang
5. wolde	wuld	would
6. lion	loine	lionn

Words That Sound Alike

Underline the words in each sentence that sound alike.

1. I will ride on the right side of the wide wagon.
2. I saw a ball fall near the wall.
3. Did the cat lick or kick the stick?
4. She will stand on dry land while the band plays.
5. Did the cook take a look at the book?
6. The bird did fill its bill at the mill.
7. We heard a dog bark at the park after dark.
8. Mr. Phillips did not hear the spear go by his ear.
9. I will neither play nor go away for the day.
10. Did you know the crow would fly low today?
11. The cowboy was given a chance to dance or prance.
12. He sat on a stool by the pool at school.
13. Did you see the dog chase the frog from the log?
14. When did the hen begin crackling?
15. I lost my luck when I paid a buck for a duck.
16. There was a bright light in the sky last night.
17. The farmer got wet when he took the pet from the net.
18. A clown went to town and bought a brown hat.
19. How did you know the wind would blow the snow?
20. The cat gave a wink as she took a drink from the sink.

Always True

"All," "every," and "no" are words that should be used carefully. Read each sentence, and find the word in the answer box that makes the sentence always true. Write the word in the blank.

books	cold	December	eggs	hot
laugh	ocean	seed	uncles	wings

1. All birds have ________.
2. All chickens come from ________.
3. All whales swim in the ________.
4. All fire is ________.
5. All ice is ________.
6. Every January follows ________.
7. No library is without ________.
8. All mother's brothers are my ________.
9. Every tree comes from a ________.
10. Every clown wants to make people ________.

baby	boy	ceiling	foot	girls
old	vines	water	winter	write

1. All aunts were ________.
2. No calf is ________.
3. All cucumbers grow on ________.
4. No donkey can ________.
5. Every fish lives in ________.
6. Every man was once a ________.
7. Every mother had a ________.
8. No room is without a ________.
9. Every shoe is for a ________.
10. Every spring comes after ________.

All Are

Read the words in each row. Think how they are alike. Find the answer in the answer box. Write the answer in the blank.

animals	birds	carpenter's tools	colors	days
drinks	frozen water	in the sky	months	trees
babies	buildings	clothes	fruit	

1. cardinal, sparrow, wren — All are ______________.
2. dog, cat, pig — All are ______________.
3. elm, oak, apple — All are ______________.
4. hammer, saw, screwdriver — All are ______________.
5. June, August, January — All are ______________.
6. Monday, Thursday, Sunday — All are ______________.
7. red, black, purple — All are ______________.
8. snow, hail, sleet — All are ______________.
9. star, moon, sun — All are ______________.
10. tea, coffee, punch — All are ______________.
11. apple, pear, peach — All are ______________.
12. kitten, calf, piglet — All are ______________.
13. shirt, pants, blouse — All are ______________.
14. house, barn, store — All are ______________.

Fun with Numbers

A Write the numerals.

1. forty 40
2. 7 tens, 0 ones ______
3. sixteen ______
4. seventy-two ______
5. 9 tens, 3 ones ______
6. 14 tens ______
7. twenty-six ______
8. eighteen ______
9. two hundred ______
10. 6 tens, 7 ones ______

B Answer the following:

1. $\begin{array}{r} 22 \\ +10 \\ \hline \end{array}$	2. $\begin{array}{r} 60 \\ +30 \\ \hline \end{array}$	3. $\begin{array}{r} 12 \\ +\ 4 \\ \hline \end{array}$	4. $\begin{array}{r} 15 \\ -\ 9 \\ \hline \end{array}$	5. $\begin{array}{r} 80 \\ -30 \\ \hline \end{array}$
6. $\begin{array}{r} 8 \\ +6 \\ \hline \end{array}$	7. $\begin{array}{r} 15 \\ +10 \\ \hline \end{array}$	8. $\begin{array}{r} 15 \\ -10 \\ \hline \end{array}$	9. $\begin{array}{r} 110 \\ +\ 20 \\ \hline \end{array}$	10. $\begin{array}{r} 90 \\ +30 \\ \hline \end{array}$
11. $\begin{array}{r} 70 \\ +20 \\ \hline \end{array}$	12. $\begin{array}{r} 80 \\ -20 \\ \hline \end{array}$	13. $\begin{array}{r} 14 \\ +\ 5 \\ \hline \end{array}$	14. $\begin{array}{r} 9 \\ -6 \\ \hline \end{array}$	15. $\begin{array}{r} 70 \\ +60 \\ \hline \end{array}$

16. ______ threes = 9
17. ______ twos = 12
18. ______ sixes = 18
19. ______ fours = 16
20. ______ twos = 8
21. ______ sevens = 21
22. ______ fives = 15
23. ______ twos = 20
24. ______ sixes = 24
25. ______ threes = 15
26. ______ sevens = 14
27. ______ sixes = 0
28. ______ fours = 12
29. ______ threes = 6
30. ______ fours = 8

Belonging Together

Read each sentence. Think how the words in the box go together. Underline the word in the parentheses that goes with the underlined word in the same way.

1. Before is to after as up is to (right, left, down).
2. Bird is to cage as pig is to (pen, box, wagon).

3. Dollar is to 100¢ as quarter is to (10¢, 25¢, 50¢).
4. Dog is to bark as cat is to (moo, chirp, meow).
5. Glasses is to eyes as hearing aid is to (feet, hand, ears).
6. Head is to foot as engine is to (caboose, gondola, hopper).
7. Whale is to water as bird is to (nest, air, mud).

8. Toe is to foot as finger is to (arm, nose, hand).
9. Ring is to finger as hat is to (heart, head, lung).
10. Hog is to pork as cow is to (beef, bacon, stew).
11. Ballet is to dancing as boxing is to (football, car, sport).
12. Sparrow is to bird as Collie is to (duck, dog, pig).

13. Pet is to dog as toy is to (doll, horse, car).
14. Hand is to glove as foot is to (pocket, shoe, shirt).
15. Cat is to kitten as cow is to (calf, colt, desk).
16. Window is to house as porthole is to (car, wagon, ship).

17. Acorn is to tree as grape is to (stump, root, vine).
18. Bird is to fly as horse is to (saddle, run, rider).
19. Cat is to animal as dress is to (paper, pencil, clothes).
20. Car is to highway as airplane is to (wing, runway, cockpit).

Read the Stories

Read each story, and answer the questions. If you have problems, read the story again.

Dress Properly

The way you dress can help you stay healthy. On a rainy day you should wear a raincoat, boots, and a hat. On a very cold day be sure to wear a warm coat, mittens, boots, and cap. To feel your best on a hot day, wear light, loose clothes. Always dress according to the weather. Your parents will help you.

1. Dressing properly will help you (a) make friends (b) learn more (c) stay healthy.
2. On a rainy day wear a (a) sun dress (b) raincoat (c) pair of sandals.
3. You should dress according to the (a) weather (b) fashions (c) school colors.
4. Who will help you decide what to wear? (a) strangers (b) baby brother (c) parents

Wheat

Wheat is a very important grain crop. Wheat is grown in many countries. Much is grown in North America. Wheat seeds are ground into flour. Bread and other products are made from flour. Countries that do not raise wheat must buy it. Wheat is a major food source for all the world.

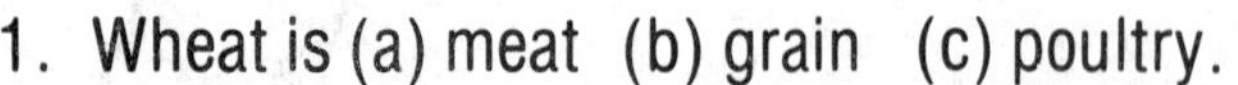

1. Wheat is (a) meat (b) grain (c) poultry.
2. North America includes (a) the United States and Canada (b) England (c) Russia.
3. Wheat is grown (a) mostly in China (b) only in Canada (c) in many countries.
4. Wheat is ground into (a) flour (b) meal (c) cornstarch.

Entertaining Stories

Read each story, and answer the questions. If you have problems, read the story again.

Friends

Do you have a best friend? You can share many things with your best friend. Sometimes it it nice to have other friends too. You need more than one friend to play most games. Several friends together can do many things. All friends are important.

1. With a best friend you can (a) be selfish (b) share (c) ignore others.
2. It is nice to have (a) more than one friend (b) only one friend (c) no friends.
3. Friends are (a) unimportant (b) important sometimes (c) important.
4. You usually need several friends to (a) play games (b) read (c) swing.

A New Puppy

Would you like to have a puppy? Only people who like animals should have dogs. If you get a puppy, it will need much care. You must feed it and give it water every day. The puppy will need a bed and should visit the veterinarian. Of course the puppy will have to be trained. With loving care your puppy will grow into a healthy dog.

1. Who should have a dog? (a) someone who likes animals (b) only a boy (c) only a girl
2. All dogs need food and water (a) once a week (b) sometimes (c) every day.
3. An animal doctor is (a) an oculist (b) a veterinarian (c) a pediatrician.
4. Good care will produce a (a) mean dog (b) lazy dog (c) healthy dog.

Answer the Questions

Read each story, and answer the questions. If you have problems, read the story again.

Food

Good food will help you grow. Breakfast is very important. A good breakfast will give you energy. You should eat four kinds of food each day. These foods will give your body the things it needs. Be sure to drink plenty of milk.

1. You need food to (a) grow (b) have energy (c) work.
2. Breakfast is (a) not important (b) very important (c) important sometimes.
3. How many kinds of food should you eat each day? (a) six (b) two (c) four
4. What should you drink with meals? (a) tea (b) milk (c) cola drinks

Teeth

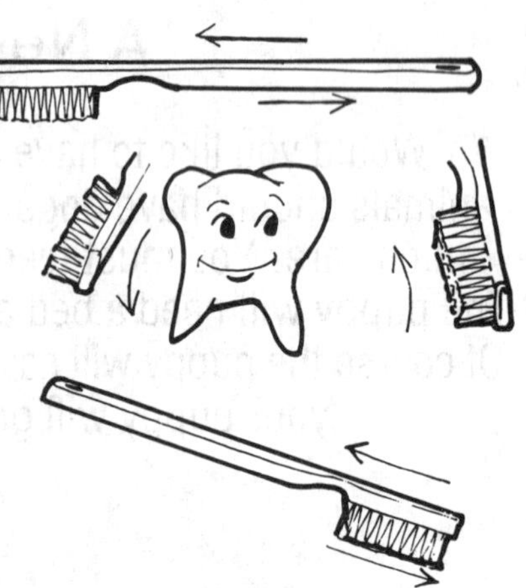

During your life you will have two sets of teeth. If you take care of both sets, your second set should last all your life. The second set is called permanent teeth.

Brush your teeth after meals and at bedtime. Floss your teeth every day. See your dentist regularly.

1. You will have (a) one set of teeth (b) two sets of teeth (c) three sets of teeth.
2. The second set is called (a) primary teeth (b) temporary teeth (c) permanent teeth.
3. Teeth should be cared for (a) weekly (b) sometimes (c) daily.
4. The specialist who cares for teeth is a (a) dentist (b) doctor (c) engineer.

Finding How Many More

Fill in the blanks.

	You Want	You Have	You Need
1.	6 apples	4	2 apples
2.	2 pencils	0	______ pencils
3.	7 bananas	3	______ bananas
4.	12 roses	7	______ roses
5.	4 shirts	3	______ shirt
6.	9 envelopes	2	______ envelopes
7.	5 candy bars	1	______ candy bars
8.	2 sandwiches	0	______ sandwiches
9.	3 books	2	______ book
10.	11 spoons	7	______ spoons
11.	8 crackers	3	______ crackers
12.	10 goldfish	4	______ goldfish
13.	9 papers	4	______ papers
14.	6 oranges	3	______ oranges
15.	1 hat	1	______ hats
16.	14 marbles	6	______ marbles
17.	7 games	2	______ games
18.	11 friends	10	______ friend
19.	5 eggs	2	______ eggs
20.	11 dolls	8	______ dolls

Choosing Words

Write the correct word in each blank.

1. is, are

   Mary ___is___ singing.

   The men ___are___ working.

2. was, were

   They ________ hiking.

   My big dog ________ barking.

3. a, an

   Will you loan me ________ dime?

   I have ________ apple.

4. gave, given

   Father ________ me his watch.

   Sue has ________ her brother a cookie.

5. saw, seen

   Have you ________ my cat?

   John and Ted ________ the bus coming.

6. did, done

   They have ________ their chores.

   ________ you go to school?

7. come, came

   Will you ________ to my house for lunch?

   She ________ to see us.

8. went, gone

   They have ________ to a movie.

   He ________ to the ball game.

9. ate, eaten

   The monkeys have ________ the peanuts.

   I ________ my ice-cream cone.

10. run, ran

    Will you ________ in the race?

    The horse ________ fast enough to win.

Noun Words

Underline each noun, or naming word.

1. The red apple is juicy.
2. My dog is very big.
3. The new car is sleek and shiny.
4. The pear is yellow.
5. The girl played with the kittens.
6. My friend put flowers on the table.
7. Why does the bird sing?
8. Icicles are cold.
9. Jane bought a new dress.
10. The movie was sad.
11. My brother is a doctor.
12. Mother baked a large chocolate cake.
13. Will Jane go to your house?
14. Marsha is learning to play the piano.
15. The band is marching in the parade.
16. Close the door, please.
17. I like steak.
18. Sue swept the floor.
19. Dad bought peaches at the store.
20. My coat is blue.

Action Words

Underline each verb, or action word.

1. Birds fly.
2. The baby sleeps in a crib.
3. John rode his new bicycle.
4. Mother cooks dinner each evening.
5. She plays the piano.
6. Many men work in large office buildings.
7. My grandparents live on a dairy farm.
8. The horse raced across the meadow.
9. Ben carried my books.
10. We will walk to the picnic.
11. Mr. Jones drives a truck.
12. The nurse gave me a pill.
13. Dad and Tom washed the car.
14. Mother and I wash the dishes.
15. At the zoo you see many animals.
16. Please eat lunch with me.
17. The children ran to the park.
18. I planned a party for Marie.
19. Dave's dog jumps over the fence.
20. Trains travel to many cities.

Underlining Words

A **Underline the words that are opposite in meaning.**

1. tall	(short, fat)	7. fat	(plump, thin)
2. early	(late, big)	8. busy	(idle, mean)
3. push	(over, pull)	9. mean	(pretty, nice)
4. run	(walk, float)	10. quick	(skip, slow)
5. happy	(polite, sad)	11. tight	(loose, small)
6. polite	(rude, thoughtful)	12. find	(lose, see)

B **Underline the rhyming words.**

1. sun	fun	two	gun
2. flea	top	sea	tea
3. milk	save	wave	pave
4. break	steak.	make	say
5. boy	joy	nod	toy

C **Underline the correct words.**

1. The wind (blew, blue) the boat across the lake.
   The girl's sweater is (blew, blue).
2. The dump truck will (hall, haul) the trash away.
   His room is at the end of the (hall, haul).
3. I have (to, too, two) cookies.
   Mother has gone (to, too, two) the store.
   Her dress is (to, too, two) big.
4. Father (ate, eight) a snack.
   Jim has (ate, eight) marbles.

Which Word?

One word in each line does not go with the other words. Draw a line under that word.

1. boy man lad girl
2. fish swim whale shark
3. shoe hat foot glove
4. ride car ship airplane
5. talk laugh think sing
6. apple drink orange lemon
7. day morning evening night
8. hail snow sleet rain
9. duck rabbit goose hen
10. dog kitten puppy calf
11. six nine number three
12. walk trot run sit
13. head woman arm leg
14. door gate glass window
15. ditch road highway trail
16. cow horse hog man
17. pen paper pencil crayon
18. whole half fourth third
19. biscuit donut cake plate
20. green black jacket blue

From "Car" to "Doll"

c a r e a d d o g

r
o
w
a
n
t
h
i
s
t
o

l l o d o o g g e r

Write the words for the following definitions that are found in order in the arrow.

1. c a r — an automobile
2. _ _ _ _ — to feel interest, be concerned
3. _ _ _ — We ___ waiting for the doctor.
4. _ _ _ _ — to get meaning from printing or writing
5. _ _ _ — two plus two
6. _ _ _ — a four-legged pet
7. _ _ _ _ — to become bigger by taking in food
8. _ _ _ — to use ores to move a boat
9. _ _ _ _ — to feel that one needs
10. _ _ _ _ — Come here ____ minute!
11. _ _ _ — belonging to him
12. _ _ — The sky __ blue.
13. _ _ _ _ _ — place where things are kept for sale
14. _ _ _ _ — ripped apart by force
15. _ _ _ — Iron ___ is found in Alabama.
16. _ _ _ — A bird laid this.
17. _ _ — to move away
18. _ _ _ _ — doing right
19. _ _ — to carry through to the end
20. _ _ _ _ — child's toy that looks like a baby

From "Came" to "Ear"

c a m e n e w a s a t h a t h e n o t o y e a r

Write the words for the following definitions that are found in order in the arrow.

1. c a m e moved toward
2. __ __ Give the ball to __ __.
3. __ __ __ Boys grow up to be __ __ __.
4. __ __ __ never having been before
5. __ __ __ I __ __ __ late for school this morning.
6. __ __ as black __ __ coal
7. __ __ __ I __ __ __ in a chair.
8. __ __ __ __ pointing to some one person or thing
9. __ __ __ covering for the head
10. __ __ by, near
11. __ __ __ I saw __ __ __ dog.
12. __ __ __ __ at that time
13. __ __ __ female chicken
14. __ __ opposite of "yes"
15. __ __ __ I will __ __ __ go.
16. __ __ in the direction of
17. __ __ __ something for a child to play with
18. __ __ (old English) you
19. __ __ __ __ 12 months
20. __ __ __ something you hear with

WELCOME TO THE WORLD OF CHILDREN

MY SECOND GRADE YEARBOOK was carefully prepared to teach seven-year-old children the basic, fundamental skills necessary to function successfully in the second grade. The materials contained in this work text were designed by experienced school curriculum planners and writers to introduce and teach those basic skills necessary to enable the average seven-year-old person to grow and mature academically according to the prescribed patterns found in most public and private schools throughout the nation.

This publication is unique in that it is the only workbook ever devised to teach a student the very same basic academic skills that the child should learn in a well-planned course of study in an organized classroom. This publication is also unique in that it is designed to be administered either by the classroom teacher or the concerned parent at home. Please notice the absence of educational terminology used in most textbooks teachers' manuals. Such language was intentionally omitted in the instructions so that parents, as well as trained teachers, would have little difficulty in administering this program. The reasoning for each teaching segment has also been omitted. This work text is organized to teach the basic academic curricula (reading; arithmetic; social studies; science; health; art; and language arts such as spelling, vocabulary, grammar, punctuation, etc.) and it intentionally omits special areas of learning such as music, drama and speech, foreign languages, and any other fringe or nonbasic subjects.

The approach taken in this work text is referred to as unified modules. The work is organized in units or lessons that contain materials that relate to other curriculum skills areas. For example, a lesson may be primarily structured to teach a specific skill, such as the short vowel sound of "a," but may also teach vocabulary, art, handwriting, and arithmetic skills at the same time. This integration of subject areas is unquestioned in quality curriculum construction. The sequential presentation of materials is the strength of this program; it is purposely designed to be presented in front-to-back order. Each lesson builds on the previous lesson. In other words, each lesson should be completely mastered before moving on to the next. Under no circumstances should a pupil be allowed to skip a lesson or skip around in the work text. If this happens, the continuity pattern will be interrupted, thus weakening the program.

In most school systems teachers follow a teaching pattern called a curriculum guide, teaching outline, course of study, or some similar name. This guide or outline provides the teacher with a day-by-day lesson plan to insure that the materials are presented in a sequential manner so that the students acquire the desired skills in the proper order of importance. Each outline or guide is usually closely tied or related to a textbook in the given academic area, such as reading or math, and the teacher has to match the suggestions of the school's course of study with the lesson presentations of the various textbooks. This is sometimes a very difficult task for the teacher who must search for extra or supplementary materials to fill the gap between the textbook and the curriculum guide. MY SECOND GRADE YEARBOOK was designed specifically to meet this need. It was prepared as a unified course of study and was especially designed to teach the basic subject-matter facts and concepts in the proper order of importance to provide the second-grade student the necessary and desired academic skills. If properly administered to its conclusion, this course should help to teach a second-grade student of average intelligence reading, writing, and standard arithmetic computations.

TO THE CLASSROOM TEACHER

The units in this student work text should, with some exceptions, coincide with your school's course of study. The sequential order of presentation is basically in agreement with the standards of the national norm. Some units may have to be used out of the order of our presentation to agree with your program. This student work text is printed offset and bound by the "perfect-binding" process. This workbook was designed to be used by one student and is consumable. However, it can be used as a reproducible book by removing pages and copying by means of any process available, including the use of thermal spirit master units. The right to reproduce the pages for the teacher's use is granted to classroom teachers purchasing one or more books. Reproduced copies cannot be sold. The pages are specially printed to enable copying. The binding enables easy removal of pages.

Each lesson is self-explanatory. The instructions to the students appear at the top of each page and should be read to the student by the teacher. Even if the student thinks the exercises are too easy for him, he should be expected to work them anyway. Being highly structured, the exercises will teach and maintain the skills necessary to progress. If a student has a problem with a unit, make sure the student locates and masters the problem before moving on. The student should not be allowed to skip around but should work each exercise in sequence. Teaching suggestions and answers are provided in this manual for some of the lessons.

TO THE PARENT-TEACHER

Congratulations! You are about to undertake the most challenging and rewarding role you have ever attempted — becoming a parent-teacher. Up to now the task has been almost insurmountable because you had no access to quality teaching materials like those used in schools. Your requests for copies of school textbooks were probably met with answers such as "it's against school policy to allow textbooks away from the school" or "you should leave the teaching to teachers." This work text is designed for you — the parent-teacher.

MY SECOND GRADE YEARBOOK is not a teaching book designed to undermine or replace the classroom teacher (because thousands of teachers use this very book in their classrooms), but it is designed to augment and fortify the very fine work done by the classroom teacher.

The role of the parent in the parent-child learning process has been simplified to as few steps as possible. However, there are some parent responsibilities that are extremely important for the success of this program. Be sure you study and follow these steps carefully.

1. Study the manual carefully and be aware of special instructions or suggestions for different lessons. Note that answers have been printed for some lessons while other answers have been omitted (because of their simplicity).

2. Special preparations must be made and strictly followed. We recommend the following:

(a) Select a specific time of day for study, such as 5:00 to 6:00 p.m. or any other time that suits your family's schedule. Allow one hour per day for study — no more, no less. Stress the importance of this time that you and your child will be working together. Be sure to inform other members of your family that this time is "sacred" and that the two of you are not to be disturbed with phone calls or other interruptions. Make it a rule that if you have to leave the room for something, the child stops working until you return. Call it a "time out" or "emergency call" or some such name to reinforce the importance of working together. Under no circumstances should you assign lessons to the child and leave the room for him/her to finish — this would defeat the purpose of the book.

(b) Provide several sharpened soft-lead pencils, preferably the primary- or large-type with erasers. Furnish a box of large color crayons of the basic colors. It is not necessary to buy the very large box of many colors — this tends to confuse the child in the selection of colors asked for in the worksheets.

(c) Select a quiet, comfortable, and pleasant part of the house in which to study and to store MY SECOND GRADE YEARBOOK and supplies. Promoting good study habits is also a goal of this program. The pleasant place should reinforce the habit to study.

(d) Tell your child's teacher of your plans, and show her MY SECOND GRADE YEARBOOK. She will be most appreciative of your concern and may even give you additional teaching tips.

3. Start at the beginning of the book and work in one-two-three order. Be sure to read the instructions for each lesson to the child, and explain in detail until you are sure he/she knows exactly what to do. Make sure the child successfully performs each task before going to the next lesson. Under no circumstances should you allow the child to go ahead or skip lessons. Each unit must be performed in order. Allow the child to do as many lessons as he/she is capable of within your alloted time span. Usually he/she will do about five lessons per hour.

4. Insist on quality work from your child. The best course is slow, neat, and deliberate. This will insure retention of the skills learned. Allow the child to erase and correct his /her own work. Help him/her at any point of difficulty, even by telling the answer. The child must experience success to remain interested.

You will be pleasantly surprised — even elated at the progress your child makes as you go from lesson to lesson. You will also notice the simplicity and similarity of learning to read, write, and count with any other learning situations, such as learning to ride a bicycle or to play a game. Learning, in all cases, must start from the beginning and progress to the difficult, one step at a time until each segment of the learning process is completed. Learning is a continuing process — it is never "over."

When MY SECOND GRADE YEARBOOK is completed, it should be preserved as a family memento to mark an outstanding achievement by your child. It may also reflect a very significant sense of pride and personal development in you as a parent.

1 The Alphabet

2 Matching Shapes

3 Lengths of Words 3. is, 4. the, 5. me, 6. and, 7. go, 8. for, 9. to, 10. not, 11. up, 12. far, 13. we, 14. red, 15. it, 16. big, 17. if, 18. toy, 19. of, 20. you, 21. at, 22. can, 23. be, 24. get, 25. in, 26. put, 27. on, 28. was, 29. or, 30. rod, 31. an, 32. pet

4 See, Say, and Write Words 2. lake, 3. pan, 4. bat, 5. barn, 6. ant, 7. head, 8. car, 9. ball, 10. flag, 11. lady, 12. star

5 Number Recognition 1—5 Help students be sure to count accurately. Do the same for similar lessons.

6 Direction Pointers Help each student. They may have difficulty with some of the more subtle drawings. Repeat for similar lessons.

7 "s" Endings

8 "m," "l" Sounds A—1. M, 2. B, 3. B, 4. E, 5. B, 6. M, 7. E, 8. E, 9. B, 10. E, 11. B, 12. M, 13. M, 14. B, 15. M, 16. M; B—1. M, 2. B, 3. M, 4. E, 5. M, 6. B, 7. M, 8. B, 9. M, 10. B, 11. E, 12. M, 13. M, 14. E, 15. M, 16. E

9 Which Are Words? 1. apple, 2. lake, 3. pan, 4. bat, 5. barn, 6. ant, 7. head, 8. car, 9. ball, 10. flag, 11. lady, 12. star

10 Geometric Figures

11 Descriptions of Words 2. b, 3. b, 4. c, 5. a

12 Size Discrimination

13 "n," "p" Sounds A—1. B, 2. B, 3. M, 4. M, 5. E, 6. E, 7. M, 8. B, 9. E, 10. M, 11. E, 12. E, 13. M, 14. B, 15. E, 16. E; B—1. M, 2. E, 3. M, 4. B, 5. B, 6. M, 7. E, 8. E, 9. B, 10. E, 11. M, 12. M, 13. B, 14. M, 15. E, 16. B

14 Word Endings

15 More Than

16 Word Meanings 2. a, 3. c, 4. a, 5. b

17 Writing Words 2. cube, 3. broom, 4. cabin, 5. bird, 6. bear, 7. bow, 8. boy, 9. comb, 10. web, 11. tub, 12. bus

18 Less Than

19 Spelling Words 1. bee, 2. cube, 3. broom, 4. cabin, 5. bird, 6. bear, 7. bow, 8. boy, 9. comb, 10. web, 11. tub, 12. bus

20 Which Is Like the First?

21 "q," "r" Sounds A—1. B, 2. B, 3. M, 4. B, 5. M, 6. B, 7. B, 8. B, 9. B, 10. M, 11. B, 12. B, 13. M, 14. M, 15. M, 16. B; B—1. M, 2. B, 3. M, 4. E, 5. B, 6. E, 7. M, 8. B, 9. M, 10. M, 11. E, 12. M, 13. B, 14. M, 15. M, 16. E

22 Word Reversals 3. nap, 4. gas, 5. saw, 6. now, 7. ton, 8. pit, 9. pot, 10. ban, 11. pat, 12. pig, 13. keep, 14. war, 15. tool, 16. dab, 17. bad, 18. tool, 19. raw, 20. peek, 21. gip, 22. tap, 23. nab, 24. top, 25. tip, 26. not, 27. won, 28. was, 29. sag, 30. pan, 31. tub, 32. wed

23 Number Recognition 6—9

24 Word Descriptions 2. c, 3. b, 4. b, 5. a

25 Matching Capital Letter Forms

26 Number Words 1—5

27 "s," "t" Sounds A—1. B, 2. B, 3. M, 4. E, 5. M, 6. E, 7. B, 8. E, 9. M, 10. B, 11. E, 12. M, 13. M, 14. B, 15. E, 16. M; B—1. E, 2. M, 3. B, 4. E, 5. B, 6. M, 7. E, 8. B, 9. M, 10. B, 11. E, 12. M, 13. B, 14. E, 15. M, 16. M

28 Defining Words 2. b, 3. a, 4. a, 5. a

29 Confusing Words 3. bread, 4. court, 5. broad, 6. dunce, 7. touch, 8. lover, 9. chow, 10. stuck, 11. clear, 12. warn, 13. soup, 14. mowed, 15. snail, 16. lion, 17. dared, 18. unite, 19. sorted, 20. broad, 21. intend, 22. bribe, 23. stable, 24. dump, 25. flap, 26. back, 27. sacred, 28. traits, 29. quiet, 30. fired, 31. horse, 32. daisy

30 Recognizing Shapes B. 8, C. 15, D. 1, E. 4, F. 12, G. 2, H. 6, I. 11, J. 9, K. 3, L. 5, M. 10, N. 13, O. 7

31 What Are the Pictures? 2. sack, 3. cap, 4. cone, 5. cake, 6. ice, 7. face, 8. tack, 9. cage, 10. cup, 11. cat, 12. sock

32 Spelling Words for Fun 1. coat, 2. sack, 3. cap, 4. cone, 5. cake, 6. ice, 7. face, 8. tack, 9. cage, 10. cup, 11. cat, 12. sock

33 Define Words 2. b, 3. a, 4. c, 5. a

34 How Many?

35 Matching Lower-Case Letters

36 "v," "x" Sounds A—1. M, 2. E, 3. M, 4. B, 5. M, 6. B, 7. E, 8. B, 9. M, 10. B, 11. M, 12. E, 13. M, 14. B, 15. M, 16. E; B—1. B, 2. M, 3. E, 4. M, 5. M, 6. B, 7. E, 8. M, 9. B, 10. E, 11. M, 12. E, 13. M, 14. B, 15. M, 16. M

37 Number Transposition C. 31, D. 41, E. 41, F. 51, G. 61, H. 71, I. 81, J. 91, K. 02, L. 32, M. 32, N. 42, O. 52, P. 62, Q. 72, R. 82, S. 92, T. 03, U. 03, V. 43, W. 53, X. 63, Y. 73, Z. 83, A. 93, B. 04, C. 54, D. 64, E. 74, F. 84

38 Number Words 6—9

39 Word Definitions 2. b, 3. c, 4. c, 5. b

40 Naming Pictures 2. door, 3. wood, 4. duck, 5. bread, 6. deer, 7. hand, 8. candy, 9. card, 10. drum, 11. end, 12. bed

41 Spelling Words Correctly 1. cold, 2. door, 3. wood, 4. duck, 5. bread, 6. deer, 7. hand, 8. candy, 9. card, 10. drum, 11. end, 12. bed

42 Addition Facts A—3, 4, 5, 6, 7, 8, 9, 10; B—3, 4, 5, 6, 7, 8, 9, 10, 11; C—4, 5, 6, 7, 8, 9, 10, 11, 12; D—5, 6, 7, 8, 9, 10, 11, 12, 13; E—6, 7, 8, 9, 10, 11, 12, 13, 14; F—7, 8, 9, 10, 11, 12, 13, 14, 15; G—8, 9, 10, 11, 12, 13, 14, 15, 16; H—9, 10, 11, 12, 13, 14, 15, 16, 17; I—10, 11, 12, 13, 14, 15, 16, 17, 18

43 Upper- and Lower-Case Matching

44 Counting Sets

45 "z," "b" Sounds A—1. B, 2. M, 3. E, 4. M, 5. E, 6. E, 7. E, 8. M, 9. B, 10. E, 11. M, 12. B, 13. E, 14. M, 15. E, 16. M; B—1. B, 2. M, 3. E, 4. M, 5. B, 6. E, 7. M, 8. E, 9. B & E, 10. M, 11. E, 12. B & E, 13. M, 14. M, 15. B & E, 16. B & M

46 Number Changes C. 123, D. 232, E. 415, F. 425, G. 188, H. 422, I. 816, J. 725, K. 454, L. 726, M. 563, N. 382, O. 485, P. 328, Q. 997, R. 359, S. 679, T. 676, U. 876, V. 245, W. 483, X. 626, Y. 424, Z. 727, A. 337, B. 191, C. 258, D. 346, E. 559, F. 272

47 Proper Positions Encourage students to practice carefully and to try to improve. Repeat for similar lessons.

48 Addition Facts 1's, 2's, and 3's B. 5, 6, 7; C. 8, 9, 10; D. 3, 4, 5; E. 6, 7, 8; F. 9, 10, 11; G. 4, 5, 6; H. 7, 8, 9; I. 10, 11, 12; J. 2, 3, 4, 5; K. 4, 5, 6, 7; L. 6, 7, 8, 9; M. 7, 8, 7, 5

49 Proper Attitudes

50 Meanings of Words 2. a, 3. b, 4. b, 5. c

51 Recognizing Pictures 2. eye, 3. ten, 4. belt, 5. key, 6. gate, 7. leg, 8. egg, 9. nose, 10. rake, 11. five, 12. ear

52 Addition 4. 2, 3, 4; 5, 6, 7; 8, 9, 10; 5. 3, 4, 5; 6, 7, 8; 9, 10, 11; 6. 4, 5, 6; 7, 8, 9; 10, 11, 12; 7. 5, 8. 10, 9. 5, 10. 11

53 Letter Discrimination

54 Underlining Answers 2. b, 3. a, 4. c, 5. a

55 Practicing Addition 1's, 2's, and 3's A—7, 6, 9, 5, 8, 7, 10, 9, 7; B—6, 7, 9, 5, 8, 5, 8, 8, 10, 4; C—7, 3, 10, 11, 6, 9, 9, 7, 10, 5; D—3, 9, 6, 8, 7, 9, 3, 4, 7, 10; E—8, 6, 10, 9, 4, 4, 7, 6, 11, 8; F—4, 8, 7, 10, 5, 5, 8, 4, 11, 9; G—7, 9, 11, 12, 7, 6, 9, 6, 8, 10; H—9, 11, 5, 10, 8, 10, 3, 10, 5, 9; I—6, 8, 2, 12, 9, 8, 9, 5, 8, 11; J—9, 3, 8, 4, 6, 8, 5, 4, 10, 9

56 "c," "d" Sounds A—1. B, 2. M, 3. B, 4. M, 5. B, 6. M, 7. M, 8. E, 9. B, 10. E, 11. B & M, 12. B & E, 13. B & M, 14. E, 15. M, 16. B; B—1. M, 2. E, 3. E, 4. B, 5. B, 6. M, 7. E, 8. M, 9. M, 10. B, 11. M, 12. E, 13. M, 14. M, 15. M, 16. B & E

57 Internal Number Changes C. 2412, D. 2639, E. 3013, F. 1984, G. 2672, H. 2478, I. 4125, J. 2159, K. 3264, L. 3271, M. 5325, N. 4652, O. 2344, P. 3786, Q. 1725, R. 2919, S. 2438, T. 3865, U. 1842, V. 2792, W. 2522, X. 3838, Y. 3124, Z. 3461, A. 2356, B. 2895, C. 1429, D. 2127, E. 2136, F. 8453

58 Addition Facts 4's, 5's, and 6's 4. 5, 6, 7; 8, 9, 10; 11, 12, 13; 5. 6, 7, 8; 9, 10, 11; 12, 13, 14; 6. 7, 8, 9; 10, 11, 12; 13, 14, 15; 7. 14, 8. 13, 9. 11, 10. 11

59 Spell the Words 1. bell, 2. eye, 3. ten, 4. belt, 5. key, 6. gate, 7. leg, 8. egg, 9. nose, 10. rake, 11. five, 12. ear

60 Can You Define the Words? 2. b, 3. c, 4. a, 5. a

61 Practicing Addition 4's, 5's, and 6's A—14, 12, 11, 8, 13, 9, 12, 13, 13; B—10, 7, 6, 13, 8, 10, 10, 9, 13, 15; C—11, 8, 15, 13, 13, 12, 12, 13, 12, 13; D—13, 11, 10, 12, 7, 11, 7, 7, 7, 8; E—13, 14, 11, 12, 7, 6, 15, 13, 12, 12; F—10, 13, 11, 12, 11, 9, 10, 8, 9, 14; G—13, 13, 15, 10, 13, 13, 7, 14, 15, 11; H—12, 15, 14, 8, 6, 13, 13, 15, 13, 11; I—12, 14, 14, 6, 8, 6, 7, 14, 12, 11; J—12, 13, 11, 8, 7, 7, 13, 6, 14, 9

62 Seeing Difference

63 "f," "g" Sounds A—1. E, 2. M, 3. B, 4. E, 5. B, 6. E, 7. M, 8. E, 9. M, 10. E, 11. M, 12. E, 13. M, 14. E, 15. E, 16. B & E; B—1. B, 2. M, 3. E, 4. E, 5. E, 6. M, 7. B, 8. E, 9. M, 10. B, 11. M, 12. E, 13. M & E, 14. M, 15. E, 16. B & M

64 Addition Facts 7's, 8's, and 9's 4. 8, 9, 10; 11, 12, 13; 14, 15, 16; 5. 9, 10, 11; 12, 13, 14; 15, 16, 17; 6. 10, 11, 12; 13, 14, 15; 16, 17, 18; 7. 16, 8. 18, 9. 15. 10. 13

65 Definitions of Words 2. a, 3. c, 4. c, 5. b

66 Write the Words 2. fist, 3. fork, 4. four, 5. calf, 6. fox, 7. fire, 8. fan, 9. safe, 10. knife, 11. fish, 12. roof

67 Practicing Addition 7's, 8's, and 9's A—12, 11, 17, 11, 13, 13, 14, 11, 11; B—12, 14, 11, 10, 13, 12, 12, 15, 15, 12; C—12, 10, 16, 17, 13, 13, 17, 11, 8, 13; D—10, 12, 12, 14, 13, 11, 13, 11, 10, 10; E—16, 12, 11, 10, 10, 11, 10, 14, 12, 11; F—12, 10, 12, 16, 12, 11, 13, 11, 10, 10; G—10, 11, 9, 10, 13, 10, 10, 15, 12, 8; H—12, 11, 10, 18, 17, 16, 13, 13, 16, 10; I—10, 10, 9, 12, 9, 10, 15, 16, 16, 13; J—17, 13, 10, 16, 14, 11, 11, 12, 12, 16

68 Letter Reversal

69 "h," "j" Sounds A—1. B, 2. M, 3. E, 4. M, 5. M, 6. E, 7. M, 8. E, 9. B, 10. M, 11. E, 12. M, 13. B, 14. M, 15. M, 16. B & E; B—1. B, 2. M, 3. E, 4. E, 5. B, 6. M, 7. B, 8. E, 9. E, 10. M, 11. E, 12. M, 13. E, 14. M, 15. E, 16. B & E

70 Addition of 4's, 5's, and 6's B. 8, 9, 10; C. 11, 12, 13; D. 6, 7, 8; E. 9, 10, 11; F. 12, 13, 14; G. 7, 8, 9; H. 10, 11, 12; I. 13, 14, 15; J. 5, 6, 7, 8; K. 10, 11, 12, 13; L. 7, 8, 9, 10; M. 12, 13, 14, 7

71 Spell 1. gift, 2. fist, 3. fork, 4. four, 5. calf, 6. fox, 7. fire, 8. fan, 9. safe, 10. knife, 11. fish, 12. roof

72 Underlining Definitions 2. a, 3. c, 4. a, 5. a

73 Addition of 7's, 8's, and 9's B. 11, 12, 13; C. 14, 15, 16; D. 9, 10, 11; E. 12, 13, 14; F. 15, 16, 17; G. 10, 11, 12; H. 13, 14, 15; I. 16, 17, 18; J. 8, 9, 10, 11; K. 13, 14, 15, 16; L. 10, 11, 12, 13; M. 15, 16, 17, 10

74 Differences in Words 2. my, 3. do, 4. em, 5. as, 6. de, 7. an, 8. bo, 9. at, 10. by, 11. jo, 12. ax, 13. me, 14. ai, 15. am, 16. ad, 17. be, 18. fa, 19. ba, 20. fe, 21. ed, 22. an, 23. at, 24. we, 25. ox, 26. go, 27. ay, 28. at, 29. do, 30. in, 31. be, 32. is

75 "k," "oy," "oi" Sounds A—1. M, 2. B, 3. E, 4. B, 5. E, 6. M, 7. B, 8. E, 9. B, 10. E, 11. M, 12. B, 13. M, 14. M, 15. M, 16. B & E; B—1. M, 2. E, 3. B, 4. M, 5. M, 6. M, 7. B, 8. E, 9. M, 10. B, 11. M, 12. E, 13. M, 14. E, 15. M, 16. M

76 Picture Problems B. 9, 12; C. 12, 12; D. 9, 13; E. 9, 12; F. 10, 14; G. 11, 13

77 Underlining Correct Answers 2. a, 3. b, 4. b, 5. b

78 Picture Names 2. wagon, 3. goat, 4. girl, 5. gun, 6. wag, 7. glass, 8. sun, 9. pig, 10. glove, 11. hang, 12. gas

79 Subtraction Facts 1's, 2's, and 3's B. 5, 4, 3; C. 2, 1, 0; D. 7, 6, 5; E. 4, 3, 2; F. 1, 0, 6; G. 5, 4, 3; H. 2, 1, 0; I. 3, 5, 1; J. 8, 7, 6, 5; K. 3, 2, 1, 0; L. 6, 5, 4, 3; M. 1, 0, 6, 5

80 Internal Letter Changes 3. rode, 4. spot, 5. hone, 6. want, 7. tine, 8. what, 9. wont, 10. mike, 11. word, 12. cake, 13. fond, 14. came, 15. give, 16. like, 17. lake, 18. gave, 19. come, 20. fond, 21. coke, 22. ward, 23. make, 24. want, 25. whit, 26. time, 27. want, 28. home, 29. spat, 30. ride, 31. then, 32. lost

81 "th," "wh" Sounds A—1. M, 2. B, 3. E, 4. M, 5. B, 6. E, 7. M, 8. B, 9. M, 10. E, 11. E, 12. M, 13. B, 14. E, 15. B, 16. M; B—1. B, 2. M, 3. B, 4. M, 5. B, 6. B, 7. M, 8. B, 9. M, 10. B, 11. M, 12. B, 13. M, 14. B, 15. M, 16. B & M

82 Combining Members of Sets B. 7, C. 6, D. 11, E. 8, F. 12, G. 11

83 Correct Spellings 1. bag, 2. wagon, 3. goat, 4. girl, 5. gun, 6. wag, 7. glass, 8. large, 9. pig, 10. glove, 11. hang, 12. gas

84 Underline the Right Answers 2. b, 3. c, 4. a, 5. a

85 Subtraction Facts 1's, 2's, and 3's 4—1, 2, 3; 4, 5, 6; 7, 8, 9; 5—1, 2, 3; 4, 5, 6; 7, 8, 9; 6—1, 2, 3; 4, 5, 6; 7, 8, 9; 7. 9, 8. 7, 9. 6, 10. 6

86 First Letter Changes 3. take, 4. bake, 5. raid, 6. rant, 7. wake, 8. time, 9. ball, 10. pump, 11. some, 12. side, 13. came, 14. sent, 15. cave, 16. dove, 17. love, 18. rave, 19. went, 20. same, 21. ride, 22. come, 23. jump, 24. tall, 25. lime, 26. make, 27. pant, 28. paid, 29. rake, 30. lake, 31. hone, 32. look

87 "ch," "sh" Sounds A—1. B, 2. E, 3. B, 4. M, 5. B, 6. E, 7. M, 8. M, 9. M, 10. E, 11. M, 12. B, 13. M, 14. M, 15. M, 16. E; B—1. E, 2. M, 3. M, 4. E, 5. M, 6. B, 7. M, 8. E, 9. B, 10. M, 11. E, 12. M, 13. M, 14. E, 15. B, 16. M

88 Practicing Subtraction 1's, 2's, and 3's A—5, 2, 7, 7, 4, 3, 4, 6, 2; B—4, 4, 5, 3, 2, 5, 3, 3, 6, 2; C—1, 1, 6, 5, 4, 3, 7, 2, 8, 3; D—1, 1, 6, 6, 3, 4, 3, 2, 5, 4; E—6, 2, 6, 7, 7, 2, 5, 1, 5, 2; F—2, 4, 3, 6, 1, 3, 2, 7, 5, 3; G—1, 3, 7, 6, 2, 4, 5, 5, 3, 8; H—5, 5, 3, 8, 2, 4, 1, 6, 2, 3; I—2, 4, 6, 6, 5, 2, 7, 1, 4, 7; J—5, 1, 2, 2, 4, 4, 3, 1, 8, 7

89 Practice Spelling Words 2. a, 3. c, 4. c, 5. b

90 Writing the Words 2. bath, 3. fight, 4. shoe, 5. house, 6. sharp, 7. three, 8. chin, 9. teeth, 10. shell, 11. horse, 12. light

91 Subtraction Facts 4's, 5's, and 6's B. 5, 6, 7; C. 4, 6, 5; D. 5, 3, 1; E. 3, 4, 2; F. 1, 2, 3; G. 9, 8, 7, 6; H. 4, 3, 2, 1; I. 8, 7, 6, 5; J. 6, 5, 4, 3; K. 7, 3, 3, 0; L. 7, 3, 6, 6,

92 Last Letter Changes 3. feed, 4. seep, 5. that, 6. held, 7. loam, 8. ball, 9. look, 10. wand, 11. pair, 12. them, 13. tale, 14. what, 15. sent, 16. fine, 17. find, 18. send, 19. wham, 20. talk, 21. then, 22. paid, 23. want, 24. loop, 25. bale, 26. loan, 27. help, 28. than, 29. seed, 30. feet, 31. seal, 32. work

93 "ng," "dr" Sounds A—1. E, 2. M, 3. E, 4. E, 5. M, 6. M, 7. E, 8. M & E, 9. M, 10. E, 11. M, 12. E, 13. M, 14. M, 15. M, 16. M; B—1. B, 2. B, 3. M, 4. M, 5. B, 6. M, 7. B, 8. B, 9. M, 10. B, 11. M, 12. B, 13. M, 14. B, 15. B, 16. M

94 Subtraction of 4's, 5's, and 6's 4. 1, 2, 3; 4, 5, 6; 7, 8, 9; 5. 1, 2, 3; 4, 5, 6; 7, 8, 9; 6. 1, 2, 3; 4, 5, 6; 7, 8, 9; 7. 8, 8. 6, 9. 9, 10. 8

95 Learn to Spell 1. ham, 2. bath, 3. fight, 4. shoe, 5. house, 6. sharp, 7. three, 8. chin, 9. teeth, 10. shell, 11. horse, 12. light

96 Practicing Spelling 2. b, 3. a, 4. c, 5. a

97 Practicing Subtraction 4's, 5's, and 6's A—2, 2, 1, 5, 1, 1, 3, 5, 3; B—2, 1, 4, 1, 4, 1, 3, 1, 6, 3; C—3, 2, 3, 3, 1, 4, 2, 5, 2, 5; D—1, 1, 4, 4, 3, 3, 5, 2, 1, 4; E—5, 2, 1, 1, 1, 4, 3, 4, 4, 6; F—2, 5, 5, 2, 3, 1, 3, 4, 2, 2; G—5, 3, 3, 6, 4, 4, 5, 2, 3, 3; H—2, 3, 2, 6, 2, 3, 5, 4, 6, 4; I—3, 4, 2, 4, 4, 2, 5, 3, 4, 3; J—4, 5, 1, 4, 1, 3, 3, 4, 4, 3

98 Add a Letter 3. your, 4. does, 5. care, 6. wind, 7. cane, 8. fund, 9. cape, 10. cute, 11. pine, 12. bite, 13. tear, 14. hate, 15. kite, 16. rate, 17. tape, 18. dote, 19. bush, 20. seat, 21. rode, 22. made, 23. hope, 24. here, 25. feed, 26. copy, 27. find, 28. ride, 29. toot, 30. sink, 31. ward, 32. book

99 "gl," "fl," "cl" Sounds A—1. E, 2. B, 3. M, 4. E, 5. E, 6. B, 7. E, 8. M, 9. E, 10. B, 11. B, 12. B, 13. M, 14. E, 15. E, 16. M; B—1. M, 2. B, 3. B, 4. E, 5. M, 6. E, 7. M, 8. B, 9. E, 10. M, 11. E, 12. B, 13. M, 14. B, 15. E, 16. E

100 Subtraction Facts 7's, 8's, and 9's A. 9, 7, 8, 5, 6; B. 9, 8, 7, 6; C. 9, 8, 7, 6; D. 9, 8, 7, 6; E. 9, 8, 7, 6; F. 0, 1, 2, 3, 4, 5, 6, 7; G. 0, 1, 2, 3, 4, 5, 6, 7; H. 0, 1, 2, 3, 4, 5, 6, 7; I. 4, 5, 2, 5, 1, 4, 9, 7

101 Write Sentences 2. b, 3. a, 4. c, 5. b

102 Word, Picture Matching 2. sit, 3. nine, 4. time, 5. train, 6. pipe, 7. hit, 8. bib, 9. pin, 10. milk, 11. chair, 12. stir

103 Subtraction Facts 4. 1, 2, 3; 4, 5, 6; 7, 8, 9; 5. 1, 2, 3; 4, 5, 6; 7, 8, 9; 6. 1, 2, 3; 4, 5, 6; 7, 8, 9; 7. 9, 8. 6, 9. 6, 10. 5

104 Number Discrimination

105 "ed," "th" Endings A—1. E, 2. E, 3. B, 4. E, 5. B, 6. E, 7. E, 8. E, 9. M, 10. E, 11. E, 12. B, 13. E, 14. M, 15. M, 16. M & E; B—1. B, 2. E, 3. M, 4. E, 5. M, 6. B, 7. M, 8. E, 9. M, 10. B, 11. E, 12. E, 13. E, 14. M, 15. B, 16. E

106 Practicing Subtraction 7's, 8's, and 9's A—6, 2, 1, 3, 1, 3, 5, 6, 5; B—6, 2, 6, 2, 5, 7, 1, 5, 8, 4; C—2, 4, 7, 8, 6, 6, 7, 2, 3, 5; D—6, 6, 2, 1, 3, 3, 3, 7, 5, 4; E—1, 5, 5, 4, 3, 8, 6, 4, 6, 6; F—6, 3, 6, 3, 1, 2, 1, 3, 4, 5; G—6, 4, 7, 6, 5, 5, 1, 4, 7, 5; H—1, 3, 8, 2, 2, 7, 5, 2, 6, 3; I—6, 5, 3, 1, 6, 1, 3, 7, 7, 5; J—2, 2, 7, 8, 3, 4, 4, 3, 1, 6

107 Improve Your Spelling 1. king, 2. sit, 3. nine, 4. clock, 5. train, 6. pipe, 7. hit, 8. bib, 9. pin 10. milk, 11. chair, 12. stir

108 Practice Spelling 2. c, 3. b, 4. a, 5. c

109 Add — Subtract Combinations Through 9's A—3, 1, 4, 4, 3, 4, 2; B—2, 7, 3, 5, 5, 5, 2, 6; C—2, 7, 1, 2, 6, 6, 3, 1; D—7, 13, 12, 4, 9, 7, 13, 7; E—6, 9, 5, 12, 10, 5, 8, 8; F—15, 11, 11, 17, 9, 11, 10, 10; G—3, 4, 4, 3; H—5, 2, 2, 3; I—6, 3, 4, 3

110 "z" Sounds and "l" Blends A—1. M, 2. E, 3. E, 4. M, 5. M, 6. M, 7. E, 8. E, 9. E, 10. E, 11. E, 12. E, 13. M, 14. E, 15. E, 16. M; B—1. S, 2. P, 3. B, 4. B, 5. P, 6. S, 7. P, 8. B, 9. S, 10. P, 11. B, 12. S, 13. P, 14. B, 15. P, 16. B

111 Underline Definitions 2. c, 3. b, 4. a, 5. a

112 Sets of Ten C. 6 + 4, D. 3 + 7, E. 2 + 8, F. 5 + 5, G. 7 + 3, H. 9 + 1, I. 3 + 3 + 4, J. 1 + 4 + 5, K. 2 + 5 + 3, L. 4 + 2 + 4, M. 3 + 2 + 5, N. 3 + 4, + 3, O. 5 + 3 + 2, P. 7 + 2 + 1, Q. 2 + 1 + 7
113 Choosing Words 2. jelly, 3. jump, 4. join, 5. jacket, 6. junk, 7. judge, 8. jar, 9. juice, 10. Jell-O, 11. jet, 12. jam
114 Long "a," Short "a" A—1. B, 2. M, 3. M, 4. M, 5. B, 6. M, 7. E, 8. E, 9. B, 10. M, 11. M, 12. E, 13. B, 14. M, 15. M, 16. M & E; B—1. B, 2. M, 3. B, 4. B, 5. M, 6. B, 7. B, 8. M, 9. M, 10 M, 11. B, 12. M, 13. B, 14. M, 15. B, 16. E
115 Supply Missing Numerals Help students by telling them not to use numerals higher than "9."
116 Correctly Spelled Words 1. jug, 2. jelly, 3. jump, 4. join, 5. jacket, 6. junk, 7. judge, 8. jar, 9. juice, 10. Jell-O, 11. jet, 12. jam
117 Underline Word Meanings 2. a, 3. b, 4. c, 5. a
118 Watch That Sign 2. 12; 3. 11, 5, 12, 5; 4. 12, 13, 13, 8; 5. 9, 7, 12, 17; 6. 4, 13, 13, 8; 7. 7, 13, 12, 4; 8. 13, 6, 10, 13; 9. 13, 9, 14, 14; 10. 7, 13, 7, 6; 11. 14, 14, 6, 5; 12. 14, 9, 7, 14; 13. 9, 7, 8, 8; 14. 9, 6, 7, 8; 15. 9, 4, 8, 6; 16. $14.00; 17. 6; 18. 15
119 Long "e," Short "e" A—1. M, 2. B, 3. E, 4. M, 5. M, 6. B, 7. M, 8. E, 9. B, 10. M, 11. M, 12. E, 13. E, 14. E, 15. M & E, 16. M & E; B—1. B, 2. B, 3. M, 4. M, 5. B, 6. M, 7. M, 8. B, 9. M, 10. M, 11. B, 12. B, 13. M, 14. B & M, 15. M, 16. B & M,
120 Underline the Definitions 2. b, 3. a, 4. a, 5. c
121 Telling Time B. 4:00, C. 9:00, D. 2:00, E. 10:00, F. 1:00, G. 5:00, H. 3:00; I. - P. Help students draw hands in the correct places.
122 Choosing and Writing Words 2. mark, 3. bike, 4. bank, 5. knee, 6. bake, 7. neck, 8. kite, 9. pond, 10. book, 11. snake, 12. dark
123 Long "i," Short "i" A—1. M, 2. B, 3. E, 4. M, 5. M, 6. B, 7. B, 8. B & M, 9. M, 10. E, 11. M, 12. E, 13. M, 14. M, 15. E, 16. E; B—1. M, 2. M, 3. M, 4. B, 5. B, 6. M, 7. M, 8. B, 9. M, 10. M, 11. B, 12. B, 13. M, 14. B, 15. B, 16. B
124 Writing Two Equations B. 8 + 5 = 13; 5 + 8 = 13; C. 7 + 6 = 13; 6 + 7 = 13; D. 5 + 7 = 12; 7 + 5 = 12; E. 4 + 8 = 12; 8 + 4 = 12; F. 9 + 3 = 12; 3 + 9 = 12; G. 6 + 5 = 11; 5 + 6 = 11; H. 7 + 4 = 11; 4 + 7 = 11; I. 3 + 8 = 11; 8 + 3 = 11; J. 9 + 2 = 11; 2 + 9 = 11; K. 2 + 8 = 10; 8 + 2 = 10
125 Spelling 1. hike, 2. mark, 3. bike, 4. bank, 5. knee, 6. bake, 7. neck, 8. kite, 9. pond, 10. book, 11. snake, 12. dark
126 Picking the Right Answers 2. c, 3. c, 4. a, 5. b
127 Writing Subtraction Equations Students should be able to complete these equations. Give help if needed.
128 Long "o," Short "o" A—1. M, 2. E, 3. E, 4. B, 5. M, 6. B, 7. B, 8. B, 9. E, 10. M, 11. B, 12. E, 13. B & M, 14. B & E, 15. B & E, 16. B; B—1. M, 2. B, 3. M, 4. B, 5. M, 6. M, 7. B, 8. B, 9. M, 10. M, 11. M, 12. B, 13. M, 14. M, 15. B, 16. B
129 Choosing the Correct Answers 2. b, 3. c, 4. c, 5. b
130 Subtract the Facts A—1, 2, 3, 4, 5, 6, 7, 8, 9; B—Each row has the same answers. Have students study these basic subtraction facts until they know them. Give the same kind of help for similar lessons.
131 Picking Proper Words 2. nail, 3. bowl, 4. plate, 5. tail, 6. smile, 7. walk, 8. lion, 9. lamp, 10. play, 11. sail, 12. pail
132 Long "u," Short "u" A—1. M, 2. B, 3. E, 4. E, 5. B, 6. M, 7. E, 8. E, 9. M, 10. B, 11. M, 12. E, 13. B, 14. E, 15. M, 16. E B—1. M, 2. B, 3. M, 4. M, 5. B, 6. M, 7. M, 8. M, 9. M, 10. B, 11. B, 12. M, 13. B, 14. M, 15. M, 16. M
133 Writing Addition Equations
134 Picture Fun 1. clown, 2. nail, 3. bowl, 4. plate, 5. tail, 6. smile, 7. walk, 8. lion, 9. lamp, 10. play, 11. sail, 12. pail
135 Can You Remember the Meanings? 2. a, 3. a, 4. c, 5. b
136 Likenesses and Differences C. 2; D. 2, 2; E. 1, F. 2; G. 3; H. 2; I. 2, 2; J. 3; K. 2; L. 2; M. 4; N. 1; O. 4; P. 3; Q. 1, 1; R. 1; S. 4; T. 2; U. 5; V. 1; W. 2; X. 3
137 Long "oo," Short "oo" 1. L, 2. L, 3. S, 4. L, 5. S, 6. L, 7. S, 8. L, 9. S, 10. L, 11. L, 12. L, 13. S, 14. S, 15. L, 16. L, 17. L, 18. L, 19. L, 20. S, 21. L, 22. S, 23. L, 24. L, 25. S, 26. L, 27. L, 28. S, 29. L, 30. S, 31. L, 32. L, 33. L, 34. L, 35. S, 36. S, 37. S, 38. L, 39. L, 40. L, 41. L, 42. S, 43. S, 44. S
138 How Is Your Vocabulary? 2. a, 3. c, 4. a, 5. b
139 Going to the Store

B.	C.	D.	E.
6¢	6¢	10¢	8¢
9¢	6¢	2¢	10¢
8¢	5¢	6¢	9¢
23¢	17¢	18¢	27¢

F.	G.	H.	I.
6¢	6¢	8¢	6¢
5¢	8¢	6¢	8¢
10¢	10¢	8¢	6¢
21¢	24¢	22¢	20¢

140 Choose the Proper Words 2. mop, 3. moon, 4. mill, 5. farm, 6. stump, 7. aim, 8. stamp, 9. smell, 10. pump, 11. mail, 12. seam
141 "aw," "au," "ow," "ou" Sounds A—1. M, 2. E, 3. M, 4. M, 5. B, 6. B, 7. M, 8. M, 9. E, 10. B, 11. M, 12. M, 13. B, 14. M, 15. M, 16. E; B—1. M, 2. B, 3. E, 4. M, 5. M, 6. M, 7. B, 8. M, 9. B, 10. B, 11. E, 12. M, 13. B, 14. M, 15. E, 16. E
142 Adding, Number Line Help students work "C" and "D" using the number line provided for each problem.; E—10, 11, 12, 13, 11; F—12, 13, 14, 13, 14; G—15, 15, 16, 17, 16; H—17, 18, 9, 10, 11; I—12, 13, 9, 10, 11; J—12, 13, 14, 5, 6; K—7, 8, 9, 10, 11; L—12, 3, 4, 5, 6; M—7, 8, 9, 10, 11; N—3, 4, 5, 6, 7; O—8, 9, 10, 3, 4; P—5, 6, 7, 8, 9
143 Can You Name the Pictures? 1. arm, 2. mop, 3. moon, 4. mill, 5. farm, 6. stump, 7. aim, 8. stamp, 9. smell, 10. pump, 11. mail, 12. seam
144 Word Description 2. b, 3. a, 4. c, 5. a
145 Money Problems C—3, 1, 1, 18¢; D—4¢, 10¢, 20¢, 34¢; E—5, 2, 3, 45¢; F—3, 7¢, 10¢, 32¢; G—4, 2, 30¢, 44¢; H—2, 3, 3, 47¢; I—3, 3, 2, 15¢; J—0, 4, 1, 0; K—5, 3, 1, 30¢; L—1, 1, 1, 5¢; M—2, 2, 2, 20¢; N—4, 3, 2, 4¢
146 "w," "y" Sounds A—1. B, 2. M, 3. B, 4. B, 5. M, 6. M, 7. E, 8. M, 9. B, 10. M, 11. B, 12. B, 13. M, 14. E, 15. B, 16. E; B—1. B, 2. M, 3. E, 4. B, 5. E, 6. B, 7. E, 8. B, 9. M, 10. B, 11. B, 12. E, 13. M, 14. E, 15. B, 16. B & M
147 Defining Words Is Fun 2. a, 3. b, 4. c, 5. a
148 Number Line Subtraction B—8, 9, 6, 7; C—14, 15, 13, 11; D—10, 11, 9, 11; E—5, 8, 10, 11; F—6, 2, 5, 2; G—9, 9, 13, 11; H—9, 7, 6, 4; I—2, 2, 2, 2; J—5, 3, 3, 8; K—8, 8, 10, 12; L—12, 8, 5, 7; M—6, 4, 3, 0; N—3, 3, 6, 4; O—6, 10, 13, 8; P—10, 4, 9, 7; Q—1, 5, 4, 7; R—2, 1, 3, 3; S—8, 5, 10, 7; T—14, 7, 3, 4; U—1, 6, 7, 4; V—7, 4, 12
149 Let's Match Words with Pictures 2. sun, 3. nest, 4. can, 5. money, 6. phone, 7. run, 8. nut, 9. horn, 10. nurse, 11. wing, 12. corn
150 Which Words Are Correct? 1. sing, 2. sun, 3. nest, 4. can, 5. money, 6. phone, 7. run, 8. nut, 9. horn, 10. nurse, 11. wing, 12. corn
151 Sets Can Help 2. 7 + 5 = 12, 5 + 7 = 12, 12 - 7 = 5, 12 - 5 = 7; 3. 9 + 4 = 13, 4 + 9 = 13, 13 - 9 = 4, 13 - 4 = 9; 4. 8 + 6 = 14, 6 + 8 = 14, 14 - 6 = 8, 14 - 8 = 6; 5. 8 + 5 = 13, 5 + 8 = 13, 13 - 5 = 8, 13 - 8 = 5; 6. 6 + 9 = 15, 9 + 6 = 15, 15 - 6 = 9, 15 - 9 = 6; 7. 8 + 4 = 12, 4 + 8 = 12, 12 - 8 = 4, 12 - 4 = 8; 8. 9 + 3 = 12, 3 + 9 = 12, 12 - 3 = 9, 12 - 9 = 3; 9. 7 + 4 = 11, 4 + 7 = 11, 11 - 7 = 4, 11 - 4 = 7; 10. 8 + 3 = 11, 3 + 8 = 11, 11 - 8 = 3, 11 - 3 = 8; 11. 6 + 7 = 13, 7 + 6 = 13, 13 - 7 = 6, 13 - 6 = 7
152 What Are the Meanings? 2. c, 3. b, 4. c, 5. a
153 Writing Time 2. 12:00, 3. 12:05, 4. 12:10, 5. 12:15, 6. 12:20, 7. 12:25, 8. 12:30, 9. 12:35, 10. 12:40, 11. 12:45, 12. 12:50, 13. 12:55, 14. 1:00, 15. 2:00, 16. 3:00, 17. 4:00, 18. 5:00, 19. 6:00, 20. 7:00, 21. 8:00, 22. 9:00, 23. 10:00, 24. 11:00, 25. 1:30, 26. 3:25, 27. 4:35, 28. 5:20, 29. 6:15, 30. 7:10, 31. 8:05, 32. 9:10, 33. 10:05, 34. 11:25, 35. 9:20
154 Write the Correct Words 2. one, 3. hoe, 4. stove, 5. pony, 6. rocks, 7. road, 8. top, 9. cow, 10. boat, 11. old, 12. owl
155 Vocabulary Development 2. c, 3. b, 4. a, 5. c
156 Words and Pictures 1. hop, 2. one, 3. hoe, 4. stove, 5. pony, 6. rocks, 7. road, 8. top, 9. cow, 10. boat, 11. old, 12. owl
157 5 + 3 Puppies Help students with this lesson if they need it. Offer help for similar lessons if needed.
158 Give the Meanings 2. a, 3. b, 4. a, 5. c
159 5 + 4 Geese
160 Pick the Proper Words 2. drop, 3. paint, 4. ape, 5. pants, 6. soap, 7. peanut, 8. rope, 9. paper, 10. map, 11. soup, 12. pear

161 What Are the Descriptions? 2. a, 3. a, 4. b, 5. c
162 Improve Your Spelling 1. drip, 2. drop, 3. paint, 4. ape, 5. pants, 6. soap, 7. peanut, 8. rope, 9. paper, 10. map, 11. soup, 12. pear
163 6 + 2 Squirrels
164 Choose the Right Answers 2. a, 3. c, 4. c, 5. b
165 6 + 3 Chicks
166 Picture, Word Matching 2. quail, 3. queen, 4. quake, 5. squid, 6. quiz, 7. quick, 8. quartet, 9. quarter, 10. quiet, 11. quart, 12. quack
167 Can You Choose the Correct Answers? 2. c, 3. c, 4. c, 5. b
168 Recognizing Correctly Spelled Words 1. question, 2. quail, 3. queen, 4. quake, 5. squid, 6. quiz, 7. quick, 8. quartet, 9. quarter, 10. quiet, 11. quart, 12. quack
169 6 + 4 Cookies
170 Give the Correct Answers 2. b, 3. a, 4. a, 5. b
171 6 + 5 Frogs
172 Matching Words with Pictures 2. pair, 3. cry, 4. rest, 5. rug, 6. draw, 7. burn, 8. dress, 9. hare, 10. crash, 11. ride, 12. tree
173 Remember the Meanings 2. c, 3. c, 4. c, 5. a
174 Fun with Pictures 1. tire, 2. pair, 3. cry, 4. rest, 5. rug, 6. draw, 7. burn, 8. dress, 9. hare, 10. crash, 11. ride, 12. tree
175 7 + 2 Kittens
176 Let's Choose the Correct Answers 2. a, 3. b, 4. c, 5. a
177 7 + 3 Pigs
178 Select the Proper Words 2. music, 3. asleep, 4. mask, 5. shine, 6. twins, 7. sea, 8. skirt, 9. brush, 10. seal, 11. last, 12. ship
179 Describe the Words 2. c, 3. b, 4. c, 5. a
180 Match Words and Pictures 1. dust, 2. music, 3. asleep, 4. mask, 5. shine, 6. twins, 7. sea, 8. skirt, 9. brush, 10. seal, 11. last, 12. ship
181 7 + 4 Ducks
182 Can You Remember the Definitions? 2. c, 3. b, 4. a, 5. a
183 7 + 5 Monkeys
184 Which Pictures Match the Words? 2. team, 3. boot, 4. tail, 5. cut, 6. toes, 7. bottle, 8. eat, 9. tool, 10. tooth, 11. fat, 12. wet
185 Developing Your Vocabulary 2. b, 3. c, 4. a, 5. a
186 Name the Pictures 1. stem, 2. team, 3. boot, 4. tail, 5. cut, 6. toes, 7. bottle, 8. eat, 9. tool, 10. tooth, 11. fat, 12. wet
187 7 + 6 Giraffes
188 Select the Correct Answers 2. b, 3. a, 4. c, 5. a
189 8 + 2 Books
190 Choosing Proper Words 2. study, 3. pour, 4. curls, 5. suit, 6. turtle, 7. fur, 8. button, 9. hunt, 10. luck, 11. buy, 12. out
191 What Are the Answers? 2. c, 3. a, 4. b, 5. b
192 Naming Objects 1. butter, 2. study, 3. pour, 4. curls, 5. suit, 6. turtle, 7. fur, 8. button, 9. hunt, 10. luck, 11. buy, 12. out
193 8 + 3 Apples
194 Give the Descriptions 2. b, 3. a, 4. c, 5. a
195 8 + 4 Lambs
196 Writing Words in Spaces 2. dive, 3. save, 4. river, 5. serve, 6. five, 7. leave, 8. weave, 9. cave, 10. waves, 11. voice, 12. vine
197 Giving Correct Answers 2. c, 3. b, 4. b, 5. b
198 Identify the Pictures 1. slave, 2. dive, 3. save, 4. river, 5. serve, 6. five, 7. leave, 8. weave, 9. cave, 10. waves, 11. voice, 12. vine
199 8 + 5 Turtles
200 Pick the Correct Answers 2. a, 3. c, 4. c, 5. a
201 8 + 6 Boats
202 Selecting Proper Words 2. snow, 3. witch, 4. wolf, 5. wheel, 6. whale, 7. elbow, 8. water, 9. swing, 10. swim, 11. flower, 12. well
203 Do You Know the Meanings? 2. c, 3. b, 4. b, 5. a
204 Learning Spelling Words 1. weight, 2. snow, 3. witch, 4. water, 5. wheel, 6. whale, 7. elbow, 8. well, 9. swing, 10. swim, 11. flower, 12. wolf
205 8 + 7 Mice
206 Can You Select the Right Answers? 2. a, 3. b, 4. a, 5. c
207 9 + 2 Children
208 Match Words with the Right Pictures 2. ox, 3. ax, 4. relax, 5. fix, 6. explode, 7. cowboy, 8. mix, 9. wax, 10. extra, 11. box, 12. six
209 Selecting Correct Answers 2. a, 3. c, 4. b, 5. c
210 Identifying Pictures 1. exercise, 2. ox, 3. ax, 4. relax, 5. fix, 6. explode, 7. cowboy, 8. mix, 9. wax, 10. extra, 11. box, 12. six
211 9 + 3 Bears
212 Selecting the Right Answers 2. a, 3. c, 4. c, 5. a
213 9 + 4 Flowers
214 Spelling Students should write each word that is printed below each picture. Help students if they need it. Be sure students use manuscript. Offer help for all similar lessons.
215 Let's Describe the Words 2. b, 3. a, 4. c, 5. b
216 Matching Words and Pictures
217 9 + 5 Candy Bars
218 Spelling
219 9 + 6 Oranges
220 Fun in Naming Pictures
221 Our Flag 2. 50; 3. state; 4. ground; 5. buildings, streets, speeches; 6. sunrise to sunset; I pledge allegiance to the flag of the United States of America and to the Republic for which it stands, one Nation under God, indivisible, with liberty and justice for all.
222 Fun with Stories My Room — 1. b, 2. a, 3. c, 4. a
Bicycle Riding — 1. c, 2. b, 3. b, 4. a
223 9 + 7 Butterflies
224 Write Words
225 The Wheat Farmer 1. breads, cakes, cookies, cereals; 2. green; 3. seeds; 4. yellow; 5. spring, fall
226 Stories Walking to School — 1. c, 2. a, 3. c, 4. b
Learning About a Hospital — 1. b, 2. b, 3. a, 4. c
227 9 + 8 Marbles
228 Writing Spelling Words
229 Neighbors That Help Us milkman, milk; laundry, clothes; baker, bakery; cobbler, shoes
230 Story Fun The Circus — 1. a, 2. c, 3. b, 4. c
Policemen — 1. b, 2. a, 3. c, 4. a
231 How Is Your Spelling?
232 Friendly Helpers Help students if needed. Do the same for similar lessons.
233 Stories of Interest Farmer Brown — 1. b, 2. a, 3. c, 4. c
A Trip to the Zoo — 1. b, 2. a, 3. c, 4. a
234 Addition and Subtraction Through 9's 4. 3, 2, 4; 2, 2, 9; 4, 15, 3; 5. 17, 8, 7; 16, 13, 5; 5, 2, 11; 6. 7, 3, 7; 8, 12, 14; 5, 4, 12; 7. 13, 8. 8, 9. 15, 10. 3
235 Fun with Spelling
236 Helpful Neighbors
237 Interesting Stories Maps — 1. b, 2. a, 3. c, 4. b
Water Systems — 1. b, 2. a, 3. c, 4. c
238 Practicing Addition & Subtraction Through 9's A—5, 9, 10, 3, 8, 10, 15, 12, 8; B—12, 4, 6, 3, 1, 16, 13, 11, 2, 9; C—10, 10, 7, 6, 9, 10, 15, 14, 7, 5; D—17, 3, 8, 16, 2, 7, 11, 2, 12, 16; E—6, 5, 11, 1, 6, 13, 3, 11, 7, 7; F—2, 14, 7, 10, 3, 4, 2, 3, 15, 12; G—9, 10, 16, 1, 13, 13, 17, 5, 6, 13; H—6, 2, 12, 16, 6, 7, 13, 12, 8, 4; I—16, 12, 7, 8, 12, 11, 8, 2, 12, 11; J—12, 10, 5, 1, 17, 11, 13, 7, 10
239 Recognizing Words
240 Doctor and Dentist
241 Enjoyable Stories My School — 1. a, 2. c, 3. b, 4. b
The Library — 1. b, 2. a, 3. b, 4. c
242 Recognizing Spelling Words
243 Firemen
244 Reading for Fun Newspapers — 1. c, 2. a, 3. b, 4. b
Vince the Bus Driver — 1. b, 2. a, 3. c, 4. a
245 Names of Tens 20, twenty; 30, thirty; 40, forty; 50, fifty; 60, sixty; 70, seventy; 80, eighty; 90, ninety; 100, hundred
246 Writing Picture Words
247 Health Review B—1. true, 2. true, 3. false, 4. true, 5. false, 6. true, 7. false, 8. false, 9. true, 10. false; C—1. gums, 2. teeth, 3. taste buds, 4. tongue
248 Understanding What You Read Bill's Garden — 1. b, 2. a, 3. c, 4. a; Helping Mother — 1. a, 2. c, 3. b, 4. c
249 Tens 3, 7; 4, 6; 5, 5; 6, 4; 7, 3; 8, 2; 9, 1; 5, 7; 6, 6; 7, 5
250 Improving Spelling
251 Exercises to Do Fire Drills — 1. a, 2. c, 3. c, 4. b
The Fourth of July Twins — 1. c, 2. c, 3. a, 4. a
252 Ears A—1. yes, 2. yes, 3. yes; B—These are the words to be underlined: sounds, whistle, music, loud, sing, hear, noise, laughter
253 Learning Words
254 More About Ears Help students with part "A" if necessary. B—1. c, 2. false, 3. c, 4. b, 5. a, 6. c
255 Enjoying Stories Tom the Mailman — 1. c, 2. b, 3. b, 4. a
A Dangerous Job — 1. a, 2. c, 3. b, 4. c

256 Completing Each Row B—88, 90, 92, 93, 95; C—0, 2, 4, 6, 8; D—14, 15, 16, 20, 21, 22; E—57, 59, 60, 62, 64, 65; F—37, 38, 42, 43, 44, 45; G—0, 1, 2, 3, 7, 8; H—93, 94, 95, 96, 100, 101; I—69, 70, 74, 75, 76, 77
257 Write the Spelling Words
258 Protecting Eyes Students should be able to answer "yes" to all six questions.
259 Puzzling Stories Germs — 1. b, 2. a, 3. c, 4. a
Airports — 1. a, 2. b, 3. a, 4. c
260 What Comes Before? B—19, 24, 27, 31, 35; C—38, 41, 44, 40, 17; D—11, 23, 28, 32, 36; E—12, 18, 25, 33, 42; F—46, 49, 16, 34, 43; G—52, 59, 63, 21, 30; H—55, 37, 15, 20, 61; I—47, 39, 22, 29, 26
261 Learn to Spell Better
262 Understanding Stories A Lady Doctor — 1. b, 2. a, 3. b, 4. c
The Dentist — 1. c, 2. a, 3. b, 4. a
263 Keeping Clean 1. water, towel, soap; 2. each day; 3. before each meal; 4. after each meal; 5. yes
264 Know the Words
265 Reading Exercises Nurse Margaret — 1. c, 2. a, 3. c, 4. b
An Orange Cat — 1. b, 2. a, 3. c, 4. b.
266 Our Best Foods milk, meat, apple, vegetables, cereal, orange
267 What Comes After? B. 8, C. 11, D. 14, E. 15, F. 20, G. 25, H. 28, I. 32, J. 36, K. 39, L. 42, M. 45, N. 41, O. 18, P. 12, Q. 24, R. 29, S. 33, T. 37, U. 13, V. 19, W. 26, X. 34, Y. 43, Z. 47, A. 50, B. 17, C. 35, D. 44, E. 53, F. 60, G. 64, H. 22, I. 31, J. 56, K. 38, L. 16, M. 21, N. 62, O. 48, P. 40, Q. 23, R. 30, S. 27
268 Writing Different Words
269 The Many Forms of Water 2. steam, Steam; 3. sleet; 4. frost; 5. snow; 6. dew
270 Questions to Answer A Good Diet — 1. a, 2. c, 3. a, 4. b
Growing — 1. c, 2. c, 3. a, 4. b
271 Even Numbers to 100
272 Knowing and Writing Words
273 Wealth from the Earth
274 Exercises We Do My Backyard — 1. a, 2. c, 3. a, 4. b
Dairy Farms — 1. b, 2. c, 3. b, 4. c
275 Odd Numbers to 100
276 Writing Many Words
277 Reading Stories Staying with a Friend — 1. c, 2. a, 3. a, 4. b
A Halloween Party — 1. b, 2. a, 3. c, 4. a
278 The Earth's Different Places 1. streams, 2. oceans, 3. Prairies, 4. Canyon, 5. Hills, 6. forests
279 Telling Time A. 9, 8, 4, 1, 11; B. 6, 10, 3, 2, 5; C. 12:30, 11:30, 9:30, 11:30, 4:30; D. 2:30, 10:00, 7:00, 5:00, 12:00
280 Learning to Spell Better
281 Water on the Earth Help students identify the uses of water shown in the pictures.
282 Choosing Correct Answers Skating — 1. b, 2. a, 3. a, 4. c
A Rainbow — 1. b, 2. a, 3. b, 4. c
283 Spelling Fun
284 Time Problems Help students with this lesson if necessary.
285 The Earth's Land Parts
286 Stories We Like The Sports Car — 1. b, 2. c, 3. a, 4. c
A Visit with Grandmother — 1. a, 2. b, 3. c, 4. b
287 Using Picture Words
288 Air Is Everywhere 2. pushes, 3. above, 4. inside, 5. turns, 6. moves
289 Using Naming Words
290 Objects of Different Colors
291 Having Fun with Stories Geese — 1. a, 2. c, 3. b, 4. b
Teri Fixes Breakfast — 1. b, 2. a, 3. a, 4. c
292 Plane Figures A—circle, rectangle, square, triangle; B—rectangle, circle, triangle, square; C—triangle, rectangle, square, circle; D—square, triangle, circle, rectangle
293 Correctly Spelled Words
294 Do You Know? A—Be sure each student writes the alphabet correctly, using manuscript. B—angry, apple, beg, cart, deliver, event, fox, golf, green, hotel, in
C—Help students write simple statements and questions.
295 Reading Comprehension Our Family — 1. c, 2. a, 3. b, 4. b
The Dictionary — 1. a, 2. b, 3. a, 4. c

296 Arithmetic Word Problems B—60, 90; C—24, 36; D—36, 54; E—14, 21; F—2; G—hat; H—25; I—2; J—"X" in first box (half dollar); K—1 mile; L—1 ton
297 The Reindeer 1. strong, 2. cold, 3. skins, 4. milk, 5. fast, 6. sleds
298 Public Places Encourage students to think about what should be on the signs. In some cases it is appropriate to remind students that safety rules may be used.
299 Arithmetic Word Problems B—20, 30, 40; C—6, 18, 24; D—36; E—26; F—26, 39, 52; G—25, 75, 100; H—70, 105, 140; I—100, 150, 200; J—22; K—12
300 Vowel Sounds A—3. blĕd, 4. mĕn, 5. mēan, 6. shāke, 7. tūbe, 8. wāke, 9. kēy, 10. nōte, 11. nīght, 12. brĕad, 13. cōat, 14. tēa, 15. fĭx. 16. māin, 17. fīnal, 18. fŭnny, 19. năp, 20. ōpen, 21. dŏctor, 22. gō, 23. fīve, 24. māde; B—3. mat, 4. mad, 5. car, 6. met, 7. lock, 8. pin, 9. track, 10. cup, 11. dim, 12. not, 13. fix, 14. man, 15. milk, 16. cot, 17. fast, 18. nap, 19. up, 20. yes; C—ā ū ē ī ō
301 How Does Jack Feel? A — 1. happy, 2. mad, 3. sleepy, 4. sad
B — 1. b, 2. d, 3. a, 4. e, 5. c
302 Counting Money A—4, 7, 9; B—15, 25, 35; C—26, 40, 13; D—11, 17, 16; E—8, 24; F—35, 40; G—80, 19; H—85, 55; I—28, 26; J—95, 35
303 Where You Live
304 The Eagle 1. golden, 2. flag, 3. money, 4. nest, 5. strong, 6. feathers
305 Two-Letter Vowel Sounds "oo" A—1. bo͞ot, 2. mo͞on, 3. wo͝od, 4 ro͞ot, 5. to͞oth, 6. fo͞od, 7. no͞on B—2. boots, 3. noon, 4. food, 5. wood, 6. roots, 7. tooth
306 Supply Rhyming Words B—meal, steal, deal; C—boy, toy, joy; D—toe, go, so; E—tree, me, see; F—head, bed, red, G—bump, thump, lump; H—nose, rose, goes; I—town, brown, down; J—hay, lay, stay; K—book, look, took; L—door, more, roar
307 Money Problems A—16, 10, 26, no; B—40, 11, 51, no; 70, 27, 97, yes; C—45, 15, 60, no; 77, 17, 94, no
308 Airplanes 1. yes, 2. yes, 3. yes, 4. yes
309 The Snake 1. skin, 2. fast, 3. mice, 4. skins, 5. tongue, 6. bigger
310 Vowel Sounds "ou," "ow," "au," "aw," "oi," "oy" A—2. ou, 3. ow, 4. ou, 5. ou, 6. ow, 7. ou, 8. ow; B—1 - 8 ow; C—1. aw, 2. aw, 3. au, 4. aw, 5. aw, 6. au, 7. aw, 8. au; D—1. oi, 2. oy, 3. oy, 4. oi, 5. oy, 6. oi, 7. oi, 8. oi
311 Listening with Eyes 2. left, 3. hello, 4. quiet, 5. love, 6. sad, 7. hurt, 8. stop, 9. happy
312 Odd Tens, Counting by 10's to 1,000
313 Buses 1. no, 2. yes, 3. yes, 4. no
314 All About Salt 1. white, 2. salt, 3. under, 4. mines, 5. deep, 6. animals
315 Recognizing Long Vowels A—1. me, 2. fly, 3. hay, 4. we, 5. so, 6. light, 7. fry, 8. go, 9. use, 10. no, 11. way, 12. sly, 13. be, 14. tray, 15. wild; B—2. fly, 3. go, 4. me, 5. sky, 6. My
316 A Listening Poster A—2. interrupt, 3. attention, 4. polite, 5. hands; B—A. 4, B. 3, C. 7, D. 1, E. 6, F. 2, G. 5
317 Counting by 10's to 1,000 (Even 10's)
318 Traveling by Train Help students as necessary.
319 Beagles 1. floppy; 2. hunting; 3. gentle, friendly; 4. rabbits; 5. Beagles, 6. watchdogs
320 Following Vowels with "R" "ir" sound—sir, skirt, girl, dirt, first, fir, stir, whirl; "ar" sound—bark, far, yard, dark, park, barn; "er" sound— term, summer, fern, hammer, every, water, her, clerk; "ur" sound—burn, nurse, purse, turn, curl, curve, church, hurt; "or" sound—north, sport, stork, or, for
321 Music for Quiet Time 2. typewriter, 3. harp, 4. bicycle, 5. banjo, 6. radio, 7. calliope, 8. clock. 9. record player, 10. guitar, 11. telephone, 12. trumpet
322 < Means "Is Less Than" C, F, G, H, I, J, L, M, O, P, Q, S, U, V, X, Y, Z, A
323 The Post Office 1. no, 2. no, 3. yes, 4. yes, 5. yes, 6. yes
324 Pictures in Caves 1. stories; 2. caves; 3. walls; 4. stores; 5. warm, dry; 6. write
325 Beginning or Final Sounds A—2. wh p, 3. str ng, 4. c rd, 5. fl g, 6. st mp, 7. f rk, 8. gl s, 9. t nt, 10. wh l, 11. thr d, 12. k ng, 13. dr m, 14. th n, 15. fl r, 16. ch ch, 17. sp n, 18. b sh, 19. cl d, 20. cl n, 21. w rm, 22. st mp; B—3. log, 4. moon, 5. lion, 6. seal, 7. bean, 8. jug, 9. mat, 10. book, 11. wood, 12. deer, 13. pail, 14. cot, 15. pear

326 Applying What You Know A—2. b; 3. c; B—1. c; 2. a; 3. a; C—1. a, b; 2. a, c; D—1. a. 1; b. 2; 2. a. 2; b. 1; E—1. 3 o'clock; 2. tea; 3. me

327 > Means "Is Greater Than" B, D, E, F, G, H, I, J, K, M, O, Q, R, S, V, W, X, Y, Z

328 The Supermarket

329 Autumn 1. frost, 2. nuts, 3. winter, 4. south, 5. Farmers, 6. Leaves

330 Consonant and Vowel Sounds A—2. ch; 3. wh; 4. th; 5. th; 6. ch; 7. th, sh; 8. sh; 9. sh; 10. th, 11. ch; 12. sh; 13. wh, ch; 14. sh, th, wh; 15. sh; 16. ch; 17. ch; 18. ch; 19. ch; 20. sh; B—3. tĕnt, 4. thĭck, 5. rŏck, 6. răg, 7. păn, 8. nŭt, 9. băt, 10. hĭs, 11. făn, 12. ŏn, 13. ăm, 14. jŭst, 15. hŏt, 16. pĭn, 17. nō, 18. răn, 19. slōw, 20. wē

331 Repeating Instructions A—2. a, 3. b, 4. b, 5. c, 6. a; B—1. ran, tan; 2. rake, cake; 3. moon, spoon; 4. car, jar; 5. top, mop; 6. cat, rat, bat; 7. box, fox; 8. fan, man, ran; 9. boat, goat; 10. wall, tall; C—1. c, 2. b, 3. a, 4. b, 5. b, 6. c, 7. a, 8. c

332 Writing Numerals D. 47, E. 49, F. 38, G. 53, H. 66, I. 31, J. 26, K. 44, L. 29, M. 51, N. 56, O. 40, P. 36, Q. 39, R. 43, S. 59, T. 61, U. 25, V. 48, W. 45, X. 28

333 Starfish 1. animals, 2. covering, 3. five, 4. sea, 5. eye, 6. starfish

334 Making Words A—3. o, 4. o, 5. y, 6. a, 7. e, 8. i, 9. o, 10. c, 11. c, 12. l, 13. t, 14. e, 15. t, 16. s, 17. l, 18. t, 19. t, 20. o, 21. a, 22. l, 23. e, 24. a; B—4. w k, 5. j n, 6. m n, 7. t p, 8. r n, 9. h r, 10. h l, 11. b d, 12. b d, 13. f r, 14. b t, 15. f r, 16. d s, 17. b d, 18. t n, 19. l d, 20. cr l, 21. s n, 22. p ty, 23. f n, 24. sh d, 25. m n, 26. p l, 27. f r, 28. t b, 29. l d, 30. t p, 31. d r, 32. t d, 33. g s, 34. n th, 35. h l

335 Selecting Best Answers A—1. a, 2. b; B—1. a, 2. c, 3. b; C—1. b, 2. b, 3. a, 4. c

336 Ten + 1, 2, 3, 4, 5 B. 12, C. 13, D. 14, F. 12, G. 14, H. 13, J. 12, K. 15, L. 11, M. 13, N. 15, O. 11, P. 10, Q. 15, R. 11, S. 10, T. 13, U. 11, V. 10, W. 13, X. 12

337 No Clothes for Animals 1. hair, 2. clothes, 3. birdbaths, 4. tongue, 5. people, 6. feathers

338 "le" Words 2. raffle, 3. eagle, 4. purple, 5. pickle, 6. wrestle, 7. candle, 8. bundle, 9. people, 10. settle, 11. Myrtle, 12. able

339 Taking Tests

A—2. e; 3. a; 4. b; 5. d

B—1. a; 2. b; 3. b; 4. a; 5. a

C—1. play, pig; 2. with, work; 3. boy, bad; 4. ride, run; 5. see, sad; 6. big, bag

D—1. 1; 2. 3; 3. 2; 4. 7; 5. 2; 6. 0

E—1. no, 2. no, 3. yes, 4. no, 5. yes, 6. no

340 Ten + 6, 7, 8, 9 B. 17, C. 18, D. 19, F. 19, G. 16, H. 18, J. 17, K. 19, L. 16, M. 19, N. 16, O. 17, P. 15, Q. 16, R. 17, S. 19, T. 18, U. 18, V. 19, W. 15, X. 17

341 The Oppossum 1. dead, 2. small, 3. pouch, 4. bees, 5. night, 6. tail

342 "er" and "est" Endings

A	2. braver	bravest
	3. riper	ripest
	4. paler	palest
	5. nicer	nicest
	6. closer	closest
	7. later	latest
	8. finer	finest
B	2. sillier	silliest
	3. fuzzier	fuzziest
	4. sleepier	sleepiest
	5. curlier	curliest
	6. saltier	saltiest
	7. furrier	furriest
	8. funnier	funniest
	9. luckier	luckiest
	10. drier	driest
	11. rockier	rockiest

343 Following Poems

A—1. school, 2. twenty, 3. green

B—1. 3 o'clock, 2. tea, 3. me

C—1. a box, 2. in a puddle, 3. the rocks

D—1. rivers, 2. seas, 3. sky

E—1. shells, 2. damp, 3. wells

344 Twenty + 6, 7, 8, 9 B. 27, C. 28, D. 29, F. 28, G. 29, H. 26, J. 29, K. 26, L. 27, M. 29, N. 26, O. 27, P. 28, Q. 28, R. 27, S. 26, T. 29, U. 26, V. 27, W. 28, X. 29

345 The Spider's Web 1. web; 2. food; 3. threads; 4. sticky; 5. Flies, sticky; 6. spider, threads

346 Final Letters and Endings A—2. e, 3. b, 4. de, 5. de, 6. w, 7. b, 8. t, 9. d, 10. d, 11. b, 12. ne; B—2. locked, 3. stared, 4. planted, 5. showed, 6. called, 7. used, 8. painted, 9. rented, 10. cared; C—2. started, 3. traded, 4. pretended, 5. ransomed, 6. threaded, 7. added, 8. shaved, 9. parted, 10. tamed, 11. ended, 12. happened

347 Practicing Directions A—2. d; 3. b, d; B—1. c; 2, a; 3. d; 4. b; C—1. a bug, 2. walk, 3. runs; D—1. b, 2. d, 3. c, 4. a; E—1. F, 2. T, 3. F

348 Recognizing Tens D. 83, E. 61, F. 24, G. 60, H. 22, I. 10, J. 90, K. 58, L. 46, M. 70, N. 7, O. 63, P. 28, Q. 49, R. 79, S. 80, T. 81, U. 11, V. 95, W. 54, X. 42, Y. 36, Z. 18, A. 39

349 Beach Hermit 1. softest, 2. claws, 3. house, 4. snails, 5. four, 6. beach

350 Making Words and Sentences A—2. quickly, 3. rainiest, 4. hilly, 5. sleeper, 6. sticky, 7. dirtiest, 8. friendly, 9. strongest, 10. softer, 11. fastest, 12. sooner, 13. soapy, 14. lately; B—2. silliest, 3. deepest, 4. curlier, 5. hilly, 6. longer,

351 Watching for Clues A—2. grapes, 3. banana, 4. orange, 5. lemon, 6. apple

All statements in 1—6 should have "X" beside them.

B—1. G, 2. E, 3. F, 4. C, 5. A, 6. H, 7. D, 8. B

352 Total Coins A 5, 10, 7; B 15, 17; C 10, 25, 8; D 14, 51; E 25, 50, 75; F 40, 60, 26; G 85, 42; H 75, 92

353 The Sand Dollar 1. round, 2. silver, 3. holes, 4. feet, 5. hairs, 6. skeleton

354 Dividing Words (Closed Syllables) B. 2, 2, 2; C. 2, 3, 2; D. 1, 2, 1; E. 2, 3, 2; F. 1, 2, 1; G. 2, 4, 2; H. 2, 2, 2; I. 1, 2, 1; J. 2, 3, 2; K. 1, 2, 1; L. 2, 3, 2; M. 1, 1, 1; N. 3, 3, 3; O. 3, 3, 3; P. 3, 4, 3; Q. 2, 2, 2; R. 3, 4, 3

355 Differences (Big) A "X" should be on: 2, 3, 5, 7, 8, 13, 15; B—1. c, 2. c, 3. a, 4. c, 5. a, 6. a, 7. a, 8. c, 9. c, 10. a

356 Counting Money (Coins)

5.	2	5	6. 2, 1	4
	2	5	10	2
	10		5	
7.	2	5	8. 20	25
	10	10	5	5
	25		2, 1	
9.	10	5	10. 10	5
	25	2	10	20
	4			

357 Caterpillars 1. worms, 2. Tent, 3. strong, 4. grown, 5. bodies, 6. leaves

358 Using Compound Words 1. afternoon, basketball; 2. butterscotch, cookbook; 3. football, softball; 4. mailbox, postman; 5. birthday; 6. playground, inside

359 Classifications 1. b, d; 2. a, d; 3. b, c; 4. a, c; 5. a, c; 6. b, c; 7. a, b; 8. b, d

360 Multiplication Properties of 0 and 1 4. zero, 5. product, 6. multiplication, 8. multiplication, 9. zero, 10. all answers are zero, 11. 1

4	2	3
7	5	6
	8	9

Review this lesson with students as often as necessary. Be sure there is complete understanding.

361 Wolves 1. dog, 2. den, 3. Coyotes, 4. one hundred, 5. wilderness, 6. tails

362 Root Words A—2. flatter, flattest; 3. longer, longest; 4. happier, happiest; 5. owner, owning; 6. covered, covering; 7. partner, parting; 8. careful, caring; 9. colder, coldest; 10. freely, freer; B—2. cover, 3. settle, 4. care, 5. sleep, 6. care, 7. free, 8. low, 9. hard, 10. cover, 11. free, 12. love, 13. like, 14. kind

363 Milk and Other Liquids A—2. butter, 3. cheese, 4. chocolate milk; bones, teeth, D; B—1. pineapples, 2. apples, 3. grapes, 4. oranges

364 Practicing Multiplication Properties of 0 and 1

E	0	1	0	0	2	2
	0	3	0	3	0	0
F	4	0	4	5	0	5
	0	0	6	0	6	0
G	7	7	0	8	0	8
	0	9	0	9	1	0
H	6	0	5	0	4	0
	0	0	2	0	0	9
I	8	0	9	3	0	0
	0	0	6	5	4	3
J	2	1	0	0	0	0
	0	0	0	0	0	9

365 Sea Shells 1. beach, 2. snail, 3. sizes, 4. round, 5. food, 6. colorful

366 Compound Words to Write 3. box, 5. man, 7. some, 9. set, 11. mill, 13. bag, 15. coat, 17. hole, 19. top, 21. tie, 23. ride, 25. be, 27. time

367 Protein Foods pork, beef, mutton; 1. pig; 2. cow; 3. chickens, turkeys; 4. sheep; 1. peas, 2. fish, 3. eggs, 4. peanut butter, 5. lobster

368 Honey 1. flowers, 2. kings, 3. energy, 4. honeybees, 5. honey, 6. ancient

369 Forming New Words A—C. item, D. other, E. brave, F. port, G. hard, H. tall, I. small, J. love, K. tall, L. hand, M. green, N. wonder, O. America, P. stupid, Q. care, R. clear, S. invent, T. auto B—2. alphabetize 3. guide, 4. lone, 5. improve, 6. care, 7. perfect, 8. act, 9. friend, 10. kind, 11. read, 12. self

370 Our Grain Foods

371 The Friendly Squirrel 1. tiny, 2. sharp, 3. hand, 4. park, 5. friends, 6. bite

372 Count Syllables 4. a vert ed, 5. bas ket, 6. tar get, 7. chil dren, 8. dis charge, 9. dic tate, 10. ex port ed, 11. rest less, 12. please, 13. pur ple, 14. ser vant, 15. dis play ing, 16. ad dress, 17. near est, 18. cir cus, 19. com bine, 20. ac count, 21. a cross, 22. un like ly, 23. dis grace, 24. un cer tain, 25. car pen ter, 26. com fort, 27. swim ming, 28. a light, 29. tel e phone, 30. tra peze

373 Fruits to Grow On 1. eat; 2. dessert; 3. snack; 4. straight, tall

374 Storks 1. birds, 2. legs, 3. voices, 4. nests, 5. babies, 6. good luck

375 Syllabication 2. ad mit, 3. de fine, 4. de fense, 5. un like ly, 6. un re al, 7. post man, 8. sud den, 9. be fore hand, 10. car pen ter, 11. mis print, 12. dis trust, 13. moun tain, 14. ac cept ed, 15. re mem ber, 16. a dop tion, 17. turn pike, 18. un fas ten, 19. un cer tain, 20. de part, 21. joy ful, 22. near est, 23. bet ter, 24. tel e graph, 25. un com mon, 26. el e phant, 27. de ter gent, 28. mon u ment, 29. oc ca sion, 30. sweet er, 31. re fund, 32. fair ness, 33. ex pen sive, 34. dis lo ca tion, 35. de frost, 36. cel e brate

376 Vegetables to Grow On 1. carbohydrates, minerals; 2. energy; 3. A, B, C; 4. Iron; 5. Calcium

377 The Eskimo Dog 1. courage; 2. hair; 3. sleds, 4. feet; 5. seals, bears; 6. cold

378 What Is a Prefix? 2. ex, expose; 3. ex, expert; 4. ex, expect, 5. re, remind; 6. in, invent; 7. de, defect; 8. dis, distrust; 9. sub, subway; 10. dis, disrobe; 11. de, depend; 12. re, reappear; 13. in, income; 14. a, about; 15. de, depart; 16. de, demand; 17. un, undone; 18. dis, disjoint; 19. dis, dislocate; 20. re, remain; 21. en, enrage; 22. a, amount; 23. re, refer; 24. pre, preview

379 Healthy Ways 2. milk; 3. vegetables, fruit; 4. water; 5. fruit; 6. grows; 7. health; 8. teeth

380 The Little Termite 1. harmful, 2. wood, 3. insects, 4. ants, 5. warm, 6. queen

381 What Is a Suffix? 2. ing, swimming; 3. est, quietest; 4. ize, rubberize; 5. ance, distance; 6. ful, colorful; 7. some, gruesome; 8. some, wholesome; 9. less, helpless; 10. ing, walking; 11. er, wider; 12. ize, Americanize; 13. most, almost; 14. ful, helpful; 15. ward, downward; 16. ness, slowness; 17. ly, lovely; 18. ance, disturbance; 19. est, fattest; 20. ly, dryly; 21. dom, freedom; 22. ment, payment; 23. ous, dangerous; 24. er, larger; 25. able, breakable; 26. itis, hepatitis; 27. ive, sportive; ly, fully; 29. ous, joyous; 30. ize, criticize

382 Eat Fresh Fruits b. banana, c. grapes, d. cherries, e. orange, f. pineapple, g. apple, h. peach, i. strawberries, j. plums

383 All About Lizards 1. scaly, 2. tail, 3. feet, 4. two, 5. tricks, 6. trees

384 Adding Prefixes and Suffixes A—2. un, 3. ex, 4. re, 5. mis; B—2. less, 3. ly, 4. ness, 5. able

385 Vegetables 1. tomato, 2. peas, 3. celery, 4. potatoes, 5. beans, 6. corn, 7. lettuce, 8. carrots, 9. beets

386 Frogs 1. insects; 2. water, land; 3. 2000; 4. tongues; 5. jump, swim; 6. enemies

387 Matching Synonyms A&B—2. T, 3. L, 4. A, 5. W, 6. Q, 7. B, 8. V, 9. X, 10. C, 11. M, 12. G, 13. D, 14. I, 15. E, 16. U, 17. P, 18. F, 19. K, 20. H, 21. R, 22. N, 23. J, 24. S; C&D—2. V, 3. S, 4. U, 5. P, 6. R, 7. N, 8. X, 9. A, 10. D, 11. F, 12. W, 13. E, 14. O, 15. M, 16. K, 17. C, 18. G, 19. J, 20. T, 21. I, 22. B, 23. L, 24. O

388 A Good Breakfast 1. cereal, 2. tomato, 3. corn, 4. ice cream, 5. celery, 6. eggs, 7. orange, 8. carrots, 9. bread, 10. soup, 11. milk, 12. cake; Help students circle the breakfast foods.

389 Salmon 1. streams; 2. food; 3. hatched; 4. eggs; 5. ocean, food; 6. die

390 Greater Than or Less Than B. greater, C. lesser, D. greater, E. lesser, F. greater, G. greater, H. lesser, I. greater, J. greater, K. greater, L. greater, M. greater, N. lesser, O. greater, P. greater, Q. greater, R. greater, S. greater, T. lesser, U. greater, V. greater, W. greater, X. lesser, Y. lesser, Z. lesser, A. greater, B. greater

391 Matching Antonyms A—2. chilly, 3. raised, 4. wise, 5. quiet; B I—2. C, 3. F, 4. H, 5. J, 6. B, 7. I, 8. A, 9. E, 10. D; B II—2. J, 3. H, 4. A, 5. I, 6. B, 7. E, 8. C, 9. G, 10. D

392 Health and Safety Quiz 14, 12, 1, 10, 4, 3, 11, 5, 13, 7, 16, 15, 6, 18, 9, 17, 8

393 Baby Animals 1. a, 2. b, 3. c, 4. a; 1. b, c; 2. a, b; 3. a, b, c; 4. a; 5. a, c; 1. puppy, 2. kitten, 3. bird, 4. bear, 5. pony, 6. calf, 7. pig, 8. chick

394 Writing Digits B. 25, C. 16, D. 37, E. 14, F. 31, G. 18, H. 24, I. 12, J. 22, K. 19, L. 28, M. 17, N. 23, O. 15, P. 33, Q. 13, R. 46, S. 57, T. 35, U. 26, V. 32, W. 49, X. 55

395 Food A—1. food; 2. hungry, disease; 3. healthy; B—1. T, 2. F, 3. F, 4. T, 5. F

396 Using the Dictionary 2. A, 3. B, 4. A, 5. B, 6. B, 7. B, 8. B, 9. B, 10. A, 11. B, 12. A, 13. B

397 Planning Our Breakfast Menu B. 6, C. 12, D. 2, E. 7, F. 13, G. 4, H. 9, I. 11, J. 18, K. 5, L. 16, M. 1, N. 17, O. 3, P. 8, Q. 10, R. 14

398 Dogs 1. a, 2. a, 3. c, 4. b; 1. c, 2. a, 3. c, 4. a, 5. b; boy—4, bell—5, box—6, baby—1, bear—2, boat—3

399 Small and Large Numbers B. 17, 12, 6; C. 13, 11, 12; D. 50, 30, 34; E. 11, 6, 18; F. 60, 89, 64; G. 40, 49, 10; H. 9, 17, 12; B. 75, 82, 83; C. 50, 69, 57; D. 90, 26, 93; E. 13, 12, 45; F. 50, 89, 31; G. 86, 20, 40; H. 82, 11, 21

400 Milk A—1. no, 2. no, 3. yes; B—A. cheese, C. butter, E. ice cream; C— hot chocolate-2, shake-4, soda pop-3, milk-1

401 Vowel Rules A—1. wrote, bone, float; 2. shoe, true, suit; 3. beat, deep, lazy; 4. winter, sister, inch, hidden; 5. fast, wag, gather; 6. mend, lead, tent; B. 3. short i, 4. long i, 5. short i, 6. short a, 7. short o, 8. short u, 9. long o, 10. short a, 11. short u, 12. short e, 13. short u, 14. long i, 15. short a, 16. long a, 17. short e, 18. long i, 19. long i, 20. short a, 21. short i, 22. short o, 23. short e, 24. long e, 25. short o, 26. long a, 27. long a, 28. long i, 29. long u, 30. long o, 31. short e

402 Fruits 1. apple, trees, green or red; 2. grapes, vine, purple or white; 3. orange, breakfast, orange; 4. banana, peel, yellow; 5. strawberry, red, green

403 Working Dogs 1. a, 2. b, 3. c, 4. b; 1. a; 2. a; 3. b, c; 4. b; 5. a, b, c; cow-5, cake-2, cap-3, cat-4, car-6, coat-1

404 Batting Lineup B. Kelly, C. Waddell, D. Banks, E. Chance, F. Cobb, G. Baker, H. Aaron, I. Ward, J. Ruth

405 Grain A—2. E, 3. A, 4. B, 5. D; B—1. C, E; 2. D; 3. B; 4. F; 5. A

406 Sentence Completion A—2. stars, 3. book, 4. dress; B—2. supper, 3. balloon, 4. garden; C—2. carpenter, 3. elephant, 4. octopus; D—2. letter, 3. mailbox, 4. sky, 5. giraffe

407 Mr. Health Food 2. M, 3. K, 4. L, 5. C, 6. I, 7. G, 8. J, 9. D, 10. F, 11. E, 12. A, 13. H

408 Cats 1. b, 2. a, 3. b, 4. c; 1. a, c; 2. a, b; 3. c; 4. b; 5. a, b; duck-1, doll-2, door-5, desk-4, deer-6, dress-3

409 Equivalent Sets A—2. d, 3. b, 4. a; B—2. e, 3. a, 4. b, 5. c

410 Beef, Pork A—1. bacon, sausage, ham; 2. hamburger; 3. steak, roast, chops; B Place "X" beside bacon, sausage, ham, chops. C Draw a box around hamburger, steak, roast.

411 Everyday Helpers 2. J, 3. A, 4. I, 5. H, 6. D, 7. C, 8. E, 9. K, 10. F, 11. B

412 Working Cats 1. b, 2. b, 3. c, 4. a; 1. a, b; 2. a, b, c; 3. b; 4. a, b, c; 5. a; fish-6, frog-4, foot-2, farmer-5, flower-3, fan-1

413 Fowl, Fish A chicken, goose, turkey; B—1. poultry, 2. meat, 3. feathers, 4. eggs, 5. on farms; C "T"-turkey, D "P"-chicken, E "W"-duck, goose; F tuna, salmon, perch, catfish; G—1. meat, 2. in water, 3. bones, 4. scales, 5. fins; H "F"-perch, catfish; I "S"-tuna, salmon

414 Halves B. 1 to 4, C. 1 to 4, D. 5 to 2, E. 1 to 5, F. 2 to 5

415 Eating a Good Breakfast Help students work this lesson. Try to reinforce good nutrition habits.

416 Turtles 1. a, 2. b, 3. a, 4. c; 1. c, 2. a, 3. b, 4. b, 5. a; giraffe-6, goat-2, girl-3, ghost-1, goose-4, guitar-5

417 Fruits B. banana, C. grapes, D. peach, E. cherries, F. grapefruit, G. strawberries, H. lemon, I. plums, J. pineapple, K. pear, L. apple; Underline 2, 4, 6, 7, 9, 12

418 What Am I? 2. soap, 3. banana, 4. egg, 5. corn, 6. comb, 7. milk, 8. apple, 9. carrots, 10. bus

419 Rabbits 1. a, 2. a, 3. b, 4. c; 1. a, b, c; 2. a; 3. c; 4. b; 5. a, b, c; horse-5, hand-6, head-2, hen-4, house-1, hat-3

420 Vegetables peas, pumpkin, lettuce, cabbage, spinach, potatoes, onions, carrots, beets

421 Health and Safety 2. I, 3. H, 4. G, 5. B, 6. E, 7. F, 8. A, 9. J, 10. D

422 Ducks 1. b, 2. a, 3. a, 4. c; 1. b; 2. a, b; 3. c; 4. a; 5. b; jar-2, jeep-3, jet-6, jelly-4, jail-5, jump-1

423 Sweets A—1. yes, 2. no, 3. yes, 4. no, 5. yes, 6. yes, 7. no, 8. yes, 9. no; B—1. sugar, 2. dessert, 3. energy, 4. tooth decay

424 Breakfast

425 Capitalization Students should be able to complete this lesson alone. If necessary, remind them of capitalizations. Students should use manuscript.

426 Geese 1. a, 2. b, 3. a, 4. c; 1. c; 2. a; 3. a; 4. b; 5. a, b, c; key-3, kite-1, knife-4, knee-2, king-6, kangaroo-5

427 Nuts A—2. H, 3. D, 4. C, 5. I, 6. B, 7. G, 8. A, 9. J, 10. E; B—1. shells, 2. trees, 3. sizes, 4. small, 5. protein

428 Writing Sentences

429 Turkeys 1. c, 2. a, 3. b, 4. a; 1. a; 2. a, b; 3. c; 4. a; 5. a, b, c; lion-1, lamb-2, light-4, leaf-5, ladder-6, lock-3

430 Clothing A—2. T, 3. F, 4. T, 5. T, 6. F, 7. T, 8. T; B—2. A, 3. D, 4. F, 5. C, 6. E

431 Forming Sentences

432 Bears 1. a, 2. c, 3. a, 4. b; 1. a, b, c; 2. b; 3. a, b, c; 4. a; 5. c; mouse-5, monkey-1, man-6, mouth-3, moon-4, money-2

433 Clothes We Wear 1. skirt, pants, shirt; 2. dresses, suits, raincoats, boots; 3. sweater, jacket, coat, gloves; 4. caps, hats, gown, pajamas

434 Creating Sentences

435 Horses 1. b; 2. a, c; 3. a; 4. c; 1. a, b, c; 2. a, b, c; 3. b, c; 4. c; 5. a; nest-2, nurse-6, needle-1, nine-5, nail-3, nut-4

436 What Clothes Are Made Of A—2. F, 3. E, 4. C, 5. A, 6. B; B. 4, C. 3, D. 2

437 Composing Sentences

438 Cows 1. a, 2. c, 3. a, 4. a; 1. a, c; 2. a, b; 3. a; 4. c; 5. b, c; puppy-6, pie-3, pencil-2, pear-5, pan-4, pony-1

439 Fibers for Thread A—1. cotton, 2. silk, 3. nylon, 4. flax, 5. wool, 6. rayon; B—2, 5; C—1, 4; D—3, 6

440 Developing Sentences

441 Sheep 1. a; 2. a; 3. a, b, c; 4. a; 1. a; 2. b; 3. c; 4. b, c; 5. a; queen-1, question-4, quarter-2, quail-5, quilt-3

442 How Thread Is Made 1. spindle, 2. spinning machine, 3. spinning wheel

443 Constructing Sentences

444 Goats 1. b, 2. a, 3. c, 4. a; 1. c; 2. c; 3. b; 4. a, b, c; 5. a, b; rat-6, rain-4, rabbit-5, rope-2, rake-1, rug-3

445 Cloth from Thread A—2. thread, 3. cloth; B—1. loom, 2. warp, 3. woof; C—A. 2, B. 3, C. 1

446 Building Sentences

447 Pigs 1. c, 2. a, 3. b, 4. c; 1. c; 2. a; 3. b; 4. c; 5. a, b; sun-5, star-2, ship-1, snake-3, sheep-6, shoe-4

448 Clothes from Cloth A—2. e, 3. d, 4. a, 5. b; B silk, cotton, wool; C—1. no, 2. yes, 3. yes, 4. no, 5. yes, 6. yes, 7. yes

449 Double Letters

450 Chickens 1. a, 2. c, 3. c, 4. a; 1. a, b; 2. c; 3. a; 4. c; 5. a; tree-1, train-5, turtle-3, truck-6, tie-4, table-2

451 Clothes for You A—1. B, 2. C, 3. D, 4. A; 2. Check (✓) should be in box 3.; B—1. B, 2. D, 3. C, 4. A; 1. B; church should be underlined.; 2. Check (✓) should be in box 3.

452 Alphabetical Order 2. cab, cent, city, cloud, cook, curl; 3. eat, echo, egg, eight, else, engine; 4. wag, wee, world, wrote; 5. gate, gentle, girl, goose, grade, guess; 6. sand, sea, shape, silk, snake, soldier

453 Map Directions 1. seven blocks, 2. five blocks east and five blocks north, 3. grandmother's, 4. Post Office, 5. twelve blocks, 6. four blocks south and one block west or one block west and four blocks south, 7. three blocks east and two blocks south, 8. four blocks east and nine blocks north or nine blocks north and four blocks east.

454 Mice 1. a, 2. b, 3. c, 4. a; 1. a, b; 2. b; 3. c; 4. c; 5. c; 1. vase, 2. violin, 3. vest, 4. van, 5. vine

455 Leather 1. jacket, 2. cap, 3. shoes, 5. belt, 6. gloves

456 Write Compound Words 2. hatbox, 3. milkman, 4. handbag, 5. upset, 6. windmill, 7. dustcloth, 8. pigpen, 9. beehive, 10. haircut, 11. cupcake, 12. pipeline, 13. beside, 14. raincoat, 15. mudhole, 16. hilltop

457 Snakes 1. b, 2. c, 3. a, 4. c; 1. b, 2. a, 3. a, 4. c, 5. a; well-5, whale-6, wing-4, worm-2, web-1, wall-3

458 Rubber 1. F; 2. C, E; 3. A; 4. B; 5. D

459 Vowels—Upper Case

460 Lizards 1. a, 2. a, 3. b, 4. c; 1. a, b; 2. a, b, c; 3. a; 4. c; 5. c; 1. xylophone, 2. box, 3. fox, 4. X ray

461 Special Holidays A—Help students fill in the appropriate blanks.; B—house, come, uncles, large, makes, funny, have, such, big, helps, wrap, some, much, happy

462 Furs A—1. b, 2. d, 3. a, 4. c, 5. f, 6. e; B—1. T, 2. F, 3. F, 4. T, 5. T; C—1. fox, 2. beaver, 3. bear, 4. seal, 5. rabbit, 6. raccoon, 7. muskrat, 8. mink

463 Vowels—Lower Case

464 Alligators 1. b, 2. b, 3. c, 4. c; 1. a, c; 2. b; 3. a; 4. b; 5. b; 1. yak, 2. yet, 3. your, 4. yellow, 5. young, 6. yarn, 7. you, 8. yes, 9. yard, 10. year, 11. yell, 12. yo-yo

465 Synthetics A—1. stockings, 2. tank top, 3. scarf, 4. bathing suit, 5. pajamas, 6. pants, 7. tennis shoes, 8. jacket; B Cross out cotton, wool, silk, fur.

466 Consonants—Upper Case

467 Lions 1.b,2.c,3.a,4.b;1.b;2.a;3.a,c;4.b;5.c;1.zipper,2.zero,3. zebra, 4. zoo

468 Shelter A—2. A, 3. F, 4. D, 5. C, 6. B; B—1. E, 2. A, 3. C, 4. B, 5. F, 6. D; C—1. tent, 2. tree house, 3. wigwam, 4. log cabin, 5. castle, 6. igloo

469 Hobbies A—1. are, is; 2. to, two; 3. has, have; 4. seen, saw; 5. go, went; 6. have, has; 7. did, done

470 Consonants—Lower Case

471 Tigers 1. a, 2. c, 3. a, 4. b; 1. a, 2. b, 3. a, 4. a, 5. b; 1. dog, 2. cat, 3. tree, 4. horse, 5. car, 6. apple, 7. fish, 8. house

472 Building Materials B—1. igloo-snow; D—2. cabin-logs; A—3. tent-cloth; E—4. wigwam-bark; C—5. castle-stone; wood, stone, brick; 1. "X" should be by tall city building.; 2. "C" should be by log cabin.
473 Root Words 2. cover, 3. run, 4. home, 5. sleep, 6. care, 7. free, 8. night, 9. hard, 10. east, 11. free, 12. love, 13. like, 14. joy, 15. kind, 16. part, 17. lock, 18. free, 19. thank, 20. slow, 21. harm, 22. deep, 23. go, 24. wonder
474 Leopards 1. a, 2. b, 3. c, 4. a; 1. b, 2. a, 3. a, 4. c, 5. c; Underline: 1, 3, 4, 6, 8, 10, 12, 13, 14, 17, 18, 19, 21, 22, 24
475 Homes A—1. T, 2. F, 3. F, 4. T, 5. T, 6. F, 7. T; B—1. D, 2. A, 3. B, 4. C
476 Writing Letters—Lower Case
477 Elephants 1. c, 2. b, 3. b, 4. a; 1. c, 2. c, 3. a, 4. a, 5. b; cake-4, flag-2, cat-1, snake-3, hat-5, train-6
478 Writing Letters—Mixed
479 Monkeys 1. b, 2. c, 3. a, 4. c; 1. a, 2. c, 3. c, 4. a, 5. b; bed-6, egg-2, seal-1, leaf-4, fence-3, teeth-5
480 Zebras 1. b, 2. c, 3. a, 4. a; 1. a; 2. b; 3. c; 4. a; 5. b, c; pig-6, fire-4, kite-1, fish-5, pie-2, bridge-3
481 Writing Synonyms 2. shy, 3. bashful, 4. moist, 5. under, 6. raced, 7. silent, 8. stay, 9. close, 10. wealthy, 11. big, 12. closed, 13. sack, 14. stone, 15. coat, 16. unhappy, 17. glad, 18. yell, 19. end, 20. jump, 21. fast, 22. high, 23. forest, 24. too
482 Deer 1. c, 2. c, 3. b, 4. b; 1. a, 2. a, 3. c, 4. a, 5. c; fox-5, frog-4, coat-6, clock-3, boat-1, nose-2
483 Proper Names
484 Giraffes 1. c, 2. b, 3. b, 4. a; 1. a; 2. a, b; 3. a; 4. c; 5. a; truck-6, bus-3, puppy-5, mule-1, fruit-2, bug-4
485 Writing Opposites 2. last, 3. fast, 4. open, 5. sad, 6. bad, 7. cry, 8. wild, 9. bottom, 10. good, 11. short, 12. push, 13. fix, 14. gentle, 15. down, 16. hot
486 A Trip to the Zoo 1. c, 2. a, 3. a, 4. c; 1. b, 2. a, 3. a, 4. c, 5. b; 1. a, 2. b, 3. b, 4. a, 5. b, 6. b, 7. b, 8. b, 9. a, 10. a, 11. b, 12. a
487 Writing Adjectives 1. pretty, 2. new, 3. big, 4. beautiful, 5. old, 6. little, 7. black, 8. tired, 9. yellow, 10. fat, 11. happy, 12. dirty, 13. tall, 14. white, 15. red
488 Animals on the Farm 1. a, 2. a, 3. c, 4. b; 1. a, b; 2. b; 3. a, c; 4. a, b, c; 5. b, c; 1. mouse, 2. pig, 3. cow, 4. cat, 5. chicken, 6. dog, 7. truck, 8. barn
489 Words That Sound the Same 2. hear, 3. to, 4. bare, 5. ate, 6. flour, 7. won, 8. road, 9. made, 10. meat, 11. knew, 12. hour, 13. sail, 14. write, 15. cent
490 Interesting Cities A—ever, city, visit, learn, will, is, made, other, means, map, river
491 A Trip to the Farm 1. c, 2. a, 3. b, 4. a; 1. a, b, c; 2. c; 3. b; 4. b; 5. c; 1. A, B, C; 2. X, Y, Z; 3. O, P, Q; 4. J, K, L; 5. A, F, Z; 6. R, S, T; 7. M, N, P; 8. D, E, F; 9. U, V, W; 10. C, L, T; 11. G, H, I; 12. B, J, R; 13. C, U, Y; 14. E, P, S; 15. D, I, W; 16. A, G, N; 17. E, I, O; 18. Q, T, X; 19. C, H, L; 20. S, U, Z; 21. A, E, R; 22. I, L, M; 23. B, S, V; 24. G, N, Z
492 Writing an Outline
493 The Pet Hospital 1. a, 2. a, 3. c, 4. a; 1. a, b; 2. a; 3. a, b, c; 4. c; 5. c; Be sure students write capital letters, using manuscript.
494 Writing Contractions 2. that's, 3. you'll, 4. she'll, 5. I'm, 6. isn't, 7. there's, 8. let's, 9. you'd, 10. hasn't, 11. didn't, 12. here's, 13. don't, 14. we're, 15. they'll, 16. won't, 17. wasn't, 18. aren't, 19. he'd, 20. couldn't, 21. it's, 22. didn't, 23. I'll, 24. there's, 25. weren't, 26. it'll, 27. we've, 28. he'll, 29. wouldn't, 30. haven't, 31. you're, 32. isn't
495 Having a Pet 1. c, 2. a, 3. b, 4. c; 1. a, b; 2. a, c; 3. c; 4. b; 5. a; 1. pet, 2. dogs, 3. cats, 4. care, 5. know, 6. fun, 7. kind, 8. are, 9. bird, 10. pony, 11. more, 12. they, 13. keep, 14. many, 15. work, 16. you, 17. play, 18. my
496 Spelling in Writing
497 Ants 1. a, 2. b, 3. c, 4. a; 1. b, 2. c, 3. b, 4. a, 5. a; 1. wet-let, 2. go-no, 3. boy-toy, 4. soon-noon, 5. look-cook, 6. give-live, 7. dish-fish, 8. say-day, 9. any-many, 10. fun-run, 11. we-see, 12. cow-how, 13. red-bed, 14. bell-fell, 15. sad-bad, 16. do-to, 17. ride-hide, 18. best-test
498 Good Health Habits 2. plenty, 3. neat, 4. meals, 5. fruit, 6. outside, 7. Floss, 8. bath, 9. teeth, 10. kind, 11. night
499 Worms 1. c, 2. a, 3. a, 4. c; 1. a, 2. b, 3. a, 4. c, 5. a; 1. The dog chased the cat. 2. You broke my pencil. 3. The car was blue. 4. I saw an airplane. 5. The moon is full. 6. May I have a cookie?
500 Writing Cities
501 Frogs 1. a, 2. b, 3. c, 4. a; 1. a, 2. c, 3. c, 4. b, 5. a; 1. book, 2. boat, 3. ball, 4. sun, 5. bird, 6. bus, 7. frog, 8. eye
502 "er" and "est" Endings 2. braver, bravest; 3. riper, ripest; 4. paler, palest; 5. nicer, nicest; 6. closer, closest; 7. later, latest; 8. finer, finest; 9. shinier, shiniest; 10. sillier, silliest, 11. fuzzier, fuzziest; 12. sleepier, sleepiest, 13. furrier, furriest; 14. saltier, saltiest; 15. curlier, curliest
503 Salamanders 1. b, 2. c, 3. a, 4. a; 1. b, c; 2. b; 3. c; 4. a, c; 5. a, b; cake-2, whale-6, rain-4, snake-3, gate-1, skate-5
504 Things About Me Give whatever help to students that is necessary. Emphasize neatness and capitalization.
505 Writing States
506 Snails 1. c, 2. a, 3. a, 4. b; 1. a; 2. a; 3. a; 4. b; 5. a, b; peach-6, teeth-5, meat-1, wheel-2, seal-3, leaf-4
507 The Prefix 2. ex, expert; 3. re, remind; 4. de, defect; 5. sub, subway; 6. de, depend; 7. de, depart; 8. un, undone; 9. dis, dislocate; 10. en, enrage; 11. un, uncommon, 12. de, demand; 13. mis, misspent; 14. re, reappear; 15. dis, disrobe; 16. dis, distrust; 17. a, about; 18. dis, dismiss; 19. dis, disjoint; 20. re, remain; 21. pre, preview; 22. a, around; 23. re, reread
508 Spiders 1. b, 2. a, 3. c, 4. b; 1. c, 2. b, 3. a, 4. a, 5. c; tie-5, dime-2, ice-6, kite-1, pie-4, knife-3
509 The Suffix 2. est, quietest; 3. ance, distance; 4. some, gruesome; 5. less, helpless; 6. er, wider; 7. most, almost; 8. ward, downward; 9. ly, lovely; 10. some, wholesome; 11. ous, dangerous; 12. able, breakable; 13. ance, disturbance; 14. ize, Americanize; 15. ful, colorful; 16. dom, freedom; 17. ing, swimming; 18. ful, helpful; 19. ness, slowness; 20. ive, sportive; 21. ly, dryly; 22. ment, payment; 23. er, larger
510 Bees 1. c, 2. a, 3. b, 4c; 1. a, 2. a, 3. c, 4. a, 5. b; boat-3, rose-6, rope-2, bone-1, nose-4, coat-5
511 Writing Letters
512 Fireflies 1. b, 2. a, 3. c, 4. c; 1. b; 2. b, c; 3. c; 4. b; 5. a; mule-1, ruler-2, fruit-3, suit-6, flute-5, glue-4
513 Writing Directions (to you)
514 Fleas 1. c, 2. a, 3. a, 4. b; 1. a; 2. b; 3. b; 4. c; 5. a, b, c; bat-2, cap-5, man-1, cat-3, flag-4, lamp-6
515 Writing Directions (from you)
516 Butterflies 1. a, 2. c, 3. b, 4. c; 1. a, 2. b, 3. a, 4. c, 5. a; desk-4, bed-6, nest-5, bell-2, hen-3, jet-1
517 Writing Stories
518 The Monarch Butterfly 1. b, 2. c, 3. a, 4. b; 1. a, 2. b, 3. c, 4. c, 5. b; pig-4, fish-2, mitt-6, ship-1, pin-5, milk-3
519 Writing Poems
520 Fish 1. b, c; 2. a; 3. a; 4. b; 1. c; 2. b; 3. c; 4. a, b; 5. a; fox-6, sock-3, frog-2, mop-5, box-1, blocks-4
521 My Family Tree Help students fill in all the blanks.
522 Writing Bulletins
523 The Octopus 1. c, 2. a, 3. a, 4. b; 1. c, 2. b, 3. c, 4. a, 5. c; bug-5, cup-3, truck-6, duck-4, bus-1, sun-2
524 Reading Your Writing
525 Goldfish 1. b, 2. c, 3. a, 4. a; 1. a; 2. b; 3. a; 4. c; 5. a, b, c; 1. red-bed, 2. so-know, 3. cat-sat, 4. tree-eat, 5. hide-hive, 6. rule-cube, 7. make-lake, 8. cut-up, 9. bike-ride, 10. desk-rest, 11. box-fox, 12. pit-sit, 13. pet-let, 14. nose-toe, 15. man-hat, 16. suit-fruit, 17. fish-pin, 18. we, me
526 The Mudskipper 1. a, 2. b, 3. c, 4. a; 1. a; 2. a, b, c; 3. a; 4. b; 5. b; 1. galloped, 2. hop, 3. fly, 4. swim, 5. walked, 6. chased, 7. drive, 8. ran, 9. crawl, 10. rolled.
527 Creative Writing Help students complete this lesson. Emphasize neatness and all areas of punctuation and capitalization.
528 Using a Comma Commas should be placed after the following: 2. cow horse, 3. spelling reading, 4. green red, 5. airport town, 6. cold wet, 7. notebook paper, 8. dog cat, 9. plants bushes, 10. closet bed, 11. eggs bacon toast, 12. balls tinsel
529 Swordfish 1. a, 2. b, 3. c, 4. c; 1. c; 2. a; 3. a, b, c; 4. b; 5. a; 1. f, 2. e, 3. h, 4. n, 5. z, 6. a, 7. t, 8. s, 9. b, 10. m, 11. e, 12. g, 13. d, 14. b, 15. o, 16. l, 17. g, 18. m, 19. b, 20. r, 21. b, 22. p, 23. r, 24. j
530 Words That Rhyme 1. clock, 2. do, 3. corn, 4. corner, 5. plum, 6. fall, 7. wives, 8. log
531 The Remora 1. b, 2. a, 3. a, 4. a; 1. b; 2. a; 3. c; 4. a, b, c; 5. a; 1. t, 2. 0, 3. p, 4. n, 5. b, 6. a, 7. e, 8. d, 9. s, 10. t, 11. i, 12. u, 13. t, 14. e, 15. r, 16. m, 17. f, 18. g, 19. d, 20. t, 21. x, 22. p, 23. e, 24. l

532 Finish a Story mother, house, beautiful, cookies, delicious, go, present, name, happy, puppy

533 The Puffer Fish 1. a, 2. b, 3. a, 4. b; 1. a, c; 2. a, b; 3. b; 4. c; 5. a; 1. all, 2. his, 3. give, 4. fly, 5. boy, 6. big, 7. you, 8. any, 9. grow, 10. cold, 11. book, 12. open, 13. bird, 14. them, 15. tree, 16. near, 17. know, 18. train

534 Rhyming Words A—2. shoe-clue, moo; 3. mouse-house; 4. loose-moose; shoes-lose; 5. flag-brag; flap-map; 6. sunny-funny, money; B—2. small, tall, fall; 3. stuff, muff, puff; 4. grouse, mouse, douse; 5. free, tee, bee; 6. my, sky, lie

535 Seals 1. c, 2. a, 3. b, 4. b; 1. a; 2. b, c; 3. a; 4. c; 5. a, b; 1. at-bat, 2. cup-sun, 3. you-too, 4. old-boat, 5. pie-try, 6. cake-rain, 7. ten-pen, 8. sea-free, 9. mud-rub, 10. dish-ring, 11. log-box, 12. time-tie, 13. car-star, 14. three-he, 15. wet-get, 16. plane-made, 17. rose-boat, 18. tube-cube

536 To, Too, Two B. two, to; C. two, too; D. to, to; E. to, too, F. to; G. two; H. too, to

537 Whales 1. b, 2. a, 3. c, 4. a; 1. b, 2. a, 3. c, 4. a, 5. a; 1. she-tree, 2. fun-sun, 3. that-hat, 4. horn-corn, 5. zoo-too, 6. nine-mine, 7. soon-noon, 8. fall-tall, 9. rest-nest, 10. fast-last, 11. do-to, 12. day-say, 13. then-when, 14. show-grow; 15. long-song, 16. fish-dish; 17. game-came, 18. thing-ring

538 Get-Well Notes Students should be able to complete this lesson.

539 Birds 1. a, c; 2. b; 3. a; 4. c; 1. c, 2. b, 3. a, 4. b, 5. a; Underline: 1, 3, 5, 8, 9, 11, 12, 13, 14, 16, 17, 20, 21, 23

540 Words That Are Opposites 2. down, 3. black, 4. straight, 5. rough, 6. loose, 7. dull, 8. good, 9. soft, 10. cool, 11. cold, 12. skinny, 13. late, 14. over, 15. work, 16. everything, 17. many, 18. long, 19. ugly, 20. opposite, 21. large, 22. listen

541 Cardinals 1. b, 2. a, 3. b, 4. c; 1. b; 2. a; 3. c; 4. c; 5. a, c; Help students complete the last section.

542 Do You Know? 1. after you get a present or something nice; 2. when a friend is sick or in the hospital; 3. short, dirty, bad, in, early, right, happy, up; 4. A—to, B—two, C—too; 5. Sunday, Monday, Tuesday, Wednesday, Thursday, Friday, Saturday; 6. sing, ring; 7. rare, bare

543 Robins 1. b, 2. a, 3. a, 4. c; 1. a, 2. b, 3. c, 4. a, 5. a; 1. he, 2. big, 3. go, 4. all, 5. man, 6. book, 7. am, 8. hill, 9. new, 10. far, 11. eat, 12. do, 13. is, 14. by, 15. not, 16. pull, 17. doll, 18. bell, 19. good, 20. ask, 21. him, 22. girl, 23. my, 24. eye

544 Rocks Are Part of the Earth 1. houses, 2. fireplaces, 3. fences, 4. roads

545 The Sandpiper 1. b, 2. c, 3. a, 4. a; 1. a, 2. c, 3. b, 4. b, 5. a; 1. i, 2. a, 3. i, 4. o, 5. a, 6. a, 7. i, 8. o, 9. e, 10. i, 11. a, 12. o, 13. a, 14. u, 15. a, 16. a, 17. e, 18. a, 19. o, 20. a

546 Owls 1. b, 2. a, 3. b, 4. c; 1. a, 2. b, 3. b, 4. c, 5. c; 1. b, 2. s, 3. f, 4. l, 5. n, 6. c, 7. g, 8. c, 9. p, 10. r, 11. t, 12. k, 13. l, 14. f, 15. s, 16. m, 17. f, 18. g, 19. c 20. h, 21. c, 22. f, 23. w, 24. r

547 Water 2. washing, 3. drinking, 4. cooking, 5. bathing, 6. washing hands clean, drinking, home, school

548 Parrots 1. b, 2. c, 3. a, 4. a; 1. a; 2. b, c; 3. b; 4. a; 5. a, b; Underline: 1, 3, 4, 5, 7, 8, 10, 11, 14, 16, 17, 18, 19, 20, 22, 24

549 How to Protect Yourself in Bad Weather 1. umbrella, 2. hat, 3. raincoat, 4. boots; A. sweater, B. boots, C. coat, D. scarf, E. gloves, F. mittens; 1. neck, 2. warm, dry, 3. Gloves, mittens, 4. umbrella, 5. ear muffs

550 Woodpeckers 1. c, 2. c, 3. a, 4. b; 1. c, 2. b, 3. b, 4. c, 5. a; 1. are, 2. who, 3. run, 4. hot, 5. ball, 6. has, 7. will, 8. home, 9. this, 10. tree, 11. made, 12. foot, 13. one, 14. try, 15. cool, 16. bird, 17. food, 18. it

551 Hands—the Tattletales A-clean, B-dirty; 1. Don't bite your nails.; 2. Wash your hands before you eat.; 3. Keep your fingers out of your mouth.; 4. Wash your hands after you go to the bathroom. Use plenty of soap.; 5. Keep your nails clean.

553 The Hummingbird 1. c, 2. b, 3. a, 4. c; 1. b, 2. a, 3. c, 4. a, 5. c; 1. same-game, 2. cute-tune, 3. hot-not, 4. jet-hen, 5. pig-pin, 6. run-nut, 7. road-bone, 8. fell-tell, 9. six-lip, 10. pot-lock, 11. ate-pay, 12. ice-nice, 13. gate-snake, 14. five-fire, 15. bat-cap, 16. desk-step, 17. more-for, 18. meat-wheel

553 Telephone Manners 1. voice, 2. smile, 3. speak, 4. apologize, 5. stop, 6. Slamming, 7. absent, 8. found

554 Bird Homes 1. c, 2. a, 3. b, 4. a; 1. b; 2. a, b, c; 3. a; 4. a; 5. a, b, c; 1. at-sat, 2. ten-pen, 3. can-ran, 4. all-ball, 5. egg-leg, 6. pop-top, 7. me-she, 8. slow-grow, 9. try-fry, 10. hand-sand, 11. they-hay, 12. door-poor, 13. make-take, 14. give-live, 15. rose-nose, 16. best-rest, 17. never-ever, 18. will-fill

555 Table Manners 1. floor, 2. elbows, 3. mouth, 4. talk, 5. mouth, 6. mouth

556 Bird Talk 1. a, 2. c, 3. a, 4. b, 1. b, 2. a, b, c; 3. a; 4. a, b; 5. c; 1. I live here.; 2. He ran away.; 3. She is pretty.; 4. Dave is at home.; 5. The dog barked.; 6. I like you.; 7. You are my friend.; 8. I saw a bird.

557 Your Dentist 1. dentist, 2. friend, 3. twice, 4. soft, 5. milk, 6. Sugar, 7. healthy, 8. pretty, 9. afraid, 10. women, 11. doctor

558 Animal Homes 1. b, 2. c, 3. c, 4. a; 1. a, b, c; 2. a; 3. c; 4. a, c; 5. a, b, c; 1. go, in; 2. bat, car; 3. boy, you; 4. day, toy; 5. cow, hill; 6. big, run; 7. get, we; 8. are, dog; 9. now, she; 10. is, one; 11. ball, who; 12. no, yes

559 Health Puzzle 2. sleep, 3. milk, 4. meals, 5. water, 6. hands, 7. breakfast

560 Animal Talk 1. c, 2. a, 3. b, 4. a; 1. a, 2. c, 3. a, 4. c, 5. b; 1. sing-ring, 2. them-pen, 3. hurt-dirt, 4. leave-eat, 5. kite-mine, 6. made-hate, 7. just-fun, 8. nice-right, 9. name-rain, 10. week-fear, 11. frog-dog, 12. car-hat, 13. kinds-try, 14. old-hold, 15. play-trade, 16. tent-head, 17. bus-rush, 18. sit-it

561 Nutritious Foods Help students work this lesson.

562 A Trip to the Bakery 1. a, 2. b, 3. b, 4. a; 1. a; 2. b; 3. b; 4. c; 5. a, b, c; 1. Fido is my dog.; 2. This is my house.; 3. The bell rang.; 4. The bird flew away.; 5. I caught a fish.; 6. The train is late.

563 Kinds of Foods

564 A Trip to the Dairy 1. b, 2. a, 3. c, 4. a; 1. b; 2. a; 3. b; 4. a; 5. a, b, c; 1—18 should all begin with capital letters.

565 Fresh Air and Sunshine A—1. healthy, 2. sunshine, 3. glowing, 4. lungs; B—1. lungs, 2. air, 3. fresh, 4. Sunshine

566 A Trip to the Airport 1. a, 2. b, 3. c, 4. c; 1 a, b; 2. b; 3. a; 4. a; 5. c; 1. car, 2. train, 3. airplane, 4. ship, 5. bus

567 Clean Hair A—2. brush, comb, shampoo, warm water; 3. no; 5. at least once a week; 6. no; 7. no; 8. no; B—1. Clean hair makes healthy hair.; 2. To clean your hair, use plenty of shampoo and warm water.

568 A Trip to the Orchard 1. b, 2. a, 3. c, 4. a; 1. a; 2. a, b, c; 3. a, b; 4. a, b; 5. a; 1. your, 2. house, 3. walk, 4. girl, 5. toy, 6. hurt, 7. show, 8. off, 9. make, 10. came, 11. they, 12. best, 13. like, 14. has, 15. nose, 16. open, 17. black, 18. over, 19. use, 20. who

569 Gateways to the Body Help students by showing them how to refer to the drawing on the right side of the paper.

570 A Trip to the Supermarket 1. c, 2. a, 3. c, 4. b; 1. c, 2. a, 3. c, 4. b, 5. a; Underline: 1, 3, 4, 6, 8, 9, 11, 13, 14, 16, 18, 19, 21, 24

571 Making Bread

572 A Trip to a Ranch 1. c, 2. a, 3. a, 4. b; 1. c, 2. a, 3. a, 4. b, 5. c; Underline: 1, 3, 5, 7, 8, 10, 14, 16, 17, 20, 21, 23

573 A Good Citizen A—polite, honest, helpful, clean, kind, truthful, thoughtful, respectful, unselfish, friendly; B—work well, never be late, get along with others, think of others, respect the flag, play safely, listen well, obey rules

574 The Police Officer 1. a, 2. a, 3. b, 4. b; 1. a, b, c; 2. a; 3. a, b, c; 4. b, 5. c; 1. you, 2. big, 3. and, 4. book, 5. up, 6. pen, 7. my, 8. tree, 9. see, 10. dog, 11. home, 12. bike, 13. sky, 14. car, 15. talk, 16. name, 17. eat, 18. foot

575 Family Helpers Test A—2. miller, 3. fireman, 4. milkman, 5. farmer, 6. dentist, 7. painter; B—1. electrician; 2. plumber; 3. cobbler; 4. bakery; 5. red, white, blue; 6. dairy; 7. family

576 The Fire Fighter 1. a, 2. b, 3. c, 4. b; 1. b, 2. a, 3. b, 4. b, 5. c; Be sure students rewrite each word and add "s."

577 A Good Citizenship Test 1. no, 2. yes, 3. yes, 4. yes, 5. yes, 6. yes, 7. no, 8. yes, 9. yes, 10. yes, 11. yes, 12. yes, 13. yes, 14. yes, 15. no, 16. yes, 17. no, 18. yes, 19. no, 20. yes

578 The Doctor 1. a, 2. b, 3. b, 4. c; 1. a; 2. a; 3. a, b, c; 4. b; 5. a, b, c; 1. son-sun, 2. to-two, 3. for-four, 4. ate-eight, 5. sea-see, 6. be-bee, 7. know-no, 8. new-knew, 9. rode-road, 10. red-read, 11. blue-blew, 12. meet-meat, 13. by-buy, 14. write-right, 15. here-hear, 16. week-weak, 17. dear-deer, 18. it's-its

579 Who Got Them? A—1. Someone took the cookies.; 2. They were in the cookie jar.; 3. They were taken at 3 o'clock.; 4. Three cookies were taken.; 5. A boy got them.

580 The Sea Horse 1. b, 2. a, 3. b, 4. b; 1. b, 2. a, 3. c, 4. c, 5. a; 1. sun, 2. hat, 3. sand, 4. we, 5. look, 6. egg, 7. yes, 8. boy, 9. stop, 10. ran, 11. milk, 12. eye, 13. bus, 14. rain, 15. girl, 16. cat, 17. ball, 18. box

581 Stars

582 Nurses 1. c, 2. a, 3. b, 4. c; 1. c; 2. a, b; 3. a; 4. b; 5. a, b, c; 1. like-ride, 2. way-hay, 3. at-cat, 4. goat-hold, 5. she-he, 6. hit-sit, 7. save-cave, 8. men-bet, 9. know-blow, 10. blue-new, 11. feet-teeth, 12. rat-fat, 13. see-eat, 14. vine-kind, 15. row-toe, 16. man-hand, 17. nurse-hurt, 18. place-face

583 Types of Flying Things

584 The Dentist 1. b, 2. a, 3. c, 4. a; 1. b, 2. a, 3. a, 4. b, 5. b; 1. d, 2. f, 3. m, 4. u, 5. n, 6.y, 7. w, 8. n, 9. n, 10. w. 11. p, 12. y, 13. r, 14. w, 15. p, 16. c, 17. k, 18. b, 19. o, 20. v, 21. h, 22. d, 23. h, 24. b

585 Colors Give help if needed for students to complete lesson.

586 The Librarian 1. a, 2. c, 3. a, 4. c; 1. a, 2. a, 3. c, 4. b, 5. a; 1—20 are all proper nouns. All should begin with capital letters.

587 Different Sounds We Hear 1. drum, 2. violin, 3. xylophone, 4. piano

588 The Teacher 1. a, 2. a, 3. b, 4. c; 1. b, c; 2. a; 3. a; 4. a; 5. a, b, c; 1. and play; 2. lion, very; 3. bird, home; 4. rose, tree; 5. fish, help; 6. shoe, wood; 7. game, pull; 8. rain, well; 9. each, fun; 10. near, worm; 11. hour, train; 12. pole, soon

589 Machines with Wheels 1. two, 2. sixteen, 3. four, 4. three, 5. one, 6. two

590 The Postal Carrier 1. a, 2. c, 3. b, 4. b; 1. a, 2. a, 3. b, 4. b, 5. c;

591 Inventions We Use 1. zipper, 2. telephone, 3. television, 4. saw

592 Bus Drivers 1. c, 2. a, 3. c, 4. b; 1. c; 2. a, b, c; 3. a; 4. b; 5. a, b, c; 1. I liked the story.; 2. We sang a song.; 3. The sky is blue.; 4. Carl is here.; 5. The water is hot.; 6. I see the puppy.; 7. Come here.; 8. Ann made the cake.

593 Electricity in Your Home 1. radio-d, 2. refrigerator-a, 3. iron-e, 4. toaster-c, 5. mixer-b

594 The Farmer 1. b, 2. c, 3. a, 4. c; 1. a; 2. a, b, c; 3. a, b, c; 4. a; 5. a; 1. word-bird, 2. long- song, 3. floor-door, 4. fly-sky, 5. keep-sleep, 6. burn-turn, 7. air-pear, 8. tax-wax, 9. look-book, 10. hand-land, 11. beg-leg, 12. wall-tall, 13. they-hay, 14. must-dust, 15. sun-run, 16. still-hill, 17. grow-so, 18. live-give

595 Birds We See 1. seeds, 2. berries, 3. worm, 4. bugs, 5. grubs

596 The Airplane Pilot 1. b, 2. a, 3. c, 4. b; 1. a; 2. a; 3. b; 4. a; 5. a, b, c; 1. b, 2. b, 3. a, 4. b, 5. b, 6. a, 7. a, 8. b, 9. a,

597 Machines Around Us 1. ladder, 2. airplane, 3. hammer, 4. truck, 5. crane, 6. tractor, 7. scissors, 8. shovel, 9. typewriter, 10. bicycle

598 People at Work 1. a, 2. c, 3. a, 4. c; 1. a; 2. a, b; 3. b, c; 4. b, c; 5. a, b, c; Underline: 1, 3, 4, 6, 8, 9, 12, 13, 14, 16, 17, 20, 22, 24

599 The Moon Offer help if needed.

600 Going on Vacation 1. c, 2. b, 3. a, 4. a; 1. b, c; 2. a, b, c; 3. a, b, c; 4. a, c; 5. a, b; Underline: 1, 2, 4, 6, 7, 8, 10, 11, 14, 16, 18, 19, 21, 23, 24

601 Choosing Breakfast B—1. fruit, 2. cereal, 3. margarine, 4. eggs, 5. milk; D—1. yes, 2. no, 3. yes, 4. yes, 5. no

602 The Sun 1. plants, 2. energy, 3. light, 4. warm

603 Christmas 1. a, 2. a, 3. c, 4. b; 1. a; 2. b; 3. a; 4. c; 5. a, b, c; 1. I, 2. me, 3. I, 4. me, 5. me, 6. I, 7. me, 8. me, 9. I, 10. I, 11. I, 12. me

604 Vacations B—1. beach, 2. camping, 3. mountains, 4. ranch; C—build, waves, beach, tent, fire, camping, long, cowboys, ranch, warm, fish, mountains

605 What We See Around Us

606 Easter 1. c, 2. a, 3. a, 4. c; 1. b; 2. c; 3. a; 4. a, b, c; 5. a, b; 1. she, 2. her, 3. she, 4. her, 5. her, 6. she, 7. her, 8. she, 9. she, 10. her, 11. she, 12. her

607 Plants

608 Halloween 1. a, 2. c, 3. c, 4. a; 1. a, b, c; 2. a; 3. a; 4. b; 5. c; 1. he, 2. him, 3. him, 4. he, 5. him, 6. he, 7. him, 8. he, 9. he, 10. him, 11. him, 12. he

609 Pets This, grandmother, keep, have, small, much, any; (Help students answer all questions.)

610 Different Sounds 2. f, 3. a, 4. e, 5. b, 6. d

611 Thanksgiving 1. a, 2. b, 3. a, 4. c; 1. a, b; 2. a, b; 3. c; 4. c; 5. a, b, c; 1. my, 2. mine, 3. my, 4. mine, 5. my, 6. my, 7. mine, 8. my, 9. mine, 10. my, 11. my, 12. mine

612 Gardening A—1. has, have; 2. are, is, is, is; 3. did, done; 4. seen, saw; C—First, help, is, must, time, to, grow, our

613 Objects Around Us That Give Light 1. flashlight, 2. sun, 3. Lightning, 4. firefly, 5. mirror, 6. moon

614 What Is a Color? 1. b, 2. a, 3. a, 4. b; 1. c, 2. b, 3. a, 4. b, 5. b; 1. find-five, 2. land-and, 3. fed-sell, 4. the-be, 5. luck-truck, 6. fruit-glue, 7. hill-fill, 8. jar-car, 9. sky-fly, 10. read-need, 11. well-web, 12. case-race, 13. beat-green, 14. yes-wet, 15. true-you, 16. rock-clock, 17. say-may, 18. nut-puppy

615 Question Time 2. truth, 3. Pledge of Allegiance, 4. every day, 5. airmail, 6. school, 7. city to city, 8. letters, 9. mailbags, 10. supermarket, 11. "Quiet Please," 12. a bookmobile, 13. not kind to others, 14. baggage, 15. a helpful shop, 16. books

616 Friends B—nice, rake, bake, taste, like; C—many, Sometimes, cookies; D—play, rake, bake, taste, play; E—friend, bridge, almost, woodcutter

617 Why We Wear Shoes 1. b, 2. b, 3. a, 4. c; 1. c; 2. a, b, c; 3. a, b, c; 4. a; 5. b; Help students use suitable words.

618 The Bookmobile

619 Why We Wear Coats 1. c, 2. a, 3. c, 4. a; 1. c; 2. b, c; 3. a, c; 4. a; 5. a, b; 1. I found a penny.; 2. Sit down.; 3. I like horses.; 4. He followed me.; 5. Wait for me.; 6. I am ready to go.; 7. You may come in.; 8. The man smiled.

620 The Library

621 Why We Wear Hats 1. c; 2. a, b, c; 3. b; 4. a; 1. c; 2. a; 3. b; 4. c; 5. a, b, c; 3. I knew that.; 4. Mrs. Sims is here.; 5. Kim looks happy.; 6. His name is R. J. Brown.; 7. Ben asked Dr. Jones.; 8. I like you.; 9. Mr. Roberts called.; 10. We watched the show.; 11. It's true.; 12. This is Ms. Fields.

622 Flying a Kite 1. a, 2. b, 3. a, 4. c; 1. c; 2. a; 3. b; 4. b; 5. b, c; 3. Who is he?; 4. Do you like it?; 5. I did my homework.; 6. What did you say?; 7. Sam rode his bike.; 8. When is the party?; 9. Which desk is yours?; 10. I'm hungry.; 11. How old are you?; 12. Will you do it?

623 Watching the Sky 1. b, 2. c, 3. b, 4. a; 1. c; 2. a, b; 3. c; 4. a, c; 5. b, c; 1. star, 2. sun, 3. you, 4. me, 5. too, 6. see, 7. sky, 8. look, 9. rain, 10. cold, 11. wind, 12. hot, 13. moon, 14. snow, 15. word, 16. line, 17. shoes, 18. coat

624 My Room B—1. time, 2. read, 3. alone, 4. toys, 5. care, 6. too; C—1. soap, 2. horse, 3. apple, 4. thing, 5. would, 6. lion

625 Words That Sound Alike 2. ball, fall, wall; 3. lick, 4. kick, stick; 4. stand, land, band; 5. cook, look, book; 6. fill, bill, mill; 7. bark, park, dark; 8. hear, spear, ear; 9. play, away, day; 10. know, crow, low; 11. chance, dance, prance; 12. stool, pool, school; 13. dog, frog, log; 14. When, hen, begin; 15. luck, buck, duck; 16. bright, light, night; 17. wet, pet, net; 18. clown, town, brown; 19. know, blow, snow; 20. wink, drink, sink

626 Always True 1. wings, 2. eggs, 3. ocean, 4. hot, 5. cold, 6. December, 7. books, 8. uncles, 9. seed, 10. laugh; 1. girls, 2. old, 3. vines, 4. write, 5. water, 6. boy, 7. baby, 8. ceiling, 9. foot, 10. winter

627 All Are 1. birds, 2. animals, 3. trees, 4. carpenter's tools, 5. months, 6. days, 7. colors, 8. frozen water, 9. in the sky, 10. drinks, 11. fruit, 12. babies, 13. clothes, 14. buildings

628 Fun with Numbers A—2. 70, 3. 16, 4. 72, 5. 93, 6. 140, 7. 26, 8. 18, 9. 200, 10. 67; B—1. 32, 2. 90, 3. 16, 4. 6, 5. 50, 6. 14, 7. 25, 8. 5, 9. 130, 10. 120, 11. 90, 12. 60, 13. 19, 14. 3, 15. 130, 16. 3, 17. 6, 18. 3, 19. 4, 20. 4, 21. 3, 22. 3, 23. 10, 24. 4, 25. 5, 26. 2, 27. 0, 28. 3, 29. 2, 30. 2

629 Belonging Together 2. pen, 3. 25 , 4. meow, 5. ears, 6. caboose, 7. air, 8. hand, 9. head, 10. beef, 11. sport, 12. dog, 13. doll, 14. shoe, 15. calf, 16. ship, 17. vine, 18. run, 19. clothes, 20. runway.

630 Read the Stories 1. c, 2. b, 3. a, 4. c; 1. b, 2. a, 3. c, 4. a

631 Entertaining Stories 1. b, 2. a, 3. c, 4. a; 1. a, 2. c, 3. b, 4. c

632 Answer the Questions 1. a, 2. b, 3. c, 4. b; 1. b, 2. c, 3. c, 4. a

633 Finding How Many More 2. 2, 3. 4, 4. 5, 5. 1, 6. 7, 7. 4, 8. 2, 9. 1, 10. 4, 11. 5, 12. 6, 13. 5, 14. 3, 15. 0, 16. 8, 17. 5, 18. 1, 19. 3, 20. 3

634 Choosing Words 2. were, was; 3. a, an; 4. gave, given; 5. seen, saw; 6. done, did; 7. come, came; 8. gone, went; 9. eaten, ate; 10. run, ran

635 Noun Words 2. dog, 3. car, 4. pear, 5. girl, 6. friend, 7. bird, 8. Icicles, 9. Jane, 10. movie, 11. brother, 12. Mother, 13. Jane, 14. Marsha, 15. band, 16. door, 17. I, 18. Sue, 19. Dad, 20. coat

636 Action Words 2. sleeps, 3. rode, 4. cooks, 5. plays, 6. work, 7. live, 8. raced, 9. carried, 10. walk, 11. drives, 12. gave, 13. washed, 14. wash, 15. see, 16. eat, 17. ran, 18. planned, 19. jumps, 20. travel

637 Underlining Words A—2. late, 3. pull, 4. walk, 5. sad, 6. rude, 7. thin, 8. idle, 9. nice, 10. slow, 11. loose, 12. lose; B—1. sun, fun, gun; 2. flea, sea, tea; 3. save, wave, pave, 4. break, steak, make; 5. boy, joy, toy; C—1. blew, blue; 2. haul, hall; 3. two, to, too; 4. ate, eight

638 Which Word? 2. swim, 3. foot, 4. ride, 5. think, 6. drink, 7. day, 8. rain, 9. rabbit, 10. kitten, 11. number, 12. sit, 13. woman, 14. glass, 15. ditch, 16. man, 17. crayon, 18. whole, 19. plate, 20. jacket

639 From "Car" to "Doll" 2. care, 3. are, 4. read, 5. add, 6. dog, 7. grow, 8. row, 9. want, 10. this, 11. his, 12. is, 13. store, 14. tore, 15. ore, 16. egg, 17. go, 18. good, 19. do, 20. doll

640 From "Came" to "Ear" 2. me, 3. men, 4. new, 5. was, 6. as, 7. sat, 8. that, 9. hat, 10. at, 11. the, 12. then, 13. hen, 14. no, 15. not, 16. to, 17. toy, 18. ye, 19. year, 20. ear